WOMEN AND THE CRIMINAL JUSTICE SYSTEM

Third Edition

WOMEN AND THE CRIMINAL JUSTICE SYSTEM

Katherine Stuart van Wormer
University of Northern Iowa

Clemens Bartollas
University of Northern Iowa

Prentice Hall
Boston   Columbus   Indianapolis   New York   San Francisco   Upper Saddle River
Amsterdam   Cape Town   Dubai   London   Madrid   Milan   Munich   Paris   Montreal   Toronto
Delhi   Mexico City   Sao Paulo   Sydney   Hong Kong   Seoul   Singapore   Taipei   Tokyo

Editor in Chief: Vernon Anthony
Acquisitions Editor: Tim Peyton
Editorial Assistant: Lynda Cramer
Director of Marketing: David Gesell
Marketing Manager: Adam Kloza
Senior Marketing Coordinator: Alicia Wozniak
Operations Specialist: Renata Butera
Creative Art Director: Jayne Conte
Cover Designer: Suzanne Duda
Cover Coordinator Permissions and Research:
    Catherine Mazzucca

Manager, Cover Visual Research & Permissions:
    Karen Sanatar
Cover Art: Brand X / SuperStock
Lead Media Project Manager: Karen Bretz
Full-Service Project Management:
    Sadagoban Balaji/Integra Software Services Pvt. Ltd.
Composition: Integra Software Services Pvt. Ltd.
Printer/Binder: Bind-Rite/Robbinsville
Cover Printer: Bind-Rite/Robbinsville
Text Font: 10/12, Times

If you purchased this book within the United States or Canada you should be aware that it has been wrongfully imported without the approval of the Publisher or the Author.

Library of Congress Cataloging-in-Publication Data
van Wormer, Katherine S.
  Women and the criminal justice system/Katherine Stuart van Wormer, Clemens Bartollas. —3rd ed.
    p. cm.
Includes bibliographical references and index.
ISBN-13: 978-0-13-700878-0 (alk. paper)
ISBN-10: 0-13-700878-3 (alk. paper)
  1. Sex discrimination in criminal justice administration—United States.   2. Women—Drug abuse—United States.
3. Female offenders—United States.   4. Women prisoners—United States.   I. Bartollas, Clemens.   II. Title.
HV9950.V38 2011
364.082—dc22

                                                                        2009029907

10 9 8 7 6 5 4

Prentice Hall
is an imprint of

www.pearsonhighered.com

ISBN 10:   0-13-700878-3
ISBN 13: 978-0-13-700878-0

Dedicated to
Flora Templeton Stuart and Natalie Stuart Moorcroft,
the sister and niece of Katherine van Wormer,
respectively—two woman lawyers in Bowling
Green, Kentucky, fighting for social justice.

CONTENTS

PREFACE

The world has changed in many ways since the second edition of *Women and the Criminal Justice System* was published in 2007. The changes with which we are concerned have special repercussions for victims and offenders in the criminal justice system, some positive and some negative. On the positive side, the pendulum is swinging toward a new progressivism characterized by a new government and a new "yes, we can" ethos. An emphasis on rehabilitation and substance abuse treatment is increasingly in evidence in the United States. At the same time, a global economic crisis of epic proportions has brought an impact to bear on every social institution in the land. With a universal rise in job insecurity and unemployment rates, a rise in domestic violence victimization including murder-suicide is in evidence. As for the future, a rise in white-collar crime and other economically based crime is predictable. Taken together, these factors have implications for girls and women at every level of the criminal justice system, including those in the professions of law, policing, and correctional work.

The continuing impact of globalization on the criminal justice system and on professionals who work in that system has been profound. Economic conditions determine which kinds of crimes will be committed and opportunities for self-fulfillment. At the global level, consider the significant gap between the rich and the poor, a fact making women from impoverished regions of the world vulnerable to recruitment into the prostitution and sex-trafficking industry. Meanwhile, the market in illegal drugs pulls immigrant women into its vortex, while the war on drugs continues to be a war against poor women and minorities.

It is in this context of globalization and the increasing feminization of poverty that the third edition of *Women and the Criminal Justice System* is shaped. Persons familiar with the earlier editions will soon note that we have made major changes, including the rewriting of two chapters and the thorough updating of the remaining twelve. We have added new updated boxed readings as well. In a nutshell, the major changes that are new to this edition are:

- The writing of a completely new chapter on women in crime to reflect changes in arrest rates for female offenders and to update information on the expanding literature on female pathways to crime;
- The replacement of a reprinted chapter on restorative justice with a chapter original to this volume that is more uniquely geared toward the needs of female offenders and victims;
- A reconceptualized theoretical framework to stress knowledge from the third wave of feminism, including heightened attention to the intersectionality of gender, race/ethnicity, and class;
- Consistent with the increasing impact of globalization in today's world, we have updated the chapter on victimization worldwide and added content on international programming;
- The addition throughout the book of sections devoted to such contemporary issues as Latina feminist theory, inmates as mothers, reentry programming, rape in the military, teen dating violence warning signs, domestic homicide, and global innovations in correctional treatment;
- Complete revamping of the chapters on domestic violence, rape, the prison environment, woman lawyers, and female correctional officers;
- The replacement of just under half of the featured boxed readings and of most of the personal narratives with new material;

The third edition continues to emphasize an empowerment perspective. Empowerment as conceptualized here starts from an understanding of power and powerlessness. Relevant to the criminal justice system, we focus on who makes the laws and who gets punished for which kind of crimes or for which drugs of choice—in short, who gets victimized by the system. Empowerment is a multidimensional construct that applies to the climate of social structures as well as to treatment of individuals. Person-centered, gender-specific initiatives, for example, can help girls and women in trouble with the law tap into their inner strengths to restore (or discover) a sense of well-being. From the victim's perspective, empowerment is about healing the wounds of crime and coming to see oneself not as a victim but as a survivor. Women professionals in the fields of criminal justice—law enforcement, law, and corrections, all of which are male-dominated, patriarchal fields—seek and often find empowerment when their voices are heard.

PLAN OF THE BOOK

The book is divided into five parts. Part One, "Introduction," lays out the theoretical framework: the empowerment perspective for understanding gender, patriarchy, and social control and how these three elements interact. Part Two, "Female Crime and Delinquency," is concerned with girls and women who have been arrested and convicted of crime. Chapter 2 examines current research on crime and delinquency, while Chapter 3 is devoted to feminist criminological theory and research. Chapter 4 examines delinquency across the life course.

Part Three, "Drug Addiction, Prison, and Restoration," takes us through women's pathway to crime when substance abuse is a factor, as it most often is. Personal and policy considerations are discussed. The final chapter in this section examines innovative processes that restore justice and promote healing and describes victim–offender conferencing as a form of restorative justice with much relevance.

Part Four, "Women as Victims and Survivors," brings an empowerment perspective to the subjects of rape, partner abuse, and the victimization of women internationally. Recent statistics and research findings help reveal the extent and magnitude of the battering, rape, and sexual exploitation of women worldwide.

Part Five, "Women as Professionals," takes us into the realm of women as they promote social justice and engage in empowerment of other women (and men). Women's contributions to policing and legal fields have been significant, the more so in recent years. However, corrections is an area in which women have moved from the helm of the profession to the periphery; prison privatization and emphasis on security over counselling are two contributing factors. Even here, however, women's contributions have been and still are substantial, including inside the prison system. In humanizing these areas of criminal justice, women often have had to confront organizational structures that were oppressive and unsuitable for their needs. Women of color have made inroads professionally but often only after challenging institutional racism and sexism simultaneously. Empowerment for women in these legally based fields has come in the form of participating in the formulation of social policy as an avenue for constructive social change, change often directed toward the empowerment of marginalized persons—the offenders and victims with whom and for whom the police officers, lawyers, and correctional staff work. The final chapter presents a summary of the book's themes and prospects of future directions.

ACKNOWLEDGMENTS

Many individuals have contributed to the writing of this book. The authors are profoundly grateful to their spouses. Robert van Wormer edited and typed materials throughout the manuscript. Linda Dippold Bartollas was a constant source of support and encouragement throughout the many phases involved in the publication of this text. We want to acknowledge our appreciation to our editors at Prentice Hall—Tim Peyton and Lynda Cramer—and to Sadagoban Balaji for an excellent job in copy editing.

The authors are very grateful to those victims, offenders, and professionals in the justice system who were willing to be interviewed.

PART

I

Introduction

This introductory chapter provides the social context necessary to examine the personal situations of women who are victims of crime, women who are convicted and sentenced for their crimes, and women who work in various agencies of the criminal justice system. That gender matters is the basic theme. This social context is the patriarchal society in which males are dominant and females experience oppression in a variety of ways. In recent years, there has been a backlash both against rehabilitation and against many aspects of the feminist movement. That this backlash is played out against poor women of color and especially women in trouble with the law are major arguments of this book. This is not to say that women, including women of color, have not made inroads into the professional worlds of corrections and criminal law, and not to overlook the many new initiatives within the criminal justice system to bring gender-specific programming for girls and women.

As a starting point in a book that considers the many roles that women play within and across the criminal justice system, we turn to various perspectives on gender, race, and class, drawing on insights from feminist theory and the writings of feminist criminologists. Feminist perspectives, which focus on explaining and responding to the oppressed position of women in society, have much to offer to our understanding of the functioning of criminal justice institutions. Chapter 1, accordingly, offers a brief overview of relevant insights provided in the feminist and feminist criminological literature. Because they place gender at the forefront of the discourse, feminist teachings and scholarship can serve as a foundation for the later chapters on crime, delinquency, and professional roles. Seven representative schools of feminism are singled out; we have divided these approaches into three categories: time-based, political, and cultural. This chapter is written in the belief that an examination of sexism, racism, ethnicity, classism, and adultism (harsh treatment of the young) is essential to understanding the **multiple marginality** that girls and women face in American society and elsewhere.

1

Theoretical Perspectives on Women and the Criminal Justice System

T he task of this chapter is to provide a theoretical overview to enhance our understanding of the criminal justice system in terms of the experiences of girls and women at various levels within the system. Forces for **oppression** and forces for empowerment will be discussed. Our discussion is informed by insights from major feminist perspectives concerning gender, female criminality, and victimization, and the interactive factors of race, class, and gender. An introduction to these perspectives is important because our task is to study the treatment of female offenders in the criminal justice system, as well as women's occupational advances in the field. A second but not secondary concern of this chapter is with women's agency and their personal and political empowerment across the landscape of criminal justice.

Because there is a lot we can learn from the art and science of feminist criminology, it is to this school of thought that we now turn to for guidance in our investigation. Committed to understanding the status of women in society and how this status impinges on women's roles within the justice system, feminist criminologists have been instrumental in shaping debates and conceptions of gender and crime, and in revealing the unique role of violence in the background of female offenders. Employing interdisciplinary theoretical frameworks, feminist criminology examines gender and gender inequality, as well as the intersections of race, ethnicity, class, gender, and age (Miller and Mullins, 2006, p. 204). Feminist criminologists also see themselves as scholar-activists in the pursuit of social justice and advocacy for change (Chesney-Lind, 2006).

In examining the challenges and obstacles faced by women offenders, victims, and workers in the justice system, this book has developed five underlying feminist themes. First, women offenders, victims, and practitioners experience sexism, racism, and classism on an ongoing basis, and these forms of oppression contribute to feelings of "multiple marginality" (Chesney-Lind and Pasko, 2003). Second, the effects of the multiple oppressions based on gender, class, and race are not merely additive, that is, simply interlocking and piled on each other (Dominelli, 2003; Littlefield, 2003), but the effects are synergistic or multiplicative. Third, this examination focuses on the social construction of knowledge and how it is typically male oriented. The study of crime itself, as the following discussion reveals, has been by males about males. The myths concerning female offenders, victims, and practitioners are vivid examples of this social construction of knowledge. Fourth, this examination of women in the justice system heavily emphasizes the importance of social context. In this social context, in which the doors have opened to women professionally, oppression still exists at many levels. Subcultures within society have varying definitions and expectations of what it means to be a woman, and these norms and values can influence a girl's pathway into crime or into seeking advanced education and a career as correctional counselor or lawyer. Finally, our attention is drawn to the theme of empowerment, a theme that is echoed throughout the chapters of this text. Such a focus is chosen in that it provides a means or a direction for how women, whether offenders, victims, or practitioners, can move from oppression to empowerment.

Beginning with how the study of crime has been dominated by males and the main feminist theories of criminology, this chapter examines the oppressions that females experience in the social context of the United States and elsewhere. These oppressions take place in a patriarchal society and are reflected in the laws defining women's place; the sexual harassment of women in criminal justice institutions; and the expressions of sexism, racism, and class bias as they affect women offenders, victims, and practitioners.

THE STUDY OF CRIME AND THE MALE PERSPECTIVE

Men commit the majority of crimes. Arrest, self-report, and victimization data all reveal that men and boys commit more frequent and serious crimes than do women and girls. Men also have a virtual monopoly on the commission of corporate, organized, and political crimes (Messerschmidt, 2004). It is for this reason that "gender has consistently been advanced by criminologists as the strongest predictor of criminal involvement" (Belknap, 2007). Gender matters. Yet, as Frances Heidensohn, British pioneer of feminist criminology, once observed, "most criminologists have resisted this obvious insight with an energy comparable to that of medieval churchmen denying Galileo or Victorian bishops attacking Darwin" (Heidensohn, 1987, p. 22).

From a historical perspective, it is apparent that major theoretical works written by male criminologists about men and boys have been alarmingly gender-blind. Virtually all the classic delinquency theories were preoccupied with why males commit delinquent acts. Girls' delinquency, according to Belknap (2007), was seen as neither interesting nor important. Criminology traditionally placed boys in the center of research and program initiatives. But exciting research inspired by feminist thought is changing all this and bringing girls and women to the forefront of criminology. As early as the 1980s, Daly and Chesney-Lind (1988) listed five aspects of feminist thought that distinguished it from the majority of criminological inquiry:

- Gender is not a natural fact but a complex social, historical, and cultural product; it is related to, but not simply derived from, biological sex difference and reproductive capacities.
- Gender and gender relations order social life and social institutions in fundamental ways.

- Gender relations and constructs of masculinity and femininity are not symmetrical but are based on an organizing principle of men's superiority and social and political-economic dominance over women.
- Systems of knowledge reflect men's views of the natural and social world: the production of knowledge is gendered.
- Women should be at the center of intellectual inquiry, not peripheral, invisible, or appendages to men. (p. 504)

Feminist criminologists have employed these elements of feminist thought to conduct investigations of girls' and women's gendered lives and experiences in terms of race, class, and sexuality (Messerschmidt, 2004). The outpouring of feminist scholarship, in the work of feminist researchers such as Susan Brownmiller and Mary Koss whose landmark work on the nature and pervasiveness of violence against women raised the national consciousness. At about the same time, the work of feminist criminology's foremothers, such as Meda Chesney-Lind and Frances Heindensohn, helped lay the foundations for what is now generally a recognized body of scholarship on gender, crime, and criminal justice. Our awareness of the challenges facing frontline workers and professionals in the field of criminal justice has been further bolstered through the work of social science researchers such as Joanne Belknap and Roslyn Muraskin. Collectively, these feminist scholars have helped move the analysis of gendered power relations to the forefront of the discussion on delinquency, crime, and corrections (Messerschmidt, 2004).

Still, while the evolution of feminist conceptualizations and activism has often been credited with important gains, there have been setbacks, regarding both the co-optation of feminist ideals and an antifeminist backlash that is pervasive in the media and in the courtrooms. The gains have been in the spread of gender-based programming in many of the nation's juvenile and adult institutions. The setbacks have been in the lawmaking and in enforcement of the law. The war on drugs is a war on women of color. This claim, which is voiced by Bloom and Chesney-Lind (2007), is based on the increasing imprisonment of impoverished minority women for involvement in drug-related crime. This situation, in conjunction with the media's showcasing of isolated episodes of girls' and women's violence and the judicial system's meting out of unduly harsh punishments, can be viewed as a counterreaction to women's successes in other areas of social life.

Oppression through a Feminist Lens

A denial of women's experiences of oppression is at the heart of the setbacks to women's advancing equality. Men and some women who deny women's experiences in this manner argue that since women (and girls) have now achieved equality, they should not request special consideration on the basis of gender. In the courtroom sentencing and correctional design, accordingly, women's bid for equality often is carried out through ever-increasingly harsh treatment. The structural and interpersonal nature of women's oppression is thus ignored. Feminist criminology has as its ultimate goal the exposure of what Dominelli (2002) refers to as "false equality traps" and what Bloom and Chesney-Lind (2007) call "equality with a vengeance." As explained by Bloom and Chesney-Lind:

> The differential treatment of women in sentencing and prison programming was challenged by an emerging "parity" perspective during the 1970s. As a result of prisoner rights' litigation based on the parity model . . . women offenders are being swept up in a system that seems bent on treating women "equally." This equity orientation translated into treatment of women prisoners as if they were men. (p. 556)

Although the victims of such strategies are often poor and minority females in trouble with the law, such strategies have been used in the workplace as well to the detriment of many women. In divorce court, the emphasis on parity in parenting has been especially hard on women due to their lack of economic resources. The Power and Control Wheel, discussed in Chapter 9, graphically illustrates the basic forms of oppression that are used in violent situations to intimidate and control women in partnerships. Use of male privilege, isolation, emotional abuse, threats, and economic abuse are some of these forms. Feminist criminology confronts such systemic oppression through making its existence known and through identifying the various strategies that are used to put a person or group in a subordinate position on the basis of gender, race, and/or class.

For a closer look at the research on oppression, we turn to the writings of Dominelli (2003), Mullaly (2002), van Wormer (2004), and van Soest (2008). Common to all these writings is the belief that a clear understanding of oppression and power relations must inform the treatment of girls and women in the system. As defined by black feminist author bell hooks (1984), oppression is the "absence of choices" (p. 5). Oppression is seen as characterized by power imbalances within a wider social system that reinforces the powerlessness of certain groups. The four kinds of oppression that we have singled out from the anti-oppression literature are:

- Psychological oppression—operates at the interpersonal level with negative consequences for one's self-identity and sense of control over one's environment;
- Social oppression—is based on divisions of class, ethnicity, race, gender, and age;
- Economic oppression—stems from the limits on the resources available to people, who are thereby excluded from full participation in the society;
- Political oppression—involves domination by a powerful group of a less powerful group.

An outstanding example of the existence of all four forms of oppression is revealed in Jody Miller's (2008) ethnographic research on violence against urban African American girls. In the economically and politically disadvantaged community she studied, virtually all the young women reported being pressured or coerced sexually; some had experienced gang rape. The absence of police or community support for such victims was a major finding. One of the most disheartening facts revealed in Miller's analysis was the extent to which young women adhered to ideologies that held female victims accountable for male violence.

Feminist criminologists are especially cognizant of those aspects of oppression that are related to the institution of justice. Concerning girls in the juvenile justice system, for example, Chesney-Lind and Pasko (2003) describe patterns of offending in girls from socially and economically deprived backgrounds who were psychologically traumatized by personal violence and who are now confined in residential treatment. These girls may have come to the attention of the authorities through running away, their drug involvement, or through involvement in prostitution on the streets. Personal and structural oppressions thus come together in the backgrounds of such individuals.

FEMINIST THEORIES

Feminist perspectives historically, as stated above, have been peripheral to the study of crime and treatment within the justice system (Parker and Reckdenwald, 2008). For example, few attempts to identify "what works" in the crime prevention and offender rehabilitation research specifically addressed gender. The extent to which correctional organizations, including work roles, are gendered generally has been ignored as well. Even as some programs for female offenders are being designed with girls and women's special needs in mind, workers within the system are embedded in organizational structures that reflect the norms of the prevailing gender-stratified society. Therefore, reflecting societal norms, many mainstream criminologists and criminal justice practitioners have yet to appreciate the significance of feminism's contributions. To address this oversight, this section reviews some of the major feminist teachings from the past to the present time.

The first point to make about feminism is that there is not one feminism but many feminisms. Feminism, in fact, consists of a collection of different theoretical perspectives, each explaining the oppression of women in a different way. We start with a historical description of the three leading waves of feminism. Then we differentiate among the various schools of thought within contemporary schools of thought.

The first feminist movement was born in 1848 at the Seneca Falls Convention, when women demanded the right to vote. Its suffrage emphasis culminated when the Nineteenth Amendment to the Constitution was ratified in 1919. The second feminist movement began in the 1960s. It was sparked by the Equal Pay Act of 1963, which required equal pay for equal work, and Title VII of the Civil Rights Act of 1964, which applied to wages as well as hiring and promotions. Another major influence in the birth of the second feminist movement was the publication of Betty Friedan's groundbreaking *The Feminine Mystique* (2001/orig. 1963). Friedan issued a call for housewives to seek their own identity through the development of themselves as full human beings.

Heidensohn (2000) differentiates the first two waves of feminism in the United Kingdom in terms of a crusade in the Victorian era against state regulation of women (allowing for the detention of prostitutes who had venereal disease), and an attempt in modern times to move the issue of victimization out of private hands and into the public arena of law enforcement. "It is not hard," she states, "to see the parallels between 'vice' in relation to first wave feminism and 'violence' in the history of the second wave" (p. 27). A number of varieties of feminism evolved in the 1970s and 1980s, with much overlap between them—for example, liberal feminism, radical feminism, postmodernism, and so on. We describe these developments in the sections below. Feminist criminology also came of age during this time of political activism and social change (Chesney-Lind, 2006). This body of scholarship exists today, according to Chesney-Lind, as a mature field within a political landscape characterized by the politics of conservatism and backlash.

Emerging in the 1980s and 1990s, the third wave of the women's movement challenged the idea that poor women, women of color, and lesbians share the same problems as white middle-class women or similarly located poor men, men of color, or gay men (Price and Sokoloff, 2004, p. 3). The privileging of white, middle-class female voices is a familiar rebuttal to the pronouncements of movers and shakers from the second wave. **Third-wave feminists**, who are also called *women of color feminists*, *womanists*, and *critical race feminists*, object to white feminists defining "women's issues" from their own standpoint without including women of color and third-world concerns. They also object to the antiracist theory that presumes that racial and ethnic minority women's experiences are the same as those of their male counterparts. These modern-day feminist theorists focus on the significant roles that sexism, racism, class bias, sexual orientation, age, and other forms of socially structured inequality have in women's lives. Central to their approach is the notion of **intersectionalities** which calls our attention to the interlocking sites of oppression inherent in the categories of race, ethnicity, class, gender, sexuality, and age. Third-wave feminism helps clarify not only those behaviors of women defined as criminal but also the many crimes against women. This approach makes clear the need to understand issues of social justice in evaluating the criminalization of women (Price and Sokoloff, 2004, p. 3). Furthermore, this form of feminist theory seeks ways for men and women to work together to eliminate racism, sexism, and class privilege. For example, bell hooks (1984), in the following passage, attacks what she perceives as the antimale stance of the early radical feminists:

> They were not eager to call attention to the fact that men do not share a common social status; that patriarchy does not negate the existence of class and race privilege or exploitation; that all men do not benefit equally from sexism. They did not want to acknowledge that bourgeois white women, though often victimized by sexism, have more power and privilege, are less likely to be exploited or oppressed, than poor, uneducated, non-white males. (p. 68)

These feminist movements, especially in the second and third formulations, have resulted in at least seven main expressions of feminist theory that are relevant to criminal justice. These are: liberal feminism, radical feminism, socialist feminism, Marxist feminism, postmodern feminism, black feminism, and Latina feminism.

Liberal Feminism

Liberal feminism, or egalitarianism, calls for women's equality of opportunity and freedom of choice. Burke (2005) traces liberal feminism to the eighteenth- and nineteenth-century social ideals of liberty and equality. Liberal feminists look to legislation to ensure the rights of women and changes in socialization practices so that children do not grow up accepting of an unequal status (Payne, 2005).

In 1972, Congress passed the Equal Rights Amendment (ERA). In the campaign to ratify it, many women were mobilized into activism, and liberal feminists were introduced to the political mainstream. However, the defeat of the ERA in 1982 was associated with a conservative backlash during which rights previously won by feminists, including affirmative action and legal abortion, were challenged (Rollins, 1996). Despite this defeat, we owe a debt to the liberal feminist movement for the extensive legislation that was enacted as a result of the activities of its members. This perspective, however, is criticized for its reluctance to confront deep-rooted gender inequality as well as its failure to acknowledge the relevance of race (Burke, 2005; Dominelli, 2002).

Radical Feminism

Radical feminists view masculine power and privilege as the root cause of all social inequality. The most important relations in any society, according to radical feminists, are found in patriarchy, a social system which is maintained through masculine control of labor, finance, and the sexuality of women (Burke, 2005).

In common with liberal feminism, proponents of the radical school argue that greater levels of inequality may lead to an elevated risk of domestic assault and homicide by placing women at a structural disadvantage (Vieraitis, Britto, and Kovandzic, 2007). In contrast with liberal feminism, this orientation focuses much more on women's oppression, while it values and even celebrates the differences between men and women (Payne, 2005). A major contribution has been the focus on victims' rights and on the prevalence of sexual violence toward women. Through the extensive documentation and grass-roots activism provided by members of this group, the national silence on the role of violence in girls' and women's lives was broken. The naming of the types and dimensions of female victimization had a significant impact on public policy (Chesney-Lind, 2006). Radical feminism has been criticized, however, for its **essentialism**, or the belief that all men are the same, as are all women (Payne, 2005).

Marxist Feminism

Marxist feminists argue that as private property evolved, males dominated all social institutions. Proponents of this belief system emphasize women's oppression as arising from their structured inequality in society (Payne, 2005). From this perspective, gender and class inequalities are viewed as closely related.

According to Marxist ideology, capitalism profits from the low-wage work of women in factories and corporations, both in the United States and elsewhere. Under capitalism, women who do not work are seen as confined in the home to domestic slavery, a form of exploitation that parallels the exploitation of the women workers.

Marxist feminists have been criticized for their overuse of economic explanations of women's opportunity to the neglect of the effect of family relationships and socialization factors (Burke, 2005). The lack of scientific proof for Marxist assumptions is another major criticism of this belief system. To challenge this argument, Vieraitis Britto, and Kovandzic. (2007) examined female homicide victimization data across counties in the United States. Their finding that counties with the highest levels of poverty had the highest homicide rates lends some support to Marxist feminist theory. Relevant to criminology, Marxist feminists explain domestic violence against women in part as related to their lack of access to resources and their relationships with men who are frustrated because of their own low economic standing (Littlefield, 2003).

Socialist Feminism

Socialist feminists, in contrast to other feminists, give neither class nor gender the highest priority. Instead, socialist feminists view both class and gender relations as equal, as they interact with and reinforce each other in society. They thus offer a synthesis of the radical and Marxist feminist schools of thought. It is important, as Dominelli (2002) asserts, to maintain a perspective that emphasizes the gendered nature of human relations that divides men and women, while also attending to other forms of oppression and differences that divide women from each other. To understand class, socialist feminists argue, it is necessary to recognize how class is structured by gender, and understanding gender requires that one see how it is structured by class.

Proponents of this position advocate for equal work opportunities as well as special provisions such as child care arrangements for employees (Barak, Leighton, and Flavin, 2006). Relevant to women's work in the criminal justice professions, socialist feminism clarifies how women tend to become excluded from the highest-paying jobs and marginalized within the professional ranks due to male dominance and bonding.

Postmodern Feminism

Postmodern feminists criticize other feminists for assuming that women are a "clearly defined and uncontroversially given interest group" (Smart, 1995, p. 10). While positivist feminists, as well as other modernists, claim that the truth can be determined, providing all agree on responsible ways of going about it, **postmodern feminism** argues for multiple truths that take contexts into account .

Postmodern feminists also question whether scientific claims are provable and reject the idea that there is a universal definition of justice true for all people all of the time. Feminists who view society through a postmodernist lens are more inclined to focus attention on power relations rather than patriarchy as their frame of reference (Moore, 2007). They emphasize the importance of alternative discourses and accounts, which frequently take the form of examining the effects of language and symbolic representation. Postmodernist perspectives are criticized for their neglect of oppression in society and their undermining of feminist notions of solidarity and collective organizing against injustice (Dominelli, 2002). A contribution to criminology is the focus on deriving knowledge from qualitative data such as personal narratives of women in the correctional system.

Black Feminism

Black Feminist Thought by Patricia Collins (2000) articulates the African American feminist position. Social change will only come, argues Collins, when the consciousness of individuals is raised—consciousness about the domination of intersecting oppressions. The historical structure of these interlocking oppressions must be acknowledged in order to transform the institutions of domination for the people's empowerment.

Hillary Potter (2006) utilizes a black feminist criminological framework that focuses on intimate-partner violence experiences of African American women. Following Collins' (2000) conceptualization of critical race theory, Potter examines women's victimization from a combined gendered and racialized standpoint.

Many African Americans concerned with the treatment of women in society prefer the term *womanism* to *feminism*. Womanism, to Littlefield (2003), "is an emergent theoretical perspective that reforms and expands mainstream feminist theory to incorporate racial and cultural differences, with a particular focus on African American women" (p. 4). Womanism, according to Littlefield, focuses on three key themes: the interlocking nature of multiple oppressions, the meaning of self-determinism for African American women, and the importance of naming and claiming African American women's culture. Moreover, writers from this school emphasize the key role that personal spirituality and religion play in African American women's cultural and personal empowerment.

The womanist and black feminist perspectives have implications for criminal justice scholars and practitioners in providing a basis for empowerment-oriented practice with racial and ethnic minorities. In bringing our attention to the intersection of race, gender, and class, African American theorists help us to recognize the political backlash is not directed at women alone but that the oppression played out in mass incarceration has had serious repercussions for black girls and women. The message for feminist criminologists is clear—to focus on only one aspect of oppression (such as gender) to the neglect of the others is to miss a vital part of the equation.

Latina Feminism

In 1972, Mirta Vidal wrote in "Chicanas Speak Out: Women: New Voice of La Raza," a chapter in *Feminism and Socialism*, that when Chicano men talk about maintaining *la familia* and the cultural heritage of *la raza*, they are in fact talking about keeping women in the kitchen, and pregnant. The real unity of men and women, as Vidal argued, is the unity forged in the course of struggle against their joint oppression: "It is by supporting, rather than opposing, the struggles of women, that Chicanos and Chicanas can genuinely unite" (p. 32).

The impact of ethnicity, gender, and class are inextricably linked in the life of the Mexican American woman. Her socioeconomic class as a Spanish-speaking, low-income Chicana woman determines her political and social position. In this way, her challenges differ from those of poor African American women and Anglo white lower-class women.

Telling to Live: Latina Feminist Testimonios is a more recent anthology selected and oganized by the Latina Feminist Group (2001). Part I of this book is entitled "Genealogies of Empowerment" and includes vignettes and personal narratives of a diverse group of Latina women, for example, a Spanish-speaking Jewish woman, an academic, and a working-class Puerto Rican. A major theme is empowerment and the mapping of individual paths to achievement despite historical displacement. Collectively, these writers bear witness to social injustice related to social barriers and those derived from gender constraints.

Relevant to criminal justice, Lorraine Gutiérrez and Edith Lewis's (1999) edited volume *Empowering Women of Color* provides the foundation for a model of empowering practice with Latina women. The two major components for such work are an understanding of power and powerlessness, and the importance of the development of a sense of self-efficacy in conjunction with a connectedness to social networks. Organizations must be transformed so that they are primarily accountable to the communities they serve.

The Rise of Feminist Criminology

The criminal justice system is a system built on human tragedy. The tragedy is found in the personal stories and case histories of girls and women who, like the William Faulkner women, have had to "endure and then endure, without rhyme or reason or hope" (1936, p. 59). The stories and case histories tell of victimization, of personal crime and addiction, and of falling in the web of too-harsh sentencing practices—and also of survival.

For many who have come to earn the unfortunate label of "female offender," their suffering began long before they got into trouble with the law. Things might have been so bad for some, in fact, that getting caught could almost be seen as a blessing, a turning point in their lives. Perhaps there was an encounter with someone in the system who cared or perhaps they were placed in an innovative program designed with gender in mind. This brings us to some remarkable stories of women on the other side of the law (from the offenders), women who went into corrections to reform the system and to help others reach their potential—among them prison wardens, probation officers, and lawyers. We are referring here to women who have served other women, working to empower others even as they themselves have been empowered.

Reform can come as well through writing. In the field of criminal justice, much credit goes to feminist criminologists who through their prolific writings have inspired reform and new ways of thinking about gender and crime. Throughout the literature, personal narratives are corroborated through empirical research and/or government data. Both forms of scholarship are consistent with feminist methodology and the goals of effecting social change. Because of the policy implications, Chesney-Lind (2006) refers to this body of research emerging from feminist criminology as an activist scholarship.

Contemporary forms of feminist criminology draw on parts or all of the traditions described above. For the feminist criminologist, as for other feminists, enabling women to tell their stories and to speak of their experiences is integral to women's ways of gathering information and understanding the world (Dominelli, 2002). This is not to the neglect of empirical research, however, or the use of statistical data from government sources such as Uniform Crime Reports. Feminist scholars, however, have insisted on research grounded in the voices of women—women, for example, who have experienced domestic violence first-hand or who have suffered the pains of imprisonment. Academic attention has also been directed toward the career paths of professional workers in the field of criminal justice and obstacles that they have encountered along the way.

These feminist researcher-activists are rightly credited with providing a rich body of research concerning girls' and women's unique pathways to crime and the need for gender-based programming. As with any reform, some of the developments have had unintended consequences, however. Zero tolerance laws for domestic violence, strongly advocated by the feminist movement, paradoxically have now resulted in a huge increase in the arrests of girls and women (see Chapter 9).

Meanwhile, media hype portraying young women as masculinized and violent, for example, in popular books such as *See Jane Hit: Why Girls Are Growing More Violent and What We Can Do About It* (Garbarino, 2007), have helped create an atmosphere in which harsh punishments are meted out to girls for relatively minor offenses. Feminist criminologists increasingly are concerned about the antifeminist backlash, a backlash that is even evidenced in many women's reluctance to identify with the term *feminist*.

Backlash to the Women's Movement

A correlation between women's liberation and crime, known as emancipation theory, as postulated by Freda Adler (1975) in her bestselling book *Sisters in Crime,* was widely accepted when it appeared, perhaps because the women's movement was so new. People didn't know what to expect. The thesis was that now that women had the same opportunities as men to commit violent crimes, they would do so. Heidensohn (2000) refers to this as the "liberation leads to violence thesis" (p. 41), an explanation that did not gain currency on the eastern side of the Atlantic. While British writers looked to economic marginalization as a key factor in female crime, some American criminologists and the media now viewed women as masculinized in their lawbreaking behavior. Their criminality was seen as an indirect result of the achievements of their feminist sisters.

Feminist criminologists shortly became outraged with this faulty proposition. Drawing on criminal justice statistics, they could easily document that the supposed increase in female violence had not materialized. Those women in trouble with the law, besides, were far from feminists, but rather they represented poor and uneducated groups who were often unemployed (Muraskin, 2007). A crackdown on welfare fraud in the 1970s had led to an increase in arrests of women for fraud. Generally, most arrests as before were for prostitution and shoplifting. Still, the media in the 1970s used the seemingly scholarly work of Adler to discredit the women's movement and to misrepresent the kinds of crimes that women were committing. We can consider this discrediting through false claims of feminist-inspired crime as the first antifeminist backlash, as far as criminal justice is concerned.

Following several decades during which little was said on the topic, another backlash against the women's movement has developed. Perhaps inevitably, the myth of the "liberated female criminal" has surfaced again. This rebounding of an unsubstantiated claim coincides with the recent harsh treatment of women in the courts of law, in both civil (child custody) and criminal litigation. The justification for rulings against women in many such cases is that women are equal now, and as equals they can no longer expect special consideration. The media have both reflected and promoted this shift in perspective.

Exaggerating feminist gains is a central feature of antifeminist men's attack (Dominelli, 2002). This is seen in fathers' rights groups, often comprised of men desiring more agreeable child custody arrangements following a divorce. These men's wives, stepmothers to the children, are often active spokespersons for these groups as well. These groups actively work in Canada, the UK, and the United States with media outlets and local legislators in an attempt to get the laws changed to their advantage.

This backlash can be viewed as well among the fervent antiabortionists for whom religion and politics are merged. It can also be seen in the sharply increased rate of incarceration of women, especially poor and minority, throughout the 1990s, despite a significant decline in violent offenses committed by women. Furthermore, it can be seen in the passing of laws by various jurisdictions across the United States that define pregnant women on drugs as criminals alleged to be delivering controlled substances to their unborn child. Finally, this ongoing backlash is viewed through the periodic reemergence of the myth that a new and more dangerous type of female criminal has come on the scene as a result of the women's movement (Price and Sokoloff, 2004, p. 5). When equality is construed as sameness, razor wire is strung around women's prisons, resources go to security instead of job training programs and treatment, and curtains, rugs, and many feminine items are removed from the premises (Morton, 2007). Media depictions of wild, bad girls and women as serial killers have fueled concerns that women are as dangerous as men and have increased legal sanctions holding offending women to a male standard. Dual arrests are now replacing arrests of the main perpetrator in domestic violence incidents reported to the police. These issues are explored in Chapters 6 and 9.

THE DEVELOPMENT OF GENDER-SPECIFIC PROGRAMMING

Consistent with most feminist perspectives of the second and third waves is the emphasis on gender and gender relations. To understand gender relations, it is necessary to examine both the structures of relationships, which involve the enduring and expected patterns of behavior that constrain practices, and the agency of individuals in learning, accommodating, navigating, and resisting these structures. Agency itself is made up of both social practices and behaviors and the configurations of gender identity that women bring to these activities. In some cases, the two correspond, as when women draw from a repertoire of behaviors in order to enact or demonstrate their gender identity; yet the relationship between gendered social practices and gender identities is sometimes much more complex (Miller and Mullins, 2006, p. 11).

We have developmental psychologist Carol Gilligan (1982) to thank for bringing researchers' attention to fundamental gender differences in moral development. Until the time of Gilligan's writing, discourse on moral development was couched in terms of formal, abstract, and male-centered concepts. Through her research on young women and their decision making, Gilligan concluded that female values centered around the development of personal and caring relationships rather than the inculcation of an ethic of justice. Gilligan argued that female voices needed to be heard and that women's belief systems and values were in no way inferior or less mature than those of men. Personal growth for the woman, as demonstrated in Gilligan's findings, involved accepting responsibility for making her own decisions. Gilligan's theoretical model has been criticized by some feminists for its "difference feminism"—its emphasis on male–female psychological differences as well as the claim that women's decisions are not based on a notion of justice.

The writings of influential criminologists today who are concerned with the obvious differences in the pathways to crime between girls and boys echo the work of Carol Gilligan.

Drawing on Gilligan's "different voice" and relational constructs, such researchers as Frances Heidensohn have investigated differences in the life course experiences in the backgrounds of male and female juvenile and adult offenders. Extensive research has been done documenting the participation of girls in gangs and on the role of physical and sexual abuse starting a girl on a path to crime.

The work of Bloom, Owen, and Covington (2003), for example, has been at the helm of the movement to shape gender-responsive theory and programming for girls and women in the criminal justice system. According to these writers, the first step is to understand gender-based characteristics and be familiar with the specific life factors that shape patterns of offending. Female offenders are more likely than their male counterparts not only to have experienced childhood and adulthood abuse but also to have distinctive physical and mental health needs. When arrested, they were often the primary caretakers of their children and posed little danger to the community.

Running away and alcohol and drug use are often intervening variables in the troubled family history of a juvenile offender. Undeniably, trauma is a key pathway to offending, especially for white girls and women. Temptations from the street more often bring African American and Latina girls into juvenile facilities and prison, according to self-reporting surveys. Some studies of crack users, reported by Belknap (2007), however, indicated that about half of them started using it in response to one or more traumatic experiences. These pathway models, as Belknap suggests, are built on some of the most useful data regarding understanding girls' and women's entries into delinquency and crime.

The National Institute of Corrections, the center of correctional learning and training, has developed a case management model for women who are incarcerated or under probation/parole supervision. This model evolved from gender-informed, evidence-based practices designed to reduce recidivism and enhance the lives of women and is based on the gender-responsive formulation as articulated by Bloom, Owen, and Covington (2003). According to the National Institute of Corrections, to help offenders become productive citizens, "we must revisit some of our efforts and acknowledge that gender makes a difference" (Sydney, 2005, p.1). The Institute makes the following recommendations for effective gender-responsiveness:

- Acknowledge and accommodate differences between men and women.
- Assess women's risk levels, needs, and strengths and construct supervision case plans accordingly.
- Acknowledge the different pathways through which women enter the community corrections system.
- Recognize the likelihood that women offenders have a significant history of victimization.
- Build on women's strengths and values, including recognizing that relationships are important to women.
- Acknowledge and accommodate the likelihood that women are primary caregivers to a child or other dependents (Sydney, p. 3).

In juvenile corrections, increasing attention is being paid to the specific needs of adolescent girls and innovative programming is being offered across the states. Another significant development is the thrust to provide gender-specific programming for female offenders, especially for juvenile offenders, in correctional institutions and in community correctional programs. The federal government's focus on gender-appropriate treatment for girls is facilitated by the current Juvenile Justice and Delinquency Prevention Act, which was reauthorized in 2002. This act requires that state plans provide needed gender-specific services for the prevention and treatment of juvenile delinquency, and provides substantial funding for such programming (Sherman, 2005).

To summarize the discussion so far, the evidence presented of male–female gender differences in behavior and values argues for specialized treatment tailored for girls' and women's special needs. A major challenge to implementing gender-responsive programming is the scope of the needed changes; so many areas within community corrections and in the larger culture need to be addressed that implementation appears overwhelming (Sydney).

Laws Defining Women's Place

The oppression of women in a male-dominated society can be clearly seen through examining the laws of that society. Taking the United States as an example, history reveals that the men who wrote and interpreted the law saw that it was necessary to secure the safety of women to protect the family and the community. Leo Kanowitz (1973) aptly expressed this position: "That God designed the sexes to occupy different spheres of action, and that it belonged to men to make, apply, and execute the laws, was regarded as an almost axiomatic truth" (p. 44). The creators of the law, then, made certain that women could enter certain areas of life only under carefully controlled circumstances. This means of protecting womanhood and motherhood sought by legislators and judges actually harmed women by restricting their ability to work and earn a living on an equal basis with men. Such protections—protecting women from danger, for example—have made having careers in criminal justice especially difficult for women (Belknap, 2007, p. 376).

This belief that women had to be protected from the sordid nature of life led to their being excluded from jury duty. In 1879, the U.S. Supreme Court lent its support to the common-law exclusion by deciding that states had the constitutional right to limit jury duty to men only. The Civil Rights Act of 1957 gave women the right to serve on federal juries, but some states continued to impose restrictions. Despite the 1975 U.S. Supreme Court decision in *Taylor v. Louisiana* that women could not be excluded from jury duty because of sex, in many states when it came to the process of voir dire to choose a jury, women were often readily dismissed (Belknap, 2007, p. 440).

The law that was quick to protect the proper woman was equally quick to punish women who were offenders. The Muncy Act of Pennsylvania is an example of discriminatory legislation that was developed to punish women offenders. This act stated that any female pleading guilty to or convicted of a crime punishable by imprisonment of one year or more "must" be sentenced to the state prison for women and that her sentence "shall be merely a general one" and the court "shall not fix or limit the duration thereof" (Kanowitz, 1969, p. 59).

Eventually, as with those prohibiting women on juries, laws similar to the Muncy Act were declared unconstitutional. In *Commonwealth v. Daniel*, Jane Daniel was convicted in Pennsylvania of robbery, an offense that carried a maximum sentence of ten years. After sentencing her to one to four years in the county prison, the judge brought Daniel back to court for resentencing under the Muncy Act, which required an indeterminate term of up to ten years at the state prison for women. Daniel won her appeal to the Pennsylvania Supreme Court in a precedent-setting case, and the Muncy Act was declared unconstitutional (*Commonwealth v. Daniel*,1968).

In *State v. Costello*, Mary A. Costello successfully argued that her constitutional right to equal protection under the Fourteenth Amendment had been violated when she received an indeterminate sentence of not more than five years for pleading guilty to a gambling offense. Under New Jersey law, a man convicted of a similar offense would have received a sentence of not more than two years and not less than one year. The New Jersey Supreme Court ruled: "These distinctions, in essence, form the basis of defendant's claim of denial of equal protection because of discrimination on the basis of sex" (*State v. Costello*, 1971).

Although some women, as these cases testify, received harsher punishments than did men, there was a parallel tradition of paternalism that affected women who presented an image of helplessness when prosecuted for misdemeanors and felonies, including homicide. White women of a certain class and background were usually given lighter sentences than men as part of a tradition of chivalry. Such a privilege was never accorded to black women, however, who could expect to be punished to the full extent of the law. And even when individual white women did benefit by preferential treatment, the attitude that they were "frail" and "nobler" than men was demeaning in its own way (Belknap, 2007). The paternalism was consistent with restrictions on women in other areas. This brings us to a consideration of legislation pertaining to women's employment.

As is widely known in feminist circles, sex was added as a protected class to the 1964 Civil Rights Act by a white Southerner in an effort to defeat its passage, since giving women equal rights was not something that was taken seriously at that time. The effort failed and women won rights that went largely unnoticed until some years later.

In recent years, employment lawsuits are filed on the basis of Title VII, a 1972 amendment of the Civil Rights Act, to ensure equal employment opportunities. Oddly enough, as Belknap indicates, the resulting legislation has more often benefited males who have sued on the basis of sex discrimination. Yet the bulk of the discrimination that takes place is against females. A special problem with this legislation is that lawsuits must be based either on race or sex; this makes it difficult for women of color whose discrimination may come from their membership in both groups. In any case, passage of laws can only go so far to ensure full acceptance of women in male-dominated professions; their work can always be undermined where their presence is resented, and if they ever file a sex discrimination claim with an organization such as the Equal Employment Opportunity Commission, future employment in that particular profession becomes problematic.

SEXUAL HARASSMENT OF WOMEN IN CRIMINAL JUSTICE INSTITUTIONS

Title IX was enacted into federal law to outlaw sex discrimination in education. This included sexual harassment. Yet, as Brown, Chesney-Lind, and Stein (2007) indicate, our nation's schools are riddled with sexual or gender-based harassment. Many of these behaviors are illegal. Yet, because of the recent anti-bullying efforts, as Brown et al. indicate, sometimes egregious behaviors are framed as bullying, a gender-neutral categorization.

The **sexual harassment of women** emerged as a critically important issue in the 1980s and 1990s. Contributing to the attention given to sexual harassment is the number of notorious cases catapulting sexual harassment onto the front pages of newspapers and magazines and onto television news programs. Sportswriter Lisa Olsen claimed that she was sexually harassed by players on the New England Patriots football team, who displayed their body parts in close proximity to her face while she attempted to conduct interviews in the players' locker room (Webb, 1994, p. 4). Dr. Frances Conley, a well-known neurosurgeon, left her position at Stanford University because of "ongoing verbal and physical harassment by her fellow surgeons" (Webb, 1994, p. 4). Three months later, the nation watched as law professor Anita Hill accused Supreme Court nominee Clarence Thomas of creating a hostile working environment laden with inappropriate sexual overtones. The alleged conduct occurred when they both worked for the Equal

Employment Opportunity Commission in the 1980s (Webb, 1994, p. 4). Three weeks before the Thomas and Hill hearing, the military's biggest sex scandal unfolded, involving aviators at the Navy's annual Tailhook Association Convention (Douglas, 2007). The convention generated nearly 150 complaints of harassment. The legacy of Tailhook still exists, but in the barracks rather than in the convention hall. The Veterans Association, in an extensive study, found that 30 percent of female veterans had been victims of sexual assault; sexual harassment in the military is rampant (Douglas, 2007).

The National Advisory Council on Women's Education Programs has categorized sexual harassment into five levels:

1. The first level includes generalized sexual remarks and behavior that are directed at a person because of his or her gender, rather than designed to elicit sexual activity. Examples might include comments about women's supposedly lesser cognitive abilities and their mythical propensity to be vindictive, jealous, and seductive.
2. The second level includes situations that involve actual sexual references. What distinguishes this level from the first level is the introduction of the request for sexual encounters, which is often accompanied by some sort of touching. These situations do not need to be blatantly offensive, just inappropriate, and take place where the woman is the subordinate and the man is the superior.
3. The third level includes a solicitation for sex and the promise of some reward. Explicit threats may be absent, but the harasser uses some kind of organizational or institutional authority to "make payment" for a sexual favor.
4. In the fourth level, the notion of punishment is introduced for failure to comply with the request for sexual favors. This is generally thought of as the quintessential type of sexual harassment and is illustrated by a failing grade in class, a negative job performance review, or dismissal from work.
5. The final type includes such extreme behaviors as indecent exposure, gross sexual imposition, and outright sexual assaults. Probably the least common type of sexual harassment, this behavior is usually the most devastating to victims (Erez and Tontodonato, 1995, pp. 231–235).

Sexual violence exists on a continuum, with sexual harassment at the lower end. The impact can be long-lasting, however, especially in cases where such harassment is almost a daily occurrence. To determine how widespread such unwanted behaviors are in society, researchers from the University of Kentucky (2008) conducted a survey of 600 girls aged 12–18. They found that 90 percent of the respondents reported experiencing sexual harassment at least once. Specifically, 67 percent of girls reported receiving unwanted romantic attention and 62 percent were exposed to demeaning gender-related comments. Whites reported more harassment than did girls of other races, and girls of lower socioeconomic status reported the most instances of this behavior.

Through in-depth interviews with 24 female officers in the Midwest, Cara Rabe-Hemp (2008) found that although the strength of "the all boys' club" in policing had declined from the early years, women still had to always be on guard to maintain whatever acceptance they personally had earned. She summarizes her findings in these words:

While the duration and the form varied widely, all female officers interviewed identified personal instances of sexual harassment, discrimination, or disrespect that impeded their successes and acceptance in police work. Surprisingly, most participants suggested the serious obstacles they faced, such as physical assault and obstacles to promotion, had occurred early in their careers and had desisted after several years experience; often to re-surface following agency or officer changes. Rather than being a level of achievement or an obstacle overcome, female officers reported acceptance by the police culture was constantly negotiated and re-negotiated throughout their careers, underscoring the need for additional research which analyzes the continuum of female officers' careers to determine the pattern of the onset and desistance of resistance. (p. 165)

Women who are lawyers, as well as those who are probation, parole, or correctional officers, also face discrimination and sexual harassment. It was a long uphill battle for women to be accepted into law school, then to find jobs as lawyers and to be appointed as judges, and, more recently, to be employed in the most desirable law firms and legal positions. Women who enter the field of corrections also have found discriminatory barriers placed before them and, on overcoming these barriers, have faced sexual harassment in one form or another. It is these forms of sexual harassment that have prevented probation and parole officers from achieving supervisory positions or being appointed directors of agencies and that have limited the upward mobility of women in correctional institutions. The antiwoman sentiment that is often present in correctional institutions for men is analyzed in considerable depth by Dana Britton (2003) in her organizational study *At Work in the Iron Cage: The prison as gendered organization.* Similarly, Jurik (2007) found that from a social and career standpoint, this working environment held some unique challenges for women, whether or not they conformed to the feminine stereotype. Because of gender pressures on female officers, women who seek to advance in the system reported that they had to try to strike a balance between a series of countervailing negative sex role stereotypes. Even when successful, the stress that they experienced in accommodating to this predominantly male work environment was substantial.

GENDER, CLASS, AND RACE AND WOMEN IN THE CRIMINAL JUSTICE SYSTEM

Women grow up in a social context of domination and control by males. In this patriarchal society, troublesome females are quickly subjected to various forms of discrimination, exploitation, and criminalization. These forms of oppression are expressions of sexism, racism, and classism. The race discussion in this section also includes ethnicity.

An understanding of the class-race-gender interactionist configuration is essential to a study of the criminal justice system. Feminist theory is increasingly committed to examining how factors such as racism, classism, sexism, and heterosexism are useful for understanding gender differences and discrimination dynamics (Belknap, 2007). Spelman accused some feminists of ignoring racial, class, ethnic, religious, and cultural differences among women. It is through examining these factors, according to Spelman, that oppression against women can be more clearly grasped and understood (Spelman, 1989). This perspective suggests that discrimination based on gender, class, and race involves interlocking forms of oppression and that the whole is greater than the sum of the parts. In other words, each minority category to which a woman belongs reinforces the others to the extent that the effect is multiplicative, not merely additive. "To fully understand the interface between patriarchal social control mechanisms and criminal justice in the United States," Chesney-Lind (2006) suggests, "we must center our analysis on the race/gender/punishment nexus" (p. 10).

The female offenders who are incarcerated in the juvenile justice system are often victims of "multiple marginality" because their gender, class, and race have placed them at the economic periphery of society (Chesney-Lind and Pasko, 2003). Labeling the troubled girl a delinquent takes place in a world, Chesney-Lind (2006) charges, where gender still shapes the lives of young people in very powerful ways; the social context of this world is not fair to women and girls, especially to those of color and those with low incomes. The detention rates of African American girls have increased more rapidly than the rates for either white girls or boys.

Gender, class, and race are the focus of attention in this text. Yet, sexuality cannot be ignored and, at times, will be included with gender, class, and race. Culture also becomes a critical component in understanding the criminal justice system's resistance to women's pursuing a police career, to women lawyers gaining employment at leading law firms, and to women correctional officers finding acceptance in prisons for men.

An examination of the gender, class, race, and sexuality literature reveals six common themes. First, these factors are contextual. They undergo change as part of the emergence of new political, economic, and ideological processes, events, and trends. Second, gender, race, class, and sexuality are socially constructed. The meaning of these social constructs develops out of group struggles over socially desired resources. Third, and perhaps most important, gender, class, race, and sexuality are power relationships that are historically specific and socially constructed hierarchies of domination. They are power hierarchies in which one group (males) exerts control over another (females), securing a position of dominance and assuming control over such material and nonmaterial resources as income, wealth, and access to health care and education. Fourth, gender, class, race, and sexuality have meaning at the micro level of individuals' lives as well as at the macro level of community and social institutions. Understanding the significance of these constructs requires grasping the meaning in both contexts. Fifth, gender, class, race, and sexuality simultaneously exist in every social situation. This fact suggests that almost everyone experiences both dominant and subordinate positions at some time and that, therefore, there are no pure oppressors or oppressed in the United States or other industrial nations. Finally, gender, race, class, and sexuality scholarship consistently emphasizes the interdependence of knowledge and activism. This process is dynamic, continually moving from understanding oppression to seeking social change and social justice.

THE EMPOWERMENT PERSPECTIVE

In April 2008, the international journal *Feminist Criminology* devoted the issue to the antifeminist backlash. This contribution was inspired by the challenge of sustaining the gains of second-wave feminism in the face of neoconservative political developments across the globe. Two examples highlighted in the issue are: the taking of equality measures to extremes in the courtroom, and the rising influence of the international men's rights movement in shaping family violence and child custody laws.

Sociological research and theory on feminism have "rediscovered" an emphasis on human agency. The term **human agency**, or **agency**, recognizes the fact that women not only are acted upon by social influences and structural constraints but also make choices and decisions based on the alternatives that they see before them. Feminist criminologists acknowledge the strength, resilience, and agency of women and strive toward the goals of female empowerment and self-determinism. The rational choice approach stresses the importance of rational decision-making in delinquent and criminal behaviors. The various perspectives on the life course all consider that individuals are "planful" and make choices among options that are available to them. It is these decisions that are so critical in constructing their life course.

The feminist and empowerment perspectives view power and powerlessness related to race, gender, and class as central to the experiences of women in poverty and women of color. Empowerment theory, sometimes called the strengths approach because of its positive approach in helping people, sees individual problems as arising not from personal deficits, but from the failure of society to meet the needs of all the people. The promotion of social justice is primary (see Parsons, 2008).

Central to the **empowerment approach** is the concept of power. Power is viewed as an attribute with consequences that may be negative or positive. Negative consequences arise from powerlessness, power imbalances in relationships, and an inability to make choices about one's life or livelihood. The subordination of women is a factor that creates violence, whether institutionally (for example, against women in prison) or within the family system. From a positive standpoint, power can be a liberating force. Gaining a sense of personal power can be a first step in assuming personal responsibility for change and for a personal journey from apathy and despair to positive social action.

Of special relevance to criminal behavior, and without which change is unlikely, is the taking of personal responsibility for one's actions and one's life. A counseling relationship can serve as a powerful tool for helping clients change cognitive misconceptions that result in self-destructive thoughts and behavior. Even in a life crushed by circumstances of time and place, there nevertheless exists the potential for actions other than those characteristically taken. This belief in potential is at the core of a healthy, therapeutic relationship.

An empowerment approach focuses on oppression and on those who suffer from its consequences. Oppressed individuals are not devoid of personal or moral strengths or resources. Help in tapping into those resources often is needed. For all of us, a sense of control over our lives and relationships is crucial. Ellen H. McWhirter (1991) captures the essence of empowerment in her inclusive definition:

> Empowerment is the process by which people, organizations, or groups who are powerless (a) become aware of the power dynamics at work in their life context, (b) develop the skills and capacity for gaining some reasonable control over their lives, (c) exercise this control without infringing upon rights of others, and (d) support the empowerment of others in their community. (p. 224)

Shoshana Pollack (2006) warns that there is a danger in prioritizing an individualistic or psychological notion of empowerment while minimizing the importance of social influences and oppression. When empowerment is viewed as an individual's subjective sense in which she can determine her own life's course, personal struggles tend to become privatized and individualized. This is particularly problematic in addressing the effects of oppression. Individualizing social issues can result in blaming women for problems that arise from being oppressed in various ways and can result in further disempowering them. In addition, perspectives that view empowerment as residing within the individual will lead to services and policies that are thought to enhance feelings of self-worth and autonomy. In contrast, perspectives assuming that an individual's autonomy is largely determined by social relationships and environment will tend to adopt a social or political analysis of empowerment, advocating critical social reflection and social change as methods of obtaining empowerment (pp. 76–77).

Until recently, the empowerment perspective has been absent from the criminal justice literature. A computer search of the criminal justice abstracts index (as of January 2009) reveals only nine listings for articles under the headings *strengths approach* and *strengths perspective.* This is four more than appeared three years ago. The word *empowerment* does appear over 200 times in the computer index as a progressive term for work with juveniles, female victims, and, occasionally, female offenders. Writing about probation, one decade ago, Clark (1998) called for a new paradigm to focus on offenders' strengths rather than on their faults and failures. This perspective, borrowed from social work, is gaining ground, according to Clark. Progress, however, has been slow.

We concur with Zavlek and Maniglia's (2007) call for a paradigm shift from society's current retributive justice response to the healing model of gender-based restorative justice. In restorative justice, the focus is on restoring individual family networks: Healing, not punishment, is emphasized. This approach, which has made much headway in juvenile corrections, reflects a renewed emphasis on rehabilitation rather than punishment. A focus on solutions rather than problems is empowering to clients and corrections workers alike.

Empowerment theory, with its focus on personal, social, educational, and political dimensions, offers a useful framework for addressing the needs of women at all levels of the criminal justice hierarchy. Just as a woman in prison or on probation can be empowered through her understanding that her situation is not just a personal problem but one related to gender, class, and racial oppression, so too can female correctional officers and lawyers be informed by a macro view that explains why affirmative action programs may be a necessary but not sufficient requisite to success.

The personal is political and the political is personal. This, in a nutshell, is the underlying theme of the feminist empowerment approach. The view of humanity underlying this approach is that humans are unique, multifaceted beings with the potential to make a contribution to their community (van Wormer, 2004). This contribution can be made unobtrusively through public consciousness-raising and networking, for example, through membership in various self-help groups or specialized professional associations. Sharing in writing and receiving newsletters is an example of educational empowerment. Political empowerment can occur through activities such as lobbying politicians and mass media campaigns. Issues relevant to women in criminal justice are lobbying for victims' rights, working toward legislative changes to protect women in prison from sexual abuse, and working to enhance affirmative action programs to increase the female-to-male ratio in policing. The empowerment of professional women in the field of criminal justice should have a ricocheting effect on women at every level of the criminal justice system.

Paradigm Shift

A **paradigm shift** is a revolution in the worldview of a social unit. It can take place on the individual, organizational, institutional, systemic, society, and scientific levels. During this time period, understanding or knowledge is perceived in a new way. This term is associated with the writings of Thomas Kuhn (1970) who suggested that changes in our construction of reality come about through a series of paradigm shifts. In science, for example, new discoveries from astronomy eventually led to an intellectual revolution in our understanding about the universe.

The history of social justice is a history of paradigm shifts related to our conception about the nature of crime and the purpose of punishment. In the 1960s and 1970s, rehabilitation was discredited and replaced by a "just deserts" philosophy and standardization of punishment (Zehr, 2002). The "get tough on crime" model continues to dominate crime policy and has led to draconian punishments in the courts and skyrocketing prison populations.

There are some signs today of a paradigm shift away from zero tolerance and one-size-fits-all laws and toward a rediscovery of the importance of rehabilitation. The proliferation of drug courts as an alternative to prison- or gender-specific programming for juveniles and reentry planning for inmates are cases in point.

A number of possible paradigm shifts in terms of how women are viewed and treated in the United States and other nations are featured in this book. Focusing on women offenders, victims, and professionals, these paradigm shifts seek to empower individuals, structures, and systems. The restorative model is one attempt to respond to victims and offenders with a more empowering approach.

Summary

As bell hooks (1998) states "We live in a world in crisis—a world governed by politics of domination, one in which the belief in a notion of superior and inferior, and its concomitant ideology—that the superior should rule over the inferior—affects the lives of all people everywhere, whether poor or privileged, literate or illiterate" (p. 19). The origin of this crisis, according to some feminist thinkers, is sexual politics. hooks adds that these feminist thinkers believe that "differentiation of status between females and males globally is an indication that patriarchal domination of the planet is the root of the problem" (p. 579). A central goal of feminist theory is a commitment to change such oppressive structures and to raise the level of awareness about the interlocking nature of sexism, racism, and classism. Great progress has taken place in this regard. A major challenge to women's progress, however, exists in the form of a backlash that is expressed both openly, aggressively, through individual attacks on girls and women, and in the guise of appeals to general cultural values (e.g., family values, fathers' rights equality under the law) to which most subscribe.

An understanding of how backlash turns the goals of feminism against women, especially marginalized women, is essential in efforts to counter its impacts. Offering women equality of opportunity does not mean policies must be gender neutral; inviting women to achieve success along with men in the work world does not mean girls and women in trouble with the law should be treated like dangerous, antisocial males. Equality, in other words, does not mean sameness; common sense should prevail. Fortunately, government initiatives to fund gender-specific programming for girls and women are a promising development in offender treatment.

This chapter, in short, has provided an overview of how male domination affects female victims, offenders, and workers in the criminal justice system. Legally and socially, women have experienced the domination of men in terms of such matters as the right to own property, to vote, to serve on a jury, and the need to be protected from sexual predators and intimate partner violence. Within the professions, we have seen that sexual harassment has been a special problem for women who work in male-dominated fields such as policing, law, and corrections. This chapter also briefly examined the categories of gender, class, and race and how they intersect in the lives of women victims and offenders. As one of the major themes of this book, an analysis of gender, class, and race/ethnicity guides the discussion in the chapters that follow.

Moreover, this chapter has proposed that there is consensus among feminist theorists on at least two basic principles—the importance of social/political context in the lives of girls and women and a focus on the goals of female empowerment and self-determination. The feminist model also acknowledges the agency and strengths of women.

Finally, this chapter has suggested that there is no single feminist perspective on the victimization of women. Feminist theories from different periods in history have been categorized as liberal, radical, socialist, Marxist, postmodernist, black, and Latina feminism, and there are differences among these perspectives. These differences may be due to the varying extent to which feminist theorists advocate for victims, identify with victims, or emphasize offender rights and treatment. Women, adds Bernat (1995), do not make up a homogenous

entity. As she aptly puts it, "we have a community of differences which need to be:

> Celebrated,
> Uncovered,
> Legitimated,
> Taught,
> Understood,
> Respected, and
> Embraced." (p. 7)

Key Terms

empowerment approach *20*
essentialism *9*
human agency *19*
intersectionalities *7*
Latina feminism *10–11*

liberal feminism *8*
Marxist feminists *9*
multiple marginality *2*
oppression *3*
paradigm shift *21*

postmodern feminism *9*
radical feminists *8*
sexual harassment of women *16*
socialist feminists *9*
third-wave feminists *7*

Critical Thinking Questions

1. What was the reason for the popularity of the class-race-gender analysis in college settings? Why was the original class-race-gender analysis in the 1990s expanded to include sexual orientation, ethnicity, and age?
2. What is the danger of making empowerment too individualistic a perspective?
3. Which form of feminist theory do you find most attractive? Why?
4. What is the importance of the class-race-gender analysis regarding the criminal justice system?
5. Does this form of analysis have different meanings for various groups of women (i.e., African American,

Latino, Native American, and white)? What is essentialism?
6. Why is this an important concept in understanding the oppressions of women?
7. What are possible avenues for feminism to have greater influence on the culture of the United States and other Western societies?
8. Why has patriarchy led to the oppression of women?
9. What are the consequences to women offenders of the backlash to the women's movement?

Web Destinations

New Web sites are being developed, while others are disappearing. Check with a search engine such as Google at www.google.com to locate information on feminism, female victims or offenders, individuals who work with women offenders or victims, and other relevant subjects, using a key word or phrase or organization.

Some sites relevant to this chapter are are follows:

African American feminist Web site: http://www.library.ucsb.edu/subjects/blackfeminism/

Chicana feminist Web site: http://www.chicanas.com/

Correctional Services Canada (2008). Women offender programs and issues:

http://www.csc-scc.gc.ca/text/pblcsbjct-eng. shtml#women

Feminist Criminology (journal): http://fcx.sage pub.com/

Feminist issues in prostitution: http://www.feminis-tissues.com/index.html

Feminist Majority Foundation: http://www. feminist.org/

Minnesota Association of Community Corrections Act Counties: http://www.maccac.org/Offender_ Programs/Female_Offenders/female_offenders.htm

References

Adler, F. (1975). *Sisters in crime: The rise of the new female criminal.* New York: McGraw-Hill.

Barak, G., Leighton, P., and Flavin, J. (2006). *Class, race, gender, and crime: The social realities of justice in America,* 2nd ed. Lanham, MD: Rowman and Littlefield.

Belknap, J. (2007). *The invisible woman: Gender, crime, and justice,* 3rd ed. Belmont, CA: Thomson.

Bernat, F. P. (1995). Opening the diaglogue: Women's culture and the criminal justice system. *Women and Criminal Justice 7*: 1–7.

Bloom, B., and Chesney-Lind, M. (2007). Women in prison. In R. Muraskin (ed.), *It's a crime: Women and justice* (pp. 542–563). Upper Saddle River, NJ: Prentice Hall.

Bloom, B., Owen, B., and Covington, S. (2003). *Gender responsive strategies: Research, practice and guiding principles for women offenders.* Washington, DC: National Institute of Corrections.

Britton, D. (2003). *At work in the iron cage: The prison as gendered organization.* New York: New York University Press.

Brown, L. M., Chesney-Lind, M., and Stein, N. (2007). Patriarchy matters: Toward a gendered theory of teen violence and victimization. *Violence Against Women 13*: 1249–1273.

Burke, R. H. (2005). *An introduction to criminological theory,* 2nd ed. Devon, UK: Willan Publishing.

Chesney-Lind, M. (2006). Patriarchy, crime, and justice: Feminist criminology in an era of backlash. *Feminist Criminology 1*: 6–26.

Chesney-Lind, M., and Pasko, L. (2003). *The female offender: Girls, women and crime.* Thousand Oaks, CA: Sage.

Clark, M. D. (1998, June). Strength-based practice: The ABC's of working with adolescents who don't want to work with you. *Federal Probation 62*: 46–53.

Collins, P. H. (2000). *Black feminist thought,* 2nd ed. New York: Routledge.

Commonwealth v. Daniel (430 Pa. 642, 243 A. 2d 400, 1968)

Daly, K., and Chesney-Lind, M. (1988). Feminism and criminology. *Justice Quarterly 5*: 497–538.

Dominelli, L. (2002). *Feminist social work theory and practice.* Hampshire, UK: Palgrave.

Dominelli, L. (2003). *Anti-oppressive social work theory and practice.* Hampshire, UK: Palgrave.

Douglas, S. (2007, May 29). The legacy of Tailhook. *In These Times.* Retrieved April 2009 from http://www.inthesetimes.com/article/3182/the_legacy_of_tailhook

Erez, E., and Tontodonato, P. (1992). Sexual harassment in the criminal justice system. In I. Moyer (ed.), *The changing roles of women in the criminal justice system: Offenders, victims, and professionals,* 2nd ed. (pp. 227–252). Prospect Heights: Waveland Press.

Faulkner, W. (1936). *Absalom, Absalom!* New York: Random House.

Friedan, B. (2001; orig. 1963). *The feminine mystique.* New York: Norton.

Garbarino, J. (2007). *See Jane hit: Why girls are growing more violent and what we can do about it.* London: Penguin.

Gilligan, C. (1982). *In a different voice: Psychological theory and women's development.* Cambridge: Harvard University Press.

Gutiérrez, L., and Lewis, E. (eds.) (1999). *Empowering women of color.* New York: Columbia University Press.

Heidensohn, F. (2000). *Sexual politics and social control.* Buckingham, UK: Open University Press.

Heidensohn, F. (1987). Women and crime: Questions for criminology. In P. Carlen and A. Worrall (eds.), *Gender, crime, and justice* (pp. 16–27). Philadelphia: Open University Press.

Hooks, B. (1984). *Feminist theory: From margin to center.* Boston, MA: South End Books.

Hooks, B. (1998). Feminism: A transformational politics. In B. Hooks (ed.), *Talking back: Thinking feminist, thinking black* (pp. 19–27). Cambridge, MA: South End Press.

Jurik, N. (2007). Striking a balance: Female correctional officers, gender role stereotypes, and male prisons. *Sociological Inquiry 58*(3): 291–305.

Kanowitz, L. (1969). *Women and the law: The unfinished revolution.* Albuquerque: University of New Mexico Press.

Kanowitz, L. (1973). *Sex roles in law and society: Cases and materials.* Albuquerque: University of New Mexico Press.

Kuhn, T. (1970). *The structure of scientific revolutions.* Chicago, IL: University of Chicago Press.

Latina Feminist Group. (2001). *Telling to live: Latina feminist testimonios.* Durham, NC: Duke University Press.

Littlefield, M. (2003). A womanist perspective for social work with African American women. *Social Thought 23*(4): 3–17.

McWhirter, E. H. (1991). Empowerment in counseling. *Journal of Counseling and Development 69*(3): 222–227.

Messerschmidt, J. (2004). *Flesh and blood: Adolescent gender diversity and violence.* Lantham, MD: Rowman & Littlefield.

Miller, J. (2008). Violence against urban African American girls: Challenges for feminist advocacy. *Journal of Contemporary Criminal Justice 24*: 148–162.

Miller, J., and Mullins, C. W. (2006). The status of feminist theories in criminology. In press. In F. Adler and W. Laufer (eds.), *Taking stock: The status of criminological theory. Vol. 15: Advances in criminological theory* (206–220), New Brunswick, NJ: Transaction Publishers.

Moore, D. (2007). Feminist criminology: Gain, loss and backlash. *Sociology Compass 2*(1): 48–61.

Morton, J. B. (2007, August). Providing gender-responsive services for women and girls. *Corrections Today 6*(2). Retrieved December 2008 from http://www.highbeam.com/doc/1G1-167889347.html

Mullaly, B. (2002). *Challenging oppression: A critical social work approach.* Don Mills, Ontario: Oxford University Press.

Muraskin, R. (2007). Feminist theories: Are they needed? In R. Muraskin (ed.), *It's a crime: Women and justice,* 4th ed. (pp. 31–43). Upper Saddle River, NJ: Prentice Hall.

Parker, K. F., and Reckdenwald, A. (2008). Women and crime in context: Examining the linkages between patriarchy and female offending across space. *Feminist Criminology 3*(1): 5–24.

Parsons, R. (2008). Empowerment practice. In National Association of Social Work (NASW), *Encyclopedia of Social Work* (pp. 123–126). New York: Oxford University Press.

Payne, M. (2005). *Modern social work theory,* 3rd ed. Chicago, IL: Lyceum.

Pollack, S. (2006). Reconceptualizing women's agency and empowerment: Challenges to self-esteem discourse and women's lawbreaking. *Women and Criminal Justice 12*: 75–89.

Potter, H. (2006). An argument for black feminist criminology: Understanding African American women's experiences with intimate partner abuse using an integrated approach. *Feminist Criminologist 1*: 106–124.

Price, B. R., and Sokoloff, N. J. (2004). The criminal law and women. In B. R. Price and N. J. Sokoloff (eds.), *The criminal justice system and women: Offenders, victims, and workers,* 3rd ed. (pp. 11–29). New York: McGraw-Hill.

Rabe-Hemp, C. (2008). Survival in an "all boys club": Policewomen and their fight for acceptance. *Policing: An International Journal of Police Strategies & Management 31*(2): 251–270.

Rollins, J. H. (1996). *Women's minds, women's bodies: The psychology of women in a biosocial context.* Upper Saddle River, NJ: Prentice-Hall.

State v. Costello. New Jersey State Supreme Court 59, 1971.

Sherman, F. T. (2005). *Pathways to juvenile detention reform—Detention reform and girls* (Vol. 13). Baltimore, MD: The Annie E. Casey Foundation.

Smart, C. (1995). *Law, crime and sexuality: Essays in feminism.* London: SAGE.

Spelman, E. V. (1989). *Inessential woman.* Boston, MA: Beacon Press.

Sydney, L. (2005). *Gender-responsive strategies for women offenders.* U.S. Department of Justice, National Institute of Corrections. Retrieved December 2008 from http://nicic.org/pubs/2005/020419.pdf

University of Kentucky (2008, May 16). Culture affects how teen girls see sexual harassment *ScienceDaily.*

Retrieved December 21, 2008, from http://www.
sciencedaily.com/releases/2008/05/080515072645.htm

Van Soest, D. (2008). Organizational development and
change. In NASW, *Encyclopedia of social work*
(pp. 324–327). New York: Oxford University Press.

van Wormer, K. (2004). *Confronting oppression,
restoring justice: From policy analysis to social
justice.* Alexandria, VA: CSWE.

Vidal, M. (1972). Chicans speak out, women: New
voice of La Raza. In *Feminism and Socialism*
(pp. 3–11). New York: Pathfinder Press.

Vieraitis, L., Britto, S., and Kovandzic, T. V. (2007).
The impact of women's status and gender inequality
on female homicide victimization rates. *Feminist
Criminology 2*: 57–73.

Webb, S. L. (1994). *Shockwaves: The global impact of
sexual harassment.* New York: MasterMedia.

Zavlek, S., and Maniglia, R. (2007). Developing
correctional facilities for female juvenile offenders: design and programmatic considerations.
Corrections Today 69(4): 58–63.

Zehr, H. (2002). *The little book of restorative justice.*
Intercourse, PA: Good Books.

PART

II

Female Crime and Delinquency

Racial, ethnic, and class diversity come together in compelling ways in the chapters of this part. Here we concentrate on the female offender, often a drug addict/alcoholic with a long history of sexual and physical abuse. The typical adjudicated female offender is a woman of color and mother of small children. Their stories reveal how social control of already oppressed people is carried out by the state and legitimized through the mass media. The ultimate inequality of U.S. society is revealed in a visit to the nation's prisons.

How do women get caught up in violating the law? Which crimes do they commit? Are women committing more crimes today, or are they being arrested and prosecuted more diligently than in the past? What are contemporary explanations of women's crime? These are among the questions considered in Chapter 2.

Chapter 3 examines both theories among feminists relating to crime, gender, and criminology and to research methods that are being utilized by feminist criminologists. This chapter builds on and expands material in Chapter 2. The focus in Chapter 3 is on gender because its study is what guides feminist theories in criminology. This chapter points out that the best feminist work remains critically engaged with gendered life situations of women and men.

Chapter 4 examines delinquency across the life course, one of the most exciting new developments in the field of juvenile delinquency. Beginning with an examination of risk factors in adolescence, the chapter compares juveniles who are early offenders with those who begin their delinquency offenses in adolescence. These adolescents are followed through part of and sometimes nearly all of their life span. Their social and criminal histories are compared with those of others in their cohort, and particular attention is given to juveniles who persist and those who desist from law-violating behaviors. Researchers want to know what factors contributed to desistance from such activities. Even though the vast majority of the research has been done on male delinquents, more attention is being given to female delinquents across the life course.

2

Women in Crime

C rime is a socially constructed category and often says more about the society's values and traditions, even hang-ups, than about the individuals whose behavior is defined as criminal. In other words, society gets the criminals it creates, and even, in a sense, deserves. In this chapter, we will see from the statistics how gender, race, and class intersect in the correctional sphere. We will see how much women's crime is directly related to their disadvantaged economic and social condition, to their pasts, and to drugs, not to mention, to their relationships with men.

Virtually every day, somewhere in the United States, Canada, and Britain, a newspaper headline pops up about the new breed of female criminals (girl or woman) who are taking their place beside their male counterparts. Stories of girl gangs, battering women, and drug-addicted mothers abound.

To evaluate the truth of these claims, we will examine recent statistics from the federal government's *Uniform Crime Reports*. That crime is gendered is a major concern of this chapter, and the next topic, even more intriguing and controversial, is the nature of female crime. How do we explain female conformity to the legal norms of society and how do we explain female lawbreaking behavior? These are the questions at the heart of this chapter. Biological, psychological, and sociological explanations for female crime will be discussed. That even a seemingly neutral offense such as theft or assault may have a different meaning to a man than to a woman is a theme of this chapter. When woman-on-boy sexual molestation occurs, normally unspoken cultural dispositions—feelings about gender and sexuality and power—are suddenly articulated and, even in the public eyes, glamorized.

ANTIFEMINIST ACCOUNTS OF FEMALE CRIME

Woman blaming has a long history; when a man errs, blame his wife, mistress, or mother. When a woman errs, she alternatively is described as a male-bashing woman or a bad mother, or even a "bad girl." In an article in *Psychology Today,* entitled simply "Bad Girls," freelance writer Barry Yeoman (1999) recounts the violent acts of several high-profile cases including Lorena Bobbit, who amputated her unfaithful husband's penis; Susan Smith, who drowned her small children; and even the born-again Christian Karla Faye Tucker. Given the "proliferation" of such cases, declares Yoeman, and the recent surge in crime, our cultural notions concerning the woman as nurturer may be off the mark. Women need greater incentive than men to express violence, according to Yeoman, but the "social changes over the years—especially the movement toward gender equality—have provided several" (p. 65). One of the experts cited in the article is Rutgers University criminal justice professor Freda Adler.

Freda Adler was catapulted to fame in 1976 during the height of the women's revolution, with her publication of the book *Sisters in Crime: The Rise of the New Female Criminal* (1976). A sudden fascination with the liberated woman as criminal was spawned. It was not the petty criminal who got the attention, of course. Public attention was drawn to the latter-day Lady Macbeths and Lizzy Bordens. A highly readable book, *Sisters in Crime* opened with examples of infamous violent female criminals such as assassins and revolutionaries. On the surface her argument was plausible: No one was interested in petty criminality, of course. Examples of infamous, dangerous, and violent female criminals such as assassins and revolutionaries are among those dramatically provided by Adler at the beginning of her book. Because of new opportunities and expectations for girls and women, she claimed, "females are cutting themselves in for a bigger slice of the pie" (p. 29). When their goals of sexual equality are denied, however, these frustrated women get involved in aggressive and violent acts. The rise in female crime, in short, must be seen in the context of women's liberation: The movement for full equality has a darker side which has been slighted even by the scientific community. The same way that women are demanding equal opportunity in fields of legitimate endeavor, a similar number of determined women are forcing their way into the world of major crimes (p. 13).

Adler's hypothesis was put to rest in the late 1970s when the reported rise in characteristically male types of crime failed to materialize. True, Adler's reasoning is logical; as women have more employment opportunities and occupy positions that require handling money, they have more opportunity to embezzle money. The increase in women's economic crime during the early 1970s, however, was occasioned not by embezzlement of large sums but by a well-publicized crackdown on welfare fraud. Middle-class women, the ones with the new opportunities, were not being arrested in large numbers. And as Adler herself conceded, female inmates are far from liberated and, in fact, more often are downright hostile to the goals of the women's movement.

Feminist critics of the 1970s generally were outraged at Adler's hypothesis, which was widely reported in exaggerated form in the media. Foremost among the critics were scholars such as Crites (1976). In her analysis of FBI crime data Crites concluded the obvious, that there was no validity to the myth of the new, violent, and aggressive female criminal. Feinman (1980) concurred. The women's rights movement had largely swept over the groups of poor, unemployed women of color who were being arrested.

What the increase in female arrests for welfare fraud and other petty crime probably reflected was an end to the so-called chivalry once extended to female criminals by virtue of their being considered the "weaker sex." Only white women of a certain class had access to such protectionist treatment, the idea of chivalry being that such women were on a pedestal (Bloom,

Owen, and Covington, 2007). But with the movement toward gender equality, men in the position of making and enforcing the laws were beginning to change their attitudes. Many who resisted the bid for equality were angry. So if women didn't want special treatment, they wouldn't get special treatment. Prosecutions of women for larceny and fraud soared.

The **liberation thesis or hypothesis** was revived in the late 1990s, about three decades later. According to this hypothesis, as women become more equal to men, their offending rates will converge with men's (Belknap, 2007). Headlines such as the ones published in the *Cincinnati Enquirer*—"Girls' Crimes Starting to Match Boys' " (Bricking, 1998), "Violence among Girls on the Rise" (Rowe, 2001), and "Women More Likely than Men to Stalk and Attack their Partner" (*Times of India,* 2006)—are typical. The *Times of India* story referred to research by U.S. criminologist Angela Gover, who claimed that relationships are different today, and that women are likely to victimize as well as become victims themselves. Appetites for misbehaving girls are seemingly insatiable, with weekly barrages of reports in the press (Ringrose, 2006). Recently, the female norm of developing close relationships has been viewed in terms of cliquishness, and unprecedented media attention is devoted to relational aggression among girls. Ringrose refers to this sensationalizing of gender difference and preoccupation with the cruelty of "mean girls" as a "way of re-pathologizing the feminine" (p. 419). In fact, such relational aggression among members of the female sex is nothing new.

In Canada, likewise, has come the sudden discovery that "Girl Bullies Strike Dubious Blows for Gender Equality." Such is the headline in an *Ottawa Citizen* story about a newfound aggression seen among girls on the playground (Enman, 1999). Without any reference to statistical data, the article attempts to link gender equality and schoolgirl violence. The book on which the article is largely based, however, *Sex, Power, and the Violent School Girl* by Canadian social scientist Sibylle Artz (1998), tells a different story: Violence in schoolgirls, the author clarifies, is a product not of independence at all but an outgrowth of social conditioning and female vulnerability. Cited in the *Toronto Star* (Landsberg, 1999), Artz explains that such girl-on-girl violence stems from competition over male attention. "This is true of oppressed groups; they commit violence horizontally—that is, on people like themselves, in the name of people with more power" (p. L1).

IS FEMALE CRIME INCREASING?

One strategy to determine if women are engaging in more criminal behavior today than formerly is to compare the female percentage of crime from earlier times with today. We can calculate from FBI statistics, which gives the male percentage, that the female percentage of all arrests in 2007 was 24.2 percent (see Table 2.1). We can compare this figure to the rate of total arrests across all offenses for 1965, a year that is significant because it was before the contemporary women's movement got underway. We learn that the female percentage of total arrests at that time was significantly less—only 10 percent. And by 1980, the female rate had risen to 15.8 percent (BJS, 1980, Table 34).

So what was happening? The media blame the rise on women's increasing liberation from traditional roles, while feminist criminologists pointed to the crackdown on welfare fraud and an increased willingness of stores to prosecute shoplifters (Chesney-Lind and Pasko, 2003; Feinman, 1980). This was indeed borne out in the statistics for arrests for fraud and minor theft, not crimes of violence. From 1987 to 1998, however, the arrest rate for crimes of violence for young adult women has increased by 80 percent, and the juvenile arrest rate has risen substantially as well (BJS, 2000). Most of the increase, as the Bureau of

TABLE 2.1   Arrests, by Sex, 2007

- Nationwide, 75.8 percent of the 10,698,310 persons arrested in 2007 were male.
- Males comprised 81.8 percent of those arrested for violent crimes and 66.6 percent of those arrested for property crimes.
- Of all persons arrested for murder in 2007, 89.8 percent were male.
- Males accounted for 81.2 percent of all persons arrested for drug abuse violations.
- Females accounted for 51.5 percent of all persons arrested for embezzlement in 2007.

Source: Crime in the United States, 2007, Table 42; U.S. Department of Justice—Federal Bureau of Investigation; released September (2008).

Justice Statistics (BJS) report indicates, was in arrests for aggravated assault "perhaps reflecting increased prosecution of women for domestic violence" (pp. 5–6). As we can calculate from the male percentage given in Table 2.1, by 2007, the female proportion of arrests for violent crimes had risen to 18.2 percent.

Looking at conviction as opposed to arrest trends shows that the offense composition among women in state prison was changing rapidly during the last two decades of the past century (BJS, 2000). The number of both men and women who had been convicted of violent and property crime decreased, while the proportion of drug and public-order offenders has been growing. These convictions were related to the emphasis during this period on the war on drugs. Between 1990 and 1998, the women's imprisonment rate increased 88 percent; the increase for male offenders was also pronounced but not as dramatic.

The most notable trend in the years since 1997 has been the continuing rise in the female share of persons arrested for the violent crimes of simple assault (without injury or use of a weapon) and aggravated assault. The Uniform Crime Reports (FBI, 2007), which calculated ten-year arrest trends from 1997 through 2006, found that the total arrest rate for adults declined around 7 percent for males during this period and rose by 4 percent for females. Women showed an increase in arrests for forgery, possession of stolen property, but above all, for simple assault. The fact that the homicide rate was down by 10.3 percent and the aggravated assault rate by 3.6 percent seems to indicate that women are not more violent than they were formerly.

Arrest and conviction rates are a function of both criminal behavior and law enforcement measures of the society. With regard to women's offending behavior, the level of tolerance of that behavior may vary from time to time, and changes in attitudes toward offending women would be reflected in the arrest and conviction rates. So how can we prove whether women are changing, for example, by engaging in more instances of less serious assault than they did in the past? One thing we can do is consult a source of crime reports that is in many ways even more accurate than the FBI arrest data. We are referring to data collected from the National Crime Victimization Survey (NCVS) that is conducted annually on a random sample of the U.S. population. Because this survey collects information directly from persons on their own victimizations, the crime of homicide is not a consideration. The NCVS results are useful, however, as an indication of the frequency and severity of other forms of violence. We can also discover from the interview data the percentage of crimes in which the perpetrators were male or female. As reported by the BJS (2006b), the interviewees identified perpetrators of violent crime as female 19.2 percent of the time; these were cases of single-offender crimes. For the crime of robbery, for example, the perpetrator was identified as female in 10.5 percent of the cases. For aggravated assault the figure was 14.1 and for simple assault, 22.7.

Steffensmeier et al. (2006) examined NCVS data over time to determine if the increasing female arrest rates reflected actual changes in women's behavior or if they reflected changes in policy. What they found was that since 1979, male and female assault rates rose through the early 1990s and declined significantly in recent years. These researchers conclude, therefore, that recent policy shifts have affected the apparent increase in women's violence, since no such increase is revealed in the survey data. In fact, victims' reports indicate sizable declines in female-perpetrated assaults since at least the mid-1990s, in contrast to the Uniform Crime Reports arrest data.

RACE AND CLASS

While nearly two-thirds of women under probation supervision are white, nearly two-thirds of those confined in local jails and prisons are minority (BJS, 2000). Hispanics account for about one in seven women confined in state prisons and nearly one in three female prisoners in federal custody. With respect to occupational status, about 60 percent of women in contrast to 40 percent of men were unemployed at the time of arrest; 30 percent of the women were receiving welfare assistance. This "racialized feminization of poverty" (Sudbury, 2004, p. 230) limits women's survival options and sometimes leads to their involvement in illegal moneymaking activities. Poor and minority women are the major casualties of America's war on drugs; many of those incarcerated in the federal sector, besides, are immigrant women who were transporters of drugs, or "mules."

The overall incarceration rate for black women was 3.8 times the rate for white women. Latina women were 1.6 times more likely than white women to be incarcerated. Across age groups, African American women were incarcerated between 2.8 and 4.3 times the rate of white women (BJS, 2007b). Since the majority of female prison inmates are women of color, the stridency of the attacks on the "new violent criminal females" can be perceived as a thinly veiled instance of institutionalized racism. The situation here is the same as that which occurred in the crackdown on women on welfare, which also had racist overtones.

EXPLANATIONS OF FEMALE CRIME

More recent explanations of female crime place much greater emphasis on sociological factors, with criminologists coming to vastly different conclusions. Some criminologists challenge whether gender-specific explanations are needed, claiming that existing sociological theories can account for both male and female crime (Mazerolle, 1998, p. 66). These comparisons of how males and females respond to traditional sociological theories are found in this section. Other criminologists still argue for gender-specific explanations because they claim that the traditional sociological theories of delinquent behavior fail to adequately explain the female experience in the United States.

Biological and Constitutional Explanations

"Most criminologists," as Vito, Maahs, and Holmes (2007) indicate, "regard biological studies of crime with a mixture of indifference and ridicule" (p. 82). The biological factors that are rejected include genetic factors in crime-related behavior, and probably drug use, gender, and age as well.

Perhaps these researchers associate biological theories of crime with the early criminologists such as Cesare Lombroso. We will bypass Lombroso. Who needs a theory about ugly, hairy women with enormous jaws, heavy eyebrows, and "neck-muscles exaggerated as in oxen" (Lombroso and Ferrrero, 1895, p. 89)? These views reflected the societal belief that a fallen woman was a lower species than a male criminal and therefore less capable of reform. More contemporary studies on sex chromosomal abnormalities in delinquent girls are of little value as well (see, for example, Gibbens, 1971). A major problem with the early biological theories of criminal behavior is that they were all created by men and were highly misogynistic.

And yet biology is a crucial component in much that is human (van Wormer, 2007). In our quest for knowledge, we cannot afford to be constrained by that false nature-versus-nurture dichotomy. Moreover, we cannot reject all biological theories of sex differences because they might seem repugnant to our ideals of equality. Feminists disparage biological research, as Pollock (1999) suggests, because the theories hark back to the days when women were told they must fill their natural role as "mother of the species" and work in the home. A biological approach accepts that there are fundamental differences between male and female and that these differences interact with cultural norms to influence differences in male/female criminality. A challenge to traditional feminist cultural determinism is provided by evolutionary theory and brain research.

Evolutionists such as Wrangham and Petersen (1996), who wrote the fascinating bestseller *Demonic Males: Apes and the Origins of Human Violence*, offer a challenge to traditional feminist cultural determinism. Their conclusions are bolstered by ape studies in which male predators attack the weak, and females (of the chimpanzee variety) often bond with the predators. "Is the frequency of male violence a mere artifact of physical strength?" they ask. For answers, they look to human society.

Examining data drawn from global crime statistics on same-sex murder (to eliminate the factor of male strength) Wranham and Peterson found the statistics to be amazingly consistent. In all societies except for Denmark, the probability that a same-sex murder has been committed by a man, not a woman, ranges from 92 to 100 percent. (In Denmark, all the female same-sex murders were cases of infanticide.) We need to remove our inhibitions based on feminist politics these researchers argue. We need to study violence such as murder and rape as biological phenomena. The origins of male violence, as Wrangham and Peterson conclude, are found in the social lives of chimpanzees and other apes, our closest living relatives.

Brain research is the province of psychologists, psychiatrists, and neurobiologists, who today are on the threshold of discoveries related to such biologically based disorders as antisocial personality, addiction, and compulsive risk taking. Antisocial personality, which used to be called psychopathy, is a mental disorder listed in the *Diagnostic and Statistical Manual of Mental Disorders, 4th edition (DSM-IV-TR)* (American Psychiatric Association, 2000). Persons who qualify for this diagnosis are impulsive, blaming of others, and seemingly unable to feel empathy or guilt. Eight times as many men as women receive this label. Research shows that the rate that this character disorder is manifest in correctional populations is around 10–15 percent among females and 25–30 percent among males (Strand and Belfrage, 2005). Traditionally, mothers have been blamed for causing this disorder through abuse. Increasingly, research is looking toward biological explanations—for example, in twin studies conducted at the University of Southern California and brain studies at the University of Iowa (Barovick, 1999). This disorder may be of some relevance to female offenders, although mostly in terms of their victimization.

The notion of the influence of testosterone levels on criminal behavior in both males and females resurfaces from time to time. The link between testosterone and aggression in animals is well established (Simpson, 2001). Much-cited research by Dabbs and Hargrove (1997) and Dabbs (1998) measured the testosterone levels via saliva samples taken from 87 female inmates of all ages. In the prison context, women who had the highest levels of testosterone tended to have been convicted of violent crimes and to evidence dominant, aggressive behavior in prison. The findings by Dabbs and Hargrove are similar to those in studies of male prisoners. Testosterone levels were highest among male inmates convicted of violent crimes such as rape, homicide, and assault. These men also violated more prison rules. Keep in mind that men have on average ten times as much testosterone as women do.

Addictions researchers, similarly, are devoting attention to brain chemistry. The research is two-directional—focused on the impact of drugs on the brain and the risk factor of addiction susceptibility. Thanks to sophisticated new imaging techniques such as positron emission tomography (PET) scans, scientists can view the brain today in ways never before imagined. On the eve of the new millennium, in fact, scientists know more about how drugs act on the brain than we do about anything else in the brain, according to Alan Leshner, director of the National Institute on Drug Abuse (cited in *Washington Post* by Squires, 2000: H01). What we know the most about is the extent to which substance abuse can cause severe, and often irreversible, damage to brain cells and to the nervous system in general.

Over the past decade, similarly, scores of American scientists have been diligently mapping the brain waves of alcoholics and their offspring. Although researchers have not been able to track down specific genes that cause alcoholism and addictive behavior, they do claim to have found telltale electrical patterns that identify those at risk of alcoholism (Vines, 1999). Low levels of the neurotransmitter serotonin are linked to both addiction and aggression. When individuals self-medicate with cocaine, for example, the brain adapts to the artificially induced highs, and an unbearable craving for the drug results. Thus the biochemistry of the brain is a factor in addiction, with regard to both its etiology and continuation.

In women's lives, the connection between addiction and crime is both direct and indirect—directly associated through uninhibited lawbreaking behavior, not to mention perhaps careless use of the illegal drug itself, and indirectly through involvement in destructive relationships, relationships with people who are involved in the criminal underworld.

Psychological Explanations

Psychological aspects of offending include psychopathic modes of thinking, a background of personal trauma, and emotions such as anger and depression. Feelings are, of course, closely linked to biology. We will consider theories relating crime to criminal thought patterns (male-oriented theories) and explanations for female offending that stress a history of trauma and victimization.

Loucks and Zamble (1999) conducted a study of 100 female inmates at the prison for women in Kingston, Ontario, to determine predictive factors in recidivism. Personality factors, rather than background factors of trauma and abuse, emerged as the key predictor of reoffending. Psychopathy (measured on the Psychopathy Checklist—Revised instrument) emerged as the preeminent measure. This attribute is also a key prediction of male recidivism, according to Loucks and Zamble. The difference is that psychopathy in women occurs far less frequently. Cognitive-behavioral techniques are recommended as the most effective treatment modality with this group.

The work of Yochelson and Samenow (1976, *The Criminal Mind*) and of Samenow (1984, *Inside the Criminal Mind*) would be of little relevance to the topic of female offending were it not for the fact that these theories and therapy techniques shape the treatment that many inmates, male and female, receive in prison. Yochelson and Samenow derived their ideas through studies of the criminally insane at St. Elizabeth's Hospital in Washington, DC. After probing the psyches of hundreds of inmates, they decided that the criminals weren't sick; they were just masters at manipulation. Accordingly, they devised a therapeutic technique for cracking the resistance, breaking the lies. Criminals are told that none of their hard-luck stories of victimization are relevant. Criminals must be made to feel total self-disgust for their actions. Change only comes through a drastic alteration in thinking patterns; however, only a few criminals are amenable to change.

A mental disorder that does occur frequently in female offenders and especially adolescent girls is depression. Obeidallah and Earls (1999), in a project from the Institute of Justice, confirmed the link between depression and delinquency. Whereas during childhood, males' and females' rates of depression are similar and relatively low, early adolescence is a time when the rates clearly diverge, with girls showing a pronounced increase. Difficulty in concentrating, loss of interest in previously enjoyable activities, feelings of hopelessness, and low self-worth—all may contribute to self-destructive acts and alliances. To document a relationship between depression and antisocial behavior in an ethnically diverse population, interviewers gathered self-report data on 754 girls in urban Chicago. Comparing the antisocial behavior of girls who were depressed with those who were not, Obeidallah and Earls found that 40 percent of nondepressed girls engaged in property crimes compared to 68 percent of girls with depression. Fifty-seven percent of depressed girls engaged in seriously aggressive behavior compared to only 13 percent of those who were not depressed. Overall, these findings suggest that depression in girls may put them at high risk for antisocial behavior. Smith, Leve, and Chamberlain (2006) further validated the role of a background of trauma and health-risking and delinquent behavior in their assessments of 88 girls referred to Oregon juvenile services.

The prevalence of physical and sexual abuse in childhood and adult backgrounds of female offenders has been consistently supported in the research literature (Bloom, Owen, and Covington, 2004). Among men and women on probation, the BJS (2000) found that six in ten women in state institutions experienced prior physical or sexual abuse. A similar rate of such abuse is reported among men and women in treatment for substance abuse (van Wormer and Davis, 2008). The Canadian rates for incarcerated women are that 68 percent suffered physical abuse and 53 percent sexual abuse at some point in their lives Comack and Brickey (2007). Among Aboriginal women, the rates are much higher.

To understand male/female differences in motivation for crime, we need to consider not only female pathways to crime but also research on masculinities and male identity. Mullins, Wright, and Jacobs (2004), in their study of young urban male offenders, found that most of men's interpersonal disputes with other men were grounded in the need to build and maintain gendered reputations. They further found that the men held gendered perceptions of appropriate and inappropriate behavior that served as a trigger for retaliations. Retaliation following a threat was practiced as a key street survival strategy.

Sociological Explanations

Beginning in the late 1970s, several studies proceeded from the assumption that sociological processes traditionally related to males could also affect the antisocial involvement of females. Researchers who examined the sociological themes of blocked opportunity theory, social control theory, masculinity hypothesis, power-control theory, and labeling theory found that they offered much more promise than biological or psychological causes. But Leonard, who focused on other sociological theories, was much less convinced of the value of sociological factors in explaining criminality among women offenders.

SOCIOLOGICAL EXPLANATIONS FOR FEMALE DELINQUENT BEHAVIOR.   *Opportunity theory* states that blocked opportunity in a society that stresses material success leads to antisocial forms of behavior. Certainly the economic marginalization of women and the feeling by those without skills or education that they will never "make it" are factors that might play into crimes such as theft, fraud, or drug dealing. Women offenders when released from prison are often not equipped with the skills to fit within the dominant economic and social structures (Failinger, 2006). Conversely, the opportunity to handle other people's money such as at banks or restaurants might lead to the property crime of embezzlement (Simon, 1975). Freda Adler (1975) offered social as opposed to psychological explanations for crime. "The entrance of women into the major leagues of crime," argued Adler, "underscores the point that the incidence and kinds of crimes are more closely associated with social than sexual factors" (p. 27). The problem is, women have never entered "the major leagues of crime" or even come close. As women become liberated, as these criminologists reasoned, they would be as prone to criminal activities as do men. Despite women's professional achievements since the 1970s, however, their criminal behavior has not followed suit.

Proponents of social control theory contend that females are less involved in crime than males because sex-role socializations result in a stronger social bond for females than for males. In addition, females may have less opportunity to engage in crime because in general they are more closely supervised by parents when they are younger and by society when they get older. Females, it is added, are also more dependent on others, whereas males are encouraged to be more independent and achievement oriented. Consequently, differences in sex-role socialization supposedly promote a greater allegiance to the social bond among females, and this allegiance insulates them from crime more than it does males. This position infers that females require a greater "push" to become involved in delinquent and criminal acts.

Labeling theory has the advantage of linking the sociological to the psychological. When kids or adults are labeled as bad, according to this theory, the label becomes a self-fulfilling prophecy. The concept is consistent with the strengths approach of social work, which shows how trust and positive rather than negative interpretations of people's acts can bring out the best in them (see Saleebey, 2006). Kai Erikson (1966) gave life to this notion in his historical analysis of records left by the early Puritans of Massachusetts Bay Colony. His investigation led him to the stories of women, rebellious in some way, who received the label of deviant and whose behavior accordingly grew more extreme. His words can still inspire us today:

> People in this society do not expect much in the way of reform from those who are labeled "deviant." And this, historically, brings us back to the Puritans, for it is then their image of deviation, their belief in the irreversibility of human nature, which may be reflected in that expectation (p. 205).

Integrated Theory of Women and Crime

The biopsychosocial framework used by social work and other counseling theorists makes a good fit for understanding the phenomenon of crime causation. A theory to be explanatory must be comprehensive; biological, psychological, and social factors all need to be included. Such a holistic approach should be able to explain male as well as female criminality, and conformity to as well as violation of the law. To take one example from the life course of a female offender: Sally, a hyperactive girl with a short attention span, can't sit still at school and drives her teacher and parents crazy. Internalizing the negativism around her, she joins a group of outcasts, experiments with drugs, and drops out of school. She may or may not gravitate toward crime and be arrested. However, she is at high risk for trouble-prone and self-destructive behavior. Biological attributes, combine with the psychological process of internalizing negative adult reactions, which combine, in turn, with social influences in her environment, including peer group culture and ultimately lead to the acquisition of a deviant, "bad girl" label. Each of us is a unique individual; our personalities and behavior can only be understood in terms of the interaction of a combination of factors. As summarized by Bloom, Owen, and Covington (2004), women's most common pathways to crime are based on survival of abuse, poverty, and substance abuse. And let me underscore the word *survival.*

Feminist criminology is an exciting new area of research. Kathleen Daly (1994) has introduced a typology of female offenders. She differentiates street women from battered women. Street women have entered a life of crime through structural circumstances and opportunity within that realm; much of their crime is economically based. Battered women have sometimes gotten into trouble through use of violence against the batterer.

Some of the theories discussed above are narrow in that they explain one kind of crime but not another. Opportunity theory, for example, is far more relevant to economic crimes such as embezzlement than to crimes of personal violence or drug possession. The fact that the crime of embezzlement has risen steadily for women since the 1970s undoubtedly relates to career changes for women as well as to their increasing involvement in gambling. The remainder of this chapter will briefly describe various types of crime, with special relevance for girls and women.

PROPERTY CRIMES

The most significant gender difference in arrest profiles is the relatively greater involvement of females in minor property crimes such as shoplifting and fraud and the relatively greater involvement of males in major property crimes and crimes against persons (Steffensmeier and Schwartz, 2004). The economic marginalization of women may help account for their relatively high involvement in larceny, theft, check and welfare fraud, and forgery. While men still dominate in property crimes, women's steadily high rate of criminality here undoubtedly is linked to the "feminization of poverty" (Belknap, 2007).

Shopping and shoplifting tend to go together for some women. The gender factor here is evidenced in the types of merchandise that is taken. Men steal items that express their manliness, to impress their peers. Girls and women, on the other hand, are drawn to take luxury items they feel they need but cannot justify spending household income on, items such as cosmetics and jewelry.

Embezzlement is a crime that, on the surface, is not related to poverty but, rather, to opportunity for women. The overwhelming majority of bank tellers today, for example, are women. In that sense, there is more opportunity for them to take money than they had before.

Women's embezzlement rate rose by 28 percent between 1997 and 2006 (FBI, 2007), compared to a minor increase in the rate for men. As we can see from Table 2.1, which was presented earlier in this chapter, women make up more than half of all arrests for embezzlement. This does not mean, however, that women are responsible for half of the money and resources that are confiscated in this manner, however, because such women rarely have access to the vast sums of money that some men do (Belknap, 2007). Studies of embezzlement reveal that most women charged with this crime most often worked as tellers or in clerical positions, whereas many of their male counterparts were in managerial positions (Daly, 1994; Steffensmeier and Schwartz, 2004).

PROSTITUTION

Described by some as the "oldest profession" for women, prostitution seemingly provides a lucrative environment for the exchange of sex for money between mutually consenting adults (Valandra, 2007). Prostitution is illegal in all states except for Nevada; about twice as many women as men are arrested for this crime. Managing prostitutes in the criminal justice system neglects the fact that for many women, their prostitution is the result of numerous and complex psychological stressors (Arnold, McNeece, and Stewart, 1999; Websdale and Chesney-Lind, 2004). The social aspect is explored in graphic terms by Vednita Nelson (1993):

> Racism makes Black women and girls especially vulnerable to sexual exploitation and keeps them trapped in the sex industry. It does this by limiting educational and career opportunities for African-Americans in this country. It does this through a welfare system that has divided the poor Black family. . . . Today, middle-class white men from the suburbs drive through the ghettos of America to pick out whatever Black women or girls they want to have sex with, as if our cities were their own private plantations (pp. 81, 82).

When we think of prostitution, most of us think of street prostitution. Street prostitution, however, is estimated to account for only about 20 percent of prostitution in major cities but for the majority of prostitution arrests (Arnold, McNeece, and Stewart, 1999). The organization COYOTE (Cast Off Your Old Tired Ethics) is a high-class prostitutes' rights group that advocates the legalization of prostitution, which they describe as sex work (Rauch, 2006). Today they are protesting recent restrictions imposed by the government's new antihuman trafficking laws. Legalization such as that exists in the Netherlands and in several other European countries provides for regulation of prostitution, health check-ups, and protection from women in this trade, who can call the police, for example, if they are victimized. In order to combat the problem with trafficked women that was rampant in Sweden, the government passed legislation that criminalized the buying of sex but not prostitution itself (De Santis, 2007). The thinking behind this law, which was strongly supported by Sweden's organization or women's shelters, is that women prostitutes are not criminals but victims. This is a shift in viewing prostitution from the male to a female perspective. Sweden chose this route over its tradition of legalization, which had only expanded the sex industry. The results in Sweden have been favorable, especially in cutting down on sex trafficking and organized crime.

In neighboring Norway, conditions for women who are imprisoned are so agreeable that the police have had to stop taking Russian prostitutes into custody. The reason was conditions were so favorable in jail that the prostitutes were not deterred from crime. Prostitution, then, has been essentially legal in Norway. Today, however, government officials have grown increasingly worried about the scores of foreign prostitutes on local streets (*Aftenposten*, 2007). They believe most are victims of human traffickers who have forced the women into prostitution and seize the vast majority of their earnings. The new proposed law forbidding the purchase of sex is aimed at prostitutes' customers and alleged white slavery operations.

The life of a street prostitute, according to Stout and McPhail (1998), is a life of pain and terror. Battering and rape from the hands of pimps and johns "goes with the territory." Pimps often take the earnings of a woman used in prostitution or stop her from seeking other employment, whereas johns use economic and physical power to make her comply with their demands. They know the prostitute has no legal protection. Prostitutes, like other women, are more at risk of contracting the AIDS virus than of spreading it; they often contract AIDS from use of dirty needles to inject heroin or cocaine into their bodies. Crack cocaine is most commonly used among African American and heroin among European American street prostitutes. Exchange of sex for drugs is common.

Many prostitutes are arrested and come into jails and prisons on drug charges. Others, however, are being prosecuted through AIDS-specific laws targeting prostitutes who receive positive test results for HIV antibodies and then are subsequently arrested for prostitution. Critics of these laws argue that this is a punitive strategy aimed at vulnerable women and that there is no epidemiological evidence that prostitutes are contributing significantly to the sexual transmission of the AIDS virus (Luxenburg and Guild, 2007).

DRUG-RELATED CRIME

The most obvious trend over the years is related to arrests for drugs and drug-related offenses (Butterfield, 2003), and often arrests and prosecutions for other crimes such as violence, robberies, and prostitution are drug related. According to the U.S. Department of Justice (BJS, 2006a), approximately half of female and male federal prison inmates were using drugs in the month before the offense. In state prisons, the numbers were 60 percent and 42.8 percent respectively. More women used methamphetamines (meth) than men during this time period— 15 percent (federal) and 17 percent (state) compared to 10 percent in both federal and state facilities for men. Interestingly, as an earlier BJS report (2000) states, nearly one in three women serving time in state prisons said they had committed the offense in order to obtain money to support their need for drugs.

The war on drugs, as stated previously, has emerged as a war on minority and poor women, a war that is packing nonviolent women into prison in record-breaking rates. Chapter 8 explores the nature of addiction in women in considerable depth. Our focus here will be on the policy side, policy driven by a frenzy of media attention to one drug in particular—"crack." Central to understanding the creation of the sentencing guidelines for crack cocaine, the cheaper, smoked alternative to powder cocaine, is the role of the media. The social reality of crack was shaped and presented by the media to the general public, at the time relatively unconcerned about the drug problem, along with President Reagan's declaration of the war on drugs in 1986 (Sudbury, 2004).

In constructing and presenting the problem of crack, the media, as Everett (1998) suggests, focused on three general themes: the claim that crack was more addictive than powder cocaine, leading to such problems as crack babies and exchange of sex for drugs; the strong link to the violent crime world of inner city gangs; and the low cost and ready supply of the drug. Immediately then, with public opinion aroused, and head on the heels of a barrage of sensational media stories such as the sudden death of basketball star Len Bias, who died of a cocaine-induced heart attack (in fact, the culprit was powder cocaine), there was a public and political outcry for action. Without the usual committee hearings, therefore, a bill swept through Congress. This bill culminated in the 1986 and 1988 Anti-Drug Abuse Acts establishing harsh mandatory minimum sentencing guidelines targeting crack cocaine. Possession of 500 grams of powder cocaine, but only 5 grams of crack, triggers a mandatory minimum sentence of five years for possession: This is the 100 to 1 ratio that people are talking about, a ratio that has been considered racist and classist by most observers. The penalty for drug dealing (trafficking) is of course higher. The states followed suit and increased their penalties as well. No wonder then that the number of black women incarcerated for drug offenses increased 828 percent between 1986 and 1991 (Bush-Baskette, 1998). This increase was more than three times that of white women. Unlike men, women typically are convicted of drug possession rather that drug dealing.

Male–female differences in drug distribution are pronounced. A study of gender differences in drug market activities that used extensive arrest data found that women's earnings in this illegal enterprise are low, that they tend to procure drugs in their own neighborhoods, and that these drugs are acquired by means of a sexual than a cash transaction (Rodriguez and Griffin, 2005). The drug market, according to these researchers, is thus highly gendered, and women are not equal partners to the men. Still, women are vulnerable to arrest and prosecution.

As noted by the American Civil Liberties Union (ACLU) (2005), women are increasingly caught up in the ever-widening net cast by current drug conspiracy laws and accomplice liability laws that extend criminal liability to the arrested offender's partners and relatives. Such sentencing laws fail to consider the many reasons—including domestic violence, economic dependence, or dependent immigrant status—that may compel a woman to remain silent. Despite a recent Supreme Court ruling to give judges more discretion, the mandatory minimum laws still are on the books in most states.

A *New York Times* article on the war on drugs presents the cases of two women victims of the antidrug hysteria: Tonya, serving ten years for mailing a package containing crack, who had to serve the maximum because of her inability to provide sufficient information about higher-ups, and Monica, who at 20 was sentenced to ten years for counting money for her boyfriend, a crack dealer (Egan, 1999). Sudbury (2004) presents a similar case of a black college student, Kemba Smith, who received a twenty-four-year sentence just for knowledge of her boyfriend's drug dealing. Kemba was pregnant and threatened by her boyfriend of whom she feared for her life. This case, according to Sudbury, represents the gender entrapment experienced by many African American women entering the criminal justice system.

Women drug dealers often wind up with a longer sentence than the drug-dealing men they're involved with because they lack the information about the drug trafficking operations the prosecutors want or they are unwilling to go undercover or snitch on family members (ACLU, 2005). Because women are socialized to "stand by their man," and thus provide assistance both as men commit crime and as they attempt to avoid being caught for it, many women get caught in the web of the law. Women engage in what would otherwise be noncriminal activity that is identified as "aiding and abetting," such as accompanying a male intimate to a drug sale, or answering the phone when a drug deal is taking place, or spending money obtained through drug sales (Failinger, 2006).

The interplay of race, class, and gender is at its most pronounced in the prosecution of drug-addicted mothers. Under the rational of protecting the fetus, poor, black, drug-addicted mothers are being hauled into court. This is part of an alarming trend toward greater state intervention into the lives of pregnant women. And poor women of color are the primary targets of government control; they are the least likely to obtain adequate prenatal care yet the most vulnerable to government monitoring, and the least able to conform to the white middle-class standard of motherhood. The prosecution of drug-addicted mothers thus becomes more than an issue of antifemale backlash. Poor black women have been selected for punishment as a result of an inseparable combination of their gender, race, and economic status.

ROBBERY

Robbery, unlike burglary, is a crime of theft that involves violence or a threat of violence against a person. As we learned earlier from Table 4.1, offenders who commit robbery are almost 90 percent male. Although the motivation of robbery—to obtain goods or cash—is the same for both genders, the male/female differences in the modus operandi of robbery has been found to be pronounced. In her in-depth interviews with 37 African American offenders operating on the streets of St. Louis, Jody Miller (2001) found that compared to women, men were more apt to view robbery as one means of expressing their masculinity. Men relied on violence, often using a gun and injuring their victims, who were usually men. Women often robbed other women whom they viewed as weak and easy targets. If their targets were men, however, they manipulated the men into thinking they were willing to engage in sex, got them off in a hotel or some other indoor setting, then robbed them when they were the most vulnerable. Sometimes the women worked with men as a team. Miller sees the urban backgrounds of poverty and lack of legitimate opportunities as powerful incentives for robbery for both genders. Belknap (2007) cites obtaining money to buy drugs as a motivation for many of the habitual criminals.

MURDER

The relative scarcity of female perpetuated murder is what makes female murderers—women such as Bonnie Parker (of Bonnie and Clyde fame), Jean Harris (a high school headmistress who killed her ex-lover), Susan Smith (who killed her children), and Karla Faye Tucker (a born-again Christian who was executed in Texas)—so intriguing.

In 2006, although both male and female homicide rates had declined significantly, the male rate of committing homicide was about ten times the female rate (FBI, 2006). Compared to men, research has revealed that women arrested for homicide are less likely to have previous criminal histories, are more likely to have committed the offense alone, and are more likely to have killed as the result of domestic conflict.

DOMESTIC HOMICIDE.   The victim–offender relationship differs substantially between female and male murders (BJS, 2007a). Whereas men are more apt to kill a stranger or be killed by a stranger, homicides by and of women generally involve intimates or other family members.

According to BJS (2007a) data, the number of intimate homicides for all race and gender groups declined between 1975 and 2005—the number of black males killed by intimates dropped by 83 percent, white males by 61 percent, black females by 52 percent, and white females by 6 percent. It should be pointed out that in previous years, the numbers of black partners and spouses killed by women was extraordinarily high; now these numbers are considerably down, although still well above the white murder rate. According to my calculations from the same BJS data, the black male spouse victimization rate is four times the comparable white rate and the boyfriend murder rate is seven times the comparable white rate. Note also that white women are still victimized at almost the same level as earlier. Across the board, guns were the most common weapon used.

In 2005, 329 males and 1,181 females were killed by their intimate partners, according to the most recent BJS report. This means that men are significantly more likely to kill their spouses and partners than are women to kill theirs. Interestingly, in the early 1970s, before domestic partner shelters and other victim protection services were introduced, about as many women killed their intimate partners as their partners killed them, and the number was well over 1,200 homicides committed by each gender. The most frequently offered explanation for the striking decline in female homicides of their male partners is that since most of these murders committed by women were done out of self-defense or anger over being beaten, now battered women have an alternative means of escape from a dangerous or otherwise intolerable situation. Wells and DeLeon-Granados (2004), for example, explain the striking decline in homicides of men by their wives/partners in terms of "exposure reduction theory" (p. 233). Exposure reduction theory is the notion that the availability of mechanisms that allow a woman to sever her ties with an abusive partner will spare her from seeking a violent solution.

Unfortunately, since men's motives for killing their wives/partners are different—that is, not for defense but for retaliation after a break-up—when the woman does escape, her life may still be at risk. Sometimes the end result is murder suicide; virtually all of murder suicides that arise out of intimate partner situations are perpetrated by men. Research shows that the individual who is dangerously violent and also prone to depression is at risk of killing his partner and himself when the threat of a break-up occurs (van Wormer and Roberts, 2009). There are almost two murder suicides a day in the United States, three-fourths of which involve domestic partner situations (Violence Policy Center, 2006).

In cases of female-on-male intimate partner homicide, the power imbalance between men and women comes into play. Women who kill, as Karlene Faith (1993) explains, generally do so when the man is in some way incapacitated—asleep or drunk, for example—and thus the defense of being in immediate danger does not apply. These women serve long prison terms, accordingly. Recent research showing that women engage in violence against their spouses to the same degree as men do are erroneous and fail to take into account women's structured vulnerabilities. Weapon availability, of course, figures in, boosting American murder rates far above that of their European and many Asian counterparts (VPC, 2006).

What are the personalities like of women who kill? Since these women likely end up serving long prison terms, they are available to be studied by sociologists and observed over the years by correctional workers. In a classic study, Ann Jones (1980), the author of *Women Who Kill*, observed that although the act of killing, especially by a woman, may be extraordinary, most women who commit this act are ordinary in every way. In fact, women convicted of murder, as it is universally acknowledged, are often the most compliant women in prison, the most middle class, and the most likely to lack criminal records (Faith, 1993). Van Wormer's prison participation observation study in Alabama confirms this observation (if we overlook the behavior of two self-proclaimed "hit ladies") (see Chapter 5).

In one of the most intriguing studies up to that time, Hamilton and Sutterfield (1998) compared a sample of 20 battered women who murdered their partners with a sample of 29 battered women at a women's shelter who did not do so. The key difference between the groups was not personality but their earlier treatment by police and whether or not they were referred to a shelter. These findings are consistent with recent statistics from the U.S. Department of Justice and Statistics Canada, which show a decline in female partner murder rates but not in women killed by their partners.

Albert Roberts (2007) examined data drawn from a sample of 105 women in prison convicted of killing their husbands and 105 battered women in a sample from the community in New Jersey. The women in prison for murdering their spouses/partners had a history of being battered. Compared to the battered women who did not kill their partners, the prison sample was far more likely to have received death threats from their partners; these threats were specific as to time and place and method. In addition to a history of partner violence, the majority of the women prisoners had a history of sexual abuse, a substance use problem, had attempted suicide, and had access to the batterer's guns.

Child Murder—Filicide

Mothers and stepmothers kill about half of all children murdered; whereas mothers tend to kill infants, fathers more often kill children age 8 or older. Mothers of course spend a great deal more time with children, especially small children, than fathers do. McKee (2006), a forensic psychologist who evaluated over 30 girls and women who have killed their infants and children, and the author of *Why Mothers Kill*, presents case histories and a typology of mothers who have killed. The following types of mother murderers are included: abusive/neglectful, psychotic/suicidal, psychopathic, detached, and retaliatory. The first three categories are self-explanatory. Detached mothers are defined as those who fail to bond with their newborn infants, and retaliatory mothers are those who kill to get revenge on someone. Actually, as McKee informs us, parents who kill their children for revenge are almost always fathers.

If women who murder their spouses are considered an anomaly, women who kill their children are regarded as downright monsters. Wilczynski (1991) examined the public images of such women; they tend to be viewed in terms of the "mad" (in Britain, where they are seen as mentally ill) and the "bad" (in North America, where they are prosecuted for homicide). Postpartum psychosis has been recognized by the law as an element in infanticide for fifty years in England. Women suffering from this condition are given intensive hospitalized treatment until they recover.

An estimated 50–80 percent of new mothers suffer from mild depression after giving birth; major postpartum depression, however, is a rare yet serious psychological issue affecting fewer than 1 percent of new mothers within the first year after giving birth (McKee, 2006). What distinguishes this condition from the milder variety is the mother's obsessive concern about hurting her baby. Because the woman is at risk of harming herself or her baby, postpartum psychosis is a medical emergency. In the United States, between 1976 and 2000, 30 percent of the child homicides were committed by the biological mother at an annual rate of over 200 (McKee, 2006). The mother who kills her newborn does not see the infant as human but more as a foreign body needing to be destroyed. McKee refers to "ignored pregnancy cases" (p. 27), who are principally young women who had denied or concealed their pregnancies. Mothers who kill older children may be acting out of anger and hatred or out of a suicidal impulse. Some women such as Susan Smith, who drowned her children in a car, kill their children and then plan to kill themselves (McKee, 2006). Susan Smith had many of the risk factors for suicidal murder. There was a high rate of suicide in her family, including her father who died when she was a child. Susan was sexually abused by her stepfather and diagnosed as having bipolar personality disorder. Her marriage was shaky and her children were very young.

In the old days, killing babies for rational reasons used to be much more common. Abortion was illegal, and children born out of wedlock and their mothers were stigmatized. Today, in India, female newborns are at least three times more likely to be the victims of neonatal murder than are boys (McKee).

Moving from the "mad" to "bad," such women are viewed not as sick but as "ruthless, selfish, cold, callous, neglectful or their children or domestic responsibilities, violent or promiscuous," in the words of Wilczynski (p. 78). McKee presents a case history of "Samantha," who killed her nine-year-old daughter while she, the mother, was impaired by heavy cocaine use. Her daughter had just been raped by Samantha's boyfriend and was threatening to tell her teacher.

Pregnant mothers who endanger their unborn children by using drugs also fall into this pejorative category of mother child killers. The shocking image of monstrously deformed "crack babies" proliferated in the mass media is the early 1990s and led to numerous prosecutions of women for "fetal abuse." We can liken the state's reaction to pregnant, drug-using mothers today to the Progressive Era's response to mothers accused of child abuse. In both historical periods, the child savers have imposed their class, ethnic, and racial biases on immigrant, poor, and African American women. At the turn of the century, then and now, women have been subjected to strict formal control and informal condemnation. In the modern period, the criminalization of pregnant drug users has resulted in prosecution of mothers in accordance with mandatory reporting laws regarding those who fail drug tests. Sanctions include loss of custody of the child; the placement of other, older children in foster homes; the loss of various welfare benefits; and arrest and imprisonment (van Wormer and Davis, 2008).

Public benefits often denied to individuals on the basis of a drug conviction or drug use include welfare, educational loans, and public housing. Although federal law authorizes these policies, several states have begun to reject such punitive measures (Drug Policy Alliance, 2007).

Fuentes (1998) describes the sad cases of two African American women in New York City whose breast-fed infants failed to thrive and who died of malnutrition. Both women were denied care for their babies although enrolled in Medicaid. Both women were arrested and charged with criminally negligent homicide; the charges against one of the mothers were eventually dropped. Although rare, this happenstance illustrates the worst elements of the health and social service system and the backlash against poor mothers of color. A related issue is the prosecution of mothers for substance abuse while pregnant; this matter is discussed under the section on drug abuse.

The Female Chronic Offender

Wolfgang, Figlio, and Sellin's (1972) cohort study in Philadelphia identified that 6 percent of the total sample had been arrested five times or more. In a second cohort study, which included female offenders were able to identify only 1 percent of the females as chronic offenders. These female offenders were involved in significantly less serious crimes than the males of the cohort. Yet, similar to males of both cohorts, the more the female offenders were arrested and the more serious their court's disposition, the more likely they were to be arrested again.

Danner et al. (1995) examined female chronic offenders from data on file for 1,076 incarcerated female offenders in Florida. They found that female chronics in comparison with female nonchronics were more likely to be younger, of minority status, substance abusers, single, and involved in spouse abuse, as well as to have committed the crimes alone. Comparing the female chronics with female nonchronics, it was found "that the process of becoming a female chronic offender appeared to be more complex than for males in that more criminogenic forces were required to overcome the crime-inhibiting effects of female socialization" (pp. 45–46). Furthermore, they found that the core variables that discriminated most strongly between the female chronics and nonchronics were age at first adult arrest, offense seriousness, substance abuse, and minority group status.

Matt DeLisi, in using the criminal records of 500 male and female adult recidivists, applied the concept of career criminality to women and described how this application had specific gendered elements. The average female offender age was 37 years, nearly three years younger than the male chronic offender. Habitual female offenders were also more ethnically diverse than their male counterparts. Chronic female offenders further had a later onset age of arrest, had shorter criminal careers, and were arrested in fewer states than their male peers. In addition, female career offenders were less migratory than men in terms of the accumulation of arrests in multiple jurisdictions (DeLisi, 2005).

PROCESSING WOMEN FOR CRIME

The belief that women receive lighter sentences than men do for similar crime and criminal histories persists; from this perspective women offenders are seen as getting away with more lenient treatment than men due to the belief that they are the weaker (and less dangerous) sex. Objective research seems to bear this belief out. Economists Sarnikar, Sorensen, and Oaxaca (2007), for example, formed this conclusion based on their analysis of data obtained from the U.S. Sentencing Commission's records. Their research, which was based on over 45,000 sentencing cases between 1996 and 2002, used sophisticated formulas to weigh variables such as prior criminal record. The results showed that women had an advantage of 9.5 months less of their sentences and therefore received more lenient sentences than did men with a similar crime and history. One serious flaw in their study, however, was these researchers used only cases of white women. This was, as stated in the article, to rule out the factor of racism. This finding is interesting in that it seems to indicate a small degree of chivalry accorded to white women. But we cannot generalize the findings as the majority of sentenced offenders are members of minority groups.

It is true that women are less likely to be sentenced to death row than are men or executed. There is firm evidence that women who are masculine and therefore not considered gender appropriate in their demeanor in court are treated more harshly than are women who seem more feminine in their appearance and behavior (Belknap, 2007). Prosecutors of women in capital cases (cases for which a death sentence is possible), for example, have been known to emphasize masculine characteristics and lesbianism to turn the jurors against them (Baker, 2007). Farr (2004), in her study of women on death row, found that the media had portrayed these offenders as "manly" and "man-hating" women who were the personification of evil. Many had engaged in felony robbery (a male-associated crime) in connection with the murder. As a result of homophobia in society and in the criminal justice system, about half of the women on death row are lesbians.

The gender of the judge is also a factor in sentencing patterns. Female judges, far from over-identifying with female defendants, may hold them to a higher standard than judges who are male. One study found the higher the proportion of female judges in a district, the less the disparity in male and female defendants' sentencing (Schanzenbach, 2005).

Although more research is needed on sentencing practices, we can probably conclude that white women who are feminine in demeanor have the best chance of receiving somewhat more lenient treatment than African American females and males of all races. As a rule, research shows that women of color, poor women, younger women, immigrants, and lesbians are accorded less leniency than other women (Bloom, Owen, and Covington, 2007). And we also know from reports throughout the literature that conspiracy laws unfairly impact persons who are minimally involved in criminal behavior but who are the partners and wives of men who are actively engaged in lives of crime. Under conspiracy laws, neither the context of the relationship nor the impact on the children of sending both parents to prison is taken into account (Gaskins, 2004). The **gender-neutral** sentencing laws fail to recognize the distinction between major players in drug organizations and minor ancillary players (Bloom et al.).

Summary

We know that the pathway to crime for a girl or woman has biological, psychological, and social components. Negative early childhood experiences involving trauma and depression coupled with addictive tendencies followed by unhealthy relationships and initiation into drug use and other illicit activities is a typical scenario. Serious problems related to poverty and perceived lack of career opportunity set the stage for the girl or woman's entry into a pattern of hardship and crime. She may shift in and out of homelessness, unemployment, and heavy drug use, and get involved in gang life and prostitution. Because racism and poverty often go hand-in-hand, females from poor, inner-city backgrounds are often forced to deal early, and on a regular basis, with problems of violence, drugs, childhood pregnancy, and rough treatment by the authorities. The intersection of gender, race, and class is thus a highly evident component in female crime, in regard to both the form that the crime takes and the punishment meted out. Chivalry for women who go against the norms of expected sex role behavior, especially concerning femininity and motherhood, is nonexistent.

The pathway to crime for a middle-class woman may involve family victimization and heavy alcohol and other drug use. Alternatively, the pathway may relate to gambling addiction and temptation to borrow money from the company and later charges of embezzlement. Murder is an act that cuts across class lines: a battered woman may kill her husband for defense or for revenge and a mother suffering from postpartum depression may take the life of her child. The conundrum of female crime and its relation to social and personal victimization are facts of life virtually ignored by the mass media. Virtually absent from the lurid media crime accounts is any serious attempt to connect the dots between the myriad variables involving race, poverty, and the key variable of relationship. In the hopes of demystifying the complex subject of female crime, we have focused on particular types of crime and viewed each (for example, robbery, murder, embezzlement, prostitution, drug-related crime) through a gender-based lens. Whether they are labeled criminal or not, sent to prison or not, female offenders do what ordinary women do; they become embroiled in family life and relationships and they try to make their world safe and habitable for their loved ones. Even when violent, and women's capacity for violence is undeniable, women are often acting within the context of highly gendered personal relationships.

Many of the facts of women's lives that form the web of circumstances of their lawbreaking are specific to women: childbirth and child care, care of the elderly, abuse by men, and dependence on men or the social system for economic aid. To lump female lawbreakers together with male lawbreakers without regard for these details in their lives, as Canadian psychologist Evelyn Sommers (2005) argues, is to blur the experiences of two disparate groups. Gender-specific counseling for troubled female adolescents and their placement in nonpunitive, nurturant group homes could perhaps save them from their worst, most self-destructive instincts.

Key Terms

feminist criminology *38*
gender-neutral *46*
liberation thesis *31*

Critical Thinking Questions

1. Which of the theoretical explanations of women and crime do you find most appealing?
2. What is the importance of gender related to adult women and crime?
3. How does social class contribute to class oppression of women in the United States?
4. What does racial discrimination contribute to our understanding of women and crime?
5. What are the most salient trends regarding women and crime?

Web Destinations

See the National Consortium on Violence Research for research reports on violence by women and minorities at: www.heinz.cmu.edu/researchers/centers.html

For research on women in the justice system, visit this site: www.ncjrs.org/pdffiles1/nij/189973.pdf

National Institute of Corrections, gender-responsive strategies: www.nicic.org/pubs/2003/018017.pdf

References

Adler, F. (1975). *Sisters in crime: The rise of the new female criminal.* New York: McGraw Hill.

Aftenposten (2007, July 4). Buying sex can yield jail term: News from Norway. *Aftenposten.* Retrieved January 2008 from http://www.aftenposten.no/english/local/article1870915.ece

American Civil Liberties Union (ACLU) (2005, May 17). *Caught in the net: The impact of drug policies on women and families.* ACLU. Retrieved November 2007 from www.civilrights.com

American Psychiatric Association (2000). *Diagnostic and Statistical Manual of Mental Disorders, Text Revision,* 4th ed. Washington, DC: American Psychiatric Association.

Arnold, E. M., McNeece, C. A., and Stewart, J. C. (1999). *A community-based intervention for female prostitutes.* A paper presented at the Criminal and Juvenile Justice Symposium. The Council on Social Work Education, March 10–13, San Francisco, USA.

Artz, S. (1998). *Sex, power, and the violent school girl.* Toronto: Trifolium Books.

Baker, D. V. (2007). Systemic white racism and the brutalization of executed black women in the United States. In R. Muraskin (ed.), *It's a crime: Women and justice,* 4th ed. (pp. 394–443). Upper Saddle River, NJ: Pearson.

Barovick, H. (1999). Bad to the bone. *Time,* pp. 130–131.

Belknap, J. (2007). *The invisible woman: Gender, crime, and justice.* Belmont, CA: Thomson.

Bloom, B., Owen, B., and Covington, S. (2004). Women offenders and the gendered effects of public policy. *Review of Policy Research 21*(1): 31–48.

Bricking, T. (1998, June 17). Girls' crimes start to match boys'. *The Cincinnati Enquirer* (p. 17). Washington, DC: Department of Justice.

Bureau of Justice Statistics (BJS). (1980). *Uniform Crime Report.* Washington DC: US Department of Justice.

Bureau of Justice Statistics (BJS). (2000, October). *Women offenders.* Washington, DC: U.S. Department of Justice.

Bureau of Justice Statistics (BJS). (2006a, December 10). *Criminal victimization in the United States—Statistical tables.* Washington, DC: U.S. Department of Justice.

Bureau of Justice Statistics (BJS). (2006b, October). *Drug use and dependence, state and federal prisoners, 2004.* Washington, DC: U.S. Department of Justice. Retrieved December 2007 from Washington, DC: U.S. Department of Justice.

Bureau of Justice Statistics (BJS). (2007a, July). *Homicide trends in the U.S.: Intimate homicide.* Washington, DC: U.S. Department of Justice. Retrieved December 2007 from http://www.ojp.usdoj.gov/bjs/homicide/intimates.htm

Bureau of Justice Statistics (BJS). (2007b, June). *Prison and jail inmates at midyear 2006.* Washington, DC: U.S. Department of Justice.

Bush-Baskette, S. (1998). The war on drugs as a war against black women. In S. L. Miller, (ed.), *Crime* control and women: Feminist implications of criminal justice police (pp. 113–129). Thousand Oaks, CA: SAGE.

Butterfield, F. (2003, December 29). Women find a new arena for equality: Prison. *The New York Times*. Retrieved November 2007 from http://query.nytimes.com/gst/fullpage.html?res=9A05E5D6123EF93AA15751C1A9659C8B63

Chesney-Lind, M., and Pasko, L. (2003). *The female offender: Girls, women, and crime*. Thousand Oaks, CA: SAGE.

Comack, E., and Brickey, S. (2007). Consituting the violence of criminalized women. *Canadian Journal of Criminology and Criminal Justice 49*: 1–37.

Crites, L. (1976). Women offenders: Myth vs reality. In Laura Crites (ed.), *The female offender* (pp. 36–39). Lexington, MA: Lexington Books.

Dabbs, J. M., Jr. (1998). Testosterone and the concept of dominance. *Behavioral and Brain Sciences 21*: 370–371.

Dabbs, J. M., and Hargrove, M. (1997). Age, testosterone, and behavior among female prison inmates. *Psychosomatic Medicine 59*(5): 477–480.

Daly, K. (1994). *Gender, crime, and punishment*. New Haven, CT: Yale University Press.

De Santis, M. (2007). Sweden's prostitution solution: Why hasn't anyone tried this before? Women's Justice Center. Retrieved December 2007 from http://www.justicewomen.com/cj_sweden.html

Drug Policy Alliance. (2007). Drugs, police, and the law. Retrieved December 2007 from http://www.drugpolicy.org/law/publicbenefi/index.cfm

Egan, T. (1999, February 28). The war on crack retreats, still taking prisoners. *New York Times*, p. A1.

Enman, C. (1999, November 14). Girl bullies strike dubious blows for gender equality. *Ottawa Citizen Online*. Retrieved December 2007 from http://www.fact.on.ca/newpaper/oc991021.htm

Erikson, K. (1966). *Wayward Puritans: A study in the sociology of deviance*. New York: John Wiley and Sons.

Everett, R. S. (1998). The evolution of the federal sentencing guidelines for crack cocaine: Social construction and social control. In E. L. Jensen and J. Gerber (eds.), *The new war on drugs: Symbolic politics and criminal justice policy* (pp. 91–106). Cincinnati, OH: Anderson.

Failinger, M. (2006). Lessons unlearned: Women offenders, the ethics of care, and the promise of restorative justice. *Fordham Urban Law Journal 33*(2): 487–527.

Faith, K. (1993). *Unruly women: The politics of confinement and resistance*. Vancouver, BC: Press Gang Publishing.

Farr, K. A. (2004). Defeminizing and dehumanizing female murderers: Depictions of lesbians on death row. In B. Price and N. Sokoloff (eds.), *The criminal justice system and women* (pp. 249–260). Boston, MA: McGraw Hill.

Federal Bureau of Investigation (FBI). (2007, September). *Uniform crime reports*. Washington, DC: U.S. Department of Justice.

Feinman, C. (1980). *Women in the criminal justice system*. New York: Praeger.

Fuentes, A. (1998, September/October). Mother charged with murder when their infants fail to thrive. *MS*, pp. 21–22.

Gaskins, S. (2004). "Women of circumstance"—the effects of mandatory minimum sentencing on women minimally involved in drug crimes. *American Criminal Law review 41*(4): 1533–1554.

Gibbens, T. C. N. (1971). Female offenders. *British Journal of Hospital Medicine 6*: 279–286.

Hamilton, G., and Sutterfield, T. (1998). Comparison study of women who have and have not murdered their abusive partners. *Women and Therapy 20*(4): 45–55.

Jones, A. (1980). *Women who kill*. New York: Holt, Rinehart and Winston.

Landsberg, M. (1999, November 13). Feminism not the link between girls and violence. *Toronto Star*, L1.

Lombroso, C., and Ferrero, W. (1895). *The female offender*. London: T. Fisher Unwin.

Loucks, A., and Zamble, E. (1999). Predictors of recidivism in serious female offenders: Canada searches for predictors to both men and women. *Corrections Today 61*(1): 26–31.

Luxenburg, J., and Guild, T. E. (2007). Women, AIDS, and the criminal justice system. In R. Muraskin (ed.), *It's a crime: Women and justice*, 4th ed. (pp. 379–391). Upper Saddle River, NJ: Pearson.

McKee, G. (2006). *Why mothers kill: A forensic psychologist's casebook*. New York: Oxford University Press.

Mullins, C. W., Wright, W. R., and Jacobs, B. A. (2004). Gender, street life and criminal retaliation. *Criminology 42*: 911–940.

Nelson, V. (1993). Prostitution: Where racism and sexism intersect. *Michigan Journal of Gender and Law 1*: 81–89.

Obeidallah, D., and Earls, F. (1999). *Adolescent girls: The role of depression in the development of delinquency* (FS000244). National Institute of Justice, Washington, DC: U.S. Government Printing Office.

Pollock, J. M. (1999). *Criminal women*. Cincinnati, OH: Anderson.

Rauch, L. (2006, July 14). Vegas sex workers demand rights, respect. *USA Today.* Retrieved December 2007 from http://www.usatoday.com/news/offbeat/2006-07-14-sexworkers-rally_x.htm

Ringrose, J. (2006). A new universal mean girl: Examining the social regulation of a new feminine pathology. *Feminism and Psychology 16*: 405.

Roberts, A. R. (2007). Domestic violence continuum, forensic assessment and crisis intervention. *Families in Society 88*(1): 42–54.

Rodriguez, N., and Griffin, M. (2005, November). Gender differences in drug market activities. An unpublished federally-funded grant final report. Retrieved December 2007 from http://www.ncjrs.gov/App/Publications/abstract.aspx?ID=233440

Saleebey, D. (2006). *The strengths perspective in social work practice,* 4th ed. Boston, MA: Allyn and Bacon.

Samenow, S. E. (1984). *Inside the criminal mind.* New York: Times Books.

Sarnikar, S., Sorensen, T., and Oaxaca, R. (2007, June). Do you receive a lighter prison sentence because you are a woman? An economic analysis of federal criminal sentencing guidelines. IZA Discussion Paper No. 2870. Retrieved December 2007 from http://ssrn.com/abstract=999358

Schanzenbach, M. (2005). Racial and sex disparities in prison sentences. *Journal of Legal Studies 34*: 57–92.

Simon, R. (1975). *Women and crime.* Lexington, MA: D.C. Heath.

Simpson, K. (2001). The role of testosterone in aggression. *McGill Journal of Medicine 6*: 32–40.

Smith, D., Leve, L., and Chamberlain, P. (2006). Adolescent girls' offending and health-risk sexual behavior: The predictive role of trauma. *Child Maltreatment 11*(4): 346–353.

Squires, S. (2000, January 12). The dope on drugs: How the most popular substances affect your brain, body and behavior. *Washington Post,* p. H01.

Steffensmeier, D., and Schwartz, J. (2004). Trends in female criminality: Is crime still a man's world? In B. Price Price and N. Sokoloff (eds.), *The criminal justice system and women,* 3rd ed. (pp. 95–111). Boston, MA: McGraw Hill.

Steffensmeier, D., Zhong, H., Ackerman, J., Schwartz, J., and Agha, S. (2006). Gender gap trends for violent crimes, 1980 to 2003: A UCR-NCVS comparison. *Feminist Criminology 1*: 72–98.

Stout, K. D., and McPhail, B. (1998). *Confronting sexism and violence against women: A challenge for social work.* New York: Longman.

Strand, S., and Belfrage, H. (2005). Gender differences in psychopathy in a Swedish offender sample. *Behavioral Sciences and the Law 23*: 837–850.

Sudbury, J. (2004). Women of color, globalization, and the politics of incarceration. In B. Price and N. Sokoloff (eds.), *The criminal justice system and women,* 3rd ed. (pp. 219–234). Boston, MA: McGraw Hill.

van Wormer, K. (2007). *Human behavior and the social environment, micro level: Individuals and families.* New York: Oxford University Press.

van Wormer, K., and Davis, D. R. (2008). *Addiction treatment: A strengths perspective,* 2nd ed. Belmont, CA: Thomson.

van Wormer, K., and Roberts, A. R. (2009). *Death by domestic violence: Preventing the murders and the murder-suicides.* Westport, CT: Praeger.

Vines, G. (1999, November 29). The gene in the bottle. *New Scientist,* 39–43.

Violence Policy Center (VPC). (2006). American roulette: The untold story of murder-suicide in the United States. VPC. Retrieved July 2007 from www.vpc.org/studyndx.htm

Vito, G., Maahs, J., and Holmes, R. (2007). *Criminology: Theory, research and policy.* Boston, MA: Jones and Bartlett.

Websdale, N., and Chesney-Lind, M. (2004). Doing violence to women: Research synthesis on the victimization of women. In B. Price and N. Sokoloff (eds.), *The criminal justice system and women* (pp. 303–322). Boston, MA: McGraw Hill.

Wells, W., and DeLeon-Granados, W. (2004, June). The intimate partner homicide decline: Disaggregated trends, theoretical explanations, and policy implications. *Criminal Justice Policy Review 15*(2): 229–246.

Wilczynski, A. (1991). Images of women who kill their infants: The mad and the bad. *Women and Criminal Justice 2*: 71–88.

Wrangham, R., and Peterson, D. (1996). *Demonic males: Apes and the origins of human violence.* Boston, MA: Houghton Mifflin.

Yeoman, B. (1999, November). Bad girls. *Psychology Today 32*(6): 54–57, 71.

Yochelson, S., and Samenow, S. E. (1976). *The criminal personality.* New York: Aronson.

3

Feminist Theory
and Research

Frances M. Heidensohn is one of those scholars who note that "women and crime" is recognized now as an important topic in criminology texts and readers (Heidensohn, 1996, pp. xiii–xiv). As part of the rapid expansion of the field, authors of many criminology texts not only devote sections to feminist perspectives and theories but also attempt to differentiate between feminist and nonfeminist analyses (Daly, 1998, p. 86). Expansion has come from two sources: (1) research by nonfeminist scholars who are interested in studies of women and crime or race and gender differences and (2) research by feminist scholars from a variety of disciplines with diverse political stances. The first source focuses on criminological debates, but its members may not have a grasp of feminist theories and research; the second source focuses on a theoretical and political analysis of women's situations, but its members may fail to grasp the limits of criminalization or be familiar with theories of crime and punishment (Daly, 1998, p. 86).

The purpose of this chapter is to bridge these sources by presenting feminist theory and research within the context of criminology and its theories of crime and punishment. Chapter 2 presented gender differences in lawbreaking, whereas this chapter examines more carefully the patterns of lawbreaking, including gender ratio of crime, gendered crime, gendered pathways, and gendered lives. In addition, this chapter considers feminist epistemologies; epistemology refers to "theories of what knowledge is, what makes it possible, and how to get it" (Harding, 1987, p. 308). Finally, Chapter 3 examines feminist research methodology. The use of feminist methodology implies a commitment to the empowerment of women, a critical examination of traditional methodology in the social sciences, and a recognition of gendered power relationships in the conduct and process of research.

KEY FEATURES THAT DISTINGUISH FEMINIST THEORIES

The discussion in this chapter begins by highlighting key features that distinguish feminist theories from other theoretical perspectives in criminology. Kathleen Daly and Meda Chesney-Lind (1988) list five aspects of feminist thought that distinguish it from traditional criminological inquiry:

1. Gender is not a natural fact but a complex social, historical, and cultural product; it is related to, but not simply derived from, biological sex difference and reproductive capacities.
2. Gender and gender relations order social life and social institutions in fundamental ways.
3. Gender relations and constructs of masculinity and femininity are not symmetrical but are based on an organizing principle of men's superiority and social and political-economic dominance over women.
4. Systems of knowledge reflect men's views of the natural and social world; the production of knowledge is gendered.
5. Women should be at the center of intellectual inquiry, not peripheral, invisible, or appendages to men. (p. 504)

In addition, as suggested in Chapter 1, feminist theorists investigate the interlocking nature of gender, race/ethnicity, class, sexuality, and age, recognizing that women's experiences of gender may vary according to their position in class and racial/ethnic hierarchies (Daly and Maher, 1998; Simpson, 1991).

Within this broad framework, Jody Miller and Christopher W. Mullins (2006a, pp. 218–219) highlight key features that distinguish feminist theories from other theoretical perspectives in criminology. First, feminist scholarship is grounded in the inquiry into the meaning and nature of gender relations. According to this perspective, gender theory is crucial to the study of criminality and crime.

Second, feminist perspectives cut across a broad range of questions within criminology and criminal justice. Feminist research has particularly emphasized juvenile/criminal justice processing, including incarceration and violence against women.

Third, feminist criminologists grapple with what has been referred to as an "intellectual double shift." As Daly and Maher note, gender operates not only within the practices and organizations of social life but also within "the discursive fields by which women [and men] are constructed or construct themselves" (1998, p. 4). To elaborate, feminist scholars face the challenge not only of examining the impact of gender and gender inequality in "real" life but also of deconstructing the intertwined ideologies about gender guiding social practices (Miller and Mullins, 2006a).

Finally, feminist criminology is best suited to the development of what Daly (1998) refers to as theories of the "middle range." These middle range theories seek to explore how broader structural forces are realized within both organizational contexts and the micro-level interactions of social actors within a specific area. Instead of creating gender theories, feminist criminology requires us to move beyond broad and global analyses. With the starting recognition that society and social life are patterned on the basis of gender, feminist criminology recognizes that **gender order** is complex and shifting.

THE PROBLEM OF GENERALIZABILITY

Chapter 2 investigated how much theories of men's crime apply to women. For the most part, these studies have received mixed results (Broidy, 2001). Candace Kruttschnitt aptly summarizes: "It appears that the factors that influence delinquent development differ for males and females in some contexts but not others" (1996, p. 141).

Peggy C. Giordano and colleagues' sample from the Ohio Serious Offender Study led them to conclude "that the either/or dichotomy suggested by the contrast between traditional and feminist frameworks is neither necessary nor helpful to the theory-building process." They suggest that the above study "indicates that the basic tenets of these seemingly opposing viewpoints are not in themselves fundamentally incompatible, and the results show that a comprehensive understanding of girls' delinquency requires a more integrated approach." They found that this was particularly true when the focus is on the small subgroup of girls with serious delinquent histories (Giordano, Deines, and Cernkovich, 2006, p. 18).

Giordano and colleagues' follow-up of their study of this subgroup of serious female offenders suggests that a comprehensive examination of their actions requires that we draw from both classic explanations of delinquency and contemporary perspectives that emphasize uniquely gendered processes. Within the life histories of these girls there is ample evidence of both types of social dynamics. Frequent themes within the narrative include disadvantaged neighborhoods, economic marginality, and "excess of definitions favourable to the violation of law," but, at the same time, parents' criminal involvement and/or severe alcohol and drug problems emerge early on and continue throughout the women's childhood and adolescent years. The adult follow-up further supports the idea that some processes associated with continued crime or desistance seem to be "generic" (that is, they have a good fit with both women and men's life experiences), while others appear to be more heavily gendered (Giordano, Deines, and Cernkovich 2006, p. 36).

One of the major problems with explanations of crime that focus on generalizability is that they cannot account for the gender ratio of offending; that is, men are disproportionately involved in crime. Much of this research also assumes that variables or constructs have the same meaning for males and females. However, recent work reveals that these factors have different influences within and across gender. Thus, as a result of the gendered nature of women's and men's lives, factors often take on different meanings and have different consequences for males and females. Thus, feminists insist that while some of the concepts found in presumably gender-neutral theories may be useful for understanding women's offending, gendered theories that take gender and gender stratification into consideration are preferable to those approaches that assume measures or constructs are gender-neutral. However, instead of assuming that "gender difference is the sole focus of feminist research, feminists question: when, how, and why does gender matter?" (Miller and Mullins, 2006a, pp. 226–227).

Important questions relate to the vastly different rates of criminal offending by gender: Why are women less likely than men to be involved in crime? Conversely, why are men more crime-prone than women? What explains these gender differences? (Daly and Chesney-Lind, 1988, p. 515). This **gender ratio of crime** issue is typically pursued by inquiring into the factors that block or limit women's involvement in crime. It can be argued that this inquiry "reflects an androcentric perspective that makes men the norm upon which women deviate through their limited offending" (Miller and Mullins, 2006a, p. 227).

Feminists tend to propose treating gender as a key element of social organization rather than as an individual trait. This approach permits a more complex examination of the gender gap. For example, data on crime trends reveal that the gender gap is more persistent for some offenses than others, fluctuates over time (Steffensmeier and Schwartz, 2004), and varies by class, race/ethnicity, and age (Sommers and Baskin, 1993). In addition, approaches that simply address a gender gap miss the opportunity to examine how causal factors shape differentially men's and women's offending across cross-cutting social positions. Miller and Mullins illustrate this point by noting that evidence exists of a link between "underclass" conditions and African American women's offending, which fails to have explanatory power for women's offending in other contexts (Miller and Mullins, 2006a, p. 228).

Karen Heimer and colleagues examine the "economic marginalization thesis," which proposes "that the gender gap in crime decreases and females account for a greater proportion of crime when women's economic well-being declines" (Heimer, Wittrock, and Unal, 2006, p. 115). They found "that the *relative* economic well-being of women and men is the key to understanding the gender gap in offending." "Not only," they add, are "women more likely to live in poverty than men but also that the gender gap in poverty rates for women in the most crime-prone group continues to increase" (Heimer, Wittrock, and Unal, 2006, p. 121). Their conclusion, which is opposite to the liberation argument, is that economic oppression, instead of economic liberation, may be at the root of the narrowing of the gender gap in crime over the previous four decades (Heimer, Wittrock, and Unal, 2006, p. 131).

The most promising avenues for exploring the complexities of the gender ratio of offending are found in Daly's (1995) conceptual scheme of these three areas of inquiry:

- *Gendered Pathways*: What trajectories bring females and males to offending? What social contexts and factors facilitate entrance to and desistance from offending, and how are they gendered?
- *Gendered Crime*: What are the ways in which street life, sex and drug markets, crime opportunities, informal economies, and crime groups are ordered by gender and other social relations? What is the variation in the sequencing and contexts of women's and men's lawbreaking?
- *Gendered Lives*: How does gender affect the daily lives of females and males? How does gender structure courses of identities and action? How do these experiences intersect with lawbreaking? (pp. 96–99)

Gendered Pathways

From the early 1990s, feminist criminologists began to examine what is now referred to as **gendered pathways**. This approach emphasized "biographical elements, life course trajectories and developmental sequences" (Daly, 1998, p. 97). The pathways approach, which will be covered more extensively in the next chapter on life course and delinquency, seeks to map out the life experiences leading girls and women to offending as well as to desistance (Giordano, Cherkovich, and Rudolf, 2002). The recognition of the "blurred boundaries" of victimization and offending is an important underpinning of this research. In a number of publications, and as articulated in her "feminist theory of delinquency," Chesney-Lind has observed how females' earlier victimization set the stage for their entry into homelessness, survival sex and sometimes prostitution, unemployment, drug use, and eventually into other criminal acts (Chesney-Lind and Pasko, 2004, p. 5).

Some feminist scholars, despite the important insights of this "blurred boundaries" approach, contend that it needs to be broadened to recognize the diversity of women's pathways to offending. For example, this exclusive emphasis on victimization as the key pathway to women's offending can overlook other aspects of women's and girls' lives that put them at risk for offending (Miller and Mullins, 2006b, p. 18). Gaarder and Belknap's (2002) analysis identified not only the importance of victimization and violence but also economic marginality and racial and structural dislocation, school experiences, and drug and alcohol use in explaining adolescent females' delinquency.

Miller and Mullins (2006b) also argue that relying only on female samples makes it difficult to specify whether and how such risks influence pathways to offending across gender. One area in which feminist pathways analysis has been used is the study of youth gangs

(Miller, 2001; Moore, 1991). This research has compared males and females in gangs and non-gangs by usually using one of two approaches: (1) an analysis of etiological risk factors from survey research and (2) a qualitative analysis focusing on juvenile females' accounts of why they joined gangs and on their life contexts prior to and at the time of joining (Miller and Mullins, 2006a, p. 230).

Gendered Crime

Attention to **gendered crime**—to situational and organizational aspects of crime that relate to gender—emerged in the 1980s with Steffensmeier's (2004) analysis of gender segregation and institutional sexism in criminal networks. As a logical extension of feminist criminology, which views gender as totally relevant to social behavior and recognizes the situational nature of gender accomplishment, some feminist scholars have examined how situational gendered-opportunity structures and gender expectations shape criminal events (Miller and Mullins, 2006a, p. 232).

There are at least two ways in which research can be conducted on gendered crime. It is possible to count the frequency of offense elements, such as the role played by and the size of the crime group; awareness exists that this may not be sufficiently nuanced to reveal the extent of crime. A second approach would be to link gender (and race, class, and age) identities to crime as a gendered line of action. Recent research on boys and men reveal ways in which masculine privileges and identities enable certain risk-taking behavior in boys (Cannon, Higginbotham, and Leung, 1991) more so than in girls (Bottcher, 2001). Daly does ask whether it may be better to start "with concrete studies of boys'/men's and girls'/women's lives, rather than with ungrounded, commonsensical assumptions in the professional rush to devise grand theory" (Daly, 1995, p. 99). This approach on gendering crime is found in studies that emphasize how women and men "do gender" in response to those beliefs about femininity and masculinity (Messerschmidt, 1993; Simpson and Ellis, 1995). The importance of this research is its ability to examine both similarities and differences between women's and men's offending.

Gendered Lives

Daly (1998, p. 98) defines the concept of **gendered lives** as the examination of the "significant differences in the ways that women experience society compared with men." Daly argues that "rather than analyze gender as a correlate of crime, one would analyze crime as a correlate of gender" (p. 99). She states that there are several ways to develop the idea of women's gendered lives in criminological research, such as by revealing how gender-related conditions of life structure delinquent and nondelinquent identities and actions (Bottcher, 2001). Jean Bottcher's interviews of youths whose brothers had been institutionally confined suggest that the social organization of gender can act as social control. The girls in this study, compared to the boys, were insulated from delinquent interest and activity. Thus, instead of the traditional approach of analyzing gender as a correlate of crime, this approach analyzes crime as a correlate of gender (Bottcher, 2001).

Another approach to the study of gendered lives is to document how methods of income generation over time vary in relation to turning points in women's lives, such as pregnancy and care of children, and to state supports for housing on welfare (Daly, 1995, p. 99). Regina Austin (1992, pp. 1801–1811) shows what can be learned by studying "hustling" as women move between the straight and street worlds. Lisa Maher (1997) also documents the connections among neighborhood conditions, declining value of sex work for women, and drug markets in New York City neighborhoods.

MASCULINITIES AND CRIME

Early feminist work, as has been stated several times, criticized existing theory and research for focusing on boys' and men's crime at the expense of girls' and women's crime. It was reasoned that given men's overrepresentation as offenders, the study of masculinities and crime could not be ignored. The early work in criminology emphasized subcultural approaches to the study of crime. Walter B. Miller (1958) argued that lower-class boys pursued such focal concerns as toughness, trouble, and independence, which clearly reflect what is now identified as masculine. Elijah Anderson's more recent research (1999) reveals the conceptualization of male identity among persistent offenders. R. Theodore Davidson's (1974) study of Chicano prisoners in San Quentin examined the concept of **machismo**, a Latino hegemonic masculinity, as the organizing principle behind the violence of the inmate world.

James W. Messerschmidt's (1993) broader attempt to situate criminal behavior within gendered social structures highlights intersectionality in examining the criminal behavior of both women and men. Although this approach sees gender norms and definitions as a product of social structure, it is through the micro-level processes of social action/interaction that gender is reproduced. Messerschmidt establishes an analytical framework for understanding the intersection of masculinity and crime. He indicates that "men do masculinity according to the social situation in which they find themselves" (p. 84).

Christopher W. Mullins, Richard Wright, and Bruce A. Jacobs's recent research (2004) revealed that most of men's interpersonal disputes with other men were grounded in the need to build and maintain gendered reputations. They further found that gendered perceptions of appropriate and inappropriate behavior served as the trigger for and the barrier against retaliations. Men viewed retaliation in violent ways as a key street survival strategy that is deeply rooted in their identities as *men*. However, if they were wronged by a woman, the path of action was more complex. Direct action against a woman, who was considered to be physically and emotionally weaker, could be seen as a subordinated masculinity. Yet at the same time, men believed they could not ignore a slight by a woman, another mark of "punkness." A more desirable solution was to enlist women to carry out the retaliation.

Andrew Hochstetler and Heith Copes (2003) provide an analysis of how the situational construction of masculinity frames acts of property crime. Their interviews with convicted property offenders explore how masculine posturing immediately prior to the criminal event frequently "boxes" offenders into a position where backing out of the crime would result in a loss of masculine capital. This study further suggests that such reputation maintenance is more likely to take place with younger than with older men.

FEMINIST EPISTEMOLOGIES

Epistemology as defined by Fonow and Cook (2005) specifies the generation of knowledge in the interpretation of the nature of reality. Women of color have raised important questions concerning epistemologies of the oppressed, such as whether or not researchers who are ethnically and racially outside of the group in question are entitled to speak for oppressed group. A key consideration for feminist methodologists is who gets to choose the research questions under investigation and the specific research techniques used.

Feminist methodology is not merely research conducted by female social scientists, nor is it merely research using qualitative methods. Instead, this school of methodology views women's individual experience in the context of gendered power relations. Feminist approaches to research often seek the involvement of subjects as co-researchers as a means of reducing the widely divergent power differentials between the researcher and the population being studied. Fonow and Cook (2005) and Williams (2004) draw on four basic principles of feminist epistemology that are relevant to research of offenders in the criminal justice systems as to victims of crime:

- The tradition of reflexivity or "the tendency of feminists to reflect on, examine critically, and explore analytically the nature of the research process" (Fonow & Cook, p.2218), with a focus on gender relations;
- Consciousness-raising—the consciousness of oppression can lead to new insights as outsiders challenge the claims of insiders;
- Collaborative scholarship which includes advocates (for example, women's shelter workers) in the research and funding;
- An action orientation or use of the results of the study for the betterment of the social world.

STANDPOINT THEORY

Standpoint theory starts with the premise that the standpoint or position in society of women provides a vantage point from which to view women's social reality. A key concept of standpoint theory is **intersectionality** or the interactive impact of membership in more than one marginalized group at a time, for example, the multiplying effect of gender plus race plus class.

Nancy Hartsock (1983), in her classic study of feminist standpoint epistemology, argued that women's cognitive styles, in their prioritizing of relationship and life-affirming goals, provide a standpoint from which one can envision possibilities for overcoming oppression and building a better society. It was Hartsock's belief that such a vision is superior to a masculine focus on hierarchy, dominance, and dichotomous, oppositional thinking. Ways of knowing informed by the motive of caring for everyone's needs will produce more valuable representations than ways of knowing informed by the interests of domination (van Wormer, 2009).

Feminist standpoint theory begins with the idea that less powerful members of society experience a different reality as a consequence of their oppression. Research that is undertaken from this perspective is political in the sense that the research is committed to social action on behalf of oppressed groups. Van Wormer (2009) considers from a standpoint feminist perspective, the application of restorative justice practices as a means of obtaining justice for victims of gendered crime such as sexual assault and domestic violence. Restorative justice, as we will see in Chapter 7, involves a professionally facilitated conferencing to bring parties to a dispute together following the commission of a crime or wrongdoing. Parallels between restorative justice and standpoint theory are most evident in the non-adversarial process itself that does not pit a lawyer on one side of a dispute against a lawyer on the other side. As in standpoint theory, truth telling through personal narrative is the mode of communication, and the process is victim-oriented. From a standpoint perspective, the victim-offender process stands out from the conventional form of justice in its reliance on the impact of victim-survivors telling their stories in their own words and styles. The restorative healing circles that are often used by Native American tribes, for example, to help members of a community heal following an outbreak of crime, are easily compatible with feminist methodologies. Consistent with standpoint theory, restorative processes are especially relevant to issues of power, marginality of minority groups, personal responses of a victim to a crime, a focus on personal choice, and a relevance to insider knowledge.

Of special relevance to women's victimization are the following standpoint feminist values: reliance on the woman's personal narrative for truth telling; acceptance of a holistic, nondichotomized view of reality including a merging of the personal and political; a focus on choice and options; an understanding of the gendered nature of power relations in the society; and an emphasis on personal empowerment and respect for one's personal dignity (van Wormer). Empowerment is defined by standpoint theorists Sprague and Hayes (2000) in terms of facilitating one's self-determination. Empowering relationships occur on both personal and structural levels.

FEMINIST RESEARCH METHODOLOGIES AND QUANTITATIVE RESEARCH

Feminists have been quite critical of quantitative research. This form of research has been questioned because it places greater value on quantifiable information than on other sources of knowledge, because it assumes a separation between the researcher and the object of study, and because it isolates the factors under study from their historical and socio-economic context (Bowman, 1992: 201). However, many feminist researchers have come to realize that quantitative research methods do have a role to play within feminist methodology (Kelly et al., 1994). See Box 3.1 for an excellent quantitative study by two female researchers.

BOX 3.1

Karen Heimer and Stacy De Coster: The Gendering of Violent Delinquency

Heimer and De Coster's study reveals the benefits that result from a complex conceptualization of gender. These researchers address two key theoretical problems of interest to feminist criminologists: (1) within-gender variability in the use of violence (2) and variability in violence across gender (i.e., the gender-ratio of offending).

Heimer and De Coster's complex theoretical model of violent delinquency is based on the differentials in the experiences of young women and men that result from gender inequality. They focus on the interplay of social structure and culture, arguing that social structural positions based on gender, social class, and race result in variations in the two cultural processes of family controls and peer associations. Heimer and De Coster contend that indirect control derived from emotional bonds to the family are the primary control over adolescent females' behavior, whereas direct controls have a stronger effect on reducing adolescent males' delinquency.

Heimer and De Coster used an analysis of the National Youth Survey to test their theoretical model. They found strong support for its ability to explain variations in adolescent females' and males' use of violence. The data also revealed strong support for variations in the use of violence within gender based on the causal pathways of social structural factors tied to gender, race, and class; the researchers also found that the cultural processes of family controls and peer associations shaped the cultural outcomes of violent definitions and gender definitions. They explain:

> In short, the conclusion of our research is that violent delinquency is "gendered" in significant ways. Adolescence violence can be seen as a product of gendered experiences, gender socialization, and the patriarchal system in which they emerge. Thus, consistent with feminist arguments, gender differences in violence are ultimately rooted in power differences.

Critical Thinking Questions: Are you surprised by the findings of Heimer and De Coster? How would class affect the way that violence is gendered? Why does race appear to be an important variable in the gendering of violence?

Source: Karen Heimer and Stacy De Coster, "The Gendering of Violent Delinquency," *Criminology 37* (1999): 277–317.

Still, feminist researchers have focused more on qualitative research methods. Although there is no single feminist approach to research methods, what they have in common is a strong emphasis on research relationships, on reflexivity, and on the protection of the researched (Sampson, Bloor, and Fincham, 2008: 921).

USE OF QUALITATIVE RESEARCH METHODS

Although feminist scholars have tended to stress qualitative research in the past, feminist methodology can draw on a variety of methodological designs, quantitative as well as qualitative, participatory as well as literature-based. The overriding purpose of feminist-based methodology is to discover useful knowledge to help empower disenfranchised groups (Fonow and Cook).

There is no one correct method of feminist research. Feminist researchers have used their research methods to answer important questions about the nature of criminological knowledge. For example, see Box 3.2 for Jody Miller's study of the difference between males and female in committing robbery.

Linda Williams (2004) stresses the importance of the use of researcher-advocate collaboration. Sound principles of scientific research, however, must be followed. She relates the principles of feminist epistemology to research on domestic violence. In engaging in funded research academically-trained researchers must be careful not to privilege one group over the other, but to recognize the expertise of the advocates and survivors as matching the expertise of the researchers. In the same way, quantitative research techniques should not be elevated in value over techniques that put the voices of women at the center of the research. Finally, as Williams indicates, a liberating methodology recognizes that the process of knowledge production is not value free, but is inevitably political. Even decisions about which questions to ask, which research methods to employ, and how findings are interpreted are part of a political process and influenced by researcher bias. Studying violence against women is both an ethical and political endeavor. Williams advocates linking activism with research and calls for researchers and practitioners to be careful to take into account the intersectionality of gender, race, socioeconomic status, and violence against women.

The narrative approach is one that is widely used in the women's literature on criminal justice. Often an empirically-based study, such as, for example, one on sexual abuse in the backgrounds of female offenders, will illustrate the statistical findings as reported in government surveys with quotes from interviews with representative women themselves. From the perspective of writers on narrative theory, reality is viewed as co-constructed in the minds of individuals in interaction with others (Kelley, in press). Narrative research is culturally sensitive in that it does not presume a way of being, but aims to discover the storyteller's meaning. This approach is closely related to feminist postmodernism in the study of verbal content for meaning. The meanings we attribute to experience, according to Kelley, are influenced and shaped by cultural beliefs and practices.

Using a feminist, intersectionalist orientation, criminologist Beth Richie (1996) developed a unique theoretical framework for understanding the pathways that lead battered African American women into the gates of prison. Without gathering extensive facts about the backgrounds of these 37 inmates, she never would have discovered the patterns, even inevitability, in their offending. What shined through their life stories, in case after case, was that gender, race/ethnicity, personal violence, poverty, and a racist social system had come together to cause the women to be susceptible to criminal involvement. Richie accordingly entitled her book

BOX 3.2
Jody Miller: Robbery as a Case Study

In Miller's secondary analysis of thirty-seven active African American offenders, she compared accounts of why men and women commit robbery. She found that gender influences these crimes in the following ways. Men use physical violence when committing robbery, but women do not. Men target other men, but women do not. Men view robbery as one means to attain their masculinity, a setting in which men complete with each other for status and money through the use of physical contact, guns, and violence. Women, on the other hand, take into consideration the gendered nature of their environment when they rob other women, who are regarded as less likely to be armed and are considered to be easily intimidated and weak. When they do rob men, women typically use their sexuality to manipulate men to be easier targets.

Men and women do share motivations for robbery. What attracts both sexes to robbery is the potential for obtaining money and experiencing excitement. These motives, Miller contends, are reminders that class, race, and gender are important, even critical, to understanding crime. She sees the urban backgrounds as a powerful pathway to street crime. She warns that it is critical to distinguish between motives and causes of crime. She goes on to examine structural elements such as unemployment, poverty, deindustralization, and the underground drug economy in this urban St. Louis neighborhood that provide the context for crime to take place.

In Miller's sample, women described three predominant ways in which they committed robberies: targeting female victims in physical confrontations, targeting male victims by appearing sexually available, and participating with males in street robberies of men. Significantly, most women described participating in two or more of these types of robberies.

Critical Thinking Questions: What do you find surprising about how men and women perceive the act of robbery? If this study were conducted with other racial groups, besides largely an African American sample, do you think the findings would be the same?

Source: Jody Miller, "Up It Up: Gender and the Accomplishment of Street Robbery," *Criminology 36* (February 1998): 37–65.

Compelled to Crime: The Gender Entrapment of Battered Black Women. Out of protective feelings for their men, women sometimes reported that they often failed to seek the help they needed before it was too late. The following excerpt is from the personal narrative of Janet, a forty-six-year-old African American woman who after being battered for ten years was detained on a homicide charge:

> When I finally went for help they asked why I waited so long. There was no police record. No counselor to testify and no family witness. I could tell that the judge didn't believe me, especially because he went on and on about how I "seemed so smart and all." Now what's that supposed to mean? That he's dumb? I don't want any white judge talking about my man that way. Or did he mean that the sisters (African American women) are dumb? Either way it was a put-down that I didn't appreciate at all. So to answer him, *that's* why I didn't go for help sooner (p.96).

Researchers who wish to see how feminist methodologies apply to studies on women and the criminal justice system are advised to conduct a search through articles that are published in

Feminist Criminology, an international journal dedicated to research related to women, girls, and crime within the context of a feminist critique of criminology. Published quarterly by the Division on Women and Crime of the American Society of Criminology, this publication highlights the gendered nature of crime and incorporates a perspective that the paths to crime differ for males and females. *Feminist Criminology,* as stated on its website, "provides a venue for articles that place women in the center of the research question, answering different questions than the mainstream approach of controlling for sex." Editors of the journal question the use of gender as a control variable that fails to illuminate the factors that predict female criminality. Typical of articles that are published in this journal are: studies of researcher-activist collaboration in the critique of mandatory arrest policies in situations of domestic violence, the teaching of principles of feminist criminology, and the connection between research findings and feminist activism.

Jody Miller (2008), whose work is widely referenced in this chapter, has published in this and similar journals. In an article devoted to feminist methodology, she argues for feminist advocacy as the overarching goal of gender-based research, regardless of the particular research method used. But research grounded in the real-life experience of women, she further suggests, has an important role to play in understanding of the causes and consequences of violence against women and in guiding social policy. Our research insights must connect with those of other stakeholders–such as the subjects of the study– and with the contexts in which they live. Miller illustrates the point with findings from a qualitative investigation she conducted on African American adolescent girls in an impoverished urban setting. These girls were at heightened risk for gendered violence.

When investigating such violence among female residents of the community, Miller chose a qualitative interviewing design that begins with listening to the voices of those whose experiences we are seeking to understand (Miller, 2008). The focus was to discover the girls' perspectives on community violence against members of their gender. How did the young women stay safe? What kinds of situations did they avoid? —These were two of the questions asked to reveal strategies of self-protection as well as the contexts that were unsafe. Public places and gatherings where alcohol and drug use were identified as places or events to avoid. Women's advocates were able to build on such information obtained by these methods to help promote community safety. Earlier research, in contrast, relied on the expertise of professional stakeholders who were inclined to overlook the structurally embedded nature of female crime (Miller, 2008).

The gender-specific programming that is now a dominant framework used in the field of female juvenile corrections owes much to the pioneering work of feminist psychologist Carol Gilligan. In an interview published in the international journal, *Forum: Qualitative Social Research,* Gilligan discusses her methodology, which centered on analysis of the transcripts of the interviews that she had conducted with young women. Gilligan famously made the discovery that young women, in making a decision, often start from a different premise than men, from an assumption of connectedness rather than separateness. She describes the process of research relationships as follows:

> Well, the research relationship . . . . became collaborative, became a relationship in a truer sense of the word. To learn from girls about girls' development, we had to come into relationship with girls in a genuine way and approach them as the authorities about their experience . . . . The process of inquiry has its own integrity

when driven by a genuine curiosity, and it differs from the process of assessment, which has more to do with judgment and ranking. (Unlike assessment, this approach) frees the voice of the researcher and engages the participant in the research process. (2009, p.9)

This methodological approach does not start with the question; the questions emerge through listening to the interviewee and developing new insights as the process moves along. To Gilligan the research starts from a position of not knowing rather than from the position of being the expert. The ethics of research becomes an ethic of relationship as the researcher listens to the voice of the person and attends not only to the story being told but to the tone of voice, the pauses, and the silences.

Summary

This chapter has suggested a variety of ways in which feminists do theory and pursue research. One of the major problems of generalization, or investigating how theories of men's crime apply to women, is the failure to account for the gender ratio of offending; that is, the reality that men are disproportionately involved in crime. This gender ratio of crime was explored in this chapter by the conceptual scheme of gendered crime, gendered pathways, and gendered lives. The section on masculinities and crime situated criminal behavior within gendered social structures in highlighting the criminal behavior of both men and women, revealing that it is through the micro-level processes of social action/interaction that gender (re)produced.

Feminist epistemologies, another concern of this chapter, feminist methodology, the study of power relations, and research collaboration. Feminist methodology (instead of empiricism) basically accepts the value of the scientific method but calls for females and their experiences to be included in the scientific process. Feminist standpoint theories challenge traditional criminology's empirical assumptions.

Key Terms

gendered crime *55*

gendered lives *55*

gendered pathways *54*

gender order *52*

gender ratio of crime *53*

intersectionality *57*

machismo *56*

Critical Thinking Questions

1. Why is this chapter important to a book on women and the criminal justice system?
2. Did this chapter present any paradigm shifts to you? If so, what were they and why are they important?
3. How does this chapter bridge the gap between traditional theory and research in criminology and research done by feminists?
4. What are the various ways that feminists can do research? Evaluate each one.

Web Destinations

Feminist Criminology, the journal: http://fcx.sagepub.com/

References

Anderson, E. (1999). *Code of the street: Decency, violence and the moral life of the inner city.* New York: W. W. Norton.

Bottcher, J. (2001). Social practices of gender: How gender relates to delinquency in the everyday lives of high-risk youths. *Criminology 39*: 893–932.

Bottcher, J. (2001). Social practices of gender: How gender relates to delinquency in the everyday lives of high-risk youths. *Criminology 39*: 893–932.

Bowman, C. (1992). The arrest experiments: A feminist critique. *Journal of Criminal Law & Criminology, 83* (1), 1992, 201–208.

Broidy, L. (2001). A test of general strain theory. *Criminology 39*: 9–32.

Cannon, L. W. W., Higginbotham, E., and Leung, M. L. A. (1991). Race and class bias in qualitative research on women. In M. M. Fonow and J. A. Cook (eds.), *Beyond methodology: Feminist scholarship as lived research* (pp. 107–118). Bloomington, IN: Indiana University Press.

Daly, K. (1994). *Gender, crime and punishment.* New Haven, CT: Yale University Press.

Daly, K. (1995). Looking back, looking forward: The promise of feminist transformation. In B. R. Price and N. J. Sokoloff (eds.), *The criminal justice system and women: Offenders, victims, and workers* (pp. 447–448). New York: McGraw-Hill.

Daly, K. (1998). Gender, crime, and criminology. In M. Tonry (ed.), *The handbook of crime and justice* (pp. 85–108). Oxford: Oxford University Press.

Daly, K., and Chesney-Lind, M. (1988). Feminism and criminology. *Justice Quarterly 5*: 497–538.

Daly, K., and Maher, L. (1998). Women pathways to felony court: Feminist theories of lawbreaking and problems of representation. *Review of Law and Women's Studies 2*: 11–52.

Davidson, R. T. (1974). *Chicano prisoners: The key to San Quentin.* Prospect Heights, IL: Waveland.

Fonow, M. M., & Cook, J. A. (2005). Feminist methodology: New applications in the academy and public policy. *Signs: Journal of Women in Culture and Society, 30* (4), 2211–2236.

Gaarder, E., and Belknap, J. (2002). Tenuous borders: Girls transferred to adult court. *Criminology 40*: 481–518.

Gilligan, C. (2009). Making oneself vulnerable to discovery: carol Gilligan in conversation with Mechthild Kiegelmann, *Qualitative Social Research, 10* (2), 1–19.

Giordano, P., Cherkovich, S. A., and Rudolf, J. (2002). Gender, crime and desistance: Toward a theory of cognitive transformation. *American Journal of Sociology 107*: 990–1064.

Giordano, P. C., Deines, J. A., and Cernkovich, S. A. (2006). In and out of crime: A life course perspective on girls' delinquency. In K. Heimer and C. Kruttschnitt (eds.), *Gender and crime: Patterns in victimization and offending* (pp. 17–40). New York: New York University Press.

Harding, S. (1987). *Feminism and methodology: Social science issues.* Bloomington, IN: Indiana University Press.

Harstock, N. (1987). The feminist standpoint: Developing the ground for a specifically feminist historical materialism. In S. Harding (Ed.), *Feminism and methodology: Social science issues* (pp.157–180). Bloomington: Indiana University Press.

Heidensohn, F. M. (1996). *Women and crime*, 2nd ed. London: Macmillan.

Heimer, K., Wittrock, S., and Unal, H. (2006). The crimes of poverty: Economic marginalization and the gender gap in crime. In K. Heimer and C. Kruttschnitt (eds.), *Gender and crime: Patterns in victimization and offending* (pp. 115–136). New York: New York University Press.

Hochstetler, A., and Copes, H. (2003). Situational construction of masculinity among male street thieves. *Journal of Contemporary Ethnography 32*: 279–303.

Jayartne, T. E., and Stewart, A. J. (1991). Quantitative and qualitative methods in the social sciences: Current feminist issues and practical strategies. In M. M. Fonow and J. A. Cook (eds.), *Beyond methodology* (pp. 86–106). Bloomington, IN: Indiana University Press.

Kelley, P. (in press). Narrative theory and social work treatment. Chapter 20. In F. Turner (Ed.), *Social work treatment* (5th ed.). New York: Oxford University Press.

Kelly, L., Burton, S. and Regan, L. (1994). Researching Women's Lives or Studying Women's Oppression? Reflections on what constitutes Feminist Research. In M. Maynard and J. Purvis (Eds), *Researching Women's Lives from a Feminist Perspective* (pp. 27–48). London: Taylor & Francis.

Kruttschnitt, C. (1996). Contributions of quantitative methods to the study of gender and crime, or bootstrapping our way into the theoretical thicket. *Journal of Quantitative Criminology 12*: 135–161.

Laub, J. H., and Sampson, R. J. (1993). Turning Points in the life course: Why change matters to the study of crime. *Criminology 31*: 301–325.

Maher, L. (1997). *Sexed work: Gender, race and resistance in a Brooklyn drug market.* Oxford: Clarendon Press.

McDermott, M. J. (1992). The personal is empirical: Feminism and research methods. *Journal of Criminal Justice Education 3*: 237–249.

Messerschmidt, J. W. (1993). *Masculinities and crime.* Lanham, MD: Rowman & Littlefield.

Mies, M. (1991). Women's research or feminist research? The debate surrounding feminist science and methodology. In M. Fonow and J. A. Cook (eds.), *Beyond methodology* (pp. 60–84). Bloomington, IN: Indiana University Press.

Miller, J. (2001). *One of the guys: Girls, gangs and gender.* New York: Oxford University Press.

Miller, W. B. (1958). Lower-class culture as a generating milieu of gang delinquency. *Journal of Social Issues 14*: 5–19.

Miller, J., and Mullins, C. W. (2006a). Taking stock: The status of feminist theories in criminology. In F. Cullen, J. P. Wright, and K. Blevins (eds.), F. Adler and W. Laufer (series eds.), *The status of criminological theory. Advances in criminological theory*, Vol. 15 (pp. 206–230). New Brunswick, NJ: Transaction. In Press.

Miller, J., and Mullins, C. W. (2006b). Stuck up, telling lies, and talking too much: The gendered context of young women's violence. In K. Heimer and C. Kruttschnitt (eds.), *Gender and crime patterns in victimization and offending* (pp. 41–66). New York: New York University Press.

Miller, J. (2008). Violence against urban African American girls: Challenges for feminist advocacy. *Journal of Contemporary Criminal Justice, 24,* 14–16.

Moore, J. (1991). *Going down to the barrio: Homeboys and homegirls in charge.* Philadelphia, PA: Temple University Press.

Mullins, C. W., Wright, W. R., and Jacobs, B. A. (2004). Gender, streetlife and criminal retaliation. *Criminology 42*: 911–940.

Owen, B. (1998). *In the mix: Struggle and survival in a woman's prison.* Albany, NY: State University of New York Press.

Richie, B. E. (1996). *Compelled to crime: The gender entrapment of battered black women.* New York: Routledge.

Sampson, H., Bloor, M., and Fincham, B., 2008 A price worth paying? Considering the 'cost' of reflexive research methods and the influence of feminist ways of 'doing.' *Sociology 42 , 919–933.*

Simpson, S. (1991). Caste, class and violent crime: Explaining differences in female offending. *Criminology 33*: 47–81.

Simpson, S. S., and Ellis, L. (1995). Doing gender: Sorting out the case and crime conundrum. *Criminology 33:* 47–81.

Sommers, I., and Baskin, D. R. (1993). The situational context of violent female offending. *Journal of Research in Crime and Delinquency 30*: 136–162.

Sprague, J., and Hayes, J. (2000). Self-determination and empowerment: A feminist standpoint analysis of talk about disability. *American Journal of Community Psychology, 28,* 671–695.

Steffensmeier, D., and Schwartz, J. (2004). Trends in female criminality: Is crime still a man's world? In B. R. Price and N. J. Sokoloff (eds.), *The criminal justice system and women: Offenders, prisoners, victims and workers,* 3rd ed. (pp. 95–111). New York: McGraw-Hill.

Tong, R. (1998). *Feminist thought*, 2nd ed. Boulder, CO: Westview Press.

van Wormer, K. (2009). Restorative justice as social justice for victims: A standpoint feminist perspective. *Social Work, 54* (2), 2009.

Williams, L. M. (2004). Researcher-advocate collaborations to end violence against women: Toward liberating methodologies for action research. *Journal of Interpersonal Violence, 19,* 1350–1357.

4

Delinquency across the Life Span

Developmental and life-course (DLC) theory, a relatively new but extremely promising theoretical orientation, represents a major change in how we think about and study lives (Elder, Johnson, and Crosnoe, 2003). Drawing on the increased numbers of longitudinal studies that examine the lives of young children, and that follow these cohorts sometimes for decades, many researchers are using the life-course perspective in the study of delinquent behavior (Laub and Sampson, 2003; Sampson and Laub, 1993).

DLC theory is concerned with three main issues in the study of delinquency: (1) the development of offending and antisocial behavior, (2) protective factors and risk at different ages, and (3) the effects of life events on the course of an individual's development. DLC theories attempt to integrate knowledge about individual, family, school, neighborhood, peer, community, and situational influences on offending. It also integrates key elements of earlier theories of delinquency, such as strain, control, differential association, and social learning (Farrington, 2005).

Beginning with an examination of risk factors in adolescents, early juvenile offenders are compared with those who begin their delinquency offenses in adolescence. Then, these adolescents are followed through part of and sometimes nearly all of their life span. Their social and criminal histories are compared with those of others in their cohort. Researchers pay particular attention to those who persist and those who desist from law-violating behaviors, as they seek to understand factors that contribute to ending law-violating activities.

It would seem that delinquency across the life course has particular relevance to an examination of women and the criminal justice system. The life-course developmental model focuses on significant life events or transitions, particularly in terms of changes in status, social roles, and relationships. However, this perspective needs to be supplemented by models that address childhood victimization and the ways that discrimination and oppression, based on a juvenile's race or sex, can shape this person's experiences, options, and identity (Gaarder and Belknap, 2004, p. 71). Juvenile female delinquents, often victims of various forms of victimization at home, turn to the use of alcohol and drugs, become involved with youth gangs, and have conflict at home. It is not unusual for these girls to run away from abusive homes and to become involved in various forms of survival on the streets, including prostitution, theft, and drug addiction.

The first half of this chapter examines delinquency across the life course, while the second half investigates the relationships among victimization, oppression, and juvenile females' pathways to crime. Beginning with an introduction to the life course, we examine the influence of patriarchy on juvenile females, the effect of human agency on decision making, and the factors dividing those who desist from crime and drug use from those who persist.

THE LIFE-COURSE PERSPECTIVE

The **life-course perspective**, a relatively new but promising theoretical orientation, represents a major change in how we think about and study lives (Elder, Johnson, and Crosnoe, 2003, p. 3). Until recently, sociological research largely neglected life histories and individual life trajectories. However, the many publications of Glen H. Elder Jr. and his colleagues have done much to stimulate the use of life-course theory as an appropriate research base in the study of individuals and groups (Elder, 1999).

John Claussen's classic study of children of the Great Depression was one of the earliest attempts to use the life-course perspective. He followed members of the Berkeley longitudinal studies for nearly fifty years—from childhood through the later years of the participants' lives. Claussen defined what he called "planful competence" as comprising the dimensions of self-confidence, intellectual investment, and dependability. He found that a youth who demonstrated planful competence was "equipped with an ability to evaluate accurately personal efforts as well as the intentions and responses of others, with an informed knowledge of self, others, and options, and with the self-discipline to pursue chosen goals" (Claussen, 1993, p. 1).

Claussen's research revealed that early competence in study participants meant fewer crises in every decade up to their fifties. Highly competent men were more likely to find the right job and to remain in this rewarding line of work. Highly competent women were more likely to find the right husband and to feel rewarded in family life. Both choice and selection were involved; a choice of attractive options, as well as the ability to be selective, permitted the most competent to take best advantage of their opportunities. Claussen compared the competent individuals with those youngsters who lacked planful competence with far different trajectories or pathways as a result. These youngsters made choices that led to job difficulties, marital breakup, and personal problems with the law and with figures in authority (Claussen, 1993, pp. 512–521).

Researchers are drawing on the increased numbers of longitudinal studies that examine the lives of young children, including their conduct disorders, and following these cohorts sometimes for decades. They are also using the life-course perspective in the study of delinquent behavior and how it affects subsequent life experiences (Laub and Sampson, 2003; Sampson and Laub, 1993).

DLC criminology is particularly concerned with documenting and explaining individual changes in offending throughout life. This paradigm has greatly increased knowledge about the measurement of criminal career features such as onset, continuation, and desistance. A major reason for the popularity of DLC during the 1990s was the enormous volume of longitudinal research on offending that was being published (Farrington, 2003, pp. 221–222). Three of the most important contributions were the self-report youth surveys in Denver, Pittsburgh, and Rochester (Browning and Huizinga, 1999; Browning and Loeber, 1999; Browning, Thornberry, and Porter, 1999). Other important longitudinal projects were the Dunedin study in New Zealand (Moffitt et al., 2001), the Seattle Social Development Project (Hawkins et al., 2003), the Montreal Longitudinal-Experimental Study (Tremblay et al., 2003), and further analysis by Robert J. Sampson and John H. Laub (1993) of the Gluecks' classic longitudinal study of 1,000 men.

Continuity of Delinquency into Adult Criminality

Sampson and Laub (1993) sought to explain both the continuity of delinquency into adult criminality and noncriminality, or change, in adulthood for those who were delinquent as children. They developed a threefold thesis:

1. Structural context mediated by informal family and school social control explains delinquency in childhood and adolescence.
2. In turn, there is continuity in antisocial behavior from childhood through adulthood in a variety of life domains.
3. Informal social bonds in adulthood to family and employment explain changes in criminality over the life span despite early childhood propensities (p. 7).

Employing life-history data from the Gluecks' longitudinal study, Laub and Sampson found that although adult crime is connected to childhood behavior, both incremental and abrupt changes still take place through changes in adult social bonds. Strong bonds to work and family among adults appear early, establishing life-long patterns. Laub and Sampson also contend that the events that trigger the formation of strong adult bonds to work and family commonly occur by chance or luck (Laub and Sampson, 1993, pp. 301–320).

The concept of a **turning point** in the life course is one of the fascinating contributions of Laub and Sampson's research. A turning point involves a gradual or dramatic change and may lead to "a modification, reshaping, or transition from one state, condition, or phase to another" (Laub and Sampson, 1993, p. 309). In seeking to unravel the mechanisms that operate at key turning points to turn a risk trajectory to a more adoptive path, Laub and Sampson found that stable employment and a good marriage, or changing roles and environments, can lead to investment of social capital or relations among persons (Laub and Sampson, 1993, p. 310).

However, not all researchers concur that there is a continuing of behaviors from childhood to adulthood. For example, Raymond Paternoster, Robert Brame, and David Farrington, using data from the Cambridge Study in Delinquent Development, investigated the relationship between adolescent and adult involvement in criminal behavior. In opposition to Sampson and Laub, Paternoster and colleagues found that adult offending "is not systematically related to events and experiences after adolescence" (Paternoster, Brame, and Farrington, 2001, p. 201). They argue that variation in adult offending is consistent with a random process and, therefore, it is impossible to conclude that relatively simple explanations, such as marriage and employment, can explain complex life-course decisions. They propose that much further study is needed to clarify the relationship between adolescent acts and adult criminal behaviors (Paternoster, Brame, and Farrington, 2001, p. 222).

DESISTANCE FROM CRIME

A final piece before moving to the life course and females, as well as the influence of gender, race, and class on women, is the matter of desistance. The age of **desistance,** or the termination of delinquent behavior, has become an important consideration of researchers. One of the problems of establishing desistance is the difficulty of distinguishing between a gap in a delinquent career and true termination. There are bound to be crime-free intervals in the course of delinquent careers (Sampson and Laub, 2001). Long-term follow-up is needed to establish the age of termination. To explain changes in offending over time, or desistance, theorists have proposed several explanations, which follow.

MATURATION AND AGING ACCOUNTS OF DESISTANCE.   The maturation process appears to be involved in desistance, as youths or adults become aware either of the desirability of pursing a conventional lifestyle or of the undesirability of continuing with unlawful pursuits. Sheldon and Eleanor Glueck drew this conclusion from the follow-up of juvenile delinquent careers: "With the passing of the years there was . . . both a decline in criminality and a decrease in the seriousness of the offences of those who continued to commit crimes" (Glueck and Glueck, 1940, p. 89). James Q. Wilson and Richard Herrnstein contend that the relatively minor gains from crime lose their power to reinforce deviant behavior as juveniles mature and develop increasing ties to conventional society. Another aspect of this maturation process, they add, is the individual's ability to delay gratification and forgo the immediate gains that delinquent or criminal acts bring (Wilson and Herrnstein, 1985, pp. 126–147).

DEVELOPMENTAL ACCOUNTS OF DESISTANCE.   One developmental explanation of desistance is that identity changes account for reduction in or cessation of crime. Edward Mulvey and John LaRosa, focusing on the period from age 17 to 20—the period they call the time of "natural" recovery—found that desistance was linked to a cognitive process taking place in the late teens when delinquents realized that they were "going nowhere" and that they had better make changes in their lives if they were going to be successful as adults (Mulvey and LaRosa, 1986, pp. 212–214). Peggy C. Giordano and colleagues, in a longitudinal study of serious female offenders, found that desistance took place when there were cognitive shifts in these offenders. Cognitive transformation provided desisters "with a detailed plan of action or a fairly elaborate *cognitive blueprint* for proceeding as a changed individual" (Giordano, Cernkovich, and Rudolph, 2002, p. 1055).

RATIONAL CHOICE ACCOUNTS OF DESISTANCE.   Theorists who hold to the rational choice framework propose that the decision to give up or continue with crime is based on a person's conscious reappraisal of the costs and benefits of criminal activity. They advance the idea that desisters are seen as "reasoned decisionmakers" (Cornich and Clark, 1986). One of the most important components of the decision to desist is the increased fear of punishment with aging. Barry Glassner and colleagues studied youths in a medium-size city in New York State and found that many youths curtailed involvement in delinquent activities at the age of 16 because they feared being jailed if they were apprehended as adults (Glassner, Ksander, and Berg, 1983, p. 221).

SOCIAL LEARNING ACCOUNTS OF DESISTANCE.   According to the social learning framework, the basic variables explaining initiation into crime are essentially the same factors that account for the desistance from crime (Akers, 1998). Michael Warr supports the social learning account of desistance because he found that changing peer relations accounted for the association between marital status and desistance from crime. The transition to marriage was followed by "a dramatic decline in time spent with friends" and "reduced exposure to delinquent peers" (Warr, 1988, pp. 183–216).

LIFE-COURSE ACCOUNT OF DESISTANCE.   The main objective of the life-course perspective on desistance is to link social history and social structure. A central element in the desistance process, according to Laub and Sampson (2004), is any change that "knifes off" individual offenders from their environment and, at the same time, offers them a new script for the future. A new "structured role stability" can emerge across various life domains (e.g., marriage, work, and/or community). The men desisting in their study shared a daily routine that provided structure and meaningful activity. Laub and Sampson add that although there are multiple pathways to desistance, they found what seem to be important general processes or mechanisms consistent with the idea of informal social control. In sum, offenders "choose to desist in response to structurally induced turning points that serve as the catalyst for sustaining long-term behavior change" (p. 11).

FEMALE DELINQUENCY ACROSS THE LIFE COURSE

There is both good news and bad news concerning an examination of the female delinquent across the life course. The bad news is that the study of delinquency has long focused on the delinquent male, and the longitudinal studies that have been done or are being done on delinquents across the life course predominantly feature the study of males. The good news is that studies of juvenile females are increasing in number, some of which follow females across the life course.

The study of female delinquents has examined several dimensions of delinquent behavior: females' involvement in offenses; their use of drugs and alcohol; their participation in types of antisocial behaviors, including gangs and prostitution; and their desistance and persistence as offenders.

Relationship between Male and Female Patterns of Delinquency

We learn from information that is provided in the *Uniform Crime Reports* (FBI, 2003), which shows the figures for male increases and decreases in arrests that occurred during the decade between 1997 and 2006, that when the female juvenile arrest rates decreased, they decreased less than male juvenile arrests in many offense categories (e.g., aggravated assault) and unlike male arrests, they increased for drug and alcohol-related offenses (e.g., driving under the influence, drug abuse violations, simple assault, and liquor law violations). As a result, while male juvenile arrests declined 26.4 percent over the period, female juvenile arrests declined by only 17.4 percent.

The early cohort studies provide some evidence of the relationship between male and female patterns of delinquency. Delinquency cohort studies usually include all people born in a particular year in a city or county and follow this group, or cohort, through part or all of their lives. The second Philadelphia cohort study examined all males and females born in 1958 in Philadelphia. It found that males in this cohort study were two and a half times more likely than females to become involved in delinquent acts. Law-violating females were much more likely to be one-time offenders and less likely to become chronic offenders (Wolfgang, Figlio, and Sellin, 1972). The Racine cohort study examined males and females born in 1942, 1949, and 1955 in Racine, Wisconsin. White females in this study had fewer contacts and less serious involvement with the police than white males or African American males or females (Shannon, 1982). The Columbus cohort study examined all males and females born between 1956 and 1960 in Columbus, Ohio. This study found that males outnumbered females by almost six to one in the delinquent population. The violent cohort consisted of 84.6 percent boys and 15.7 percent girls (Hamparian et al., 1980).

Terrie E. Moffitt and her colleagues have proposed a developmental taxonomy differentiating a small group of **early-onset, persistent offenders** (LCP) from the much larger category of **adolescence-limited delinquent males** (AL). These researchers found that these two groups differ both in age-related profiles of offending and in patterns of early risk. For persistent offenders, risks center on individual vulnerabilities that were evident early in childhood. In contrast, later-onset, AL groups are characterized by more marginal levels of psychosocial and individual risks. Their adolescent difficulties are perceived to be prompted by frustrations associated with an adolescent maturity gap and by coping with the behavior of antisocial peers (Moffitt, 1993, pp. 674–701)

Moffitt, Lynam, and Silva, in their examination of the neuropsychological status of several hundred New Zealand males between the ages of thirteen and eighteen, found that poor neuropsychological scores "were associated with early onset of delinquency" but were "unrelated to delinquency that began in adolescence" (Moffitt, Lynam, and Silva, 1994, p. 277). Moffitt's developmental theory views delinquency as proceeding along two developmental paths. On one path, children develop a lifelong course of delinquency and crime at as early as age 3. They may begin to bite and hit at age 4, shoplift and be truant at 10, sell drugs and steal cars at 16, rob and rape at 22, and commit fraud and child abuse at 30 (Moffitt, 1993; Moffitt et al., 1996, pp. 399–424).

On the other path, the majority of male delinquents begin offending during the adolescent years and desist from delinquent behaviors around the eighteenth birthday. Moffitt refers to these youthful offenders as "adolescence-limited" delinquents. The early and persistent problems found with members of the LCP group are not found with the AL delinquents. Yet the frequency of offending and even the violence of offending of the AL group during the adolescent years may be as high as with the LCP delinquents. Moffitt notes that AL antisocial behavior is learned from peers and sustained through peer-based rewards and reinforcements. AL delinquents continue in delinquent acts as long as such behaviors appear profitable or rewarding to them, but they have the ability to abandon those behaviors when prosocial styles become more rewarding (Moffitt, 1993; Moffitt et al., 1996, pp. 399–424). See Box 4.1, which followed a sample of 1,000 males and females from age three to age twenty-one.

Female Use of Drugs and Alcohol

The abuse of alcohol and other drugs are identified, along with juvenile unlawful behavior, as two of the most serious problems of adolescents. Figure 4.1 shows, for a one-month period, the illicit use of drugs of any kind in a national household sample of juveniles and adults. Young people are clearly the leaders in illicit drug use in the United States. After age 18, drug use tends to drop off, with only 2.6 percent of persons over age 50 using illicit drugs of any kind. Somewhat surprising to some, a few studies are now beginning to focus on the long-known fact that elementary students are using various types of drugs. Most research today, unfortunately, focuses on youths ages 12 and older. Our attention here, of course, is focused on the use of alcohol and other drugs by juveniles.

BOX 4.1
Gender Differences in the Dunedin Longitudinal Study

In *Sex Differences in Antisocial Behavior*, Moffitt and her colleagues report on the findings of the Dunedin Longitudinal Study. The basic findings indicate that youths develop antisocial behavior for two reasons. One form of antisocial behavior may be understood as a disorder with neurodevelopmental origins—a disorder that, like hyperactivity, autism, and dyslexia, shows a strong male preponderance and low prevalence in the population. Extreme gender differences are apparent in this form of antisocial behavior. The other form of antisocial behavior represents the bulk of such behavior, especially by females. This form is best understood as a social phenomenon originating in the context of social relationships, with onset in adolescence and high prevalence across the population. Gender differences in antisocial behaviors, according to this study, are negligible. Males' and females' antisocial behaviors are particularly alike when alcohol and drugs are involved, near the time of female puberty, and when females are yoked with males in intimate relationships. Other important insights were:

• Increasing numbers of symptoms of conduct disorder predict increasingly poor young adult outcomes, regardless of gender.
• Antisocial behavior has disruptive effects on both females and males as they make the transition from adolescence to adulthood.

• The life-course-persistent antisocial female is extremely rare; approximately 1 in 100 females in a birth cohort seem to be on the life-course-persistent path.
• Females and males on the life-course-persistent path share similar risk factors of family adversity, poor discipline, cognitive deficits, hyperactivity, undercontrolled temperament, and rejection by peers.
• Almost all females who engage in antisocial behavior best fit the AL type. Among AL delinquency, the gender ratio is 1.5 males to 1 female.
• Males on the life-course-persistent path suffer from multiple poor outcomes as young adults, and youth on the AL path also have some poor outcomes.

Critical Thinking Questions: Why do you think so few females in this study became life-course-persistent offenders? What predicted offending among male and female offenders? Did you find any of the findings of this study surprising?

Source: Terrie E. Moffitt, Avshalom Caspi, Michael Rutter, and Phil A. Silva, *Sex Differences in Antisocial Behavior* (Cambridge, England: Cambridge University Press, 2001).

The data for *Monitoring the Future Project* for 2008 indicate that the upturn in drug use that started in the early 1980s has reversed modestly and has continued to drop in recent years. Amphetamines showed a significant decline in lifetime, annual, and the 30-day prevalence rates for the 8th, 10th, and 12th graders surveyed. Other significant declines took place with the annual prevalence of cocaine and crack and for the 30-day prevalence of any illicit drug other than marijuana. Inhalants, hallucinogens, LSD, PCP, ecstasy, sedatives (barbiturates), and tranquilizers held steady in use in 2008 in at least two of the grades (Johnston et al., 2008). Even with this recent drop, rates of drug use are higher than anyone would like.

These and other studies have shown a marked decrease in gender differences among drug users. Female high school students are slightly more likely than high school males to smoke cigarettes and to use some illicit drugs, including amphetamines; they use alcohol and marijuana at about the same rates as male high school seniors. Yet male adolescents are more likely to be involved in heavy, or binge, drinking than female adolescents. African American females have a

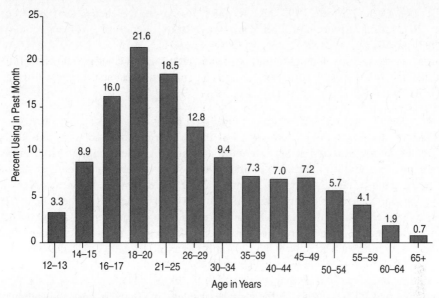

FIGURE 4.1   Past Month Illicit Drug Use among Persons Aged 12 or Older, by Age 2007
Source: Substance Abuse and Mental Health Services Administration, Office of
Applied Studies, *Results from the 2007 National Survey on Drug Use and Health:
National Findings* (Rockville, MD: Substance Abuse and Mental Health Services
Administration, 2008), Table 2.1.

disproportionately low rate of drug referrals compared white females, at only 10 percent. This is
below their percentage of the juvenile population, which is 16 percent (Substance Abuse and
Mental Health Services Administration, 2008).

Gang Behavior among Female Adolescents

Recent decades have brought increased awareness of adolescent girls who are involved in gangs.
     According to the National Youth Gang Center survey (2007), it was found that one in five of
gangs in the cities contained female members, compared to about one in three of rural area gangs.
The research on girls from the 1980s and 1990s came up with a number of findings:

- Juvenile females in male gangs do not usually plan a gang activity. But they may participate in violent crimes and drug-related activities (Bowker and Klein, 1980).
- Juvenile females often become part of gangs that have a connection to male gangs and
  derive their name from their male counterparts (Quicker, 1983).
- Adolescent females typically are not coerced into the gang, but they still need to prove
  their loyalty and undergo an initiation procedure (Quicker, 1983).
- Loyalty to the gang rivals loyalty to the family and most friends came from within
  the gang. The gang offers "warmth, friends, loyalty, and socialization" as it insulated its
  members from the harsh environment of the barrio or the neighborhood (Quicker).
- Some adolescent female gangs are independent of male gangs (Harris, 1988, p. 172).
- Girl gang participants typically commit a wide variety of offenses, including selling crack
  cocaine, and at only a slightly lower frequency than boys involved in this survey

(Bjerregaard and Smith, 1993, pp. 347–348; Esbensen, Deschenes, and Winfree, 1998, pp. 20–21; Joan Moore and John Hagedorn's 2001; Lauderback, Hansen, and Waldorf, 1992, pp. 57–72).

• Girls usually age out of gangs before boys and that girls receive more emotional fulfillment from their involvement with gang activity (Esbensen, Deschenes, and Winfree, 1998, pp. 20–21).

More recently, Jody Miller, in several published papers and in her 2001 book *One of the Guys*, provides an update and close analysis of the gender dynamics of gang membership in mixed-gender gangs. She found that a female in a mixed-gender gang, an environment that supports gender hierarchies and the exploitation of young women, must learn to negotiate to survive in the gang milieu (Miller and Brunson, 2000, pp. 443–445). Gang involvement does expose young women to risks of victimization. Young women can choose to be "one of the guys" and expose themselves to higher risks of being arrested, injured, or even killed in conflicts with rival gangs. Or they can use gender to decrease their risk of being harmed by not participating in "masculine" activities such as fighting and committing crime. However, females who opt out of violence and crime are then viewed as lesser members and may expose themselves to greater risks of victimization within their gangs (Miller, 1998, 2001).

Eghigian and Kirby (2006), in their study of gangs in Chicago, describe roles that girls may play in gangs, including holding and transporting drugs and guns; transporting contraband to and from prison; acting as lures with rival gang members to secure information or set them up for murder or violence; and supporting criminal acts such as selling drugs, engaging in robbery, and burglary. Leaving a gang is difficult because gang members fear leak of intelligence; if she leaves, then she probably has to move far away for her protection.

In sum, most studies have found that girl gangs still serve as adjuncts to boy gangs. Yet an increasing number of studies show that female gangs provide girls with the necessary skills to survive in their harsh communities while allowing them a temporary escape from the dismal future awaiting them. These studies reveal that girls join gangs for the same reasons that boys do and share with boys in their neighborhood the hopelessness and powerlessness of the urban underclass (Joe and Chesney-Lind, 1993, p. 9).

Prostitution

Eleanor M. Miller's *Street Women*, which is based on intensive interviews with sixty-four Milwaukee prostitutes, contends that prostitution evolves out of the profound social and economic problems confronting adolescent females, especially young women of color (Miller, 1986). For African American women, constituting over half of Miller's sample, movement into prostitution took place as a consequence of exposure to deviant street networks. Usually recruited by older African American males with long criminal records, these women organized themselves into "pseudo families" and engaged primarily though not exclusively in prostitution. These women viewed prostitution as an alternative to boring and low-paying jobs and as a means to relieve the burdens of pregnancy and single motherhood. Although they were attracted by the excitement and money involved in prostitution, they soon learned that the life was not nearly as glamorous or remunerative as they had anticipated (Miller, 1986).

For whites, Miller found that street prostitution was not so much a hustle into which one drifted as it was a survival strategy. For this group there was often a direct link between prostitution and difficulties with parents, runaway behavior, and contact with the juvenile justice system.

Interviewees described family lives that were characterized by disorganization and extremely high levels of violence and abuse. But running away from these chaotic settings resulted in the girls' arrest and lengthy detention as status offenders (Miller, 1986).

Considerable research supports the conclusion that adolescent female delinquents frequently have histories of abuse and victimization. Mimi Silbert and Ayala M. Pines found that 60 percent of the street prostitutes they interviewed had been sexually abused as juveniles (Silbert and Pines, 1982, p. 476). R. J. Phelps and colleagues' survey of 192 female youths in the Wisconsin juvenile justice system discovered that 79 percent of these youths (most of whom were in the system for petty larceny and status offenses) had been subjected to physical abuse that resulted in some form of injury (cited in Chesney-Lind, 1997). Chesney-Lind and Rodriquez's investigation of the backgrounds of adult women in prison underscored the links between their victimization as children and their later criminal careers. Interviews revealed that virtually all of these women were victims of physical and/or sexual abuse as youngsters; more than 60 percent had been sexually abused and about half had been raped (cited in Chesney-Lind, 1997, p. 19).

Jennifer, aged 12 (interviewed by Barbu on November 9, 2009), sadly is typical of girls who have gone into prostitution:

> My mother chooses men over my sister and me. That's why we are all messed up. I started prostituting myself. I didn't care. I already felt like crap—I might as well make some money. Now, I feel a little better about myself, here [juvenile institution]. I told my mom she has to make my sister and me a priority not the man currently in her life.
>
> I don't know why I'm always hungry. I do get regular meals here. At home my mom would be at work and there would not be a thing to eat in the house. I wouldn't have any money. My step Dad would get up at 2:00 p.m. He worked the night shift. He would order a pizza or something for himself and eat it in front of us kids. He would not share. He said we didn't need it because we were fat and lazy (Personal interview of November 9, 2008).

Adolescent Females and Violent Behavior

The media, especially in the last few years, have been quick to identify the rise of violence among juvenile girls when reporting increased arrest trends. As Table 4.1 shows, juvenile girls' official arrest rates for violence have risen, while juvenile males' rates for violence has gone down. The juvenile arrest rate for simple assaults is more than three times greater than the rate for aggravated assaults. Again, the arrest rate of girls for simple assault in 2003 was more than three times the rate in 1980 (Zahn et al., 2008). See Box 4.2 for a discussion of the rise of violence among juvenile females.

M. Brown, M. Chesney-Lind, L. Mikel, and Nan Stein, in their article, "Patriarchy Matters: Toward a Gendered Theory of Teen Violence and Victimization," challenge this notion of a rise of violence among juvenile females. They claim that self-report data sources reveal that juvenile boys' and girls' violence has *decreased* dramatically in the late 1990s. They also refer to the findings of the Youth Risk Behavior Survey, the biennial survey of the Centers for Disease Control (CDC). In 1991, while 34.4 percent of girls surveyed said that they had been in a physical fight in the last year, this figure had dropped to 23.9 percent in 2001, a 30.5 percent decrease in girls' fighting. Furthermore, these researchers are skeptical of arrest data reporting rises in

TABLE 4.1   Percent Change in Male and Female Juvenile Arrests for Violent Crimes, 1966–2005

Type	Girls	Boys
Aggravated assault	−5.4 percent	-23.4 percent
Simple assault	24.0	-4.1
Violent crime index	−10.2	-27.9
All crimes	−14.3	-26.7

Source: Crime in the United States, 2005, Table 33 (Washington, DC: FBI, 2006).

BOX 4.2

Violence on the Rise among Juvenile Girls

Toledo, IA. For years, 15-year-old Chantal Steeg handled anger by striking and screaming at people. She punched staff members and others at detention centers and foster homes. She threw furniture. She spewed verbal threats on other youths.

"It's a snowball effect—if you're angry at one thing and then another and you don't deal with it, you're going to explode," said Chantal, whose actions caused her to be removed from several foster homes and detention centers.

Violent behavior like Chantal's is on the increase among juvenile females, data from the Iowa Department of Public Safety show.

In 2003, 3,897 females younger than 18 were arrested, up 19 percent from the 3,283 arrested in 1998. Robbery, aggravated and simple assault, larceny, and vandalism were among the crimes showing increased occurrences among female juveniles.

Arrest rates for juvenile males during the same period fell 6 percent.

The numbers don't surprise Deb Hanus, treatment director at the Iowa Juvenile Home and State Training School for Girls in Toledo. An increasing percentage of the home's residents are there for committing violent crimes, she said.

In 2004, 37 percent of the home's residents had been charged with assault, up from 16 percent in 2000, Hanus said. . . .

Two teenage females were arrested this month after a teacher trying to stop a fight was pushed through a plate glass window at Mason City High School. The teacher suffered minor injuries, police said.

Ashley Ashby, 17, and Kedejsia Caples, 16, both students at the Mason City school, were arguing. When the teacher intervened, she was pushed through the window, officials said. . . .

Jamie Gilley, a social worker at Des Moines' East High School, recalls several fights among teenage females that resulted in serious injuries. "These are all-out brawls—I think (females) are more violent in their fighting. It's a level of difference that used to not exist," she said.

Valley High School sophomore Lyndsey Bohall agrees. She said the females she has seen fighting are very physical in their aggression.

"It is really aggressive; they just like, attack each other," she said.

Bohall said she thinks females hit harder and fight longer than boys. She said, males tend to hit each other once, and the fight is over.

"Girls go behind each other's backs—they're more secretive than boys, and that makes girls more angry," she said.

Critical Thinking Questions: According to this article, in what ways has aggressiveness among female offenders recently increased? In this article, how is the media involved in the social construction of knowledge? •

Source: Jessica Graham, "Violence on the rise among juvenile girls," *The Register's Iowa Weekly* (March 22, 2005), p. 14.

violence among young women, because studies of other systems that monitor injury and mortality do not show dramatic increases in violent victimization. For example, hospital admission data, as well as vital statistics maintained by the health department over the past decades in San Francisco note decreases, rather than increases in girls' injuries and mortality rates. Finally, in considering other forms of violence, such as robbery and murder, there is no trend indicated here that girls are becoming more violent. Instead, arrests of juvenile girls for other crimes of violence, including the most lethal, have shown decreases, rather than increases (Brown et al., 2004, p. 4).

Brown, Chesney-Lind, Mikel, and Stein conclude that "someone's behavior has been changing, but it is likely not the behavior of girls, but rather those that police and monitor youthful behavior, including the behavior of girls" (Brown et al., 2004, p. 6). They believe that three factors are at work in this social construction of crime data for juvenile females' increased rates of violence.

The first is "relabeling," often called "bootstrapping," of female girls' status offense behavior from noncriminal charges like "incorrigibility" to assaultive charges. This practice is taking place, these researchers reason, partly because of parents being advised to do so if they wish their defiant daughters arrested and detained and partly as a result of changing police procedures or practices (Brown et al., 2004, p. 6).

The second factor involves a "rediscovery of girls' violence," especially in the arrests of both girls and women for domestic violence. For example, in California, arrests of girls and women for domestic violence increased from 6 percent of the total in 1988 to 16.5 percent in 1998. Race also appears to be significant here, because African American girls and women had arrest rates for domestic violence about three times that of white girls and women. In citing one study, which assessed 1,000 girls' files from different points in the juvenile justice system, the findings revealed that about one-third of these girls were charged with "person offenses," the majority of which involved assault. A closer reading of these files revealed that most of those girls charged with assault were "the result of nonserious, mutual combat, situations with parents" (cited in Brown et al., 2004, p. 6).

The third factor, according to Brown, Chesney-Lind, Mikel, and Stein, is the "upcriming" of minor forms of youth violence (including juvenile females' physical aggression). "Upcriming" refers to policies, such as "zero tolerance policies," which have the effect of increasing the severity of criminal penalties associated with particular offenses, such as minor forms of fighting and school bullying. It was not that long ago that schoolyard fights and other instances of bullying were largely ignored or handled informally by parents and schools. But today, with the official concern about youth violence and with the proliferation of "zero tolerance" policies, school principals are increasingly willing to call police onto their campuses (Brown et al., 2004, p. 8).

Brown, Chesney-Lind, Mikel, and Stein conclude:

> In short, criminalizing girls' violence, like the justice system's earlier efforts to criminalize their sexuality, has had an enormous impact on girls. . . . But while the earlier policing of girls was justified by gender difference, today's pattern is masked as gender equity. The results of what might be called "vengeful equity," though, are clearly as disadvantageous to girls as the earlier pattern of inequality. In both systems, girls are the clear losers, and neither affords them the justice promised by a system that purports to seek the "best interest of the child" (pp. 8–9).

GENDER ACROSS THE LIFE COURSE

Jean Bottcher's study of brothers and sisters of incarcerated teenagers conceptualized gender as social practices and used these practices as the unit of analysis. Her study revealed six social factors that intertwined with delinquent activities, limiting female delinquency, while at the same time enabling and rewarding male delinquency. These factors included male dominance, differences in routine daily activities, variations in sexual interests and transition to adulthood, and an ideology that defined crime as male activity and child care as female activity (Bottcher, 2001, pp. 905–925).

Longitudinal studies usually reveal that delinquent careers differ by gender. Male careers tend to begin earlier and to extend longer into the adult years. Studies of youth gangs show that female members are more likely than male members to leave the gang if they have a child. Conventional life patterns—especially marriage, parenting, and work—draw both males and females away from gangs and delinquency but do so more completely and quickly for females (Bottcher, 2001, p. 899).

Amy C. D'Unger, Kenneth C. Land, and Patricia L. McCall's follow-up of the second Philadelphia cohort study found both life-course-persistent and AL delinquency (see Moffit's classification scheme earlier in the chapter) among the males, with a high and lower category for each group. Among the females in this study, there were comparable AL groups, though with lower overall offending levels. The high-rate AL female offenders did share marked similarities with low-rate chronic male offenders. Yet the chronic or persistent category of offenders was less prominent among the females (D'Unger, Land, and McCall, 2002, pp. 371–373).

Rebecca S. Katz, using waves 1 and 7 of the National Longitudinal Study of Youth, found that much as in other studies, childhood victimization, sexual discrimination, adult racial discrimination, and the experience of domestic violence largely explained women's involvement in crime and deviance. Katz found some support for revised strain theory as an explanation for female involvement in criminal behavior, but she concluded that female crime may require a unique theoretical model that more directly takes into account females' social and emotional development in a racist and patriarchal society (Katz, 2000, pp. 652–655).

John Hagan and Holly Foster state that American youth experience high levels of violence, and the U.S. public policy response is increasingly to punish the perpetrators of violence through waivers and transfer from juvenile to adult court. Adolescence is a time of expanding vulnerabilities and exposures to violence that can be destructive to self as well as to others. Such violence can involve intimate relationships or strangers. In addition to being perpetrators or victims, juveniles are often bystanders and witnesses to violence. The authors found from an analysis of data from the first two waves of the National Longitudinal Study of Adolescent Health that the life-course consequences of experiences with violence, especially violence in intimate adolescent relations, result in special difficulties for female juveniles, including depression and teenage pregnancy (Hagan and Foster, 2001, pp. 874–900).

Desistance from Crime

There have been at least three studies that have examined the desistance process among women. Ira Sommers, Debrorah R. Baskin, and John Fagan found that quality marriages led women to desist from crime, with some variation depending on the class and race of the women being studied (Sommers, Baskin, and Fagan, 1994, pp. 125–149). A later study by Sommers and Baskin revealed that the desistance process was quite different for inner-city women of color. These women were more likely to desist as the result of receiving alcohol and drug treatment or because they grew tired or fearful of repeated imprisonments (Sommers and Baskin, 1997, pp. 833–849).

Peggy C. Giordano and her colleagues developed a theory of cognitive transformation to explain desistance in their follow-up of a sample of serious adolescent female delinquents. They found neither marital attachment nor job stability to be strongly related to female desistance. Instead, desisters underwent a cognitive shift, or transformation. These researchers found that four types of cognitive transformations take place as an integral part of the desistance process: (1) There is a shift in the actor's openness to change; (2) the individual is exposed to a hook or set of hooks for change; (3) the individual begins to envision and fashion an appealing and conventional "replacement self"; and (4) a transformation takes place in the way the actor views the former deviant behavior or lifestyle. These various cognitive transformations or shifts not only influence receptivity to one or more hooks of change but also inspire and direct behavior. These hooks "facilitated the development of an alternative view of self that was seen as fundamentally incompatible with criminal behavior" (Giordano, Cernkovich, and Rudolph, 2002, pp. 1000, 1003; Giordano, Deines, and Cernkovich, 2006, p. 35).

A FEMINIST THEORY OF DELINQUENCY

The **feminist theory of delinquency**, an expression of radical feminism, contends that girls' victimization and the relationship between that experience and girls' crime have been systematically ignored. Chesney-Lind, one of the main proponents of this position, stated that it has long been understood that a major reason for girls' presence in juvenile courts is their parents' insistence on their arrest. Researchers, as well as those who work with female status offenders, are discovering today that a substantial number are victims of both physical and sexual abuse (Chesney-Lind, 1989, pp. 5–29).

Chesney-Lind proposed that a feminist perspective on the causes of female delinquency includes the following propositions: First, girls are frequently the victims of violence and sexual abuse (estimates are that three-quarters of sexual-abuse victims are girls); but, unlike boys, girls' victimization and their response to that victimization are shaped by their status as young women. Second, their victimizers (usually fathers or stepfathers) have the ability to invoke official agencies of social control to keep daughters at home and vulnerable. Third, as girls run away from abusive homes characterized by sexual abuse and parental neglect, they are forced into the life of an escaped convict. Unable to enroll in school or take a job to support themselves because they fear detection, female runaways are forced to engage in panhandling, petty theft, and sometimes prostitution to survive. Finally, it is no accident that girls on the run from abusive homes or on the streets because of impoverished homes become involved in criminal activities that exploit their sexuality. Because U.S. society has defined physically "perfect" young women as desirable, girls on the streets, who have little else of value to trade, are encouraged to utilize their bodies as a resource. The criminal subculture also views them from this perspective (Chesney-Lind, 1989, pp. 5–29). In Box 4.3, Chesney-Lind expands on this notion of the feminist theory of delinquency.

Emily Gaarder and Joanne Belknap interviewed twenty-two girls adjudicated and sentenced as adults in a large Midwestern state. They examined their lives before they were imprisoned and their perceptions of being tried and convicted as adults. The interviewees described lives filled with victimization and violence, sexism, racism, and economic marginalization. Significantly, the offending pattern of these girls was found to be similar to that of girls who remained in the juvenile justice system. Status offenses played a major role in this group of girls tried as adults (Gaarder and Belknap, 2004, p. 69).

BOX 4.3
Meda Chesney-Lind on the Feminist Theory of Delinquency

The question now is whether the theories of delinquent behavior can be used to understand female crime, delinquency, and victimization. Will the "add women and stir" approach be sufficient to rescue traditional delinquency theories? My research convinces me that it will not work. Gender stratification or the patriarchal context within which both male and female delinquency is lodged has been totally neglected by conventional delinquency theory. This omission means that a total rethinking of delinquency as a social problem is necessary.

The exclusion of girls from delinquency theory might lead one to conclude that girls are almost never delinquent and that they have far fewer problems than boys. Some might even suspect that the juvenile justice system treats the few girls who find their way into it more gently than it does the boys. Both of these assumptions are wrong.

Current work on female delinquency is uncovering the special pains that girls growing up in male-dominated society face. The price one pays for being born female is upped when it is combined with poverty and minority status, but it is always colored by gender. Consequently, sexual abuse is a major theme in girls' lives, and many girls on the run are running away from abusive and violent homes. They run to streets that are themselves sexist, and they are often forced to survive as women—to sell themselves as commodities. All of this is shaped by their gender as well as by their class and their color.

You might ask: How about the system's response to girls' delinquency? First there has been almost no concern about girls' victimization. Instead, large numbers of girls are brought into juvenile courts across America for noncriminal status offenses—running away from home, curfew, truancy, and so on. Traditionally, no one in the juvenile justice system asked these girls why they were in conflict with their parents; no one looked for reasons why girls might run away from home. They simply tried to force them to return home or sentenced them to training schools. The juvenile justice system, then, has neglected girls' victimization, and it has acted to enforce parental authority over girls, even when the parents were abusive. Clearly, the pattern described above requires an explanation that places girls' delinquent behavior in the context of their lives as girls in a male-dominated society—a feminist model of delinquency if you will. That's what I'm working on these days.

Critical Thinking Questions: Is it as hard for girls to grow up in male-dominated society as Chesney-Lind suggests? What do you think of other feminist theories of delinquency?

Source: Interviewed in 1988 and found in Clemens Bartollas, *Juvenile Delinquency*, 7th ed. (Boston, MA: Allyn & Bacon, 2005), p. 212.

This article shows the lack of a sound basis and the social construction that takes place in this serious act of transferring girls to the adult court. The researchers titled their chapter "Tenuous Borders" because they found there was a fine line between being retained in the juvenile court and being transferred to the adult court. The authors call for a more complex model of the relationship between victimization, agency, and responsibility, and a greater understanding of the social structural limitations and constraints placed on individual female offenders (Gaarder and Belknap, 2004).

Mary E. Gilfus (1992), in her analysis of life history interviews with incarcerated female offenders, further found that these women's childhoods and adolescence were plagued with neglect and abuse. Many responded by running away from home. Once they were on the streets, they became involved in an onset of drug use, stealing, and truancy, following which a large minority entered into juvenile prostitution as a survival strategy. These offenders participated in this illegal work simply as a survival strategy, but it further enmeshed them in criminal networks.

As they transitioned into adulthood, the vast majority experienced continued victimization and many developed drug addictions.

In sum, the research findings of Chesney-Lind, Gaarder and Belknap, and Gilfus reveal that girls can have a different pathway to crime than do boys. This means that the life-course developmental model examined in the past section is only partly adequate in understanding female delinquency. The life-course model focuses on significant life events or transitions, particularly in terms of changes in status, social roles, and relationships. This developmental approach, as identified by Sampson and Laub (1990), makes two hypotheses—first, problems in adult development are a result of childhood antisocial behaviors and, second, changes in offending behavior and development over the life course can be explained by social bonds to family and work in adulthood. However, as Gaarder and Belknap point out, life-course developmental models do not adequately address childhood victimizations, such as physical abuse, neglect, and sexual abuse, including those perpetrated by children's parents. Furthermore, the life-course perspective does not adequately address how discrimination and oppression, such as those based on a juvenile's race or sex, can shape this person's experiences, options, and identity (Gaarder and Belknap, 2004, p. 71).

The remainder of this chapter places emphasis on gender relations, influence of class, and racial discrimination and how they affect the processing of the female delinquent. It will be seen that delinquency across the life course, as proposed by Gaarder and Belknap, needs to be supplanted by an understanding of the victimizations of young women, as well as the discrimination and oppression they experience, to more fully understand how they process through their life transitions, including juvenile and criminal activities.

HOW GENDER BIAS AFFECTS THE PROCESSING OF THE FEMALE DELINQUENT

The fundamental theme of this section is that adolescent females grow up in a particular social context of domination and control by males (Spelman, 1989, p. 85). In this patriarchal society, troublesome juvenile females are quickly viewed through the lens of discrimination, exploitation, and oppression (Spelman, 1989, p. 51). Sexism, classism, and racism, several forms of oppression girls experience, affect the processing of the female delinquent in the juvenile justice system.

Gender Relations

The oppression of gender on adolescent females can be viewed in several ways.

- **Adolescent females receive discriminatory treatment because of society's disapproval of sexual activity** (Anderson, 1976, pp. 350–357). Krohn, Curry, and Nelson-Kilger's analysis of 10,000 police contacts in a Midwestern city over a thirty-year period found that adolescent females who were suspected of status offenses were more likely than their male counterparts to be referred to juvenile court for such offenses during all three decades (Krohn, Curry, and Nelson-Kiger, 1983, pp. 417–439). Some studies have found that police officers adopt a more paternalistic and harsher attitude toward younger females to deter any further violation or inappropriate sex-role behavior (Chesney-Lind, 1973, pp. 57–59; Visher, 1983, pp. 5–28). Several studies have indicated that juvenile females are treated more harshly than boys because of their sexual history (Chesney-Lind, 1973, pp. 57–59; Cohn, 1963, pp. 272–275; Rogers, 1973, pp. 223–246; Schaffner, 1998; Strouse, 1972, p. 84).
- **Second, offering another perspective, Rosemary C. Sarri concluded that juvenile law has long penalized females.** She claimed that although the law may not be discriminatory on

its face, the attitudes and ideologies of juvenile justice practitioners administering it may result in violations of the equal protection clause of the Fourteenth Amendment, by leading them to commit females to longer sentences than males under the guise of "protecting" the female juveniles (Sarri, 1976, pp. 68–69). She added that "females have a greater probability of being detained and held for longer periods than males, even though the overwhelming majority of females are charged with status offenses" (Sarri, 1976, p. 76).

- **Third, juvenile females receive punitive processing through the juvenile justice system.** Randall G. Sheldon and John Horvath further found that adolescent females who were reported to court for status offenses were more likely than their male counterparts to receive formal processing or a court hearing (Sheldon and Horvath, 1986). C. R. Mann's research on runaway youths found that juvenile females were more likely than adolescent males to be detained and to receive harsh sentences (Mann, 1984). Chesney-Lind also concluded that adolescent females are more likely than adolescent males to be held for long periods of time in detention centers (Chesney-Lind, 1989, p. 152). Randall R. Beger and Harry Hoffman's study of case files of juveniles ordered into detention by an Illinois juvenile court for technical probation violations found that females are confined in detention longer than males for disobeying probation rules (Beger and Hoffman, 1998, p. 173). Robert Terry's study of 9,000 youths apprehended by police in a Midwestern city found that females were more likely to be referred to the juvenile court than males and, if referred, were more likely to receive an institutional commitment (Terry, 1967, p. 218). K. O. Rogers found that females' average period of confinement in Connecticut was longer than that of males (Rogers, 1973, pp. 243–246). Clemens Bartollas and Christopher M. Sieverdes, in a study of institutionalized youths in North Carolina, found that 80 percent of the confined females had committed status offenses and that they had longer institutional stays than males (Bartollas and Sieverdes, 1985).

- **Fourth, according to another perspective, the oppressive treatment of adolescent females is hidden in the juvenile justice system.** Following the decriminalization of status offenses in 1979, Anne R. Mahoney and Carol Fenster reported that many girls appeared in court for criminal-type offenses that had previously been classified as status offenses. They suggested that juvenile justice officials may have redefined these girls to be eligible for the kinds of protectionist sanctions that have been traditionally applied (Mahoney and Fenster, 1982). Following the decriminalization of status offenses in 1979, Anne R. Mahoney and Carol Fenster reported that many girls appeared in court for criminal-type offenses that had previously been classified as status offenses. They suggested that juvenile justice officials may have redefined these girls to be eligible for the kinds of protectionist sanctions that have been traditionally applied (Mahoney and Fenster, 1982).

- **Fifth, another expression of the gender bias found in this "hidden justice" is that certain provisions of the Juvenile Justice and Delinquency Prevention Act provide that status offenders found in contempt of court for violating a valid court order may be placed in secure detention facilities. This permits juvenile judges to use their contempt power to confine repeat status offenders.** If a runaway girl, for example, was ordered by the court to remain at home, and she chose to run away again, she might be found in contempt of court—a criminal-type offense. There is reason to believe that juvenile judges apply their contempt power more often to female status offenders than to their male counterparts (Bishop and Frazier, 1992, p. 1167).

- **Finally, the early studies, especially, found that police officers, intake personnel, and judges supported a sexual double standard.** Female status offenders, as previously indicated, were more likely than their male counterparts to be petitioned to formal court proceedings, to be placed in preadjudicatory detention confinements, and to be confined in juvenile institutions. But at the same time, males who committed delinquent acts frequently received harsher treatment than their female counterparts. Consistent with what is known as the "chivalry" or "paternalism" thesis, police were less likely to arrest females suspected of property or person crimes. If arrested, female delinquents were less likely than male delinquents to be formally charged with criminal offenses, and, if charged, they were less likely than males to be incarcerated for their offenses (Bishop and Frazier, 1992, p. 1164). See Box 4.4 for a critical examination of gender-specific services in the juvenile justice system.

BOX 4.4

Sara Goodkind: Gender-Specific Services in the Juvenile Justice System: A Critical Examination

Goodkind refers to the 1992 Juvenile Justice and Delinquency Prevention Appropriations Authorizations (JJDPA) that states that "the term 'gender-specific services' means services designed to address needs unique to the gender of the individual to whom such services are provided." She adds that "the term *gender specific* has been interpreted to mean 'for girls' and that gender-specific programming refers to a comprehensive approach to female delinquency rooted in the experience of girls."

Goodkind found four fundamental critiques of the literature of gender-specific programming for female delinquency.

1. The need for gender-specific services is demonstrated and justified by frequent citations of increased rates of arrest and confinement for girls. However, Goodkind concludes that self-report and other sources have indicated that girls' delinquent behavior may not be on the rise.
2. An essentialized notion of gender is used that serves to reify socially constructed categories and ignore intersections of gender with race, ethnicity, class, sexuality, and other axes of difference.
3. Her third critique is that there is too great a focus on the individual. Interventions focus primarily on changing individuals, with few efforts geared toward institutional or structural change.
4. Her final critique is that girls' delinquency is frequently tied to their victimization, especially physical and sexual abuse. This approach ignores girls' agency and neglects the fact that girls

continue to be punished for behavior that is considered to be acceptable among boys.

Goodkind's concern is to shift the way that treatment agents, such as social workers, think about and engage gender. She is proposing an understanding of gender that is part of a framework for designing services for boys and girls that address their differential social locations without reifying socially constructed gender differences. This framework is based on the following eight principles, which she developed through her critical review:

- Deconstruct and move beyond false dichotomies;
- Adopt an interpretivist or constructionist epistemology that recognizes categories as socially constructed and presents a vision for social change;
- Uncover assumptions and identify interests and goals;
- Attend to the importance of context;
- Balance structure and agency and think in terms of interdependence;
- Focus on progress; and
- Rethink difference.

Critical Thinking Questions: What is your evaluation of Goodkind's article? Do you believe that her recommendations would improve the services for adolescent females involved in the juvenile justice system?

Source: Sara Goodkind, "Gender-Specific Services in the Juvenile Justice System: A Critical Examination," *Affilia 20* (Spring 2005): 52–70.

On balance, some evidence does exist that the discriminatory treatment of female status offenders may be declining since passage of the Juvenile and Delinquency Prevention Act (Bishop and Frazier, 1992, p. 1165). No longer do many states send status offenders to training schools with delinquents. But the long tradition of sexism in juvenile justice will be difficult to change. Due process safeguards for female delinquents, as well as for female status offenders, must be established to ensure them greater social justice in the juvenile justice system. The intrusion of extralegal factors into the decision-making process in the juvenile court has led to discrimination against the adolescent female that must become a relic of the past.

The Issue of Race

Young women of color, as well as other minority girls, often grow up in contexts much different from those of their white counterparts. Anthropolist Signithia Fordeham's article "Those Loud Black Girls" showed that young African American women resisted accepting the Anglo norm of femininity by being loud or asserting themselves through their voices. This behavior led to negative school experiences, and it did not take long for these juvenile females to discover that it is the quiet ones who do well in school. Some of this underachieving population decided to "pass for white" or to adopt more acceptable norms of femininity in order to be successful in the school experience. Others refused to adopt this survival strategy and their tool for liberation contributed to isolating or alienating them from school success (Fordham, 1997, pp. 81–111).

Pugh-Lilly, Neville, and Poulin (2001) explored African American adolescent girls' perceptions of delinquent behaviors in interviews with eleven girls enrolled in an alternative school.

Some had been expelled from the regular school for fighting. All of the girls indicated that they used aggressive behaviors to protect themselves from perceived threats and physical attacks. The environment that they inhabited was perceived as hostile and nonsupportive. They also perceived a high degree of racism in society.

A national survey of youths conducted by the Centers for Disease Control and Prevention (CDCP, 2002) found that physical violence in the form of fighting was more common among male than female high school students and more common among African American and Latina females than among whites. Males and minority groups were more likely than white students to be injured in the fights. Girls of color were by far more likely than other groups to feel unsafe going to school.

In self-report surveys, another relevant measure of problem behavior—drug and alcohol use—was shown to be in a higher proportion of males than females, especially heavy use, and African Americans were shown to have lower drug, alcohol, and tobacco use rates than whites or Hispanics (OSJJDP). Consistent with these findings, African American females have disproportionately low rates of drug referrals compared to white females, at only 10 percent. This is below their percentage of the juvenile population, which is 16 percent.

And yet, young African American women are picked up by police at three times the rate of young white women (Marks, 2003). Among females referred to juvenile court in 2002 for person offenses, African Americans accounted for 38 percent of cases—a clear overrepresentation of this population (Snyder and Sickmund, 2004). This was about the same racial breakdown as occurred among males. The Latina rate is not provided separately but rather included in the rate for whites.

These official statistics combined with qualitative observations of the concerns and behavior of African American girls from poor backgrounds is suggestive of the possibility of a different pathway to delinquency for many African American girls due to the reality of their lives. Belknap and Holsinger (2006) refers to cross-racial research that shows socialization of African American girls stresses resourcefulness, self-reliance, independence, and little sex-role segration. This upbringing is contrasted to that typical for white females who are more likely to be socialized to be subordinate. This more stereotypically masculine pattern of upbringing may provide strength for African American girls, particularly in regard to self-esteem but one that is not appreciated by the juvenile justice system. Belknap and Holsinger suggest that the pathway to delinquency unique to African American females may be shaped by negative experiences in a racist and often inadequate school system.

Katz (2000) found that a background of sexual abuse had different consequences for African American and white women. For African American women, the psychological reaction to childhood abuse was associated with externalization of the anger in outbursts of violence and for white women with drinking. Belknap and Holsinger, similarly, found a link between abuse and poor mental health among white delinquent girls and abuse and violence among African American delinquent girls. Given the racial differences in socialization and self-esteem, they note that these differences are not surprising.

Because racism and poverty often go hand in hand, African American girls are forced by their minority status and poverty to deal early and on a regular basis with problems of abuse, drugs, and violence (Chesney-Lind, 1997, p. 23). They also are likely to be attracted to gang membership (Esbensen and Winfree, 1998, p. 510). H. C. Covey, Scott Menard, and R. Franzese summarized the effect of ethnicity on gang membership:

> Racial difference in the frequency of gang formation such as the relative scarcity of non-Hispanic, white, ethnic gangs may be explainable in terms of the smaller proportion of the non-Hispanic European American population that live in neighborhoods characterized by high rates of poverty, welfare dependency, single-parent households, and other symptoms that characterize social disorganization (Covey, Menard, and Franzese, 1997, p. 240).

Minority girls' strategies for coping with the problems of abuse, drugs, violence, and gang membership, as Chesney-Lind has noted, "tend to place them outside the conventional expectations of white girls," and it also increases the likelihood that they will come to the attention of the juvenile justice system (Chesney-Lind, 1997, p. 23).

Influence of Class

As part of the female delinquent's "multiple marginality," class oppression is another form of exploitation experienced by this young person (Chesney-Lind, 1997, p. 4). In a number of ways, powerful and serious problems of childhood and adolescence related to poverty set the stage for the young person's entry into homelessness, unemployment, drug use, survival sex and prostitution, and, ultimately, even more serious delinquent and criminal acts. Even those adolescents coming from middle-class homes may be thrust into situations of economic survival if they choose to run away from abusive environments.

Poverty is a major risk factor for delinquency and frequently is accompanied by other risk factors related to family disruption (Snyder and Sickmund, 2004). Lower-class girls tend to confront higher risk levels than youth from the higher echelons, to live in tougher neighborhoods where there is more crime and victimization, and to have unsatisfactory experiences at school, to need to deal with risks of pregnancy and premature motherhood, and to lack supportive networks at home. According to Marks, "Many live in neighborhoods where guns, gangs, and drugs are common" (Marks, 2003). "And many come from families with at least one relative in jail, making prison terms more of a norm than a social rarity." (Marks, 2003, p. 2). For all races, middle-class children from stable backgrounds do not typically have problems of the frequency or magnitude as those described here:

In the criminalizing of juvenile offenses, therefore, the issues of gender, race, and crime are paramount. The impact of the criminalizing of girls' offenses has a significant impact on girls, especially on minorities and girls from dysfunctional and impoverished backgrounds. When children from families from the middle and upper classes get into trouble, their parents can often persuade the courts to sentence them to probation with a referral to outpatient mental health or substance abuse treatment (Chesney-Lind and Shelden, 2004).

The Whole Is Greater than the Sum of the Parts

The examination of the experience of African American juvenile girls reveals, as it does with adult women, that it is not as though one form of oppression is piled on another. That is, the effects of the multiple expressions of gender, class, and race are more than merely additive. This suggests that gender, class, and race are interlocking forms of oppression and that the whole is greater than the sum of its parts. Thus, female delinquents, like adult women, suffer the consequences of multiple oppressions as more than some form of simple additive experience (Spelman, 1989, p. 123).

Summary

This chapter, in examining the female delinquent across the life course, discussed the ways in which the female delinquent is expected in her culture to think, feel, and act (Spelman, 1989, p. 14). Female delinquency, like all other social behaviors, takes place in a world where gender still shapes the lives of adolescents in powerful ways (Chesney-Lind, 1977, p. 5). The value of feminist theory ultimately is based on accepting the notion that juvenile females are positioned in society in ways that produce vulnerability to victimization by males, including abuse and the negative effects of poverty. This position assumes, then, that behavior is gender-contextualized and that it should be examined from this perspective (Shoemaker, 2005, p. 242). Patriarchal society places a moral chastity belt around the behavior of adolescent females at home, in school, and in the community. Contextual analysis is helpful in understanding females' acceptance or rejection of their expected social norms and roles.

The problems of sexism, racism, and class and their influence on female delinquency have been generally ignored by criminologists. As a result, writers on female delinquency have often been more concerned with the adjustment of the adolescent female to society than with the extent and consequences of oppression in their lives. An examination of how the categories of gender, class, and race are interlocked and influence delinquency across the life course will lead to needed insight about the problems female delinquents face in U.S. society.

Key Terms

adolescence-limited delinquent
   males *71*
desistance *69*
developmental and life-course
   (DLC) theory *66*

early-onset, persistent
   offenders *71*
feminist theory of delinquency
   79

life-course perspective *67*
turning point *68*

Critical Thinking Questions

1. Why is the interlocking nature of gender, class, and race so important in understanding female delinquency?
2. Why has society been so sensitive to the sexual behavior of adolescent girls?
3. What is the relationship between victimization and oppression and the life course of female delinquents?

4. Do you believe that it would be more difficult for males or females to desist from delinquency in their late teens? How about in their mid-thirties? Why do you feel the way you do?

Web Destinations

Check out Meda Chesney-Lind's homepage at this site: http://home.hawaii.rr.com/chesneylind/

Girls and gangs: www.knowgangs.com/school_resources/menu_026.htm

Building blocks for youth: www.buildingblocksforyouth.org/issues/girls

Texas youth commission, adolescent girls with co-occurring disorders: www.tyc.state.tx.us/prevention/adolescent_girls.html

American Bar Association; girls in the juvenile justice system: www.abanet.org/crimjust/juvjus/girls.html

References

Akers, R. L. (1998). *Social learning and social structure: A general theory of crime and deviance.* Boston, MA: Northeastern University Press.

Anderson, E. A. (1976). The chivalrous treatment of the female offender in the arms of the criminal justice system: A review of the literature. *Social Problems 23*: 350–357.

Bartollas, C., and Sieverdes, C. M. (1985). Games juveniles play: How they get their way. Unpublished manuscript.

Beger, R. R., and Hoffman, H. (1998). The role of gender in detention dispositioning of juvenile probation violators. *Journal of Crime and Justice 21*: 173–186.

Bishop, D. M., and Frazier, C. E. (1992). Gender bias in juvenile justice processes: Implications of the JJDP Act. *Journal of Criminal Law and Criminology 82*: 1132–1152.

Bjerregaard, B., and Smith, C. (1993). Gender differences in gang participation, delinquency, and substance abuse. *Journal of Quantitative Criminology 9*: 329–348.

Bottcher, J. (2001). Social practices of gender: How gender relates to delinquency in the everyday lives of high-risk youths. *Criminology 39*: 905–925.

Bowker, L., and Klein, M. W. (1980). Female participation in delinquent gang activities. *Adolescence 15*: 509–519.

Brown, M., Chesney-Lind, M., Stein, N., and Mikel, L. (2004). *Patriarchy matters: Toward a gendered theory of teen violence and victimization* (Wellesley Centers for Women Working Paper No. 417). Center for Research on Women, Wellesley College, Wellesley, MA.

Browning, K., and Huizinga, D. (1999). *Highlights from the Denver Youth Survey. OJJDP Fact Sheet.* Washington, DC: Office of Juvenile Justice and Delinquency Prevention.

Browning, K., and Loeber, R. (1999). Highlights from the Pittsburgh Youth Study. *OJJDP Fact Sheet.* Washington, DC: Office of Juvenile Justice and Delinquency Prevention.

Browning, K., Thornberry, T. P., and Porter, P. K. (1999). *Highlights of findings from the Rochester Youth Development Study. OJJDP Fact Sheet.* Washington, DC: Office of Juvenile Justice and Delinquency Prevention.

Centers for Disease Control and Prevention (CDCP). (2002). *Youth risk behavior surveillance—United States 1991–2001.* Atlanta, GA: U.S. Department of Health and Human Services.

Chesney-Lind, M. (1973). Judicial enforcement of the female sex role: The family court and female delinquency. *Issues in Criminology 8*: 57–59.

Chesney-Lind, M. (1989). Girls, crime and women's place. *Crime and Delinquency 35*: 5–29.

Chesney-Lind, M. (2004). *The female offender: Girls, women, and crime.* Thousand Oaks, CA: Sage Publications.

Chesney-Lind, M., and Shelden, R. C. (2004). Girls, delinquency, and juvenile justice. Belmond, CA: Wadsworth.

Claussen, J. A. (1993). *American lives: Looking back at the children of the Great Depression.* New York: The Free Press.

Cohn, Y. (1963). Criteria for probation officers' recommendations to juvenile court. *Crime and Delinquency 1*: 272–275.

Cornich, D. B., and Clark, R. V. (1986). *The reasoning criminal: Rational choice perspectives on offending.* New York: Springer Verlag.

Covey, H. C., Menard, S., and Franzese, R. (1997). *Juvenile gangs*, 2nd ed. Springfield, IL: C. C. Thomas.

D'Unger, A. V., Land, K. C., and McCall, P. L. (2002). Sex differences in age patterns of delinquent/criminal careers: Results from Poisson latent class analyses of the Philadelphia cohort study. *Journal of Quantitative Criminology 18*: 349–375.

Eghigian, M., and Kirby, K.(2006). Girls in Gangs: On the Rise in America. Corrections Today, 68: 48–50.

Elder, Jr., G. H. (1999). *Children of the great depression: Social change in life experience, 25th anniversary edition.* Boulder, CO: Westview Press.

Elder, Jr., G. H., Johnson, M. K. K., and Crosnoe, R. (2003). The emergence and development of life course theory. In J. T. Mortimer and M. J. Shanahan (eds.), *Handbook of the life course*, New York: Kluwer Academic/Plenum Publishers.

Esbensen, F. A., Deschenes, E. P., and Winfree, Jr., L. T. (1998). *Differences between gang girls and gang boys: Results from a multi-site survey.* Paper presented at the annual meeting of the Academy of Criminal Justice Science in Albuquerque, New Mexico.

Esbensen, F. A., and Winfree, L. T. (1998). Race and gender differences between gang and nongang youths: Results from a multisite survey. *Justice Quarterly 15*: 505–526.

Farrington, D. P. (2003). Developmental and life-course criminology: Key theoretical and empirical issues: The 2002 Sutherland Award Address. *Criminology 41*: 221–247.

Farrington, D. P. (2005). Introduction to Integrated Developmental and Life-Course Theories of Offending. In D. P. Farrington (ed.), *Integrated Developmental and Life-Course Theories of Offending.* New Brunswick and London: Transaction Publishers.

Federal Bureau of Investigation (FBI). (2003). *Uniform crime reports.* Washington, DC: U.S. Government Printing Office.

Fordham, S. (1997). Those loud black girls: (Black) women, silence and gender "passing" in the academy. In M. Seller and L. Weis (eds.), *Beyond black and white: New faces and voices in U.S. schools* (pp. 81–111). Albany, NY: University of New York Press.

Gaarder, E., and Belknap, J. (2004). Tenuous borders: Girls transferred to adult court. *Criminology 40*: 481–517.

Gilfus, M. E. (1992). From victims to survivors to offenders: Women's routes of entry and immersion into street crime. *Women and Criminal Justice 4*: 63–89.

Giordano, P. C., Cernkovich, S. A., and Rudolph, J. L. (2002). Gender, crime, and desistance: Toward a theory of cognitive transformation. *American Journal of Sociology 107*: 990–1064.

Giordano, P. C., Deines, J. A., and Cernkovich, S. A. (2006). In and out of crime: A life course perspective on girls' delinquency. In Karen Heimer and Candace Kruttschnitt (eds.), *Gender and crime: Patterns in victimization and offending* (pp. 17–40). New York: New York University Press.

Glassner, B., Ksander, M., and Berg, B. (1983). A note on the deterrent effect of juvenile vs. adult jurisdiction. *Social Problems 31*: 219–221.

Glueck, S., and Glueck, E. (1940). *Juvenile delinquents grown up.* New York: Commonwealth Fund.

Hagan, J., and Foster, H. (2001). Youth violence and the end of adolescence. *American Sociological Review 66*: 874–900.

Hamparian, D., Schuster, R., Dinitz, S., and Conrad, J. P. (1980). *A violent few: A study of dangerous juveniles.* Lexington, MA: D.C. Heath and Company.

Harris, M. G. (1988). *Cholas: Latin girls and gangs.* New York: AMS Press.

Hawkins, D. J., Smith, B. H., Hill, K. G., Kosterman, R., Catalano, R. J., and Abbott, R. D. (2003). Understanding and preventing crime and violence: Findings from the Seattle Social Development Project. In T. P. Thornberry and M. D. Krohn (eds.), *Taking stock of delinquency: An overview of findings from contemporary longitudinal studies* (pp. 255–303). New York: Plenum.

Joe, K., and Chesney-Lind, M. (1993). *Just every mother's angel: An analysis of gender and ethnic variations in youth gang membership*. Paper presented at the annual meeting of the American Society of Criminology in Phoenix, Arizona.

Johnston, L. D., O'Malley, P. M., Bachman, J. G., and Schulenberg, J. E. (2004). *Monitoring the future national results on adolescent drug use: Overview of key findings*. Bethesda, MD: National Institute on Drug Abuse.

Katz, R. S. (2000). Explaining girls' and women's crime and desistance in the context of their victimization experiences. *Violence against Women 6*: 633–660.

Krohn, M. D., Curry, J. P., and Nelson-Kilger, S. (1983). Is chivalry dead? *Criminology 21*: 417–439.

Laub, John H., and Sampson, R. J. (1993). Turning Points in the life course: Why change matters to the study of crime. *Criminology 31*: 301–325.

Laub, J. H., and Sampson, R. J. (2004). *Shared beginnings, divergent lives: Delinquent boys to age 70*. Cambridge, MA: Harvard University Press.

Lauderback, D., Hansen, J., and Waldorf, D. (1992). Sisters are doin' it for themselves: Black gang in San Francisco. *Gang Journal 1*: 57–72.

Mahoney, A. R., and Fenster, C. (1982). Family delinquents in a suburban courts. In N. Hahn and E. A. Stanko (eds.), *Judge, lawyer, victim, thief: Women, gender roles and criminal justice*. Boston, MA: Northeastern University Press.

Mann, C. (1984). *Female crime and delinquency*. University, AL: University of Alabama Press.

Marks, A. (March 7, 2003). For more black girls, a violent cycle. *Christian Science Monitor*, p. 2.

Miller, E. (1986). *Street women*. Philadelphia, PA: Temple University Press.

Miller, J. (1998). Gender and victimization risk among young women in gangs. *The Journal of Research in Crime and Delinquency 35*: 429–454.

Miller, J. (2001). *One of these guys: Girls, gangs, and gender*. New York: Oxford University Press.

Miller, J., and Brunson, R. K. (2000). Gender dynamics in youth gangs: A comparison of males' and females' accounts. *Justice Quarterly 17*: 419–449.

Moffitt, T. E. (1993). Adolescent-limited and life-course persistent antisocial behavior: A developmental taxonomy. *Psychological Review 100*: 674–701.

Moffitt, T. E., Caspi, A., Dickson, N., Silva, P. A., and Stanton, W. (1996). Childhood-onset versus adolescent-onset antisocial conduct problems in males: Natural history from ages 3 to 18. *Development and Psychopathology 8*: 399–424.

Moffitt, T. E., Caspi, A., Rutter, M., and Silva, P. A. (2001). *Sex differences in antisocial behavior: Conduct disorder, delinquency, and violence in the Dunedin Longitudinal Study*. Cambridge, England: Cambridge University Press.

Moffitt, T. E., Lynam, D. R., and Silva, P. A. (1994). Neuropsychological tests predicted persistent male delinquency. *Criminology 32*: 247–275.

Moore, J., and Hagedorn, J. (2001). Female gangs: A focus on research. *Juvenile Justice Bulletin*. Washington, DC: Office of Juvenile Justice and Delinquency Prevention.

Mulvey, E., and LaRosa, J. (1986). Delinquency cessation and adolescent development: Preliminary data. *American Journal of Orthopsychiatry 56*: 212–224.

Paternoster, R., Brame, R., and Farrington, D. P. (2001). On the relationship between adolescent and adult conviction frequencies. *Journal of Quantitative Criminology 17*: 201–225.

Quicker, J. C. (1983). *Home girls: Characterizing Chicano gangs*. San Pedro, CA: International University Press.

Rogers, K. O. (1973). For her own protection: Conditions of incarceration for female juvenile offenders in the state of connecticut. *Law and Society Review 7*: 223–246.

Sampson, R. J., and Laub, J. H. (1990). Crime and deviance over the life course: The salience of adult social bonds. *American Sociological Review 55*: 609–627.

Sampson, R. J., and Laub, J. H. (1993). *Crime in the making: Pathways and turning points through life*. Cambridge, MA: Harvard University Press.

Sampson, R. J., and Laub, J. H. (2001). Understanding desistance from crime. In M. Tonry (ed.), *Crime and Justice*, Vol. 28. Chicago, IL: University of Chicago Press.

Sarri, R. C. (1976). Juvenile law: How it penalizes females. In Laura Crites (ed.), *The female offender*. Lexington, MA: Lexington Books.

Schaffner, L. (1998). *Female juvenile delinquency: Sexual solutions and gender bias in juvenile justice*. Paper presented at the annual meeting of the American Society of Criminology in Washington, DC.

Shannon, L. (1982). *Assessing the relationships of adult criminal careers to juvenile careers: A summary*. Washington, DC: U.S. Government Printing Office.

Sheldon, R. G., and Horvath, J. (1986). *Processing offenders in juvenile court: A comparison of males and females*. Paper presented at the annual meeting of the Western Society of Criminology in Newport, CA.

Shoemaker, D. J. (2005). *Theories of delinquency: An examination of delinquent behavior*, 5th ed. New York: Oxford University Press.

Silbert, M., and Pines, A. M. (1982). Entrance into prostitution. *Youth and Society 13*: 471–500.

Sommers, I., and Baskin, D. R. (1997). Situational or generalized violence in drug dealing networks. *Journal of Drug Issues 27*: 833–849.

Sommers, I., Baskin, D. R., and Fagan, J. (1994). Getting out of the life: Crime desistance by female street offenders. *Deviant Behavior 15*: 125–149.

Spelman, E. (1989). *Inessential woman*. Boston, MA: Beacon Press.

Strouse, J. (1972). To be a minor and female: The legal rights of women under twenty-one. *Ms. 1*: 116, 70–75.

Terry, R. (1967). Discrimination in the police handling of juvenile offenders by social control agencies. *Journal of Research in Crime and Delinquency 14*: 218–230.

Tremblay, R. E., Vitaro, F., Nagin, D., Pagani, L., and Seguin, J. R. (2003). The Montreal Longitudinal and Experimental Study: Rediscovering the power of description. In T. P. Thornberry and M. D. Krohn (eds.), *Taking stock of delinquency: An overview of findings from contemporary longitudinal studies* (pp. 205–254). New York: Plenum.

Visher, C. A. (1983). Gender, police arrest decisions, and notion of chivalry. *Criminology 21*: 417–439.

Warr, M. (1998). Life course transitions and desistance from crime. *Criminology 36*: 183–216.

Wilson, J. Q., and Herrnstein, R. (1985). *Crime and human nature*. New York: Simon and Schuster.

Wolfgang, W. E., Figlio, R. M., and Sellin, T. (1972). *Delinquency in a birth cohort*. Chicago, IL: University of Chicago Press.

PART

III

Drug Addiction, Prison, and Restoration

The title of this section of the book could spell out the journey of one woman or of many women in trouble with the law—the journey from drug use to incarceration to redemption. Common to all these chapters is the focus on the female offender. Chapter 5 presents research on the biology, psychology, and sociology of substance use and addiction. The emphasis is on the brain, trauma, and the societal response, respectively. Drugs and alcohol are involved not only in the commission of crime and women's involvement in the criminal justice system in that regard but also in women's victimization and criminal justice involvement.

Chapter 6, The Prison Environment, takes us into the world of the prison. Despite being a small proportion of the U.S. prison population, women and especially women of color have seen their numbers rise drastically over the past decade. Modeled on medium-security prisons for antisocial men, women's prisons are not hospitable places. Research shows that behind bars, women's treatment needs—in the areas of substance abuse, mental health, and prior victimization—are not being met. Many of the women in prison could lead productive lives in the community and at tremendous savings to the state if alternative intensive supervision programs were provided.

A promising new development (based on old traditions) is restorative justice. Chapter 7 reveals how the processes that are included under the rubric of restorative justice have special relevance for women, offenders as well as victims. Victim–offender conferencing is a form of peacemaking between the wrongdoer and the victim that is a process of empowerment for the offender, the victim, and the community.

5

Women, Substance Abuse, and Criminal Justice

T he decision to include a separate chapter on substance abuse problems in female offenders and victims is based on the following considerations:

- The war on drugs and its disproportionate impact on women;
- The extent to which substance abuse is associated with criminal activity of all sorts—for example, prostitution, child abuse, assault, manslaughter, and burglary;
- The considerable extent to which female offenders suffer from addictive tendencies and addiction;
- The implication of drugs and alcohol directly and indirectly for women's victimization.

Exploring the link between female crime and women's involvement with substance abuse is the first and major task of this chapter. This link will be examined through a look at relevant statistics and a description of typical pathways to crime. The **war on drugs** has been most influential in the nationwide expansion of the prison population, having a particularly devastating impact on women over the past twenty-five years. According to the Sentencing Project (2007), a research advocacy group that promotes sentencing reform, women are now more likely than men to serve time for drug offenses and are subject to increasingly punitive law enforcement and sentencing practices, despite the fact that women are less likely than men to play a central role in the drug trade. That the war on drugs (and drug users) has drastic repercussions for poor women of color is one of the basic assumptions of this chapter. The effects of this war are seen in the increased rate of arrest and imprisonment of minority women.

To prepare students and staff to work with persons with substance abuse and addictive problems, we have chosen a bio-psycho-social framework. This framework entails a study of the **biology of addiction** and substance abuse, including co-occurring mental disorders. Involvement in the criminal justice system often results from drug-seeking behavior and participation in illegal activities to acquire the drugs. Some of this and other high-risk and destructive behavior may stem from disrupted thought processes, according to a recent article in the *Journal of the American Medical Association* (Chandler, Fletcher, and Volkow, 2009). Such disrupted thinking is related to brain changes associated with long-term substance use. When an individual has a serious mental disorder as well, the combination compounds the problem and increases one's chances of getting into trouble with the law. Because so many offenders, especially those who are incarcerated, have both a diagnosable mental disorder and a substance dependency problem, a section of this chapter is devoted to co-occurring disorders, sometimes known as dual diagnoses.

In the discussion of *psychological factors*, we review facts concerning the pathway through which personal factors, including childhood trauma, can lead girls and women into unhealthy patterns of peer group alliances and relationships characterized by heavy alcohol and other drug use. Turning to the policy level, *social factors* in this context encompass the legal response to the lawbreaking behavior; the prosecution can be seen as a form of victimization in itself. The enforcement of antidrug conspiracy laws and prosecution of mothers who consumed drugs prenatally are among the topics discussed.

A woman does not have to break the law or have a substance abuse problem to find her life controlled by alcohol and other drug use or to be involved in the criminal justice system. Her involvement may be indirect, for example, through victimization by a drunken spouse or partner. Alcoholic- and drug-abusing women are highly vulnerable to all forms of victimization—robbery, rape, and physical abuse. Such victimization stems from their frequenting of dangerous places and their personal involvement with others who live a life characterized by antisocial behavior and sporadic violence. In summary, this chapter will consider these multiple dimensions of substance abuse with a special emphasis on gender. We begin with a statistically based overview.

FIRST, THE STATISTICS

According to the annual report *Crimes in the United States* (FBI, 2008), the percentages of the total of the most obvious drug-related arrests that were females are:

Drug abuse violations: 10.1

DUI 8.5

Disorderly conduct: 5.5

Liquor laws 5.1

Drunkenness: 2.8

Derived from Table 42, Arrests by Sex, 2007

Table 5.1 from the Bureau of Justice Statistics (BJS) is reproduced in full so that readers can examine the particular crimes that brought inmates with substance use problems into the jail facility. These data were collected by Karberg and James (2005) based on interviews that were conducted previously in more than 400 jails through the Census Bureau. As well as proving a breakdown by crimes committed by substance abusing and substance-dependent inmates, Table 5.1 also provides a breakdown by gender for substance dependence and abuse.

TABLE 5.1   Substance Dependence or Abuse among Jail Inmates, by Selected Characteristics, 2002

Characteristic	Percent of Jail Inmates		
	All	Dependence	Abuse Only
All jail inmates	68.0%	45.2%	22.9%
Gender			
Male	67.9%	44.3%	23.6%
Female	69.2	51.8	17.4
Race/Hispanic origin[a]			
White[b]	77.7%	55.4%	22.3%
Black[b]	64.1	40.4	23.7
Hispanic	58.7	35.7	23.0
Other[c]	66.0	45.4	20.7
Age			
24 or younger	66.1%	40.3%	25.8%
25–34	70.5	48.1	22.4
35–44	71.4	50.4	21.0
45–54	61.9	41.7	20.3
55 or older	46.2	23.1	23.1
Most serious offense			
Violent	63.1%	40.8%	22.3%
Property	71.7	50.6	21.1
Drug	72.1	49.6	22.4
Public-order	67.0	41.3	25.7

[a]Excludes inmates who did not specify a race.

[b]Excludes persons of Hispanic origin.

[c]Includes Asians, American Indians, Alaska Natives, Native Hawaiians, other Pacific Islanders, and inmates who specified more than one race.

Source: BJS (2005). *Substance Dependence, Abuse, and Treatment of Jail Inmates* (Washington, DC: U.S. Department of Justice).

We see from this table that there was little difference in the overall prevalence of substance dependence or abuse between men (68 percent) and women (69 percent) in jails. This means that over half suffered from alcohol or drug addiction (see the next section on biology). Convicted female inmates in jail had a higher rate of previous drug use (61 percent) compared to a comparable male sample (54 percent). As also revealed in the same research source, although not shown in this table, alcohol or drugs were a factor for both genders (predominantly male) in about 67 percent of violent crimes and almost 73 percent of property offenses. Clearly the national interview survey data show significant alcohol/drug involvement among this criminal justice population.

Note in Table 5.1 that approximately 45 percent of female inmates met the criteria for a diagnosis of substance dependence. How about a comparable figure for residents of state prisons? According to official estimates, 60 percent of women in state prison have a history of drug dependence (BJS, 2007b). The implications of these figures are that these female inmates are in need of intensive substance abuse treatment to help them later be successfully reintegrated into the community, and that had these women received substance abuse treatment in the first place, they might not have been brought to the attention of the criminal justice system at all.

Treating substance dependence as a public health problem instead of a problem for law enforcement would have benefits for these women and for the society as a whole. Yet, even though crime rates for both men and women have steadily declined over the past decade, the nation's war on drugs coupled with punitive sentencing practices continue to create harm. Significantly, women have been hurt in multiple ways: They have been hurt through incarceration and separation from their families, and through the siphoning of public resources away from health and treatment programs into prison construction and maintenance (Sentencing Project, 2007). Let us see what the statistics reveal about the nature of female crime and the extent of drug and alcohol involvement in such crime.

Keep in mind that other crimes for which the women were sentenced, including property crime and public order (DWI, or driving while intoxicated), also might have been alcohol/drug related. According to *The Sourcebook of Criminal Justice Statistics* (Office of Justice Programs, 2005), just over 12 percent of federally sentenced drug offenders were women. As this source further informs us:

- Approximately two out of three women (66.6 percent white, 64.8 percent black, 46.6 percent other) serving federal prison terms in 2002 were convicted of drug crimes.
- The breakdown of female federal drug offenders sentenced in 2003 shows 16.4 percent incarcerated on heroin charges, 14.1 percent on **methamphetamine** (**meth**), 11.5 percent on powder cocaine, 13.1 percent on marijuana, 8.7 percent on crack cocaine, and 14.4 percent on charges for other drug types. (*2003 Sourcebook of Federal Sentencing Statistics, U.S. Sentencing Commission, Table 35*)

In her examination of statistics such as these, Wallace (2005) argues that the extent of alcohol/drug involvement is even more pervasive than the raw statistics indicate. The process of plea bargaining, as she indicates, distorts the picture in that offenders are often sentenced for a lesser nondrug offense to clear the docket. Wallace cites evidence from a New York City study in which urinalysis tests showed that 28 percent of women tested positive for drugs when only 19 percent had been arrested on drug charges.

In Iowa, and increasingly in other states, meth is listed as the drug of choice among female but not male inmates. In 2002, for example, 43 percent of women entering prison said meth was their drug of choice (*USA Today,* 2002). Although there is no racial breakdown by gender in tabular form, BJS statisticians Karberg and James (2005) inform us that the cohort of white females, like white males, had a slightly higher rate of women who had substance dependence or abuse than did others in the jail population. White females were the minority at 43 percent of women in jail.

We learn further, as stated in the BJS substance dependence report, that convicted women offenders were more likely to have been under the influence of drugs (34 percent) than alcohol (22 percent) at the time of the offense. In contrast, alcohol involvement was more prevalent among the men. The high incidence of meth use and the tightening of laws intended to deal with this problem are only beginning to be reflected in the statistics. Results from a survey of 500 local officials conducted by the National Association of Counties declared meth to be the nation's leading law enforcement scourge and blamed it for crowding jails and fueling increases in theft and violence (Zernike, 2005). Meth is associated with Mexicans in terms of its transport and with rural whites in its manufacture and use. Since meth predominantly is a white problem, one could expect an increase in the numbers of white women sentenced for the use and manu-facture of this drug.

The most recent figures available from the government on meth use among inmates is presented in the BJS (2007a) report *Drug Use and Dependence, State and Federal Prisoners* as follows:

Profile of Methamphetamine Users among State and Federal Prisoners, 2004

Among state prisoners in 2004

- Female inmates (17 percent) were more likely than males (10 percent) to report use of meth in the month before their offense.
- White inmate (20 percent) were almost twice as likely as Hispanics (12 percent) to have used meth. Around 1 percent of black inmates reported using meth in the month before the offense.

Similar patterns emerged among federal inmates:

- Females (15 percent) were more likely than males (10 percent) to have used meth in the month before the offense.
- White inmates (29 percent) were six times more likely than Hispanics (5 percent) to report using meth. Black inmates (1 percent) reported low use of meth. (BJS, p. 3)

How about treatment for substance abuse problems? Most prison surveys show that a majority of inmates with substance abuse problems have access to treatment. But we must keep in mind that treatment included attendance at self-help groups such as Alcoholics Anonymous (AA) or Narcotics Anonymous (NA). As far as enrollment in professional substance abuse treatment programming, fewer than 20 percent receive the attention they need (Chandler, Fletcher, and Volkow, 2009).

The obvious relationship between substance abuse and crime suggests a strong role for treatment in crime prevention. Yet while the extent of the treatment needs among state and federal inmates has risen, due to the continuing prosecutions of drug users, the number receiving treatment has actually dropped. We will look at the policy implications under the treatment section of this chapter.

The Meaning of the Statistics

Many different data sources establish a correlation between drug/alcohol use and other criminal offenses. But correlation does not mean causation. MacCoun, Kilmer, and Reuter (2003), adopting Goldstein's (1985) framework of drug–violence connections, offer a three-part classification scheme. This scheme posits that the connection is (1) psychopharmacological, (2) economic-compulsive, or (3) systemic (territorial fights over drug markets). These explanations can serve to explain the link between substance use and the commission of property crimes (stealing to support the habit or embezzlement related to gambling) or crime of an economic nature. With regard to the third category, the violence–drug use link, the psychopharmacological properties of some drugs—especially alcohol and stimulants such as meth and cocaine—may induce violence or bellicosity in certain individuals. As MacCoun, Kilmer, and Reuter explain, such substances can amplify the psychological and situational facilitations of aggression. A combination of suppression of normal inhibitions may lead to impulses that normally are controlled. At the same time, impaired cognitive functioning caused by the influence of the substance on the brain creates a situation ripe for some form of explosive behavior. For example, in a report on violence, suicide, and risky behavior, SAMHSA (2003) reveals a high rate of delinquent behaviors in girls under the influence of alcohol or other drugs. Fighting among girls at school or work, engagement in group-on-group fights, and stealing in older girls were behaviors closely associated with substance abuse. We now take a closer look at biological factors relevant to women's substance use.

BIOLOGICAL FACTORS

Before examining the alcohol/drug crime link, let us examine some of the gender differences in the effect on the body of alcohol/drug consumption. Starting with research on girls, we learn from the National Center on Addiction and Substance Abuse (CASA) at Columbia University (2006) studies that:

- Girls and young women from the ages of eight to twenty-two face increased risk during early puberty and transitions to middle school, high school, and college.
- Adult women from twenty-three to fifty-nine years of age face increased risk of divorce, the burden of caring for elderly parents, and concerns about the effects of aging.
- Girls and young women are likelier than boys and young men to abuse substances in order to lose weight, relieve stress or boredom, improve their mood, reduce sexual inhibitions, self-medicate depression, and increase confidence.
- Women in substance abuse treatment are more than five times likelier than men (69 percent vs. 12 percent) to have been sexually abused as children, and girls and women are likelier than men to suffer eating disorders, both of which are major risk factors for substance abuse.
- Girls exhibit symptoms of nicotine dependence more rapidly than boys. Females have greater smoking-related lung damage than males; a single cigarette smoked by a woman has nearly the same carcinogenic effect as two smoked by a man.
- Females have greater susceptibility to alcohol-induced brain damage, cardiac problems, and liver disease than males; because their bodies contain less water and more fatty tissue and because of decreased activity of the enzyme ADH that breaks down alcohol, one drink for a woman commonly has the impact of two drinks for a man.
- Females are more susceptible to Ecstasy-induced brain damage than males;
- Women who use sedatives, antianxiety drugs and hypnotics are almost twice as likely as men to become addicted to such drugs.
- Teenage girls are likelier than boys to be hospitalized due to the misuse of medications such as Tylenol, which affects the liver, and antidepressants.

Similarly, research studies on alcohol abuse from the National Institute on Alcohol Abuse and Alcoholism (NIAAA, 2004) show that, compared to men, women

- Have a much shorter interval between onset of drinking-related problems and entry into treatment;
- Become intoxicated after drinking smaller amounts of alcohol, even when compared to men of the same weight;
- Experience a higher rate of physiological impairment earlier in their drinking careers;
- Have a much higher mortality rate from alcohol abuse, with increased death stemming from organ damage, especially of the liver, brain, and heart.

Holly Johnson (2004), a researcher for the Australian government, has delved into the difficult research question of the extent to which pharmaceutical qualities play a key role in criminal behavior in women. Her literature review, which is international in scope, is bolstered by extensive data from interviews with Australian women in the criminal justice system. Women's criminality is apt to be more drug involved than men's, as Johnson reminds us.

Biological effects on human behavior discussed by Johnson include being high, drunk, or craving for drugs at the time of the offense. The process of intoxication is clearly biological; the short-term effects of chemical substances on the brain, liver, and other parts of the body are seen in delayed (or speeded up) reflexes, slurred speech, inability to concentrate, flushed face, or dilated pupils of the eye, and so on. The impact of such a physiological state in combination with situational factors (such as provocation) can be a risk factor for crimes of violence. Johnson found, for example, that 58 percent of women were intoxicated by alcohol when they committed murder. In regard to property and driving offenses, intoxication increases the probability of getting caught.

A few choice descriptions provided by offenders in Johnson's sample are revealing:

Drugs, speed made me crazy. You live in an unreal space. I was quite psychotic when I did my armed robbery.
 Drugs give me courage and I think I can do anything, so I do crime.
 It made me feel good and happy, but my decisions between right and wrong were cloudy. (p. 5)

A second key biological factor emphasized by Johnson is the nature of addiction. The role of addiction is implicated in the motivation for crime—for example, committing burglary or engaging in prostitution to support a habit. Drug dependency was found in Johnson's sample to be highest among sex workers (at 84 percent) and individuals who committed property offenses (74 percent) and lowest for violent offenders (58 percent). The strikingly high dependency rate is no doubt related to the high proportions of aboriginal inmates in the Australian sample. In Australia, 34 percent of the female prison population is aboriginal (they are 2 percent of the total population) (Yehia, 2003). Aboriginal inmates in Australia, like other indigenous populations in Canada and the United States, have a high alcoholism susceptibility and are imprisoned disproportionately to their numbers (Collins and McNair, 2003; van Wormer and Davis, 2008). Women of the Sioux tribe, for example, have drinking rates that match those of the men. Let us digress somewhat to look more closely at the chemistry of alcohol/drug craving and addiction and the particular susceptibility of girls and women to substance dependence. We start with the brain.

The Brain on Drugs

Thanks to advances in technology, namely the development of functional magnetic resonance imaging (**fMRI**), scientists can capture chemical images of the brain at work. They can also observe not only structures but also actual functions of the living brain. Although brain research is in its infancy, new knowledge about the role of **neurotransmitters**, the chemicals that carry messages between nerve cells, have captivated the interest of persons concerned with all forms of substance abuse and addiction. The defining features of drug intoxication and addiction can be traced to disruptions in cell-to-cell signaling (Sherman, 2007).

Researchers are now recording brain changes that occur as a person experiences a high or rush from the drug as well as the low associated with craving, as happens with cocaine. The pleasure circuits have been identified. Through the use of fMRI, alterations in the brain register as activity when craving is induced through various means such as showing the individual addict pictures of drug paraphernalia related to his or her addiction. Gamblers who play poker might be shown a deck of cards, for example. Neurotransmitters have been linked to normal emotions and also to mental disorders, including substance dependence.

Cocaine's chief biological activity is in preventing the reabsorption of the neurotransmitter dopamine. **Dopamine** is the "feel-good" transmitter that triggers a drug user's high. Too much dopamine causes the bizarre thoughts of schizophrenia, and too little is implicated in the tremors of Parkinson's disease. **Serotonin**, associated with sleep and low anxiety, is the neurotransmitter most closely linked with alcohol use. Decreased levels have been linked to depression, anxiety, and aggression.

The fact that addiction runs in families and has been shown to manifest itself dispro-portionately in the offspring of children put up for adoption who had alcoholic fathers provides some evidence of a hereditary component. Recent research on brain structure has identified a genetic factor that may predispose young people to harmful drinking habits. According to medical scientists Chandler and her colleagues (2009), addiction is a chronic brain disease with a strong genetic component. We now know that use of many addictive substances over time depletes the brain of these natural feel-good chemicals (NIDA, 2008). This is what addiction is all about—the compulsion to get back to feeling high or even, when tolerance sets in, to simply feeling good. The individual heavy drug user eventually loses the ability to feel pleasure normally.

Meth can affect lots of brain structures, but the ones it affects the most are those that contain the chemical dopamine. The reason for this is that the shape, size, and chemical struc-ture of meth and dopamine are similar. Because meth is a high-energy drug that reduces the need for sleep, many of its users began using it to reduce feelings of exhaustion from the long hours of work necessary in today's competitive job market. Recent studies in chronic meth abusers have also revealed severe structural and functional changes in areas of the brain asso-ciated with emotion and memory, which may account for many of the emotional and cognitive problems observed in chronic meth abusers (NIDA, 2008). A depletion of dopamine following cocaine and meth use probably accounts for the binges, development of tolerance, craving, and the obsessive behavior characteristic of meth users. (View the photographs of brain injuries at http://www.drugabuse.gov.)

Recent research on recovering meth addicts, summarized by Zickler (2004) of the National Institute of Drug Abuse (NIDA) in a small sample of men and women, shows some modest improvement in memory function after nine months of sobriety. Another part of the brain, that related to motivation, future planning, and ability to feel pleasure, however, showed no recovery after abstinence. This fact explains why a long period of inpatient treatment is needed. What we know about meth recovery from anecdotal reports is that a very long time is required for physiological recovery.

What do brain studies show about male/female differences in neurological damage caused by drug/alcohol use? With regard to alcohol abuse, women who drink to excess experience more and earlier brain damage and sooner than males who drink a comparable amount. The effect is a result of the kind of brain shrinkage associated with dementia. From brain research, we learn that women process cocaine cues differently than men do (Whitten, 2004). As women listened to a script about cocaine, the blood flow in their brains was measured. In women as with men, the pleasure centers of the brain were activated. During this craving period, however, the brain study showed that part of the emotional response to the craving was inhibited. The significance of this difference requires further study; the findings could have important treatment implications because craving is a key factor in relapse.

Co-occurring Disorders

In the general population, women with substance use disorders are more likely to have mental disorders compared with their male counterparts. The most common disorders in these women are posttraumatic stress disorder (PTSD), depression, anxiety, and eating disorders (SAMHSA, 2005). Research indicates that many women who enter the criminal justice system not only have substance abuse problems but also accompanying mental disorders and HIV/AIDS. According to the BJS (2006) special report on mental health problems among prison and jail inmates, female inmates reported higher rates of mental health problems than male inmates—in state prisons: 73 percent vs. 55 percent; in federal prisons: 61 percent vs. 44 percent; and in local jails: 75 percent vs. 63 percent. These rates seem unrealistically high, but keep in mind that these mental health problems include neuroses as well as very disabling mental illness. Major depression and mania were the most commonly reported problems; around 15 percent of the incarcerated men and women had psychoses. Around one-fourth of females in state prisons as in local jails stated they had been diagnosed with a mental disorder in the past year by a mental health professional. This was almost three times the rate of male inmates (around 8 percent) who had been told they had a mental health problem.

The BJS researchers compared female inmates with mental health problems with those who did not report such problems. They found that female state prisoners who had a mental health problem were more likely than the other inmates to:

- meet criteria for substance dependence or abuse (74 percent compared with 54 percent),
- have a current or past violent offense (40 percent compared with 32 percent),
- have used cocaine or crack in the month before arrest (34 percent compared with 24 percent), have been homeless in the year before arrest (17 percent compared with 9 percent).

They were also more likely to report—

- three or more sentences prior to probation or incarceration (36 percent compared with 29 percent),
- past physical or sexual abuse (68 percent compared with 44 percent),
- parental abuse of alcohol or drugs (47 percent compared with 29 percent),
- a physical or verbal assault charge since admission (17 percent compared with 6 percent). Bureau of Justice Statistics (2006)

A study commissioned by the Canadian government and focused on mental health needs of female inmates reported that federally incarcerated women were three times as likely as men to have received mental health treatment in the community (Laishes, 2002). They were also three times more likely to suffer from depression. Self-mutilation was common among the women but not the men. Compared to community samples, women in the Canadian prison system are about twice as likely to have experienced childhood sexual abuse and two-and-a-half times more likely to have been physically abused as an adult.

Mental disorders are biological in their origins, genetically and constitutionally. Serious mental illnesses are believed to be caused by abnormality of brain chemistry; therefore they can be expected to respond to medication and often do. Evidence of a physical basis of mental disorders such as schizophrenia comes from neuroimaging of the brain, which reveals structural abnormalities. The new technologies also reveal the fact that drugs that block certain dopamine receptors reduce the symptoms of the disease (Ginsberg, Nackerud, and Larrison, 2004). It is a convention in correctional psychiatry to identify as serious mental illness only certain Axis I disorders of the *Diagnostic and Statistical Manual of Mental Disorders-IV-Text Revised* (*DSM-IV-TR*) (American Psychiatric Association [APA], 2000) such as bipolar disorder, major depression, and schizophrenia, and to limit mental health treatment to prisoners with these disorders only (Human Rights Watch, 2003).

A growing body of evidence from specialized scientific studies implicates common neurological pathways and abnormalities involved in addiction and a number of psychiatric disorders (Brady and Sinha, 2005). Bipolar (manic-depressive) disorder, for example, has a close association with chemical dependency. Friedman and colleagues (Friedman et al., 2005) collected criminal history data on dually diagnosed men and women. The majority of both the men and women in the sample of 132 reported that they had been charged with a crime, and half of those had been incarcerated. The authors concluded that the addition of substance abuse to bipolar disorder has a greater influence on criminal behavior in women than in men, especially when the drug used was cocaine. This research helps explain the overrepresentation of women with bipolar disorder in the corrections system.

Because of their past life trauma, large numbers of women in prison with a history of substance abuse problems also are diagnosable, that is, they meet the criteria for current PTSD. Kubiak (2004) found in a study of 60 participants in a prison-based substance abuse treatment program, that over half were diagnosed with PTSD. Most had suffered early childhood sexual abuse and/or later battering and rape experiences. The dually diagnosed women had a higher rate of drug relapse upon release than did the women with substance abuse problems only.

PTSD is listed in the *DSM-IV-TR* as a mental disorder. Whereas with schizophrenia, brain abnormality precedes the development of the disease, with PTSD the mental disorder itself leads to the changes in brain chemistry. The major symptoms of PTSD are denial of event, numbing, flashbacks, intrusive thoughts, guilt feelings, sleep disturbances, jumpiness, and preoccupation. Instead of a diagnosis of PTSD, correctional mental health staff more often give female offenders a diagnosis of borderline personality. This diagnosis, which is described in the *DSM* as a personality disorder characterized by volatile behavior is clearly a pejorative one; it is likely to be given to a woman who is considered too difficult for treatment, with the end result that her treatment needs are ignored (Human Rights Watch, 2003).

Neurobiologists, who are pioneering studies using brain imaging to learn how traumatic events are imprinted on the brain through altered brain chemistry, now know there is an organic basis to psychological trauma (Jackson, 2003). In other words, when people who have been victimized by a horrifying event or series of events, such as by rape or combat, experience trauma, the changes in brain chemistry may be long-lasting. These changes are often manifested in depression (probably related to the impact on serotonin levels in the brain). Reduced brain activity of dopamine, a naturally occurring substance that moderates feelings of pleasure, may contribute to obesity as well as to drug addiction. Mathias (2001) reports in *NIDA Notes* of a NIDA-funded study that found dopamine deficiencies in the brains of individuals who were compulsive overeaters. A high incidence of obesity is seen in female prison populations.

The Role of Early Childhood Trauma

Early childhood sex abuse is widely recognized to be a major factor in the later development of substance abuse problems (Laishes, 2002; Lapham, 2004/2005; Mullings, Marquart, and Hartley, 2003; van Wormer and Davis, 2008). Survivors of such extreme stress who now have depression or anxiety disorder are apt to suffer an abnormal stress response. One of the bridging constructs, in fact, between psychiatric and substance use disorders is the role of stress in the development of substance use disorders (and relapse) and other psychiatric disorders such as PTSD (Brady and Sinha, 2005). This link between trauma and excessive stress reactions was examined by Heim and colleagues (2000) in relation to child abuse.

Published in the *Journal of the American Medical Association*, this article is touted as the first human study to find persistent changes in stress reactivity in adult survivors of early trauma. A comparative study of forty-nine healthy women revealed detectable biochemical abnormalities in those who had been severely abused in childhood. In a laboratory situation women survivors were four times more likely than other women to develop excessive stress response to mild stimuli. Those who were abused and now have anxiety disorder or depression are six times more likely than other women to suffer an abnormal stress response. The significance of this study for our purposes is that it helps explain the drive to self-medicate due to their inability to cope with psychological stress, an inability that derived from early childhood trauma. (We know from animal studies that stress and alcohol consumption levels are highly correlated [Spear, 2001].)

Epidemiological studies report rates of co-occurrence of major depression with nicotine, alcohol, and illicit drug abuse ranging from 32 to 54 percent (Brady and Sinha, 2005). Individuals with major depression are more likely to develop substance use disorders, and individuals with substance use disorders are at greater risk for the development of major depression, compared to the general population. Because of the weakened stress response, the stage is set for future psychological problems, especially under conditions of repeated stress. PTSD occurs because of the impact of an extreme stress response on memory. The stress hormones such as cortisol act on the brain, creating a state of heightened alertness and supercharging the circuitry involved in memory formation (Cowley, 2003). Then, even years later, when confronted with stress in adulthood, the adult brain might regress to an infantile state. Fight/flight reactions to stress are common due to the power of the "body memory," as Basham and Miehls (2004) explain. Such memory is often triggered by sights, sounds, touch, or smells. (Recent news reports of extreme overreactions to such stimulus by soldiers recently home from Iraq are relevant here.)

Because memories run on chemicals, they can be altered by chemicals. In an experiment reported by Begley (2005), emergency room patients who were given beta blockers had subdued memories of extremely disturbing events compared to a control group.

These scientific findings concerning the trauma–stress link help explain the close interconnection between women's criminal behavior (often through a link with a drug-involved man) and an earlier history of abuse. Women who have been sexually abused are more likely to engage in behavior placing them at risk for HIV/AIDS infection through such practices as getting intoxicated, trading sex for drugs, and using shared needles in drug use injection (Mullings, Marquart, and Hartley, 2003). According to Mullings and colleagues, the rate of HIV infection among female prisoners has increased by almost 90 percent compared to 28 percent for males. It appears that the high prevalence of HIV infections among female inmates is directly related to risky drug activities. The rate is now 3 percent for female inmates in state prisons compared to 1.9 percent for males. This is far higher than the rate for the population as a whole. Most of the inmates with HIV/AIDS are African American and Hispanic (BJS, 2004).

The HIV rate is higher among female than male inmates for a number of reasons (Lanier and Zaitzow, 2007). Women who smoke crack tend to have more sexual partners and are likelier to engage in prostitution than nondrug users. Incarcerated women are more likely than men to be serving time for drug offenses, especially for cocaine. Women who are sexually involved with long-term drug-using men further increase their susceptibility. The high rates of HIV/AIDS in the African American and Latino inner cities are reflected in the prison population.

As we take a closer look at the psychological pathway leading a girl or woman into the criminal justice system, keep in mind the fact that a significant percentage of girls and women who get into trouble with the law have experienced physical and/or sexual abuse in the past by a family member, and that many of these were revictimized by a boyfriend or spouse in adulthood.

PSYCHOLOGICAL FACTORS

In this section, we focus on victimization. We first look at the situations of women whose problems with the law were related at least in part to their personal background of childhood victimization. Then we consider situations of women whose involvement in the criminal justice system is as witness and victim—a victim of domestic violence, for example. In both types of cases our concern remains with the role of alcohol and other drugs in the victimization. For women, victimization and criminalization typically are intertwined.

Pathways to Crime

In women's lives, the connection between addiction and crime is manifest both directly through drug-induced lawbreaking and indirectly through involvement in destructive relationships with people involved in the criminal underworld. Poverty compounds a woman's dependency on drug-abusing, often battering, men. The racial dimension is reflected in the fact that African American women are more likely than white or Latina women to be recruited to deviant street networks through domestic ties, whereas white and Latina women are more likely to be recruited into these networks through running away, drug use, or both—behaviors often associated with physical and sexual abuse in their families of origin (Farr, 2000). The typical pattern or **pathway to crime** is for the girl who runs away from a violent or sexually abusive family to join other runaways on the streets. Once there, she learns how to survive through various illegal means.

In their review of the literature, Covington and Bloom (2006) found that women's pathways into crime indicates that gender matters, that there are profound differences between men's and women's lives that shape their patterns of criminal offending. Some women come into contact with the law through their life on the social and economic margins, as they struggle to survive outside legitimate enterprises. Because of their gender, women are also at greater risk for experiences such as sexual abuse, sexual assault, and domestic violence. Among women, the most common pathways to crime therefore are based on survival (of abuse and poverty) and substance abuse.

Mullings and colleagues (2003) conducted personal interviews with a sample of women prisoners in the Texas system. Their purpose was to study HIV sexual risks and HIV drug risk in terms of the independent variable, which was whether the woman had ever been sexually abused prior to age eighteen. The results echoed those reported elsewhere in the literature. The women who had been victimized in childhood were significantly younger at admission to prison, likely to be white, and from an unstable family background. Overall, the sexually abused groups experienced child neglect at greater frequency than did non-abused women. This fact, of course, explained in part how they became vulnerable to sexual exploitation. Trauma theory that suggests sexually abused girls suffer from low self-esteem and engage in high-risk-taking behavior (Downs and Rindels, 2004) is given some support by these findings.

Compared to male offenders, female offenders have a disproportionately high rate of multiple victimization. According to the BJS (2006) investigation on mental health problems in inmates, 44 percent of the female inmates who were interviewed reported that they had been victims of physical and/or sexual abuse prior to their imprisonment. Much of this abuse, as we know from other reports, occurred in childhood.

Chesney-Lind and Pakso (2004) map out the pathway that would lead a girl—desperate to escape the sexual and physical abuse at home—to run away; seek solace in drugs and the company of drug users, gang members, and the like; and survive on the streets through prostitution. This pattern is highlighted in inner-city females for whom prostitution may serve as a means of survival in circumstances of extreme economic hardship. Belknap (2007) and Enos (2001) similarly stress the role of poverty and sexual and physical abuse in women who assist the men in the commission of crime.

Surveys of women in trouble with the law indicate that early childhood victimization—for example, sexual molestation—is highly correlated with later involvement in prostitution (Belknap, 2007). Victimization during childhood is associated with feelings of distress and low self-esteem. To dull the pain, the woman may use drugs such as alcohol, cocaine, heroin, or meths. Sometimes the drugs are introduced to the woman by her boyfriend. Many female addicts were initiated into drug abuse by a drug-using partner; and once involved with an alcohol- or drug-dependent man, it is very hard for a recovering woman to maintain sobriety.

Enos (2001), who gathered interview data based on fieldwork in a northeastern women's prison, discusses paths to prison in terms of racial and ethnic differences. For white women, the most typical route to prison was the run-away-to-the-streets path. The white inmate mothers in Enos's study grew up in homes they found dysfunctional and fled as soon as they were able to, often becoming involved in drugs and crime through the influence of a boyfriend or male partner. Most lost contact with their families and were forced to rely on foster care for their children if there was no father in the picture. Looking back, the women characterized their parents as abusive. Sexual abuse was also part of the history, as reported by this inmate:

> My parents were really bad alcoholics. I spent most of my childhood in foster care.
> I got molested by one of my uncles and nobody wanted to hear about it. (p. 49)

Other white women in Enos's study, however, were from supportive middle-class backgrounds with limited exposure to street crime. While these women spoke highly of their normal upbringings, other white women linked their drug involvement to poor parenting and child neglect.

The pathways for African American women mostly involved introduction to the drug scene through relatives and domestic networks. When the women were arrested, family caretakers often were found to take care of their children if family resources were depleted. The African American women in the study had greater access to help from their mothers than did white women, but less access to help from husbands or boyfriends to care for their children. In the interviews, black women seldom connected their involvement in crime and drugs to bad parenting.

Latina women's paths to prison often exclusively involve drug charges. In Enos's sample, two of the women, recent immigrants, were serving long sentences for drug trafficking and had no prior involvement in the criminal justice system. Two others were serving time for drug-related property crimes. Their pathways to crime were through running away to the streets. In interviews, they attributed the lure of quick money through drug sales as a key factor. Most did not place blame on their parents. They were able to rely on family members, including the children's fathers, for child care.

Early-Life Physical and Sexual Abuse

Statistics on prior abuse reported by incarcerated women enhance our awareness of the child abuse/substance abuse configuration. To put a human face on these data, read about the compelling case of Amanda Peterson, who was introduced to meth by her father and who became completely hooked on the drug. Her story is presented in the Des Moines Register (Leys, 2005):

> Following the classic pattern of addiction, she ate or smoked more and more of the drug, gaining less and less effect.
>
> She willingly recounts the facts behind the drug charges and assault arrests that littered her teenage years. She speaks more reluctantly about an earlier incident, for which court papers listed her as "victim." Authorities referred to her then as "Jane Doe," because the 1998 crime was so awful. And after all, she was just a kid. In the "defendant" space, the court papers list a man's name. Peterson barely recognizes it, because she only knew him by his nickname, Satan.
>
> Satan threw drug parties at his house, and he let kids participate. When Peterson was wasted, he would have sex with her on a couch. Police found out about it, and they arrested him on charges of sex abuse and running a drug house. Peterson didn't understand, at first, what was wrong. She thought he loved her. She was thirteen. He was thirty-two. She sees the truth now. "He didn't love me," she said. "He was just a damned pedophile." (p. 2)

This brief biography of one woman could be a composite drawn from all the stories of meth addiction. The drug-infested household, the predatory sexual abuse, the drug-induced fighting, the drug tolerance leading to demands for more extreme forms of drug ingestion— all are here.

The opiate drug, Oxycontin, is a highly addictive substance prescribed to cancer patients and persons recovering from surgery for pain relief. Washington State is reporting a widespread problem with persons who get hooked on this drug. The following case is reported in a news story by Pawloski (2009):

> Black Hills High School graduate Samantha Studebaker, 22, became addicted to OxyContin two years ago, after a co-worker's offer of a quick—and free—fix for her headache while she worked a shift at the Tumwater Costco.
>
> Soon, Studebaker says, she was paying up to $40 or $80 a pill—$1 a milligram— to that same co-worker to feed her addiction to the painkiller.
>
> At first, Studebaker used her credit cards to pay for the pills. Then she began stealing. In September, Studebaker was caught after embezzling more than $32,000 from Costco over about five months to pay for the OxyContin pills that her co-worker sold at increasingly high prices. Studebaker, who worked in Costco's returns department, said she entered fraudulent returns for items, then pocketed the cash.
>
> Studebaker's story is part of a nationwide epidemic of prescription-drug abuse. In the late 1990s, OxyContin abuse ravaged communities in the East, particularly in New England and parts of the South, where it earned the name "hillbilly heroin."
>
> Studebaker said she had never been in trouble with the law before her September arrest, and she wouldn't have started stealing if not for her addiction. . . .
>
> Studebaker said that at the height of her addiction, she was taking up to eight or nine 80-milligram OxyContin pills a day.
>
> "They're so addictive," she said during an interview behind the glass at the visitor's room at the Thurston County Jail before she was shipped off to the women's prison in Purdy. ". . . If I'm paying forty and eighty dollars a pill, you better believe I'm addicted."

Samantha Studebaker said she and others who abuse the drug can easily defeat OxyContin's timed-release coating by crushing the pills and snorting or smoking them for a quicker high.

An earlier study by SAMHSA (1997), *Substance Use among Women in the United States*, found the association between drug use and crime is stronger for women than for men, according to self-reports. While about a third of the drug-using women reported committing any criminal activity during the past year, only around 5–6 percent of women not using drugs did so. Women who were heavy alcohol users had rates of criminal activity as high as those of comparable male drinkers; this included driving while intoxicated offenses. Adult women who used any illicit drugs in the past year were six times as likely as women who had not used any illicit drugs to have been arrested. In a comparison of their sample of more than 1,000 Texas female inmates, Mullings, Pollock, and Crouch (2002) found that about twice as many women with drug problems committed other crimes (theft, forgery, robbery, prostitution, etc.) in their lifetimes. One drug that may have involved theft but not prostitution was meth. In their survey of sixty-four female offenders in mandated treatment for meth, Strauss and Falkin (2001) found that the women typically had earned money through the dealing and manufacture of the drug and did not resort to prostitution.

More detailed information concerning drug use is available from the Arrestee Drug Abuse Monitoring (ADAM) program *Annual Report* (Taylor, Newton, and Brownstein, 2003). ADAM conducts extensive interviews at sites throughout the United States and validates results with urinalysis tests. A majority of the women arrested tested positive for an illicit drug. The following were their findings:

- Of the three drugs analyzed, cocaine was used most frequently, followed by marijuana, meth, and the opiates.
- Meth was most prevalent in the western states, at almost half of users in Honolulu.
- Polydrug use was rare.
- Arrestees were 40 percent white, 39.7 percent black, and 4 percent Hispanic, and the rest were "other."
- About one-third had no high school diploma.
- One half of the women and around 18 percent of the women obtained marijuana and crack cocaine, respectively, through noncash means (usually sex).
- Forty-two percent of the women were at risk of drug dependence.

Partner Violence

We now turn from the topic of pathways to crime to adulthood victimization, still focusing on the alcohol/drug connection. It is a myth believed in some domestic violence circles that heavy drinking and drug use are not a significant factor in domestic partner violence, that substance use is just an excuse used by batterers. The truth is otherwise. It is true that some individuals who engage in bad behavior claim they were drunk or high on drugs as an excuse for their behavior. In his interviews with male inmates who had murdered their wives, David Adams (2007), for example, found that most of them claimed they had been drinking or using drugs. And indeed this could have been only an excuse.

To obtain more objective results, Adams interviewed twenty women who had narrowly escaped being murdered. Three-fourths of these survivors characterized their attackers as heavy substance abusers. Other research confirms a relationship between substance use and intimate partner violence. Fals-Stewart, Leonard, and Birchler (2005) found that in men who drank, violence escalated on drinking days in proportion to the amount of alcohol consumed.

Additionally, these researchers found that among men in a domestic violence intervention program who had a diagnosis of antisocial personality disorder, heavy drinking was strongly associated with severe intimate partner violence.

These substances are known to be most closely associated with aggression—the depressant, alcohol, and the stimulants, cocaine and methamphetamine (van Wormer and Davis, 2008). If batterers who had substance abuse problems abstained from alcohol and other drug use, we could predict their rate of violence would decrease. And at least one study has found that male batterers who were receiving substance abuse treatment improved their behavior markedly as a result of the treatment. This was true even though the interventions did not directly focus on domestic violence (Stuart, 2005). More research is needed on this point.

How about substance abuse in battered women? A recent study by Call and Nelsen (2007) of 30 mostly low-income women of color who were in treatment for substance abuse problems and who also reported partner abuse revealed a close association between the violence and the use of substances. Drinks and illicit drugs were often taken after being beaten because these substances "helped them deal with it or because substances 'kept them blind' to it" (p. 341).

A minority of the women stated that they were physically abused because of their alcohol and other drug use. In any case, alcohol and other drugs consistently have been found to be a major factor in intimate-partner violence.

That women who are drug addicted are highly susceptible to partner violence is revealed in a study of heroin-addicted women in methadone maintenance (methadone is a synthetic substitute for heroin that can be legally prescribed by specially qualified physicians). Research by Engstrom et al. (2008) found in a sample of over 400 women receiving treatment at a methadone clinic that over half had been sexually abused in childhood, that just under 90 percent had been beaten by their partners and almost one-third were suffering from PTSD. These findings have implications for treatment interventions with women who are former heroin addicts.

The extent of family violence associated with meth use, as mentioned previously, is a reality highlighted in the media nationwide. A search through www.google.com for recent reports from small-town newspapers revealed a tremendous upsurge in domestic violence related to meth. For example, Harris (2005), a British journalist who visited a small town in Tennessee, wrote of the stranglehold that meth has taken on rural America. The impact he found was substantial as evidenced in the sixty recent "meth orphans" from Cumberland County, in the increase in sexual abuse associated with a drug that gives sex drives a powerful boost, and in the 500 percent increase in domestic violence in this one small county. Significantly, as reported in the article, jails that used to have minority majorities now have white majorities inasmuch as meth is the drug of choice among rural whites. Because women are more likely to use meth than other illegal drugs (many start using it for weight loss), child neglect and abuse are a real part of the scenario (Knickerbocker, 2005).

An earlier scholarly study that examined the history of abuse and violence in more than 1,000 meth users (Cohen et al., 2003) provides validation to the media accounts. In the research on men and women in treatment for meth addiction, the reporting of violence was extensive, with 80 percent of women reporting partner violence. Experiences of early-life violence were commonly recounted as well. Men also experienced violence, more commonly from friends and acquaintances.

The long-term consequences of psychological abuse can include anger and hostility toward others. In their review of the literature, Mullings and colleagues (2003) found "distrust of authority and adults, alienation from others, a negative self-view, substance abuse (for self-medication), emotional volatility (either overreacting or numb approach to life), inappropriate use of sex and sexuality, and distant or dysfunctional family relationships" (p. 77). The cycle of victimization, substance abuse, unhealthy relationships, and victimization goes round and round.

Concerning this substance abuse connection, we learn from victimization surveys from the offices of the U.S. Department of Justice (BJS, 2007b) that victims reported the presence of alcohol or other drugs in about 42 percent of all cases of intimate-partner violence. For further information concerning the battering-substance abuse link, we turn to clinical studies. For a start, here is a summary of findings gleaned from the domestic violence literature:

- Approximately one-half of batterers in batterer education programs have significant alcohol problems.
- Over one-half of married male alcoholics in treatment were physically aggressive toward their partners in the previous year.
- Cocaine, meth, and alcohol in high doses are all associated with a man's hyperactivity and violence; marijuana and heroin have not been proven to induce violence.
- Military studies on alcohol consumption in the army show that soldiers who drink heavily have a high rate of partner violence even when they are not drinking (Thompson and Kingree, 2006, pp. 252–253).

The reason for the correlation between alcohol and other drugs and any type of violence is generally attributed to the fact that intoxication lowers the person's inhibitions and the ability to think rationally; sometimes a state of paranoia results. The effect of alcohol, for example, contributes to a misreading of social cues through a cognitive impairment, and violent outbursts may result.

Researchers from the National Institute on Alcohol Abuse and Alcoholism today are testing people who are intoxicated at a blood alcohol level of 0.08 to determine their levels of sensitivity to stimuli related to danger (National Public Radio, 2008). The tests are fairly simple, thanks to the new fMRI techniques for directly observing the brain at work. In an experiment devised by Jodi Gilman, intoxicated subjects view photographs of neutral and threatening faces. Under the influence of alcohol, the subjects fail to react. As the researchers conclude, intoxication decreases one's sensitivity to danger. This means that a person who is drunk might not know when to stop because he or she would not pick up on the warning signs.

A woman's substance use often parallels her partner's. Women arrested for battering—often fighting back—commonly are found to have been intoxicated at the time (Dutton, 2007). Furthermore, research on women incarcerated for the murder of their partners shows they often had been drinking along with their partners just before they fired the fatal shots (Serran and Firestone, 2004). Women whose partners have been drinking are significantly more likely to be injured than are women whose partners have not been drinking (Thompson and Kingree, 2006).

SOCIAL/SOCIETAL FACTORS

Policies, programs, and services need to respond specifically to women's unique pathways in and out of crime and to the contexts of their lives that support criminal behavior (Covington and Bloom, 2006). Instead, public policy through the so-called war on drugs has punished women as victimizers with little consideration of their personal histories of victimization. Female offenders' ties to their children, as Bloom and Chesney-Lind (2007) point out, are often compromised in harsh zero tolerance policies. Such policies are discussed in the following section under the social aspects of women's involvement in drug/alcohol abuse and dependence.

We are talking here of responses to women's drug and alcohol use by the criminal justice system. Violence and victimization, as Mullings and colleagues (2003) indicate, carry over into the adult lives of women offenders as they enter the criminal justice system. Once criminalized, women are revictimized by the state through coercive laws and their "one-size-fits-all" enforcement. Because their involvement with drug dealing, if this is their charge, was typically at a low level with limited involvement with other dealers, their cooperation with prosecutors (in turning in others) is necessarily limited. There may be threats of abuse from a crime partner, or as often happens, the woman may be charged with conspiracy to deliver drugs when her partner or spouse turns her in as the only way he has to reduce his own sentence. This is how the war on drugs is being played out, with the strongest impact inflicted on the poor and vulnerable.

The treatment of substance abuse as a criminal justice rather than a public health problem has led to a situation in which incarceration, instead of a policy of last resort, has become the first-order response for both men and women. Women alcoholics and drug users, especially when they are mothers, minority, and poor, are highly stigmatized in the system. Those who are caught using street-level drugs, and, increasingly, meth, are demonized in ways tied to their drug of choice. Because chivalry (the view that women, especially white women, are weak and need to be protected) was a casualty, as well it should have been, of the women's movement, the judicial system seems to have gone in the opposite direction, and no longer takes into account situational factors related to gender. Gender-neutral (treating men and women the same) laws and standardized treatment now predominate. Policies and procedures developed to subdue potentially violent and highly dangerous male offenders were, in response to gender-equality laws, thrust on women as well. The very architecture of women's prisons was redesigned to stress security over livability. The situation that comes to mind is the reporting throughout the correctional system of women forced to give birth in handcuffs and, until the last minute, leg shackles. These facts are explored in more depth in Chapter 6.

Central to understanding the creation of the sentencing guidelines for crimes involving crack cocaine—the cheaper smoked alternative to powder cocaine—are the roles of the media and racism in constructing and presenting the problem of crack. The media focused on three general themes: the claim that crack was more addictive than powder cocaine and a cause of such problems as "crack babies" and exchange of sex for drugs; the strong link to the violent crime world of inner-city gangs; and the low cost and ready supply of the drug. Media coverage by the TV networks and other news accounts in the 1980s and early 1990s presented an extremely negative and racially charged image to poor black mothers who had used crack and were thought to be destroying lives (Sagatun-Edwards, 2007). At the same time, other possibly more severe risk factors such as alcohol and tobacco used were not condemned in the same moral tones. Although the crack epidemic is over, and the horror stories of serious mental defects in infants exposed in utero to crack cocaine discounted, the legacy of the earlier media hype is still with us, evident in our prisons and in the continuing enforcement of mandatory minimum laws.

In a surprise development, in 2005 the U.S. Supreme Court struck down a part of the mandatory laws to make them advisory but no longer binding on judges (Cornell University Law School, 2008). The laws are still on the books in most states, and defendants still have little protection when facing harsh sentencing judges. Time will tell what the impact of the decision will be.

The war on drugs is considered one of the most serious obstacles to achieving racial justice in the United States and internationally. This fact was argued in a petition signed by more than one hundred U.S. civil rights and religious leaders and presented to the U.N. World Conference against Racism. The group cited statistics showing that African Americans constitute 57 percent of the drug offenders in U.S. prisons and Latinos account for 22 percent ("Petition Asks U.N. Racism Conference to Take Up U.S. War on Drugs," 2001).

Black and Latina women started being herded into prison following the passage of the 1986 and 1988 Anti-Drug Abuse Acts, which established harsh mandatory-minimum sentencing guidelines targeting crack cocaine. This is the drug associated in the public mind with inner-city crime. The war on drugs, as stated previously, emerged as a war on minority and poor women, and it is still packing nonviolent women into prison at a record-breaking rate. The 100-to-1 ratio in punishment for crack cocaine compared with powder cocaine has been considered racist and classist by most observers. One of the results of this federal law, which was modeled at the state level, was that the number of women incarcerated for drug offenses has increased exponentially over the past two decades. The increase for African American women was more than three times that of white women.

The interplay of race, class, and gender is at its most pronounced in the prosecution of drug-addicted mothers. Under the rationale of protecting the fetus, poor, black, drug-addicted mothers are being hauled into court. This is part of an alarming trend toward greater state intervention into the lives of pregnant women. Poor women of color are the primary targets of government control; they are the least likely to obtain adequate prenatal care, yet the most vulnerable to government monitoring and the least able to conform to the white middle-class standard of motherhood. The prosecution of drug-addicted mothers thus becomes more than an issue of antifemale backlash. Poor black women have been selected for punishment as a result of an inseparable combination of their gender, race, and economic status.

Punishment of Pregnant Drug Addicts

The media hype over "crack babies" that appeared in the early 1990s, later found to be scientifically untenable (Sagatun-Edwards, 2007), was embodied into law due to a landmark case, *Whitner v. South Carolina*, which became law in 1997. This case upheld the prosecution of an African American woman who ingested crack cocaine during the third trimester of her pregnancy. After the baby was found to have cocaine in his bloodstream, the mother was prosecuted under child-abuse and endangerment statutes. On appeal, the South Carolina Supreme Court upheld the conviction based on laws recognizing a viable (defined as past twenty-four weeks of gestation) fetus as a person for the purpose of homicide laws and wrongful death statutes (Sagatun-Edwards, 2007). Maternal substance abuse during pregnancy, in effect, was outlawed, and some women have found themselves shackled to their hospital beds immediately after giving birth.

By 2004, hundreds of women had been arrested nationwide for their addictive behavior while pregnant (Paltrow, 2004). Some of the cases have since been overturned, for example, in the landmark South Carolina mentioned above. After she served eight years in prison for homicide by child abuse, the court finally recognized that the woman's conviction had been based on "outdated" research and that her trial counsel had failed to call experts who would have testified about recent studies showing that cocaine is no more harmful to a fetus than nicotine use, poor nutrition, lack of prenatal care, or other conditions commonly associated with the urban poor, according to court documents (Paltrow, 2008). These cases are not going away, however, because of the determination of the fetal rights advocates. Paltrow's organization, National Advocates for Pregnant Women, has documented hundreds of cases in which fetal rights have been used to justify denying human rights to women when it comes to making medical decisions concerning their pregnancies, for example, to choose to give birth at home. Many more have lost custody of their children because some states now consider "child neglect" to include prenatal exposure to controlled substances. Mandatory reporting of cases of suspected child abuse and neglect involving drug use are now increasingly common in many states. Since drug testing occurs only in publicly funded health care facilities, such laws, needless to say, fall chiefly on the poor and minority women. There has been no effort to use a newborn's toxicology screen to check for the role of sperm (damaged by drug use) in causing birth defects.

Attorney Lynn Paltrow (2004), who specializes in laws that punish pregnant women for potential harm to the fetus, brings to our attention the significance of a new law passed and signed by President Bush in 2004—the Unborn Victims of Violence Act. This law, which was a product of the antiabortion movement, makes it a crime to cause harm to a "child in utero." More than thirty states have similar laws on the books. Paradoxically, as Paltrow indicates, this federal law does not make it a federal crime to physically attack pregnant women, yet homicide is the number-one killer of pregnant women.

Although in many states, such as Maryland and New Mexico, the states' higher courts are throwing out convictions of women who endangered their unborn children, the district attorney in a southern county in Alabama has gone all out to punish mothers whose babies are found to have drugs in their bloodstreams. As reported in a *New York Times* article, (Nossiter, 2008), at least eight women have been prosecuted for this offense over an eighteen-month period.

Significantly, today, the media hyperbole that played into the crackdown on mothers who used crack while pregnant is now being directed toward meth. In response to the barrage of stories that appeared in the media concerning an epidemic of birth defects caused by meth use in pregnant women, over ninety leading doctors, scientists, and treatment specialists released a public letter calling on the media to stop the use of terms such as "meth babies" (Lewis, 2005). The use of such terms, they said, harms the children to which they are applied and lowers expectations for their academic success and is without scientific basis. The suggestion that treatment will not work for people dependent upon meth, particularly mothers, also lacks any scientific basis. The scientists further fault news reports and policy makers for not consulting experts to obtain information about the effects of prenatal exposure and about the efficacy of treatment.

Both pregnancy and drug "epidemics" are issues ripe for government exploitation, a way of diverting the people's attention away from the major, structural problems onto issues of "morality" of individuals. Drug wars (whether inner-city blacks and Latinos associated with crack cocaine or poor rural whites involved in meth production) lend themselves to scapegoating, and the international war on drugs can be justified on the basis of images of people strung out on drugs. The increase in the prison population and huge expenditures on the prison industrial complex take billions of dollars that otherwise could be spent on housing, health care, and substance abuse treatment on demand.

TREATMENT ISSUES

Despite the fact that an estimated 60 percent of female state prisoners (and 43 percent of federal prisoners) are dependent on or abusing drugs at the time of arrest, only around 9 or 10 percent of these inmates are in treatment at one time (BJS, 2006). Surveys show that more white than black female offenders have alcohol and other drug problems; today, meth involvement is bringing large numbers of white women into prison.

Were substance abuse treatment offerings more prevalent in the community and more inviting, it is likely that many of the girl runaways and women who got into so much trouble with their addictive behavior could have been spared the full force of the law. Consider the fact that the majority of women arrested for drug use violations do not have health care coverage and do not have access to affordable treatment (Taylor, Newton, and Brownstein, 2003). Inpatient treatment is largely unavailable.

Although drug-addicted women might benefit more from residential treatment provided in the community, with such programming out of reach, many do benefit from the treatment they receive behind prison bars. Research reported in the Journal of the American Association shows that for each dollar spent per inmate on treatment, $2–$6 would be saved, a calculation based on the reduction in crime and child welfare costs associated with continued drug use (Chandler, Fletcher, and Volkow, 2009). Given this cost-savings benefit, not to mention the tremendous benefit to women's lives, treatment offerings should be expanded accordingly.

To document the availability of substance abuse treatment program offerings across all correctional settings, the National Criminal Justice Treatment Practices Survey was conducted nationwide. Taxman (2008) summarizes the results. The findings are not encouraging. The survey found overall that:

- Access to treatment services within correctional settings is minimal—less than 10 percent of adult offenders and about 20 percent of juvenile offenders across all settings receive the treatment that they need.
- Less than half of the administrators report using a standardized tool to screen for substance abuse disorders.
- Inadequate numbers of treatment staff, and types of training for the staff, make effective implementation of programs and services difficult.
- Substance abuse treatment services are reported to be offered in 65 percent of the adult correctional programs (e.g., work release, intensive supervision), but the most frequently provided services are educationally oriented or low-intensive group therapy (less than four hours a week), which are unlikely to facilitate behavior change.
- Most of the substance abuse services are less than the ninety days recommended by the literature.
- Treatment providers report using some of the consensus-driven, evidence-based practices, but in general, correctional administrators are unaware of these practices occurring in the programs offered to offenders.

The only mention of gender in the report was the statement that 31 percent of males and 50 percent of females in correctional facilities are in need of intensive services. When the report speaks of evidence-based services, the focus is on the behavioral-cognitive approach; there is no mention of gender-based services. Despite this serious omission in the report, there is every likelihood that an expansion of substance abuse treatment services in female institutions will be designed, as is recommended in other government-based reports, with gender issues in mind. Clinical services for addiction treatment that focus on women's specific issues and needs have been shown to be more effective for women than traditional programs originally designed for men (Covington and Bloom, 2006).

Empirical evidence indicates as well that treatment for drug-abusing women is effective and that its effectiveness is not diminished when women offenders are coerced into treatment by the criminal justice system as a condition of probation or parole (Springer, McNeece, and Arnold, 2003). Within prison walls, women are usually eager for services, and there may be a waiting list to attend. The benefits of group treatment within the prison setting are that the members are eager for an outsider to talk to, absences are rare, and the women often have an extended period of sobriety. On the negative side, there is no family or community involvement, nor is there a chance for women to become independently resourceful. Moreover, there is no testing ground for inmates to learn to resist temptation—there is little or no temptation to resist. The outpatient setting is just the opposite in terms of advantages and disadvantages: clients relapse and disappear, and they may resent being forced to attend when they have pressing family and work demands to attend to. Their support system may still be intact, however, and family members' involvement in the program enhances the addict's chances of recovery. Referral to nearby resources, such as community treatment and self-help groups, can reinforce social skills learned in treatment.

The treatment program at Mitchellville women's prison in Iowa is immensely popular with meth addicts; unfortunately, the waiting list is long. Read Box 5.1 for a glimpse at a successful intensive treatment program. Note the comment by one inmate: "It's really sad that you have to come to prison to get into this kind of program."

BOX 5.1
Addicts Battle Back

The brain damage it causes makes meth hard to kick. But success rates are rising, and long-term recovery prospects are looking better.

—by Tony Leys, *Des Moines Register* staff writer

Inside the razor-wire fences and brick walls of the Mitchellville women's prison, forty inmates sit in a circle, clapping, stomping, and singing their way into a new day.

". . . A group of women living right," one of them chants.

"A GROUP OF WOMEN LIVING RIGHT," the rest respond. "That's the way we live our lives."

"THAT'S THE WAY WE LIVE OUR LIVES."

The prisoners are enrolled in an intensive treatment program for addictions. More than half of them were hooked on meth, which led to the crimes that brought them to prison.

The room is full of examples of how difficult the struggle can be. Doctors say meth is even tougher to kick than most other drugs, because it causes such profound damage to the brain. Treatment methods are improving, and new research increases hope that the brains of nearly all addicts can heal over time. But the biggest initial hurdle is that many people trying to recover can't think straight enough to succeed without intense help.

Few of the women here know the scientific details, but they can describe the results. Many went through treatment for a few weeks on the outside, only to return to the pipe or needle. They say being clean left them miserable beyond description. The drug was the only thing that made them feel even close to normal.

Here, they spend at least nine months in the program, constantly surrounded by other women in treatment. They live together in a big, open area. They eat together, work together, take counseling together. They praise each other for becoming more confident and vocal. They criticize each other for slipping back into the anger and self-pity that helped bring them here. They share wishes for strength, which they will need when they return to Iowa neighborhoods riddled with meth.

"It's really sad that you have to come to prison to get into this kind of program," says Rikki Thornton of Des Moines, a 31-year-old serving time for drug trafficking. Thornton has completed the program and now mentors other participants. She acknowledges that few of them would have volunteered for the intensely controlled treatment, even if it had been offered to them before they were arrested.

That fact fits with the reality of the addiction. Counselors say meth users rarely come in for treatment unless they're forced to do so.

Alcoholics and people hooked on many other kinds of drugs are more likely to seek help when they see their habits threatening their marriages, jobs, or children, says John Mathias, who helps run Des Moines' Bridges of Iowa center. Meth quickly strips away such concerns.

"All you want to do is crank up and sleep, crank up and sleep, crank up and sleep," he says. "Nothing else matters."

(Continued)

(*continued*)

Iowa's jails and prisons hold plenty of people who have gone back to meth after undergoing treatment on the outside. The successes are plentiful, too, but they're nearly invisible.

A northern Iowa woman explains why. The 38-year-old mother of four knows that many residents of her hometown are trying to beat the habit, as she did. She would like to step into the spotlight as an example of a person who is making it. She wishes that meth addiction could lose some of its devastating stigma, the way related problems have.

"I know how people are when someone goes into treatment for alcoholism. Everyone thinks they're the greatest for doing it," she says. "But for meth, I don't know. . . . "

Michael Edens is an exception. He will tell you exactly how meth grabbed him, and how he's managing to stay away from it. Edens will only hint at his past during the addiction-information sessions he holds in an Ames conference room. If you're the ponytailed teenage boy, the college-age guy in the Budweiser T-shirt, the young woman with the squawking toddler son, you've probably come to his class because your probation officer told you to. You don't want to hear why the muscular young man in front of you became an addictions counselor. So this is what he'll tell you: "Don't think addicts could quit taking drugs if they simply had more willpower."

Scientists know that abuse of alcohol or other drugs damages people's brains, he says, leaving them with an overpowering urge to get more. He poses a challenge to anyone who believes addicts can simply make themselves stop: Take an entire box of Ex-Lax, he says, then tell yourself that you simply won't let the powerful laxative affect you.

"I'm here to tell you," Edens says, "once that chemical change happens in your body, you're going to need to go to the bathroom. I don't care how much willpower you've got."

Edens shows a video, "The Hijacked Brain," explaining the science of addiction. The class members learn how drugs cause brain cells to release huge amounts of dopamine, a chemical that causes pleasurable feelings. They learn how the brain adapts to the drug use by decreasing dopamine production. That leaves addicts feeling dreadful when they're sober.

After a while, they need the drugs just to feel halfway normal. The cycle continues, causing insatiable cravings for the drugs, even though they no longer deliver the euphoria that first pulled in the users.

If you ask him outside the class, Edens will talk about how he first tried meth as a thirteen-year-old in California. He didn't really want to, he says, but he had a crush on the girl who offered it to him, and he didn't want to disappoint her. He describes how the drug gave him energy, helped him finish his homework, and allowed him to open up to other people. By 15, he'd become nothing but trouble, and his family sent him to a strict school for boys. As soon as he got out, he went back to tweaking. The habit wound up costing him a marriage and custody of his son. It also led to a stint in prison. "I said, 'Wild horses couldn't drag me back to meth,'" he says.

His father, who lived in Iowa, invited him to move here to make a new start. Edens recalls being stunned at how many Iowans knew how to make meth using anhydrous ammonia, an easily stolen farm chemical. For two years, he resisted the temptation to partake. Then he drank a liter of Black Velvet whiskey at a party one night, and suddenly it didn't seem like such a bad idea to try some of the meth people were passing around.

Eight weeks later, totally hooked again, he was arrested at a farmer's co-op, trying to steal anhydrous ammonia. He was too messed up to figure out how to flee. He spent five months in jail, then went to a halfway house and started going to treatment sessions. "I was so ready to do something different," he says. "I swore I was not going to use meth again."

That was three years ago, and he's kept his promise. He's trained as a counselor and is helping others get clean. He says people can succeed, but they must pay a steep price. By the time they quit, many have nothing positive left in their lives. They're broke, unemployed, and friendless. The reality compounds the chemical depression caused by the drug's aftermath. "I learned to expect life to be crappy for the next few months."

Researchers believe that if they could reduce the number of months recovering meth addicts feel crappy, they could greatly increase the chances of success. Des Moines is one of five sites nationally for a study on whether medications could help the brain heal faster and ease the cravings and depression that drive people back to drug use. Dr. Richard Rawson, a California psychologist overseeing the study, is optimistic. Doctors had feared that meth caused permanent devastation inside brain cells, he says. But recent studies on monkeys show that many of the cells repair themselves eventually. Relatively little research has been done on possible medications, because drug manufacturers don't foresee potential profits from helping meth addicts.

"There is not going to be a Xanax or a Prozac or a Viagra for drug abuse," Rawson says. But he predicts at least some benefit from the medications his program is testing—including some already used by people trying to quit smoking cigarettes. A small percentage of meth users suffer permanent psychosis, similar to schizophrenia patients. Years after they stop using the drug, they still hear voices in their heads, and they're paralyzed by feelings of paranoia.

"It's clear that they've done something to their brains that's not going to get better. Those are the most heart-wrenching cases," says Rawson, who works at the University of California-Los Angeles.

Most addicts can recover, however. One key is that they stay away from all addictive drugs—including alcohol. Even for patients who never had serious drinking problems, the odds of relapsing into meth use quintuple if they resume any alcohol use, Rawson says. "That's one of the few things we can tell you for sure."

Another key is to find a treatment program specializing in meth addicts. Older programs designed mainly for alcoholics aren't nearly as effective, he says. Most programs keep patients overnight for the first few days, then help them rebuild their lives in the community. To be effective, treatment must be done several times a week for many months, he says. "You need to be taught how not to use methamphetamine today. Then you need to be taught how not to use it tomorrow."

Dr. Dennis Weis, who runs one of Des Moines' largest treatment programs, says people trying to kick meth have to overcome daunting hurdles. "Rehabilitation" often is an irrelevant concept. The word implies that patients used to have decent lives, which they hope to resume.

Many patients at the Powell Chemical Dependency Center grew up around meth-using parents or even grandparents. They've never known anything else. They've never succeeded at school, worked steady jobs, or maintained healthy friendships.

Weis oversees the Des Moines portion of Rawson's medication study. He is optimistic about the prospects of new medications, and he sees benefits from using current antidepressant drugs with some patients. Those medicines are no cure-all, he says, and they shouldn't be taken until a person is totally off meth. "Taking antidepressants while you're on meth is like building a sand castle with a teaspoon while the waves keep crashing in."

Counselors also must deal with an unusual twist to the addiction: Many patients have become obsessed with making and selling the drug. It fits well with the compulsive behavior meth induces, and it's often one of the only things they've ever succeeded in. The production also gives them a sense of power over other addicts. The temptations will be pervasive throughout their lives. Every time they walk through a store and see batteries, cold medicine, or drain cleaner, they'll be reminded of how easy it was to make money, impress others, and get high.

Even with those complications, Weis and his colleagues stress that success is increasingly possible. Early in the meth epidemic, success rates commonly were reported at 15 percent. Nowadays, carefully tailored programs are seeing 40 percent of their patients stay sober for at least a year, Weis says. Those numbers should continue to climb, and many people who fail at first go on to find success after a second or third try. Society doesn't give up on people who struggle to recover from cancer, heart attacks, or diabetes, counselors say, and it shouldn't give up on people who relapse into addiction. The road to sobriety will always be hard, but never impossible, Weis says. "You don't just walk into treatment and suddenly you're drug-free for life."

Critical Thinking Questions: Consider the statement in this reading that recovery is not about willpower in light of the women meth addicts in prison. How can treatment take into account brain studies on addiction?

Source: Des Moines Register (November 26, 2003). Reprinted with permission of the Des Moines Register.

Many prisons (and some jails) subcontract out with substance abuse treatment centers for the provision of counseling services. This approach provides the counseling staff with more professional freedom than would otherwise be the case if their first loyalty were to the correctional authorities. In addition, confidentiality is better maintained by having practitioners answer to their own agencies, not to the correctional system. In any case, inmates—so in need of a friendly professional to talk to, and usually with time on their hands—often are highly motivated for treatment, and they welcome the individual attention to their needs. Mullings and colleagues (2003) agree. Additionally, they make the point that women with a history of abuse who know little else may require prison-based interventions to reduce their HIV risk and other risk-taking behaviors. And they require post-prison supervision as well until they map out the kind of life they want to, need to, live. In fact, extensive services are needed to help a woman during the tough transitional period to the community as she begins to seek work and housing and to regain custody of her children.

The challenge of delivering treatment in a correctional setting requires the cooperation of disparate cultures: the justice system designed to punish and the professional treatment team trained to treat (Chandler, Fletcher, and Volkow, 2009). One system is geared to protect society, beyond all else; the other system to protect the client. Everywhere the bureaucracy interferes with creative treatment initiatives. Then there is potential conflict as well between mental health treatment and substance abuse treatment staff. Within prisons, substance abuse and psychiatric services tend, as on the outside, to be separate (Kubiak and Rose, 2007). And yet, integrated psychological services are required to address the combination of mental health disorders that co-occur with addictive behavior and cravings for mood altering substances (van Wormer and Davis, 2008).

Substance abuse counselors often fear that addressing past trauma, as mental health professionals regularly do, will open a Pandora's box, contributing to increased psychological symptoms. To test this assumption, Killeen et al. (2009) conducted a large-scale clinical trial that provided trauma therapy with substance abuse treatment for one group and found there were no adverse consequences from this approach. This is an important finding because inattention to co-existing disorders such as PTSD may negate the success of substance abuse treatment. Women need help to heal from their wounds to enhance their overall life adjustment.

Addiction, according to Covington and Bloom (2006), comprises a piece of a larger mosaic that includes a woman's individual background and the social, economic, psychological, and cultural forces that shape the context of her substance use. Treatment, to be effective, needs to address these various aspects of a woman addict or alcoholic's life.

A 172-page report from the U.S. Department of Health and Human Services written by Kassebaum (1999) documents the results of several demonstration programs funded by the Center for Substance Abuse Treatment to address the complex needs of drug-dependent female offenders. These model programs provide intensive all-female in-house therapy geared toward meeting women's special needs with regard to their backgrounds of childhood and partner victimization, low self-esteem and shame, and parenting skills. Examples of exemplary programs described in this research document are: the Forever Free Program at the women's prison at Frontera, California; the six-month pre-release Focus Program at Salem, Oregon; and the Stepping Out in-custody treatment project, with a strong after-care component, at San Diego, California. To this end, the programs modified the male-model, confrontational therapeutic community into a nurturing, family-like setting, and adapted the traditional twelve-step model to suit the needs of women who already felt powerless over most aspects of their lives. In one program, official ceremonies to honor women clients are affirming events to celebrate graduation and follow-up achievements, which serve to bring the community together as a bonding experience.

Preliminary evaluation studies of client retention and abstinence following treatment, as summarized in the Kassebaum report, revealed that women did well only if released from custodial facilities to residential centers for a transitional period, preferably for over five months. Themes common to successful programs are: the provision of a holistic continuum of care built on extensive networking referring women for job placement and sober-living houses (e.g., San Diego County); the avoidance of a move from a woman-specific center (women in Delaware showed that they were not ready for this abrupt transition); continuity in treatment approach so that clients don't get conflicting messages; residential care for pregnant and parenting women and their children; and the presence of a care manager to continue monitoring the women to help keep them from drifting into old patterns.

What we can learn from the compilation of research offered in the Kassebaum document is the key role of a case management system in providing adequate supervision of women who have graduated from treatment to assist them with referrals and track their progress. Case managers need to be able to serve as a linkage among criminal justice, child welfare, and substance abuse agencies. The cost savings to their communities of innovative treatment programs include prevention of the spread of HIV/AIDS and fetal alcohol syndrome, tremendous savings in welfare and foster care costs, and a significant reduction in crime rates.

Consistent with these guidelines for offender treatment, Stephanie Covington (2008) has produced a broad-based treatment curriculum, *A Woman's Journal: Helping Women Recover*, designed for women who are recovering from substance abuse and psychological trauma. This curriculum is well suited to twelve-step work in correctional settings and yet is eclectic in design. A guiding principle of this book and of Covington and Bloom's (2006) earlier article is that substance abuse, trauma, and mental health issues must be addressed through integrated and culturally relevant services. These three therapeutically interrelated issues are constants in the lives of female offenders. Trauma and addiction theories provide a critical element in the integration of and foundation for gender-responsive services in the criminal justice system.

The program that treated Amanda Petersen, the meth addict whose story was described earlier in the chapter, the Sisters Together Achieving Recovery program, is housed in a separate building; treatment lasts for nine months on average. Thanks to a large grant from the federal government, each counselor can spend a great deal of time with the fifteen or fewer inmates assigned to her. Fewer than 10 percent of the 220 graduates have been rearrested.

PROMISING DEVELOPMENTS

Increasingly, research is highlighting the superiority of substance abuse programs delivered in the community over those conducted in correctional institutional settings (van Wormer and Davis, 2008). A major problem with shutting women away from society for extended periods, and especially of women with a history of substance abuse, is that the shock of readjustment to society may be too much for them.

Not surprisingly, a review of the literature suggests that most of the women who are released from jail or prison are likely to return to the same difficult conditions that played into their legal problems in the first place (Richie, 2004). When unaccustomed child care responsibilities of children who have their own serious problems and resentments are thrust upon them and with few financial resources to provide proper care, the challenges can be tremendous. Relapse and recidivism risks are major public health problems that echo the original risks that were the cause of grief to the women and their families in the first place. In some instances, society is avoiding this change of events through sentencing women to community supervision under the authority of the drug court.

Drug Courts and Community Treatment

One of the most promising developments in recent years is the **drug court**, an alternative to prison that was first launched in Florida. These new courts, which divert nonviolent drug offenders from the prison system into treatment, prove that such programs are cost-effective to society and still allow people to obtain treatment and maintain their work and family roles. Today, there are just under 2,000 drug courts across the states (National Institute of Justice, 2008). For women, their effectiveness is enhanced because of the continuum of services provided and the close partnerships linking community-based organizations. Federally funded drug courts have been set up in Kentucky, Hawaii, and elsewhere especially to deal with the meth crisis. Intensive case management services are provided, mental health disorders are treated simultaneously with drug treatment, and medication is prescribed where appropriate (van Wormer and Davis, 2008). The results have been very favorable for both the offender and the community.

Because many women offenders are mothers of small children, correctional programs delivered in the community are particularly important. Community centers that house mothers together with their children are especially valuable, as they can provide counselors who model appropriate parenting skills as issues arise spontaneously in the common living situation. Knowing that jail time awaits them if they begin abusing drugs again can offer women a strong incentive to change. By the same token, without help and the educational and vocational skills necessary to survive on their own, some women seem to deliberately get themselves in trouble in order to return to the safety of the prison environment.

Empowerment and Gender-Responsive Approaches

A gendered policy approach calls for a new vision for the criminal justice system, one that recognizes the behavioral and social differences between female and male offenders that have specific implications for **gender-responsive policy** and practice (Covington and Bloom, 2006). Gender-responsive policy provides effective interventions that address the intersecting issues of substance abuse, trauma, mental health, and economic oppression, as Bloom and colleagues indicate. A focus on women's relationships with their family members is paramount as well.

In light of the stigmatizing impact of women's experiences in the criminal justice system, and the relationship between low self-esteem and chemical dependency in the first place, empowerment and consciousness-raising approaches are vital. Programs that use such approaches describe women's success as being linked to their ability to shift their point of view from self-blame to self-responsibility for one's family and neighborhood (Richie, 2004). Since much of consciousness-raising helps women develop critical insight into the structural influences on their lives, as Richie suggests, it is perhaps understandable that prison systems do not very often endorse such programs.

Mental health practitioners desiring to promote women's empowerment and healing should be wary of a widely used model throughout all levels of the correctional system that is anything but empowering. Designed for work with male psychopaths, this approach is built around correcting inmates' errors in thinking. The goal of what is appropriately termed a moral-cognitive approach is to encourage inmates' awareness of how they have hurt the people in their lives; the purpose, as originally described by its founding proponents, is to arouse feelings of guilt and self-disgust. In Yochelson and Samenow's (1976) influential work on "the criminal personality," narcissism or self-centeredness is taken as the central theme of the criminal's psychological makeup. Environmental factors and structural inequalities are considered irrelevant in the "criminal mind" formulation (Pollack, 2005).

Correctional Service of Canada does not use the psychopathology or antisocial personality diagnosis for women, seeing it as irrelevant to the lives of women (Laishes, 2002). Pollack (2004) cautions that relying on individualizing discourses from psychiatry often dilutes a more appropriate structural analysis of female inmates' problems. Women's mental health needs, she further argues, should be addressed within a wider social context. Pollack is especially critical of the borderline personality disorder diagnosis, a psychiatric diagnosis given disproportionately to women thought to be manipulative and angry. Models of this sort, argues Pollack, are congruent with notions of criminalized women and consistent with the present conservative political climate. Unfortunately, they encourage women to internalize their oppression rather than to legitimately protest the system.

We present this description of these gender-neutral (as opposed to gender-responsive) frameworks that permeate the substance abuse treatment programming for offenders because these models are incongruous with a strengths-based perspective designed to meet the female offenders' special needs. Key elements of an empowerment gender-specific counseling perspective are: a focus on dialogue and relationships; consciousness-raising to recognize one's own power to change things; motivational work to enhance motivation for change and promote a sense of responsibility; therapy to promote healing from earlier victimization; and the instilling of hope. Because empowerment methods initially were developed to address the needs and conditions of women and people of color (Gutiérrez, Parsons, and Cox, 1997), this kind of practice has always centered on the experiences of marginalized populations.

One exemplary program that deserves recognition is the new program for pregnant and parenting women offenders with substance abuse histories in California. The women are sentenced directly to the family foundations facility for one year, where they receive a range of special services to prepare for community reentry. Preliminary results have been highly favorable according to Wiewel and Mosley (2006).

Summary

In this chapter, we have examined the key role that biological and psychological aspects of addiction play in women's criminality. Emphasis was placed on the brain and the role of the neurotransmitters, serotonin, and dopamine, both in substance dependency and in one's susceptibility to the development of mental disorders. New developments in neurobiology show the extent to which the brain on drugs is an injured brain; a long period of abstinence may be required before the brain can regenerate itself and healing takes place. The length of treatment needs to parallel the length of time it takes for the "feel-good" brain chemicals to be replenished. This chapter reviewed recent literature on brain and other biologically-based research to help show gender differences in alcohol/drug users' physiological responses to the chemicals they consume.

The psychology of substance use differs by gender as well. Women in the criminal justice system come into the system in ways different from those of men. This is due, in a large part, to a background of early and late victimization as a key factor in the female pathway into drug-related crime. The pathway to crime for a girl or woman, therefore, can be seen to have biological, psychological, and social roots. Addictive or depressive tendencies, magnified by early childhood sexual or physical abuse, leading to affiliations with abusive and lawbreaking companions is the typical pattern. Serious problems related to poverty and perceived lack of opportunity set the stage for the girl's or woman's entry into homelessness, unemployment, drug use, fraud, gang life, and prostitution. Drugs are a part of a relationship network, a part of their lifestyle shared with boyfriends and others in their company. Because racism and poverty often go hand in hand, girls from poor, inner-city backgrounds are forced to deal early, and on a regular basis, with problems of abuse, drugs, childhood pregnancy, and rough treatment by the authorities. The intersection of gender, race, and class is thus highly evident in female crime, both in regard to the form that the crime takes and the punishment meted out. The configuration is changed only somewhat with the influx of meth addicts into the system and a shift in media attention from crack cocaine to meth as the most frightening drug on the market.

Within the correctional system, a "one-size-fits-all" philosophy operates to the extent that women's particular circumstances, if they exist, are rarely taken into account. There is little allowance, for example, for the kind of specialized health care needs that accrue to reproduction. Accordingly, the situation of women delivering babies while tied to the bed and in handcuffs has been the logical result. Not only are pregnant inmates mistreated under rules meant for men, but specialized laws are directed at women's reproductive rights: The prosecution of addicts who are pregnant or who have given birth to drug-affected babies is another repressive side effect of the war on drugs.

Ignored by the media is the conundrum of female crime and its relation to social and personal victimization. Virtually absent from the lurid media crime accounts is any serious attempt to connect the dots between the myriad variables involving race, poverty, mental disorders, especially PTSD and mood disorders, and the unhealthy sexual relationships often associated with the heavy drinking and/or other drug use.

Sadly, treatment opportunities often come too late to spare the drug user from family breakups. Much of the substance abuse treatment that women offenders are receiving for addiction problems is taking place through the criminal justice system, offered in highly punitive settings behind prison walls. Yet even in the disempowering environment of prison, effective counseling programs can help women learn healthier ways of coping than using drugs or getting entangled in destructive relationships. To prepare women to make a successful transition into the community and to resume their parenting duties and work roles, halfway houses with professional supervision can be an invaluable aid.

Gender-specific rather than gender-neutral is empowering because it reflects an understanding of the realities of women's lives and their unique needs. Clearly it costs far less money to treat a woman offender for addiction than to incarcerate her. The cost savings of innovative treatment programs are incalculable; they include prevention of the spread of HIV/AIDS and fetal alcohol syndrome, and reduction of crime rates and of extensive welfare and foster care costs. In short, what is good for both mothers and children is good for the society as a whole. Most women who are incarcerated will one day be returned to society. How well they are prepared—psychologically, educationally, and emotionally—for life in the community will depend on the level of investment that our society is willing to make in their care.

Key Terms

biology of addiction *93*	gender-responsive policy *118*	PTSD *101*
dopamine *99*	methamphetamine (meth) *95*	serotonin *99*
drug court *118*	neurotransmitters *98*	
fMRI *98*	pathway to crime *103*	

Critical Thinking Questions

1. How can the war on drugs be conceived as a war on minorities and women?
2. Describe the empirical findings on the drug-crime link for women.
3. Some people claim addiction is a brain disease. What is the evidence for this claim?
4. How are the media accounts of the crack cocaine crisis and the meth crisis similar?

5. Discuss the link between PTSD and a girl's pathway to crime.
6. Contrast the principles of gender-responsive treatment with gender-neutral approaches used in offender treatment.

Web Destinations

Canadian Association of Elizabeth Fry Societies: www.elizabethfry.ca

National Center for Injury Prevention and Control: www.cdc.gov/ncipc/factsheets

National Institute on Drug Abuse: www.nida.nih.gov

National Institute on Alcohol Abuse and Alcoholism: www.niaaa.nih.gov

National Institute of Mental Health: www.nimh.nih.gov

Substance Abuse and Gun Violence Resource: www.jointogether.org

Harm Reduction Coalition: www.harmreduction.org

National Center on Addiction and Substance Abuse at Columbia University: www.casacolumbia.org

Women and sentencing policy: www.sentencing project.org

References

Adams, D. (2007). *Why do they kill? Men who murder their intimate partners.* Nashville, TN: Vanderbilt University Press.

American Psychiatric Association (APA). (2000). *Diagnostic and statistical manual of mental disorders* (text revision). Washington, DC: APA.

Basham, K., and Miehls, D. (2004). *Transforming the legacy: Couple therapy with survivors of childhood trauma.* New York: Columbia University Press.

Begley, S. (2005, August 19). Science Journal: A spotless mind may ease pain, but erase identity. *Wall Street Journal.* Retrieved from www.post-gazette.com

Belknap, J. (2007). *The invisible woman: Gender, crime, and justice*, 3rd ed. Belmont, CA: Wadsworth.

Bloom, B., and Chesney-Lind, M. (2007). Women in prison: Vengeful equality. In R. Muraskin (ed.), *It's a crime: Women and justice*, 4th ed. (pp. 542–563). Upper Saddle River, NJ: Prentice Hall.

Brady, K., and Sinha, R. (2005). Co-occurring mental and substance use disorders: The effects of chronic stress. *American Journal of Psychiatry 162:* 1483–1493.

Bureau of Justice Statistics (BJS). (2004). *HIV in prisons and jails, 2002.* Washington, DC: U.S. Department of Justice.

Bureau of Justice Statistics (BJS). (2006). *Mental health problems of prison and jail inmates.* Washington, DC: U.S. Department of Justice. Retrieved June 2008 from http://www.ojp.usdoj.gov/bjs/pub/pdf/mhppji.pdf

Bureau of Justice Statistics (BJS). (2007a, January 19). *Drug use and dependence, state and local prisoners, 2004.* Washington, DC: U.S. Department of Justice. Retrieved February 2009 from http:// www.ojp.gov/bjs/pub/pdf/dudsfp04.pdf

Bureau of Justice Statistics (BJS). (2007b, December 19). *Intimate partner violence in the U.S.: Victim characteristics.* Washington, DC: U.S. Department of Justice. Retrieved February 2009 from http:// www.ojp.usdoj.gov/bjs/intimate/victims.htm#gender

Call, C., and Nelsen, J. (2007). Partner abuse and women's substance problems: From vulnerability to strength. *Affilia 22:* 334–346.

Chandler, R., Fletcher, B., and Volkow, N. (2009). Treating drug abuse and addiction in the criminal justice system; Improving public health and safety. *Journal of the American Medical Association* 301(2): 183–190

Chesney-Lind, M., and Pakso, L. (2004). *The female offender: Girls, women, and crime*, 2nd ed. Thousand Oaks, CA: Sage.

Cohen, J., Dickow, A., Horner, K., Zweben, J., Balabis, J., Vandersloot, D., et al. (2003). Abuse and violence history of men and women in treatment for methamphetamine dependence. *American Journal on Addictions* 12(5): 377–385.

Collins, R. L., and McNair, L. D. (2003). Minority women and alcohol use. National Institute on Alcohol Abuse and Alcoholism (NIAAA). Retrieved from www.niaaa.nih.gov

Cornell University Law School. (2008). Supreme Court collection. Legal Information Institute. Retrieved February 2009 from http://www.law.cornell.edu/supct/08highlts.html

Covington, S. (2008). *A woman's journal*: *Helping women recover*, revised. San Francisco, CA: Jossey-Bass.

Covington, S., and Bloom, B. (2006). Gender responsive treatment and services in correctional settings. *Women & Therapy* 29(3): 9–33.

Cowley, G. (2003, February 24). Our bodies, our fears. *Newsweek*, pp. 43–46.

Downs, W., and Rindels, B. (2004). Adulthood, anxiety, and trauma symptoms: A comparison of women with nonabusive, abusive, and absent father figures in childhood. *Violence and Victims* 19(6): 659–672.

Dutton, D. (2007). *Rethinking domestic violence.* Vancouver, Canada: University of British Columbia Press.

Engstrom, M., El-Bassel, N., Go, H., and Gilbert, L. (2008). Childhood sexual abuse and intimate partner violence among women in methadone treatment. *Journal of Family Violence* 23(7): 605–617.

Enos, S. (2001). *Mothering from the inside: Parenting in a women's prison.* Albany, NY: State University of New York Press.

Fals-Stewart, W., Leonard, K. and Birchler, G. (2005). The occurrence of male-to-female intimate partner violence on days of men's drinking: The moderating effects of antisocial personality disorder. *Journal of Consulting and Clinical Psychology* 73(2): 239–248.

Farr, K. (2000). Classification for female inmates: Moving forward. *Crime and Delinquency* 46(1): 3–17.

Federal Bureau of Investigation (FBI). (2008). *Crimes in the United States.* Arrests by sex. Retrieved February 2009 from http://www.fbi.gov/ucr/cius2007/data/table_42.html

Friedman, S., Shelton, M., Elhaj, O., Youngstrom, E., Rapport, D., Packer, K., et al. (2005). Gender differences in criminality: Bipolar disorder with co-occurring substance abuse. *The Journal of the American Academy of Psychiatry and the Law 33*: 188–195.

Ginsberg, L., Nackerud, L., and Larrison, C. (2004). *Human biology for social workers: Development, ecology, genetics, and health.* Boston, MA: Allyn & Bacon.

Goldstein, P. (1985). The drugs/violence nexus: A tripartite conceptual framework. *Journal of Drug Issues 39*: 143–174.

Gutiérrez, L., Parsons, R., and Cox, E. (1997). *Empowerment in social work practice: A sourcebook.* Belmont, CA: Brooks/Cole.

Harris, P. (2005, August 14). Tragedy of US drugs craze orphans. *The Guardian Unlimited.* Retrieved from http://observer.guardian.co.uk

Heim, C., Newport, D., Heit, S., Graham, Y., Wilcox, M., Bonsall, R., et al. (2000). Pituitary-adrenal and autonomic responses to stress in women after sexual and physical abuse in childhood. *Journal of the American Medical Association 284*(5): 592–597.

Human Rights Watch. (2003). *Ill-equipped: U.S. prisons and offenders with mental illness.* New York: Human Rights Watch.

Jackson, K. (2003, June). Trauma and the national psyche. *Social Work Today:* 20–23.

Johnson, H. (2004). *Drugs and crime: A study of incarcerated female offenders.* Research and Public Policy Series, Australian government. Canberra, Australia: Australian Institute of Criminology.

Karberg, J., and James, D. (2005). *Substance dependence, abuse, and treatment of jail inmates, 2002.* Bureau of Justice Statistics. Washington, DC: U.S. Department of Justice.

Kassebaum, P. A. (1999). *Substance abuse treatment for women offenders: Guide to promising practices.* Rockville, MD: U.S. Department of Health and Human Services.

Killeen, T., Hien, D., Campbell, A., Brown, C., Hansen, C., Jiang, H., et al. (2009). Adverse events in an integrated trauma-focused intervention for women in community substance abuse treatment. *Journal of Substance Abuse Treatment 35*(3): 304–311.

Knickerbocker, B. (2005, July 15). Meth's rising US impact. *Christian Science Monitor.* Retrieved from www.csmonitor.com

Kubiak, S. (2004). The effects of PTSD on treatment adherence, drug relapse, and criminal recidivism in a sample of incarcerated men and women. *Research on Social Work Practice 14*(6): 434–433.

Kubiak, S., and Rose, I. (2007). Trauma and posttraumatic stress disorder in inmates with histories of substance use. In D. W. Springer and A. R. Roberts (eds.), *Handbook of forensic mental health with victims and offenders* (pp. 445–466). New York: Springer Publishing.

Laishes, J. (2002). *The 2002 mental health strategy for women offenders.* Ottawa, Canada: Correctional Service of Canada.

Lanier, M., and Zaitzow, B. (2007). Living and dying with HIV/AIDS. In R. Muraskin (ed.), *It's a crime: Women and justice* (pp. 363–391). Upper Saddle River, NJ: Prentice Hall.

Lapham, S. (2004/2005). Screening and brief intervention in the criminal justice system. *Alcohol Research and Health 28*(2). Retrieved from www.niaaa.nih.gov

Lewis, D. (2005, July 27). Top medical doctors, scientists and specialists urge major media outlets not to create "meth baby" myth. Public letter reprinted by National Advocates for Pregnant Women. Retrieved from www.advocatesforpregnantwomen.org

Leys, T. (2005, January 30). Dad's drug runner. *Des Moines Register*, pp. 1a, 6a.

MacCoun, R., Kilmer, B., and Reuter, P. (2003). *Research on drugs-crime linkages: The next generation.* Washington, DC: U.S. Department of Justice. Retrieved from www.ojp.usdoj.gov

Mathias, R. (2001, October). Pathological obesity and drug addiction share common brain characteristics. *NIDA Notes 16*(4). Retrieved from www.drugabuse.gov/NIDA_Notes

Mullings, J., Marquart, J. W., and Hartley, D. J. (2003). Exploring the effects of childhood sexual abuse and its impact on HIV/AIDS risk-taking behavior among women prisoners. *The Prison Journal 83*(4): 442–463.

Mullings, J., Pollock, J., and Crouch, B. (2002). Drugs and criminality: Results from the Texas women inmate study. *Women & Criminal Justice 13*(4): 69–96.

National Center on Addiction and Substance Abuse (CASA) at Columbia University (2006). *Women under the Influence.* Baltimore, MD: Johns Hopkins University Press.

National Institute of Justice. (2008, December). Drug courts. Washington, DC: U.S. Department of Justice. Retrieved February 2009 from http://www.ojp.usdoj.gov/nij/topics/courts/drug-courts/welcome.htm

National Institute on Alcohol Abuse and Alcoholism (NIAAA). (2004, July). Alcohol—An important women's health issue. *Alcohol Alert, no. 62.* Retrieved February 2009 from http://pubs.niaaa.nih.gov/publications/aa62/aa62.htm

National Institute on Drug Abuse (NIDA). (2008, June). *InfoFacts: Methamphetamine.* Washington, DC: NIDA. Retrieved Februay 2009 from http://www.drugabuse.gov/pdf/infofacts/Methamphetamine08.pdf

National Public Radio (NPR). (2008, May 2). Peering into the human brain with fMRI techniques. Talk of the Nation.

Nossiter, A. (2008, March 15). In Alabama, a crackdown on pregnant drug users. New York Times. Retrieved February 2009 from http://www.nytimes.com/2008/03/15/us/15mothers.html?_r=1&hp

Office of Justice Programs. (2005). *Sourcebook of Criminal Justice Statistics.* Washington, DC: U.S. Department of Justice, Bureau of Justice Statistics.

Paltrow, L. M. (2004, April 5). The pregnancy police. *AlterNet.* Retrieved from www.alternet.org

Paltrow, L. M. (2008, October 23). Can there be justice for pregnant women if the unborn have "human rights?" Reproductive Health Reality Check. Retrieved February 2009 from http://www.rhrealitycheck.org/blog/2008/10/22/can-there-be-justice-pregnant-women-if-unborn-have-human-rights

Pawloski, J. (2009, January 18). The fight against Oxycontin. *The Olympian* (Washington State). Retrieved February 2009 from http://www.thenewstribune.com/front/topstories/story/599029.html

"Petition Asks U.N. Racism Conference to Take Up U.S. War on Drugs" (2001, August 22). Retrieved from www.drugwarinjustice.org

Pollack, S. (2004). Anti-oppressive social work practice with women in prison: Discursive reconstructions and alternative practices. *British Journal of Social Work 34*: 693–707.

Pollack, S. (2005). Taming the shrew: Regulating prisoners through women-centered mental health programming. *Critical Criminology 13*: 71–87.

Richie, B. E. (2004). Challenges incarcerated women face as they return to their communities. In M. Chesney-Lind and L. Pakso (eds.), *Girls, women, and crime: Selected readings* (pp. 231–245). Thousand Oaks, CA: Sage.

Sagatun-Edwards, I. (2007). Legal and social welfare response to substance abuse during pregnancy. In R. Muraskin (ed.), *It's a crime: Women and justice,*

4th ed. (pp. 346–362). Upper Saddle River, NJ: Prentice Hall.

Sherman, C. (2007). Impact of drugs on neurotransmission. National Institute of Drug Abuse (NIDA). *NIDA Notes 21*(4): 1–4.

Substance Abuse and Mental Health Services Administration (SAMHSA). (1997) Substance use among women in the United States. The Center for Substance Abuse Treatment. Retrieved from www.samhsa.gov/csat

Substance Abuse and Mental Health Services Administration (SAMHSA). (2003). *Violence, suicide and risky behavior.* Office of Applied Studies. The Center for Substance Abuse Treatment. Retrieved from www.samhsa.gov/csat

Substance Abuse and Mental Health Services Administration (SAMHSA). (2005). *Substance abuse treatment for persons with co-occurring disorders: A treatment improvement protocol* (TIP) 42. The Center for Substance Abuse Treatment. Retrieved from www.samhsa.gov/csat

Sentencing Project (2007, May). *Women in the criminal justice system.* Washington, DC. Retrieved February 2009 from http://www.sentencingproject.org/Admin/Documents/publications/womenincj_total.pdf

Serran, G., and Firestone, P. (2004). Intimate partner homicide: A review of the male proprietaryness and the self-defense theories. *Aggression and Violent Behavior 9*: 1–15.

Spear, L. (2000). Modeling adolescent development and alcohol use in animals. *Alcohol Research & Health 24*(2): 115–123.

Springer, D. W., McNeece, C. A., and Arnold, E. M. (2003). *Substance abuse treatment for criminal offenders: An evil-based guide for practitioners.* Washington, DC: American Psychological Association.

Strauss, S., and Falkin, G. P. (2001). Women offenders who use and deal methamphetamine: Implications for mandated drug treatment. *Women and Criminal Justice 12*: 77–97.

Stuart, G. L. (2005). Improving violence intervention outcomes by integrating alcohol treatment. *Journal of Interpersonal Violence 20*: 388–393.

Taxman, F. (2008, April 28). *Findings from a national survey of correctional agencies on substance abuse treatment and health services.* Washington, DC: National Institute on Drug Abuse. Retrieved July 2009 from http://www.drugabuse.gov/whatsnew/meetings/translatinginsights/drugabuse_treatment.html

Taylor, B., Newton, P., and Brownstein, H. (2003). Drug use among adult female arrestees. *ADAM (Arrestee Drug Abuse Monitoring) 2000 Annual Report.* Washington, DC: U.S. Department of Justice.

Thompson, M. P., and Kingree, J. B. (2006). The roles of victim and perpetrator alcohol use in intimate partner violence outcomes. *Journal of Interpersonal Violence 21*(2):163–178.

USA Today (2002, June 10). Meth use among women tough to detect. *USA Today.* Retrieved from www.usatoday.com

van Wormer, K., and Davis, D. R. (2008). *Addiction treatment: A strengths perspective*, 2nd ed. Belmont, CA: Cengage.

Wallace, B. (2005). *Making mandated addiction treatment work.* Lanham, MD: Rowan & Littlefield Publishers.

Whitten, L. (2004). Men and women process cocaine cues differently. National Institute on Drug Abuse (NIDA). *NIDA Notes 19*(4). Retrieved February 2009 from www.nida.nih.gov

Wiewel, B., and Mosley, T. (2006). Family foundations: A new program for pregnant and parenting women offenders with substance abuse histories. *Journal of Offender Rehabilitation 43*(1): 65–82.

Yehia, D. (2003, July). Sentencing aboriginal offenders. Law Link. Retrieved May 2007 from www.lawlink.nsw. gov.au

Yochelson, S., and Samenow, S. (1976). *The criminal personality,* Vol. 1. New York: Jason Aronson.

Zernike, K. (2005, July 6). Officials across U.S. describe drug woes. *The New York Times.* Retrieved May 2007 from www.nytimes.com

Zickler, P. (2004). Long-term abstinence brings partial recovery from methamphetamine damage. *NIDA Notes 19*(4): 1.

6

The Prison Environment

In the United States, the thrust toward prison reform and rehabilitation has been in decline for so many years, it has come to be accepted as the American way. For over two decades, politicians have typically run "law and order" and "zero tolerance" campaigns. The public mood, fired up by mass media rabid for stories, cried out for vengeance against people perceived as a threat—specifically, inner-city males engaging in street crime and illegal drug users. The war against single mothers on welfare in the "free world" is matched by an increasing severity in the treatment of women within prison walls. Today, paradoxically, during a time when concerns about crime are low, women of color are bearing the brunt of the "lock 'em up and throw away the key" mentality. This pattern is echoed in Birmingham, England, as well as Birmingham, Alabama; a harshness against women offenders is seen in Tokyo, Japan, as well. Throughout the world, the antifeminist backlash is palpable: If women want to be equal to men, or so the thinking goes, they can be punished like men—put on chain gangs, in boot camps, and even executed. And, at the employee level, if female guards can be assigned to a full range of duties in men's prisons (because of affirmative-action mandates), then male guards can operate unrestricted in women's prisons as well.

And yet attitudes about some of the toughest anticrime legislation from the 1980s may be changing. In a recent poll, some 60 percent of respondents opposed mandatory minimum sentencing for nonviolent crimes (Paulson, 2008). The criminal laws have not caught up with the public sentiment, however, so there is a cultural lag of sorts between practice and attitudes.

This chapter looks at the end result of the harsh sentencing of the last two decades, the end result as seen in the nation's correctional institutions. The major purpose of this chapter is to present the reality and context of life for women in confinement so that budding correctional counselors, social workers and other treatment providers will be prepared, intellectually, at least, for the major challenges awaiting them in this line of work.

We begin our exploration of the topic of women in prison with a brief history of the imprisonment of women and of theoretical frameworks concerning their criminality. We then construct a profile of the typical female inmate based on statistics involving race, ethnicity, drug involvement, and other demographic criteria available from government sources. Turning our attention to the *internal* dynamics of prison society, we ponder the way in which women of various ages and ethnicities construct a social world that is unique in itself. A related discussion on prison "play" families and sexual role-playing follows. One grim topic—women on death row—and one positive topic—innovative treatment programs—conclude this chapter.

The theme that binds these seemingly disparate topics is that of empowering feminism. *Empowering feminism* is the term we use for a perspective that engenders pride in women through recognition of their unique needs, gifts, and vulnerabilities. Another major theme is the war on drugs, which has become a war against African American and Latina women. A third major theme, equally disturbing, is the susceptibility of women behind bars to sexual abuse and harassment by male guards.

HISTORY OF THE WOMEN'S PRISON

To the extent that prisons do indeed represent a social barometer of a nation's health and level of civilization, as Dostoevsky (1864) believed they did, the punishment of female offenders can be viewed as a mirror for the treatment of women in a society. If we view female offenders' treatment historically, as well as culturally, we will realize the connection between the punishment of women who deviated from the norms of society and the patriarchal social structure of the day. In a book written in her prison cell, Jean Harris (1988) (famous for the murder of her unfaithful lover, Dr. Herman Tarnower) summarized the history of women's prison succinctly: "From a woman depraved, to a woman wronged, to a woman who now says she wants to be treated equally with men, we've spanned two hundred years, and we're more ambivalent today than we ever were" (p. 40).

In the early days of prison history, women—like men—suffered in filth, overcrowding, and harsh conditions. They were confined in separate quarters in men's prisons (Rathbone, 2005). In the 1920s, at Auburn Penitentiary in New York, women were lodged together; they were subject to beating and sexual abuse by the male guards. African American and poor women were, as always, disproportionately incarcerated in all parts of the United States. Following the passage of strict Jim Crow laws in the Southern states, which were designed to keep blacks "in their place," Southern prison populations became almost all black overnight.

Despite retrogressive laws and harsh punishments affecting women as well as men, the roots of feminism lie deep within the prison reform movement. Even before the end of slavery, Quaker abolitionists and suffragists were at the forefront of this movement. Elizabeth Fry of England helped organize the women confined at London's Newgate Gaol in the early 1800s (Craig, 2009). Her brave and innovative work at Newgate with incarcerated women and their children was testimony to the fact that, with decent treatment, women convicts were redeemable, that a single light could dispel the darkness. She challenged the rampant sexual abuse of institutionalized women, advocated as one of her key principles that women should be under the authority of women and in their own institution, and sought to substitute the Quakers' system of absolute silence with one in which inmates could communicate with each other and help each other reform. Working indefatigably until her death in 1845 to transform the lives of inmate women, Fry managed to instill hope and dignity where there was only despair (American Friends Service Committee, 1971). Today, in Canada, the Elizabeth Fry associations play an active role in exposing abuses in prisons for women.

On becoming matron of the woman's prison at Sing Sing in 1844, Eliza Farnham stirred up controversy with the new techniques that she implemented and with her articulate defense of them. Farnham strove in many ways to brighten the tone of inmate life during the period of her tenure (Craig, 2009). But the charge of pampering criminals had already become an easy one to level, and Farnham was finally forced to resign in 1848 (Rathbone, 2005). Across the state, women were sent back to the unsupervised section of men's prisons.

The first separate prison for women, the Indiana Women's Prison was founded by a Quaker couple and opened in 1873. Massachusetts followed four years later with the building of an all-female state reformatory. Another American Quaker cited by Jean Harris (1988) helped found the progressive women's reformatory at Bedford Hills. Gradually, other states followed, until unisexual institutions for men and women became the basic, though not exclusive, pattern. Fry's program, which consisted of women helping women and emphasized rehabilitation, obedience, and religious education, became instituted throughout North America. In the ensuing "matriarchy in corrections," the staffs, architectural designs, and programs reflected the culturally valued norms for women's behavior (Feinman, 1994, p. 44). At the administrative level, the women's prison was to remain, for a considerable time, a domain of female guidance for control and leadership.

Many significant aspects of contemporary corrections were, in fact, pioneered by female administrators in charge of institutions for female offenders. Correctional innovations such as educational instruction, work release programs, and vocational activities were initiated in an atmosphere that was female. Women's prisons, as Walker (1980) notes, became a testing ground for the new penology: prison reformers regarded women as good candidates for rehabilitation, probably because they were considered less dangerous than their male counterparts.

To speak only of the reformatory tradition in women's prisons and to neglect the existence of harsh, disciplinary institutions, such as the State Prison for Women at Auburn, New York, is to overlook the origins of what is the women's prison as we know it today, a wall built around society's problems. In 1844, New York prison authorities voiced little concern for their charges:

> The opinion seems to have been entertained, that the female convicts were beyond
> the reach of reformation, and it seems to have been regarded as a sufficient perform-
> ance of the object of punishment, to turn them loose within the pen of the prison and
> there leave them to feed upon and destroy each other. (Lewis, 1965, p. 159)

And then there was the racial factor. Chivalry for white women figured into the picture in the form of "cottage-style" reformatories, establishments that proliferated in the Northeast and Midwest during the Progressive Era as an alternative to the harsh custodial institutions. Whereas the custodial (mainly African American) prisons were characterized by filth and violence inflicted by male guards, "reformatories" were usually staffed by women and stressed correcting women's moral behavior. There were no comparable reformatories for men. Women were sentenced to these prisons for various sexual offenses, drunkenness, unwed pregnancies, and unlawful sexual intercourse (Craig, 2009). By the 1930s, the Framingham, Massachusetts, prison was regarded as one of the most progressive in the United States. Without fences and with education and reform at a premium, Framingham was a show place for gender-specific policies.

The prison's farm provided produce for the entire state correctional system. Rathbone contrasts this history with Framingham today—"an arid, isolated place" (p. 21) that is modeled on high security prisons for men. The nursery has been closed; the farm no longer exists.

By 1935, the Progressive Era was over, and the reformatories and custodial prisons were merged. The legacy of the "cottage system" still prevails at the women's federal prison at Alderson, West Virginia, and in many state prisons, such as Bedford Hills in New York State.

The 1960s and 1970s, that period of civil rights awareness and protest by various oppressed groups in the society—minorities, women, gays, and lesbians—was also a time of much feminist reformist zeal concerning women in prison. Although compassion was expressed for women who had killed their husbands in self-defense and were charged with murder, there was also a huge outcry over political prisoners, such as Angela Davis and Joan Little. Davis was charged with abetting a violent prisoner escape, and Little was tried for killing her jailer in the act of rape. Within prison walls, similarly, this period marked the beginning of much prisoner-generated litigation (mostly initiated from men's prisons), protesting inhumane conditions and the violation of human rights.

The period of retrenchment of social services and the **war on drugs**, which got under way in the 1980s and continues at the turn of the century, parallels a mass media campaign dramatizing crimes of violence. As noted in Chapter 5, women of color have been the most adversely affected by the new mandatory drug-sentencing laws, namely, the harsh sentencing for crack cocaine, the drug associated with inner-city drug abuse and violence. In Canada, native women (3 percent of the population) are disproportionately locked up (29 percent of federally sentenced women are aboriginal) (Canadian Human Rights Commission, 2004), as are minorities of African and Latin American origin. A further factor affecting all prisoners, as Chesney-Lind and Pasko (2004) indicate, is the vested interest of major corporations, the **prison industrial complex**, which has become a component of many local communities that depend on the building and maintenance of prisons for economic stability. The new surge in prison privatization has made the operation of prisons, as well as their construction, a typical capitalist venture. It is difficult, therefore, to alter priorities, such as, for example, to put money into substance abuse treatment and subsidized housing to prevent crime, when the dividends of crimes are so profitable to outside interest groups.

According to the 2000 Census of State and Federal Correctional Facilities, a total of 120 privately operated facilities are authorized to house women. Thirty-seven of these facilities are exclusively female. Entries on the 2000 Census range from the Des Moines Women's Residential Center, which has an excellent reputation in Iowa for gender-specific programming, to the notorious correctional center at Florence, Arizona. Operated by the privately owned Corrections Corporation of America, this facility has been the subject of several successful lawsuits on behalf of the sexually violated women.

The prison privatization movement has enormous implications for female offenders, first with regard to the increase in the number of women being incarcerated, and second, in light of the recent history in private prisons of sexual abuse by male guards. When commercial enterprises take over the hiring and supervision of correctional staff, standards are inevitably lowered. At the same time, as the state relinquishes responsibility for the running of the prisons, public accountability for the abuses inflicted on female inmates has been even further reduced.

In summary, if women at times have been given special consideration throughout correctional history by virtue of their gender, they also have been treated badly. They have been simultaneously protected and punished. A temporal perspective emphasizes that women in society at large, like women in criminal justice, have been thought of in terms of the Madonna/whore duality so aptly spelled out by Feinman (1994).

The **Madonna image** personified women who were faithful and submissive as good women and who, therefore, might be dealt with leniently by the courts. The whore image portrayed women as seductive temptresses of men (Morash and Schram, 2002). Women of color have not historically been placed in these dichotomous categories but rather treated as tough and likely to break the law. (The term "lady" in the old South tellingly was reserved for white women of a certain class.)

The women-centeredness of the early women's prisons no longer exists under the influence of the twin forces of women's equality and the new punitiveness in North American society. In the nation's imagination, a criminal is a criminal, but the strict mandatory penalties are usually set with a hardened male street criminal in mind. Whereas women in prison are significantly less violent than men in prison, women's prisons are constructed on a correctional model based on assumptions about violent men (Muraskin, 2007). Male gangs thrive in prison; women create small families. Men are territorial and fight to maintain positions of power. Women fight because of jealousy, but more often they take out their hostility on themselves through self-mutilation. Men tend to congregate by race; women create their "families" across racial lines. Women relate to each other, too, across security-level lines, whereas men's prisons are divided by classification of dangerousness of crime and criminality. The women are all incarcerated in one location and, for the most part, mix freely.

THE POPULATION PROFILE

A key background characteristic of women is their history of lifetime victimization. National surveys of women in different correctional settings find that more than one-half of incarcerated women report childhood abuse or intimate partner physical abuse, and more than one-third report past sexual assault (Whaley et al., 2007). Although most victims of childhood abuse do not become offenders, a link between victimization and offending is apparent in the lives of many who do get involved in crime. This may occur through illicit drug use to self-medicate and directly from unhealthy relationships with abusive men who are also criminally involved. In interviews with a sample of women on probation and parole, Whaley et al. found complex but consistent connections between histories of partner victimization and childhood abuse, substance abuse, and adult offending.

To provide a detailed account of the types of sexual abuse that such women have endured, McDaniels-Wilson and Belknap (2008) conducted a survey of 391 incarcerated women at all three Ohio prisons for women. One striking aspect of the findings was the fact that 11.5 percent of the women reported having been gang raped. More than half of the women reported they had been raped; others who did not claim they had been raped reported forced oral and/or anal penetration, which they did not recognize as rape. Sum total, 70 percent of the respondents reported at least one violation that legally would have been rape. Perpetrators ranged from strangers to family members. Many reported multiple instances of sexual abuse. This study, according to the researchers, provides some support for the pathways theory of female crime and for the need to provide counseling to children who experience sexual victimization to help prevent them from pursuing a self-destructive life course. These research findings also lend support to proponents of gender-informed treatment of female offenders, so many of whom have histories of significant victimization.

Influx of Women into Prison

State and county departments of corrections are no longer focused on rehabilitation but are forced to warehouse people and to worry over finding the next cell. Jail and prison construction has become the major expense in counties across the United States. Ironically, the prison-building boom is occurring at the same time that the crime rate is steadily decreasing, especially the rates of the crimes of violence so often sensationalized in the news. The more prisons that are built, inevitably the more people will be sentenced to fill them. "Build them and they will convict" is the common refrain. States that once managed with one or no prisons for women now are building several. Bloom, Owen, and Covington (2004) provide documentation to show that in the 1970s, nearly two-thirds of the women convicted of federal felonies were granted probation, but twenty years later only 28 percent were given straight probation.

For years, women have been only a tiny fraction of the total prison population. Part of the reason, of course, is women's relatively low crime rate compared to that of men. Historically, women were much less likely to be imprisoned unless the female offender did not fit the stereo-typical female role. Such differential treatment of women, sometimes referred to as chivalry, seems to have become a thing of the past, as Chesney-Lind and Pasko (2004) observe.

While women's crime rate for serious crimes continues to be low, the rapid growth in the incarceration of women continues unabated. The profiles of women in prison, in contradiction to the myth of the new, violent female offender, confirm the detrimental impact of mandatory sentencing guidelines rather than any change in female behavior (Laughlin et al., 2008).

Whereas women were only 4 percent of the U.S. incarcerated population in 1980, by 2007, women comprised 7.2 percent of the prison total (BJS, 2008d). The growth rate from 2000 to 2006 was 3.2 percent for females and 2 percent for males (BJS, 2008c), but the following year the growth rate was only 2.5 percent and 1.5 percent, respectively. In Australia, the female percentage of the prison population has expanded, similarly, from 3.9 percent in 1984 to 7 percent in 2004 (Australia Bureau of Statistics, 2006). With a prison population rate of 148 per 100,000, England and Wales lock up more prisoners per capita than any other country in Western Europe, apart from Luxembourg, and far in excess of countries such as France, Germany, Italy, Belgium, and Ireland. The prison total (in England and Wales) has increased by 18 percent in the last five years (King's College London, 2007). The largest increases in Europe in the last five years (other than in small countries such as Cyprus and Luxembourg) are in the Netherlands (up 40 percent) and in Spain (up 36 percent). Notable increases elsewhere over the same period include Indonesia, where the increase has been 87 percent, Brazil (55 percent), Japan and Mexico (both 30 percent), according to the report from King's College London. According to World Health Organization (2009), although women constitute only between 4% and 5% of prisoners in Europe, the number of women in prison is increasing rapidly. The majority of offences for which women are imprisoned are nonviolent, property, or drug related. These trends are universal.

Prisoner and jail inmate profiles can be best revealed through statistics from the U.S. Bureau of Justice Statistics (BJS) (2000) and (2008) and the American Civil Liberties Union (ACLU) (2005). From these respected sources, we learn that:

- White women were one-third as likely as black women to be incarcerated and slightly more than half as likely as Hispanic women to be incarcerated in 2007 (BJS, 2008d). This actually represents a decline in the numbers of black women incarcerated and a significant increase in the numbers of white women sentenced to prison.
- Approximately 65 percent of women in state prisons have young children; about two-thirds of the women lived with their children before entering prison (BJS, 2000).

- Nearly 60 percent of the women reported they had ever been physically or sexually abused (BJS, 2000).
- About six in ten women in state prison were using drugs in the month before their offense (BJS, 2000).
- In most cases, when a woman is imprisoned, her child is displaced; when the father is incarcerated, the child is more likely to live with the mother and not be displaced (ACLU, 2005).

These statistics provide documentation of the racism, sexism, and classism that exist in contemporary society. At every level of the social system, the effects of racism and classism leave their imprint indelibly on the later stages. Today, as Chesney-Lind and Pasko (2004) suggest, street crime has become a code word for race.

Drugs, Race, and Ethnicity

Part of the reason for the racial lopsidedness, as we have seen in Chapter 2, is the harsh mandatory sentencing that punishes users and dealers of crack cocaine, a drug associated in the public mind with inner-city crime. The past mandated minimum sentencing for involvement with this drug has filled up jail and prison cells with African American and Latina women. Then the singling out of the one drug used most frequently in the inner city for harsh penalties creates a situation with desperate consequences for black and Latino women. Women of color singularly bear the brunt of the new mandatory drug-sentencing laws. Sexism, as we have also seen, is played out in the harsh sentencing of women for conspiracy to deal in drug sales without taking into account the context of actions. Sexism is also apparent in the removal of female inmates to prisons far from their homes and their children. Classism is evidenced in the poor educational backgrounds and high poverty rates of these women as well as in harsh sentencing for drug-related crimes involving drugs that are cheap and more likely used by poor people—for example, crack cocaine and methamphetamines (known as "poor man's cocaine").

Approximately 60 percent of women in U.S. state prisons and almost two-thirds of women in Canadian prisons have a serious problem with drugs or alcohol, and substance abuse is associated with their crime in some way. Related problems are eating disorders, other mental health problems such as depression and high anxiety, and self-mutilation. The profile of Canadian women in prison is more or less comparable to that of their contemporaries south of the border. Approximately 70 percent of these women have had serious problems with alcohol and other drug-related problems and eating disorders (Canadian Human Rights Commission, 2004). Around 80 percent had a history of abuse.

Reports from the United Kingdom revealed similar problems in British prisons for women, mainly because of overcrowding, the incarceration of juveniles for lack of female juvenile institutions, drug problems, and the shortage of professionally trained personnel. In recognition of the problems, the UK parliament (2004) in its House of Lords took up the matter of women in prison and presented the following facts:

- There were three times as many women prisoners in the UK in 2003 as in 1993, yet the crime rate is not rising;
- Nearly 50 percent of the women are mothers of young children;
- The women increasingly are dependent on medication;
- Many have neurotic disorders and are suicidal;
- Almost half of the women were imprisoned for drug offenses;

- Research from abroad shows that in Germany mothers are housed in nearby units with their children; women in Russia are given suspended sentences until the child is 14; women in France are imprisoned far less than in the UK
- Some 18 percent of the women in UK prisons are foreign, often serving drug sentences for having been used as drug carriers or "mules."

One reason for the increasingly multicultural composition of prison populations is the result of the international war on drugs. In England, Canada, and elsewhere, women who have been convicted for their work as "mules" in international drug trafficking are being held in countries far from home. Women are forced or talked into doing this work by international drug smugglers. Because they are generally ignorant of the overall operations and criminal justice policies, women often plead guilty and receive extensive mandatory minimum sentences. The sex-neutral lengthy sentences, as Pollock (1998) argues, do not take into account that many of the seemingly hardened female criminals may have been acting on behalf of male drug traffickers, who are often their boyfriends and partners. In conjunction with the high profits in the drug trade, increasing numbers of female drug smugglers are caught while passing through customs in Washington, DC, New York, and London. In private correspondence (with van Wormer on January 31, 2009), Kim Pate of the Elizabeth Fry Association of Canada describes the situation befalling foreign women in Canada:

> We have a few Latina women in prison, but more women from the Caribbean, and increasingly, women from Southeast Asia for drug importation and/or trafficking charges. Most have no contact with their families for fear of repercussions on them if it is known that their sister/mother/daughter/etc. is in prison abroad. They are terribly isolated as a result, all the more so if they do not speak English or French. We used to be able to try to get them early parole for the purposes of deportation, but legislative changes in 1992 stopped this. . . . Now the women have to serve their entire prison sentences prior to deportation.

The influx of women filling America's prisons significantly eclipses the male incarceration increase. The repercussions of the upsurge in women's incarceration will be felt well beyond prison walls. Experts point, in particular, to the children of inmates who are far more likely than other children to end up in the juvenile justice system or prison.

The rapid increase in the numbers of women in the United States who are sentenced means that departments of corrections are not able to focus on treatment and rehabilitation but, rather, on the warehousing of people; worry over finding the next cell is the predominant concern. Jail and prison construction has become the major expense to counties all across the nation. (Petersilia, 2003).

Inmates as Mothers

According to the BJS (2008b):

> The nation's prisons held approximately 744,200 fathers and 65,600 mothers at midyear 2007. Fathers in prison reported having 1,559,200 children; mothers reported 147,400. Since 1991, the number of children with a mother in prison has more than doubled, up 131%. The number of children with a father in prison has grown by 77%. This finding reflects a faster rate of growth in the number of mothers held in

state and federal prisons (up 122%), compared to the number of fathers (up 76%) between 1991 and midyear 2007. (p. 2)

Almost half (48%) of all mothers held in the nation's prisons at midyear 2007 were white, 28% were black, and 17% were Hispanic. (p. 3)

Social worker Renee Barbu (in private correspondence with van Wormer on December 8, 2008) provides the following remarks concerning girls whom she worked with at a residential facility:

While I was working at the center, two girls told me that their mothers were sentenced to prison. The first mother, sentenced for selling drugs, was a single parent and her daughter was first sent to a foster home. There this girl was sexually abused for two and a half years before it was discovered. The girl said she had told her foster mom about her husband but the woman did not believe her so the girl did not trust anyone well enough to tell for a while. Since then this girl bounced from foster home to foster home and then was finally sent to this place to get her ready for independent living. She does not want to have a relationship with her mother because the mother seems to continue selling and using drugs.

The second girl's mother was sent to prison for repeatedly writing bad checks and stealing checkbooks and forging the name. She had two daughters and was divorced, but the father was able to have the girls live with him. The oldest daughter was doing well. The younger daughter was a self-identified juvenile delinquent. Sometimes when I would give her a compliment, she would snap back and say, "I'm a criminal just like my mamma." This girl very much wants to continue a relationship with her mother.

A large majority of mothers in prison, like the majority of women prisoners in the United States, are serving time for nonviolent offenses (BJS, 2008b). Mandatory minimum sentences provide the same punishments for conspiracy to commit crimes, such as driving the getaway car, as for the instigator of the crime itself. Accordingly, a substantial number of women in prison today under these mandatory sentencing laws have been convicted of conspiracy; this is guilt by association (Evans, 2006). According to the ACLU (2005), women are increasingly caught up in the ever-widening net cast by current drug-related **conspiracy laws** and accomplice liability laws that extend criminal liability to the arrested offender's partners and relatives. Sentencing laws fail to consider the many reasons—including domestic violence, economic dependence, or dependent immigrant status—that may compel women to remain silent. The mandatory minimum laws, despite a recent Supreme Court ruling to give the judge more sentencing leeway, still often subject women to the same, or in some cases, harsher sentences than the principals in the drug trade who are ostensibly the target of those policies (ACLU, 2005). This is an example of what we might call "equality with a vengeance," an equality of punishment meted out to women who violate the law.

In Canada, property crimes bring most women to prison. Canada relies heavily on short sentences for minor offenses such as for public intoxication, shoplifting, and theft. And a large percentage of the sentences are for fourteen days or less. The lack of alternative sentencing options seems to be a factor in these brief incarcerations. The high percentage of women who have small children is similar to that south of the border (Correctional Service Canada, 2007).

Poor women locked in Canadian prisons often have been driven into "underground economies," such as prostitution and drug dealing as a way to make ends meet.

The United States' war on drugs, combined with the backlash against affirmative action, sometimes is played out in the form of "zero tolerance" for women who violate drug use laws. Mandatory minimum sentencing laws tie the hands of judges who personally might favor probation in sympathetic cases. Kemba Smith (2008), a woman who was convicted of a conspiracy charge and whose sentence eventually was commuted by President Clinton, describes her experience as a convicted felon:

> I am one of those people. If I had not received a commutation, my first-time conviction for a non-violent offense would have kept me in prison until 2016 (with good behavior) because of the harsh mandatory sentencing laws for crack cocaine. My 1994 prison sentence grew out of my boyfriend's trafficking in crack. After he was murdered, the government charged me with conspiracy to distribute the crack that his drug ring distributed. During my court hearings, prosecutors acknowledged that I never sold, handled or used any of the drugs involved in the conspiracy. . . .
>
> Today, I could be in federal prison still serving my 24-year sentence. Instead, I've been raising my now 13-year-old son, graduated from college in 2002 and completed a year of law school. I own a home and speak to youth about the importance of their choices and the consequences that can affect their lives forever. (p. 11A)

Today, Smith heads a nonprofit foundation that focuses on providing children of incarcerated parents with a mentor. Unfortunately, very few of the relatively innocent women sentenced on conspiracy charges have been freed.

The new hostility toward drug users is also signaled by the bringing of child-abuse charges against women who have used drugs, even before the birth of their children (Belknap, 2007). The criminalizing of pregnancy during which drugs or alcohol were consumed is a fairly recent development that illustrates the power of the political right (see Chapter 5).

In media accounts, including fictional movies and TV documentaries, Cecil (2008) conducted a content analysis of the best known of these films and discovered a sensationalized and damaging image of women behind bars. Designed to excite the viewers with shocking content, the programs focused on several of inmates with a history of violence. The presentation of these "babes behind bars" films, according to Cecil, serves to reinforce society's beliefs that these women deserve to be locked away. Even the references to the inmates as mothers leave the impression that these women were uncaring and neglectful, and that the children are better off without them. In the media portrayals, the significance of motherhood, abuse, and addiction in the lives of these women are downplayed. Even the risks of victimization of women at the hands of male correctional officers tend to be overlooked in these broadcasts. It is little wonder therefore that the general public has a lack of understanding about the women's pathways to crime and their struggles to survive emotionally in a prison setting. We need to give voice to the stories of such women, as Cecil suggests, to provide a true picture of the reality they face and to arouse empathy for their plight.

Because of the intergenerational costs of locking up mothers and paying for foster care for their children, women are far more expensive to the state to imprison than men. Such a willingness to spend millions of dollars incarcerating women stands, of course, in stark contrast to the paucity of resources made available to other women's programs.

When a mother is imprisoned, often merely held in jail awaiting trial, the separation from her children can be traumatic for them all. Prisons, and especially women's prisons, generally are located in remote, rural areas far away from home and community. Family ties, over time, are broken. Yet prisoner's family relationships are very important not only for mental health considerations but also in terms of postrelease success (Sandifer, 2008).

The Children of Mothers in Prison

While the children of imprisoned fathers also experience loss, there is a tremendous difference in the disruption that imprisonment brings to the children of imprisoned women, as compared to the children of imprisoned men (Pollock, 2002). According to a new federal report, *Parents in Prison and their Minor Children* (BJS, 2008b), prior to incarceration, women were more likely than men to live with their children and to be the primary caregiver. A fact to keep in mind is that nine out of ten times, when the father is imprisoned, the mother carries on the responsibility of child care alone, but when the mother is incarcerated, only 28 percent of the fathers care for their children (Reed and Reed, 2004). Therefore, the children of incarcerated mothers are much more likely than the children of incarcerated fathers to be placed in foster care or to live with their grandmothers. Moreover, a large majority of the children are African American and Latino, so the burden of caring for these "prison orphans" falls disproportionately on families of color. In her research on mothering in a women's prison, Sandra Enos (2001) found that white women, compared to women of color, were less likely to even want their children to be cared for by relatives, first from a belief that these homes were not healthy places, and second from not wanting to feel obligated to reciprocate. In fact, there are serious risks to children who have to be placed when the mother is sentenced to prison. Sharp and Marcus-Mendoza (2001), in their survey of approximately 100 female inmates sentenced for drug violations, found that the women's children were often at serious risk of abuse in their placements. Not surprisingly, van Wormer (2001) found, in her nationwide survey of administrators of women's prisons, that practically all of the respondents listed the welfare of children as the primary concern of these mothers. Many such mothers face termination of their legal rights today due to the Adoption and Safe Families Act of 1997 that mandates the termination of parental rights once a child has been in foster care for fifteen or more of the past twenty-two months (Belknap, 2007).

One of the most painful problems confronting mothers who have been convicted of a crime is the fear of losing control over their children's lives and loss of custody to the fathers or state. Over half of the mothers in prison never see their children during their incarceration (Golden, 2005). The adoption law which was intended to help children of incarcerated parents has resulted in a major crisis for the women who face the permanent loss of their children. Because this policy limits possibilities for family bonding and for the establishment of meaningful relationships between mothers and their children, Laughlin et al. (2008) call for a reevaluation of the Adoption and Safe Families Act and a requirement that prison mothers give consent for the permanent adoption of their children.

A key advantage of community correctional programming such as drug courts, as discussed in Chapter 5, is in keeping families intact, providing much needed treatment and supervision, and preventing the next generation from following the pathway to substance abuse, sick relationships, and crime.

When incarceration is a given, family ties can still be maintained through regular contact and supervised home visits or furloughs. Contact by telephone should be encouraged; one of the most unnecessarily callous correctional policies is the lack of access to the telephone. Prison phone systems invariably have been privatized with additional fees sometimes tacked on. Communication with loved ones on the outside is therefore very difficult. Severe visitation restrictions are also a part of the typical prison scene.

Yet continuing connectedness with loved ones during incarceration is a major benefit to institutionalized populations. Such maintenance of family ties has been shown to result in decreased recidivism rates and improved mental health of inmates and other family members (Reed and Reed, 2004). An empirically based study by Sandifer (2008) found that the impact of a parenting program on prison mothers at a Southern correctional institution was demonstrably positive. The parenting program had significant benefits in terms of mothers' parenting knowledge and healthy attitudes toward parenting. Unfortunately, most internal prison policies as well as traditional public policies have provided minimal support for the maintenance of family relationships for individuals involved in the criminal justice system.

An encouraging development is the offering of parenting educational programs in prison. Such programs have even been helpful in teaching mothers how to handle encounters with difficult teenagers in family visits (Rathbone, 2005). Parenting programs range from parenting classes to prison nurseries. We describe the nursery program at Bedford Hills in a later section of this chapter.

When their spouses and partners are arrested for drug dealing, the women are often brought down with them. Equality under the law may thus not correctly take into account the inequality in most of these male/female relationships. In any case, today's harsh sentencing practices weigh heavily among the young women of color, most of them mothers, who are serving time in the nation's prisons.

PRISON STRUCTURE

Belknap (2007) argues convincingly that women's imprisonment is different from men's and that their special needs have been systematically ignored by prisoner advocates as well as prison administrators. As elsewhere, the major stumbling block in substantial reform is the persistent punitiveness, which is an outgrowth of a climate of fear and resentment toward the deviant poor and nonworking single mothers living on welfare.

Compounding the problem, women have been thrust into a system designed for men who are defined as a high security risk to society. It was for the sake of controlling a population of violent male predators that the whole correctional apparatus, this military-style system of command run by officers given the ranks of lieutenant, captain, and sergeant, originally was set up. This framework, designed for the 93 or so percent of inmates who are the majority of (male) prisoners, was superimposed on the female minority, for whom its suitability is questionable. Some allowance is made for women's particular needs, admittedly, such as the establishment of nurseries for inmate children in a few select places; to date no one has argued for placing a nursery in a men's prison.

The formal structure of the women's prison in many ways belies the informal treatment women receive within the prison walls. At the personal level, women are treated not as tough men, but as children; they are infantilized. Harsh punishments are meted out for cursing, disrespect, and other minor violations. Called "girls" by staff or "ladies" as at New Bedford (as the title of Harris's book, *They Always Call Us Ladies* indicates), but never "women," female prisoners are encouraged to display "good" passive behavior by prison officials. Independent thinking, much less grassroots organizing for social change, is severely punished. As Linda Evans (2006) describes her experience:

> There was no question I was entering another universe—a tiny world surrounded by double razor wire fences and high concrete walls, where the guards had absolute control over every aspect of prisoners' lives.
> Prisons are designed to make a person feel like a caged animal. (p. 294)

The Social World of the Women's Prison

The complex and diverse histories of women incarcerated in prison produce a prison culture that is itself complex and diverse in many ways. We now consider three critical dimensions of life that constitute the culture of women's prisons: the social and cultural background of the women themselves, the cliques or families that develop in prison, and prison sexuality.

Any attempt to comprehend the social organization of prisons must address the contemporary prisoner experience in light of what John Irwin (1980) calls the "cultural baggage" that inmates import into the prison setting with them. Much of this cultural baggage today is the end product of the drug wars on the streets and the war on drugs in society. Caught up in the war on drugs are minority women involved with male gang members (Latino and African American), foreigners arrested at airports as drug "couriers" for international syndicates, and the usual array of violent and nonviolent offenders arrested for crimes that are indirectly related to drug use. Race and class intersect in predictable ways to ensure that the persons most feared and resented by society will be those who are shut away. Racial tensions in the community, as Chesney-Lind and Pasko (2004) suggest, lay the groundwork for ethnic differences and resentments behind prison bars.

Sometimes the resentments, as Jean Harris (1988) reports, are taken out on "honkie," or white, correctional officers. Sometimes prisoners take them out on each other. Former prison inmate Linda Evans (2006) describes how racial tensions over scarce resources such as use of the telephone can erupt; one such argument led to two women being placed in solitary confinement. In one earlier study, as reported by Feinman (1994), observers noted that overt problems occur more often between African American and Latina women than between white and African American women. More studies are needed to confirm this phenomenon throughout the prison system. Research does tell us that the kind of race wars and gang warfare that characterize the social structure in men's prisons seem to have no counterpart in women's institutions.

Two aspects of the social structure with which we are concerned in the following section are prison homosexuality and kinship ties. These elements of female prison culture, although usually addressed separately in the correctional literature, are inextricably linked.

Prison Families

One can expect that like men a woman's orientation to prison life will be based on her pre-prison identity. So when they are moved to rural areas miles far away from their own families, and inaccessible in any case because of financial and legal restrictions, women in prisons tend to develop their own networks for familial ties. In sharp contrast to the male prison society organized around power, women prisoners, at least in the United States, often replicate the family patterns they knew on the outside for life on the inside. Linda Evans, who was a prisoner for sixteen years in federal institutions, writes movingly of the caring relationships that developed among the women. Regarding an inmate who had lung cancer:

> A whole team of women prisoners took care of her. We developed a schedule of tasks for her care such as—cleaning her cell, keeping her company, making and bringing her food . . . In prison we also comforted each other when someone got news of a family member's death, and on visiting days when children were torn away from their mothers' sides at the end of the allotted hours. (p. 288)

Sometimes the family ties are more overt with inmates playing out specific role relationships such as sister or "Mom." "Married" couples may head such families and even occasionally include a father figure. Lesbians often assume the male role within the prison environment. Prison "mamas" keep their "children" in line and provide emotional support (see Giallombardo, 1966; van Wormer, 2001). Although these inmates generally live in a world dominated by pettiness, gossip, and much regressive behavior, a lot of love and nurturing goes on in such a society of women; care and respect for the elderly and mothering of the very young (or retarded) are common themes.

In her study of the Federal Reformatory for Women at Alderson, West Virginia, Giallombardo discovered that the major difference between male and female prisons is that the women's inmate society establishes a substitute world in which women can identify or construct family patterns similar to those in the free world, whereas male prisoners design a social system to combat the social and physical deprivations of imprisonment. Family life—with "mothers and fathers," "grandparents," and "aunts and uncles"—was at the very center of inmate life at Alderson. Research shows that women who recreate their family lives in prison derive much meaning from these relationships, and it helps the time go faster. Such commitments to pre-prison identities continue to shape the social world of the women's prison (Bloom and Chesney-Lind, 2007).

Considerable controversy surrounds the viability of these family forms and whether or not they even exist. As Pollock (1998) suggests, "Although it seems clear that women do form affectional ties that have some similarity to familial relationships, it is not clear that the extensive kinship networks were or are anywhere near as defined as one might believe reading the early studies" (p. 38). Faith (1993) and Belknap (2007) concur in the view that early researchers exaggerated the centrality of family forms.

Among the witnesses to the prison "kinship" scene are Owen (1998), who studied the subculture on the prison yard in a California institution; and Jean Harris (1988), who spent eight years in residence at Bedford Hills, New York; In her survey of women's prison's administrators, van Wormer and Kaplan (2006) found that thirty-one of thirty-five respondents said that the women in their prison assumed family roles. Significantly, the administrators did not approve of this role playing, for the most part, and thought the intensity of the relationships interfered with the inmates working on their own issues.

The open expression of affection among women is highly visible, in contrast to relations among men in prison. Dana Britton (2003), who wrote of the prison as a gendered organization, found that correctional officers' views were shaped by heterosexist perceptions of such interactions as "sickening" and saw dealing with them as a serious management problem. A major theme of Britton's book, in fact, was the near-universal disdain especially by male officers for working in a women's institution and dealing with the emotions of women and their unpredictable outbursts.

As long as women are shut away from the outside world and from the close, caring (and scolding) relationships to which they are accustomed, the argument can be made that the familiar relationship pattern of the outside world will be replayed in the prison world with a different cast, that family ties will be created to replace the ties that were lost. From a strengths perspective, we can appreciate women's bonding, their recreation of the life they had known and valued in "the free world." The differences between male and female social organization are revealed most tellingly in the inner social structure of the unisexual environment.

Because there has never been any consensus concerning the percentage of inmates involved in **prison play-families**, it is hard to conclude whether they are, in fact, on the decline, as contemporary writers such as Fox (1984), Harris (1988), and Diaz-Cotto (1996) contend. Diaz-Cotto argues that the degree to which family groupings are growing less common may be the result of increasing access to family, friends, and outside volunteers. Her description of the Latina prisoners' active involvement in these adoptive families and of the tremendous emotional investment in these relationships is consistent with descriptions in the classic studies. A difference is the ethnic cliquishness of these bondings. Because Latina inmates come from families with strong extended kinship ties and in many cases are incarcerated in a foreign country, their need to recreate familiar role relationships is greater.

Far from viewing these family forms and even the homosexual aspects of jail house relationships as negative, we can view them from a strengths perspective, as a means of psychological survival in a situation that is extreme and abnormal. The functions of prison families are many: They offer mutual support and protection in a strange and often bewildering environment; they provide a mutual aid network in an atmosphere of deprivation; they are often encouraged by the administration for their social control aspect—keeping family members out of trouble; and above all, they create situations for fun and laughter.

Pollack (2004), in her research in Canadian prisons, found the close prison relationships to be multifaceted, complex, and in many ways supportive and sustaining. For example, an underground network of peers helped bandage the wounds of inmates who self-injured. Gaarder and Belknap (2004) interviewed juveniles sentenced to a women's prison, finding that although these girls were housed separately from the women, they intermingled all day with women of all ages and, in many cases, were mothered and nurtured by them. Through such relationships, women acquire an increase in self-esteem. The training of peer counselors can build on such nurturing relationships.

Another possible advantage of clearly defined family roles for women who live in close quarters is that relationships can become very intimate and include touching and hugging without taking on sexual connotations. In same-sex institutions, where sexual tensions often are played out as homophobia, a clarification of one's relationship in terms of sister-to-sister and mother-to-daughter ties can serve to legitimize the bonding between unrelated women (see van Wormer, 2001). Pollack (2004) reached the same conclusion that institutional homophobia serves to perpetuate these normative familial ties.

Prison Sexuality

In men's prisons, homophobia is played out in a different way. A men's prison is a world of untempered masculinity where the strong preserve their sense of manhood through sexual conquest of the weak. Sexual threats, taunting, and assault dominate the scene into which the new inmate is initiated. Under a ruthless inmate code that enables carefully executed schemes of smuggling and escape to go undetected, predators subdue their prey. Young men, especially nonstreetwise white males, are especially vulnerable to sexual harassment and physical attack. In the male prison society, rape or the threat of rape serves as a form of peer group social control exerted by the aggressors and leaders in the facility. While the rapist wields power and respect, the victim is shamed and feminized. The aggressor is never considered anything other than heterosexual; his "punk" is a mere woman substitute. Among men, rape is about power and dominance as well as sexual gratification. Once victimized, a man is ranked as a target for sexual exploitation and subject to gang rapes; one escape avenue is to become more or less a prostitute to one "protector" (Donaldson, 1995; *Prison Legal News*, 1995). Interestingly, a similar pattern prevailed among the convict laborers in colonial Australia as described in disturbing detail in the epic history *The Fatal Shore* (Hughes, 1987).

Behind bars, women recreate a world of the familiar. Many seek out strong types of women with whom to relate and to play their accustomed roles. The father or brother role in the family is usually assumed by the studs or butches; these "players" generally are not lesbians but women playing at being men. Their popularity in a house of femmes exceeds all expectations. Referred to by the pronouns "he" and "him," butches are sought after by male-starved women who provide them with cigarettes and all kinds of other enticements. It is a myth perpetuated in Hollywood B grade movies that butches have to resort to force against unwilling parties.

Hensley, Tewksbury, and Koscheski (2002) conducted a survey of 245 inmates in a southern correctional facility. Their purpose was to study the motivations behind female prison sex. Almost half of the women acknowledged engagement in homosexual activities including kissing and oral sex. White women were less sexually active than were women of other races/ethnicities. Similarly, in her review of the recent literature on women's prisons, Severance (2004) found that estimates are that about one-third of women inmates are sexually active with other inmates. In her own interviews with forty incarcerated women in Ohio, some respondents who were sexually involved saw their involvements as limited to prison, while others were questioning their sexual identity and thought they might continue the same or other same-sex relationships on the outside. Reasons given for the prison sexual involvement were a past of abusive relationships with men, loneliness, curiosity, and deprivation of sexual contact. Many were uncertain why they got involved and there was much confusion over their sexual identity as a result of their behavior. Jean Harris (1988) described the role-playing at the New York State facility:

> Many of the butches make a concentrated effort to emulate the behavior of young black males, the hip-walking, cool-talking model of masculinity. Some cut their hair short or shave their heads. . . . I've watched many a woman wash, iron, and cook for her "butch," "dike," "bulldagger," and I've heard one stand outside a cell door, begging forgiveness for some wrongdoing she couldn't identify. Inside, as well as outside, it's the woman who pays. (pp. 136, 139)

In personal correspondence with Katherine van Wormer, Kathy Tyler (1998), who was sentenced to life at the Iowa Correctional Institution for Women at Mitchellville, shares her reactions to the author's earlier research:

> I was rather astonished to learn of the mother/sister/brother/cousin, whatever, that you have researched. I have not seen that at all here. What I have seen, and sadly, lots of it is the homosexual relationships. I find them sad because they are so counterproductive in many ways. First, the women fight—it is strange relationships, almost like they fight

between each other to ease the boredom. Secondly, I think the relationships prevent them from doing things they would otherwise do because they always do things in tandem. And thirdly, they are transient, and each time a breakup occurs and a new one takes the place, I think something is lost within each of them. (pp. 1–2)

The prison sex role-playing, even though it says more about female heterosexuality than about homosexuality, in all probability makes the homophobia that much worse by increasing sexual tensions in crowded institutions. Hence, as we have seen, one finds the tendency throughout the prison system for women to define themselves as kin—as sisters, mainly, or as mother/daughters. As kin, they can maintain a certain closeness while avoiding all the gossip that would flow from a less clearly defined relationship. The prison counselor is well advised to recognize the centrality of family relationships to women and to advocate for strengthening family ties with relatives on the outside. A good example is found at Bedford Hills, one of comparatively few prisons in the United States to permit family visits overnight. Trailers on the prison grounds make such extended visits possible.

In summary, taken together, these dimensions—ethnicity, prison family construction, and sexual relationships—compose the prison culture typical of many U.S. prisons for women. An inmate's participation in this culture is determined by many factors, as Owen (1998) informs us, including time spent in prison, social and cultural background, and commitment to a deviant lawbreaking lifestyle.

ATTITUDES TOWARD WOMEN IN PRISON

It is now clear to all researchers, as it was always clear to feminist theorists, that the notion that Women's Liberation was associated with a new type of female criminal was false (Chesney-Lind and Pasko, 2004; Crites, 1976). The now exponential increase in the numbers of women in prison is a political fact, a result of a societal backlash against poor and minority women who become involved with drugs, often through their men. Typically, these women get caught up in legal violations, through drug possession, drug transporting, or drug trafficking. Far from being liberated, such women are doubly dependent—dependent on drugs and dependent on the men who supply them.

Despite women inmates' relatively low level of criminality (compared to male offenders), female correctional officers are very often biased against their female charges (Lutze, 2003). They see "the girls" they supervise as immature, overemotional, and quarrelsome. It has been van Wormer's experience in her prison study, confirmed by Rasche (2007), that female correctional officers overwhelmingly prefer to work with male offenders, who are considered less difficult. The negative attitude is often mutual. Women inmates resent female officers enforcing rules, many of them quite petty. Compared to male prisoners, women are more likely to receive numerous citations and for less serious rule infractions than those received by men (Bloom and Chesney-Lind, 2007). Total compliance with every rule is required. Infantilization is thus enforced throughout the system in sanctions for petty violations (Lutze, 2003).

In her chapter, appropriately entitled "The Dislike of Female Offenders among Correctional Officers," Rasche suggests that the almost unanimous desire on the part of correctional officers, male and female, to avoid working with female offenders or in women's prisons is probably due to a lack of specialized training for correctional officers. Indeed, as she further states, the very inmate supervisory techniques that are taught emphasize intimidating tactics which may backfire when applied to female prisoners.

In Canada during the 1980s, women's groups succeeded in persuading criminal justice agencies to refer to convicted female lawbreakers as "women in conflict with the law," as a less pejorative term (Faith, 1993). Nevertheless, the prejudice against women offenders persists. Women in Canadian as in U.S. prisons are punished much more readily than men for minor offenses such as disrespect and use of strong language, as Faith indicates.

Prison Health Care

Approximately twice as many female as male inmates report having three or more medical problems (BJS, 2008a). The most frequent problems reported are arthritis, asthma, and hypertension. From a human rights perspective, Sodja (2006) considers the mistreatment of women prisoners in terms of health care. Women are especially vulnerable for several reasons as indicated by Sodfa. These are: women's unique health care issues related to pregnancy, childbirth, and other gynecological needs; women have a higher rate of drug-related health problems; and women often have histories of being abused prior to incarceration.

The failure of the state to provide adequate medical care to meet the special needs of female prisoners was highlighted in the earlier report by the General Accounting Office (1999) *Women in Prison: Issues and Challenges Confronting U.S. Correctional Systems.* Focusing on the nation's three largest correctional systems—the federal prisons, the California Department of Corrections, and the Texas Department of Criminal Justice—that together hold more than one-third of the nation's female inmates, the report found serious deficiencies in the areas of treatment for substance abuse, mental health problems, and HIV infection. Compared with men, women in prison have higher rates of illness in all three areas. For mental illness, for example, 13 percent of female inmates in federal prisons and 24 percent in state prisons report having a mental disorder or having spent time in a mental hospital (compared with 7 and 16 percent of men).

In her investigative book *Crazy in America*, Mary Beth Pfeiffer (2007) records the tragic case that received much publicity in Iowa. This was the case of Shayne Eggen, a woman diagnosed with paranoid schizophrenia who was prone to self-mutilation and who had a pattern of violent outbursts. In an earlier confinement in jail, she gouged one of her eyes out. Since she was also subject to such outbursts in prison, she spent her time in solitary confinement where she gouged out the other eye. Pfeiffer used Shayne's story to illustrate the impact on mentally ill individuals and the prison system of the closing of hospital beds across the nation after the federal Supplemental Security Income Law was passed to support ex-mental patients living in communities and cutbacks in Medicaid for institutional care for psychiatric patients. The discovery of new antipsychotic medications prompted these changes. So while hospital closings pushed mentally ill women onto the streets, their behavior (such as illicit drug use) sometimes drove them into prison and kept them there. Psychiatric treatment, apart from the providing of medications, is rare within the prison setting. Protecting the public from crime and maintaining discipline within prison walls are the major goals of prison, not healing the sick.

That little has been done since the 1999 report was published is revealed in the following recent news account: "Third Death in Two Months at Tutwiler Raises More Questions." This more recent headline refers to the scandal concerning medical treatment inadequacies at the Julia Tutwiler correctional facility in Wetumpka, Alabama (Associated Press, 2005). The news report provides the results of a federal lawsuit brought against the prison following the death through negligent care of three inmates. Earlier, the prison health services had been privatized. An appointed court monitor cited the lack of a treatment plan and failure to watch vital signs in seriously ill inmates as responsible for unnecessary deaths at the prison. Throughout the prison system, the growing trend toward privatization of prison services with its undeniable profit motive rather than a goal to help inmates receive better health care has exacerbated the problem of poor quality health care. For some women in prison, their ten- and twenty-year sentences become death sentences, as chronic illnesses become terminal.

In their in-depth study of medical care through the eyes of inmates at a detention center in Arizona, Moe and Ferraro (2003) found that although some women were pleased to get any health care available because none had been available to them on the outside, many provided chilling stories of near-fatal neglect. Fear of contracting diseases in the enclosed space of the prison was a constant among the women.

Two of the most life-threatening diseases for prisoners are HIV/AIDS and Hepatitis C. Two and three-tenths percent of all female inmates in state and federal prisons (compared with 1.7 percent of male inmates) are HIV-positive (BJS, 2007). This rate has declined steadily since its peak in 1999. The decline reflects a decline in the general population. In some states such as New York, Texas, and Maryland the rates are much higher. A high correlation exists between HIV cases and tuberculosis, and being HIV-positive and having Hepatitis C.

Hepatitis C, which is spread through infected blood and can lead to chronic liver disease affects one-fifth to one-half of women's jail and prison populations (Talvi, 2007). Hepatitis C is especially prevalent among women incarcerated for crimes related to sex work and drug addiction (Correctional Association of New York, 2008). Because unlike HIV medications which are often subsidized, Hepatitis C medications are highly expensive, some prison systems fail to test for this disease. In New York facilities, for example, around 62 percent of women who test positive for HIV receive medical treatment, while only 4 percent of inmates with Hepatitis C receive comparable medical treatment (Correctional Association of New York). At the Bedford Hills facility, 23 percent of the inmates have Hepatitis C.

With the dismantling of public mental health hospitals in the 1960s and the incarceration boom of the past decade, prisons have become home for alarming numbers of the mentally ill. Jails and prison today have become the poor person's mental hospitals, the dumping grounds for people whose bizarre behavior lands them behind bars. According to Moe and Ferraro (2003) in their Arizona study, it appeared that the only time inmates received treatment for their mental problems was when they threatened suicide. But then they were locked in solitary confinement on "suicide watch."

Due to the abysmal health care conditions at Taycheedah Correctional Institution, the ACLU (2006) filed a lawsuit on behalf of female prisoners. The lawsuit described the human suffering resulting from the breakdown of an understaffed, underfunded and dangerously dysfunctional health care system in Wisconsin's prisons. One of the plaintiffs was not seen by a gynecologist for seven years after arriving at Taycheedah, despite a diagnosis of chronic endometriosis and progressively worsening vaginal bleeding. Ramos ultimately needed a hysterectomy that might have been avoided by timely care. Another prisoner developed painful, bleeding sores on her scalp. In fact, it was a highly contagious form of staph infection. Because of the neglect, the infection spread throughout the institution. In Wisconsin, following eight years of lawsuits and media exposés, Taycheedah Correctional Institution agreed to federal demands to make widespread improvements to mental health care for women confined there. Federal investigators had found mentally ill prisoners—some as young as 15—locked in isolation cells and given psychotropic drugs for months without a doctor's oversight. In a prelude to a federal lawsuit, the U.S. Attorney General signed a complaint that said Wisconsin has shown "deliberate indifference" to the mental health needs of women in the prison (Diedrich, 2008).

Elaine Lord (2008), former superintendent of Bedford Hills Correctional Institution, describes the difficulty of running an institution in which a large percentage of the population are seriously mentally ill. The wild behavior of some of the most disturbed inmates occupied the time of prison staff and resulted in many injuries including self-harm cutting and attacks on staff and other inmates. As the population exploded at Bedford Hills, giving attention to the needs of these seriously ill women was not possible. In the segregated units, women were continuously yelling and banging on the walls. A lawsuit was brought against the institution for the havoc that existed in the disciplinary unit. "Legal action is not always bad news for superintendents," as Lord states, "in some cases it actually forces necessary changes in procedure that open new ways of reacting to incidents or groups or provides funding for staff and space for new programs" (p. 937). Thanks to the court case, additional mental health staff members were added and special therapy groups were run in the segregated unit. However, as all the critics and commentators agree, a more appropriate setting for the treatment of persons with mental illness must be found.

The Bad Mother Image

Women who are mothers have always been judged especially harshly when they get into trouble with the law. If they cared about their children, the reasoning goes, they would be more careful and protective of the children. This attitude is reflected in conviction and sentencing practices. In situations where a stepfather kills a child, the mother who failed to protect her child sometimes gets a longer sentence than the man who struck the fatal blows. So it was in a recent case that was tried in Brooklyn, New York, where the mother was sentenced to seventeen years longer in prison than her husband. According to the *New York Times* report, the sentence disparity occurred because the woman had failed in her duty to be a good mother (Fahim and Zraick, 2008).

One of the most painful stigmas attached to imprisonment is that of being a bad mother. Even when the crime had nothing to do with child abuse or neglect, incarcerated mothers are often blamed for getting themselves into trouble and thus being unable to care for their children. They are judged in a way that fathers are not.

For prison mothers as we have seen, visits with children are rare, and when they do occur, the visits are often painful. Physical contact between parent and child is generally not allowed. Keeping in contact by telephone is limited, and email correspondence usually forbidden. Whether out of shame or to keep children from "blabbing" about where their mothers are, small children are often told, especially by their grandparents, that the prison they are visiting is a hospital. If the children are in foster care, there is little incentive to take them for what could be a disturbing institutional visit.

Especially in divorce proceedings, women are often declared to be unfit mothers by virtue of their imprisonment. If they retain custody, after they serve their time their role as mother is difficult in every way. Among the major challenges are children who feel abandoned, foster parents or grandparents who may not want to let go, and a society that has little compassion for a woman who took drugs or stole or killed, much less a mother who did these things. Females convicted of infanticide occupy the lowest rung on the female convict ladder (Rathbone, 2005). Because most women in prison are mothers who sincerely miss their children, they have little understanding of a mother who would harm her baby. Women who take the lives of their young are often highly suicidal and act out of extreme hopelessness.

DEGRADING PRACTICES

The history of women in conflict with the law is the history of male oppression. Society is afraid of both the feminist and the female criminal, for each of them in her own way tests society's established boundaries (Jones, 1980; 2009). The interconnectedness of feminist advances and harsh punishment of female criminality noted by Ann Jones in her book *Women Who Kill* is apparent in current sentencing practices. Not surprisingly, the political interests of feminist and criminal, therefore, sometimes coincide. The sexual harassment of women in prison by male guards is clearly a women's political issue, however reluctant women prisoners are to unite their cause with that of "liberated" women on the outside.

Increased sexual harassment of women prisoners has come about, ironically, because of the push for women's equality to work as correctional officers in men's prisons and to engage in body-pat frisks and other close contact searches the same as men do. This has led to a situation in which men are allowed the same responsibilities in female institutions. Because of men's greater proclivity than women to be sexually aroused by visual stimuli, the results are entirely predictable (Moir and Jessel, 1991).

Whether the guard is a man or a woman, loss of control over privacy and the most intimate access to one's body are among the most disturbing aspects of imprisonment for women. So disturbing that they can be defined as sexual abuse are invasive body cavity searches, use of strip searches for punishment, women giving birth in chairs and leg shackles, gynecological medical neglect, gynecological procedures performed with male guards present, and women's suscepti-bility to sexual abuse by male guards.

What Erving Goffman (1961) said about the functions of degradation ceremonies and mortification of the self in total institutions as a means of establishing control certainly rings true in women's prisons. The prisoner must surrender again and again to degrading rituals in which the state has taken ownership of the body/self (Rathbone, 2005). Prisoners who do not submit readily to body-part searches, which may be performed by male guards, typically are forced to strip for more thorough searches. This is how power is negotiated, how the new prisoner is moved into the status of "nonperson" as a passive recipient of whatever the guards choose to mete out. This is not to impugn the motives of the prison employees but rather to show, in the Goffman tradition, how a total institution keeps its charges in line.

Between 3 and 4 percent of women in state and federal custody are pregnant when they enter prison. Pregnancy poses special difficulties. Delivery is often an ordeal for women who, if drug addicted, commonly are deprived of sufficient pain medication. During the delivery, they may even be shackled to the delivery table and then be whisked back to the prison away from the baby and health care (Schwartzapfel, 2008). This shoddy medical care of women in childbirth is duplicated in all areas of health care. Gynecological care, for example, is poor to nonexistent.

Taking into account that about half the women in U.S. and Canadian prisons have been victimized sexually in the past, the forced body searches are especially disturbing. Indeed, for many women, prison literally recalls the arbitrary, self-eroding terror of life in previous violent relationships. Inmates may be stripped naked at any time and made to kneel on all fours for rectal/vaginal searches. Male or female guards are often required by institutional policy to probe inmates' body cavities for contraband.

The public got a rare look at the racist and sexist brutality in the women's federal prison when the Canadian Broadcasting Company aired a videotape of male guards roughing up crying women in a forced strip search. The outcry that ensued and the resulting follow-up inves-tigations have done a lot to force the prison to take remedial action and to get the women removed to regional institutions (Dreidger, 1997). Faith (2004), however, cautions that much of the progressive decarceration rhetoric has not been heeded. The fact that the numbers of women confined to prison has tripled during this "reform" period parallels the conservative political mood of the times even while some improvements have occurred.

Prison Sexual Abuse

All rape is an exercise in power, but some rapists have an edge that is more than physical; they operate within an institutionalized setting (Brownmiller, 1975). Rape in slavery, rape in the military, and rape in prison are three such examples.

The scandals involving sexual harassment of women in the military, most recently among soldiers in the Iraq war, has been highlighted in the mass media (see, e.g., Corbett, 2007). Relatively little attention has been paid until recently to the sexual assaults on female prisoners by their male guards. In 1996, extensive documentation was provided by the Human Rights Watch Women's Rights Project (1996), an international NGO, which revealed that the extent of guard-on-inmate abuse behind the closed doors of prisons is staggering. This 347-page report, drawn from firsthand interviews, court records, and records of guards' disciplinary hearings, is astonishing in its graphic detail of everyday experiences of women in our state prisons. As one would expect of a cross-gender power imbalance such as exists between male guards and female inmates, sexual misconduct has been rampant. Here is a summary of the report's findings

> The custodial sexual misconduct documented in this report takes many forms. We found that male correctional employees have vaginally, anally, and orally raped female prisoners and sexually assaulted and abused them. We found that in the course of committing such gross misconduct, male officers have not only used actual or threatened physical force, but have also used their near total authority to provide or deny goods and privileges to female prisoners to compel them to have sex or, in other cases, to reward them for having done so. In other cases, male officers have violated their most basic professional duty and engaged in sexual contact with female prisoners absent the use of threat of force or any material exchange. In addition to engaging in sexual relations with prisoners, male officers have used mandatory pat-frisks or room searches to grope women's breasts, buttocks, and vaginal areas and to view them inappropriately while in a state of undress in the housing or bathroom areas. Male correctional officers and staff have also engaged in regular verbal degradation and harassment of female prisoners, thus contributing to a custodial environment in the state prisons for women which is often highly sexualized and excessively hostile. (p. 1)

Human Rights Watch (1996) and **Amnesty International** (1999) took the U.S. government to task for failing to protect the women who are subjected to institutionalized rape by prison authorities. The placing of male officers in contact positions over female prisoners is in violation of the United Nations Standard Minimum Rules for the Treatment of Prisoners.

Law professor Brenda Smith (2006) offers psychological insights into the power dynamics of controlling women who were enslaved in the nineteenth century and the norms of imprisonment today, which she views as "a modern corollary of slavery":

> At base, both slave owners and correction officers used sexual domination and coercion of women to reinforce notions of domination and authority over the powerless. Like women slaves, women prisoners are seen as untrustworthy, promiscuous, and seductive. (p. 571)

The persons who are most vulnerable to sexual abuse are first-time offenders, women who are young or mentally ill, and lesbian and transgendered persons. The gripping prison Hollywood drama *Love Child*, produced in 1982, tells the true story of an inmate who became pregnant by a guard in Florida and fought for her right to keep the baby. Many times female inmates willingly trade sex for favors; male guards who have been involved in sexual relations with inmates are transferred to men's prisons rather than being fired. Prisoners, such as those in Georgia who are not given a stipend for their work, have no means of purchasing the many supplies they need or the cigarettes they so badly crave. This dependency enhances their vulnerability to sexual exploitation (Human Rights Watch, 1996). In many instances, women have been impregnated as a result of sexual misconduct, placed in segregation if they filed a complaint, and sometimes pressured to get an abortion (Human Rights Watch, 1996). In a recent follow-up, Human Rights Watch (2007) states that the sexual abuse of prisoners still is rampant in our prisons.

According to psychologist Louis Rothenstein, who worked for six years in the federal prison in Dublin, California, it was not uncommon for guards to go into women's cells and have sex (cited in Stein, 1996). Complaints by women inmates and their advocates were ignored. "You would be blackballed if you were thought of as an advocate for the inmates," he said (p. 24). A code of silence within the prison industry shields it from public scrutiny, he added. In 1998, at the U.S. District Court in San Francisco, a settlement was reached providing $500,000 for three female inmates who filed a grievance after being raped by male inmates while housed at the male facility at Dublin, California (*Prison Legal News*, 1998). The inmates reportedly had been given access to women after bribing a male officer.

According to Stop Prisoner Rape (2003), the sexual abuse of female inmates at the Ohio Reformatory for Women was widespread and persistent. Reports of such abuse were brought by a therapist and confirmed by a nurse administrator and former inmates at the facility. The extensive investigation conducted by Stop Prisoner Rape, which was bolstered by widespread media coverage in Ohio, further revealed that female inmates who complained were locked in solitary confinement.

Examples from some representative news reports highlight the issue of sexual abuse of female inmates by correctional staff:

- "City to Pay Damages for Strip-Searches" (Feuer, 2007), *The New York Times*
- "Red Tape Lets Guards Rape Women Prisoner, Suit Argues" (Lydersen, 2007), *The NewStandard*.
- "Female Inmate Described Rapes in Lawsuit Against State" (Seidel, 2009), *Detroit Free Press*.

The above reports were all retrieved on www.google.com under the category news and the typed-in heading, "sexual abuse, inmates." The frequency of such reports and of those still emerging from U.S. prisons reveals that rampant abuse of women continues to take place.

Rathbone's (2005) interviews with women confined in the Massachusetts women's prison at Framingham provide details of sexual relationships between inmates and guards, often the trading of sex for small privileges. A further account of prison scandals from the popular literature is provided by Amy Fisher (2004), who at age sixteen shot her lover's wife at his request. In prison, as a celebrity murderer, Fisher was sexually abused by correctional officers. Now a free woman, she is active today in prison reform.

Official reports both echo those from the scholarly and popular literature and provide additional information. Survey results from the sexual violence report conducted by the U.S. Department of Justice and analyzed by BJS statisticians Beck and Hughes (2005) provide some rather startling information about sexual misconduct in the nation's jails and prisons. Female staff members were frequently reported for sexual misconduct in men's prisons. The statistics are these: with regard to inmate-on-inmate nonconsensual sexual acts in prison and jail, males comprised 90 percent of the victims and perpetrators. In local jails, 70 percent of victims were female, and 65 percent of perpetrators were male. In state prisons, however, 67 percent of those involved in sexual misconduct were female, as perpetrators, and 69 percent of the victims were male. No specific illustrations are given, but one can speculate from other studies in the literature that some female officers who work in men's prisons might be psychologically susceptible to being manipulated by men in their charge.

To understand this phenomenon, we turn to a special report from the U.S. Department of Justice (2005). This inquiry, the first of its kind, was undertaken as a requirement of the Prison Rape Elimination Act passed by Congress and signed into law in 2003. Among the cases it described: a female psychologist overheard discussing her sexual relationship with an inmate; a letter that was intercepted describing a female teacher's sexual relationship with a male inmate; a male officer who raped a male inmate; and a female inmate who reported to authorities that she had had sexual relations twelve times with a guard. What stands out in these cases is that the male inmates were not the ones filing the complaints, whereas we know from other reports many of the women who get sexually involved with their male correctional officers do feel victimized and do complain. Although the female officers who violate the boundaries are clearly behaving in an unprofessional manner and could be expected to be sanctioned by the prison, accordingly, one wonders if criminal prosecution is appropriate for female officers who engage in sexual conduct with their male charges. Gender differences in human sexuality, including who takes the initiative, perhaps should be considered in these cases. Few prosecutors, in fact, prosecute such cases, perhaps in light of an intuitive understanding that sex with a female officer may have a different meaning for a male inmate than sex with a male guard for a female inmate. To our knowledge, there is no discussion in the academic literature on this matter; hopefully, future BJS victim reports will provide further clarification about this behavior.

How about inmate-to-inmate sexual coercion among women? Hensley, Castle, and Tewksbury (2003) explored that issue via questionnaires completed by 245 inmates in a southern correctional facility. Over 4 percent of the 245 inmates reported that they had been sexually coerced by other female inmates and 2 percent admitted they had sexually coerced another inmate. The incidents included genital touching or attempts at sexual contact. Although African Americans were more heavily represented among perpetrators than as victims, whites were sometimes perpetrators as well. Interestingly, for some, a perceived change in sexual orientation occurred. Over half of the victims and perpetrators stated that they had identified as heterosexual prior to incarceration. However, the sample size of perpetrators was extremely small, only 5 inmates out of the 245 who filled out questionnaires, however, so further research is needed on this subject.

INMATE LITIGATION

We begin by summarizing litigative events at the notorious women's prison in Georgia. These events have special meaning for van Wormer; she was personally escorted out of the Milledgeville facility in 1973 by a correctional officer speaking on behalf of the warden (this prison had gone through five wardens in that one year), who said, "It has been decided that you cannot consider your [dissertation] study here; you might see some things you don't understand."

The New York Times (Applebome, 1992) described some of the things that might, in truth, have been understood by the investigator only too well: Although women in Georgia's prison sued the prison for sexual abuse in 1984, they had to wait eight years to win their case in November 1992. In the end, fourteen former employees—ten men, including the deputy warden, and four women—were indicted on sexual abuse charges, including rape, sexual assault, and sodomy in "one of the worst episodes of its kind in the history of the nation's women's prisons" (p. 1). The incidents took place in the warden's house, in a prison rest room, and in other areas.

These indictments at the Georgia Penitentiary were only the tip of the iceberg at the penitentiary. Whether brought about through trade-offs or coerced through violence between male guards and female inmates, sexual involvement was not deviant behavior in that setting; it was the norm. Even female staff members were implicated in sexual abusive behavior, according to court records cited in the Human Rights Watch (1996) report. There is no way to begin to estimate the number of inmates involved before the lawsuit was filed in 1992. Between 1992 and 1996 (Human Rights Watch, 1996), when better records were kept owing to the investigations taking place, attorney Bob Cullen told Human Rights Watch that he had learned of approximately 370 reported incidents during this period. Some of the cases have been publicized in the media.

Legislation in the form of the Prison Litigation Reform Act was passed by the U.S. Congress and signed into law in 1996 (Human Rights Watch, 1996). The intent was to stifle the spate of frivolous lawsuits coming from prisons and mainly from men's prisons. Unfortunately, the ability of women inmates and their legal advocates to sue over human rights violations is now drastically curtailed, according to the Human Rights Watch.

Regarding Sexual Abuse

Not surprisingly, extensive litigation concerns the sexual mistreatment of female inmates. According to Chesney-Lind and Pasko (2004), scandals have erupted in California, Georgia, Hawaii, Ohio, Louisiana, Michigan, Tennessee, New York, and New Mexico. "Perhaps there is something inevitable about guard-on-inmate sex," declares Rathbone (2005), "when you have a building full of constitutionally disempowered women ruled over by uniformed male guards" (p. 45). In her investigation of the situation at the Framington institution in Massachusetts, Rathbone got an earful of stories about the officers' demands: "There were the officers who liked to be touched, and the officers who liked to touch; officers who dared only to kiss and officers who liked to go the whole way" (p. 45). Very few of these activities ever come to light.

The women themselves, according to Rathbone, have little incentive to report their liaisons with the men. Many of the women get special favors from the guards, using sex as a trade-off for prison supplies such as gum, cigarettes, and even pills. Those who want to complain risk being sent into solitary confinement while the claim is investigated, and such claims are hard to substantiate. Most of the scandals that have come to light publicly have occurred only because of publicity surrounding legal suits. The past decades may portend a new trend in the nature of legal action taken against the criminal justice system. Van Wormer (2001) in her survey of prison administrators asked if media reporting of sexual abuse of inmates was blown out of proportion or reflective of reality. The responses were equally divided on this issue. On the question of whether or not male correctional officers performed all the same tasks as female officers, two left the question blank, two said yes, and twenty-six said no. The exceptions were said to be with regard to routine strip searches. Most indicated that with regard to pat-down searches, shower duties, emergency strip searches, and dorm assignments, men were still unrestricted as before.

These practices, although improved in that some restrictions are imposed on male officers, are still below the standard recommended by Amnesty International (1999). The organization declared that the sexual abuse of women inmates was a form of torture and called for female inmates to be supervised by female staff only in accordance with international standards.

A recent report from the Detroit Free Press is one of a five-part series chronicling a civil trial that resulted from a lawsuit against the state of Michigan. This well-publicized case represents the tip of the iceberg in what had been taking place for decades in Michigan's prisons for women (see Human Rights Watch, 1996). In connection with the recent lawsuit, over 500 female prisoners have come forward to say they were raped and molested by male officers, many repeatedly (Seidel, 2009). At the civil trial that lasted three weeks, ten women shared their experiences. Not only were the wrenching stories of the women provided but also testimony from a female officer who had observed her fellow officers engaging in unprofessional incidents. The state did not dispute the women's stories, only faulted them for their failure to report the incidents. The women who have been awarded $50 million in damages have to await the state's appeal.

Efforts to minimize staff misconduct have led to a revamping of the environment at the Denver Women's Correctional Facility (Shoemaker, 2007). The focus is on developing a positive culture. To achieve this end, gender-responsive training is provided by the warden and supervisory staff. Offenders are allowed to file grievances, and all allegations of misconduct are taken seriously. The simple act of having supervisors walk around in the living units helps enhance the flow of information as well as providing monitoring of other staff members. As a result of these initiatives, staff conduct and morale have improved considerably.

In addition to sexual abuse, female prisoners are raising issues of clemency for battered women who killed in self-defense, drug treatment, prison nurseries, decent dental care, and health care for the aged and for those with HIV/AIDS. Much of the litigation concerns the lack of employment and vocational training opportunities for women, compared to men, in prison. Correctional policy makers often justify the poor training options in light of the numbers of women in prison being too small to provide many options, the fact that few of the female inmates have marketable skills and that interest in men's prison programs such as auto mechanics is minimal (Feinman, 1994). Accordingly, most work in prison relates to the everyday running of the prison—washing, cleaning, and cooking.

Concerning Employment Opportunities

Angela Davis (2003) argues that prison life is a form of slavery, and that it is no coincidence that such a high percentage of the women being sent to prison today are African American. It is significant to note also, as Davis correctly indicates, that the Thirteenth Amendment to the Constitution, which outlawed slavery, did allow for "involuntary servitude" for those who had been convicted of a crime. Following the Civil War, in the South, prisoners were leased to white plantation owners to do the work of the former slaves. Most, in fact, were former slaves. Today work conditions in many prisons, including work on chain gangs, bear some resemblance to the conditions of long ago. And there is little legal recourse given the lack of ambiguity in the Constitution. Interestingly, the United Nations Universal Declaration of Human Rights, which was passed in 1948, outlaws slavery in all forms. Perhaps some day the United States will be found out of compliance with this document and in violation of international law. In the meantime, the present inhumane work conditions persist.

The operation of the prison industry at Carswell Prison for women in Texas provides an illustration of the exploitation of prison labor for profit. Contracts with the government corporation

Federal Prison Industries exempt the prison from fair labor practices. Challenges have come from private industry and Congress due to competition from cheap labor. According to an inmate informant, "This prison is making huge profits off of nothing more than slave labor and then making up prices by as much as 50% in the commissary making even more profit off of all of us" (Brink, 2008, p. 44). The women are paid as little as twenty-three cents an hour.

A major problem with the litigation to equalize employment training opportunities for men and women is that male prisoners are heavily exploited as a source of cheap labor, making only a few dollars per hour, at the most. Employers are enticed by ads promoting cheap labor—no health insurance, no benefits, no workers' compensation. Instead of going to Mexico, many private companies are relying on this state-subsidized program to get inmates to work. The issues are the same as with the exploitation of cheap labor overseas: wages for regular labor can be driven down and work opportunities are provided for persons in no position to bargain.

Concerning Medical Abuse

Legal cases based on medical abuse and neglect abound. Whereas prison administrators insist they are doing their job, health-care-related allegations from female inmates and their legal advocates indicate otherwise. The denial of adequate medicine for chronic diseases, lack of timely treatment for spreading cancers, and dangerous delays in care for pulmonary and cardiac problems are among the allegations made (Talvi, 2007). At the California Women's Facility at Chowchilla with a population of over 4,000 inmates, for example, come reports of mentally ill prisoners locked in solitary confinement twenty-three hours a day, a rash of suicides, a total lack of privacy even when women are on the toilet, and brutal "cell extractions" of noncompliant inmates.

Convicted for selling drugs, Linda Fenton spent almost seven years in Carswell's psychiatric unit (Brink, 2008). Two days before her release she was found comatose with a sheet wrapped around her neck. The postmortem, however, indicated the inmate had died of a lethal choke hold. A wrongful death lawsuit was recently filed by the bereaved family of Fenton. This case is reminiscent of one case known personally by van Wormer that took place at the Pewee Valley women's prison in Kentucky (see van Wormer, 2004). Again there was a mentally ill woman killed under questionable circumstances and an autopsy report that contradicted the prison's claims concerning cause of death.

Historically, almost all the legal action for prisoner rights was pursued on behalf of men. Suggested reasons for gender differences in filing litigation are women's general passivity, their prisons' locations far from urban centers and legal aid attorneys, and the scarcity of jailhouse lawyers among them (Feinman, 1994; Rathbone, 2005). A unique explanation is that the female inmate tendency to form play-families and to pair off as "married couples" serves inadvertently to suppress troublemakers and absorb women's energies, while having a subduing effect on their activism (see Giallombardo, 1966; van Wormer, 2001).

In other countries, although there has been litigation, corrections reform for women has come more often from highly publicized efforts on their account and a concerned public enlightened by sympathetic press accounts. In Canada, for example, a 1990 task force report on federally sentenced women led to construction of model prisons designed for the offenders' well-being. In 1994, a Canadian federal inquiry into strip searches by a male riot squad at the women's federal prison resulted in a castigating report written by Madam Justice Louise Arbour Faith (2004). A human rights issue desperately in need of litigation, but that seems unlikely to benefit from court action, is the extremely brutal treatment of detained political refugees who, because they are not U.S. citizens, are considered to be outside the jurisdiction of the Constitution. Kassindja's harrowing memoir, *Do They Hear You When You Cry?* (1998), graphically recounts the horrors of her oppression during confinement by the Immigration and Naturalization Service. Kassindja, who arrived in the United States as a refugee from forced genital mutilation in Togo, Africa, was successful only because her story received rare national press coverage.

WOMEN ON DEATH ROW

In 2008, the world moved even closer toward abolition of the death penalty. Recently, the United Nations General Assembly adopted by a large majority a second resolution calling for a moratorium with a view to abolish the death penalty. This resolution, according to Amnesty International (2009), consolidates three decades of steady progress toward complete abolition of the death penalty. The trend globally and in the U.S. is toward abolition of this primitive form of punishment.

After 1976, when the death penalty was reinstated in the United States, there was a lull in the executions of women. In chronological order, here are the women whom the states punished in this way:

November 2, 1984: Velma Barfield, 52, lethal injection in North Carolina for poisoning her fiancé for insurance money. She had poisoned other men in her life and is sometimes referred to as a serial killer.

February 3, 1998: Karla Faye Tucker, 38, lethal injection in Texas for killing two people.

March 30, 1998: Judy Buenoano, 54, electrocution in Florida for killing her son and husband.

February 24, 2000: Betty Lou Beets, 62, lethal injection in Texas for killing one of her husbands.

May 2, 2000: Christina Riggs, 28, lethal injection in Arkansas for smothering her two small children.

January 11, 2001: Wanda Jean Allen, 41, lethal injection in Oklahoma for killing two women.

May 1, 2001: Marilyn Plantz, 40, lethal injection in Oklahoma for having her husband killed.

December 4, 2001: Lois Nadean Smith, 61, lethal injection in Oklahoma for killing her son's ex-girlfriend.

May 10, 2002: Lynda Lyon Block, 54, electrocution in Alabama for murdering a policeman.

October 9, 2002: Aileen Wournos, 46, by lethal injection in Florida for murdering six men.

September 15, 2005: Frances Newton, 40, by lethal injection in Texas for killing her two children and husband.

Velma Barfield's (1985) autobiography, *Women on Death Row*, describes her religious conversion in depth and her efforts to spread the word to other women to whom she talked through the walls. Of these ten women who were executed in recent years, the public outcry was the strongest against the execution of born-again Christian, Karla Fay Tucker, whose interviews on national TV captivated the nation and public opinion in her support. In Europe, in early February 1998, editorial writers called the execution of Karla Fay Tucker a "barbaric act." The *Irish Times* featured the story on page one for two consecutive days (Carroll, 1998; *Irish Times*, 1998). Entreaties from all over the world and from the Pope failed to gain clemency for Tucker, the first woman executed in Texas since 1863. Tucker, despite being an admitted axe murderer who had killed strangers in a drug-induced rage, galvanized the sympathy of the world.

Following Tucker's execution, but this time without much fanfare, Judias Buenoano, an unrepentant woman prisoner known as the Black Widow, was executed in Florida's electric chair in March 1998. More recently, with Texas preparing to execute the first black woman in the state since the Civil War, the British news carried a story raising questions about her guilt. Frances Newton, forty years old, was convicted for killing her husband and two children. Like other women who are charged with murdering their husbands, Newton, it was claimed, killed him to get his insurance. (Since men often carry life insurance, this charge is commonly made in such cases.) Newton never confessed and always said an intruder committed the murders. New evidence uncovered the existence of a second gun at the scene (Luscombe, 2005). Nevertheless, Newton was executed on September 15, 2005, an act witnessed by her grieving parents (Turner and Ganza, 2005).

Sentencing

The deaths of these women, like all executions, are highly political. The message sent to the public by the state execution of these women is that justice is without mercy and, as for women, that if they want equality of opportunity they can also have equality of punishment. Laster's (1994) astute analysis of women executed in Australia between 1842 and 1967 demonstrates that politics rather than law influences the sentencing outcome for women. Women were hanged in Victoria not for what they did but for what they were. They were not hardened criminals or a threat to society; their crimes were different from those of their male counterparts. Overwhelmingly, their victims were intimates. Execution of women, as Laster argues, is a kind of social control in a society stressing traditional family values. In a twisted irony, in today's world, the insistence of feminists for equal treatment is used against them as a way of advancing antifeminist political agendas.

As of January 2008, there were fifty-six women on death row; this constitutes 1.69 percent of the total death row population of about 3,309 persons (Death Penalty Information, 2008). In the past 100 years, over forty women have been executed in the United States, including eleven since 1976. In recent years, almost all of those executed were white; most on death row, however, are black. About half killed their husbands or boyfriends and half killed their children; two killed both their husbands and children.

Of all the women who commit murder, only a small fraction end up on death row. The figures give some indication that race played some role in this. We can surmise that all the women were poor. One thing that we probably did not consider though was how many were lesbian or otherwise failed to conform to sex role expectations. Kathryn Ann Farr (2000) argues that the masculinized portrayal of female evil affects sentencing decisions pertaining to an already heinous crime. The unfeminine image of women such as Buenoano, portrayed as a man-hater, the "black widow" reduces any sympathy for such women who are seen as deserving of their fate, in contrast to Karla Fay Tucker, described in the media as pretty and married to her prison chaplain, who aroused national sympathy in her passing. Farr's article relates the experiences of thirty-five women who were sent to death row in part because they are lesbians and were seen as being in defiance of appropriate gender roles. Her findings showed that lesbians are overrepresented in death sentence cases, and that the playing up of nonfeminine personality traits by prosecutors and the media undoubtedly influenced the juries or judges when it came to imposing the maximum penalty. A study by the ACLU (2004) confirmed that prosecutors used sexual orientation and images of masculinization to prejudice juries in at least three cases of female death row inmates.

To explore the possibility of discrimination against women who break from traditional gender roles in the commission of homicide, Messing and Heeren (2009) analyzed data from newspaper articles reporting cases of multiple domestic or family member homicides. In the decade studied, the researchers located sixty-nine perpetrators who were eligible for the death penalty. Of these, 18 percent were women. Most had killed their children; many unsuccessfully attempted suicide. Comparisons by gender showed that women who kill their children using a knife or firearm are disproportionately sentenced to death, whereas men who kill in the context of a separation are granted leniency in regard to the death penalty.

Living on Death Row

Death row conditions vary from state to state. Some states allow the women to mingle for visits and yard time, but most allow no contact visits (only visits behind glass, by means of a telephone), no work, and solitary confinement for twenty-three hours per day. Death row inmates have some limited contact with correctional officers, prison chaplains, and treatment staff.

There are few books describing conditions for women confined to death row. Barfield (1985), in her autobiography, provided this picture of her routine at the Raleigh, North Carolina, penitentiary:

> I was put in an end cell that, like all the others, contained four bunks. "No one else," the officer said, "will ever occupy the cell with you."
>
> I didn't realize it then, but for the next four and a half years, my world would consist of a room ten feet by ten feet, with bars for two sides and concrete walls for the other two. Little natural light penetrated the cell. . . . A guard led me out of my cell every day for one hour of exercise. Aside from that daily hour and occasional trips to the administrative building or to the mental health unit or when I was taken to court, I never moved outside my cell. (p. 106)

Probably the best-known woman who was executed in recent years was Aileen Wuornos, who, unlike other women in her category, killed complete strangers—men who solicited her as a prostitute (Schulberg, 2007). Called the first female serial killer, Wuornos opposed all appeals on her behalf and was executed in 2005.

Kathleen O'Shea, a former nun, has made it her life's work to publicize conditions for women sentenced to die. In a newspaper interview, O'Shea (interviewed by Loper, 2004) described the grim circumstances of life on death row:

> Many women's prisons do not have "death rows" per se and so the women are held in isolation in areas generally known as "the hole." Very few of these prisons have any women working in these areas. The men in charge of women on death row have total control over what goes on there . . . women on death row frequently lack even the basic necessities . . . like underpants . . . I recently wrote a letter for a woman on death row who was asking the Commissioner of Prisons if they (the women on death row) could have one pair of underpants a day, instead of only three pairs a week as they are allowed now—These women aren't asking to be free—they are asking to be recognized as humans.

Recently, *The Sunday Times* (2009) of London featured an article on correctional officers who work with women on death row at the Muncy, Pennsylvania, prison. The cells are described as very small:

> They are little more than 6 feet wide, eight feet high and 12 feet long. Everything is fastened to the wall, toilet and bed included. The cells are airless and smell pungent and institutional. The sound of steel doors closing is amplified. It is an atmosphere heavy with despair, remorse, anger, and loneliness. (p. 1 of 7)
>
>   The women put their hands through an opening in the door to be cuffed when leaving the cell. They are allowed outside for "yard" for an hour once a day, first thing in the morning (p. 2 of 7)

The three women on death row at Muncy prison live in single cells in the Restricted Housing Unit in Charlie pod. Other inmates nearby can be heard screaming that they will kill themselves. The inmates on death row have Bible studies once a week with a priest. Other privileges include ice cream once a week and the right to have TV sets inside their cells. Preventing suicide is one of the duties of the correctional officer who was interviewed for the *Sunday Times* story. The irony of this—making sure the inmates don't kill themselves before the state can kill them—was acknowledged by the officer.

It is impossible to discuss the death penalty as the ultimate cruelty without revealing its curious attraction to suicidal inmates. Chaplain Kopatich (1998) describes the scene for women inmates in Iowa, a state without the death penalty:

> I have heard that over and over again, they wish that they could end this agony. And they would like to have the death penalty. But that is probably cyclical too because the urge for life is very strong. So when they first come in I hear that a lot, "I wish that I would have gotten the death penalty." But they haven't faced death row so I'm not sure about that. But I just know it's very harsh to face life in prison. (p. 3)

INNOVATIVE PROGRAMS

To move from the grimmest aspect of penal policy—executions—to the brightest, we now briefly review some laudable innovations within the context of women's imprisonment. Some of the innovations are holistic and structural and woman-centered from top to bottom. The others discussed in this section are piecemeal, positive programs operating against a backdrop of punitiveness and antifeminism. We could refer to these as beacons of light. These types of programs are family centered, cultural, specific, and educational.

We start with international approaches provided in Denmark, Germany, Canada, Australia, and the Netherlands. Denmark, a country with a strong social welfare state and a nonpunitive philosophy toward offenders, maintains a state prison at Ringe that is the proto-type of progressivism. In contrast to the Canadian approach described below, a gender-neutral model is exemplified in Denmark's prison programming, which emphasizes gender equality. As described by Feinman (1994) and the International Centre for Prison Studies (2008), Denmark's prison accommodates young men and young women in totally integrated housing. A man and woman are permitted to be alone in each other's rooms but they must be recognized as a couple to avoid prostitution; inmates also may entertain spouses or lovers from the outside in their rooms. All prison activities are completely integrated, including cooking. Inmates buy their own food and prepare their meals together. There are a large number of professional staff; although there are a few guards, there are no heavy fences, no riot equipment, no guns, and no uniforms (International Centre for Prison Studies, 2008). The prisoners are required to attend school or work in the daytime. To maintain family ties, even the inmates with the longest sentences can go home once every three weeks. Escapes are extremely rare. The Denmark example typifies Scandinavian cultural values, values that promote sexual equality and fewer restrictions on sexuality.

Conditions in Germany are even more amazing. According to the International Centre for Prison Studies (2008):

> In Frondenberg Prison in the State of North Rhine-Westphalia in North West Germany the State prison service runs an open unit for women with children up to the age of six. It only holds 16 mothers as it is quite expensive. Mothers live with their children in self contained flats which consist of a kitchen, bathroom, one bedroom and a living room. They do not have the appearance of cells but look more like well equipped family houses. The building also does not look like a prison but more like a student flat from the outside. The majority of women are there for theft or fraud. According to a prisoner, children do not notice that they are in a prison. (p. 42)

At the Amerswiel women's prison in the Netherlands, the authorities attempt to follow the U.N. Standard Minimum Rules for the Treatment of Prisoners. As reported by the European Commission (2002), Amerswiel prison in the Netherlands consists of women housed in eleven group dwellings of eight women prisoners each, in the form of ordinary housing blocks where each prisoner has a key to her own bedroom and the staff only lock the front-door in the evenings.

Australia has just constructed a new prison, the Alexamder Maconochie Centre, built according to principles of conserving human dignitiy. Both men and women will be confined there; many will be transferred from stark traditional institutions to this setting surrounded by views of grass and mountains. A replica of a small town is contained within the enclosed space where trees are planted and one can see kangaroos grazing. As described in a radio broadcast (Gorman, 2009):

> Almost 50 percent of the accommodation in the Centre is cottage-style housing, where inmates will live together in small groups. This includes a mothers' and babies' unit with a communal kitchen and solar-powered hot water. The Centre also has a town square where inmates can gather for concerts or public events.

For our fifth example, we look north to Canada. Canadian culture, although having much in common with that of the United States, is generally regarded as having a more humane social welfare system (see Adams, 2003). Not surprisingly, therefore, Canada's prison system is less harsh than that south of the border, but the Canadian Correctional Service has had to answer to a barrage of criticisms from human rights groups. A major objection concerns the dispropor-tionate confinement of aboriginal women in maximum security prisons and the continued use of male guards in women's prisons (Cordon, 2005). Nevertheless, the correctional service that placed female offenders in small regional, woman-centered facilities to help integrate inmates into the environment has now pledged to make further improvements. As described in a glowing New Jersey newspaper account (Peet, 2004):

> Arguably the most progressive corrections system in North America, Canada is the only place that offers a healing lodge for Native American women offenders, nontraditional job training off-site, a certified trade school and, it was announced this month, prison tattoo parlors to lower the risk of spreading hepatitis through self-inflicted jailhouse body art. . . . Unlike U.S. states that are just now developing gender-specific inmate programs, Canada operates under a Strategy for Women Offenders established in 1994. (p. 1)

The Canadian approach follows a "special-needs" model as opposed to a gender-neutral one. The special-needs approach for women prisoners caters to women's special needs, such as privacy, self-esteem work, and maintenance of family ties. Recently, Canadian correctional authorities have drawn upon a branch of feminist psychology called relational psychology as a foundation of gender-specific programming. Pollack (2007) warns that knowledge of women's victimization may be used against them when it comes to risk assessments; in other words, women's self-disclosures that help them receive gendered treatment may be turned against them when it comes to assessments of women's risks of reoffending.

In the United States, female inmates have experienced a history of neglect in the development of correctional programming targeted to their particular situations (Bloom and Chesney-Lind, 2007). Here, the outgrowth of feminist-inspired court cases demanding equality of opportunity (in jobs and vocational training) for female inmates has been beneficial and the enforcement of the gender-neutral concept in other ways has led to solutions in providing employment opportunities for women in men's institutions. But, this, in turn, has had unintended consequences. Bloom and Chesney-Lind (2007) bring our attention to the placing of girls and women in military-style boot camps and even in Alabama, for a time, on chain gangs. Another development that seemed progressive when it was introduced was placing women with men in co-correctional establishments. These co-correctional (often called coeducational) prisons have subjected women, who are in the minority, to exploitation by male inmates and guards and to special restrictions on their freedom of movement to prevent sexual activity among inmates.

A progressive development in the UK is the setting up of modern juvenile homes with professionally trained staff and specialized treatment services for girls. In all the women's prisons, the plan is soon to have methadone maintenance programs in place as well as extensive mental health and substance abuse treatment. And special community centers are being set up to develop an integrated approach to link women to mental health and substance abuse services as needed (Petrillo, 2007). Still, much more work needs to be done to meet the special needs of women.

What would be the most beneficial for women, in light of their specialized needs, would be placement in highly structured community settings. Fortunately, there are some promising developments in this direction. Nationwide, programs are being developed that use an empowerment model of skill building to help women move toward independence and stability in their family lives (Bloom and Chesney-Lind).

Family Programs

Exemplary prison programs for mothers of small children are few and far between. Only nine programs in the United States allow incarcerated women to keep their infants with them after they give birth (Schwartzapfel, 2008). South Dakota allows babies to stay for just thirty days; Washington State allows children to stay up for three years and offers a Head Start program. Of the programs, Bedford Hills in New York State is the most prominent (see, e.g., Boudin, 1998; Pollack, 2004). The Bedford Hills program provides a nursery where babies up to eighteen months old can live with their mothers. A playroom is available for older children, who are encouraged to come and visit their moms. The mother–child bonding has been excellent in this program; mothers learn child-care skills from child development experts. The theoretical foundations for the program were drawn from feminist consciousness-raising groups, group psychology, and the trauma recovery process. This peer support program is facilitated by the incarcerated mothers themselves. Pollack (2004) describes the philosophy as anti-oppressive in its acknowledgement of structural oppression and its impact on the women, and as empowering in its building on the women's initiative and autonomy. Pollack correctly concludes that the task of progressive mental health services for this population is to counter constructions of women offenders as having personality and thinking disorders. Rather, she says, we need to tap into women's strengths and acknowledge their varied and skillful modes of coping. Ohio, Indiana, Illinois, and California are among the states that let inmates who meet the requirements live with their newborns (Women's Prison Association, 2009). The Shakopee program in Minnesota allows for twenty-four-hour visits with mother and child. The child sleeps on a trundle bed that pulls out from under the mother's bed in her cell.

Washington state allows children to stay for up to three years with their mothers in a separate wing of the women's prison (Schwartzapfel, 2008). A federally funded Early Head Start program for prenatal health and infant-toddler development is provided as well as doula services to the women during and after pregnancies. Advocates say that programs that help mothers behind bars to maintain relationships with children are key to reducing crime over the long run (Women's Prison Association, 2009). Cost savings of such nursery programs not only are reflected in reduced foster care expenses, but also in the reduced likelihood that the incarcerated mother's children will be incarcerated themselves (Office of Performance Evaluations, 2003). Still, as the report by the Women's Prison Association suggests, many women parenting their infants in prison nurseries could be doing so in the community with better results.

Although little positive has been said about the overcrowded California system and its treatment of women in years past, hope is on the horizon as the California Legislative Women's Caucus has made this issue of the treatment of women in prison a top priority (Warren, 2005). Now, new rules are to be applied; in the future, for example, male guards will no longer conduct pat searches of women. The intense focus on security for women, who typically have been convicted of survival crimes, who are little or no security threat, is at last being questioned. This questioning is perhaps a reflection of the realization that equality does not have to mean sameness, that to take into account gender differences is not to belittle women. Attention to the importance of the role of motherhood to most of the women is to be given more attention in the future. The California Department of Corrections is looking to innovative programs in other states as models, to Indiana that keeps women convicts heavily involved in their children's lives, to Missouri that emphasizes a transition to parole, and to Minnesota in its focus on alternatives to prison close to the women's homes.

A European organization, Committee for Children of Imprisoned Parents (Eurochips) advocates the needs of children in maintaining ties with their incarcerated parents. The Swedish Prison and Probation Service ordered the following for all prisons in Sweden:

- Special leave will be granted for important events concerning children.
- Children should be allowed to telephone and speak directly to the parent. (In the past, children could only leave a message and ask the parent to call back, which frequently occurred several hours later.)
- Each new prisoner should be asked about his/her children.
- Flexible visiting hours for children need to be provided (Eurochips, 2005).

In Australia, inmate mothers can usually care for their children until they reach the age of two or three. New Zealand recently passed a law that babies can now stay in jail with their mothers until they are two years old. Applicants will be screened for mental health and substance abuse problems (National Business Review, 2008). In Western Europe, except for Norway (a country that makes extensive use of long-term foster care), children are kept at the prison for up to several years. The UK provides eighty places for babies with their mothers in seven women's prisons. The upper age limit for the infant is eighteen months at open prisons and nine months (11 Million, 2008). Germany has, perhaps, the most outstanding prison nursery system in the world. In this program, described by Harris (1988), teachers and social workers help mothers learn how to be good mothers. According to a BBC broadcast (2001), mothers of small children who have been sentenced to prison can keep their children until the children are six years old. The facility at Frondenberg in northwest Germany has no bars in the windows; the mothers can go outside and play with the children and can visit the town. The mothers go to work after the child is two years old, and they can go on leave from the grounds for twenty one days of vacation per year. The children attend a regular nursery school and kindergarten. It has been found that mothers in this program have a much lower reoffending rate than a comparable group of mothers who do not have their children with them. A California state program allows female prisoners with small children a chance to move to one of seven homes in the state where they can live with their children and take parenting classes. Several hundred women, only a fraction of the mothers in California's prison system, have graduated from the program.

Other family programs involve conjugal rights for prisoners and their spouses. Russian women are entitled to a couple of three-day visits a year with their husbands. In the United States, only a handful of states allow conjugal visits, including California and New York. At Bedford Hills, families can spend forty-eight-hour periods together in trailers on the campus. California now allows for such private family visits for gay and lesbian as well as heterosexual couples (McKinley, 2007).

Ethnic-Specific Programs

The Correctional Service of Canada has now endorsed Native Canadians' right to practice Native ceremonies and healing circles. With help from spiritual teachers, Native women have formed healing circles and have revived such practices as fasting; having potlatches; burning sweetgrass, sage, and cedar; and holding medicine bundles (Faith, 1993). Correctional Service of Canada (2008) has incorporated an Elder consultation program to provide personal support to aboriginal women. Native liaison officers also consult with Elders, who are older, respected members of the community, regarding their clients. The Elders not only provide ceremony but also impart ongoing wisdom to the group. They also participate in Elder-assisted parole hearings and the reintroduction of women to the community.

Increasingly, Spanish-language radio and television programming is available for the influx of Hispanic women entering prison for drug-related offenses. A great deal more needs to be done for Latina inmates with culturally specific programming. For African Americans, also, Afrocentric consciousness-raising is helpful in engendering pride. Many of the newly developed substance abuse programs, imported from the outside by substance counselors, offer cultural-sensitive group counseling sessions for inmates. My Sister's Keeper, a Chicago-based program that is a division of the Black on Black Love Organization, is a complete after-care program that helps women who have been released from prison to lead productive lives. This **ethnic-specific program** promotes drug education, life-skills and parenting training, cultural enrichment activities, and help with housing and legal services (Samuel, 2003). To prevent recidivism, such services are vital.

Reentry

Planning for reentry should begin as soon as an inmate with a less-than-life sentence arrives at the institution. The planning process, as Covington (2006) recommends, should not be reserved for the final phase of incarceration as is the current practice. Ideally, the classification or evaluation process should determine which interventions are needed to help direct a woman on a journey to successful community membership. This might include substance abuse counseling, mental health treatment, and educational and vocational programming. Parenting education and encouragement of family ties are vital. There is a crucial need as well to develop a system of support from within the community to provide assistance to women transitioning from jails and prisons back to community life. In place of the fragmented services that are now offered, Covington recommends a continuum of care to help women find safe and affordable housing, access health care, and in many cases, maintain recovery from addiction.

In their investigation of the effects of poverty and state programming on recidivism, Holtfreter, Reisig, and Morash (2004) studied factors leading to re-arrest in a sample of 134 female felony offenders in community corrections in Oregon and Minnesota. They found that poverty status after prison increased the odds of re-arrest by about five times and the odds of supervision violation by about thirteen times. Their recommendation is for policy reforms that provide state-sponsored resources in the areas of childcare, education, health care, and job training, all of which address the causes of economic marginalization associated with crime. Washington State's Department of Correction emphasizes work release programs as a way to help inmates make a successful transition into life on the outside (Fehr, 2004). In addition, residential parenting programs are provided to women on work release who have children. Case managers work with these families to monitor their progress and refer them to other services as needed.

Inmates who pursue a college education while they are in prison have a head start in finding a job upon their release. In 1994, when Congress removed prison inmates from eligibility for Pell Grants, most of these programs came to an abrupt end. A few prisons, such as that at Bedford Hills, restarted a college education program with private money (Fried, 2006). Some can connect upon their release with the Prisoner Re-entry Institute, which fosters the College Initiative program at John Jay College of Criminal Justice in Manhattan to get the courses, monitoring, and financing they need. Such programs, however, are rare.

In 1996, the government strengthened the anti-drug abuse act by authorizing the public housing authorities to evict tenants for drug-related activities. Another law that was passed gave the housing authorities the right to deny public and other federally assisted housing to anyone who has any involvement in a drug-related or violent crime regardless of time passed since the offense (The Sentencing Project, 2007).

Punitive policies such as this and restrictions on financial aid for college students with drug convictions are counterproductive in terms of helping people who were convicted of drug-related offenses get back on their feet. Evans (2006) describes her personal shock in returning to a world that, like her, had changed:

> At the time of my release I had never seen a CD or DVD, had never owned a phone answering machine, and had never seen a cordless phone, much less a cell phone. My computer skills were minimal, and I had no experience with the Internet. . . . I felt overwhelmed by the technology, disoriented, as if I were from another planet. I had difficulty communicating what my life had been like to people around me, and I often felt overwhelmed with feelings of sorrow and separation from the friends I had left in prison. (p. 298)

Summary

Today, women make up 6.9 percent of the prison population, and 12.9 percent of those are confined in jail cells. Although their percentage of the total is small, the increase in the numbers of female inmates has well exceeded the increase for male prisoners, as a study of the latest U.S. government statistics shows.

Race, gender, and class, as we have seen in this chapter, intersect in the reality, indeed, the tragedy, of women's prisons. Viewed another way, one could easily make the argument that the antifeminist and antiwelfare movements are being played out in the courtrooms and prisons of the United States. The war on drugs has taken its toll on poor minority women and on their children, who are destined to grow up in foster homes while their mothers serve their time. The antidrug laws bring their effects to bear disproportionately on persons without political and legal leverage in U.S. society

The euphemisms "sentencing reform" and "welfare reform" are not a threat to rich, white women. The few rich, white women one finds behind prison walls are generally there for murder.

In this chapter, we have seen the circumstances for women in prison come full circle—from confinement in overcrowded, male-run prisons, to removal into maternal reformatories focusing on inmates' moral development, to confinement once again in overcrowded, punitive prisons run by a predominantly male staff. We have turned our attention to two developments in the administration of women's institutions since the 1970s: the rise of prisoner litigation, and the replacement of matrons with male officers.

Today's scandals, which center around sexual abuse and exploitation of female inmates, echo those days gone by when females were originally placed under male authority. Surprisingly, the media, which in the United States have concentrated on the drug war and harsher sentencing laws, seem to have largely overlooked the shocking developments as revealed in the international investigations conducted by Human Rights Watch. In Canada, in contrast, there has been considerable local media coverage of rough treatment of women by male prison officers. In any case, in both countries current litigation has offered prisoners some protection they might not otherwise have had.

In the 1980s, equality for women was the word. In the field of corrections, the focus was on equality of opportunity for female correctional officers in men's prisons and equality of educational and vocational opportunity for male and female offenders. In light of some unintended consequences of the bid for equality, namely, the widespread sexual harassment of female prisoners by male correctional officers (the counterpart of female officers who work without restriction in men's prisons) and the mandatory harsh minimum sentences for drug possession and dealing, women's advocates today are arguing for an empowering feminist approach geared toward women's special needs. We agree with Bloom and Chesney-Lind (2007) that changes in public policy are needed so that the response to women's offending will be one that emphasizes human needs over punitive sanctions.

In conclusion to this chapter, we would like to argue forcefully against the placing of women in male-oriented facilities. For empowerment of women to occur, she suggests, male and female inmates need programs especially geared toward their needs. Ignoring women's reality is not the way to sexual equality, and the whole notion of incarceration for women needs to be carefully evaluated.

Key Terms

Amnesty International *146*
conspiracy laws *133*
ethnic-specific program *160*

Madonna image *129*
prison industrial complex *128*

prison play-families *139*
war on drugs *128*

Critical Thinking Questions

1. Consider prison construction and management as a big business enterprise. What are the ramifications for residents? Why are states privatizing? Discuss advantages and disadvantages.
2. Is there such a thing as the "Madonna image"? Discuss this concept with regard to historical racial differences.
3. How do conspiracy laws hurt women? Make up a situation in which a woman who is innocent of drug dealing can get caught up in the criminal justice net as a result of these laws.
4. How is the war on drugs played out as a war against poor women and minorities?
5. The text briefly theorizes that homophobia in prison may cause inmates to declare themselves to be sisters and mother and daughter. Discuss how this process operates.
6. Discuss advantages and disadvantages to female inmates in forming pseudofamily bonds.
7. Compare the expression of sexuality in men's and women's prison institutions.
8. Describe the pathways by which some women in prison come to adopt different sexual identities.

How do you think this new identity will or will not affect their homecoming?

9. Discuss how the sexual abuse of women came about due to legal factors. Compare the situation in which male officers sexually abuse female inmates and female officers get into trouble with male inmates. Are these offenses exactly the same in terms of gender factors?
10. How does the case for equality not have to entail sameness?
11. Compare two scenarios, one in which a drug user gets treatment in the community and one in which she is sent to serve a prison term. Consider economic costs and consequences for her and her children's lives.
12. Discuss the death penalty in terms of how it is carried out. Does the death penalty bring about justice in our society?
13. Design a women's prison in which you would like to work. Would the way the women's prison in Denmark is run work in the United States?
14. Do small children belong in prison? If so, up to what age? Discuss advantages and disadvantages of prison nurseries.

Web Destinations

Amnesty International: www.amnesty.org

California Coalition for Women Prisoners: www.womenprisoners.org

Canadian Service Canada: www.csc-scc.gc.ca

Children of Incarcerated Parents: http://www.eurochips.org

Death Penalty Information: www.deathpenaltyinfo.org

Elizabeth Fry Societies: www.elizabethfry.ca

Human Rights Watch: www.hrw.org

Stop Prisoner Rape: www.spr.org/pdf

U.S. Department of Justice: www.usdoj.gov

References

Adams, M. (2003). *Fire and ice: The United States, Canada and the myth of converging values.* Toronto: Penguin Press.

American Civil Liberties Union (ACLU). (2004, December). *The forgotten population: A look at death row in the United States through the experiences of women.* Retrieved April 2009 from http://www.aclu.org/capital/women/10627pub20041129.html

American Civil Liberties Union (ACLU). (2005, May 17). *Caught in the net: The impact of drug policies on women and families.* ACLU. Retrieved April 2009 from http://www.aclu.org/images/asset_upload_file393_23513.pdf

American Civil Liberties Union (ACLU). (2006, May 2). *Women at Wisconsin's Taycheedah Prison suffer medical neglect and receive worse mental health care than men.* ACLU. Retrieved January 2009 from http://acluwi.org/wisconsin/police_prisons/Taycheedah/20060502_press_taycheedah.pdf

American Friends Service Committee. (1971). *Struggle for justice: A report on crime and punishment in America.* New York: Hill & Wang.

Amnesty International. (1999). *Not a part of my sentence—Violation of the human rights of women in custody.* New York: Amnesty International.

Amnesty International. (2009). *Death Sentences and Executions in 2008.* Retrieved April 2009 from http://www.amnesty.org/en/library/asset/ACT50/003/2009/en/0b789cb1-baa8-4c1b-bc35-58b606309836/act500032009en.pdf

Applebome, P. (1992, November 14). Jailers charged with sex abuse of 119 women. *New York Times.* Retrieved April 2009 from http://www.nytimes.com/1992/11/14/us/jailers-charged-with-sex-abuse-of-119-women.html

Associated Press. (2005, May 7). Third death in two months at Tutwiler raises more questions. Retrieved August 2009 from http://www.privateci.org/may_05.htm

Australia Bureau of Statistics. (2006, December). Prison population increased 40% over last ten years. Retrieved July 2009 from http://www.abs.gov.au/AUSSTATS/abs@.nsf/Previousproducts/4517.0Media%20Release12004?opendocument&tabname=Summary&prodno=4517.0&issue=2004&num=&view=

Barfield, V. (1985). *Woman on death row.* Minneapolis, MN: World Wide Publications.

Beck, A., and Hughes, T. (2005). *Sexual violence reported by correctional authorities, 2004.* Washington, DC: U.S. Department of Justice, Bureau of Justice Statistics.

Belknap, J. (2007). *The invisible woman: Gender, crime, and justice*, 3rd ed. Belmont, CA: Thomson.

Bloom, B., and Chesney-Lind, M. (2007). Women in prison. In R. Muraskin (ed.), *It's a crime: Women and justice*, 4th ed. (pp. 542–563). Upper Saddle River, NJ: Prentice Hall.

Bloom, B., Owen, B., and Covington, S. (2004). Women offenders and the gendered effects of public policy. *The Review of Policy Research 21*(1): 31–49.

Boudin, K. (1998). Lessons from a mother's program in prison: A psychosocial approach supports women and their children. *Women and Therapy 21*(1): 103–125.

Brink, B. (2008, Summer). Carswell prison blues. *MS*, pp. 40–45.

British Broadcasting Company (BBC). (2001, November 20). Mothers in prison. Woman's Hour. Retrieved July 2009 from http://www.bbc.co.uk/radio4/womanshour/2001_47_tue_03.shtml Britton, D. (2003). *At work in the iron cage: The prison as gendered organization.* New York: New York University Press.

Brownmiller, S. (1975). *Against our will: Men, women, and rape.* New York: Bantam Books.

Bureau of Justice Statistics (BJS). (2000). *Women offenders.* Washington, DC: U.S. Department of Justice.

Bureau of Justice Statistics (BJS). (2007, September). *HIV in prisons, 2005.* Washington, DC: U.S. Department of Justice.

Bureau of Justice Statistics (BJS). (2008a, April 22). *Medical problems of prisoners.* Washington, DC: U.S. Department of Justice. Retrieved January 2009 from http://www.ojp.gov/bjs/pub/html/mpp/mpp.htm

Bureau of Justice Statistics (BJS). (2008b, August). *Parents in prison and their minor children.* BJS. Retrieved January 2009 from http://www.ojp.gov/bjs/pub/pdf/pptmc.pdf

Bureau of Justice Statistics (BJS). (2008c, June). *Prison inmates at midyear 2007.* Washington, DC: U.S. Department of Justice.

Bureau of Justice Statistics (BJS). (2008d, December). *Prisoners in 2007.* Washington, DC: U.S. Department of Justice. Retrieved January 2009 from http://www.ojp.gov/bjs/pub/pdf/p07.pdf

Canadian Human Rights Commission. (2004, March 19). *Protecting their rights.* Retrieved from http://www.chrc-ccdp.ca/legislation_policies/chapter1-en.asp?highlight=1

Carroll, J. (1998, February 4). Tucker executed by lethal injection. *The Irish Times*, p. 1.

Cecil, D. K. (2008). Looking beyond Caged Heat: Media images of women in prison. *Feminist Criminology 2*: 304–326.

Chesney-Lind, M., and Pasko, L. (2004). *The female offender: Girls, women, and crime*, 2nd ed. Thousand Oaks, CA: Sage.

Children of Imprisoned Parents (Eurochips). (2005, March). News: Sweden. Eurochips. Retrieved July 2009 from http://www.eurochips.org/uk_news.html

Corbett, S. (2007, March 18). The women's war. *New York Times Magazine*. Cover story.

Cordon, S. (2005, February 17). Correctional service promises changes in women's jails. *The Canadian Press*. Retrieved July 2009 from http://www.thecanadianpress.com/news_and_information.aspx?id=1600

Correctional Association of New York. (2008, March). Women and HIV/Hepatitis C fact sheet. Women in Prison Project. Retrieved January 2009 from http://correctionalassociation.org/publications/download/wipp/factsheets/HIV_Hep_C_Fact_Sheet_2008.pdf

Correctional Service Canada (CSC). (2007). *CSC action plan in response to the report of the Canadian human rights commission*. Ottawa, Canada: CSC. Retrieved January 2009 from http://www.csc-scc.gc.ca/text/prgrm/fsw/gender4/CHRC_response-eng.shtml

Correctional Service of Canada. (2008, December 18). Aboriginal offenders. Retrieved August 2009 from http://www.csc-scc.gc.ca/text/plcy/cdshtm/702-cde-eng.shtml

Covington, S. (2006). *A woman's journey home: Challenges for offenders and their children*. Washington, DC: U.S. Department of Health and Human Services. Retrieved August 2009 from http://aspe.hhs.gov/hsp/prison2home02/Covington.htm

Craig, S. C. (2009). A historical review of mother and child programs for incarcerated women. *The Prison Journal*. Doi:10:1177/0032885508329768

Crites, L. (1976). *The female offender*. Lexington, MA: Lexington Books.

Davis, A. (2003). *Are prisons obsolete?* New York: Seven Stories Press.

Death Penalty Information. (2008). *Women and the death penalty*. Retrieved January 2009 from http://www.deathpenaltyinfo.org/node/2311

Diaz-Cotto, J. (1996). *Gender, ethnicity, and the state: Latina and Latino prison politics*. Albany, NY: New York State University Press.

Donaldson, S. (1995, May). Can we put an end to inmate rape? *USA Today 123*: 41–42.

Dostoevsky, F. (1969) [1864]. *Notes from the underground*. Washington, DC: University Press of America.

Dreidger, S. D. (1997, January, 27). Showdown of P4W: Women are being moved into men's prisons. *Maclean's 110*, p. 4.

Enos, S. (2001). *Mothering from the inside: Parenting in a women's prison*. Albany, NY: State University of New York Press.

European Commission (2002, February 28). Is the commission aware of the progress of the experiment at Amerswiel prison? Section 26.9. Official Journal of the European Communities. Retrieved August 2009 from http://eur-lex.europa.eu/LexUriServ/LexUriServ.do?uri=OJ:C:2002:229E:0054:0055:EN:PDF

Evans, L. (2006). Locked up, then locked out: Women coming out of prison. *Women & Therapy, 29* (3/4), 285–308.

Fahim, K., and Zraick, K. (2008, November 17). Seeing failure as mother as factor in sentencing. *The New York Times*. Retrieved January 2008 from www.nytimes.com/2008/11/17/nyregion/17nixzmary.html

Faith, K. (1993). *Unruly women: The politics of confinement and resistance*. Vancouver, British Columbia: Press Gang Publishing.

Faith, K. (2004). Progressive rhetoric, regressive policies: Canadian prisons for women. In B. Price and N. Sokoloff (eds.), *The criminal justice system and women: Offenders, victims, and workers* (pp. 281–288). New York: McGraw Hill.

Farr, K. A. (2000). Defeminizing and dehumanizing female murderers: Depictions of lesbians on death row. *Women and Criminal Justice 11*(1): 49–66.

Fehr, L. (2004, October). *Corrections Today 66*(6): 82–85.

Feinman, C. (1994). *Women in the criminal justice system*, 3rd ed. Westport, CT: Praeger.

Feuer, A. (2007). City to pay damages for strip searches. *New York Times*. Retrieved January 2009 from http://www.nytimes.com/2007/10/05/nyregion/05strip.html

Fisher, A. (2004). *If I knew then*. Lincoln, Nebraska: iUniverse.

Fox, J. G. (1984, March). Women's prison policy, prisoner activism, and the impact of the contemporary feminist movement: A case study. *The Prison Journal 64*: 25.

Fried, J. (2006, October 18). Leaving prison doors behind, some find new doors open. *New York Times*. Retrieved January 2009 from http://www.nytimes.com/2006/10/18/education/18convict.html

Gaarder, E., and Belknap, J. (2004). Little women: Girls in adult prison. *Women and Criminal Justice 15*(2): 51–80.

General Accounting Office. (1999). *Women in prison: Issues and challenges confronting U.S. correctional systems.* Washington, DC: U.S. Department of Justice.

Giallombardo, R. (1966). *Society of women: A study of a woman's prison.* New York: Wiley.

Goffman, E. (1961). *Asylums: Essays on the social situation of mental patients and other inmates.* Garden City, NY: Doubleday.

Golden, R. (2005). *War on the family: Mothers in prison and the families they leave behind.* New York: Routledge.

Gorman, C. (2009, January 15). The ultimate prison? Radio Netherlands. Retrieved January 2009 from http://www.radionetherlands.nl/thestatewerein/otherstates/tswi-090115-ultimate-prison

Harris, J. (1988). *They always call us ladies: Stories from prison.* New York: Zebra Books.

Hensley, C., Castle, T., and Tewksbury, R. (2003). Inmate-to-inmate sexual coercion in a prison for women. *Journal of Offender Rehabilitation* 37(2): 77–87.

Hensley, C., Tewksbury, R., and Koscheski, M. (2002). *Women and Criminal Justice* 13(2/3): 125–139.

Holtfreter, K., Reisig, M., and Morash, M. (2004). Poverty, state capital, and recidivism among women. *Criminology and Public Policy* 3(2): 185–209.

Hughes, R. (1987). *The fatal shore: The epic of Australia's founding.* New York: Alfred A. Knopf.

Human Rights Watch Women's Rights Project. (1996). *All too familiar: Sexual abuse of women in U.S. state prisons.* New York: Human Rights Watch.

Human Rights Watch (HWR). (2007, December 16). New report by justice department under scores need for zero tolerance. HWR. Retrieved January 2008 from http://www.hrw.org/en/news/2007/12/15/us-federal-statistics-show-widespread-prison-rape

International Centre for Prison Studies. (2008, April). King's College, London Retrieved January 2009 from http://www.hmprisonservice.gov.uk/assets/documents/10003BB3womens_prisons_int_review_final_report.pdf

Irish Times. (1998, February 5). Robinson critical of U.S. execution of double killer.

Irwin, J. (1980). *Prisons in turmoil.* Boston, MA: Little, Brown.

Jones, A. (1980). *Women who kill.* New York: Holt, Rinehart & Winston.

Jones, A. (2009). *Women who kill*, 2nd ed. City University of New York: Feminist Press.

Kassindja, F. (1998). *Do they hear you when you cry?* New York: Delacorte Press.

King's College London (2007). World prison population still growing. News archive 2007. Retrieved August 2009 from http://www.kcl.ac.uk/news/news_details.php?news_id=507&year=2007

Kopatich, K. (1998, May 8). Interviewed by social work student Lynette Keefe at the women's prison in Mitchellville, Iowa.

Laster, K. (1994). Arbitrary chivalry: Women and capital punishment in Victoria, Australia 1842–1967. *Women and Criminal Justice* 6(1): 67–95.

Laughlin, J. S., Arrigo, B., Blevins, K., and Coston, T. (2008). Incarcerated mothers and child visitation. *Criminal Justice Policy Review* 19(2): 215–138.

Lewis, W. D. (1965). *From Newgate to Dannemora.* Ithaca, NY: Cornell University Press.

Loper, G. E. (2004, February). Seen around town: Sister Kathleen A. O'Shea. The Home Page of George Edward Loper. Retrieved January 2009 from http://george.loper.org/trends/2004/Feb/928.html

Lord, E. A. (2008). The challenges of mentally ill female offenders in prison. *Criminal Justice and Behavior* 35(8): 928–942.

Luscombe, R. (2005, August 26). Fight to stop Texas woman's execution. *The Guardian.* Retrieved at www.guardian.co.uk

Lutze, F. (2003). Ultramasculine stereotypes and violence in the control of women inmates. In B. Zaitzow and J. Thomas (eds.), *Women in prison: Gender and social control* (pp. 183–203). Boulder, CO: Lynne Rienner Publishers.

Lydersen, K. (2007). Red tape lets guards rape women prisoners, suit argues. *The NewStandard.* Retrieved August 2009 from http://www.november.org/stayinfo/breaking06/RapeSuit.html.

McDaniels-Wilson, C., and Belknap, J. (2008). The extensive sexual violation and sexual abuse histories of incarcerated women. *Violence against Women 14*: 1090–1127.

McKinley, J. (2007, June 3). Gay inmates to be granted conjugal visits in California. *New York Times.* Retrieved January 2009 from http://www.nytimes.com/2007/06/03/us/03visit.html?th&emc=th

Messing, J., and Heeren, J. (2009). Gendered justice: Domestic homicide and the death penalty. *Feminist Criminology* 4(2): 170–188.

Moe, A., and Ferraro, K. (2003). Malign neglect or benign respect: Women's health care in a carceral setting. *Women and Criminal Justice* 14(4): 53–80.

Moir, A., and Jessel, D. (1991). *Brain sex: The real difference between men and women.* New York: Delta.

Morash, M., and Schram, P. (2002). *The prison experience: Special issues of women in prison.* Prospect Heights, IL: Waveland Press.

Muraskin, R. (2007). Disparate treatment in correctional facilities: Women incarcerated. In R. Muraskin (ed.), *It's a crime: Women and justice*, 4th ed. (pp. 493–506). Upper Saddle River, NJ: Prentice Hall.

National Business Review. (2008, September 11). Parliament passes babies in prison law change. Retrieved January 2009 from http://www.nbr.co.nz/article/parliament-passes-babies-prison-law-change-35118

Office of Performance Evaluations. (2003, February). *Programs for incarcerated mothers*. State of Idaho Legislature. Retrieved from www.legislature.idaho.gov/ope

Owen, B. (1998). *In the mix: Struggle and survival in a women's prison*. Albany, NY: State University of New York Press.

Paulson, A. (2008, September 25). Poll: 60 percent of Americans oppose mandatory minimum sentences. *Christian Science Monitor*, p. 1.

Peet, J. (2004, May 25). *Canada's system specializes in unusual solutions*. Trenton, NJ: The Star-Ledger. Retrieved from www.starledger.com

Petersilia, J. (2003). *When prisoners come home: Parole and prisoner reentry*. New York: Oxford University Press.

Petrillo, M. (2007). The Corston Report: A review of women with particular vulnerabilities in the criminal justice system. *Probation Journal 54*: 284–287.

Pfeiffer, M. B. (2007). *Crazy in America: The hidden tragedy of our criminal mentally ill*. New York: Carroll & Graf Publishers.

Pollack, S. (2004). Anti-oppressive social work practice with women in prison: Discursive reconstructions and alternative practices. *British Journal of Social Work 34*(5): 693–707.

Pollack, S. (2007). "I'm just not good in relationships": Victimization discourses and the gendered regulation of criminalized women. *Feminist Criminology 2*: 158–174.

Pollock, J. M. (1998). *Counseling women in prison*. Thousand Oaks, CA: Sage.

Pollock, J. M. (2002). Parenting programs in women's prisons. *Women and Criminal Justice 14*(1): 131–148.

Prison Legal News. (1995). New stateside data show prison rape a widespread problem. *Prison Legal News 6*(11): 17.

Prison Legal News. (1998, May). Bureau of prisons sexual abuse suit settled for $500,000. *Prison Legal News*, p. 9.

Rasche, C. (2007). The dislike of female offenders among correctional officers: A need for specialized training. In R. Muraskin (ed.), *It's a crime: Women and justice*, 4th ed. (pp. 689–706). Upper Saddle River, NJ: Pearson.

Rathbone, C. (2005). *A world apart: Women, prison and life behind bars*. New York: Random House.

Reed, D., and Reed, E. (2004). Mothers in prison and their children. In B. Price and N. Sokoloff (eds.), *The criminal justice system and women: Offenders, victims, and workers*, 3rd ed. (pp. 261–279). New York: McGraw-Hill.

Samuel, L. (2003, October). Nowhere to go. *The Chicago Reporter*. Retrieved from www.chicagoreporter.com

Sandifer, J. (2008). Evaluating the efficacy of a parenting program for incarcerated mothers. The *Prison Journal 88*: 423–445.

Schulberg, D. (2007). Dying to get out. In R. Muraskin (ed.), *It's a crime: Women and justice*, 4th ed. (pp. 572–591). Upper Saddle River, NJ: Prentice Hall.

Schwartzapfel, B. (2008, Fall). Lullabies behind bars. *MS*, pp. 16–17.

Seidel, J. (2009, January 6). Female inmate described rapes in lawsuit against state. Detroit Free Press. Retrieved January 2009 from http://www.freep.com/article/20090106/NEWS06/901060369

Sentencing Project. (2007, May). *Women in the criminal justice system*. Washington, DC: The Sentencing Project. Retrieved January 2009 from www.sentencingproject.org

Severance, T. (2004). The prison lesbian revisited. *Journal of Gay and Lesbian Social Services 17*(3): 39–57.

Sharp, S., and Marcus-Mendoza, S. (2001). It's a family affair: Incarcerated women and their families. *Women and Criminal Justice 12*(4): 21–49.

Shoemaker, J. (2007). Meeting the challenge: Positive culture in women's facilities. *Corrections Today 69*(40): 68–71.

Smith, B. V. (2006). Sexual abuse of women in United States prisons: a modern corollary of slavery. *Fordham Urban Law Journal 33*(2): 571–608.

Smith, K. (2008, December 17). The wisdom of pardons. *USA Today*, p.11A.

Sodja, Z. (2006). Human rights and U.S. female prisoners. *Women and Therapy 29*(3/4): 57–72.

Stein, B. (1996, July). Life in prison: Sexual abuse. *The Progressive*, pp. 23–24.

Stop Prisoner Rape (2003, December). *The sexual abuse of female inmates of Ohio*. Stop Prisoner Rape. Retrieved from www.spr.org/pdf/sexabuseohio

Sunday Times (2009, August 31). *The pink mile: Women on death row*. London: Sunday Times. Retrieved April 2009 from http://women.timesonline.co.uk/tol/life_and_style/women/article4619390.ece

Talvi, S. (2007). *Women behind bars: The crisis of women in the U.S. prison system*. Emerville, CA: Seal Press.

Taycheedah Correctional Institution agrees to federal demands: It's ordered to improve mental health care for women Milwaukee. (2008, September 6). *Journal Sentinel*. Retrieved January 2009 from http://www.jsonline.com/news/wisconsin/32563439.html

Turner, A., and Ganza, C. (2005). Newton is executed for slaying her family. *Houston Chronicle*. Retrieved from www.chron.com/cs/CDA

Tyler, K. (1998, June 10). Personal correspondence from Iowa Correctional Institute for Women.

United Kingdom Parliament. (2004, October 28). *Debate, House of Lords*. London. Retrieved from www.publications.parliament.uk

U.S. Department of Justice Office of Inspector General (OIG). (2005, May 13). Sex abuse of federal inmates by guards "a significant problem." OIG. Retrieved from www.november.org

van Wormer, K. (2001). *Counseling female offenders and victims: A strengths-restorative perspective*. New York: Springer Publishing.

Van Wormer, K. (2004). *Confronting oppression, restoring justice: From policy analysis to social action*. Alexandria, VA: Council on Social Work Education.

van Wormer, K., and Kaplan, L. (2006). Results of a national survey of women's prison wardens: The case for gender specific treatment. *Women and Therapy 29*(1/2): 133–151.

Walker, S. (1980). *Popular justice: A history of American criminal justice*. New York: Oxford University Press.

Warren, J. (2005, June 19). Rethinking treatment of female prisoners. *Los Angeles Times*. Retrieved from www.latimes.com/news/local

Whaley, R., Moe, A., Eddy, J., and Daugherty, J. (2007). The domestic violence experiences of women in community corrections. *Women & Criminal Justice 18*(3): 25–45.

Women's Prison Association. (2009, July 13). Prison nursery programs a growing trend. Retrieved July 2009 from http://www.corrections.com/news/article/21644

World Health Organization. (2009, June 24). Ten things to know about women and prisons. Regional Office for Europe. Retrieved July 2009 from http://www.euro.who.int/prisons/topics/20080617_1

7

Restorative Justice for Female Victims and Offenders

Restorative justice is an umbrella term that comprises a series of strategies for restoring justice when a wrong has been committed; this could be to one person, a group of people, or an entire community. Restorative justice is the attempt to provide social justice through healing encounters between victims and offenders within a community context (Presser and Gaarder, 2004).

The roots of restorative-justice theory can be found in the practices of indigenous peoples throughout the world from ancient times, and in more modern times in Canadian Mennonites (van Wormer, 2004; Zehr, 2002). Restorative justice focuses on a philosophical belief that crime should be redefined as harm done to specific victims (including a community) rather than as a violation of arbitrary state laws that identify particular behavior as criminal. Reparation for the harm done is central to the restorative process.

Among the restorative interventions that are most commonly applied today are **victim–offender conferencing** or dialoguing, family group conferencing, healing circles, and community reparations. These are all forms of resolving conflict; all of them have relevance to female offending and victimization. To get an idea of how the processes work, consider the case examples below. The first is based on a personal interview that van Wormer had with the murder victim's mother; the second summarizes a case found on a restorative justice Web site; the third is a description taken from a news account that appeared on a Canadian Internet rape survivors' Web site.

1. When first contacted by the Iowa Administrator of Victim and Restorative Justice Programs to participate in a meeting with her daughter's murderer, who was now in prison serving out her sentence, Cindy refused to participate in the meeting. Her daughter had been killed by another woman, Tara Krause, after a dispute over a man. The crime had been horribly brutal: Tara had run over the victim with her car, which had dragged her body, caught underneath the car, for several blocks. The reason Cindy refused this meeting was that the way it was told to her, she felt that the young woman was using the fact that she had been drinking as an excuse. However, when she read Tara's letter requesting the meeting, she was impressed that the inmate was taking responsibility for the crime. Both women received counseling to prepare them for the encounter. At the prison, the women met for three and a half hours, each expressing her feelings about the crime. In the end, Cindy told Tara that she wished the best for her, that her daughter would have wanted that for her, that she live a good life, and avoid the bad company she had been in before. Since Tara was soon to be paroled, the meeting took on a special significance for both of the participants and resolved a number of difficult issues.

2. On probation and unable to function in school, Alyssa (not her real name), 18, was in and out of alternative programs, youth detention facilities, and group homes as a result of her continuing delinquency. With the approval of the Bucks County Juvenile Court in Pennsylvania and family members and Alyssa, a Family Group Decision Making conference was set up. Twenty people, including the probation officer and family group conferencing facilitator, attended the conference; many were invited by family members. Following the opening prayer in which all present held hands and instructions by the facilitator, family members were left alone to come up with a solution. Two and a half hours later, the professionals were asked to rejoin the group. The family had come up with a plan for Alyssa, outlining solutions for her living situation, education and work requirements, and legal obligations, and stressing reconciliation with family, church, and community. All present were satisfied with the process (Welden, 2007).

3. Alkali Lake in British Columbia is well known in the alcoholism literature for the wonderful work that was done to bring recovery to virtually the entire tribal community through the persistence of a few AA (Alcoholics Anonymous) members. Because of the tribal bonding that took place there, Alkali Lake was an appropriate setting for the healing circle that occurred between a Catholic bishop and the woman he had wronged years before. Marilyn Belleau chose this healing ceremony to provide a sense of "freedom" to herself and other natives who had been wronged. In taking this course, Belleau was closing the door on legal remedies, which had resulted in an overturning of the bishop's conviction on appeal. During the healing circle, O'Connor was required to listen while Belleau and other complainants spoke in detail about how his sexual advances hurt them, their families, and communities. Belleau described how, while an 18-year-old employee at the residential school, the bishop had had sexual intercourse with her. One of the complainants said that O'Connor had fathered her baby. Altogether there were thirty-eight participants at the ceremony, including federal government officials and the current bishop of the parish. The ceremony was divided into three parts, each part of which began with the lighting of a sacred sage pipe. The circle provided the possibility of healing between individuals as well as between British Columbia's natives and the Catholic Church. Although the bishop's apology seemed less than sincere to some, from all accounts, the process did much to bring the community and church together (Bucci, 1998).

Common to all the above illustrations is a conception of justice that is caring of the victim-survivors even as it stresses individual responsibility on the part of the offenders. The goal of this interactive and informal means of resolution of conflict is to restore all the participants to healthy and productive functioning within the community (Van Ness, 2004). In the above situations, this goal was accomplished.

INTRODUCTION

How does restorative justice compare to standard forms of criminal justice and how does it meet the needs of female victims and offenders? Unlike the Anglo-Saxon-derived system, which harks back to primitive practices related to combat, restorative justice can be considered to be on the feminine end of the masculinity–femininity continuum of sex role behavior. Unlike conventional processes, restorative justice is more about making amends and providing **restitution** than about punishment. Representing a paradigm shift in judicial philosophy, this new vision focuses more attention on the harm to victims and communities and less on the act of lawbreaking (Van Ness, 2004; Zehr, 2002). At the macro level, restorative justice is about peacemaking, at the micro level about relationship. In both instances, people come together from various sides of the law and from various backgrounds and lifestyles. From the point of view of the offender, restorative justice is about change and redemption; from the view of the victim it is about healing. Above all, this form of justice is about empowerment.

Restorative justice requires a new way of thinking about crime and other forms of wrongdoing, a way of thinking that is victim- not offender-centered, and a way of thinking that is concerned with getting at the truth when a crime is committed rather than putting the burden of proof on the victim and the state and rewarding pleas of not guilty over honest and humbling admission of guilt. From a feminist standpoint, restorative justice is a process consistent with women's "ways of knowing" and communication through storytelling. Feminist criminologists generally are welcoming of this new vision as a relatively informal, community-oriented form of justice that is focused on victims and allows offenders to "come clean" about what they have done and why (Failinger, 2006). The lack of legalism and chance to get away from a winner-take-all mentality are appealing qualities to feminists who seek a caring, interactive process. By the same token, feminist criminologists are correct to be skeptical of any process that involves dialoguing in cases of domestic violence.

This chapter provides an overview of restorative justice as a process and shows its relevance to girls and women in trouble for wrongdoing. The criminal justice system, with its roots in masculine practices of obtaining justice, is contrasted with the teachings of restorative justice, which are much more on the feminine, caring side of the equation. The focus of the chapter is on victim–offender conferencing. The subject of the first half of the chapter is programming for juvenile and adult offenders, with the emphasis on gender-sensitive restorative programs. More controversially, the second half of the chapter tackles the relevance of the restorative justice format to situations of gendered violence—partner battering and rape.

A major argument of this chapter is that restorative principles are consistent with those of feminist criminology, both in terms of core values and areas of interest. The core values of restorative justice, as succinctly summarized by Adams (2002), are healing rather than hurting, moral learning, community participation and caring, respectful dialogue, apology, and making amends to the victim. Consistent with feminist values, restorative philosophy is holistic in its concern with the whole person; the emphasis is on non-dichotomous communication (as opposed to adversarial litigation); and the process is responsive to the voices of people whose voices are rarely heard.

Women who have been victimized by crime frequently find the criminal justice system disempowering. This is especially true in situations of family violence. In cases of sexual assault as well, the victim-survivors are often re-victimized as they seek justice through the criminal justice system. Rape victims rarely report the crime to police in anticipation of courtroom censure and brutal cross-examination on the witness stand. Victims of acquaintance or date rape are especially reluctant to undergo this courtroom process. Part of the problem may be that the laws that were framed to protect citizens from violence by strangers do not easily lend themselves to the demands of interpersonal situations (Frisch, 2003). Part of the problem too may lie in our adversarial system of justice.

THE ADVERSARY SYSTEM

The adversarial process dominates Anglo-Saxon justice today. This process has its roots in the Middle Ages in England when hired combatants fought duels on behalf of accused individuals. It was a decidedly masculine system in every respect. Then, as now, it was a case of "may the strong man win." Crime eventually became defined as an offense against the state. The role of judge emerged as a sort of referee between the disputing parties.

Today, deliberation takes place according to standardized, one-size-fits-all courtroom procedures or more commonly a plea-bargaining arrangement in which the victim's input tends to be minimal (Van Ness and Strong, 2002). In the atmosphere of warring forces that ensues, families and friends of the accused are torn apart from families and friends on the other side of the law. Such court processes and plea bargaining behind closed doors do little to enhance communication and healing among members of the community.

The failure of the criminal justice system in meeting the needs of victims of crime and the failure to provide an atmosphere in which the offender is rewarded for expressing remorse are common themes in the literature (see Rozee and Koss, 2001; van Wormer, 2004; Zehr, 2002). The first advice any competent lawyer gives his or her clients accused of a crime is to keep quiet and admit to nothing because anything they say will be used against them in the judicial process. Truth-telling, in contrast, is a primary quality of restorative justice (Zehr, 2002). In contrast to standard criminal justice practices, restorative justice processes are highly consistent with women's ways of knowing and feminist theory as articulated by Gilligan, 1982 and Van Den Bergh, 1995. These processes are people-centered, victim-centered, and conducive to open communication (van Wormer, 2004; van Wormer, 2009).

MODELS OF RESTORATIVE JUSTICE

The four models most relevant to women's issues are victim–offender conferencing, family group conferencing, healing circles, and community reparations. *Victim–offender conferencing*, sometimes incorrectly referred to as victim–offender mediation, brings together parties where one person has injured another for the sake of resolution, if possible, righting the wrong. Unlike the mediation model, restorative justice recognizes its participants as victim and offender, rather than as disputants (Presser and Gaarder, 2004). Victim–offender conferencing remains the most widely examined and empirically grounded of the restorative justice formats (Umbreit et al., 2006). The practice of providing victims a chance to meet with offenders began in 1974 in Kitchener,

Ontario, when Mennonite probation officers developed an initiative that was based on providing restitution directly to the individuals who were harmed, in this case by vandalism. The early efforts involved youthful offenders. Today there are over 300 victim–offender programs in the United States and 1,400 worldwide. The largest programs to date have been offered through victim assistance services of state departments of corrections (Umbreit et al., 2006).

The typical format is this: A trained professional opens the conference and provides a brief description of the situation. Let's imagine a situation where an adolescent male has endangered his life or that of his neighbors in some way. The victims, since they are the central focus of this event, will begin by describing the harm that was done to them and their emotional reactions to the incident. Their family members likely will have a say as well. The offender, with his supporters at his side, describes the background pertaining to his misdeed and acknowledges the depth of the harm he has caused. His supporters might provide some positive facts about the offender that speak of his moral character. They might describe some personal difficulties the offender has been having; for example, if the individual is of an immigrant status or if he was having some adjustment problems at school, this fact might be brought out. In answer to questions by the participants, the offender typically will describe his or her part in the incident that took place, taking full responsibility for his or her behavior. Following further informal discussion, the offender acknowledges the damage that was done, offers restitution of some sort, expresses remorse, and issues an apology.

This format of victim–offender conferencing has special resonance for female victims and offenders. A review of the restorative justice literature shows that practically all the case illustrations involve women one way or the other, directly or indirectly. Women as family members of a car crash victim, for example, might seek to meet with the driver of the vehicle that hit their loved one. Mothers and grandmothers actively participate in family conferencing as part of the juvenile restorative justice process, and female crime victims might form a panel to speak to groups of offenders. This latter strategy closely relates to women's issues in that the individual participants who share their personal stories of victimization with offenders are most often women, and the offenders are most often men. Typically, the speakers are survivors of crimes like rape, robbery, and attempted murder. The participants are not the victims of the particular offenders in the audience. Victim–offender panels are used as a means of getting male abusers to feel the victims' pain and to feel remorse for the harm they have done.

In the early days of the growth of restorative justice in the United States, practically all the cases involved crimes such as theft, vandalism, and destruction caused by negligence. No one foresaw that such processes would be applied to situations such as attempted murder and homicide, not to mention rape and domestic assault. But when requests to expand the service into these more serious areas came from the victims themselves, facilitators of victim–offender conferencing began to ponder the possibility (Umbreit et al., 2006). Today, one hears of restorative justice processes used behind prison walls in the aftermath of murder and of death row residents meeting in formal sessions with their victims' families. Reflecting the seriousness of these situations, the facilitators and participants require longer case preparation and counseling. Special attention must be paid to survivors' expectations and feelings about the encounter, screening of offenders who are psychopathic or otherwise unsuitable, finding facilitators with extensive training and experience, and the clarification of boundary issues for all parties. Negotiation with correctional officials unfamiliar with principles of restorative justice may be necessary as well.

Family group conferencing (*FGC*) is an outgrowth of both (New Zealand) indigenous and feminist practice concerns stemming from the international women's and children's rights movements of the late 1980s and beyond. This solutions-based process most often is used by child welfare departments in cases of child abuse and neglect. Despite differences among jurisdictions, one common theme is overriding: **family group conferences** are more likely than traditional forms of dispute resolution to give effective voice to those who are traditionally disadvantaged. Unlike victim–offender conferencing, the focus here is not on the harm done so much as on the welfare of an abused or neglected child and of the family as a whole. This approach is appropriate to the needs of women in that the focus is often on parenting and helping the mother with problems in care giving to take better care of the child, often through support from other relatives and direct help in child care responsibilities. This model works well in close-knit, minority communities with extended family ties (Burford and Hudson, 2000; Kemp, Whittaker, and Tracy, 2000).

Healing circles offer a format borrowed from North American native rituals that is especially relevant for work with victims/survivors in providing family and/or community support. Such support is often needed following the trauma caused by a crime of violence such as rape. This innovative approach is ideal for recovering alcoholics/addicts who wish to be reconciled to loved ones as well. The Toronto District School Board has adopted this approach for situations in which students have victimized others at school (*Toronto Star*, 2001).

In the healing circle, the people touched by the offense gather together, review the incident or incidents, try to make sense of it, and hopefully reach a peaceful resolution. In order for consensus to be achieved, all participants must have a voice. In addition to the use of consensus for decision making, several aspects of the circle process reinforce the democratic ideal of equal voice and equal responsibility (Pranis, 2001). A talking piece, which may be a giant bird feather, has an equalizing effect in structuring dialogue as it is passed from speaker to speaker to provide an opportunity for everyone present to speak. The community's role is to engage in discussion and to identify the factors that led to the offending behavior and to seek ways to eliminate those problems (Doerner and Lab, 2005).

Restorative initiatives are not limited to work with individuals and families but can also be successfully applied to the unjust treatment of whole populations. At the macro level, *community reparation* is the form of restorative justice that occurs outside of the boundaries of criminal justice. The violator here is the state. Unlike traditional courts of law, truth and reconciliation commissions focus primarily on victims and on their testimony. The Truth Commission held in South Africa in the 1990s to address the wounds inflicted by apartheid is one of the most powerful examples of restoration. The mandate was unprecedented: to provide public acknowledgment of the massive wrongdoings that had been inflicted upon black and mixed race people by the previous governments. Compensation came in the form of public testimony and apology.

Wartime persecutions, rape of the land and the people, slave labor, and mass murder are forms of crimes against humanity that demand some form of compensation for survivors and their families, even generations later, as long as the wounds are palpable. Over thirty truth commissions have been established to officially investigate and provide a record of the pattern of abuses that were committed against a people (Reddy, 2004). Healing the woundedness of whole populations of people is the ultimate goal of reparative justice. **Community reparation** generally involves public acknowledgement of responsibility for the crimes against humanity and sometimes monetary compensation (Braithwaite, 2002, p.207). When the state is the culprit, restorative justice means reparations for the human rights violations that occurred. Reparations may take the form of governmental acceptance of responsibility for the wrongs done, often following a national inquiry.

A landmark decision for women's rights occurred when sexual violence was included as a war crime by International Criminal Tribunals for former Yugoslavia and Rwanda, where large numbers of women had been raped as an act of war. Then again in Peru, the Truth and Reconciliation Commission investigated sexual violence against women as a human rights violation (Falcón, 2005). Sisters and daughters of detained men during a civil war had been systematically raped and subjected to other forms of sexual abuse to force the men to talk. The Commission's final report provided appropriate recognition of the women's victimization and recognition of sexual violence in such cases as crimes against humanity.

On the international stage, the thrust for a restorative vision has been embraced through the role of the United Nations. Following consultation with nongovernmental organizations, the UN, through its Commission on Crime Prevention and Criminal Justice, approved a Canadian resolution that encourages countries to use the basic principles of restorative justice and to incorporate restorative justice programming in their criminal justice processes (see Van Ness, 2002, "UN Crime Commission Acts on Basic Principles"). Sadly, the United States did not participate in the drawing up of these guidelines.

Having reviewed the four basic models of restorative justice, we now turn to the population with whom it has been the most widely and successfully used—youthful offenders.

IN THE JUVENILE JUSTICE SYSTEM

Restorative justice practices have become popular in state juvenile justice systems in recent years, with many adopting new practices for handling crime and punishment (Zavlek and Maniglia, 2007). Because of the importance of intimacy and relationships to the growing girl, restorative strategies offer an ideal gendered form of conflict resolution. Typically girls are better able than boys to accept accountability for their harmful actions to others and to confront the difficulties they have experienced in their own interpersonal relationships when they are given the opportunity to connect relationally with service providers (Zavlek and Maniglia). For girls and young women, adopting a female-responsive philosophy means allowing them the opportunity to both experience meaningful accountability to their victims and restore their own broken relationships (Zavlek and Maniglia). To prepare them for this process, the girls often need to get in touch with their own earlier victimizations and the feelings that were aroused at the time, and probably repressed or transformed into anger. This therapy process is all about helping the juvenile offenders develop empathy skills for persons they have harmed and to repair broken relationships in need of restoration.

Miriam DiBiase (2000) makes the case for gender-specific treatment programs combined with a restorative philosophy to meet girls' developmental needs. Programs such as the Alternative Rehabilitative Communities Program at Harrisburg, Pennsylvania, address personal and romantic relationships, abuse issues, victimization, self-esteem, and sexual responsibility. The programs also emphasize victim empathy and community restitution. Restorative programming speaks to the victim–offender nexus. Since many of the girls have been victimized themselves, they often can come to appreciate the impact of their behavior on others, and the need to move beyond excusing themselves from irresponsible behaviors due to their own histories of victimization.

Minnesota in particular has infused restorative justice strategies within its Department of Corrections and has also developed gender-specific programming within its juvenile and adult institutions. The department awards model program grants to community-based programs that provide gender-specific services. Under the auspices of such activities, the state has become a leader of gender-specific programming for serious and chronic juvenile offenders. The Minnesota Department of Corrections additionally employs restorative justice planners to train people at the county level for diversionary conferencing (to divert offenders from prison), emphasizing above all a spirit of dialogue and healing.

AMICUS in Minneapolis is an exemplary program for troubled girls for its unique combination of gender-specific concepts and restorative justice principles (Gaarder and Hesselton, 2008). AMICUS has admirably faced the challenge of trying to counter what the girls, hardened by their experiences with the criminal justice system, have learned: Don't trust anyone; don't admit your offenses; the victim is out to get you. Sitting in a circle with victims, family members (their own and the victims'), and their supportive probation officers, the girls are now asked to trust that healing and truth will emerge from the circle. Although the individuals level with the offender about how her behavior has caused them harm, a spirit of empathy, dialogue, and healing prevails. At-risk girls are empowered through this process and support is provided to family members and communities in ways that reduce the likelihood of juvenile offending. Recently the program's name was changed to RADIUS.

The following case example of a victim–offender process is provided on the program's Web site by Gordon (2004). This passage below is based on personal testimonies from school officials as they reacted to the student's offense. (Sarah was serving time in a long-term residential juvenile facility after she had threatened a police officer [who had been summoned to the school] with a knife).

> Sarah then responded. She said she was very sorry. She said that she never thought about what a serious offense bringing a knife to school was, and that she would never do it again. She said that she really wants to be home again, but agreed that she was getting what she needed right now. She also agreed that when she is on her meds, her life goes much better.
>
> The Circle Keeper then asked the group if there were any ideas of what Sarah could do to repair the harm. There was a silence, and then one teacher said that the apology was all she needed. The principal agreed and said that he felt that it was over. Another teacher asked if Sarah would keep her informed of her doings. "The best thing you could do," she said, "would be to promise us you will stay on your meds. And, when you are out and about, let us know how you're doing! Send me a card." Sarah promised to do those things. Then the adults wanted to know her plans, so she told them. They applauded her ideas.
>
> She then thanked everyone for coming and we ended the conference, 32 minutes later. (p. 16)

Restorative justice concepts focus not only on criminal offenses and war crimes but also on preventive measures such as education and community awareness. Restorative justice, in its focus on repairing the harm done to people and communities, above all emphasizes communication and reconciliation. Peacemaking circles operate at both the level of responding to personal crime and other wrongdoing and at the community level to make peace between factions (Pranis, Wedge, and Stuart, 2003). The healing circle is a form of interactive conferencing used in the Toronto and Waterloo, Canada, school systems, and it seems ideally suited to the needs of teenage girls in conflict. Facilitated by a social worker, the healing circle brings offenders and their victims face to face, forcing them to listen to each other and to grasp the impact of their behavior—such as threats, rumor mongering, teasing, and holding grudges. As indicated in the *Toronto Star*, the use of the circle has been highly effective in healing wounds and reducing animosities ("Healing circle shows offenders their human toll," 2001).

IN ADULT CORRECTIONS

Like many discussions in the field of criminal justice, in restorative justice, the special needs of female offenders are not taken into account. And as we know, when we treat female offenders generically, we often confuse the goals of equality and sameness—being gender blind, in other words. Gender-blind treatment of girls and women in the criminal justice system subjects them to discipline designed for antisocial men, without making allowance either for the role of motherhood or for a history of personal victimization. Addiction and dependency on drug-using and often violent men are other common themes on the pathway to crime.

Within prison walls, some powerful encounters are taking place between offenders and their victims. Encounters occur, however, only after the facilitator has provided a great deal of preparation for both parties. Often, as at the Kentucky Correctional Institute for Women, the starting point for offenders is participation in the Impact of Crime on Victims seminar. What is unique in this program is that the focus is on inmates convicted of murder. Preliminary reports from some of the inmates who attended the seminar indicate a reduction in anger and more acceptance of responsibility (Tereshkova, 2000). If inmates later desire a meeting with the homicide victim's family, facilitators act through local victim advocates or through the church to gauge the survivors' desire for such an encounter. If family members so wish, volunteers prepare them for a face-to-face meeting.

Out of such sessions, there will most likely be an apology by the offender. In rare cases, forgiveness from the victim's family may result, although it can never be forced. Whether or not they are involved in personal meetings with those they have harmed, female inmates are often especially plagued by feelings of grief, loss, and self-denigration. A particularly meaningful class offered by Transformation House professionals and volunteers to inmates deals with shame and self-forgiveness. Among the questions pondered in small group discussion are these:

- How hard are you on yourself?
- What qualities or behaviors do you think are your "gifts to the world"?
- What are some ways you can nurture your growth and well-being? (Harvey, 2002)

Efforts have been made at Transformation House and elsewhere to reach the families of homicide victims as well as the family members of the murderers. Social work educators Beck, Britto, and Andrews (2007) and authors of *In the Shadow of Death: Restorative Justice and Death Row Families* have all personally worked with defense attorneys on sentence mitigation of people facing a death sentence. Based on their work with families of individuals who have committed horrible crimes, the authors show how the family members of death row inmates are vilified by society. In addition to telling their compelling stories, Beck and her coauthors show how the application of restorative justice principles to capital crimes can help break the cycle of violence.

Restorative justice initiatives are being introduced increasingly into women's prisons. (The first case example from Iowa illustrated such a meeting between a female inmate and the murder victim's mother.) Because of its sensitivity to communication between parties and the feelings evoked by the wrongdoing and the process to advance the healing, restorative justice has a special resonance for women. Legal scholar Marie Failinger (2006), who was inspired by Gilligan's gender-based relational model of moral development, sees restorative approaches as especially appropriate in responding to women's "circles of care" or relationship issues. In bringing the individual face to face with the victim and others who have also endured pain on the victim's behalf, the restorative process can initiate healing among the participants. Secondly, restorative processes identify offenders as persons worthy of support by the community and of being restored to functioning community citizens. Third, as Failinger further suggests, restorative justice strategies respond to all participants in the process as moral agents who need to take responsibility for their actions. This is particularly important for women whose offenses are closely tied to their relationships with others.

Recognition of relevance of restorative justice to the needs of female offenders, grassroots organizers are receiving training in restorative interventions and spreading the word. This is occurring at the state and local levels. In Minnesota, several community groups and a nonprofit criminal justice agency helped spread these ideas through organizing a conference for criminal justice practitioners and policy makers. Statewide conferences and involvement of key leaders from all parts of the corrections system followed. Today, the Minnesota Department of Corrections Initiative provides technical assistance throughout the state for designing applications related to the restorative vision.

Minnesota has infused gender-specific programming within its juvenile and adult institutions, programming that is built on restorative justice principles. The Minnesota Department of Corrections furthermore employs restorative justice planners to train people at the county level for diversionary conferencing, emphasizing above all a spirit of dialogue and healing. Burns (2001), a researcher at the Center for Restorative Justice and Peacemaking, describes a process that is a combination of victim–offender conferencing, panels, and healing circles. Meetings held in a circle format at the women's prison at Shakopee were conducted with five crime victims (members of the Parents of Murdered Children support group), six inmates, two facilitators, a neutral advocate, and an observer. Participants who did not know each other before the meetings signed up for certain nights when they would tell their personal stories of victimization. Before the conferencing, the crime victims had favored harsh penalties for female offenders such as those they met at the facility, but after meeting with them, they saw these women as people and victims too in their own way. Much empathy and remorse was expressed in these exchanges.

How about the effectiveness of such exchanges and conferencing? Are lives altered thereby? Does healing of the participants—victims and offenders—take place? To discover the impact, the Minnesota Department of Corrections (2006) collects a wealth of survey data on the perceptions of offenders, victims, and community members who have participated in restorative justice initiatives. Pre- and posttest surveys are conducted on participants immediately before and after the restorative event and another survey somewhat later. During 2004 and 2005, survey data collected on thousands of participants indicated a high degree of satisfaction with the fairness of the process, especially by offenders. This finding is significant since most of the research in the literature measures victim satisfaction only.

What does the literature show us about the long-term effectiveness of these restorative justice models? An extensive review of 63 empirically based follow-up surveys of restorative events conducted by Umbreit et al. (2006) showed a high level of satisfaction with the process by participants.

A comprehensive report prepared for the Canadian Department of Justice revealed similar results. A meta-analysis of all available data conducted by Latimer, Dowden, and Muise (2001) revealed that compared to usual courtroom processes, restorative programs were found to be significantly more effective on the basis of all criteria studied. This included victim and offender satisfaction and follow-through with restitution agreements.

Of special significance to gendered violence is research on victim–offender conferencing in cases of severe violence, crimes for which it was originally believed that restorative processes would be contraindicated because of safety concerns (Grauwiler and Mills, 2004). The vast majority of such cases take place within prison walls. Similar to findings from research on victim satisfaction in cases of less serious crimes, research in cases of severe violence shows that here too the process tends to be well received by both victims and offenders. Parents of murdered children, for example, have expressed their sense of relief after meeting the inmate and sharing their pain and developing a better understanding about what happened. Some participants report they are able to let go of their hatred after coming to see the offender as a human being (Umbreit et al., 2006.)

Programming for Reentry

In New Zealand and Canada, indigenously based programs are directed toward the needs of Native women in confinement. The Sycamore Tree Project in New Zealand follows the principle of restorative justice in helping female inmates move toward reintegration into the community (Williams and Clarke, 2005). This victim awareness program is covered in six sessions. The goal is to enable prisoners to understand the impact of their crime on victims, families, and the community. Surrogate victims help in this process by coming to the prison to share their stories on victim–offender panels. At the end of the program, prisoners are given the opportunity to take part in symbolic acts of restitution, taking the first step toward making amends for their past behavior. Follow-up studies reveal an improvement in the level of empathy inmates have for their victims.

The Tree of Creation project introduced into the women's prison in Northwestern Canada focuses on the spiritual process of healing (Lambert, 1998). The symbol used for this nature-based program is a large model of a tree, the branches of which take female inmates from the past to the present. The particular focus of that exchange is on healthful practices to prevent the spread of HIV/AIDS. In common with the Sycamore project, the goal is to help prepare inmates for their eventual return to society.

From Iowa, we learn from victim and restorative justice program director Mary Roche:

Reentry is the big word in corrections today. Finally, victim assistance and restorative justice coordinators are getting involved in helping prepare inmates for reentry into the community. There are a lot of programs available, some of which are faith based and provide mentoring services. Due to budget cuts, prisons today, such as the Mitchellville Correctional Institution for women in Iowa, rely on church and other community support systems to work with prerelease inmates. Mitchellville does offer an inmate victim impact class that is taught by a qualified restorative justice facilitator. The goal is to impress offenders with the harm their actions have caused. Healing circles are highly effective with youthful offenders who talk about the crimes they have committed and how they plan to repair the harm. (Personal interview with van Wormer on December 8, 2008)

A highly developed reentry program in Hawaii provides restorative justice practices for healing relationships. Walker is the former Deputy Attorney General of the State of Hawaii and presently a public health educator and restorative justice trainer. The program with which she is involved is based on indigenous traditions and is described by Lorenn Walker in Box 7.1.

BOX 7.1
You're gonna make it: Reentry Planning at a Hawaii Women's Prison

"I've been clean for over four years, and I quit smoking two and a half years ago," says Penny, her eyes looking up, off to the left corner, with a furrowed forehead. She is trying to remember all the things she has accomplished since being in prison this time around. "Oh, yeah, I made amends with my oldest daughter, and have a good relationship with my youngest one now," she adds with a confident smile.

Penny is around thirty-five years old. She is *hapa*, part Hawaiian and part Portuguese. Her family is from the Wai'anae Coast of O'ahu, which is 51 percent Hawaiian and the most economically depressed area on O'ahu (U.S. Bureau of the Census, 2000).

Penny's black shiny hair is neatly pulled into a tight ponytail. She could pass for a grown-up cheerleader except for the homemade tattoos on her hands. She is dressed in clean blue hospital scrubs, the required uniform at the prison where she has been incarcerated for the last four years. She is in prison for selling drugs, an occupation mainly used to support her former drug habit.

Penny sits in a circle of twelve other incarcerated women who are participating in her *Modified Restorative Circle* (Walker, 2009). The Circle is a group reentry planning process designed in Hawaii for an incarcerated individual to make a transition plan for successful reintegration back into the community. The Modified Restorative Circle process is slightly different from the *Restorative Circle* process developed in 2005 in Hawaii (Walker, Sakai, and Brady, 2006).

In the original Restorative Circle, loved ones are invited and attend the group meeting, while the Modified Circle is for people whose loved ones are unable or unwilling to attend a Circle. Instead other incarcerated people attend the Modified Circles as supporters.

The Modified Circle grew out of providing a *Restorative and Solution-Focused Problem Solving Training* program for incarcerated people (Walker and Sakai, 2006). It was developed to demonstrate restorative justice and the power of reconciliation to people in the training program.

Since the first Modified Restorative Circle in 2006, thirty more, including Penny's, have been provided for both women and men. Currently, the Hawaii prison system only allows the Modified Circles for demonstration purposes only during the training program. The Modified Circle process, however, is a positive alternative to the Restorative Circle process, and hopefully it will eventually be allowed by Hawaii's prison administration.

The original Restorative Circle and the Modified Restorative Circle (Circles) give individual imprisoned people the opportunity to explore what is needed for them to live a healthy and happy life. For most imprisoned people in Hawaii, as elsewhere in the United States, this includes being drug-free.

The incarcerated individual who discusses, makes decisions, and plans for her life, after gaining information generated by a group of caring supporters, drives the Circle process. Both types of Circles meet criteria necessary for promoting *desistance* (Walker, 2009).

Desistance is the phenomenon where most people who commit crime naturally and eventually stop doing it later in life (Maruna, 2006; Rumgay, 2004). Desistance is an ongoing process and "sustained desistance most likely requires a fundamental and intentional shift in a person's sense of self" (Maruna, 2006, p. 17).

The Circles use *solution-focused brief therapy* language skills that identify a person's abilities to create peaceful and happy lives and helps people set goals for themselves (Walker, in Dejong and Berg, 2008). The Circles provide the elements that can successfully assist incarcerated people in rescripting their life stories, including assisting them in reconciling with loved ones and the community. The Circles help imprisoned people find ways to meet their needs for reintegration into the community (Walker, 2009). These positive results promote desistance by helping shift a person's image and sense of self.

Restorative Circles address an incarcerated person's needs, and their first need considered is the need for reconciliation. Here reconciliation does not require that any repaired or continued relationships be achieved. Reconciliation can merely be "the process of making consistent or compatible" (Dictionary.com, 2007), and coming to terms with

(continued)

(continued)

the fact the person is in prison, had a drug problem, lost custody of her children to child welfare, and so on.

The major difference between the two Circle processes is that the reconciliation piece is much richer when loved ones participate because they provide how they were affected and what can be done to repair the harm that they suffered. Without loved ones participating, incarcerated people having a Modified Circle can only speculate about how they have harmed others and what they might do to repair that harm. This critical thinking while done in a group, however, can be meaningful.

Usually in the Modified Circles, the incarcerated people decide that "walking the talk" and living a "clean and sober life," where they are independent, are steps toward reconciliation, which they can take regardless of others participating.

During a Modified Circle, some incarcerated people address their need for reconciling with themselves, and what they need to do to forgive themselves. Often they decide that walking-the-talk also works for reconciling with and forgiving themselves.

Sometimes if they believe it will not upset victims, they write apology letters asking what they might do to repair the harm. In some cases where others have custody of their children, they may write a letter and say that it is sent in good faith for the sake of the children. In these cases, often their prison counselor reviews and signs the letter indicating this is true.

The incarcerated people in this program are quick to recognize that they have created trust problems with others and that only they have the power to rebuild it. Writing a letter as a result of a Modified Circle in at least one case led to an incarcerated person being restored into the family after his mother contacted him in response to a letter he wrote his former girlfriend's grandmother. The grandmother contacted his mother in praise of the man writing her and thanking her for all she had done for him previously. His mother was moved by his newly found gratitude and contacted him.

Penny has waited twelve weeks to have her Modified Circle. Two other women who wanted one cannot because the training program is ending.

After Penny lists what she is most proud of having accomplished, each woman supporting her in the Circle, says what they like most about Penny and what her strengths are. The list of positive attributes eventually grows to 63 items including: "Honest, speaks up, loving, giving, productive, determined, creative, willing, visionary, humble."

The Circle is a moving experience. Not only is Penny hearing what other people like about her for the first time, but her incarcerated friends are emotionally touched too. Some have tears in their eyes, including one who says, "You're determined and loving. I know you're gonna make it."

The Circles generate inspiration, positive thoughts, and emotions, something that the current system fails at providing because it focuses almost exclusively on deficits and what is wrong with people.

People need positive emotional experiences to change (Kast, 1994). The Circles are a welcome and needed intervention. We are requesting another grant to continue the Restorative and Solution-Focused Problem Solving Training because the women strongly advocated for it, saying they "learned things in it to help keep me out of prison."

We have also been successful in gaining state legislative support for the Restorative Circle program (Brady and Walker, 2008). Although the current governor has refused to fund it, we are confident eventually we can get the Modified Circles institutionalized in Hawaii.

References

Brady, K., and Walker, L. (2008, Summer). Restorative justice is a mandated component of Hawai'i's reentry system. *Justice Connections* Issue 6.

Dictionary.com Unabridged (v 1.1). Retrieved December 27, 2007, from Dictionary.com Website: http://dictionary.reference.com/browse/reconciliation

Kast, V. (1994). *Joy, inspiration, and hope*. New York: Fromm International Publishing Company.

Maruna, S. (2006). *Making good: How ex-convicts reform and rebuild their lives*. Washington, DC: American Psychology Association

Rumgay, J. (2004). Scripts for safer survival: Pathways out of female crime. *Howard Journal of Criminal Justice 43*(4): 405–419.

U.S. Bureau of the Census (2000).

Walker, L. (2008). Implementation of solution-focused skills in a Hawaii prison. In P. Dejong and I. K. Berg's (eds.), *Interviewing for solutions*. Belmont, California: Thompson.

Walker, L. (2009). Modified restorative circles: A reintegration group planning process that promotes desistance, publication forthcoming. *Contemporary Justice Review*.

Walker, L., and Sakai, T. (2006). A Gift of Listening for Hawaii's Inmates, *Corrections Today*, http://findarticles.com/p/articles/mi_hb6399/is_7_68/ai_n29318719 (last visited March 14, 2009).

Walker, L., Sakai, T., and Brady, K. (2006). Restorative circles: A reentry planning process for Hawaii inmates. *Federal Probation Journal 70*(1): 33–37 (2006), http://www.uscourts.gov/fedprob/June_2006/circles.html (last visited June 1, 2008).

Source: Personal contribution—Printed with permission of Lorenn Walker.

IN SITUATIONS OF GENDERED VIOLENCE

Because rape and domestic violence are major women's issues and because restorative justice models increasingly are being considered as having something to offer to these situations, we have included this review of the relevant literature. We start with the most controversial application of restorative justice—in situations of domestic violence. Unlike rape, this form of interpersonal violence may have been ongoing, and there is a risk that it will continue to occur. Any formal or informal process which involves communication is therefore risky. Common to situations of both domestic and sexual assault is a history of victim dissatisfaction with standard criminal justice procedures and outcomes.

In Battering Situations

A major theme of empowerment and the related strengths perspective concerns the need for personal control—*choice*. Choice is the hallmark of social work's strengths model; its aim is to help clients find their own way, to carve out their own paths to wholeness (see Rapp and Goscha, 2006). The focus of empowerment theory, similarly, is on the process rather than simply on outcomes (Gutiérrez and Suarez, 1999) and on means rather than ends. Mills (2003) found, in a study of battered women that most of them had little faith in the criminal justice system and expressed a desire to retain choice and be treated as individuals in any attempt to stop the abuse. Victims of family violence often regret the loss of influence that can go with exercising their rights to get protection and help from the legal authorities (Burford and Adams, 2004).

The dilemma facing battered women's advocates is whether the process—giving the battered woman a choice in how to proceed—or whether the outcome—pursuing domestic violence cases to the full extent of the law, regardless of the victim's wishes—is more important. The criminalization of domestic violence following the Duluth model represented the most progressive thinking of the 1970s through the 1990s. Arrest of batterers was mandatory; often jail terms were mandatory too, and victims who filed charges were not allowed to later drop them. Sometimes victims were forced to testify against partners. All this was done for the victim's protection and it seemed to make a lot of sense at the time. Such coercion of victims, however, was inconsistent with the feminist movement's goal of self-determination (Presser and Gaarder, 2004). Complicating the mandatory arrest policy has been the widespread use of dual arrests—arrest of both partners, of both the aggressor and the one who fought back. If the case comes to trial, and the victim is forced to testify, what she says against her partner may compromise her safety later. Moreover, child protective services may start investigating a mother for her failure to protect the children even if they just witnessed the violence. Perhaps for these reasons, only one quarter of all physical assaults, as indicated in the Violence Against Women Survey, are reported to the police (Tjaden and Thoennes, 2000).

A postmodern view of justice has developed, which, according to Presser and Gaarder (2004), has called into question the ideology of absolute justice—policies such as forcing the victim to testify in open court against her partner or spouse who assaulted her. Research in the 1990s, as these writers inform us, found that battered victims who have a say in legal or less formal proceedings may feel more empowered to get help, if not to terminate the abusive relationship. Women of color often see both the courts and social services as adversaries rather than allies, so an emphasis on judicial intervention may turn them away. Many women, moreover, are dependent on a man for financial support; others have drug problems or undocumented immigration status, which make them wary of pursuing criminal prosecution.

Inasmuch as practices in the realm of domestic violence have always started at the grass-roots level, it is time, as Grauwiler and Mills (2004) argue, to expand our efforts to focus the needs of women who avoid or wish to avoid getting involved in standard criminal justice procedures. Community-based interventions are required as an option that does not rely on criminal prosecution. Duley (2006) concurs that increased reliance on the police and mandatory processes to control violence against women reduces the exploration of more community-based long-term solutions. Within the context of restorative justice, the recommended policy is to attempt to reduce domestic violence through an emphasis on rehabilitation, rather than on prosecution, although the threat of prosecution can effectively serve as an incentive for participation in the programs. The key point here is that women in battering situations need options so that they are in control of the situation. A victim needs to be advised of all options so that she can choose the one which most closely represents her needs.

One approach in the prevention of domestic violence is the requirement that battering men receive treatment. The aim is to teach offenders new ways of viewing relationships and manhood, and new ways of handling stress and feelings of insecurity. Restorative justice here often takes the form of teaching empathy by having a group of survivors of domestic violence tell their stories, relating what it feels like to be violently victimized by one's spouse or partner. In hearing the stories of pain and suffering that the crimes of violence engendered, those offenders who can be reached will not only feel for the victims as people who were hurt by the careless or cruel behavior of others, but often will get in tune with their own past victimization. Getting in touch with their own feelings may prepare them for the humanization/rehabilitation process. In short, two themes—offender accountability and the empowerment of crime victims—ideally come together in the victim–offender initiatives. Just as offenders, in these encounters, see the human face of victims, so the survivors come to see the human face of offenders.

The process of community conferencing as a way of effecting justice for victims of rape and battering is practiced in New Zealand with favorable results (Braithwaite and Daly, 1998). Sentencing in such a system is handled by community groups that include the victim and her family, as well as the offender and individuals from his support system. Power imbalances are addressed in various ways, such as limiting the right of the offender to speak on his own behalf, and including community members in a sort of surveillance team to monitor the offender's compliance. Braithwaite and Daly see the potential to use such methods safely by including them in a "regulatory pyramid," utilizing interventions of escalating intensity in refractory cases. While more conventional interventions such as imprisonment may still be used for offenders who do not respond, they see community involvement in decision making, as well as in rituals of shaming and community reintegration, as potentially more beneficial. The victim and other members of the community are given voice and are able to bring social pressures to bear on the offender while both protecting the victim and offering the option of rehabilitation to the offender.

Other reports involving successful community conferencing in cases of severe family violence have come from Canada from traditional native community ceremonies. These are unlike traditional mediation methods used with divorcing couples in that community involvement changes the balance of power. Griffiths (1999), for example, presents the case of a Canadian aboriginal **sentencing circle** that took up the case of a man who, when drunk, beat his wife. Seated in a circle, the victim and her family told of their distress, and a young man spoke of the contributions the offender had made to the community. The judge suspended sentencing until the offender entered alcoholism treatment and fulfilled the expectations of the victim and of her support group. The ceremony concluded with a prayer and a shared meal. After a period of time, the woman who had been victimized voiced her satisfaction with the process. This case, as Griffiths explains, was clearly linked to the criminal justice system. Others may be handled more quietly, by tribal members. Griffiths concludes on a note of caution: Victims must play a key role throughout the process to ensure that their needs are met and that they are not re-victimized. This is a process we can expect to be hearing much more about in the future. The emphasis on restoration rather than retribution can be empowering to all parties involved.

Feminist researcher Mary Koss (2000) advocates what she terms *communitarian justice*, a victim-sensitive model derived from the community-based approaches of New Zealand's Maori people. Such methods are apt to be effective, notes Koss, because they draw on sanctions abusive men fear most: family stigma and broad social disapproval. Such conferencing, as Koss further indicates, is recommended for young offenders without extensive histories of violence.

The goal of such an approach is to help violence-prone men take responsibility for their actions while at the same time developing empathy for their victims. Like restorative justice, the aim is to build on positives so as to facilitate the offender's restoration to the community rather than their further estrangement from it.

In ongoing relationships, an end to the violence is of course crucial. Treatment coupled with close supervision of men who have engaged in battering is an important element in curbing further family violence. Sometimes restorative justice initiatives at the community level take the form of community conferencing, as discussed in the previous section. Participation by all parties is strictly voluntary and intensive preparation precedes all such conferencing. Issues of power and control for the victim must be addressed (Umbreit, 2000). Hearing directly from the offender of his guilt and remorse while receiving support from family members can help the victim heal while reducing feelings of self-blame. In contrast, few traditional programs address the psychological needs of victims in any meaningful way. Even in situations of violent crime, community conferencing can help victims by bringing the gravity of the violence that they have experienced out into the open. The message to all concerned is that any form of family violence is unacceptable. Such conferencing can attend to the psychological as well as physical abuse a survivor has experienced and counter her sense of helplessness by involving her as an active participant in the process (Koss, 2000). Measures can be taken, moreover, to reduce the survivor's vulnerability such as in providing access to an individual bank account or transportation, for example.

Rashmi Goel (2005) believes that restorative justice options are ill-suited to application among immigrant South Asian communities for domestic violence cases. Her reasoning is that women from South Asian culture might be placated by the familiar values of community, cooperation, and forgiveness into seeking restorative justice solutions and ultimately into staying in an abusive situation. Restorative justice is based on the premise that participants are equal and can speak freely in a consensus-based proceeding. But in the South Asian (Indian) cultural tradition, such an assumption cannot be made. Tradition portrays the husband as the sole source of status and support, and Indian women are likely to feel responsible for pain inflicted by the husband. The exact opposite argument is made by Grauwiler and Mills (2004). Their recommendation is for what they call Intimate Abuse Circles as a culturally sensitive alternative to the criminal justice system's response to domestic violence. Such Circles are especially helpful, they suggest, to immigrant, minority, and religious families, where it is more likely that the family will remain intact. This model acknowledges that many people seek to end the violence but not the relationship. Such restorative processes help partners as well those who would like to separate in a more amicable fashion than through standard avenues.

In Situations of Rape

Rozee and Koss (2001) criticize the handling and outcomes of acquaintance rape at every level of the criminal justice system right from police officers' treatment to the prosecutor's reluctance to take the case to court to courtroom antics, if it comes to this, geared to demolish the credibility of the victim as chief witness for the prosecution. Racial-ethnic differences between state officials and the victim compound the lack of consideration and respect. Additionally, as Rozee and Koss further suggest, adversarial justice is experienced as "white imposed" (p. 306); women of color must contend with tension between their needs for justice and felt obligations to buffer racism in the criminal justice system. Black and Latina women may avoid seeking help from the criminal justice system or women's shelters to protect the image held of minority group in a racist society (Presser and Gaarder, 2004). Women of color are well aware of the brutal and prejudicial treatment inflicted upon their men folk by the criminal justice system, and they might not want to turn to that system for justice.

If criminal justice treatment of victims of crime in general leaves much to be desired, treatment of rape victims is unconscionable. Three main failings of the conventional system are discussed by Daly (2006). The first of these is the low rate of accountability in the system due to lack of reporting by victim-survivors. The low prosecution rate even when a charge is filed is related to perceived lack of credibility of victims of any crime involving sex coupled with the awareness of authorities of the low conviction rate even if the case does come to trial. Secondly, rapists who are sentenced to prison are often guilty of repeated offenses that they got away with and therefore are likely to re-offend upon release. Third, women are revictimized under cross-examination by defense attorneys in the courtroom, especially if they were drinking at the time of the offense, in an unsafe place late at night, or if anything could be uncovered from their past that would seem to shed light on their veracity.

Restorative justice responses are consistent with the community focus of women's grass-roots movements. Within this context, Rozee and Koss describe an American project based on community conferencing principles to redress the harm to the victim-survivor in date-rape cases. An additional focus is on restoring justice to the community. Only after successful conferencing to meet the needs of the victim do the offender-focused goals of rehabilitation and reintegration come into play.

The project was introduced experimentally at the University of Arizona to handle several categories of rape and sexual assault, those for which the standard system of justice was the least able or willing to deal with—sexual intercourse between a young woman of sixteen to eighteen years old and a young man slightly older; alcohol-related rape; date and acquaintance rape; and sexual offenses not involving penetration. Law enforcement is involved initially in the reporting of the crime; the County Attorney in cases appropriate for conferencing meets separately with accuser and accused to inform each party of the benefits and risks of the community justice model and to gain consent to refer the case. Next, the facilitator meets with the parties and family members if desired to arrange for a conference and for the participation of support systems from each side. A trained male advocate may attend on behalf of either the victim or the offender.

Daly (2006) discusses the aims of restorative justice in situations of rape. As with other crimes, the aims are to hold offenders accountable to provide information for the victim about the reasons for the crime and to give voice to her experience of victimization and a say in the penalty that is provided. Hopefully, the process will deter the offender from further violations. The goal of reconciliation which applies in some dialoguing of course does not apply here.

The conference on the college campus, as described by Rozee and Koss, is led by a facilitator, generally, a mental health professional, who is trained in restorative justice strategies. The offender begins by describing what he did; the victim-survivor speaks next about her experiences, while family and friends on both sides express the impact of the offense on them. The perpetrator admits to the violation and responds to what he has heard, often with an apology. Options include a formal apology, payment of expenses including counseling for the victim, substance abuse and/or sex offender treatment for the offender, and community service. A written record of the proceedings is provided, which includes plans for follow-up accountability. The matter is confidential but only as long as there is no re-offense, in which case, the results of the conference can be used as evidence in any future adjudication.

Advantages of this format as indicated by Rozee and Koss are the strengthening of community trust; empowerment of the victim-survivor; release of legal authorities from pressure to take action under difficult circumstances; volunteer advocates gain a forum from which to offer anti-rape messages; and a student offender is forced to take responsibility for his behavior but still has a chance to avoid a stigma that could follow him for life. Community conferencing provides a platform for describing a background of racial/economic oppression without framing such issues as excuses for the bad behavior. Above all, the woman has been listened to, been given community support, and has received justice. As with all forms of restorative justice, truth-telling rather than denial of the truth is encouraged in the process. Although this innovative university program is too new for the long-term results to be clear, the prospects are good in light of the proven effectiveness of similar programming in New Zealand. Presumably, the fact that the university has leverage in terms of the student's academic future is a strong point in facilitating a successful outcome in such a case. For all parties involved, this process should be empowering.

Canadian attorney Ross Green (1998), in his book *Justice in Aboriginal Communities*, conducted research on sentencing practices in cases that are sometimes considered too serious for handling outside the normal judicial route. And yet, we could equally argue that such situations are of too great a magnitude for ordinary adversarial methods, especially when members of Indian tribes are involved. The clash between the Anglo-Saxon way of handling criminal matters and aboriginal values is palpable. Photographs provided in the book show large numbers of people seated in a circle at one gathering concerning parents who pleaded guilty to incest. Part I of the book focuses on the conventional Canadian justice system and the clash between this formal adversarial system and Aboriginal values. In contrast to modern Euro-American forms of justice, Aboriginal justice is about restoring balance to the community. Native peoples have difficulty in standard proceedings as they are apt to feel intimidated and to lack remorse if found guilty. The victim plays a limited role in the formal process as well.

A rather extraordinary use of circle conferencing occurred in the Hollow Water (Manitoba) community. In this community, a cycle of sexual abuse had been perpetuated for generations. Because the problem was communitywide, if the victims had gone through normal channels, virtually all the male members of the community would have been removed. The process of circle sentencing was thus chosen as the pragmatic and culturally sensitive approach to an almost overwhelming situation. In the circle, offenders acknowledged the truth of their behavior. Healing Contracts and a concluding Cleansing Ceremony provided a spiritual dimension to the proceedings. Strong community pressures followed the sessions to keep the offenders in treatment. The process was empowering for all the parties involved, and instead of being divisive, pulled the community together for concerted action toward social change.

Empirical research on restorative justice in cases of sexual assault is scarce. One exception is Kathleen Daly's (2006) archival study of nearly 400 cases of youth sexual assault in South Australia. The research team gathered data from Adelaide Youth Court for several months. Some cases were referred to court and others were not. The court cases and conferencing cases were of similar severity. A comparison of the two differing responses to the alleged sexual assault revealed that only about half of them were proven in court; a good deal of natural attrition occurred. Where guilt was found, rehabilitation was not a concern; the emphasis, rather, was on scaring the youth. The court cases, besides, took a very long time to be processed.

The restorative justice resolution of the case, in contrast, focused on a youth's development of a sense of responsibility and respect for himself and others. A second major difference between the two forms of procedures was that conference youth had admitted that they committed the offence to the police. For victims, this provided some degree of vindication. For the youths, conferencing removed much of the uncertainty about what would take place—there would be an apology followed by treatment and some form of supervision. Sum total, the results of the comparative study show there is a definite place for restorative justice strategies as an option in cases of youth sexual assault.

Feminist Critique

Sometimes there is not satisfaction, however, following the handling of serious cases through circles, as Cameron (2008) suggests. Complaints have come from women that Aboriginal justice had been too lenient in a number of cases and that the victims' interests had not been represented in the decisions that were reached. Rubin (2003), in her examination of women's experiences in restorative processes in Nova Scotia, cautions critics from being overly positive in assessing these alternative forms of justice, and in ignoring family and community roles in the reinforcement of male control of women. Her recommendations include close attention to women's safety concerns and guarantees for their safety in domestic violence situations.

Women's advocates have been skeptical of the application of informal processes to deal with men who abuse and women who are abused (Cameron, 2008), and they have every right to be so. Unless it is done properly through joint decision making with the victim-survivor, the informal process can be worse than nothing at all, especially in cases of partner violence.

The process is only as good as the people who conduct it in this less structured format. In situations of gendered violence, active participation by women at all levels is crucial. Victim-survivors are at risk of having their needs neglected under conditions of gender insensitivity or predominantly male authority. In Canada, which has an extensive history with such practices under tribal law, Aboriginal women's interests have not always been represented. Sometimes the emphasis is more on the offender than the victim, and the women have been revictimized by this process (Cameron). An article in *Canadian Dimension* describes a controversial case known as the Morris case that took place in a small town in the Yukon (Pope, 2004). The judge who passed on the sentencing to the Aboriginal male leadership was himself constrained by a system that favored this form of community justice. The case involved the brutal rape at gunpoint of a woman by her common law husband. The woman had almost been killed but was saved by the police. The women of the community were outraged; forty-nine women called for a prison sentence for this dangerous man. The judge, however, under instructions to take into account cultural factors such as attendance at a Native mission boarding school focused on the offender rather than the victim. Even the fact that the accused blamed the victim and blasted women in a speech claiming they controlled the money, everything, while men have nothing was not taken into account. In the end, Morris was placed on probation by the tribal Council. All across Canada, voices were raised for a review of the case, and in fact, it is being appealed by the Attorney General of British Columbia.

Earlier, a non-Native Catholic Bishop who had sexually assaulted Native women bargained for a talking circle. He escaped sentencing altogether. The Aboriginal Women's Action Network is calling for a moratorium on restorative justice processes in cases of violence against women until the system is free of racism and sexism.

Restorative processes are inappropriate in situations involving a high level of violence and danger for the victim. An important research question that has not been adequately explored is this: For whom, for which type of batterers, would a restorative justice approach be effective? More precise knowledge of batterer typologies may ultimately be used to discriminate between offenders who might reasonably be expected to benefit from such an approach and those who are unlikely to benefit, or who pose too great a safety threat. While batterer typology systems currently have limited clinical utility (Langhinrichsen-Rohling, Huss, and Ramsey, 2000), mental health practitioners are able through psychological testing to screen out those who show antisocial tendencies, severe depression, or who have a history of violence directed toward others outside the family.

Summary

The restorative justice model, as we have seen in this chapter, is especially relevant to work with women and indeed to all marginalized persons and groups where wrongs have been committed that need to be rectified. Restorative justice can be conceived of as a form of social justice inasmuch as every effort is made to help repair the harm that was done to the victim-survivor and to restore a sense of well-being that might have been lost. The processes described in this chapter have the potential to respect the human dignity of all parties involved in the process. We have described four of the basic restorative models—victim–offender conferencing, family group conferencing, healing circles, and community reparations, and variations thereof. Common to all these models is an emphasis on the needs of the victim, on truth-telling in one's own voice, direct communication, and accountability of the offender to the victim. Restorative justice is a process designed to bring out the best in people regardless of what they have done or to what degree they have been wronged.

In light of the shortcomings of standard courtroom practices in getting at the truth of the situation and meeting the needs of the victim, while encouraging the offender to take responsibility for the crime or other wrongdoing, we propose more reliance on restorative justice strategies as an option to the usual criminal justice procedures, an option that would need to be suitable to and agreeable to all parties involved in the situation.

Restorative justice is a form of justice that we believe to be highly compatible with feminist values. The ethics of caring and sharing are common to both. We agree with Burford and Adams (2004) that the adoption of restorative principles can help bridge the gaps between formal and informal helping, between care and control, and between empowerment and coercion. The victim of crime has much to gain in receiving an honest admission of guilt from the offender and some form of compensation for the harm that was done.

For the female offender, advantages of this process are in helping restore her to the community in good standing in offering a way to make amends to the people who were wronged. Restorative justice, in short, has much to offer girls and women. In the restorative practices we have discussed, human relationships, the opportunity to speak and express feelings, support system involvement, and consensus-style decision making are central. Innovations in gender-specific programming for female juvenile offenders are especially promising.

From grassroots activity to the highest level of government, change is in the wind. With healing the wounds of crime as our goal, there is no end to the imaginative possibilities for advancing social justice and bringing people together for the common good. There is a groundswell of support out there, voiced by a diverse group of dedicated professionals and volunteers striving to foster a form of justice that provides real social justice more interested in helping people than in processing them, and more interested in restoration than in retribution.

Key Terms

community reparation *173*
family group conference *173*

restitution *170*
restorative justice *168*

sentencing circles *183*
victim–offender conferencing *168*

Critical Thinking Questions

1. Considering issues such as truth telling and expression of remorse by the offender, discuss the conventional process of criminal justice compared with restorative justice.
2. Discuss the need for restorative strategies from the point of view of the victim.
3. What are some of the difficult issues that might be raised in work in bringing together the murder victim's families with the victim's murderer who is now in prison or on death row?
4. Consider the possible uses and abuses of circle sentencing laws in cases of sexual abuse.
5. Discuss family group conferencing and how such conferencing could be used in situations of family violence.
6. How can restorative strategies address a youthful female offender's background of victimization?
7. What kind of advocacy work could be done in your area to institute or reinforce restorative justice programming?

Web Destinations

AMICUS (now RADIUS): http://www.amicususa.org

Center for Justice and Peacebuilding: www.emu.edu/ctp/ctp.html

Center for Restorative Justice and Peacemaking: http://www.emu.edu/cjp

Restorative Justice Consortium: www.restorativejustice.org.uk

Restorative Justice Online: www.restorativejustice.org

Youth Justice Reports New Zealand: http://www.cyf.govt.nz/487.htm#Youth%20justice%20reports

References

Adams, P. (2002, February 24–27). Learning from indigenous practices: A radical tradition. Paper presented at the Council on Social Work Education Conference, Nashville, TN.

Beck, E., Britto, S., and Andrews, A. (2007). *In the shadow of death: Restorative justice and death row families*. New York: Oxford University Press.

Braithwaite, J. (2002). *Restorative justice and responsive regulation*. Oxford, England: Oxford University Press.

Braithwaite, J., and Daly, K. (1998). Masculinity, violence and communitarian control. In S. Miller (ed.), *Crime control and women* (pp. 151–180). Thousand Oaks, CA: Sage.

Bucci, L. (1998, June 18). Bishop O'Connor diverted. *Vancouver Sun*. Retrieved from the Vancouver Rape Relief and Women's Shelter. Retrieved December 2008 from www.rapereliefshelter.bc.ca/issues/oconnor.html

Burford, G., and Adams, P. (2004). Restorative justice, responsive regulation and social work. *Journal of Sociology and Social Work 31*(1): 20–27.

Burford, G., and Hudson, J. (eds.). (2000). *Family group conferencing: New directions in community centered child and family practice*. New York: Aldine de Gruyter.

Burns, H. (2001, January 23). *Citizens, victims, and offenders restoring justice project*. St. Paul, MN: Center for Restorative Justice and Peacemaking.

Cameron, A. (2008). Sentencing circles and intimate violence: A Canadian feminist perspective. *Women and the Law 18*(2): 479–512.

Daly, K. (2006). Restorative justice and sexual assault: An archival study of court and conference cases. *British Journal of Criminology 46*: 334–356.

DiBiase, M. (2000). Psychology and justice working together: Addressing the needs of female juvenile offenders. *Healing Magazine 5*(2): 4–10.

Doerner, W., and Lab, S. (2005). *Victimology*, 4th ed. Dayton, OH: Anderson Publishing.

Duley, K. (2006). Un-domesticating violence: Criminalizing survivors and U.S. mass incarceration. *Women and Therapy 29*(3/4): 75–96.

Failinger, M. A. (2006). Lessons unlearned: Women offenders, the ethics of care, and the promise of restorative justice. *Fordham Urban Law Journal 33*(2): 487–527.

Falcón, J. M. (2005). The Peruvian truth and reconciliation commission's treatment of sexual violence against women. *Human Rights Brief 12*(2): 1–4.

Frisch, L. (2003). The justice response to woman battering. In A. Roberts (ed.), *Critical issues in crime and justice*, 2nd ed. (pp. 161–175). Thousand Oaks, CA: Sage.

Gaarder, E., and Hesselton, D. (2008, November 9). Connecting restorative justice with gender-responsive programming. Paper presented at the annual meeting of the American Society of Criminology. Retrieved January 2009 from http://www.allacademic.com/meta/p127720_index.html

Gilligan, C. (1982). *In a different voice: Psychological theory and women's development*. Cambridge, MA: Harvard University Press.

Goel, R. (2005, May). Sita's trousseau: Restorative justice, domestic violence, and South Asian Culture. *Violence Against Women 11*(5): 639–665.

Gordon, K. G. (2004, January). From corrections to connections: A report on the AMICUS girls restorative program. AMICUS. Retrieved January 2009 from http://www.amicususa.org/pubs/Girls%20Final%20Report%20-%20Jan%2004.pdf

Grauwiler, P., and Mills, L. (2004). Moving beyond the criminal justice paradigm: A radical restorative justice approach to intimate abuse. *Journal of Sociology and Social Welfare 31*(1): 49–62.

Green, R. G. (1998). *Justice in Aboriginal Communities: Sentencing Alternatives*. Saskatoon, Saskatchewan, Canada: Purich Publishing.

Griffiths, C. T. (1999). The victims of crime and restorative justice: The Canadian experience. *International Review of Victimology 6*: 279–294.

Gutiérrez, L., and Suarez, Z. (1999). Empowerment with Latinas. In L. A. Gutiérrez and E. A. Lewis (eds.), *Empowerment of women of color* (pp. 167–186). New York: Columbia University Press.

Harvey, L. (2002, January 12). Personal interview with Katherine van Wormer, Elizabethtown, KY.

"Healing circle shows offenders their human toll" (2001). *Toronto Star*, NE4.

Kemp, S., Whittaker, J. K., and Tracy, E. M. (2000). Family group conferencing as a person-environment practice. In G. Burford and J. Hudson (eds.). *Family group conferencing: New directions in community-centered child and family practice* (pp. 72–85). New York: Aldine de Gruyter.

Koss, M. (2000). Blame, shame, and community: Justice responses to violence against women. *American Psychologist 55*(11): 1332–1343.

Lambert, D. (1998, June 20). Tree of creation: Aboriginal HIV prevention strategy. Paper presentation at the annual meeting of the Canadian Association of Social Workers. Edmonton, Canada.

Langhinrichsen-Rohling, J., Huss, M. T., and Ramsey, S. (2000). The clinical utility of batterer typologies. *Journal of Family Violence 15*(1): 37–53.

Latimer, J., Dowden, C., and Muise, D. (2001). *The effectiveness of restorative justice practices: A meta-analysis.* Ottawa, Canada: Research and Statistics Division, Department of Justice Canada.

Mills, L. G. (2003). *Insult to injury: Rethinking our responses to intimate abuse.* Princeton, NJ: Princeton University Press.

Minnesota Department of Corrections. (2006). *Restorative Justice Program Evaluation: Fiscal Year 2005 Report.* St. Paul, Minnesota: Minnesota Department of Corrections.

Pope, A. (2004, May/June). B.C. court ignores Aboriginal women's plea. *Canadian Dimension 38*(3): 10–12.

Pranis, K. (2001). Restorative justice, social justice, and the empowerment of marginalized populations. In G. Bazemore and M. Schiff (eds.), *Restorative community justice: Repairing harm and transforming communities* (pp. 287–306). Cincinnati, OH: Anderson.

Pranis, K., Wedge, M., and Stuart, B. (2003). *Peacemaking circles: From crime to community.* St. Paul, MN: Living Justice Press.

Presser, L., and Gaarder, E. (2004). Can restorative justice reduce battering? In B. Price and N. Sokoloff (eds.), *The criminal justice system and women: Offenders, prisoners, victims, and workers*, 3rd ed. (pp. 403–418). New York: McGraw Hill.

Reddy, P. (2004). Truth and reconciliation commissions: Instruments for ending impunity and building lasing peace. *UN Chronicle 4*: 19.

Rozee, P., and Koss, M. (2001). Rape: A century of resistance. *Psychology of Women Quarterly 25*: 295–311.

Rubin, P. (2003). *Restorative justice in Nova Scotia: Women's experience and recommendations for positive policy development and implementation.* Report and Recommendations. Ottawa, Canada: National Association of Women and the Law. Retrieved from www.restorativejustice.org

Tjaden, P., and Thoennes, N. (2000). *Full report of the prevalence, incidence, and consequences of violence against women: Findings from the National Violence Against Women Survey.* Research Report. Washington, DC: National Institute of Justice and the Centers for Disease Control and Prevention.

Toronto Star (2001, May 26). Healing circle shows offenders their human toll. *Toronto Star*, p. N01.

Rapp, C., and Goscha, R. J. (2006). *The strengths model: Case management with people with psychiatric disabilities.* New York: Oxford University Press.

Roche, M. (2008, December). *Restorative justice. Presentation before graduate social work class.* Cedar Falls, IA: University of Northern Iowa.

Tereshkova, Z. (2000, March 15). Lexington-based group brings inmates, their victims together for mutual healing. *Lexington Herald-Leader*, p. A1.

Umbreit, M. (2000). *Family group conferencing: Implications for crime victims.* Washington, DC: U. S. Department of Justice.

Umbreit, M., Vos, B., Coates, R., and Armour, M. (2006). Victims of severe violence in mediated dialogue with offender: The impact of the first multi-site study in the U.S. *International Review of Victimology 13*: 27–48.

Van Den Bergh, N. (ed.). (1995). Feminist practice in the 21st century. Washington, DC: NASW Press.

Van Ness, D. (2002). UN crime commission acts on basic principles. Restorative Justice Online. Retrieved January 2009 from http://www.restorativejustice.org/editions/2002/May2002/UN%20Crime%20Commission%20Acts

Van Ness, D. (2004). Justice that restores: From impersonal to personal justice. In E. H. Judah and M. Bryant (eds.), *Criminal justice: Retribution vs. restoration* (pp. 93–109). Binghamton, NY: Haworth.

Van Ness, D., and Strong, K. H. (2002). *Restoring justice*, 2nd ed. Cincinnati, OH: Anderson.

van Wormer, K. (2004). *Confronting oppression, restoring justice: From policy analysis to social action: From policy analysis to social action.* Alexandria, VA: Council on Social Work Education.

van Wormer, K. (2009). Restorative justice as social justice for victims: A standpoint feminist perspective. *Social Work 54*(2): 107–117.

Welden, L. (2007, October 10). A family plan forged out of commitment and love: Restorative Practices: E Forum. Retrieved August 2009 from http://www.iirp.org/pdf/csffgdm.pdf

Williams, P., and Clarke, R. (2005). An evaluation of the prison fellowship Sycamore Tree Programme. Research Centre for Community Justice. Retrieved January 2009 from http://www.restorativejustice.org.uk/RJ_&_the_CJS/pdf/Sycamore_tree_evaluation.pdf

Zavlek, S., and Maniglia, R. (2007, August). Developing correctional facilities for female juvenile offenders: Design and programmatic considerations. *Corrections Today*, pp. 58–63.

Zehr, H. (2002). *The little book of restorative justice.* Intercourse, PA: Good Books.

PART
IV

Women as Victims and Survivors

Whether a woman is subjected to one-time rape by a stranger or to a pattern of brutality by a family member, the emotional scars will be with her always. Although women have more social and legal rights now than at any other time in history, vestiges of the old attitudes still prevail. Given the natural tendency to blame the victim, combined with a backlash against women's advancement, these antiwoman, antivictim attitudes continue to rear their ugly heads.

The victimization of women at the personal level is matched by the oppression of women in the wider society. Chapter 8 focuses on the crime of rape. The very existence of this crime has unique ramifications for all girls and women everywhere. The amount of compassion and respect accorded the victims of this crime is a barometer of a society's regard for women in general. Woman hating is at the heart of both rape and battering; rape can be construed as assault that is sexualized, and partner violence often includes sexual abuse.

Chapter 9 examines victimization closer to home and more enduring—battering or wife (partner) abuse. Both forms of victimization—rape and battering—are about power and humiliation; they are both about male dominance and female subordination. The essence of the male power structure is further reflected in paternalistic courtroom practices concerning these crimes. The criminal justice system itself can be seen as an instrument of control and one that reflects women's economic and political station in society. It is through the great awakening that took place among women of the 1970s, women who had been seasoned through protests for peace and social justice of that era, that we recognize rape and battering for what they are. Before that time, women were consistently blamed for causing their own victimization. Many are still blamed and blame themselves for their mistreatment.

Consistent with our awareness of the forces of globalization and the extent to which transnational crime victimizes women, we have included Chapter 10, Women's Victimization: Global Perspectives. This chapter explores domestic violence in terms of the brutalizing and exploitative treatment of women in parts of the world where male privilege is most entrenched. We look at both violence against girls and women in the home and outside the home, as institutionalized by the state. Genital mutilation and the mass rape of the enemy's women in war are examples of the latter. Sex trafficking, a major industry involving the selling of women's bodies, is discussed in some detail as well. The chapter concludes on a brighter note, with a description of innovative practices from across the world to prevent and counter female victimization.

An empowerment approach is crucial to helping such women find their own voices, in the first instance to articulate their pain, and in the second, to share their insights with others. Consistent with feminist tradition, the word *victim* is used to denote a person who has sustained an injury and *survivor* for one who has lived through and is attempting to heal from an assault. Survivorship is a state of empowerment; victimhood is not. Together, these chapters offer a framework for empowerment therapy, a framework for helping people move from a position of "I am a victim" to "I am a survivor" or, better yet, "We are survivors."

8

Rape

In Chapter 5, we learned of the tremendous overlap between early childhood sexual abuse and the later development of addiction in women. Women under the influence of intoxication are especially vulnerable to sexual exploitation and rape. Chapters 5 and 6 also explored the link between women's victimization in society—sexually, economically, and personally—and their criminality. Then we saw how once in prison many women become retraumatized by the invasive strip searches sometimes performed by male guards that are a part of the prison regime. Direct incidents of guard–inmate violations were described. Now, in this chapter, we come to look at rape in the community, a crime that is often antiwoman, even when it is practiced by men against men. We begin with some representative descriptions of alleged or proven cases of sexual assault found from across the United States during one week in March, 2009. The search of media stories yielded the following reports of sexual assault:

From Oroville, California: A registered sex offender, according to court testimony, lured a developmentally disabled woman into his motor home, after offering her a ride. "I did not touch that fat girl," the defendant had told the police. On the witness stand, the young woman had problems remembering the events. In light of her mental condition, the judge allowed the prosecutor to guide her through the questioning. Then she told how she was woken up by the man who she tried to fight off and that she was "hurt down below" (Dell, 2009).

From Coos Bay, Oregon: When an 18-year-old high school honor student and popular football player was arrested for raping and sodomizing a 14-year-old girl, students rallied in his support (Ross, 2009). Around forty students came to school wearing T-shirts containing slogans such as "Free Marcus" and "Liar, liar." A "Support Marcus" dance was planned in April.

Victims' advocate groups have been shocked by the demonstrations of public support for an accused rapist and fear this outcry will hinder future sexual assault victims from coming forward.

And from Oklahoma City: A former sheriff was sentenced to seventy-nine years in prison for using his power over female drug court participants and inmates to force them to have sex with him (Associated Press, 2009). He apologized to two of the defendants but his sentence is being appealed on the basis of its harshness. According to witnesses at the trial, he sexually assaulted one woman in his car after arresting her and another whom he took to a motel. The allegations against the sheriff surfaced after a federal lawsuit was filed against him on behalf of twelve former jail inmates in 2007. The lawsuit alleged that sheriff's employees had inmates flash their breasts in exchange for cigarettes.

These incidents, drawn from popular literature, offer just a glimpse of the many ramifications of sexual abuse. In every case, the male had power over the female, whether physically or by virtue of his position. Consider that all survivors in the above examples were forced to undergo a kind of public humiliation, whether in the courtroom, or by members of the community. Keep in mind that the survivor of rape has probably already wrestled with the terror of the attack itself, considerations of her susceptibility to contracting AIDS and other diseases, awareness of the possibility of pregnancy, and the reality of living with the aftermath of rape—the intrusive fears and nightmares, and the enduring sexual problems.

The word *rape* comes by way of the Anglo-Norman *raper* from the Latin *rapere*, to seize by force (Shorter Oxford English Dictionary, 2007, p. 2463). This definition with its emphasis on force is strikingly similar to our understanding today. Legally, the definition of rape varies by state and nation. The National Crime Victimization Survey (BJS, 2007), the most reliable source of data on this highly unreported crime, defines **rape** as "forced sexual intercourse including both psychological coercion as well as physical force. Forced sexual intercourse means vaginal, anal or oral penetration by the offender(s). . . . Includes attempted rapes, male as well as female victims and both heterosexual and homosexual rape. Attempted rape includes threats of rape." The Federal Bureau of Investigation (FBI, 2008) defines "forcible rape" more specifically as "the carnal knowledge of a female forcibly against her will. Assaults and attempts to commit rape by force or threat of force are also included; however, statutory rape (without force) and other sex offenses are excluded." Some states continue to restrict the definition of rape to crimes against a female. *Sexual assault* includes a wide range of victimizations involving attacks in which unwanted sexual contact occurs between the victim and the offender. Sexual assault includes verbal threats.

Raped as a college freshman, Alice Sebold (2002), who tells her story in the book *Lucky*, did not receive the sensitive treatment she needed immediately following the rape. Instead she was told by the police officer that she was lucky, lucky she wasn't murdered like the girl before her. This, her first sexual experience, was the beginning of a journey that would become a struggle with posttraumatic stress disorder and heroin addiction.

To the victim, rape is a painful violation of the self. The humiliation of the act leads to a secrecy that, in itself, can further maximize a sense of shame in the person violated. To be raped is to enter unwittingly the bizarre sisterhood of the victimized, a sisterhood in which the membership is secret, often even among individual victims. The reality of having been unable to fight the attacker off is haunting. The reality of being physically defiled and sexually scarred may stay with a woman forever. The trial, if there is one, instead of bringing catharsis or even closure, reopens the old wounds and subjects the victim to new wounds of public accusation and labeling. To offset the trauma and promote healing, intensive counseling should be provided to all rape victims, especially in the early period of the aftermath of the crime.

Because victims of this type of crime often find the circumstances unmentionable—no one wants to hear about it—survivor self-help groups can be a godsend. Fortunately today, through the work of rape crisis lines and victim assistance programs, the help that is needed, at least for adults, is widely available.

To glimpse how rape victims were treated yesterday versus the way they are treated today, we begin this chapter with a historical overview. Then, the prevalence of rape and the impact of the mass media are discussed. From the victim's standpoint, we look at types of rape, including acquaintance rape, mass rape, and child sexual abuse. The chapter concludes by revealing the criminal justice response and with a discussion of an empowerment approach for work with survivors of this type of crime.

HISTORICAL OVERVIEW

In terms of official treatment, there has never been a time of greater sensitivity to the needs of rape victims than today. Campaigns by women's groups and rape crisis centers worldwide have resulted in significant changes in the law and legal procedures in relation to sexual offenses against women. To know how much better the climate is now, let us look at how things were before the mid-1970s, when feminist voices began to make themselves heard. After that time, victims of rape still had it rough, but never again would they be so alone.

We begin with the law. The law tends to reflect social values. In our recent past, a rape victim's behavior before the claim of rape, her behavior during the sexual encounter, and her relationship to the perpetrator were often all taken into consideration by legal officials in deciding whether a "real" rape occurred. Until the 1970s, the law in most states recognized that a rape occurred only when a man forced a woman to have sex under the threat of injury, when she had resisted strenuously, and when there was outside corroboration (Muraskin, 2007).

To understand these traditions we need to go back centuries to a time when a man who wanted a woman simply raped her and brought her into his tribe. Later, the status of women as property was embodied in custom and law. Rape entered the law as a property crime of man against man; women were the property (Belknap, 2007). Indeed, as a crime of one group of enemies against another, rape has been a part of war in most societies throughout history (Brownmiller, 1975). Rape within marriage, of course, was considered an oxymoron. Only in recent years, in fact, has marital rape come to be recognized in some nations as a crime (Bourke, 2007).

In the decades before feminist researchers revolutionized the concept of rape by desexualizing it (e.g., Brownmiller, 1975; Burgess and Holmstrom, 1974; Griffin, 1971), virtually no research was done on this form of female victimization. In the 1960s, there were a few studies on sexual deviance that focused exclusively on the stranger-rapist and rarely on the impact of rape on victims at all. Most theories that attempted to explain rape treated it as a single phenomenon—as a sexual attack by a man on a woman whom he has never met (Sigler, Johnson, and Morgan, 2007). The rapist was characterized as a mentally defective person who was unable to control his urges. The word *rape* was not often used in polite circles; the fact might have been alluded to in some way, but then only rarely. From the earliest age, for example, girls were warned in hushed tones against strangers who might try to lure them away with candy to "do terrible things to them." At the same time, the double standard decreed virginity in the unmarried female and an acceptance of sexual-experience by the unmarried male—experience with a woman who was not considered marriage material. Women who were sexually violated were said to be "ruined" and "damaged goods."

Compounding the problem, psychoanalytical theory maintained that girls and women unconsciously desired to be raped (Bourke, 2007; Brownmiller, 1975). Women who made rape accusations were seen as suffering from a form of neurotic hysteria in which they deluded themselves into believing they were sexually attacked or they were deliberately lying. Female pathology and their overly active fantasy lives were two prominent explanations for the belief that girls and women were prone to make false accusations (Bourke). Before the 1970s, accordingly, women's stories of sexual victimization were rarely believed. An example of a typical joke of the 1960s (recalled by van Wormer) is this: "A nun tells Mother Superior that she has been raped. Mother Superior tells her to go get a lemon to suck on. 'Will that help?' asks the nun. Mother Superior answers, 'No, but it will wipe the smile off your face.'"

African American Women and Rape

Whether they were raped by white men as a legacy of slavery (there was no way a slave could resist a master's advances) or by their black brothers, African American women have learned to be silent about sexual assault. Stereotypes of hypersexual African Americans grew out of the slavery era ethos (Robinson, 1997). Black men accused of assaulting white women rarely escaped punishment; such crime was construed as a direct assault on white civilization and the social order (Dorr, 2004). Historian Fay Yarbrough (2005) examined interracial sex in her content analysis of the fascinating interviews of ex-slaves collected by the Works Progress Administration (WPA) in the 1930s. The reminiscences of former slaves revealed that they viewed the relations between slaves and the whites as coercive or exploitative. Relationships between blacks and American Indians, in contrast, were perceived as more equal and consensual. The protection of the white woman's virtue became the rationalization for brutalizing black men and women. The rape of African American women historically has been given little or no attention by the larger society. In cases of inner-city black-on-black gendered crime, according to Jody Miller (2008) who studied African American girls in spaces where victimization has become a normalized feature of neighborhood life, the authorities are inclined to look the other way. Even the youths caught up in these violent contexts fail to recognize acts of sexual violence for what they are.

For a black woman to accuse a black man of raping or sexually harassing her (as Anita Hill did Clarence Thomas) is to risk attack within her own community for speaking out against one of her own kind. As a survivor wanting to end this legacy of silence in the black community, Lori Robinson courageously tells us:

> I guess more than anything, what I carry with me and walk out of this valley in my life is a commitment to help end the silence. A close male mentor of my family could not bring himself to speak to me about my rape for an entire year. The last time we were both together was at Spelman on my graduation day.
>
> I have learned that he cried when told about my rape. I wonder how it would have been if we had cried—and healed—together. (p. 53)

It is generally conceded that in the African American community, acts of sexual violence are reported even less frequently than is true among whites. A distrust of authorities is not the only reason. A workshop for rape survivors described in *Los Angeles Times* confirms the existence of a code of silence imposed upon black women when sexually abused by a "brother." As described by Pollard-Terry (2004):

> At her workshop, CeCe Norwood, a counselor from Toledo, Ohio, gets right to the point . . . "Black culture makes it different," she says. "Our culture makes us less

likely to report." She bases this explanation on her own experiences as a sexual abuse survivor "three times over," years of counseling and surveying others, and federal statistics.

The black culture she refers to is a storytelling culture, rooted in the South before the decline of American apartheid. It comes with its own set of rules. "Blackisms," Norwood calls them during her presentation. She cites a few, as many black workshop participants chant along with her, such as: "What goes on in this house, stays in this house." (p. E-1)

Reconceptualization of Rape

Until recent times, a woman who engaged in sex outside marriage, even against her will, was considered a "fallen" woman and often was blamed for her own victimization (Bourke, 2007; Caringella, 2009. An unmarried woman who wished to prosecute her rapist had to have a good reputation without any previous sexual experience to get a conviction for the rapist. The victim, not the defendant, was on trial; the typical caution to the jury was that the charge of rape was easy to make and hard to disprove. Few cases were prosecuted, and for those that were, the conviction rate was very low. In 1972, in Chicago, for example, of more than 3,000 reported rapes fewer than 1 percent resulted in jail terms (Deckard, 1983). The laws at this time defining rape were much more restrictive than the laws today; prosecutors rarely would have considered taking a case in which the victim and offender had a previous consensual sexual relationship or if the woman had been picked up from a bar.

Some of the early research on rape, even after 1970, played into victim blaming. The publication of Menachem Amir's *Patterns in Forcible Rape* (1971) marked the first sociological study of its kind. This investigation of *victim-precipitated* crime was very influential in criminological circles and much studied throughout the next decade. Arguments about women's "complicity" in their own victimization were strongly influenced by psychoanalytical thinking that still dominated this period (Bourke, 2007). The women's movement was even held partially responsible for an increase in reports of rape that occurred in the 1970s, which was purported to be caused by the increasing permissiveness and for encouraging women to put themselves in more dangerous situations such as going alone to a bar.

About the same time, the feminist movement offered a framework for viewing male-on-female violence that was to turn the conceptualization of rape upside-down and to be a complete eye-opener for both men and women. For the first time, sexual assault was redefined from the victim's and society's perspective. Rape was seen as the violence that it is. Through the efforts of the antirape movement, it would soon become clear that such violence against women is one more mechanism for male social control (McPhail, 2002). In a landmark article entitled "Rape—The All American Crime," Susan Griffin (1971) articulated for the theory how rape and the fear of rape work to keep women dependent on men. Rape was recognized in this article, among others, as an act about domination and control, not sex. Down to the present time, some feminist writers wish to remove the sexual connotations from the concept of rape. As Bourke (2007), however, points out, such a conceptualization "would constitute a denial of the lived experience of many victims and perpetrators" (p. 408).

The work of well-known feminists such as Brownmiller and Griffin has further helped us to conceive of rape not in either-or terms but as a series of acts along a continuum. Far from being an isolated event that could be rooted out from the society at large, the crime of rape was now seen as only the logical extension of what was there already. When viewed as a continuum, commonplace sexual offenses could be seen as the "little rapes" that ranged from teasing and innuendos to making unwelcome sexual advances. Considered fair game, women were targeted as legitimate objects of sexual aggression. Unless protected by a man, a woman's personal territory could be violated by suggestion and intimidation. In her memoir, *Strange Piece of Paradise*, which described in graphic detail an attempted ax murder that occurred thirty years earlier, Terri Jentz (2007) describes the "little rapes" with which most young women are familiar:

> Categories of male violence against women and children are not distinct: beating a wife or girlfriend is not distinct from raping or murdering strangers, not distinct from molesting a niece or nephew. A guy who slaps his wife around is along the same continuum as rape and incest and murder, which are merely situations farther along this spectrum. Street harassment is on this same continuum. Pioneering feminists in the early seventies had a name for such hectoring as wolf whistles and animals noises. They called them 'little rapes'. My body knew this all along, the primal fear I felt in my early twenties when I heard hissing on the street—like a rattlesnake in the grass. (p. 397)

According to the feminist school, the violation to the self caused by everyday whistles and unsolicited greetings on the street is but one aspect of the cultural perspective that defines women as objects and men as possessors (Sigler, Johnson, and Morgan, 2007). And in the spectrum of male behavior, rape violence is the penultimate violent act.

Thanks to the influence of the women's movement and female lawyers and policy makers, the rape laws have been changed to make prosecution easier. Lawyers are restricted from introducing evidence about the victim's previous sexual experiences if these experiences were with someone other than the defendant. The rape-shield laws include broad exceptions, however, and are sometimes ignored as happened in the much publicized case against basketball star, Kobe Bryant (Caringella, 2009). The charges were later dropped when the alleged victim refused to testify; her name and details of her sexual life were leaked out to the press. According to Caringella (2009), the impact of legislative reform has fallen short of the expectations, because convictions in rape cases are still hard to obtain, especially in cases of acquaintance or date rape.

Rape reform laws have limited the ordeal of the trial and allowed many more cases to be prosecuted. Bourke (2007) lists the advances as an end to the exemption of husbands from rape accusations; the acceptance of date and acquaintance as prosecutable; inclusion of other areas of the body in addition to the vagina as violable; no longer allowing judges to admonish the jury of the need for corroboration or to issue a cautionary instruction; and the limits placed on the cross examination of the victim.

Changes in the conceptualization of rape have been reflected in significant changes in the treatment of victims. Women's group counseling centers and rape crisis centers were developed by grassroots organizations in local communities, at medical centers, and on college campuses. Numerous magazine and newspaper articles appeared, chronicling the reality of rape and its aftermath and especially the courtroom denigration of the victim's character and insinuations about her sexual history. Federal funding for a time poured into rape crisis centers and other crisis intervention programs for victims. Perhaps the most noteworthy outcome of the rape reform movement was the progress made on the legal front. Law enforcement officers gradually became more sensitized to the feelings of women who had been sexually abused. We consider the criminal justice response to rape later in this chapter.

When the federal government allocated millions of dollars to make rape kits available that included evidence for DNA testing, the prosecution of rape cases was given a major boost. Now there would be proof that sexual contact had taken place between the accused and the victim; conversely, innocent suspects could be exonerated if the evidence implicated someone else. Some police departments, however, have been slow to apply for or to use the funds to test the rape kits. While Los Angeles was remiss and failed to test thousands of the rape kits, New York City has faithfully done the testing with excellent results, as have many other cities (Pelisek, 2009).

PREVALENCE

Thanks to recent incentives to gather extensive data on sexual offenses, the Centers for Disease Control and Prevention (CDC, 2008) through the National Center for Injury and Prevention and Control has prepared fact sheets on sexual violence, while the Bureau of Justice Statistics (BJS, 2008) has accumulated data on criminal victimization. The CDC draws on scientific research, while both sources collect data from crimes known to the police as well as reports from the national victimization surveys. We need to take into account the fact that only a fraction of the rapes that take place are reported to the police, and that even in the self-reporting surveys, the interviewers ask about assault and do not directly ask about sexual offenses (Belknap, 2007). As the CDC summarizes significant findings for the literature on sexual abuse:

- In a nationally representative survey of 9,684 adults: 10.6 percent of women reported experiencing forced sex at some time in their lives; 2.1 percent of men reported experiencing forced sex at some time in their lives, and; 2.5 percent of women surveyed and 0.9 percent of men surveyed said they experienced unwanted sexual activity in the previous 12 months.
- 20–25 percent of women in college reported experiencing an attempted or a completed rape in college.
- A 2005 survey of high school students found that 10.8 percent of girls and 4.2 percent of boys from grades 9 to 12 were forced to have sexual intercourse at some time in their lives.
- In the first rape experience of female victims, perpetrators were reported to be intimate partners (30.4 percent), family members (23.7 percent), and acquaintances (20 percent).
- Among high school students, 9.3 percent of black students, 7.8 percent of Hispanic students, and 6.9 percent of white students reported that they were forced to have sexual intercourse at some time in their lives.
- Among sexual violence victims raped since their eighteenth birthday, 31.5 percent of women and 16.1 percent of men reported a physical injury as a result of a rape.

College students are especially vulnerable to rape and attempted rape because they typically are within the age range within which sexual assault is most prevalent and because of the heavy drinking that is characteristic of college life. First-year students are the most at risk of both binge drinking and victimization by acquaintance rape (Belknap, 2007; van Wormer and Davis, 2008).

In many states, criminal justice systems allow sex offenders to plead guilty to nonsex crimes such as aggravated assault or criminal trespass (see, for example, DeSantis, 2005; Gershman, 2006; Troxler, 2005). This course of action has several advantages, first to the victim, who can avoid the public humiliation of an adversarial trial, and secondly to the perpetrator, who can get off with a lighter sentence than the one he might receive at trial. The relatively low conviction rate for sexual crimes against adult women is a further factor in the prosecutor's willingness to settle such a case through negotiations with the accused's attorney.

To further our understanding of violence against women, the National Violence Against Women Survey, under the sponsorship of the federal government, conducted a national survey of 8,000 men and 8,000 women. Unlike other government victimization reports, this one looks at victimization over one's lifetime. Among the key findings: one out of six women and one out of thirty-three men has been raped over his or her lifetime; twice as many girls raped before age 18 were raped after the age of 18 as women who were not raped in childhood; and the typical female rape victim is a child (Tjaden and Thoennes, 2000). More than half of the female victims and nearly three-quarters of the male victims were raped before their 18th birthday. Women who reported being raped as minors were twice as likely to report being raped as adults.

Other significant findings were:

- Female victims are significantly more likely than male victims to be raped by a current or former intimate partner and to sustain an injury during a rape.
- Many rape victims suffer serious mental health consequences.
- Only one in five adult women report their rape to the police. About half of the women raped as adults who had contact with police and about half who had contact with the courts were satisfied with their treatment.

The National Violence Against Women Survey also clarified racial and ethnic differences. American Indians disclosed a higher rate of rape and physical assault than women of other racial/ethnic backgrounds, while Asian/Pacific Islander women were significantly less likely to report rape and physical assault. However, among Asian Americans, sexual assault may be underreported because of the sense of shame this crime brings to the victims and their families.

Kilpatrick, Saunders, and Smith (2003) report high rates of victimization among African Americans compared with youth of different ethnicities. Since the official rates from BJS (2006) are more or less equal across black/white racial lines, one is left to speculate that fewer blacks than whites are willing to report the crime to the police. To get a more detailed study of different kinds of sexual victimization among young African American women and the link with several background factors, Cecil and Matsen (2005) interviewed 249 patients who received services from an adolescent health care facility and who were sexually active. The background factors consisted of reports of family dysfunction, depression, and substance abuse problems. Results showed that 32 percent of the participants reported that they had been raped, and 11 percent that they had experienced attempted rape. Keep in mind that this sample was of inner-city health care patients, so making generalization difficult. The study does show within this sample that a background of mental health problems and family dysfunction were closely correlated with reported victimization of all kinds. The rape survivors had significantly lower levels of self-esteem than did adolescents who had experienced consensual sex.

Vulnerability factors as spelled out in the statistics presented above are: young age, prior history of sexual violence, multiple sexual partners, and poverty. Poverty, according to CDC (2008), is a high-risk factor that forces study participants into certain high-risk occupations, including prostitution. We would add high-crime neighborhoods, unsafe forms of transportation, and the need to work the night shift. But these factors relate to attacks by a stranger, the less frequent form of rape. As Pazzani (2007) indicates, the circumstances surrounding stranger rape and acquaintance or date rape differ. Their research which analyzed data from a national interview sample showed that increased gender equality in a community is related to a reduction in acquaintance rape but not stranger rape. A heavy rate of subscription to pornography in a community is associated with higher rates of attacks by a stranger. Pazzani noted a striking finding that victims of child abuse and previous sexual assaults were more likely to be victims of acquaintance than of stranger rape. We can speculate that heavy drinking is involved, since child abuse victims tend to have high rates of substance use problems, and heavy drinking in social situations increases one's vulnerability to sexual exploitation.

How about personality characteristics of the rapists? Pardue and Arrigo (2007) provide an overview of the research that reveals three basic types of rapists: power, anger, and sadistic. Power rapists desire control over their victims to accommodate their own feelings of inadequacy. There is no intent to injure the victims, although they may well do so to carry out their goal. Anger rapists coerce sex as a means of punishing their victims; some in this group are physically aroused by the violence, and assaults may last for hours. Sadistic rapists are also sexually aroused by the physical suffering of the victims; these offenders use excessive force such as bondage and torture (2007). Research reveals that around 70 percent of known rapists meet the diagnostic criteria for antisocial personality disorder. Note that Pardue and Arrigo are mainly concerned with offenders within the criminal justice system.

The World Health Organization (WHO) data presented by Krug et al. (2004) single out the following individual risk factors in sexual offending on the part of the perpetrator—substance abuse, coercive sexual fantasies, antisocial tendencies, hostility toward women, history of childhood sexual abuse, witnessing family violence, association with a sexually aggressive peer group, and exposure to societal norms that support male superiority and sexual entitlement.

Hispanic women in the national survey reported a lower rate of rape victimization than did non-Hispanic women. Previous studies have produced contradictory findings on this score. A survey of Mexican Americans in Los Angeles found that Anglos had two and one-half times the rate of sexual assault as Mexican Americans (Sorenson and Siegel, 1992). Reasons given for the lower rate were the greater sense of community as well as the protective restrictions on Mexican American females.

A review of literature reveals that, not surprisingly, more men than women subscribe to rape myths. Among women, rape myth acceptance, such as that one of the causes of rape is that women act or dress inappropriately, varies by ethnicity. European Americans are the least accepting of these beliefs, while first generation Asian American women are the most accepting of them (Devdas and Rubin, 2007). Latino Americans tend to be more accepting of the myths than African Americans. Sexually aggressive men are more inclined than others to subscribe to victim-blaming beliefs (Belknap, 2007).

Rape myths are so engrained in our society that even many victims of sexual assault are apt to subscribe to them. This is what Karen Weiss (2009) found in her examination of qualitative data that were made available to her from the NCVS collection of almost a thousand victim narratives. Three basic forms of denial of harm emerged from the accounts: denial of injury ("it was no big deal"); denial of offender responsibility ("he just got carried away"); and denial of themselves as victims ("I had too much to drink"). Twenty percent of the victims' reports contained at least one of these types of excuses; five percent of the rape victims denied that they were "real victims." These patterns of denial, as Weiss suggests, draw primarily from two commonly held myths about rape, (1) that male sexual aggression is natural and to some extent uncontrollable and (2) that the offender is not responsible due to diminished capacity from drugs or alcohol. See Box 8.1 for a list of typical rape myths commonly believed in the society.

BOX 8.1
Rape Myths

What are rape myths? Basically they are false beliefs that are refuted by the statistics provided in this chapter. Typical rape myths are:

- Most rape claims are false; women feel guilty about sex and redefine the situation later.
- Rape happens only to bad women such as prostitutes.
- Unconsciously, women want to be raped.
- Most rape is committed by a stranger in a dark alley.

- When women say no, they mean yes.
- Woman's wearing of seductive clothes and acting in a flirtatious manner sets her up for an attack that she somehow deserves.
- Rapes are impulsive acts committed by men unable to control their passions.
- Rapes are often interracial crimes committed against white victims.
- Rape is caused by male deviance and pathology.

IMPACT OF THE MASS MEDIA

Positive Developments

The impact of the television drama *Something about Amelia*, first shown on MTV in 1984, is hard to describe. The subject was incest in a middle-class family. Extensive coverage was given to this production in the general mass media and in specialized newsletters for the counseling professions. The interest of professionals was heightened, no doubt because of the central role given to family therapy in the film. In the drama, when the incest is discovered, the father, not the daughter, is removed from the home. Then intensive professional attention is devoted to this family in crisis. Following the broadcast, there was a flurry of phone calls to hotlines and children protective services. A few years later when Israeli television aired this startling and well-acted program, the impact was similarly sensational (Oppenheimer, 1998).

When the movie *The Accused* hit the screens in 1988, it was another first of sorts: at last, a portrayal of the difficulty of prosecuting a gang-rape case from the point of view of the victim! Portrayed convincingly by Jodie Foster, the victim meets her fate while she is drinking at a bar. *The Accused* is based on a true story of a working-class Portuguese woman from New Bedford, Massachusetts, who brought criminal charges against Portuguese onlookers who cheered as she was raped. In her heroic fight for justice, the survivor emerges as victor, and the prosecutor learns something about courage and determination. It is a sad commentary that when the movie was first shown, some young men in the audience hooted and cheered at the rape scene (Faludi, 1991). The real victim on whom *The Accused* was based was condemned by her community for the negative attention brought on them by the crime. She died of alcoholism several years later.

As Faludi suggested in her book *Backlash* (1991), it is a sad day when a sympathetic portrait of a rape victim is hailed as a daring feminist statement. Yet this portrayal is certainly an improvement over the way Hollywood dealt with rape in the past. In *Gone With the Wind*, which was released in 1939, Rhett Butler forces his attentions on Scarlett, who has been "getting out of hand." Although frightened at the time, the next day she wakes up in her luxurious bed humming. Mammy comments that she looks extra cheerful this morning, and Scarlett grins ear to ear. Contrast this with *A Streetcar Named Desire*, the Tennessee Williams masterpiece that was produced as a movie in 1951. The class and sexual tensions between Stanley (played by Marlon Brando) and Blanche (Vivien Leigh) result in a climactic rape scene. (This scene was watered down for the movie.)

Sinking into the chasm of mental illness, the violated sister-in-law is taken away. Perhaps because of his sexual orientation or artistry, Tennessee Williams handled the rape with a rare sensitivity.

Newspaper coverage of rape cases has tended to be sensationalized when they involve celebrities, fraternity members, or athletic teams. In recent years, some women have courageously identified themselves publicly and spoken out, an event practically unheard of before the 1980s. Rape victims, in fact, have been "in the closet" far more than gays and lesbians have been, and male victims remain the most hidden of all. Rape is a crime unlike any other; the sordidness of the crime somehow attaches to the unwilling party as much as to the instigator, and sometimes even more so.

Racism is evident not only in the reduced prosecution of cases of African American victimization but also in mass media accounts. Media attention rarely focuses on African American victims of crime (Rollins, 1996). Outrage seems to be reserved for white victims, especially those of high socioeconomic status. Rollins cites the widely publicized case of a white jogger who was raped and set on fire allegedly by a group of black youths. (Note: In 2003, the judge threw out the conviction.) Meanwhile, comparable cases of inner-city victimization were largely ignored.

Paralleling the growth of two revolutionary developments from the late 1970s—feminism and the self-help movement—reports of childhood sexual abuse rose to prominence. A deluge of newspaper articles, books, and television movies appeared in North America and Western Europe. Political progress in child welfare has historically been linked to the success of feminism, and the fact that women are disproportionately victims of sexual abuse has cemented the linkage in the modern period (Finkelhor, 1994). When feminists joined forces with child welfare professionals, who tend for the most part to be trained in social work, child protection advocacy got off the ground. Despite a formidable backlash against false accusations in recent years (most notably, the false accusation by a stripper against the 2006 Duke University Lacrosse team), there is a public and professional awareness of the exploitation of children that did not exist in previous decades. The U.S., Canadian, and Irish press has been inundated with reports of court cases involving child molesters who were in positions of authority, such as priests and teachers.

A promising development in media history occurred several years ago as the cable network Lifetime Television made women's advocacy campaigns a top priority. The network operates a Web site http://www.mylifetime.com/my-lifetime-commitment/endviolence devoted to stopping violence against women. Unlike other networks, cable TV has the freedom to endorse public policy campaigns, so their potential should not be underestimated.

Rape in a Small Town: The Florence Holway Story (HBO, 2005) is a fairly recent television documentary that chronicles an elderly woman's heroic, twelve-year struggle for justice following an intruder rape in her rural New Hampshire home. Holway, as revealed in the documentary, felt she had been brutalized twice—first by the rapist and then by a flawed legal system that offered the rapist a plea bargain to a lesser sentence without consulting her. Holway, remarkably, launched a solo campaign to force her attacker to trial. When her story was picked up by big-city media, she became a national figure. Eventually, her campaign paid off, with the state legislature ushering in reforms to rape law. The TV broadcast incited much interest in Australia when it aired there on a major TV station.

Negative, Antiwoman Messages

Although crime survivors can gain strength in reading the details of others who have had the courage to prosecute their victimizers, others are intimidated by lurid media accounts. One problem is the stories are rarely about empowerment and offender accountability. Instead they focus on a victim's trauma (Formosa, 2007). News coverage of rape trials additionally are apt to focus on lapses in the rape victim's judgment more than on the abusive strategies of the accused rapist. Rare cases of false allegations are big media events (Bourke, 2007).

Much media attention was paid in the UK recently to a case in which an accused man was acquitted in an ambiguous drunken sexual situation. The woman's complaint is only parodied rather than presented in the media accounts and readers' comments to the story. Consider this excerpt from *Sunday Times* columnist India Knight (2009) concerning a case that admittedly was not suited for traditional courtroom justice. This column predictably aroused a flood of antifeminist sentiments in the online comments that followed. Here is a sample from the column:

> Is it too much to hope that men falsely accused of rape by drunken women might one day be treated with ordinary courtesy and remain anonymous until proven guilty? Last week it took a jury a mere 45 minutes to throw out an accusation made by a woman in her forties, whom we must, maddeningly—because she is automatically guaranteed anonymity—refer to as Miss X, against Peter Bacon, a 26-year-old student and chef from Canterbury, Kent. After an evening at the woman's house, during which Miss X, Bacon and a friend had drunk at least five bottles of wine, Bacon and Miss X retired to bed and had sex. Next morning Miss X, a solicitor, was so hungover she did not even remember what had happened, then claimed Bacon had raped her because she was too drunk to have consented to sex. The way Bacon tells it, Miss X was "giving me the come-on". When they started kissing, "she did not say no. There was never any indication of her saying, 'What are you doing?' She had plenty of time to say, 'Oi!,'" he told the jury.

Belknap (2007) provides an overview of rape images in film and in cyber space. Many top-grossing films encourage stereotypes that rapists are predominantly sadistic and deviant. Depictions of rape on the Internet rely on graphic enactments of situations of violence and domination, with gang rape prominently featured. Labels such as "bitch" and "slut" indicate the victim's need to be punished. Aggressive sex is also prominently featured in television movie videos; in these depictions, the females are shown to enjoy the aggressive sex. Finally, video games sometimes promote images of extreme violence; one even encourages players to commit virtual murder and rape of prostitutes.

Blaming the Victim

A counterforce to feminist awareness of the personal as political, one related to society's antifeminist backlash, is the societal propensity for victim blaming when it comes to sexual assault (Neame, 2004). Women who deviate from societal norms are often blamed if they are raped. So even as feminist researchers and scholars have sought to create public awareness about the prevalence of sexual assault in the society, the popular literature has sought to refute it by various means. The very act of launching primary prevention campaigns on disturbing social issues has the capacity, as Neame (2004) indicates, to provoke a backlash. Members of society with vested interests in maintaining the status quo, accordingly, are apt to challenge research indicating, for example, that high rates of rape in dating relationships exist. Roiphe's (1994) *The Morning After: Sex, Fear and Feminism* became a bestseller within this context. The thesis of her book was that if women did not define the forced sex they experienced as rape, then it was not rape but just a misunderstanding. "Someone's rape," she famously claimed, "may be another person's bad night" (p. 54). Karmen (2004), in contrast, argues that to view date rape as a terrible misunderstanding in "he said-she said" terms is a form of victim blaming.

A recent offering that is less well known but that takes a similar tack is *The Decline of Men: How the American Male is Tuning Out, Giving Up, and Flipping off His Future* by Garcia (2008). A more prominently featured piece of writing à la Roiphe is that by journalist Heather Mac Donald (2008). Entitled, "The Campus Rape Myth: The Bogus Statistics, Feminist Victimology, and University-Approved Sex Toys," Mac Donald's article appeared in the quarterly magazine of urban affairs *City Journal*. In the following excerpts, the writer equates date rape on the college campus with promiscuity:

> The campus rape movement highlights the current condition of radical feminism, from its self-indulgent bathos to its embrace of ever more vulnerable female victimhood. But the movement is an even more important barometer of academia itself. In a delicious historical irony, the baby boomers who dismantled the university's intellectual architecture in favor of unbridled sex and protest have now bureaucratized both. While women's studies professors bang pots and blow whistles at antirape rallies, in the dorm next door, freshman counselors and deans pass out tips for better orgasms and the use of sex toys. The academic bureaucracy is roomy enough to sponsor both the dour anti-male feminism of the college rape movement and the promiscuous hookup culture of student life. . . .
>
> So what reality does lie behind the campus rape industry? A booze-fueled hookup culture of one-night, or sometimes just partial-night, stands. . . .
>
> Modern feminists defined the right to be promiscuous as a cornerstone of female equality. Understandably, they now hesitate to acknowledge that sex is a more complicated force than was foreseen. Rather than recognizing that no-consequences sex may be a contradiction in terms, however, the campus rape industry claims that what it calls campus rape is about not sex but rather politics—the male desire to subordinate women. (pp. 1–3)

Denial of the reality of rape crime victimhood can be understood not only in terms of current trends, but also because the natural social–psychological tendency has been always to belittle the load that others carry and to look away from others' pain. We do not want to see the homeless, hear the complaints of those on welfare, and certainly not hear of bad things happening to good people. A concept derived from social psychology, **victim blaming** refers to a fundamental tendency in American culture to hold the downtrodden or underdogs of society responsible for creating their own distress (Zastrow, 2007). Because of the reciprocity involved, the victim tends to internalize the blame attached to his or her condition ("I have failed"), and the negativity may become a self-fulfilling prophecy ("I am a tainted person").

The appeal of victim blaming lies in its apparently reassuring message (to outside observers) that a just world exists (Karmen, 2004). Victim blaming can be conceived as a validation of the offender's point of view because it shifts some of the burden of responsibility from the perpetrator to his or her target. The fact is that the closer we try to identify ourselves with victims, the more vulnerable we are to their suffering. Although we have a tendency to put ourselves in the place of someone who is suffering, there is also the countertendency to believe that the unfortunate victim in some sense merited his or her fate. In the case of crimes of personal violation, we attach a stigma to the victim almost out of fear of contamination. Accordingly, we may develop an unfavorable perception of a rape victim and are apt to reject her.

Compounding the victim-blaming ethos is the social-psychological phenomenon called *erotophobia*, or fear and ambivalence concerning sex. Erotophobia is unconsciously conveyed to children so that they will have the socially acceptable inhibitions to keep them from being a source of embarrassment to their parents in polite company. Foremost among the challenging tasks of growing up is to unlearn some of the inhibitions that one so conscientiously has been taught. Even learning the language of sexuality presents difficulties; one must employ a different vocabulary in different circles. In adulthood, a vague feeling that sex is dirty may persist. In their review of the literature concerning college women's experiences of sexual coercion, Adams-Curtis and Forbes (2004) found that erotophobia contributed toward the possession of negative attitudes toward women and to victim support groups as well.

Victim blaming falls the hardest on victims who had dated or previously knew the perpetrator. Because of the myth that the typical rapist looks like a rapist—rough and disheveled in appearance—blame is transferred to the victim if the accused rapist defies the stereotype. This is what happened in the crime documentary *Our Guys* (Lefkowitz, 1997), a work that stirred up much talk in criminology circles. *Our Guys* stands as an indictment of suburbia where when the high school jocks are charged with sexual crimes, the entire community turns the other way. What is not surprising, given our knowledge of victim blaming, is that the town rallied around the accused jocks, "our guys." Following the arrests, the townspeople spoke of the tragedy that had befallen these boys, a tragedy that would scar them forever: "In the bosom of their home-town, they were greeted like returning warriors who had prevailed in a noble crusade. Or, if you prefer, martyred heroes" (p. 5). Refer to Chapter 12 in this book, which describes a similar, more recent case in which six female athletes sued the school district and a popular softball and bas-ketball coach. The town of Warrensburg, Missouri, was divided; at school, the girls were called liars, bullies, and white trash (Zagier, 2008).

Some have argued that the tremendous effort we put into teaching aggression to athletes leads to an increase in aggressive behavior off the field (Kimmel, 2008; Schwartz and DeKeseredy, 1997). Surveys have shown that student athletes tend to endorse rape myths more than others, and that members of sports teams such as football and basketball have a disproportionately high level of participation in arrests for sexual assault (Adams-Curtis and Forbes, 2004). In an age of sports hero idolatry, star athletes get the message that they can break the law with impunity and that a certain amount of violence against women will be tolerated. This message protects star athletes from taking responsibility. It sets girls and women up for abuse and denigration. We are, as these sociologists term it, a **rape-supportive culture**.

Guyland: The Perilous World Where Boys Become Men by Michael Kimmel has been highlighted prominently on talk shows. Among the topics discussed relevant to this book are "predatory sex" and "party rape." The guy code, as he suggests, is characteristic of high school- and college-age males, especially those who are bonded through athletics and sport teams. This code is supported by a culture of silence and homophobia. For entertainment, furious rap and heavy metal music are favored, what Kimmel calls "entertainment with a vengeance." The pornography favored by these youths is contemptuous of women. The dominant emotion that drives "guyland" is anger—anger that can lead to violence. If the "guys" do get into trouble through heavy drinking or otherwise, they can count on a "culture of protection" by parents and the community.

Dating patterns in the United States set up situations that are ambiguous and can lead to misunderstandings. Belknap describes the role of male expectations in creating difficulties:

> There are . . . unwritten assumptions adopted by some men (and women): If he pays for dinner, movies, and so on, then she owes him sex; if she drinks or uses drugs with him, she is giving up her right to say no to sex; if she consensually goes to one level of sexual intimacy, she must continue; or if she once had a sexual relationship with someone, she has no right to say no to such a relationship in the future. (p. 287)

Let us digress briefly to consider the perceived contrast of rape-prone and rape-free culture. Within American society there are enclaves where male dominance reigns. Consider, for example, the male prison, the street gang, sports teams, and fraternities. Here, conditions are conducive to male dominance and sexual violence. In a rape-prone culture, dominance and control over women become aspects of achieving and experiencing masculinity to the extent that rape, while not condoned, becomes part of the cultural ethos (Watson-Franke, 2003).

What do cross-cultural data say about the opposite pattern—societies that are **rape free** or relatively so? Watson-Franke, in her survey of anthropological research from matrilineal cultures, did find some instances of societies where rape was unknown. Among the Iroquois, for example, rape was reported by European explorers to be unknown; in several societies such as the Apache, a man would have been considered less than human if he attacked a woman in this way. Watson-Franke's explanation for the absence of rape in such matrilineal societies is that biological paternity is not a concern and, typically, the role of maternal uncle is as important as the role of father. In her research on rape-free societies, Sanday (2007) found that societies characterized by sexual equality, peacefulness, and women in positions of authority tend to have relatively low levels of rape.

Strides are being made in alternative socialization for men by men. Leading the way are male educators and well-known theorists such as Michael Kimmel (work described above) and Jackson Katz. In *The Macho Paradox*, Katz (2006) contends that through daunting determination, society's mentors and other leaders can reverse the socially constructed perspectives on gender roles that are associated with male-on-female violence. Central to his argument is the assertion that sexual harassment and other forms of gendered abuse are not problems of sick individuals but social problems rooted in cultural norms. Katz is a cofounder of the Mentors in Violence Prevention Program that recruits high school and college student leaders such as athletes and members of student government to play a significant role in challenging attitudes and behaviors that demean women.

Instead of focusing on instructions for women on how to protect themselves from stranger rape, newer college prevention strategies are focusing on changing attitudes of male privilege, to sensitize men to the reality of sexual misconduct. Rape prevention programming aimed at first-year fraternity men has had success in changing male behavior by changing their attitudes (Louwagie, 2008). A study of long-term attitude and behavioral change in fraternity members and athletes following an intervention revealed that viewing a video of male-on-male rape elicited feeling of empathy in these college men and that this knowledge of how rape would feel was effective (Foubert and Perry, 2007). Participants later reported that they refrained from telling jokes about rape and discouraged others from doing so as well. About ninety campuses today receive Department of Justice grants to establish antirape programming aimed at men's attitudes (Louwagie). The Army too is initiating programming to encourage soldiers to intervene if they see signs of activity that can lead to sexual assault.

Problems on the college campus may be substantial, but they pale in contrast to the extent of sexual abuse of women serving in the military. In 2006, Congress broadened the definition of rape in the Military Code of Justice, changing it from an act of sexual intercourse "by force and without consent" to one that can include causing a person to engage in sex by using force, causing bodily harm, invoking fear of death, harm or kidnapping, rendering unconscious, or administering drugs or intoxicants to impair a victim's conduct (Wehrman and Carr, 2008). The change was instituted to help rectify an earlier situation in which acquaintance rape was not included as an offense under military law. But the problem of rape in war continues unabated. There were 2,923 reports of sexual assault across the military in the twelve months ending in September 30, 2008 (*Washington Post*, 2009). Among the cases reported, only a small number resulted in court martials. Estimates are that only 10–20 percent of sexual assaults are ever reported.

For the first time today, the Veterans Affairs (VA) is screening veterans for sexual assault and harassment in military service and is providing treatment for sexual trauma, as mandated by Congress. According to the first data of its kind stemming from the treatment, one out of seven female veterans of the war in Iraq or Afghanistan reports that she has been a victim of sexual assault or harassment during military duty (Elias, 2008). Of these, more than half have the symptoms of **posttraumatic stress disorder (PTSD)**. Such trauma raises the odds of women having other mental health problems as well. Few of the women who come to the VA for help after an assault have reported the problem to military officials. The women fear they will be ostracized by others in the military unit if they do so. Writing in *The Lonely Soldier, The Private War of Women Serving in Iraq*, Helen Benedict (2009) reveals just how isolated women in combat zones are and how vulnerable they are to sexual harassment, attempted rape, and rape. Drawing on interviews with forty soldiers who have been there, Benedict provides portraits of women who have faced the "hostility of their male comrades" (p. 5), a hostility that is happening because "the military is still permeated with stereotypes of women as weak, passive sex objects" (p. 5).

TYPES OF RAPE

The types of rape that occur most frequently are acquaintance rape, mass rape, and child abuse or sexual abuse. (Marital rape is discussed in connection with wife abuse in Chapter 9.)

Acquaintance Rape

Acquaintance rape is any rape in which the parties know one another. Included in this definition are date rape, campus rape, and partner or marital rape. Stranger rape was thought at one time to be the most common form of sexual violence. Yet, thanks to self-report surveys of both men and women, we now know that most victims know their rapists. Acquaintance rape is extremely common on college campuses.

Because practically all the studies of acquaintance rape use college samples, not much is known about this phenomenon, apart from BJS statistics on non-stranger rape. Another major problem in data gathering, as noted by Koss et al. (1985), is that so many victims of rape by their dates or boyfriends feel responsible themselves for their own vulnerability and, even in surveys, don't define what happened to them as rape. The statistics therefore vastly underestimate the prevalence of rape/sexual assault.

As reported by the NCVC (2008), research shows that almost four out of five rapes are committed by someone known to the victim, a fact true of around 85 percent of such attacks on a college campus. Only about 2 percent of these cases are reported to the police. Friends, neighbors, boyfriends, husbands, ex-husbands, and relatives headed the list of perpetrators.

When rape occurs in a dating relationship, it does not necessarily lead to the breakup of the relationship. The likelihood of multiple experiences of forced sex increases substantially if the rapist is a woman's husband or lover. In many women's minds, the boundaries between rape and strong pressure to have sex are unclear. For this reason, for greater accuracy in results rape surveys often ask if respondents were "forced to have sex" instead of "raped" (Koss et al., 1985).

Estrich (1987), in her groundbreaking *Real Rape*, alerted our attention to the seriousness of the form of rape that takes place in a relationship of trust—acquaintance rape. Taking a historical perspective, Estrich shows how this form of rape by a non-stranger frequently has been characterized by the courts and by the general public as not "real rape." The male-dominated system, as Estrich indicates, is reluctant to classify rape as violence because violence is construed as getting beaten up, while rape is viewed in sexual terms. Consider the following case, admittedly extreme, of the badgering that a survivor of date rape endured at the hands of her abusive husband to whom she had confided several years before of the rape by a man who she thought was her friend:

> I truly believed my husband requested these things because of his pain. However, I soon found out that this was a lie. One day B. asked me to talk about how I had been raped. I tried to explain that the Panamanian man took off my clothes and I told him, "no" as he was doing it, but he refused to listen. B. told me he thought I "wanted it" because, after all, I went in his dorm room when I was visiting my sister (who was attending college at the time and I was in high school). I told B. that I went to this man's room (a dorm room) because I thought we were friends and we could practice Spanish together. This explanation was not sufficient for B. He insisted I give him explicit details about the rape from beginning to end, focusing on details such as "how he went in and out" and "how I liked it." B. would badger me for hours (sometimes up to eight hours at a time) about the rape and would not stop until I convinced him that I really did not want to be raped and that I did not like it. (Confided to van Wormer in private correspondence on October 5, 2005)

As in the United States, in Britain, the public still believes the stereotype of what constitutes "real rape," which is the rape by a stranger of a victim who resists and who reports the crime immediately to the police. The saliency of this belief system is reflected in results from an analysis by criminologist Liz Kelly (cited in a British news release by Sawyer, 2005) who studied relevant court documents. In 1985, there was a 24 percent conviction rate in rape trials; in 2003, only 5 percent of rape allegations ended in a guilty verdict. "Twenty years ago," according to Kelly's report, "if a woman wore a short skirt she was deemed to be 'asking for it.' These days alcohol is the equivalent of that miniskirt" (p. 2). Prosecutors in the United Kingdom, as in the United States, only take a case to court if they have a reasonable chance of winning. Often the prospects of a harsh cross-examination and reliving the trauma over and over are enough to dissuade the victim from pursuing justice. Yet American prosecutors receive special training to prepare them to prosecute rape cases, and their conviction rate is substantially higher than that of their British counterparts (Sawyer).

McDonald and Kline (2004) presented vignettes to 300 college students and had the students recommend appropriate sanctions in cases of date rape. The results showed, as predicted, that women chose harsher sanctions for the violators than did the men.

Cases of forced sex when there have previously been sexual relations are rarely reported and, if they are reported, they are rarely prosecuted. Many campus rapes are handled internally through student conduct board hearings. One advantage of this process is that the perpetrator is forced to admit his bad behavior under threat of otherwise having the matter turned over to the police. This may spare victims the agony of the adversarial process and allow the perpetrator to "come clean." Typical in-house punishments are probation, suspension, and substance abuse counseling. Disadvantages are that the student offender generally remains on campus, which puts other women at risk, the offense is not viewed as a crime, and the victim-survivor is apt to be the one to leave the campus, in the end.

In the backlash rhetoric of some of the popular press, **date rape**, as Neame (2004) suggests, is commonly viewed as less serious and less traumatic than rape by a stranger. Yet research shows that date rape has significant consequences for women. Victims of acquaintance rape frequently blame themselves for a violent crime in a situation over which they lost control. According to the National Center for Victims of Crime (NCVC, 2008), because the assailants are previously known to them, many victims hold themselves accountable for not having better judged the character of their perpetrators. A sense of violation of trust is characteristic. Survivors of attacks by a date or boyfriend can suffer trauma just as do victims who were attacked by a stranger. Victims can suffer physically, emotionally, and financially. Rape-related PTSD, a condition suffered by almost one-third of all rape victims, includes sleeping and eating disorders, nervousness, fatigue, withdrawal from society, and distrust of others (NCVC).

Who is vulnerable to rape, and how can rape be avoided? In fact, all women are vulnerable to rape. Factors associated with avoiding stranger rape, according to Rollins (1996), are being tall, having been the oldest daughter, and having had major household responsibilities, all factors associated with assertiveness. Based on a survey of studies of women who escaped their attackers, Bourke (2007) recommends physical resistance, screaming, and reasoning with the rapist, but not pleading or arguing with him. African American women, notes Rollins, are most likely to avoid rape by having been "street smart" in dangerous situations. Surveys of convicted rapists indicate they stalk potential victims first, noting how women carry themselves as they walk. Those who seem weak and fearful are singled out as likely targets. Self-defense trainings are becoming popular to teach women how to resist physically and to escape rape threats. However, according to Hollander (2009), such trainings are controversial both because they might expose the potential victim to further risk and because of the implications of victim blaming in the message sent to women who have been unable to get away.

One area of much public concern has been the growing use of the drugs Rohypnol ("roofies") and gamma hydroxybutyric acid (GHB) to sedate women in order to take sexual advantage of them. Rohypnol resembles Valium in its properties; sedation occurs twenty to thirty minutes after ingestion. GHB can have intoxicating effects. Both are dangerous when consumed with alcohol. In Las Vegas, use of the so-called date-rape drugs was reported in about 100 cases; in the United States, there have been just under 200 fatalities so far with GHB, mostly from deliberate recreational use (Glauber, 2005). Prosecution is difficult because the victim typically suffers from drug-induced amnesia. Actually, alcohol has been used successfully by men for years to achieve similarly disabling results. "Candy is dandy, but liquor is quicker" goes the saying.

The fact that acquaintance rape is rampant on college campuses and that stereotypical stranger rape is relatively rare outside so-called high-crime areas has important implications for prevention. College rape prevention efforts are devoted to blue lights all over the campus, student escort services, and warnings to women about how to avoid rape. Campus authorities pay relatively little attention to party and date rape, however, which will not be deterred by protection remedies such as escort services and alarm systems that are designed to prevent stranger rape, even in safe campus communities. Efforts would be better spent on education and on men educating men about the risks of aggressive masculinity and objectification of women. Because of the alcohol abuse typically present on college campuses, stepped-up substance abuse prevention efforts could be immensely helpful as well.

Mass Rape

Susan Brownmiller's landmark study, *Against Our Will: Men, Women, and Rape* (1975) put the crime in an international and cultural perspective. She defined rape controversially as "a conscious process of intimidation by which all men keep all women in a state of fear" (p. 5). As a collective act, rape can promote male bonding. Among adolescent boys and gangs of bikers, rape sometimes serves as a ritual of manhood. A review of the literature on instances of fraternity gang rape shows that the sexual and drinking practices of many fraternities on American university campuses encourage gang rape (Adams-Curtis and Forbes, 2004; Sanday, 2007). Sorority women therefore are at heightened risk for attack.

Peggy Sanday discusses the demeaning attitudes about women characteristic of college fraternities in *Fraternity Gang Rape: Sex, Brotherhood, and Privilege on Campus*. Similar to the earlier book, *Sexual Assault on the College Campus* by Schwartz and DeKeseredy (1997), Sanday probes the "hypererotic subculture" that permeates the college scene. Men socialized into this subculture regard sex in terms of gaining possession of a woman. Fraternities, in their secretive nature, place a high value on loyalty to the group, a loyalty reinforced by the initiation rituals associated with hazing. Adams-Curtis (2004) differentiates high-risk fraternities in which drinking is rampant from low-risk fraternities in which membership is not associated with exploitative attitudes toward women.

"Frat" house conformity combined with strong peer-group pressure to "score" leads some to experience a sense of relative deprivation. As Schwartz and DeKeseredy suggest, "the frustration caused by a reference group–anchored sex drive often results in predatory sexual conduct" (p. 35). All-male alliances can reduce sexual intercourse to a violent power game, one that says more about relationships between men and their brothers than between men and women (Sanday, 2007).

Where there is hostility between enemies, women are particularly subject to predatory attack. War rape and sexual violence have a history as long as the practice of war itself (Benedict, 2009; Farwell, 2004). General George Patton is quoted by Brownmiller (1975) as follows, "I then told them that, in spite of my most diligent efforts, there would unquestionably be some raping" (p. 23). General Patton was speaking from experience and from his knowledge of history. Rape is more than an accident of war. Its widespread use under military occupation reflects the special terror it holds for the enemy's women. It also reflects the inequalities and discrimination women face in their everyday lives in peacetime. For an extensive discussion of mass rape of women in war, see Chapter 10, Women's Victimization, Global Perspectives. From the information presented in that chapter, drawn from historians and the United Nations, rape in war serves as an act of patriotism, an act of misogyny, and an expression of lust rolled into one (van Wormer, 2007). This form of rape can be viewed as a deliberate act of defilement not only of the individual woman but of a whole culture, and as an attack on the male enemy through rendering him helpless to protect the women in his family. The International Criminal Court today recognizes these violations against women in war as crimes against humanity.

Child Sexual Abuse

Child sexual abuse was rediscovered in the late 1970s and early 1980s when a deluge of newspaper articles, books, and television movies about this subject appeared in North America and western Europe. The percentage of women in the general population who report having been sexually abused as children varies from study to study. In their review of accumulated data,

Freyd et al. (2005) produced the estimate of 20 percent of women and 5–10 percent of men sexually victimized worldwide. Such surveys, as the authors point out, likely underestimate prevalence because of underreporting and memory failure. Because the overwhelming majority of cases are not known to authorities and national crime statistics do not include crimes against children, the only measures available are small-sample retrospective surveys.

We do have some data based on reports of child abuse and neglect from the U.S. Department of Health and Human Services (DHHS, 2009). (Keep in mind the small percentage of abuse and neglect cases that are reported.) Of all child victims in 2007, around 2.2 percent of children were reported for abuse and neglect, most of which were cases of neglect, and a smaller proportion—7.6 percent—were cases of sexual abuse. Girls are two to three times more likely than boys to be victims; the risk of this abuse increases with the child's age. Most victims are in the 12- to 15-year-old age range; the next most common age range is 8–11. Just over half of these cases involve white victims, and another half children of color. Most child sexual abuse is committed by a relative or someone known to the child; yet the media focus is on a few rare stranger child kidnapping cases (Cheit and Freyd, 2005).

Incest, usually differentiated from other forms of sexual assault, is defined as sexual acts performed within a family by an adult or an older family member against a child. Incest is the ultimate violation of a child's trust and love. Because of the child welfare issues involved, these cases are often handled by departments of human services, and prosecution is waived in lieu of treatment and reform. In both clinical and nonclinical American samples, perpetrators are predominantly male. Most of the perpetrators of incest are relatives other than parents. Boys are more likely than girls to be abused by nonfamily members. All types of sexual acts occur, and attempted or completed intercourse is reported in a large minority of the cases. Because of the secrecy and shame attached to incest, its prevalence is hard to determine.

The words of Maya Angelou (1969), who, at the age of eight, was raped by her mother's boyfriend, resonate:

> Then there was the pain. A breaking and entering when even the senses are torn apart. The act of rape is a matter of the needle giving because the camel can't. The child gives, because the body can, and the mind of the violator cannot.
>
> I thought I had died—I woke up in a white-walled world, and it had to be heaven. But Mr. Freeman was there and he was washing me. His hands shook, but he held me upright in the tub and washed my legs. "I didn't mean to hurt you, Ritie. I didn't mean it. But don't you tell . . . Remember, don't tell a soul." (p. 76)

From research we learn that father–daughter incest is associated with extreme power imbalance. In many instances the daughter is paying with her body for affection and care (Belknap, 2007). The presence of a stepfather in the household may be a further precipitating factor. The issues facing a girl pregnant by her father are horrendous, as is the public horror at children conceived under these circumstances.

The classic pattern of incest is a progression from fondling of breasts, buttocks, and genitals to mutual masturbation to full intercourse. The ongoing need for secrecy is handled through a combination of threats and bribery. Typically, the pattern continues until the child runs away or otherwise escapes the situation. If the family discovers what is going on, often through a teacher or doctor, there may be disbelief and strong pressure on the child to keep her mouth shut. "It didn't happen and don't tell anyone" is the typical twisted message given. Years later the adult is left to try to pick up the pieces from a stolen childhood.

To survive psychologically, children in a continuing incest situation may dissociate their moods from their bodies during sex. Such altered consciousness can result in clouded memories of the abuse. The survival skills may take the child out of connection with reality. The unconscious, unresolved trauma may result in symptoms both in childhood and much later, such as phobias, which appear to be meaningless in themselves (McCarthy and Kennedy, 2007). Therapists who work with children who have been sexually abused note that they typically have heightened and often troubling sexual acting out behavior (Belknap, 2007).

In the 1990s, a great deal of media attention in North America was given to false reports. The fact that innocent persons actually were sentenced to prison based on flimsy evidence is undeniable. Some false reports were promoted through suggestion by therapists with a fixed agenda. In carefully controlled laboratory experiments, children were shown to be highly suggestible as they try to make sense of their psychological distress. The use of questionable therapies served to undermine belief in the genuine memories of abuse and to increase the skepticism concerning actual suffering. The phrase "recovered memory" quickly changed to "false memory" in the public consciousness (Bourke, 2007). The risk is that because some children were too readily believed in the past, too few will be believed in the future. Cheit and Freyd (2005) discuss the fallout from the handful of highly publicized cases of false memories. Now truly guilty perpetrators, they argue, can be represented by attorneys who present evidence of false accusations that were made in the past. Meanwhile, extended societal denial coupled with the belief that child sexual abuse is rare thwarts the healing process and leaves other children vulnerable to predators. To protect children's welfare, Cheit and Freyd call for the creation of a new Institute of Child Abuse and Interpersonal Violence to exist within the Institute of Health and for research funding to be drastically increased.

We close this section with a brief description of a case that will possibly be one of the best known historically and certainly one of the most bizarre. Although hardly representative, the case of Josef Fritzl was catapulted across the world news headlines, when the depravity of his crimes came to light in an Austrian courtroom (Naughton, 2009). The facts that have come to light are these: Elisabeth, who is now 43, was kidnapped by her father as a teenager and locked in a dungeon downstairs to her home; Elisabeth was raped two to three times a day by her father on whom she was dependent for food; over the years she gave birth to seven children, one of whom died at birth, while three were raised in the home upstairs by the grandparents. Today the three who were raised in a dungeon are being provided with intensive therapy to teach them how to survive in the world outside. The court sentenced Fritz to a life in prison for psychologically disturbed criminality.

Now we turn our attention to a form of child abuse that was little known to the world until the past decade, the church's dark and shameful secret.

Priest Abuse

Thousands of Catholic priests have been accused of sexual misconduct with children and youths in incidents that go back to the 1960s. This is referred to in the media as **priest abuse** or clergy abuse. The focus in media accounts and the limited scholarly research on the topic has been on the harm done to boys and young men. Yet there are a large number of cases involving girls and young women as well.

The most comprehensive study on the prevalence of Catholic clergy abuse was undertaken by the John Jay College of Criminal Justice (2004) in a survey of dioceses across the United States. The research was authorized by the U.S. Conference of Catholic Bishops

(Bunson, 2009), so cooperation by the dioceses was assured. Findings from the survey revealed that from 1950 to 2002, 3–6 percent of priests had allegations made against them. Altogether there were over 11,500 claims filed. Direct costs to the Catholic Church in settling the cases was 2–3 billion dollars. Most of the incidents had taken place in the 1970s when the highest percentage of the perpetrators were in their 30s. Approximately 80 percent of the victims were male.

In 2006, an award-winning film, *Deliver Us from Evil*, was produced by Liongate films. The film contained extensive interviews with the former priest Father O'Grady, who honestly revealed his attraction for little girls. According to the film, there are today over 100,000 victims of priest abuse. Personal narratives record the pain endured by the survivors. The denial of the members of the hierarchy of Catholic Church to address the problem is shown to be a major source of anger by those who were wronged.

Catholicism will have a hard time righting its wrongs, wrote Kennedy (2001), a former priest and author of *The Unhealed Wound*, because so much of the church's institutional power depends on keeping its members in a dependent state. The "unhealed wound" in the title of Kennedy's book refers to Catholicism's failure to deal with sexuality in a mature fashion. Kennedy made a strong case for ending the unnatural mandate for celibacy by priests. Such a requirement, he suggested, attracts young men who are psychologically and emotionally immature.

The priest holds a position of sacred trust and is generally viewed by Catholics as God's representative on earth. Sexual abuse by such a trusted figure may lead to low self-esteem and disillusionment in the victim. To obtain personal narratives from women who had been through molestation by a priest and who were working on healing years later, van Wormer and Berns (2004) conducted an analysis of in-depth interviews of women survivors. The sample of nine women was available through workshops for survivors of priest sexual misconduct. All the women had been heavily active in church affairs and rituals; all lacked a close relationship with their fathers. Several of the women had experienced earlier sexual violation, a fact that probably increased their vulnerability, as research on childhood sexual trauma has demonstrated (Fieldman and Crespi, 2002). One of the survivors had even gone to her priest for help in coping with her experience of childhood abuse. The sense of pain and personal anguish was considerable. Moreover, because the priest represents the church, and the church represents religion in a devout Catholic family, the child or adolescent who is fondled or otherwise sexually exploited by a priest has nowhere to turn. In addition, if she (or he) successfully exposes the priest as a predator, many church attendees will be disillusioned.

In the media coverage and lawsuits, the plight of the female victims of clergy abuse has largely gone unnoticed. Yet the evidence is that the suffering engendered by their victimization is pronounced. Compared with male victims who have had to wrestle with the homosexuality dimension, women, according to what evidence we have, report that they undergo a major crisis in religious faith. Additionally, as van Wormer and Berns discovered, these girls and young women received little community support when they sought help from their friends and other confidantes; most typically, they were silenced. Such healing as did occur took place through social and therapeutic support, often years later.

A perusal of the narratives provided by these survivors reveals that the aftermath of the sexual victimization involved a second victimization. Instead of the support they needed, their needs were brushed away; often their reputations were besmirched. As we know from studies of rape survivors, a crucial factor in their recovery is the immediate response from significant others and authorities. And if trauma is to be prevented, early intervention is essential.

CRIMINAL JUSTICE RESPONSE

Because of the work of the women's movement, the contemporary understanding of rape and the legal response to this crime have undergone significant revision. Most police officers today view rape as a serious crime. A nationwide survey of almost 900 law enforcement officers revealed that officers who were college educated, were experienced with rape investigations, and had received specialized training were less likely than others to subscribe to myths about rape (Page, 2007). The entry of increasing numbers of women into this field has further promoted change from within the system. Yet, considering the long cultural tradition of women bearing the guilt for sexual victimization, it is not surprising that the legacy of the past is with us still.

The legacy of antiquated concepts that have been translated into law and custom and an innate distaste for this type of crime by all parties often cause the victim of sexual assault to feel victimized a second time. The woman's problem in confronting the law stems from three sources: attitudes of the police, the difficulty of answering questions of an intensely personal nature, and treatment by the courts. In some prosecutors' offices, rape victims are routinely asked to take lie detector tests.

An investigative report by journalists of the police department practices in the major cities of St. Louis and Philadelphia revealed that a large number of reported rapes were not officially recorded (Kohler, 2005). These cases instead were relegated to informal memos and eventually shredded. These were cases that were believed to be not proven; in other words, the victim had to prove the offense occurred. One woman had her case dismissed, as noted on the memo, because she could not stop crying long enough to answer the detective's questions.

Rape is a unique crime both in the low rate at which it is reported to the police and in the low conviction rate if it is prosecuted. It is the only crime in which the victim, at least in part, is considered guilty until proven innocent. From the first police encounter, the victim is gauged in terms of respectability and believability, and these attributes may be judged on a racial and class basis. Abused hitchhikers or women who went alone to a bar can expect to have marks against them from the start.

Why is rape so rarely reported? More to the point, why is it *ever* reported? In light of the feared mistreatment by justice officials of sexual assault victims and the ordeal of continually reliving the crime, it is remarkable that it is reported at all. Perhaps persons who have experienced crime go to the law for protection as a matter of course. Perhaps a vague sense of responsibility or a determination to get justice guides them. Caring and sensitive treatment by law enforcement officers can instill in the survivor a sense of not wanting to let them down by failing to follow through with prosecution. Sometimes the aim is to expiate the shame by publicly declaring it to have been a crime, the desire of the victim for some sort of vindication. Because what the victim really wants is for someone, an expert in these matters, to tell her, "You handled it well; you were fighting for your life. There was no other way."

Immediately after the attack, the victim approaches the authorities in an extreme state of emotional vulnerability. Because of her heightened awareness, words spoken to her at this time may stay with her forever. Rough treatment during the medical exam can cause physical pain and retraumatize the victim. As we hear from one victim advocate who was appalled at the attitudes expressed about her clients by nurses at a local hospital ER:

> A lot of times they don't say things in front of the [victims]. But out of the room, nurses and law enforcement would make comments to me that always are out of line, they say too much to me and that's when I get really frustrated. It happens a lot of

times where nurses are revictimizing my clients, saying, "Girl, what are you thinking? What were you doing like at 9:00 at night up there?" (interview provided by Ullman and Townsend, 2007, p. 436)

And yet, medical advocacy may help mitigate these emotional responses to the exam (Macy and Ermentrout, 2008). Even if victims decide not to follow through with prosecution, sensitively performed medical treatment is essential to provide needed medical treatment such as medications to prevent the contraction of venereal diseases, medication to help calm a person down, a referral to counseling resources, medication to prevent trauma (Kilpatrick et al. recommend one of the selective serotonin reuptake inhibiters [SSRIs]), and a rape kit, in case the woman changes her mind later, or for DNA collection purposes.

Due to the availability of new technologies such as the use of DNA evidence, prosecutors can be more certain they have the right person and more convincing in court. Many other factors go into a successful conviction of the accused sexual offender, some of which have nothing to do with the commission of the crime itself. We are talking of such factors as the social class and respectability of the victim, her ability to speak plain English, and blameless behavior at the time of the crime (Hope, 2005). Even though the defense attorneys are prevented in most states from cross-examining the victim concerning her previous sexual activities, there are other strategies they can use to undermine the witness's testimony. Rather than try to counter this evidence, defense attorneys attempt to frighten witnesses away with threats to reveal personal information drawn from medical and counseling records. Personal details about drinking habits, mental health history, clothing worn at the time of the incident, and so on, may be presented to play on the biases of the jurors. The fact is that rape victims are held to a higher standard of proof than victims of other crime, so without strong evidence, a conviction is hard to get. A woman named Mary, who was interviewed by Hope for *The New York Sun*, said that it took three years for her case to come to trial; when it did, the accused represented himself. This brought the victim face-to-face with the person who had terrorized her. The defendant used the occasion to grill his victim for hours about the experience. Today, Mary works for the Sexual Assault Intervention Program at Mount Sinai Hospital to help others get through the ordeal that follows the rape.

Victims' Rights

In the United States, the jury selection process, whereby each opposing side can eliminate a certain number of prospective jurors, is unique. Whole trials can be won or lost on the basis of who occupies the jury seats. In rape trials, in which victim blaming is a common component, a key question is whether men or women are the most likely to vote to convict an accused rapist. In the past, it was commonly believed that women would be harsher on other women. New York Assistant District Attorney Linda Fairstein (1993) contends that getting a conviction in a date-rape case is especially difficult. According to Fairstein, people have a fixed image of how a rapist should look. "But he doesn't look like a rapist" is the typical comment of jurors in date-rape cases, which Fairstein has tried (p. 155). More recent research is mixed. Savino, Turvey, and Baeza (2004) in their *Rape Investigation Handbook* said that research showed women over age 35 were more likely than younger women to blame the victim for putting herself in a vulnerable situation, while Batchelder, Koski, and Byxbe (2004) found in their investigation that female jurors are more likely than male jurors to disbelieve female complainants, and so acquit defendants in greater numbers. Female jurors also typically establish themselves as the primary spokespersons during deliberations, and sway male jurors who initially intend to vote guilty to vote not guilty.

Out of recognition that so many rapists are acquitted, even when the evidence is strongly against them, federal and state laws have been passed to expand the rights of crime victims. At the same time internationally, human rights law and international criminal law has brought new understandings of the sexual assault, which replaced outdated ideas about rape being a normal if regrettable aspect of conflict (Amnesty International, 2009). Although the concern of the international criminal court is with rape in war, as the United Nations comes to clarify the definition of what constitutes rape, we can hope that the concept will generalize to other parts of the world, where as we will see in Chapter 10, rape victims are actually punished for the "crime" of having been sexually attacked.

In the United States and Canada, one heralded change is the introduction in court proceedings of victim impact statements. In the United States, uniquely, victims play an active role in the plea-bargaining process. In both countries, evidence about the sex life of victims is generally excluded from sexual offense cases where it could be used to imply consent by the woman in the present case. Denmark and Scotland have recently revised their laws, for example, to provide some protection to victims in sexual assault cases from being cross-examined on irrelevant matters to the case at hand. In North America and Britain, more protection is being granted to children in sexual abuse cases by allowing them to testify on videotape or behind a screen away from the accused molester.

A favorable development is the allotment of financial compensation by the government for pain and suffering as a result of crime. Some Canadian provinces cover the maintenance of a child born as a result of rape. In the United States, victims may receive financial assistance from state victims' compensation programs. Victims must, however, demonstrate financial need.

Canadian laws are very strict concerning protection of the assault victim's right to privacy (see Canadian Resource Centre for Victims of Crime, 2006). A federal ombudsman is available to protect the rights of crime victims. The witness, if she so desires, can apply for a ban on the release of her identity, and her identity will be protected. In the United States, half of the states restrict the publication of victims' names. In the other states, the newspapers usually do not publish the names out of custom. In Britain, the anonymity of rape victims who is commonly referred to as "Miss X" is strictly maintained.

Despite all the obstacles described in North America and Europe, participation in the criminal justice process can be cathartic for the survivor, a way of getting beyond the pain. As Fairstein (1993) describes one woman's experience, "She had courageously faced her attacker and accused him with confidence and dignity. No one had humiliated or debased her, and none of the 'myths' of a complaining witness's ordeal had befallen her" (p. 261).

Hate crime law has the potential to help in the prosecution of cases on the basis of gender bias. Unfortunately, as McPhail (2002) indicates, there is a strong resistance to recognizing violence against women as a hate crime. The fact that many female victims know their attackers precludes some policy makers from fitting rape and domestic violence into a hate crime model. Recently Congressman Maloney (U.S. Congress, 2005) has introduced a bill, the Hate Crimes Statistics Improvement Act, to ensure that hate crimes motivated by gender are accounted for by the FBI and local law enforcement agencies. If a gang only beat up people of a certain race, that would be recognized as a hate crime; targeting a group based on their gender is a hate crime too, according to the Representative. Although nineteen states have included gender-based hate crimes in their hate crimes laws, the Federal Hate Crimes Statistics Act does not require the FBI to collect data on this important category.

PSYCHOLOGICAL TRAUMA

In an extensive review of international studies that looked at long-term effects, Finkelhor (1994) found an association between early sexual abuse and adult mental health impairments. Symptoms of anxiety and fear that are consistent with PTSD are found in approximately one-third of sexually abused victims (Kilpatrick et al., 2007). This compares to around 9 percent of persons who are traumatized from a very frightening event such as a serious car crash. PTSD symptoms include intrusive, unpleasant recollections of the event and avoidance and numbing symptoms. These symptoms are more likely to be present when victims perceive the attack as life threatening. For all victims of sexual assault, guilt feelings and a generalized sense of feeling dirty and damaged are common. Long-term sexual dysfunction is a corollary of childhood abuse. Repressed memories may be associated with phobias of a disabling sort (Cardwell and Flanagan, 2003). In short, the harm associated with stolen childhoods and the wreckage of adult lives in the wake of child abuse is monumental.

Increasing evidence shows that childhood trauma significantly alters the biochemistry of the brain (Ginsberg, Nackereed, and Larrison, 2004). Adaptation to trauma, such as hyper-vigilance, prepares the victim for fight-or-flight responses and may become biochemically ingrained when triggered again and again (Basham and Miehls, 2004). Cognitive and neuro-logical mechanisms that may underlie the forgetting of abuse have been identified (Cheit and Freyd, 2005). Today, we are learning much more about how childhood trauma affects brain chemistry and how the tendency toward depression and addiction figure into the equation.

For women who suffer from addictive problems and who get involved in criminal behavior, a history of early childhood sexual abuse is prominent. A history of abuse seems to predispose women to adult victimization such as rape or battering. Even the early teenage pregnancy phenomenon so derided by the media and politicians is associated with a history of childhood sexual abuse. In their analysis of school surveys, Saewyc, Magee, and Pettingell (2004) found that methods of coping with abuse—for example, substance abuse and running away from home—may put a teenager at risk for pregnancy involvement.

Maya Angelou shares with us—in her moving autobiography *I Know Why the Caged Bird Sings* (1969), in speeches, and in interviews—the trauma that rape produced in her life. In the years following the rape, she did not speak. The fact that her family killed the perpetrator made a bad situation worse. Maya was a victim with blood on her hands. Only the efforts of a lovely English teacher who introduced her to the world of literature brought out her gifts of self-expression. Today she is one of America's foremost poets.

On top of the normal reaction to what may have been a near-death assault, the person who has been victimized suffers from her involvement in a hideously sordid sexual activity, an involvement that may be known by the entire community. For this reason the victim may have to not only change jobs but leave town as well. Even marriages do not always survive such an attack, because long after the wife is ready to forget (and she *will* want to go on to other things) her husband may not be able to.

Approximately 5 percent of rape victims become pregnant as a result of the rape. Today, some emergency rooms dispense morning-after pills to prevent pregnancy. If the rapist is of a different race from the victim, child-rearing problems and difficulties in explanation abound. A recent award-winning British film, *Secrets and Lies*, portrays the stirring reunion between a white working-class woman and the mixed-race daughter she gave up for adoption years earlier in the aftermath of interracial rape. In this film, a young woman who gave birth to a son as a result of rape describes her feelings, which were exacerbated by thoughtless initial reactions by her family.

The concept of "the rape trauma syndrome" was first identified by Burgess and Holmstrom (1974). This syndrome is now considered a part of PTSD (see the American Psychiatric Association [APA], 2000). Based on their emergency room work with rape victims, Burgess and Holmstrom identified two stages of adjustment to rape. The initial or acute stage, lasting approximately two weeks, involves shock and disbelief and some seeming acceptance of what has taken place. A common coping mechanism at this stage is deliberate forgetting or repression by the unconscious of the horror of the event. These acute reactions are a normal response to an abnormal situation. Over time, when the survivor is better able to cope, often the memory returns.

In the second phase of adjustment to the rape, the survivor may begin to experience physical and emotional turmoil—insomnia, unexpected crying fits, and extreme fear related to the violence of the attack. Survivors may complain of intrusive flashbacks that hark back to the scene of the crime. The fear might be compounded if the attacker was an ex-boyfriend or ex-spouse. Such a man, who used rape to punish a woman for the breakup of their relationship, would occasionally strike again. Sometimes the harassment is so bad that the woman, feeling utterly helpless, will return to her abuser.

Many women feel anger during this second stage, anger at the police, the courts, their families, and the offender. The losses that a girl or women may experience as a result of sexual violence are many. Among them are sense of safety, independence, control, self-esteem, memories, trust, positive feelings about sex, support networks, and health. Sexually inexperienced victims experience loss of virginity and a linking in their minds of sex and violence. The association may be long-lasting.

TREATMENT AND EMPOWERMENT

Recovery from trauma occurs when the child or woman who has been victimized is transformed into a survivor who is able to integrate the catastrophe into her life history and see it as a source of strength. Recovery takes place when the world seems a beautiful and trusting place again and your body feels whole and like yours alone.

Research shows that the initial meeting and relationship between a rape victim and the first person-friend or authority figure who responds has more impact on the victim's eventual recovery than anything else. The initial response by a trusted individual also determines the extent to which the survivor will blame herself and even whether or not she will acknowledge that what happened to her was a crime. A study of college rape victims, cited by Schwartz and DeKeseredy (1997), revealed that if the victims got the message that they were loved no matter what they had undergone, they tended to blame themselves. But if survivors got the message that it was not their fault, they tended to shift the blame to the perpetrator. Society's reaction to a woman's victimization, therefore, has long-term consequences.

The need for expert help is crucial following victimization. Empirical research has shown that to prevent lifelong problems, the sooner one gets professional counseling, the better is the recovery (Kilpatrick et al., 2007). See Box 8.2 for a description of services offered in Blackhawk County, Iowa.

From van Wormer's experience counseling adult survivors of rape and incest and from the literature, we have filtered out four phases of adjustment to the shock and horror of forced sexual contact. In reality, the stages overlap and many survivors get stuck at one stage or bypass it altogether. This model represents an ideal type, in short, for the purpose of constructing a working intervention scheme. We must always recognize, however, that each survivor experiences a unique crime under unique circumstances and that her constitutional and environmental contingencies

BOX 8.2
Support Victim Service Agencies

A woman had been in a happy marriage, but after the birth of their third child, her husband became physically abusive. He began forcing her into sexual activities that she found disgusting and wrong, so she resisted them. He beat and strangled her to punish her for "refusing his right as her husband to have sex whenever he wanted." If she still refused, he raped her, again and again.

She began drinking heavily to cope with her partner's physical and sexual assaults on her. She eventually sought treatment for alcoholism. She met an advocate from Seeds of Hope who leads a victims of domestic violence and sexual assault support group at that agency.

She worked hard with the advocate and developed a plan to leave. She got a no-contact order, a divorce, and an apartment. Seeds of Hope helped her with education and job training, to furnish her new apartment, and get clothes, books, and toys for her children.

One year later, she continues to attend the support group and is involved with public awareness activities to educate the public about sexual assault and domestic violence. She has been clean and sober since. She is very happy in her new life and being a good mother to her three children.

April is Sexual Assault Awareness Month. Sexual assault crosses all class, race, lifestyle, and religious lines. According to a study conducted by the National Victim Center; 1.3 women (age 18 and older) in the United States are forcibly raped each minute. That translates to 78 per hour, 1,871 per day, or 683,000 per year. Over the course of their lifetime, one in six American women will be victims of sexual assault. We encourage local citizens to become more aware of this very serious issue and support the local efforts of Seeds of Hope and Cedar Valley Friends of the Family to positively address this issue in our community.

Contrary to popular belief, most rapists are not strangers hiding in the shadows of the parking garage or behind trees. Almost two-thirds of all rapes are committed by someone who is known to the victim: 38 percent by friends or acquaintances, 28 percent by partners, and 6 percent by a relative.

Numerous studies have shown that from 27 percent to more than 40 percent of girls are sexually abused during childhood. The Journal of the American Medical Association reviewed 166 studies of sexual abuse in boys and found that:

- Approximately 16 percent reported childhood sexual abuse
- 53–94 percent of perpetrators were men
- 98 percent of these men self-identified as heterosexual
- Women on university campuses are at high risk for sexual assault and its effects on their academic career:
- 20–25 percent of college women are raped during their college career
- 13 percent of women are stalked during the academic year, and each stalking episode lasts an average of sixty days
- 42 percent of raped women expect to be raped again
- In nearly every case, victims cannot perform at the same academic levels that they did prior to the attack
- Victims face lifelong and life-altering impacts on health, mental health, academic achievement, and more because of the sexual abuse and assault they experience as children or adults or both, including fear that it will happen again.

Cedar Valley Friends of the Family and Seeds of Hope, the Cedar Valley's victim service agencies, provide court and medical advocacy, shelter, support groups, and prevention education to Black Hawk, Bremer, Butler, Chickasaw, Grundy, and Hardin counties. Medical advocacy includes going with women to the rape exam and any follow-up medical or other services that women might need (40 percent of raped women get a sexually transmitted disease from the rape).

In the past year, our combined staff has served more than 1,000 unduplicated victims of abuse, responded to almost 12,000 crisis calls, and provided prevention education and awareness to more than 15,000 people, primarily youth in local schools in each county. Seeds of Hope and Cedar Valley Friends of the Family also meet individually with sexual assault victims, provide support groups for victims, and work with victims who have long-term issues from experiences of childhood sexual abuse.

Source: Cedar Falls Mayor Jon Crews and Ronelle Crews, board members of Seeds of Hope, Cedar Falls. Published in *The Courier* (Waterloo/Cedar Falls, Iowa), April 5, 2009 p. F2. Reprinted with permission of Nancy Newhoff, editor of *The Courier.*

will have a strong bearing on her resolution of the crisis. The duration of the abuse, the degree of violence and terror experienced, the age of the victim, and the initial reactions of the authorities and significant others all fall into play in determining the course of the recovery process. These are the four phases: denial-avoidance, guilt and sexualization, reexperience and rage, and finally, healing.

At the political level, empowerment practice helps survivors redefine personal experiences as political. Klaw et al. (2005) describe an intensive semester-long rape prevention training for college students to develop acquaintance rape consciousness to parallel feminist consciousness. The authors concluded after completion of the program that such sustained efforts can play a vital role in dismantling rape-supportive culture. For women who had been personally victimized, the course seemed to facilitate the healing process by countering internalized messages of self-blame. Men, for their part, developed an awareness of how a rape experience could affect someone close to them.

Denial-Avoidance

In denying the gravity of the event and minimizing the difficulties ahead—"I'm alive; I'm all right"—the recent victim enables herself to handle as much as she can at that time. **Denial-avoidance** or repression of some of the most disturbing aspects, coupled with dissociation of the self from the act, allows victims to cope with experiences they are not yet ready to absorb into their reality. Feelings of detachment and emotional withdrawal from others are common.

To enhance long-term recovery, referral to crisis counseling services should be made at the earliest possible moment. Much personal tragedy and self-destructiveness can be avoided if the survivor can receive support during the critical early period of trauma. Brief crisis intervention early on may offset the need for intensive in-depth psychotherapy at a later stage. The worst thing that can happen to a child who has been abused is to leave her or him to sort out these experiences alone. Key elements of counseling during this initial period are psychological support—listening, caring, nurturing the strengths in the survivor as they manifest themselves—and education. Education includes providing information about the criminal justice process if the client chooses to get involved in this system and health care information if the client has not yet received medical care for the attack.

Victim/witness assistance programs, usually situated in local county prosecutors' offices or nearby court buildings, are designed to boost witness cooperation and to provide advocacy for their needs. For victims of rape and domestic violence, however, more specialized treatment is needed. The ideal arrangement is the provision of crisis intervention programs, which may be lodged in police departments, hospitals, or nonprofit agencies and are prepared to act within the first twenty-four hours after the victimization. Help is given in filling out victim compensation forms, and crisis counseling and referral to extended counseling and psychotherapy are provided. Treatment in both short- and long-term counseling consists of a great deal of reassurance that the victim did not precipitate in or deserve the assault. The counselor needs to be aware that suicide is a real risk. According to the U.S. Department of Veteran Affairs (2008), estimates are that one-third of women who are raped contemplate suicide, and 17 percent of rape victims actually attempt suicide. In light of the risk, survivors need to be informed about actions to take to seek immediate help such as hot-line numbers to call if they have any self-destructive urges.

Above all, it is vital for criminal justice personnel to communicate that they believe the victim and that they are sorry about what has happened. This simple acknowledgment can mean a great deal to a recently traumatized person; it can bring tears of relief. One helpful approach is to ask the victim about her fears and concerns and always to validate and not disregard or dispute her feelings (Zastrow and Kirst-Ashman, 2010).

Guilt and Sexualization

The greatest irony is that the sexual offender often feels no remorse at all, while the victim is left with a sense of uncleanness and even guilt. The guilt feelings that are internalized by the child victim and that may remain with her until adulthood seem to make little sense on the surface. Sexual trauma survivors, however, feel guilty because they have engaged in forbidden sex often under sordid and horrible circumstances.

In adults, **traumatic sexualization** can also occur (see Child Welfare Information Gateway, 2009). Problems can range from negatively charged sexuality or association of all aspects of sex with self-loathing and disgust to inappropriately compulsive eroticism. Often the problems do not emerge until the survivor enters or tries to enter a committed relationship; only then does the seriousness of the trauma become apparent. *Stigmatization*, according to the same source, is associated with shame and guilt feelings that are internalized by the abused individual, especially if this individual is a child. The child may believe she is tainted forever by a bad experience, as we have seen.

The survivor therapy approach utilizes the strengths perspective to help reempower the client. Reestablishing trust in herself and the world and rediscovering her sense of personal control are primary goals in recovery from victimization. Group therapy is an invaluable technique for helping survivors let go of their self-blaming thoughts and regain their self-confidence. As group members, each of whom may unconsciously blame herself for her own suffering, come to share each other's stories of brutalization, a revelation may take place. In conjunction with an emerging sense of *we* instead of *I*, the revelation "We did not deserve this to happen to us" may come to light.

Reexperience and Rage

Adult survivors can benefit from intensive thinking and feeling work at any stage in the recovery process. Implicit in the philosophy of feeling work is the belief that feeling and thinking are in constant interaction with each other, that it is not the *event* itself that is significant but one's view of the event that shapes its impact. Whether a person is a victim or a survivor may be shaped more by the *definition* of the situation than by the situation itself.

The primary tasks of treatment for sex trauma survivors are to help them develop a sense of safety and beginning to reprocess their trauma and to integrate it into their lives to resolve symptoms and related issues. In responding to trauma, Manning (2007) recommends an empowerment approach in which the therapist in collaboration with the survivor helps her move through the following stages—safety, remembrance and mourning, and reconnection. The process is dynamic and spiraling rather than linear. For some clients, group exercises ranged from reading relevant poetry, prose, or a chapter in *The Courage to Heal* (Bass and Davis, 2008), which can be empowering. Group leaders can gently and in a noncoercive way encourage each woman to talk about what happened to her as a way of relieving the burden of the "secret."

An effective approach toward empowerment is to affirm the resourcefulness and competence of women who managed to use all the wiles at their disposal to survive and who have continued to survive ever since. In recovery, the survivor reviews a situation in which she seemed to have been completely overtaken yet, in fact, used many creative maneuvers for her own protection. In this way, a new meaning can be given to the trauma of rape or childhood sexual abuse. Some individuals, as they discard their sense of a damaged self, embrace instead the belief that the misfortune they endured made them stronger and more compassionate. The process of respectful listening, consistency, and caring is crucial in a therapeutic relationship. It is within this process that healing occurs (McCarthy and Kennedy, 2007).

Healing

Healing is simply the inner change, the sense of peace that may result from therapy work on labeling feelings and controlling them through cognitive techniques, reframing troubling events in one's life, and recognizing how past events influence present feelings, thoughts, and behavior. Reclaiming lost and damaged childhood selves may occur through the joint effort of treatment and support group relationships.

The aim of such memory retrieval work is to place the past in the past and to realize the role that past events play in shaping one's present life. Through sharing a painful and conflict-ridden episode in her life with a concerned professional, the survivor begins to perceive events increasingly through the eyes of the listener-observer. bell hooks (1993) speaks eloquently of the joy of reconciliation, the gift of healing. Referring to Alice Walker's (1982) novel *The Color Purple*, hooks recalls how Celie, the black heroine, begins to recover from her traumatic experiences of incest/rape, domestic violence, and marital rape only when she is able to tell her story, to be open and honest. Telling one's story in any form, giving voice to the unmentionable, is the first step, according to hooks, in releasing the bitterness and in healing the inner wounds, which make reconciliation possible.

Summary

Childhood sexual abuse, incest, and rape are predatory acts that constitute serious problems for society and have long-lasting consequences for victims. In this chapter, we viewed this problem from a feminist/strengths approach; the emphasis was structural, on the power dynamics of a male-dominated society in which the threat of rape can serve, as Brownmiller (1975) suggests, to keep all women in a state of fear. Rape is thus at once both a personal and a political phenomenon. At the personal level, as we have seen, women are not only susceptible to being raped but also to being blamed for their own vulnerability.

To understand the political dimensions of rape, we looked to history, to the European American heritage. Considered the property of men, of their fathers and husbands, women who were attacked were considered ruined and contaminated; the attack itself was conceived as an attack on their menfolk. In wartime, the victor has access to his enemy's women. Under the institution of slavery, access to slave women was a given.

Today, although rape in war and sexual slavery persist, there is growing international recognition, through the United Nations, of the human rights of women. The right to exercise control over one's sexuality is an important basic right. Without protection from physical and sexual violation in the home or elsewhere, previous guarantees of political and economic equality remain hollow.

The theoretical approach presented in this chapter, consistent with contemporary feminist theory, conceives of sexual aggression and abuse as a continuum or series of behaviors ranging from ordinary harassment to full-blown violent, life-threatening attacks. The common thread of dehumanization is the unifying element. Surveys show that although stranger rape is the prototype of rape, date rape and marital rape are far more common. Self-reports of college males and of women in national victim surveys reveal that sexual aggression by peers on the college campus is commonplace.

Rape victims suffer psychological as well as physical trauma. Because of the stigma attached to this crime, survivors often feel torn between the desire to talk about it, even years later, and a reluctance to tell people what they probably don't want to hear. Society's tendency to blame the victim, especially the victim of a sexual crime, effectively silences the survivor of rape. In cases of stranger rape, the omission of the victim's name from newspaper accounts, although advisable, prevents people from reaching out to the woman who has survived a life-threatening experience. Such an individual may forever wonder who knows and who doesn't know about this unmentionable crime. Shrouded in silence and internalizing society's blame, the survivor desperately needs someone to talk to. The importance of a rape crisis telephone line, rape advocates, and victim assistance programs cannot be underestimated. The choices and problems facing a recently victimized woman will seem insurmountable: whether to report the crime, how to endure the medical procedures, whom to tell, and how to go forward are just a few of the immediate concerns. Victimized children and their families need help most of all. Participation in group counseling sessions can reinforce girls' and women's self-worth and keep any self-destructive tendency that may arise in check.

Personal empowerment of women has its counterpart in political empowerment. We have the feminist movement to thank for both the recognition that violence against women is a public issue and the funding for prevention and intervention efforts to curb the impact of this type of crime. Women's interests and the state's political interests coinciding at this time of heightened attention to victims of crime provides an opportunity that should not be overlooked. To end the widespread rape and sexual harassment of women, we must continue our work toward legislative reform, educational initiatives, improved child-rearing practices, and better-funded advocacy/ counseling services.

Key Terms

acquaintance rape (also date rape) *208*
child sexual abuse *211*
denial-avoidance *221*
incest *212*

mass rape *211*
posttraumatic stress disorder (PTSD) *208*
priest abuse *213*
rape *194*

rape-free culture *207*
rape-supportive culture *206*
traumatic sexualization *222*
victim blaming *205*

Critical Thinking Questions

1. Discuss the historical connection between laws against rape and property laws.
2. Account for the differences in African American reaction to having white versus American Indian ancestors.
3. How has rape victimization been reconceptualized over time?

4. What are "little rapes"? What is their impact on young women?
5. Some say the victimization rates are exaggerated. Discuss Roiphe's arguments on this point.
6. Discuss rape myths and the resistance to treating rape by an acquaintance the same as stranger rape.
7. Discuss the concept of rape-supportive culture.

8. What would rape-free culture be like?
9. Discuss the particular violation and spiritual repercussions of priest abuse.
10. Account for the common occurrence of rape in war. Pick a particular war in history and research the extent and consequences of rape during that period.
11. Compare PTSD with regard to rape trauma and to war trauma.
12. Consider ways that survivors of rape can be empowered.

Web Destinations

Bureau of Justice Statistics: Rape Rates: http://www.ojp.usdoj.gov/bjs/glance/rape.htm

The Institute on Violence, Abuse and Trauma: http://www.alliant.edu/wps/wcm/connect/website/Home/Research+and+Public+Services/Research+Institutes/IVAT+&+FVSAI/

Latina Alliance Against Sexual Aggression: www.arte-sana.com

Rape, Abuse, and Incest National Network: www.rainn.org

Survivors of Incest Anonymous: www.siawso.org

Human Rights Watch: www.hrw.org

References

Adams-Curtis, L., and Forbes, G. (2004). College women's experiences of sexual coercion. *Trauma, Violence, and Abuse* 5(2): 91–122.

American Psychiatric Association (APA). (2000). *Diagnostic and statistical manual of mental disorders*, 4th ed. (DSM-IV-TR) (Text Revision). Arlington, VA: APA.

Amir, M. (1971). *Patterns in forcible rape*. Chicago, IL: University of Chicago Press.

Amnesty International. (2009, January 13).*Document— International Criminal Court: Clarifying the scope of the crime of rape*. Retrieved April 2009 from http://www.amnesty.org/en/library/asset/IOR53/001/2009/en/5b0b34ab-e17f-11dd-9f8a-a19d21ac1fa4/ior530012009en.html

Angelou, M. (1969). *I know why the caged bird sings*. New York: Random House.

Associated Press (AP). (2009, March 24). Ex-sheriff sentenced in sex abuse scandal. Oklahoma City: AP. Retrieved March 2009 from http://www.cbsnews.com/stories/2009/03/24/national/main4889548.shtml

Basham, K., and Miehls, D. (2004). *Transforming the legacy: Couple therapy with survivors of childhood trauma*. New York: Columbia University Press.

Bass, E., and Davis, L. (2008). *The courage to heal: A guide for women survivors of child sexual abuse*, 4th ed. New York: HarperCollins.

Batchelder, J. S., Koski, D. D., and Byxbe, F. R. (2004). Women's hostility toward women in rape trials: Testing the intra-female gender hostility thesis. *American Journal of Criminal Justice* 28: 181–200.

Belknap, J. (2007). *The invisible woman: Gender, crime, and justice*, 3rd ed. Belmont, CA: Cengage.

Benedict, H. (2009). *The lonely soldier: The private war of women serving in Iraq*. Boston, MA: Beacon Press.

Bourke, J. (2007). *Rape: Sex violence history*. Berkeley, CA: Shoemaker Hoard.

Brownmiller, S. (1975). *Against our will: Men, women and rape*. New York: Bantam.

Bunson, M. (2009). *Catholic almanac 2009* (pp. 78–79). Huntington, IN: Our Sunday Visitor.

Bureau of Justice Statistics (BJS) (2006, June). Personal crimes of violence, 2004. Criminal victimization in the United States, 2004, statistical tables. Washington, D.C.:U.S. Department of Justice. Retrieved August 2009 from http://www.ojp.usdoj.gov/bjs/pub/pdf/cvus0402.pdf

Bureau of Justice Statistics (BJS). (2007, December 19). *Definitions* . Washington, DC: U.S. Department of Justice. Retrieved from http://www.ojp.usdoj.gov/bjs/intimate/definitions.htm

Bureau of Justice Statistics (BJS). (2008, August 29). *Criminal victimization in the United States*. Washington, DC: U.S. Department of Justice. Retrieved March 2009 from http://www.ojp.usdoj.gov/bjs/abstract/cvus/rape_sexual_assault.htm

Burgess, A. W., and Holmstrom, L. L. (1974). Rape trauma syndrome. *American Journal of Psychiatry* 131: 981–986.

Canadian Resource Centre for Victims of Crime (2006, February). The devastation of sexual assault.

Retrieved April 2009 from http://www.crcvc.ca/docs/sexual_assault.pdf

Cardwell, M., and Flanagan, C. (2003). *Psychology AS—The complete companion: "A" specification*. Cheltenham, UK: Nelson Thornes.

Caringella, S. (2009). *Addressing rape reform in law and practice*. New York: Columbia University Press.

Cecil, H., and Matson, S. (2005). Differences in psychological health and family dysfunction by sexual victimization type in a clinical sample of African American adolescent women. *The Journal of Sex Research 42*(3): 203–228.

Centers for Disease Control and Prevention (CDC). (2008). *Sexual violence: Facts at a glance*. National Center for Injury Prevention and Control. Retrieved August 2009 from http://www.cdc.gov/Violence Prevention/pdf/SV-DataSheet-a.pdf

Cheit, R., and Freyd, J. (2005). Let's have an honest fight against child sex abuse. *The Brown University Child and Adolescent Behavior Letter 21*(6): 8.

Child Welfare Information Gateway. (2009). *Sexual abuse*. Washington, DC: U.S. Department of Health and Human Services. Retrieved April 2009 from http://www.enotalone.com/article/9930.html

Deckard, B. S. (1983). *The woman's movement: Political, socioeconomic, and psychological issues*, 3rd ed. New York: Harper and Row.

Dell, T. V. (2009, March 28). Developmentally disabled women testifies at rape trial. Northern California area: Chico Enterprise Record. Retrieved March 29, 2009 from http://www.chicoer.com/news/ci_12018089

DeSantis, J. (2005, June 26). When "no" is not enough. *Star News* (Wilmington, NC), pp. 1A, 4A.

Devdas, N., and Rubin, L. (2007). Rape myth acceptance among first- and second- generation South Asian women. *Sex Roles 56*(9–10): 701–705.

Dorr, L. L. (2004). *White women, rape, and the power of race in Virginia, 1900–1960*. Chapel Hill, NC: University of North Carolina Press.

Elias, M. (2008, October 28). Fifteen % of female veterans tell of sexual trauma. *USA Today*, p. 6D.

Estrich, S. (1987). *Real rape*. Cambridge, MA: Harvard University Press.

Fairstein, L. (1993). *Sexual violence: Our war against rape*. New York: Morrow.

Faludi, S. (1991). *Backlash: The undeclared war on American women*. New York: Doubleday.

Farwell, N. (2004). War rape: New conceptualizations and responses. *Affilia 19*(4): 389–403.

Federal Bureau of Investigation (FBI). (2008, September). *Crime in the United States 2007*. FBI. Retrieved April 2009 from http://www.fbi.gov/ucr/cius2007/offenses/violent_crime/forcible_rape.html

Fieldman, J. P., and Crespi, T. D. (2002). Child sexual abuse: Offenders disclosure, and school-based initiative. *Adolescence 37*: 151–160.

Finkelhor, D. (1994). The international epidemiology of child sexual abuse. *Child Abuse and Neglect 18*: 409–417.

Formosa, N. (2007, January 23). Media coverage of domestic violence, sexual assault cases have mixed effects on victims. *Summit Daily News* (Colorado). Retrieved August 2009 from http://www.summitdaily.com/article/2007101230054

Foubert, J., and Perry, B. (2007). Creating lasting attitude and behavior change in fraternity members and male student athletes. *Violence Against Women 13*: 70–86.

Freyd, J., Putnam, F., Lyon, T., Becker-Blease, K., Chiet, R., Siegel, N., et al. (2005, April 22). The science of child sexual abuse. *Science 308*: 501. Retrieved from www.sciencemag.org.

Garcia, G. (2008). *The decline of men: How the American male is tuning out, giving up, flipping off his future*. New York: Harper.

Gershman, J. (2006, February 10). Putting sex predators in mental facilities may impact plea bargains. *The New York Sun 4*.

Ginsberg, L., Nackereed, L., and Larrison, C. (2004). *Human biology for social workers: Development, ecology, genetics and health*. Boston, MA: Allyn & Bacon.

Glauber, B. (2005, August 28). Women now practice defensive drinking. *Chicago Tribune*. Retrieved from www.chicagotribune.com

Griffin, S. (1971). Rape: The all-American crime. *Ramparts 10*(3): 26–35.

Hollander, J. (2009). The roots of resistance to women's self-definition. *Violence Against Women 15*(5): 574–594.

Home Box Office (HBO). (2005, May 30). Rape in a small town: The Florence Holway Story. ABC Network, Australia. Retrieved from www.abc.net.au/4corners/content/20

hooks, b. (1993). *Sisters of the yam: Black women and self-recovery*. Boston, MA: South End Press.

Hope, B. (2005). Treatment, conviction rates vary by borough. *The New York Sun 1*.

Jentz, T. (2007). *Strange piece of paradise*. New York: Picador.

John Jay College of Criminal Justice. (2004). *The nature and scope of the problem of sexual abuse of minors by Catholic priests and deacons in the United States*. New York: John Jay College of Criminal Justice. Retrieved August 2009 from http://www.usccb.org/nrb/johnjaystudy/

Karmen, A. (2004). The victimization of girls and women by boys and men: Competing analytical frameworks. In B. Price and N. Sokoloff (eds.), *The criminal justice system and women offenders: Prisoners, victims, and workers* (pp. 289–301). New York: McGraw-Hill.

Katz, J. (2006). *The macho paradox: Why some men hurt women and how all men can help*. Naperville, IL: Sourcebooks.

Kennedy, E. (2001). *The unhealed wound: The church and human sexuality*. New York: St. Martin's.

Kilpatrick, D., Amstadter, A., Resnick, H., and Ruggiero, K. (2007). Rape-related PTSD: Issues and interventions.*Psychiatric Times 24*(7): 50–52.

Kilpatrick, D., Saunders, B. E., and Smith, D. W. (2003). Youth victimization: Prevalence and implications. *Research in brief* (NCJ 194972). Washington, DC: U.S. Department of Justice, Office of Justice Programs, National Institute of Justice. Retrieved from http://www.ojp.usdoj.gov/nij

Kimmel, M. (2008). *Guyland: The perilous world where boys become men*. New York: Harper.

Klaw, E., Lonsway, K., Berg, D., Waldo, C., Kothari, C., Mazurek, C., et al. (2005). Challenging rape culture: Awareness, emotion and action through campus acquaintance rape education. *Women & Therapy 28*(2): 47–63.

Knight, I. (2009, March 29). Face it, girls—a drunken romp isn't a rape. London: *Sunday Times*. Retrieved April 2009 from http://www.timesonline.co.uk/tol/comment/columnists/india_knight/article5993008.ece

Kohler, J. (2005). Abused by the system. *St. Louis Post-Dispatch*, p. A1.

Koss, M. P., Leonard, K. D., Beezley, D. A., and Oros, C. J. (1985). Nonstranger sexual aggression: A discriminant analysis of the psychological characteristics of undetected offenders. *Sex Roles 12*: 981–992.

Krug, E. G., Dahlberg, L., Mercy, J. A., Awi, A., and Lozano, R. (eds.) (2004). *World report on health and violence*. World Health Organization. Retrieved from www.who.int/violence_injury_prevention

Lefkowitz, B. (1997). *Our guys*. Berkeley, CA: University of California Press.

Louwagie, P. (2008, November 9). Sexual assault on campus: Culture change 101. Retrieved Minneapolis: *Star Tribune*. Retrieved April 2009 from http://www.startribune.com/local/34129724.html

Mac Donald, H. (2008). The campus rape myth: The bogus statistics, feminist victimology, and university-approved sex toys. *City Journal*. Retrieved April 2009 from http://www.city-journal.org/2008/18_1_campus_rape.html

Macy, R., and Ermentrout, D. (2008). *Consensus practices in the provision of services to survivors of domestic violence and sexual assault*. Chapel Hill, NC: University of North Carolina, School of Social Work. Retrieved April 2009 from http://ssw.unc.edu/dvsaservices.pdf

Manning, S. (2007). Transforming trauma responses to women with serious and persistent psychiatric disability. In M. Bussey and J. Wise (eds.), *Trauma transformed: An empowerment response* (pp. 51–76). New York: Columbia University Press.

McCarthy, C. J., and Kennedy, J. (2007). Transforming trauma responses to sexual abuse in adolescents. In M. Bussey and J. Wise (eds.), *Trauma transformed: An empowerment response*. (pp. 35–50). New York: Columbia University Press.

McDonald, T., and Kline, L. (2004, March). Perceptions of appropriate punishment for committing date rape: Male college students recommend lenient punishments. *College Student Journal 38*(1): 44–57.

McPhail, B. (2002, April). Gender-bias hate crimes: A review. *Trauma, Violence, & Abuse 3*(2): 125–143.

Miller, J. (2008). *Getting played: African American girls, urban inequality, and gendered violence*. New York: New York University Press.

Muraskin, R. (2007). The crime of rape. In R. Muraskin (ed.), *It's a crime: Women and justice*, 4th ed. (pp. 181–186). Upper Saddle River, NJ: Prentice Hall.

Naughton, P. (2009, March 20). Josef Fritzl "relieved" dungeon incest trial is over. London: *The Times*. Retrieved April 2009 from http://www.timesonline.co.uk/tol/news/world/europe/article5944703.ece#cid=OTC-RSS&attr=797093

National Center for Victims of Crime (NCVC). (2008). Acquaintance rape. Retrieved April 2009 from http://www.ncvc.org/ncvc/main.aspx?dbName=DocumentViewer&DocumentID=32306

Neame, A. (2004, Winter). Revisiting America's "date rape" controversy. *Family Matters 68:* 50–55.

Oppenheimer, J. (1998). Politicizing survivors of incest and sexual abuse: Another facet of healing. *Women and Therapy 21*(2): 79–87.

Page, A. D. (2007). Behind the blue line: Investigating police officers' attitudes toward rape. *Journal of Police Criminal Psychology 22*(1): 22–32.

Pardue, A., and Arrigo, B. (2007). Power, anger, and sadistic rapists. *International Journal of Offender Therapy and Comparative Criminology 52*: 378–400.

Pazzani, L. (2007). The factors affecting sexual assaults committed by strangers and acquaintances. *Violence Against Women 13*: 717–749.

Pelisek, C. (2009, March 18). DNA deep freeze.*Los Angeles Weekly*. Retrieved March 2009 from http://www.laweekly.com/2009-03-19/news/dna-deep-feeze/

Pollard-Terry, G. (2004, July 20). For African American rape victims, culture of silence. *Los Angeles Times*. Retrieved August 2009 from http://articles.latimes.com/2004/jul/20/entertainment/et-pollard20

Robinson, L. (1997). "I was raped." *Emerge 8*(7): 42–53.

Roiphe, K. (1994). *The morning after: Sex, fear and feminism*. Boston, MA: Little, Brown & Co.

Rollins, J. H. (1996). *Women's minds, women's bodies: The psychology of women in a biosocial context*. Upper Saddle River, NJ: Prentice-Hall.

Ross, W. (2009, March 21). *Students choose sides as teen faces charges* (p. A8). Eugene, OR: The Register-Guard.

Saewyc, E., Magee, L., and Pettingell, S. (2004). Teenage pregnancy and associated risk behaviors among sexually abused adolescents. *Perspectives on Sexual and Reproductive Health 36*(3): 98–105.

Sanday, P. R. (2007). *Fraternity gang rape: Sex, brotherhood, and privilege on campus*, 2nd ed. New York: New York University Press.

Savino, J., Turvey, B., and Baeza, J. (2004). *Rape investigation handbook*. Burlington, MA: Elsevier Academic Press.

Sawyer, M. (2005, July 31). 50,000 rapes each year but only 600 rapists sent to jail. *The Observer*. Retrieved from http://observer.guardian.co.uk.

Schwartz, M. D., and DeKeseredy, W. S. (1997). *Sexual assault on the college campus: The role of male peer support*. Thousand Oaks, CA: Sage.

Sebold, A. (2002). *Lucky*. Philadelphia, PA: Bay Books.

Shorter Oxford English Dictionary. (2007). Rape. New York: Oxford University Press.

Sigler, R., Johnson, I., and Morgan, E. (2007). Forced sexual intercourse: Contemporary views. In R. Muraskin (ed.), *It's a crime: Women and justice*, 3rd ed. (pp. 187–216). Upper Saddle River, NJ: Prentice-Hall.

Sorenson, S. B., and Siegel, J. M. (1992). Gender, ethnicity, and sexual assault: Findings from a Los Angeles study. *Journal of Social Issues 48:* 93–104.

Tjaden, P., and Thoennes, N. (2000). *Prevalence, incidence, and consequences of violence against women: Findings from the national violence against women survey*. Washington, DC: U.S. Department of Justice.

Troxler, H. (2005, April 19). Tough talk, tough laws, but no easy answers. *St. Petersburg Times*, p. 1B.

Ullman, S., and Townsend, S. (2007). Barriers to working with sexual assault survivors: A qualitative study of rape crisis center workers. *Violence Against Women 13*: 412–443.

U.S. Congress (2005, March 9). Press release: Rep. Maloney: "Include women in hate crime statistics." Retrieved from www.house.gov/maloney/press/109th

U.S. Department of Human and Health Services (DHHS). (2009). *Child maltreatment 2007*. Administration for Children and Families. Retrieved April 2009 from http://www.acf.hhs.gov/programs/cb/pubs/cm07/cm07.pdfwww.acf.dhhs.gov

U.S. Department of Veteran Affairs. (2008). National Center for PTSD. Sexual assault against females. Retrieved April 2009 from http://www.ncptsd.va.gov/ncmain/doclist.jsp?opm=3

van Wormer, K. (2007). Human behavior and the social environment, micro level. New York: Oxford University Press.

van Wormer, K., and Berns, L. (2004). The impact of priest sexual abuse: Female survivors' narratives. *Affilia 19*(1): 53–67.

van Wormer, K., and Davis, D.R. (2008). *Addiction treatment: A strengths perspective*. Belmont, CA: Cengage.

Walker, A. (1982). *The color purple*. New York: Harcourt Brace Jovanovich.

Washington Post. (2009, March 19). Military reports of sex assaults rose in 2008. *Washington Post*, p. A07.

Watson-Franke, M.-B. (2003). A world in which women move freely without fear of men: An anthropological perspective on rape. *Women's Studies International Forum 25*(6): 599–606.

Wehrman, J., and Carr, R. (2008, April 22). Congress weighs safeguards in military rape cases. Dayton Daily News. Retrieved April 2009 from www.daytondailynews.com/o/content/shared/news/stories/2008/04/MILITARY_RAPE20_PBP.html+senate+law+military+acquaintance+rape&cd=6&hl=en&ct=clnk&gl=us&client=firefox-a

Weiss, K. (2009). "Boys will be boys" and other gendered accounts. *Violence Against Women*. Released in advance of publication.

Yarbrough, F. (2005, August). Power, perception, and interracial sex: Former slaves recall a multiracial south. *Journal of Southern History 71*(3): 559–589.

Zagier, A. (2008, January 18). Abuse claims divide small town. *Boston Globe*. Retrieved August 2009 from http://www.boston.com/news/education/higher/articles/2008/01/18/abuse_claims_divide_small_town/

Zastrow, C. (2007). *Introduction to social work and social welfare*, 8th ed. Belmont, CA: Brooks/Cole.

Zastrow, C., and Kirst-Ashman, K. (2010). *Understanding human behavior and the social environment*, 8th ed. Belmont, CA: Brooks/Cole.

9

Wife and Partner Abuse

With regard to violence, which is the single most dangerous place for women?

The family home.

What is the leading cause of death for women at work?

Homicide by a spouse or partner.

When is the battered woman most likely to get killed?

When she leaves the relationship.

Who overwhelmingly are the victims of murder-suicides?

Women.

Evidence for these and other statements concerning the intimate victimization of women is provided in this chapter. We begin with an overview of this crime, including definitions.

Intimate partner abuse consists of intentional acts to cause injury in a spouse or partner or ex-spouse or ex-partner. Such violence of *battering* is physical aggression with a purpose to control, intimidate, and subjugate another human being. Intimate partner violence is always accompanied by emotional abuse, and in a battered woman generally arouses fear. *Domestic violence* is another commonly used term that we will use in this chapter. According to the Office on Violence Against Women (2009), domestic violence can be physical, sexual, emotional, economic, or psychological actions or threats of actions that influence another person. This includes any behaviors that intimidate, manipulate, humiliate, isolate, frighten, terrorize, coerce, threaten, blame, hurt, injure, or wound someone. *Domestic violence* is a term that came into common usage in the 1970s; this term is gender neutral and encompasses a wide range of abuse within families.

Research on intimate partner violence is provided by the U.S. Department of Justice; this resource collects data that are analyzed by scholars and are the source for mass media attention paid to this serious social problem. Across the United States, from California to New Jersey to New York, a rash of male-on-female murder-suicides have been featured in regional news reports, and in Canada the media attention has focused on cutbacks in funding for women's shelters in a time in which violent sexual attacks against women are prominent. Meanwhile, throughout North America, the death toll of women at the hands of their partners continues to mount, although at a slower pace than formerly (Rennison, Bureau of Justice Statistics [BJS], 2003). A frightening recent development highlighted in news reports is the proliferation of mass killing possibly related to economic hardship. Characterized as suicidal rampages, news reports from across the country carried stories of men who killed their own children, committed mass slaughter in a nursing home, and wiped out whole families (see, e.g., Breed, 2009; Britt, 2009).

Our emphasis in this second chapter on female victimization is on the kind of violence that takes place in intimate relationships. The issues of authority and control by men over women, both physically and emotionally, are explored first, with a historical overview and later by an examination of theories of partner abuse. To dispel the myths about partner violence, we consider statistical data from both national police reports and crime victimization surveys. Special attention is devoted to several areas often neglected in the literature: the substance abuse connection, marital rape, suicide-murder, and the relationship between battering and child abuse. In the final sections of these pages, we consider the criminal justice response and successful treatment interventions for both the batterer and the battered. Throughout this discussion, variables of race, ethnicity, and class are considered.

The continuum of violence against girls and women in our society includes sexist and degrading language, pornography, trafficking, stalking, economic deprivation, threatening behavior, child abuse, rape, assault, and murder. Violence used by men against women who are their intimate partners has its historic roots in centuries of institutionally sanctioned dominance of one gender over the other in key spheres of heterosexual relationships, such as economic, sexual, intellectual, cultural, spiritual, and emotional (Pence and Dasgupta, 2006). From the perspective of this book, domestic assault is seen as one behavior on a continuum of behaviors that serve the purpose of maintaining domination and power over a vulnerable individual. Some victims are beaten down over time; others enter into an unhealthy relationship with considerable baggage from early life experiences. Read Box 9.1 in which a survivor condenses her early life experiences into a few poignant passages.

HISTORICAL OVERVIEW

In the United States today, men who beat their wives are going against cultural norms and the law. Historically a man's right to chastise his wife was affirmed in church doctrine as well as in early Roman law and English common law. Under English common law, which influenced law on this side of the Atlantic, to be a wife meant becoming the property of one's husband. There was some effort, however, to prevent excessive violence. Men could give their wives "moderate correction" under the doctrine of coverture—the legal doctrine that held that a married woman's identity was subsumed under her husband's (Blackstone, 1979). All through the years, even after physical punishment of one's wife was outlawed (in the late 1800s), domestic violence was

BOX 9.1
Domestic Violence: A Personal Narrative

I heard: My boyfriend screaming at me as he rummaged through the closet. He kept yelling, "You are going to die, you bitch."

I saw: Him running toward me with a look of hate on his face, fire in his eyes, and a tie in his hand.

I felt: Panic as his hands squeezed the tie tightly around my neck. I felt my breath leaving me and saw my life flash before me as I lost consciousness.

I smelled: Like urine as I woke up and made my way cautiously to the bathroom in fear that he was still in the house. I changed my clothes, put some ointment on my neck and called my roommate. Two months later this same man and I got married.

This was to me: Love. I grew up in a violent home. My father beat my mother, my mother beat us.

Explanation: My boyfriend was mad at me because I had ripped up a picture we had taken together. I had deep tie burns around my neck, and open sores for several months. I could not wear a necklace or high neck sweaters for over thirty years. I never went to the police because he would be sent back to prison and I was pregnant.

Critical Thinking Questions: What does this say about intergenerational violence and victimization? Does the writer's explanation tell the full story of why she didn't seek the help she needed? What other factors do you think were involved?

Source: Rose Jansson. Printed with permission of Rose Jansson (November, 2008).

considered a private matter, not one for intervention by the state (Presser and Gaarder, 2004). One may recall testimony in the O. J. Simpson trial that when Nicole Simpson called the police for help, her husband persuaded the authorities that the problem was "a family matter" (see Ingrassia and Beck, 1994). So the legacy of the past is with us still.

In the 1970s, when the women's liberation movement took hold, and attention was drawn to rape as a crime of power, the very threat of which frightened all women and restricted their movements, women became acutely aware of how pervasive was victim-blaming in our society. Exposing such victim-blaming not only produced new theoretical understandings but also laid the groundwork for pushing institutions to change the treatment of victims of domestic violence as well as of rape by providing victim assistance programming (Smith, 2003). It laid the groundwork as well for collective political action and social support. The efforts of this movement culminated in the landmark **Violence Against Women Act (VAWA)** of 1994, federal legislation providing for improved prevention and prosecution of violent crimes against women and children and for the care of victims. The law also provided funding for prevention, shelter services, and legal advocacy. Unfortunately, however, simultaneously the new welfare "reform" legislation passed in the same year has put indigent women who were eagerly trying to escape an abusive situation at grave risk. Forcing mothers to seek child support from violent men puts them in jeopardy, and the scarcity of affordable housing and long waiting periods to qualify for subsidized housing means that large numbers of families escaping abuse have ended up in transitional housing or homeless.

In its recent reauthorizations, the VAWA has included protections for immigrant, rural, disabled, and older women as well as for immigrant children caught up in battering situations

(Family Violence Prevention Fund, 2008). In its 2005 reauthorization, for example, funding was increased for programs that offer help to victims of dating violence, human trafficking into the United States, sexual assault, and stalking.

NATURE AND SCOPE OF THE PROBLEM

Women often experience their greatest risk of violence from their intimate male partners and spouses. Although this is one of the most underestimated and underreported crimes in the United States and the single most significant cause of injury to women, intimate partner violence has received increased national attention in recent years. Research informs us that about one woman in four will be physically assaulted by a partner or ex-partner in her lifetime (National Institute of Justice [NIJ], 2004). The Bureau of Justice Statistics special reports *Intimate Partner Violence, 1993–2001* (Rennison, 2003) and *Full Report of the Prevalence, Incidence, and Consequences of Violence Against Women* (Tjaden and Thoennes, 2000) provide the most comprehensive data on reported victimization. From *Intimate Partner Violence*, we learn that:

- Between 1976 and 2000, the number of women murdered by intimates (spouses, partners, or dates) fell 22 percent, from 1,600 to 1,247;
- The number of men murdered by intimates during that period dropped 68 percent, from 1,357 to 440.

These figures are startling in their implications. What they seem to indicate is that the effect of recent efforts to curb domestic violence—the police protection, battered women's advocates, greater hospital sensitivity, and women's shelters—seems to be succeeding more in saving the lives of men than of women. Later in the chapter, we will look at this phenomenon more closely.

From Tjaden and Thoennes's *Full Report*, we learn that:

- Women experience more **intimate partner violence** than do men: 22.1 percent of surveyed women, compared with 7.4 percent of surveyed men, reported they were physically assaulted by a current or former spouse, cohabiting partner, boyfriend, girlfriend, or date in their lifetime; 1.3 percent of surveyed women and 0.9 percent of surveyed men reported experiencing such violence in the previous twelve months. Approximately 1.3 million women and 835,000 men are physically assaulted by an intimate partner annually in the United States;
- Women are significantly more likely than men to be injured during an assault: 31.5 percent of female rape victims, compared with 16.1 percent of male rape victims, reported being injured during their most recent rape; 39.0 percent of female physical assault victims, compared with 24.8 percent of male physical assault victims, reported being injured during their most recent physical assault;
- Most injuries to women were inflicted in the home; in almost half of the cases the perpetrator and victim had used drugs or alcohol;
- Stalking is more prevalent than previously thought: 8.1 percent of surveyed women and 2.2 percent of surveyed men reported being stalked at some time in their life.

Stalking is a danger sign of possible future violence because the behavior usually is a sign in North American culture of obsession with someone who has spurned the stalker. According to a recent first-of-its-kind report from the U.S. Department of Justice (2009), an estimated 3.4 million persons age 18 or older were victims of stalking. Females experienced twenty stalking victimizations per 1,000 females age 18 or older compared with 7 per 1,000 victimizations of males. Persons age 18–19 and 20–24 experienced the highest rates of stalking victimization. By the tens of thousands, victims of stalking lose their jobs, flee their homes and fear for their safety, according to this recent federal survey.

From further governmental and other sources we learn that:

- A woman's attempt to leave a relationship was the precipitating factor in 45 percent of the murders of a woman by a man (Block, 2003);
- Sexual assault or forced sex occurs in approximately 40–45 percent of battering relationships (Campbell et al., 2003).

Another way to consider gender differences is to compare violence rates in relationships that are exclusively male and exclusively female. According to the Bureau of Justice Statistics (BJS) (2007b) report on intimate partner violence:

- About 96 percent of females experiencing nonfatal intimate partner violence were victimized by a male and about 3 percent reported that the offender was another female.
- About 82 percent of males experiencing nonfatal intimate partner violence were victimized by a female and about 16 percent of males reported that the offender was another male.

Significantly, same-sex homicide rates are predominantly male perpetrated, with the gay male rate of killing at about twelve times the lesbian rate (Garcia, Soria, and Hurwitz, 2007).These figures on gay–lesbian violence are significant in what they say about violence and gender. Even taking into account the fact that there are more gay than lesbian intimate partner relationships, we can conclude that fighting among male couples is more frequent than fighting among female couples.

In one of the largest studies of its kind, a survey of 3,455 women interviewed at rural and urban emergency rooms in California and Pennsylvania found that nearly 14 percent of the women reported sexual and physical abuse at the hands of an intimate partner (Dearwater et al., 1998). Only 2.2 percent of the patients, however, over the preceding year were treated at that time for acute trauma for the abuse. Women who had ended a relationship within the previous year were seven times more likely to report abuse than women who had not. Reports of domestic abuse were more frequent in California than in Pennsylvania; those most at risk were young women with children who had extremely low incomes.

Claims by social scientists such as Donald Dutton (2007) that women assault men as much as men assault women, consistent with media reports highlighting women's active role in domestic violence, are given little support in the national (or global) crime statistics. The survey data on which the media reports purportedly showing symmetry in partner violence are based go back several decades to research conducted by Straus and Gelles (1986). In the survey, women reported hitting men even slightly more often than men reported they hit women. The National Institute of Justice (2007) warns against such studies that find that women abuse men equally or even more than men abuse women. These studies are based on data compiled through the Conflict Tactics Scale, a survey tool that may not be appropriate for intimate partner violence research because it does not measure control, coercion, or the motives for conflict tactics; it also leaves out sexual assault and violence by ex-spouses or partners and does not determine who initiated the violence. The instrument used, the Conflict Tactics Scale, as Miller and White (2003) indicate, is also problematic because its exclusive focus is on acts performed rather than the context and meaning. The use of such acts-based measures may err in equating a self-protective maneuver such as pushing the man away with the initiation of violence (Downs, Rindels, and Atkinson, 2007). These data are obtained from a national survey of households on incidents of victimization over the past year. The finding of a large gender gap is similar to that found in the government's arrest statistics.

The claim that girls and women are more violent today than formerly is a claim that pops up in the media every decade or so; then it is challenged by criminologists and forgotten for awhile, only to surface again. The perception that girls' aggression and violence have never been higher is generated by extensive media coverage of isolated incidents such as a hazing event at a Chicago high school and a video-taping of girls beating up another girl. Most media treatments link such incidents to girls becoming more like boys, the "dark side" of women's quest for equality (Brown, Chesney-Lind, and Stein, 2007). Yet looking at the official data, there is nothing to sustain the claims of an increase in female youth violence. Studies of hospital admission data and vital statistics maintained by health departments show no rise in girls' injuries, such as from fighting, as Brown et al. indicate. Nor do data from other official sources. From the FBI's Uniform Crime Reports (2008), we learn:

- The number of persons arrested in 2007 for violent crimes dropped 10.5 percent for males and 1.1 percent for females when compared with the numbers arrested a decade earlier (1998).
- When compared with data from 1998, the number of juveniles arrested in 2007 for violent crimes declined for both genders. Arrests of males under age 18 declined 14.3 percent, and arrests of females under age 18 decreased 12.7 percent.

It is true that the arrest rates are up for girls and women charged with simple assault and, surprisingly, robbery. The assault rates are about one-third of the male rates and the robbery rates about one-eighth of the male rates. Homicide rates are significantly down as are the more serious assault rates. How do we explain this discrepancy between the FBI arrest figures and data from the Conflict Tactic Scale research? This discrepancy is often explained by the fact that men are less likely to call the police when attacked by a partner than are women. Another way to look at this is to consider that the police are more likely to be called for serious assaults than for the less serious assaults where no injury results and when the victim is in fear of further violence. Women are more likely than men to be injured and more likely to be afraid and therefore to call the police for help.

Criminologists attribute the increase in simple assault for girls and women (up around 10 percent for each) to a shift in the law and in the enforcement of domestic violence laws rather than a change in female behavior (see Chesney-Lind, 2006; Menard, Anderson, and Godboldt, 2009). The laws now mandate arrest when it is determined that an act of domestic violence has taken place. Instead of just arresting the perpetrator, victims who fight back are arrested as well. Within the family, teens who become violent are now arrested where formerly police gave them warnings. Again a policy change is reflected in the statistics which are then accepted at face value.

Were women more violent today, this fact would be reflected in the national household surveys that take into account serious as well as minor crimes; no such increase is evident here (Rennison, 2003). According to the government's National Victimization Survey, 85 percent of all intimate assault victims are female (Rennison, 2003). The discrepancy between this and the Conflict Tactics surveys can be explained in part by the fact that the federal survey includes sexual assault and even robbery of an intimate person. (An intimate person is defined as a spouse or ex-spouse, and partner or ex-partner.) Women do report in the Conflict Tactics surveys that they commit a large number of acts of minor violence such as hitting and slapping. Even these acts of violence may be committed in response to men's violence.

To check out this supposition, we need to discover the context of female physical assault. Three recent empirically based studies are instructive in this regard. The first study by Downs, Rindels, and Atkinson (2007) relied on in-depth interviews with women concerning 180 incidents of domestic violence that had been reported in a previous questionnaire. The women who were interviewed were either receiving domestic violence services or substance abuse treatment. The question that was addressed was how they protected themselves from abuse when they were attacked. Most women used nonphysical strategies such as running away, locking herself up in a room, threatening to call the police, and trying to talk their partner into calming down. Of the domestic violence group, a majority (57 percent) used nonviolent strategies only. Of the substance abuse sample, 26.4 percent used nonviolent strategies only and about the same amount used both nonviolent and violent strategies. Violent strategies were only used when the other approaches failed to work. Rarely did the women initiate the violence, although a minority of women in the substance abuse sample did initiate the violence, presumably under the influence of alcohol and other drugs. This research is unique in filling in explanations of the context in which female domestic assault occurs.

These research findings by Downs and his colleagues are bolstered by those of Miller and Meloy (2006) who conducted interviews with ninety-five female offenders in batterer treatment programs. Only five of the women exhibited preemptive, aggressive violence; the remaining ninety women used violence either to defend themselves or their children or out of frustration with an abusive situation that seemed beyond their control.

The difference in male–female domestic violence patterns is further revealed in recidivism studies in individuals previously arrested for domestic assault. Menard, Anderson, and Godboldt (2009) conducted a five-year follow-up study to examine recidivism rates among such individuals. Examination of most court records involving intimate partner violence revealed that 15.5 percent of the acts of violence were perpetrated by women. Women who were arrested were likely to be in connection with dual arrests much more than were men. Significantly, none of these women re-offended, a fact that shows these women's violence was probably a self-defense or responsive maneuver. Overall, around 19 percent of the women were rearrested compared to just under half of the men. Among both men and women, whites and nondrug users were least likely to re-offend. For men, previous arrests predicted recidivism, and for women, severity of the assault and the threat of a breakup predicted recidivism.

The problem may not be female offending as highlighted in media reports, but female victimization. Let us look at an area of legitimate concern—patterns of partner violence. Such episodes of partner violence of which we speak often begin with intense dating relationships. The roots of male-on-female violence and gender conflict in relationships may be found in these earlier patterns of behavior.

Teen Dating Violence

Texas recently adopted a law that requires school districts to define dating violence in school safety codes, after the 2003 stabbing death of Ortralla Mosley, 15, in a hallway of her Austin high school and the shooting death of Jennifer Ann Crecente, 18, two years ago. In 2007, Rhode Island adopted the Lindsay Ann Burke Act—prompted by the murder of a young woman by a former boyfriend—requiring school districts to teach students in grades 7 through

12 about dating abuse. These extreme cases are described in a recent story in the *New York Times* (Olson, 2009). Harassment by phone calls, text messages, and email, are commonly experienced forms of gendered abuse, according to the article. Although there are no definitive estimates on the prevalence of abuse in dating relationships, the following statistics are the best estimates available.

Dating Violence Statistics

Adolescents and adults are often unaware of how regularly dating violence occurs. The Centers for Disease Control and Prevention (CDC) (2006) includes these statistics on dating violence:

- one in eleven adolescents reports being a victim of physical dating violence.
- one in four adolescents reports verbal, physical, emotional, or sexual violence each year.
- one in five adolescents reports being a victim of emotional violence.
- one in five high school girls has been physically or sexually abused by a dating partner.
- Dating violence occurs more frequently among black students than among Hispanic or white students.
- 72 percent of eighth and ninth graders reportedly "date"; by the time they are in high school, 54 percent of students report dating violence among their peers.

Academic research based on a focus group study of Mexican American youth shows that the use of violence in dating relationships in that population is similarly widespread (Black and Weisz, 2005).

According to the BJS (2007b) report on intimate partner violence, young women ages 16–24 experience the highest rates of relationship violence. Thanks in part to results of a much publicized teen and preteen dating survey conducted by the National Domestic Violence Hotline, much attention has been paid recently to the risks of violence in early dating relationships. A major finding of the study was that one in three teens who were having sex by age 14 said that they had been physically abused by an angry partner. For those who were not sexually active until later, the abuse rate was significantly lower, at 9 percent. This seems to indicate that teens who get involved in serious dating relationships while they are still immature are at high risk for violence. Concern about the issue prompted the National Association of Attorneys General to pass a resolution encouraging school districts to implement teen dating violence education policies (Washington Times, 2008).

In a study of gay, lesbian, and bisexual adolescents, youths involved in same-sex dating are just as likely to experience dating violence as youths involved in opposite-sex dating (Halpern et al., 2004).

Surveys on domestic violence that include slapping and hitting find that young males, like their older counterparts, are at the receiving end of much of this violence. The CDC's (2008) national youth behavior risk survey, for example, found that during the twelve months before the survey, the prevalence of dating violence victimization was higher among male (11.0 percent) than female (8.8 percent) students. The rate of dating violence was higher among black (14.2 percent) and Hispanic (11.1 percent) than white (8.4 percent) students, and higher among black female (13.2 percent) and Hispanic female (10.1 percent) than white female (7.4 percent) students, and higher among black male (15.2 percent) than white male (9.3 percent) students. A breakdown according to the severity of the assaults and the context would have been helpful.

Among older teens, we learn from government statistics that the percentage of violent crime involving an intimate partner is ten times higher for females than males (9 percent versus 0.6 percent) (Baum, 2005).

In their review of the literature on adolescent dating violence, Mulford and Giordano (2008) found that the rates of reported acts of mutual aggression generally are similar for boys and girls. However, when it comes to severe teen dating violence—including sexual and physical assault—girls are disproportionately the victims. Mulford and Giordano also report from their literature review that:

> Although both boys and girls report that anger is the primary motivating factor for using violence, girls also commonly report self-defense as a motivating factor, and boys also commonly cite the need to exert control. Boys are also more likely to react with laughter when their partner is physically aggressive. Girls experiencing teen dating violence are more likely than boys to suffer long-term negative behavioral and health consequences, including suicide attempts, depression, cigarette smoking, and marijuana use. (pp. 35–36)

In their in-depth interviews with African American adolescents, Miller and White (2003) found that girls' violence was interpreted as out-of-control behavior, but not seen as physically threatening, while boys' violence was seen as dangerous. To get some indication of the context in which male youths were abusive toward their girlfriends, Reed et al. (2008) conducted in-depth interviews with nineteen boys, ages 14–20, with known histories of perpetrating intimate partner violence. The boys lived in mostly urban neighborhoods in metropolitan Boston. Common themes that emerged from the interviews included problematic home environments, problems at school, community contexts characterized by violence and peer pressure to sexually exploit girls. Intervention programs that aim to address boys' abusive behaviors toward their girlfriends would do well, according to the authors, to address the broad array of difficulties faced within boys' lives.

Miller and White (2003), drawing from personal narratives with African American teens, provide a personal dimension to attitudes toward violence that goes beyond the statistical data. Youths described strong norms against male violence, making it likely that many men would be reticent to admit such activity. A number of young men said they were taught by their mothers not to hit girls. But both males and females justified a violent response when a young woman initiated violence or if the young woman seemed to have "forgotten her place." As one young woman explained, "If you be big enough to hit a man, you big enough to take that lick back" and a young man said, "Certain times I feel that if a girl is man enough to hit you she man enough to get hit back" (p. 1237). Male youths also defined females as deserving violence when they "runnin' they mouth" (p. 1239). Young females' violence was typically minor, but seen as posing a threat to the young men. For young women, jealousy and anger over infidelities were key factors.

A key factor that distinguishes adult relationships from adolescent relationships is the lack of experience teens have in negotiating romantic relationships. Inexperience in communicating and relating to a romantic partner may lead to the use of poor coping strategies, including verbal and physical aggression (Mulford and Giordano, 2008). A teen who has difficulty expressing himself or herself may use physically aggressive behaviors to show affection, frustration, or jealousy. The 2008 CDC youth survey included a section on sexual abuse (being forced to have sexual intercourse). Nationwide, 7.8 percent of students had ever been physically forced to have sexual intercourse when they did not want to. Overall, the prevalence of having been forced to have sexual intercourse was higher among female (11.3 percent) than male (4.5 percent) students; at 11 percent among white female, 13.3 percent among black female, and 11.4 percent among Hispanic female students; among males, it was 3.2 percent, 7.8 percent, and 6.2 percent, respectively.

Sexual abuse is often a part of the pattern of long-term relationships characterized by violence. In general, adolescent girls involved in serious relationships are more likely than adult women to be victims of interpersonal violence and to suffer both minor and severe injuries as a result. The death of a sixteen-year-old girl, shot and killed by her seventeen-year-old boyfriend in Oakland, California, epitomizes the potential of this form of violence to escalate to a tragic extreme (Davis, 2008). Another high risk facing girls who are regularly victimized by their boyfriends occurs in the form of suicide attempts and suicide. Exposure to interpersonal violence often begins in early adolescence and continues into adulthood.

Teens can learn much about healthy relationships from mature role models and in sex education classes at school. Adolescents can be taught to be alert to signs of behaviors that may put their lives at risk (see Box 9.2)

BOX 9.2
Dating Abuse: Warning Signs

Based on the literature on domestic violence, van Wormer and Roberts (2009) developed the following list of warning signs that a young woman should consider to determine if the relationship is likely to become violent. The warning signs are geared toward heterosexual female teens but can be adjusted to pertain to same-sex or male respondents.

_____1. Does your date or boyfriend brag about beating up or intimidating people?

_____2. Does he ever suggest that he knows how to kill, for example, by playfully putting his hands on your neck, then say he was only joking?

_____3. Does he own or have access to a gun, or show a fascination with weapons?

_____4. Has he ever forced you to kiss or have sex? Does he show an awareness of your wishes and feelings?

_____5. Does he use illegal drugs, especially amphetamines, speed, meth, or crack?

_____6. Does he get drunk on a regular basis or brag about his high tolerance for alcohol?

Does he push you to drink alcoholic beverages or take illicit drugs?

_____7. When you are with him, does he control how you spend your time? Is he always the one to drive or criticize you severely if you take the wheel?

_____8. Is he constantly jealous? Does he control your friendships with other people and seem to want to have you all to himself?

_____9. Is he rapidly becoming emotionally dependent on you; for instance, does he say things like "I can't live without you?" Is his thinking of an all-or-nothing pattern (either you are his best friend or his worst enemy) often about past relationships)?

_____10. Do you have the feeling that only you understand him, that others do not or cannot?

_____11. Note the relationship between his parents. Is his mother very submissive to his father? Is there heavy drinking and/or lots of tension in his family?

(continued)

(continued)

_____12. Is there a history of past victimization by his father?

_____13. Is there a history of animal abuse in his background?

_____14. Has he ever struck you? Have you known him to lose control of his anger for certain periods of time?

_____15. Has he ever threatened or tried to commit suicide?

_____16. Does he get out of patience quickly with children or is he verbally abusive toward them?

_____ Total "Yes" answers.

If you have answered yes to two or more of these items, you should talk to a mature person before pursuing this relationship further.

Critical Thinking Questions. Before getting romantically involved with someone, consider what it would be like to break up with this person. Would you be able to cool the relationship and still remain friends or end the relationship if you wanted to? Consider how your partner would handle this. Your answer provides clues to the healthiness or unhealthiness in the relationship. (Remember it's a lot easier to get out of a potentially dangerous relationship in the early stages than to wait and see how things turn out, or to see if you can change a person.)

Source: Death by Domestic Violence: Preventing the Murders and the Murder-Suicides (2009), pp. 154–155.

Lesbian and Gay Couples

Women living with female partners experience less partner violence than do women living with male partners. Slightly more than 11 percent of the women who had lived with a woman as part of a couple reported being raped, physically assaulted, and/or stalked by a female cohabitant, but 21.7 percent of the women who had married or lived with a man as part of a couple reported such violence by a husband or male cohabitant (Tjaden and Thoennes, 2000). These findings suggest that lesbian couples experience less intimate partner violence than do heterosexual couples; however, more research is needed to support or refute this conclusion.

Men living with male partners experience more partner violence than do men who live with female partners. Approximately 23 percent of the men who had lived with a man as a couple reported being raped, physically assaulted, and/or stalked by a male cohabitant, while 7.4 percent of the men who had married or lived with a woman as a couple reported such violence by a wife or female cohabitant (Tjaden and Thoennes, 2000). These findings provide further evidence that intimate partner violence is perpetrated primarily by men, whether against male or female intimates.

This same-sex violence is linked to violence in the family of origin, homophobia in the society, and alcohol abuse (Kulkin et al., 2007). Uniquely to gay–lesbian couples, some of the conflict arises from arguments over the coming-out issue. Getting help by either domestic violence services or law enforcement can be especially difficult, more so for gay men.

DOMESTIC VIOLENCE AMONG ETHNIC MINORITIES

Women living in cultures that value community over individuality, as well as those that hold women responsible for holding the community together, face enormous barriers when it comes to reporting abuse. This reluctance to bring shame on the community is strongest among Asian Americans. African American and American Indian women also may want to protect their men from law enforcement contact due to a history of discrimination. For these defensive reasons, comprehensive data on ethnic and racial minorities are hard to come by.

Rates of partner violence are higher among African Americans than for their white counterparts (Tjaden and Thoennes, 2000). These data, based on the **National Violence Against Women (NVAW)** survey, also reveal that Asian/Pacific Islander women and men tend to report lower rates of intimate partner violence than do women and men from minority backgrounds, while Indian/Alaska Native women and men report higher rates than all other groups. However, differences among minority groups diminish when other sociodemographic and relationship variables are controlled. Dugan and Apel (2003) enlighten us on the details of incidents of violence in their statistical analysis of the NVAW data. Their analysis reveals that risk factors for all forms of violence against women include moving frequently, living in an urban setting, going out at night, living in a low-income household, having no job, and having little education. Marriage is a protective factor. Significantly, Asian women are at high risk for victimization outside the home and by multiple attackers. They are least likely to report victimization to the police; African American women are most likely to contact the police. This group is also most likely to be victimized by a boyfriend at home and with a weapon. Native American women are most likely to be victimized by someone they know and by a person using drugs or alcohol.

Surveys show that around half of immigrant Latina women report that they have experienced physical abuse in their marriage (Brabeck and Guzmán, 2008). Lauritsen and White (2001) bring our attention to the role of socioeconomic disadvantage in increasing the risk for nonlethal violence. Using the NVAW data, these researchers found that controlling for socioeconomic status, the differences between black and white women would no longer be significant and that the rate for Latinos would be somewhat less if all lived in similar communities. Ingram (2007), similarly, found that controlling for educational and family income levels that victimization rates are less among Latinos than non-Latinos.

Mexican Americans, compared to other ethnic populations, tend to stay in abusive families longer, return home more frequently, and are less likely to seek formal help. Despite this fact, Brabeck and Guzmán found that these women use other proactive strategies such as trying to placate the abuser and turning to religious faith for strength.

Many South Asian Indian women in America are facing the terror of being trapped in abusive relationships, staying with their spouse to protect their immigration status and avoid deportation (Schakowsky, 2005). According to Lee and Au (2007), Chinese battered women experience tremendous pressures as foreign-born women trying to break through the abusive cycle within their cultural milieu. Because the family name has to be protected at all costs and because individual well-being should be subordinated to the common good, Chinese women do not admit to the occurrence of abuse. In a survey of directors of women's shelters in cities in the United States and Canada with large Chinese populations, Lee and Au discovered that women of Chinese origin endured much abuse in silence, that they perceived marriage as a license for the man to have sex with his wife whenever or however he desired, and that they did not consider divorce an option to escape physical abuse. Unique to the Chinese culture, gambling, rather than alcohol or drugs, was associated with violence. A second culturally specific aspect of Chinese North American wife abuse is the conjoint physical and emotional abuse by the husband's parents along with the husband.

West (1998) summarized partner violence research on American Indian groups by indicating that all the studies cited show a very high rate of battering in American Indian couples. He also indicated that the relatively small nonrandom sample sizes make it difficult to reach definitive conclusions. Much of the violence among Native American groups is alcoholism related.

Interventions to be effective must be culturally sensitive; best results are obtained when the counselors are from the same cultural and linguistic background as those receiving services. In her work with a group of African American survivors, for example, Gillum (2008) found that an agency geared to stress community values was highly effective in engaging the women. The successful intervention, which was praised by the participants, was in a predominantly African American neighborhood and used an Afrocentric curriculum. This curriculum emphasized black culture and history, a family-centered approach, and a focus on religious concepts.

To summarize, we can say of ethnic/cultural variations in domestic abuse that essentially, the universal, underlying dynamic in battering is male control and dominance, but that violence also is correlated with stress factors in the environment. Thus, the manifestation of violence in a relationship is influenced by cultural and contextual factors.

Now we turn to a look at homicide rates as the most reliable of the criminal justice data; more than other crimes they are reported to the police and they are taken the most seriously by legal authorities.

DOMESTIC HOMICIDE

Each year, about 33 percent of all women and 3 percent of all men who are murdered in the United States are killed by a so-called "intimate," a spouse, partner, or lover (van Wormer and Roberts, 2009). Nationwide, murder by an intimate is the number one cause of death for pregnant women. Not surprisingly, murder by an intimate is not just an American problem. A European task force recently found domestic violence accounts for 25 percent of all homicides in London and 35 percent across England and Wales.

Turning to domestic homicide, and to the most recent BJS (2007a) report, here is the official breakdown for 2005: 329 males and 1,181 females were killed in that year by their intimate partners. Clearly men are much more likely to kill their partners than women are to kill theirs. The character of the homicide differs by gender as well (BJS, 2007a). Whereas men are more apt to kill a stranger or be killed by a stranger, female homicides (whether the woman is the perpetrator or victim) generally involve intimates or other family members.

About one-third of female homicide victims were killed by an intimate partner compared to only 3 percent of male victims (BJS, 2007a). Researchers that use city- and State-generated databases for analysis, however, attribute 40–50 percent of female homicides to intimate partners. This discrepancy likely results from omission of ex-boyfriends and ex-girlfriends from the Federal Supplementary Homicide Reports (National Institute of Justice, 2007).

According to the BJS (2007a), overall the homicide rate from previous decades shows a significant decline. As far as race is concerned, for unknown reasons the number of African American partners and spouses killed by women has declined significantly. In the past, the rate of men so murdered was substantial. Despite the decline, the homicide rate for African Americans of both genders is still well above the white rate. The nonfatal victimization rate is quite high as well.

The homicide rate:

- for white girlfriends was higher in 2005 than it was in 1976.
- for white wives and ex-wives has declined but not as much as that for white husbands and ex-husbands.
- for black husbands and ex-husbands was twenty times greater in 1976 than it was in 2005.
- is higher for black girlfriends than any other group in 2005, although it has declined 66 percent since 1976.

Using our own calculations from the BJS (2007b) statistical tables, we find that the black male spouse victimization rate is four times the comparable white rate, and the black boyfriend murder rate is seven times the comparable white rate. Still, noteworthy in these figures is a significant decrease in the homicide rate among African Americans. One explanation for the decline is that it is attributable to a decline in marriages and long-term relationships (Dawson, Bunge, and Balde, 2009). We think a better explanation relates to the decline in use of the drug, crack cocaine in the black community, a drug that is associated with violence. In any case, it should also be noted from these data that white women are still being victimized at almost the same level as in previous years.

The claims mentioned earlier that women assault men as much as men assault women (such as by Dutton, 2007) fail to take into account women's physical vulnerabilities. Pregnant and recently pregnant women are extremely vulnerable and at high risk of domestic violence. Further, they are more likely to be victims of homicide (at the hands of their partners) than to die of any other cause. Homicide is a leading cause of traumatic death for pregnant and postpartum women in the United States, accounting for 31 percent of maternal injury deaths (Family Violence Prevention Fund, 2008). Throughout the world, pregnancy is a period of high risk for both battering and homicide.

If women truly were becoming more violent, the homicide rates would be up. Yet, according to the most comprehensive data available (BJS, 2007a), the rates for intimate homicide are down for women as well as men: Between 1975 and 2005, the number of intimate homicides for all race and gender groups declined by 75 percent. More specifically, the number of black males killed by intimates dropped by 83 percent, white males killed by 61 percent, black females by 52 percent, and white females by 6 percent.

Interestingly, in the early 1970s (not shown on these charts), before domestic partner shelters and other victim protection services were introduced, about as many women killed their intimate partners as male partners killed the women. There were well over a thousand homicides committed by each gender at this time. One could speculate that many of the women who resorted to homicide did so because they felt trapped; they could see no way out. Then when domestic violence hotlines and other services were introduced, the battered women had an alternative means of escape other than taking the life of the man.

Statistics Canada reveals that in recent years the rate of male spouses killed by their wives had declined, but the number of women killed by their husbands had stayed about the same (Dawson, Bunge, and Balde, 2009). This is similar to what is happening in the United States. One could speculate that the growth in women's domestic violence services is saving *men's* lives more than women's lives by providing a way out for battered women besides murder. The fact that women's professional opportunities and economic independence have increased may give women more confidence to escape domestic violence as well.

Men Who Kill Their Wives/Partners

The statistics discussed above, like the brief accounts contained in the media of male-on-female homicide, tell us little about the build up of the violence, the dangers facing the victims before they were killed, or the everyday assaults that would have preceded the ultimate attack. So what is it like on a daily basis living with a potential killer? What are these men like?

In search of the answers, we can listen to the stories of potential murder victims who have gotten away. We can turn to insights offered by Kathryn Ann Farr (2002) in interviews with a sample of women, all of whom survived an attempted domestic homicide. Most typically, as described by these women and confirmed by Farr in police reports, the perpetrator drank heavily and/or used illicit drugs, was an alcoholic or drug addict, was a gun owner, and, if the victim had left him, was her stalker. One victim described the attacks as so terrifying that she was certain she was going to die.

To personalize this description of offender traits with one survivor's story, read the following chilling account of life with a potential murderer. This narrative was obtained in an interview (by van Wormer, October 6, 2007) with a survivor (who is also a volunteer) at a domestic advocacy organization. In the survivor's words,

> Steve would buy my clothes for me; he told me who I could talk to, what I could eat—the whole nine yards. When I put on makeup, he would approve and watch. I tried to escape but couldn't get away. I tried to commit suicide—three or four times. I remember pointing the gun at my chin, and just when I was going to pull the trigger someone got the gun. I took pills and once slept for 24 hours.
>
> The beatings went on and on. "If you tell," he said, "I will kill you." The last time I saw him he said, "Do you want to say good-bye now? Because I'm going to kill you." I grabbed my son and we ran. That was 2003; he's still looking for me.

Lack of employment, the escalation of violence, forced sex, substance abuse, access to a gun, a pending breakup: these are among the key ingredients leading up to domestic homicide in the United States (Adams, 2007). The build-up to murder may be gradual, but to persons outside of the immediate family, the tragedy seems to have come about very suddenly. Bang, bang, and it is all over; the tell-tale yellow police tape is placed around the house. "They stayed to themselves," the neighbors say. Some lives are snuffed out, while the lives of those who remain behind may be damaged forever.

Patriarchal dominance, explosive violence, extreme possessiveness, jealousy, and a pathological fear of rejection by his wife or partner—these are among the key features of male-on-female domestic homicide (Harper and Voigt, 2007). Substance abuse and job loss are other factors that figure in.

Women Who Kill Their Husbands/Partners

Stalking is acknowledged to be a high risk for homicide (Campbell et al., 2007). Although most stalkers are men, consider this unusual case from Des Moines, Iowa (Associated Press, 2009). Debi Joy Olson readily admitted she stalked her ex-husband across the United States, then found him at work in a mall in Davenport, where she stabbed him to death. She is denying legal representation in court and says her one regret is that she can't be executed, as Iowa has no death penalty. She is requesting life imprisonment instead. In her words as contained in a note to the judge: "I gave up my country, my relatives, my friends for him 25 years ago. I will give up the rest of my life for Him now" (p. 1A).

Albert Roberts's (2007) research provides some support for the claim that much of women's killing of their partners is related to their feelings of terror and desperation. In his comparison of a sample of 105 women in prison who had been convicted of killing their partners with an equal sample of battered women from the community, Roberts found that virtually all of the women in prison had a history of being battered. Compared to the battered women who did not kill their partners, women in the prison sample were far more likely to have received death threats from their partners, threats that were specific as to time and place and method. Also in contrast to the comparison group, the majority of the women prisoners had a history of sexual abuse, a substance use problem, had attempted suicide, and had access to the batterers' guns. Noteworthy in these findings was the woman's desperation to escape, first through chemical abuse, then through suicide, and finally through a direct attack on the source of the problem.

As we have seen, in about three-fourths of intimate murders, the woman is the victim. This still leaves a substantial number of cases, a few hundred each year, in which the woman killed her spouse or boyfriend. Since 1976, the number of male spouses and other intimates killed was cut by around two-thirds while the decline in the number of female victims was cut only by about one-fourth. A logical explanation is that the increase in the availability of shelters for battered women has helped to reduce the numbers of women who kill their abusers by removing them from an extremely volatile situation.

Wells and DeLeon-Granados (2004) explain the striking decline in male homicides by their wives/partners in terms of "exposure reduction theory" (p. 233). **Exposure reduction theory** is the notion that the availability of mechanisms that allow a woman to sever ties with an abusive partner will spare her from seeking a violent solution. This theory is based on the body of evidence supporting the view that when women resort to using lethal partner violence, it is most likely a protective mechanism. An added consideration is that since most females arrested for murder are involved in substance abuse in some way, we can further speculate that removal from the drug scene in the home into the more sober shelter atmosphere gives women the chance to think more clearly about the consequences of their actions and prevents them from committing a rash and desperate act. Most women who do decide to leave manage to do so safely. Leaving is not without serious risks, however. When the woman does escape, the man may seek revenge, a fact that puts her life at risk following the breakup. About three-quarters of **murder-suicide** victims were killed by an intimate partner or ex-partner, and the majority of these murders occurred in relation to estrangement or a break-up (Campbell et al., 2007). Virtually all of the incidents involved female victims killed by a male partner.

Because battering men are, in all probability, active substance abusers who are not getting the help they need (whether in prison or in the community), their homicide rates against their partners have not declined. The paradox could be expressed in the following imaginary promotion ad: "Save men's lives; increase funding for women's shelters."

Despite occasional well-publicized cases of battered women who kill and are acquitted of murder or manslaughter, in many cases women who have killed under such circumstances receive harsh sentences. One reason may be the fact that battered women who have killed will cooperate with the police, making no attempt to cover up their crime. Men who kill their wives, on the other hand, can often afford a lawyer, and since they did not confess, they are in a position to enter a plea of guilty to a lesser charge. The plea of self-defense for a battered woman is often not believed, since she typically will kill her spouse while he is asleep or drunk or otherwise vulnerable. A woman who kills during a fight likely will use a weapon. It is hard for the jury in such cases to appreciate the danger the woman may have been in. The judicial system is based on a male model of how to determine fact in cases of self-defense.

In a politicized battered woman's murder trial, expert witnesses often rely on a battered woman syndrome self-defense argument. According to this argument—derived from Lenore Walker's (1979) theory of "learned helplessness"—repeatedly beaten women lose their faith in themselves and their judgment becomes impaired. They perceive use of force as their only means of escape. Walker (2009) recently reiterated this phenomenon and suggested a likely link in many women with a background of child abuse. One criticism of the "learned helplessness" concept is that its success depends on portraying women as passive victims

(Rothenberg, 2003). The inherent contradiction between a "learned helplessness" argument and a woman who took the direct action of committing murder is likely to leave the jury unconvinced. We must keep in mind that many victims do not survive; they are murdered by their batterers: These murder victims are the true victims of a long period of domestic abuse. For the ones who kill their assaulters, a more relevant and empowering defense than learned helplessness must be found. (The "learned helplessness" defense additionally may be used against battered mothers fighting for custody of their children; such women are often seen as incapable of protecting their children in their helplessness. Conversely, it may be used in a battered woman's favor when she is charged with not protecting her child from abuse by the man with whom she lived in terror.)

Our recommendation regarding homicide cases is that the law be changed to help women argue realistically that danger need not be immediate to be present and to also recognize that a woman beaten in her home has no duty to retreat when this is her home. Canadian law has been revised accordingly. Following a decision by the Canadian Supreme Court, judges must instruct jurors in battered women's cases that the woman is not required to leave the home (Geddes, 1998).

Specialized domestic violence or family violence courts have been established throughout Canada to address the unique nature of violence that occurs within the family, as opposed to violence between strangers or casual acquaintances. Some of the challenges with hearing family violence cases in mainstream criminal courtrooms include a high proportion of recanting and reluctant victims and witnesses (Public Health Agency in Canada, 2009). The primary objectives of the domestic violence courts are to: facilitate early intervention and prosecution of violence directed at family members; provide appropriate support to victims; and increase offender accountability. In the United States, in some large jurisdictions such as in Denver, Colorado, judges have set up special domestic violence courts working in conjunction with community agencies to hear and adjudicate cases of domestic violence (Walker, 2009).

In the UK, following much criticism of the gender sentence disparities in cases of domestic homicide, new sentencing guidelines were finally introduced. Under the guidelines, men who killed their wives or partners in a jealous rage after discovering they have been unfaithful would receive tougher sentences (Dyer, 2005). In contrast, women who killed their violent husbands or lovers would be treated more leniently. This belated change in the law helped address concerns that women who snapped and killed violent partners after years of abuse were receiving heavier sentences than men who claimed they were provoked by a partner's nagging or infidelity.

MURDER-SUICIDE

Anyone who reads or watches local or national news reports is aware that a spate of murder-suicides is taking place. In recent months, in the national news, we have learned of horrible whole family slayings committed by fathers, as well as numerous intimate partner homicides—all ending in suicide or attempted suicide. But most such cases are not reported nationally; they appear in headlines in the local paper.

Guns are by far the most common weapon used in these crimes (Violence Policy Center [VPC], 2008). One could speculate that if you shoot someone, it is relatively easy to then turn the gun on yourself. If you stab or strangle someone, however, suicide becomes much more difficult.

The most recent study by VPC (2008) reported fifty-four murder-suicide deaths nationwide between January 1 and June 30, 2007. This averages out to nine murder-suicide events each week.

Of those, Texas had twenty-four cases and Florida had twenty-four. Other statistics from the VPC include:

- cases with male offenders: 95 percent;
- cases involving an intimate partner: 73 percent;
- cases that occurred in the home: 75 percent;
- case involving a firearm: 88.5 percent;
- average age difference between offender and primary victim: six years.

In Iowa, a Midwestern state with a relatively low crime rate, between 1995 and 2005, 106 Iowans killed a partner or spouse in a domestic situation. The main factor appeared to be a pending breakup. Ninety-six of the killers were men; about half committed suicide shortly afterward. In Pennsylvania, of the 122 domestic homicide incidents in 2005, 100 of the perpe- trators were male; 68 of the victims were shot; and 45 of the perpetrators committed suicide (Pennsylvania Coalition Against Domestic Violence, 2006).

From Statistics Canada (2005) we learn that over the past forty years, one in ten solved homicides were cases in which the suspect took his or her own life following the homicide. About three-quarters of these victims were killed by a family member. Virtually all of the incidents (97 percent) involved female victims killed by a male spouse.

In the first epidemiological study of homicide-suicides in England and Wales, Barrachlough and Harris (2002) studied death certificates for all murders-suicide over a four-year time span. They found that 3 percent of male, 11 percent of female, and 19 percent of child homicides were of this type. Similarly, of all suicides, 0.8 percent male and 0.4 percent female deaths occurred in homicide-suicide incidents. The typical cases involved families of low socioeconomic status. The fact that the UK has strict gun control laws probably reduces the numbers of murder-suicides in that nation.

Palermo (1994) analyzed the psyche of the jealous, paranoid perpetrator who kills both his partner and himself. The twin nature of murder and suicide were recognized in Palermo's concept, *extended suicide*. Palermo argued that it is plausible to assume that the individual who is danger- ously violent and also prone to depression will kill his partner and himself when the relationship goes sour. Virtually all such tragic male murder-suicide cases that he studied followed a breakup or the threat of a breakup and are of the "if I can't have you, no one can" variety.

As reported by the VPC, the pattern of the domestic murder-suicide is predictable: a male perpetrator, female victim, decision by the woman to leave the man, and a gun. The typical Florida pattern involves an elderly male caregiver overwhelmed by his inability to care for an infirm wife.

Today, as of 2008, a different pattern in the murder-suicides has come into prominence. Given the recent headlines of horrific whole family slaughter, and reports from experts cited in the media, our attention is brought to a form of murder-suicide associated not with a pending breakup but with economics. Despair borne out of personal unemployment and debt is the apparent motive in these situations, as the following recent headlines indicate:

- "North Las Vegas Murder/Suicide a Result of Economic Stress" (Hernandez, 2008)
- "Killer Santa Lost His Job, Wife Before Gory Attack" (Associated Press, 2008)
- "Man Kills His Wife and Five Children" (Cathcart and Archibold, 2009)
- "Recession to Fuel More Family Murder, Suicide" (Britt, 2009)

These cases took place in the space of a few months. And they are only a sample. These cases made the headlines because they were whole family killings. Even when murder-suicide only involves the man and his partner, this type of suicide is never a solitary act in its consequences. Children in the family are orphaned, and others are left in a state of shock and despair.

How do the characteristics of a murderer who does not commit suicide differ from the one who does? In their review of the literature, Campbell et al. (2007) singled out the following characteristics as associated with this form of femicide: prior acts of partner abuse, a history of depression, estrangement in the relationship, being white, married and unemployed, and having a stepchild in the house.

In a comparison of seventy-eight cases of homicide alone and forty-six homicides followed by suicide that took place in New Mexico over a ten-year period, Banks et al. (2008) found striking differences. In contrast to the homicide-alone cases, the homicide-suicide cases involved premeditation, use of a gun (in forty-one out of forty-six cases) compared to less than half of the others, less evidence of substance use, both partners older, and a history of depression by the perpetrator. Treatment of depression and removal of guns from the households of seriously depressed individuals could help prevent the situation from escalating into violence.

Generally these killings, whether committed by youths or older people, and whether related to obsessive love gone wrong or economic crisis, are suicide-driven; hence they are referred elsewhere as **suicide-murders**. There are four basic types of homicide followed by suicide of which suicide is seemingly the primary motive. First, and easiest to comprehend, is the elderly couple situation. The typical case is that of a frail elderly man who cares for a wife with dementia; he does not want either of them to go to a nursing home. Suffering from depression, he chooses suicide instead and takes his wife with him. Their earlier relationship was typically a healthy, close one. They have no support system with the children living far away.

Far different is the mass school shooting, a highly publicized but rare event. The usual scenario is this: the boy was teased and bullied at school. He hates himself and is seething with anger. Influenced by media accounts of mass killings about which he obsesses, he gets a gun and goes on a rampage before killing himself.

The third kind is represented in the recent surge of economically based extended suicides that occur in the face of debt, foreclosures, and job loss. Here the main breadwinner in the family apparently feels compelled to end it all. In the cases that have come to light in the media reports, other factors such as substance abuse and mental illness did not seem to be in evidence.

The fourth and most common variety of suicide-murder is the case of intimate partner violence. From the dozens of cases van Wormer found in news reports, a consistent pattern emerges. The intimate couple is usually in the twenty- to thirty-five-years-old age range. The man is abusive, psychologically and/or physically. Obsessed with the woman to the extent he feels he can't live without her, he is fiercely jealous and determined to isolate her. Characteristically, suicidal murderers have little regard for the lives of other people; they would be considered, in mental health jargon, to be antisocial. So dependent are these men on their wives or girlfriends that they would sooner be dead than live without them. But for them, suicide is hard—they can't get the nerve—so they have to find a way to force themselves to do it.

Some choose suicide-by-cop, hoping to get the police officer to end their misery. Some even, in death penalty states, kill some strangers for the sole reason of qualifying for the death penalty (van Wormer recorded 20 such cases elsewhere—see http://www.katherinevanwormer.com).

In the intimate-partner situation, the girlfriend/wife makes a move to leave. Her partner is absolutely distraught in the belief that he can't live without her. These types of men, when rejected, often have a history of stalking. He either decides to kill himself and take her with him or, in another possible scenario, can't get the nerve to kill himself but realizes that if he commits a homicide first, the suicide will then be the only way out. The pattern here is the notion that after you've killed another, it's easier to get the nerve to kill yourself. In any case, the urge to commit suicide is primary.

A key factor in suicide-murders across the states is the power of suggestion and contagion. When one high-profile case is in the headlines, there is another, and another, and another. Consider the fact that in the two years following the Columbine High massacre there were nineteen incidents of school violence (half of them foiled), that were clearly imitative. So it is with intimate partner suicide-murders. A second key factor is, of course, access to a gun.

Let us differentiate this pattern of suicide from that of the suicide bombers such as Arab terrorists. These terrorist situations are truly *murder*-suicides because the impetus to kill and destroy takes precedence over suicide; suicide is simply the escape or necessity to get the job done or desire for martyrdom. In testimony given before the Senate Armed Services Committee Professor of Psychiatry, Jerrod Post presented the results of his thirty-five interviews with incarcerated terrorists in Israeli prisons (reported on CNNFN, October 1, 2001, "The Mind of a Suicide Bomber"). These individuals were failed suicide bombers whose suicide missions had failed because of unforeseen circumstances. In their interviews, they consistently spoke of the need to defend "the land of their honor," their willingness to become martyrs to a sacrificial act, and the fact that these were not acts of suicide but actions performed in service to Allah.

Are such men weak emotionally; are they sick? "No," declares Post. "Such men are fortified by religion. As a result of ruthless indoctrination, these men have subordinated their own individuality to the group. Emotionally disturbed individuals are expelled from these quasi-military units as a security risk." Unlike solitary terrorists in the United States, the members of these terrorist cells tend to have close relationships with their families, who support them in their efforts to kill the Zionist or American enemy.

Post's research on the suicide bombers could be replicated through interviews with American men convicted of murder whose suicide attempts had failed. Then our analysis of their motivation would be more complete, especially regarding the role of contagion.

DYNAMICS OF INTIMATE ABUSE

Since physical abuse of a woman or a man in a gay battering situation is about power and control, it is accompanied emotionally by psychological abuse. Psychological or emotional abuse, in other words, is the *context* within which the slaps, hits, kicks, and so forth occur. Emotional abuse can include verbal assaults, ridicule, isolation from family and friends, unwarranted accusations about infidelity, control of finances, damage to property, stealing, torture or killing of pets, and threats to harm children and others. Jentz (2006) describes the captor as proceeding with threats which escalate from acts of degradation to "accomplish the total annihilation of the will, until the victim is convinced that she cannot escape and survive" (p. 369). The effect of these acts is to attack the person's sense of self-worth. A kind of brainwashing occurs as the victim internalizes the insinuations and accusations of his or her attacker, gradually coming to believe them. Psychological abuse among lesbians may include the threat of "outing" a partner to her boss or family. See Figure 9.1 for a visual representation in the **Power and Control Wheel** of the interplay between power and control in an abusive relationship.

In any country, when psychological abuse moves on to physical abuse, the added element is terror. Women who are beaten know that they are at high risk of being killed if they try to leave. The director of crime-victim assistance of the Iowa attorney general's office, Marti Anderson, suggests that victims of such domestic terror live in perpetual fear of the next attack, of losing their children and their home, of being stalked, of losing their lives.

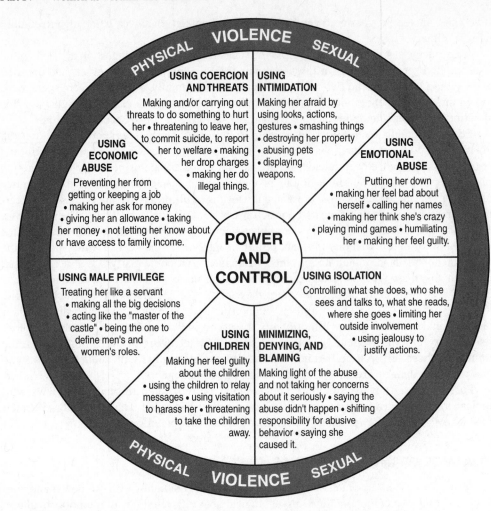

FIGURE 9.1   Power and Control Wheel   *Source:* Domestic Abuse Violence Project, 202 E. Superior Street, Duluth, MN 55802. Printed with permission of the Domestic Abuse Intervention Project.

"And yet people ask," she writes, "Why doesn't she leave?" (Anderson, 1997, p. 4AA). Protection orders, safety plans, and divorces do not stop an attack, a bullet, or a knife. These attempts at self-protection, in fact, often precipitate an attack by paranoid individuals with a history of out-of-control violence.

Instead of asking the question so resented by battered women, "Why don't you leave?" we will consider the practical and psychological barriers to escape. This approach is consistent with the empowerment/strengths-based perspective. Angela Browne (2004) summarizes the barriers in terms of practical realities, fear of retaliation, and the shock reactions of victims to constant danger. The practical barriers include such issues as finding a place to live, fear of losing one's children, and difficulty in receiving public assistance while married. The woman who works cannot hide, nor can she protect her children who are in school and day care from being taken for ransom. The woman who does not work has no means of support. Moving into a shelter is only for a brief period of time. If the woman gets a legal separation, her spouse will have visitation rights with the children.

Fear of reprisal is made more compelling by death threats. Browne compared forty-two battered women who killed their abusers with 205 women who did not kill their abusers. In the homicide group, many of the women stayed out of terror of further victimization or because they had tried to escape and were beaten for it. Expecting to get killed, they saw no way out of the danger. In fact, violent men do search out the women after they leave. And as their husbands, they know all the hiding places.

Research on victims of trauma helps explain how women cope in the height of danger by denying the threat, by being extremely suggestible, or by withdrawing emotionally so that they can survive. Chronic fatigue and tension coupled with sleep disturbances keep the victim in a state of confusion. Typically, little anger is shown toward the victimizers who are seen as all-powerful and even admired. Browne's theories are reminiscent of social psychological studies of brainwashed prisoners of war who, over time, submit to their captors and even come to admire them. Referred to as the **Stockholm syndrome**, this phenomenon is named for an incident in Stockholm, Sweden, where four bank employees were held hostage in the bank's vault for four days. Following the ordeal, the women's expressions of gratitude toward the offenders was disturbing to many people. The Stockholm syndrome is understandable as a predictable and normal response to abnormal circumstances. The development of an emotional bond between persons who share a life-threatening experience, a bond that can unite them against outsiders, can be seen as an adaptive human response to the violent scenarios played out with them as hapless, reluctant, and helpless players (Slatkin, 2008). It is known from studies in social psychology that people who are exposed to intermittent kindnesses by the captor—kindnesses that emerge within the context of a life-and-death situation from which there is only limited possibility of escape—may bond with the captor and even testify on his behalf in the eventual court proceedings. Basically, one's identity with powerful individuals who can exact terrible punishments and withhold the necessities of life can be understood as a regression to a dependent, childlike state. Bettleheim (1943) defined this phenomenon in his classic study of concentration camp survivors. Instead of anger, many prisoners identified with the SS troops and tried to emulate them.

Dutton and Painter (1993) developed the **traumatic bonding theory** to explain why battered women stay in abusive relationships. Power imbalance in combination with intermittent good–bad treatment was predicted to increase the emotional attachment in an abusive situation, a prediction based on classical social psychological theory (see, e.g., Bettleheim, 1943; Roberts and Burman, 2007). (Note that we are not talking about gender here. The Bettelheim and Zimbardo et al. studies concerned mostly men.) Dutton and Painter empirically tested this theory concerning a high level of attachment toward one's victimizer. In their assessments conducted on seventy-five women who had recently left abusive situations, they found that emotional involvement was strong. Follow-up measures six months later revealed some decrease in the level of attachment but showed that prolonged effects of the abuse were still evident.

An understanding of the dynamics of social psychology is crucial if we are to make sense of situations and reactions that may seem irrational on the surface, especially for victim service counselors who have not experienced such long-term abuse firsthand. Much criminal behavior by accomplices who are forced into it by their abusers, moreover, can be understood in the context of traumatic bonding. The story of Patty Hearst, kidnap victim, a woman locked in a closet and periodically raped over a period of many long months, is well known. Hearst inevitably fell in love with one of her captors and joined their gang—the Symbionese Liberation Front—to commit robberies (Graebner, 2008). Unfortunately, at her trial, the jury was not convinced of the phenomenon of psychological traumatizing that can occur in such cases, and Hearst was sentenced to a lengthy prison term for her crimes. The story of teenager Elizabeth Smart, also beaten, raped, and held captive for months, is similar. When the police came to rescue her, she gave a false name. It was later revealed that she had conformed to the lifestyle of her captors (Browning, 2003). There are many women in prison today whose abuse impaired their judgment in a similar vein.

Leaving is a process that may involve many attempts to be successful. Stages in the process of breaking loose involve changes in one's level of self-awareness combined with a reevaluation of the relationship as dangerous. During this gradual process of awareness, survivors build up their courage to retreat from the danger. Research shows that social support from family and friends is a crucial factor in a woman's managing to get away (Khng and Ow, 2009).

The concept of the **battered woman syndrome** was introduced by Walker (1979). As Rothenberg (2003) correctly indicates, this term, like codependency, is one we might want to avoid in that it puts the stress on women's helplessness rather than on agency and resilience. The model of an active survivor has been embraced by feminists in its emphasis on competent decision making and safety-seeking behavior.

MARITAL RAPE

The laws regarding marital rape offer a clear picture of how society has viewed this phenomenon. Historically, following British law, it was decreed that husbands were exempt from any rape laws (Jerin and Moriarty, 1998). After all, the marriage contract stipulated that a wife must submit willingly to her husband. She could not legally refuse him, therefore. The first wave of feminists argued for a definition of manliness that emphasized restraint rather than sexual appetite. As historian Joanna Bourke (2007), in her history of sexual violence, indicates, this was a crucial point in the days before reliable birth control as a woman's health was at stake. From the 1920s to the 1970s, however, consistent with a new concept of domesticity interest in speaking out against marital rape waned. The fact that divorce gradually became easier to get, provided one form of escape that wasn't available before.

In the United States, it was not until 1977 that Oregon became the first state to repeal the marital rape exemption. The controversy that arose in Oregon over its first marital rape case prompted a great deal of mass media coverage and public ridicule of the young woman who had the audacity to charge her husband with this crime. Yet by 1990, forty-eight states had marital rape laws; today, this is a crime in all states (Miller, 2005). Still about half the states treat spousal rape differently from other types of rape. Arizona briefly considered revising its laws in response to a public outcry over the lenient treatment of spousal rapists (*USA Today*, 2005).In 1983, a Canadian law recognized that any sexual contact without consent within a marriage is sexual assault. But in most other countries, such as Mexico which recently declared rape in marriage legal, wife rape is viewed as an oxymoron. Statistics Canada (2005) reports that 8 percent of ever-married women in their national telephone survey were forced into sexual activity against their will.

Marital rape did not become a criminal offence in the Republic of Ireland until 1990, which was ahead of England and Wales by two years, but twenty-five years behind Sweden. Of the 10,317 instances of abuse reported to the Irish Women's Aid in 2003, 1,352 were reported to involve sexual abuse, of which 511 were rapes (Staff Reporter, 2005). According to a government survey of sexual violence in the UK, 45 percent of women who reported they were raped were raped by their domestic partner (Myhill and Allen, 2002).

Because marital rape is rarely differentiated from rape in general in victimization surveys and because victim/survivors of this kind of rape are reluctant to acknowledge its existence even to themselves, the prevalence of marital rape is hard to determine. In the Bureau of Justice Statistics survey (Tjaden and Thoennes, 2000), the term "intimate partner rape" was used. It was found that 7.7 percent of women surveyed and 0.3 percent of men surveyed had experienced this form of abuse. Approximately 75 percent who reported they had been raped in adulthood had been raped by a current or former spouse or boyfriend (Family Violence Prevention Fund 2009). In a survey of 229 men enrolled in batterers' intervention education, over half had sexually assaulted their partner at least once as well as beaten their partner (Raquel and Bukovec, 2006).

Whereas a woman raped by a stranger has to live with the bad memory, a women raped by her husband has to live with the rapist. Bergen (1998) conducted in-depth interviews with a sample of forty survivors of wife rape who had contacted a rape crisis center or women's shelter for help. Based on her findings she divided the causes of wife rape into four categories: entitlement to sex attitudes, sexual jealousy, rape as punishment, and rape as a form of control. The majority of rapes were battering rapes in which the woman was beaten and then raped. Nine of the men performed sadistic rapes on the women, often in connection with porno films. Unlike stranger-rape experiences, marital rape occurs frequently to women who are attacked in this way by their husbands. Like battered women, marital rape victims develop strategies of resistance—going to bed late, spending the night out, getting the husband too drunk for sex, physically resisting, and saving enough money to leave. Above all, when rape seemed inevitable, the women tried to manage the violence by giving in to avoid serious injury. Emotionally, many of the women "tuned out" during the rape. Afterward they would bathe and act as if nothing had happened. Yet only one-third of the women in Bergen's sample defined their experience as rape. Emotionally, the word *disgust* came up over and over in the interviews. In the end, all but three of the women were traumatized; over half considered or attempted suicide. Sexual dysfunction and distrust of other men were among the long-term consequences. Although we can't generalize from these findings because the sample was drawn from women who sought help, the interviews do show the seriousness of the crime of marital rape. The number of women who go to the police under these circumstances and have their husbands criminally charged is minuscule (Bourke, 2007). The risk of being killed in such situations is real.

THEORIES OF PARTNER ABUSE

Consider a battered woman who is catering to her partner's every demand, preoccupied with her partner's needs and moods, consistently covering up for him after outbursts, and alternately protective of her children and neglectful of their needs. Is she a codependent woman who was bred for a self-sacrificial, self-destructive role, or has her seemingly bizarre response developed out of the abnormal demands of the situation? We will not answer this rhetorical question now but will instead look at several broad-based theories to explain domestic violence.

Societal Stress

Roberts and Burman (2007) consider a variety of stresses that can increase the potential for violence by men of women. Among them are the birth of children, fear of job loss and work-related problems, financial instability, and a pattern of alcohol abuse. The use of alcohol on the part of highly stressed men can magnify negative feelings, which may be redirected onto family members as a form of displaced aggression. Research confirms a correlation between stress factors such as unemployment and wife abuse (Ringel, cited in Kohn, 2008). With domestic homicide, the correlation with unemployment is especially strong (Campbell et al., 2007). Today, as the economic situation at the national level spirals downward, reports of increased calls to national hotlines and even whole family murder-suicides, are soaring in news reports (Cathcart and Archibold, 2009; Kohn, 2008). In Los Angeles, for example, two horrible killings apparently had economic roots:

> Last October, a man in Los Angeles, beset by financial troubles, shot his wife, mother-in-law, and three sons before turning the gun on himself. An eerily similar scene replayed itself this week, when another Los Angeles resident apparently killed his wife and five children—an 8-year-old girl, twin 5-year-old girls, and twin 2-year-old boys—before faxing a letter to a local television station and then killing himself. "This was a financial and job-related issue that led to the slayings," said Deputy Chief Kenneth Garner. (Turse, 2009)

Psychological Viewpoints

The question one asks, to a large extent, determines the answer. Instead of asking, "Why do they (the women) stay?" we should ask, as psychologist Hara Marano (1993) suggests, "What makes them (the men) so dependent, so vulnerable?" To understand the dynamics of male-on-female violence, we need to consider biological as well as cognitive and social-psychological influences. In his study of battering men, Marano links intrapsychic deficits—a hypersensitivity to abandonment, inability to control negative emotions, and poor impulse control—with biological deficits—low serotonin levels in the brain, high testosterone production, and brain damage from head injury—and with cultural contributions such as traditional gender-role attitudes.

Jacobson and Gottman (1998) monitored 140 couples with electric sensors while they discussed marital problems. The researchers were surprised to find that the ones they eventually labeled **cobras**, the most violent men who sounded and looked aggressive, were actually internally calm. Those labeled **pit bulls** became internally aroused with heart rates that increased with their anger; they never let up. The wives of pit bulls often took the risk of arguing back. If the women ever left the relationship, such men tended to stalk them. So self-centered were the cobras that, once their women were out of the way, they tended to let go of the relationship. The danger of violence with cobras occurs during the initial separation, whereas pit bulls become more dangerous following separation due to their ambivalent feelings of love. The cobras, about 20 percent of the total of the most violent husbands, are sadistic, prone to death threats, and belong in prison. Because these men have a certain charisma, as Jacobson and Gottman note, their wives tend to find them hard to resist.

A biological proclivity toward rage does not mean control is totally absent in most cases. In analyzing the rationales of eighteen batterers involved in group therapy, Ptacek (1997) found that although most of the men complained of totally losing control, usually in response to their wives' disturbing remarks, their violence was very selective. For example, these men did not attack people outside their family. Waltz et al. (2000), however, did identify one type of battering male, a psychopathic batterer, that did sometimes explode into violent rages outside of the home.

Virtually every study of the psychology of male batterers points to their low self-esteem (van Wormer and Roberts, 2009). Mills (2008) embraces a childhood exposure theory of abuse, in which a background of family violence duplicates itself in a later generation of "insecure attachment" (pp. 85–87) and pathological dependence in adult relationships. Afflicted with an inability to compromise with others, they see themselves as powerless victims. Because of their underlying feelings of insecurity, jealousy is an emotion with special meaning for battering men. Marano (1993) summarizes research linking wife abuse with difficulty handling jealousy reactions. Violent men were found, in hypothetical jealousy-provoking situations, to consistently misinterpret their wives' motives as intentionally hostile. Nonviolent men in a comparison group did not feel personally threatened by the scenarios presented. Abusive men, according to Marano, may go into a rage when their wives go out with friends. Treatment consists of helping abusers to see that as long as they give their spouses undue power over their emotions and behavior, they will continue to abuse them. Their own overdependence on their spouses causes these men to resent and hate them. This is why murderers may say things like, "I loved my wife so much that I ended up killing her."

We should not overgeneralize, however, as batterers like other offenders are a heterogeneous group. Echeburua and Fernandez-Montalvo's (2007) research on batterers in a Spanish prison found that around 12 percent of them exhibited traits of psychopathy. These men were similar in personality to the cobras in the Jacobson and Gottman's study described above. The characteristics that described the Spanish sample were suspiciousness, lack of self-esteem, and little empathy for others. Others who were not psychopathic did have hostile feelings against women, abused alcohol or other drugs, and, in some cases, had exploded in a fit of rage or jealousy.

Systems Theory

Systems theory offers a multidimensional view of reality. The concept of interactionism, which is central to systems theory, describes the influence of people's feedback on each other simultaneously. Cause and effect under this formulation are viewed as in constant and dynamic interaction with each other.

However useful this framework may be in counseling troubled families and in helping family members improve their skills in communication, when applied to a battering situation, therapy from a systems perspective is fraught with risks. According to this model, both partners may contribute to the escalation of conflict, with each attempting to dominate the other. From this perspective, interactions produce violence; therefore, no one is considered to be a perpetrator or victim. Viewing faulty family interaction as the source of the problem is one step removed from asking questions such as, What is the woman's role in perpetrating the violence? In gender-blind systems theory, each partner is held responsible for his or her contribution to the violence dynamic and for changing his or her behavior accordingly. Within this context, systems theory encourages a denial of the reality of victimization. Under conditions of violence, family counseling can be downright dangerous. Following the sessions, the batterer, in his own insecurity, may attack his wife for revelations made to the therapist.

A concept related to classical systems theory and widely applied in the field of substance abuse treatment is *codependency*. The prefix "co-" implies shared responsibility for the behavior of another. So-called codependents are said to have gravitated toward a relationship with an abuser because of an unconscious desire to be enmeshed in an unhealthy relationship (van Wormer and Davis, 2008). Codependency theory suggests that women remain in an unhealthy situation because of some early deficit in the woman herself. Such a conceptualization overlooks the fact that women who are beaten by a violent man and who successfully get away are likely to be replaced with another vulnerable woman who will also be beaten. The fact that such a woman may be competent and confident at the beginning of the relationship is no insurance against her subsequent victimization or increasing loss of sense of confidence.

Feminist Explanations and the Antifeminist Backlash

Are we looking at a codependent woman, feminists will ask, or are we looking at the results of traditional feminine training? Are we seeing poor communication skills among partners, or are we seeing the effect of severe power imbalance in our society? Because the structure of our male-supportive, woman-blaming society is founded on a history of male entitlement, men collectively have eluded taking responsibility for much of the family violence that has occurred.

Feminists perceive the violent family as a microcosm of a society that oppresses and keeps women in their place. In expressing such views and in focusing on the reality and impact of male-on-female violence, the movement is perceived in certain quarters as "male bashing" (Mann, 2008). As they peruse the literature and popular media sources, researchers need to discover the facts, recognizing female-on-male violence where it exists, while being wary of the misuse of statistics to promote a certain cause. There is no need to inflate the findings on the extent of violence against women. By the same token, we need to draw on the comprehensive data from official sources to challenge misleading claims by the media, often promoted by the influence of the antifeminist, fathers' rights groups one of the goals of which is to defeat many of the advances in women's legal history. Murray Straus, who is responsible for devising the Conflict Tactic Scale that seemingly reveals the true extent of female violence against males, applauds the challenge to feminism and the fact that a "small but increasingly influential men's movement is starting to change the political climate" (p. 1091). Straus (2006) looks forward to an end to the "gender-inclusive research and programming that feminism has imposed" (p. 1091). Articles such as his, which is titled "Future Research on Gender Symmetry in Physical Assaults on Partners," indeed are doing much to impede the progress of women in raising awareness of the impact of intimate partner violence on the family and to restrict the funding for domestic violence services.

Today, in myriad ways, the advances of the women's movement and actions to stop violence have been appropriated by law enforcement and fathers' rights associations to defeat these accomplishments (Bumiller, 2008). In Canada, men's rights advocacy groups regularly denounce women's domestic violence organizations for falsely framing domestic violence as a gendered rather than a human problem and for fostering a moral panic (Mann, 2008). In their arguments against feminist women's claims, these groups cite statistics by Murray Straus of gender symmetry in violence. Central to the rhetoric of the fathers' rights groups are: denial of the extent of domestic violence against women and the portrayal of women as perpetrators of domestic abuse, the promotion of joint custody of children, and the challenging of child support arrangements.

A major challenge to feminist theorists is how to explain the often irrational attachment of battered women to their abusers. Most writers of the feminist school focus on structural and rational aspects (such as economic considerations and death threats) in a battered woman's decision to stay with her man.

In her book *Loving to Survive*, Graham (1994) extends the concept of Stockholm syndrome to describe what she calls the societal Stockholm syndrome. Because male violence so permeates our society, as Graham and her associates argue, this engenders a societal response whereby some women are rendered isolated, powerless, and subject to male domination as a survival tactic. The captive bonds to the captor over time and may even experience love in the midst of fear. This response is viewed in the book as not related to gender but as a normal human response to an abnormal situation.

BOX 9.3
The Tombstone Project

The stories of fifty-two women killed by domestic violence over the past five years are etched on tombstones in front of the lawn at Valley View Baptist Church, Cedar Falls, Iowa. It is a blustery night in late October. Twenty to thirty of us, all women, are holding candles to commemorate those who did not survive partner violence. Each of us, in turn, reads the story of one victim, then places the lit candle before the wooden tombstone. In the eerie quiet, one woman reads:

"Laura Garrison, 30, of Waterloo, died July 7, 1990. She was shot to death in front of her small children by a man she had dated. The man then shot himself and later died."

She places the candle before the tombstone. Now it is my turn: I read: "Loretta Ellen Foster, 29, of Waterloo, died November 21, 1991. Foster was shot to death by the man she lived with and the father of her children in front of their 5-year-old daughter and 7-year-old son. He then killed himself."

After all fifty-two of the slain women are remembered in this fashion, we all stand in a circle and read in unison a closing poem composed for the occasion by women's shelter advocates Sharon Spring, Mary Langholz, and Mary Roche:

Oh Connectedness of Life
Of that we cannot see
As air we breathe
and wind we feel
Embrace us in this moment
As we stand here to
Remember
Honor
And give name to all women
Whose voices have been silenced.
May we know they are us
And we are them.
In this month of remembering
Affirm us as we
Remember their names
Remember our own
And give voice to both.

Critical thinking question: What are the implications of an annual ceremony such as this one for victims of domestic violence?

From the feminist perspective, cultural norms that support and maintain violence against women are the central culprit in partner abuse. Structural change (e.g., instituting policies that increase victim safety and personal empowerment) is the focus, along with the reeducation of batterers and of other men in their use of power and male privilege. Consciousness raising is vital to help women in situations of abuse overcome their oppression, personally and collectively.

See Box 9.3 to learn about an annual ritual performed by women who care.

THE SUBSTANCE ABUSE CONNECTION

The relationship between substance abuse and family violence is best conceived of as interactive rather than causative. Persons prone toward violence are also likely to be risk takers, impulsive, and apt to indulge in the use of a variety of substances. At the same time, their victims, being in a high state of stress and agitation, are apt to self-medicate with mood-altering substances as well. Research has shown that men (or women) who perpetrate partner violence or are victims are more likely than companion groups to have alcohol problems (Stuart et al., 2004). Heavy drinking and the use of certain drugs such as cocaine and methamphetamine lower one's inhibitions and ability to think rationally and often produce a state of paranoia. So the stage is set for violent outbursts. In Mason City, Iowa, the executive director of Crisis Intervention Services estimates that probably close to 65 percent of their clients in shelters have partners who are using meth or another drug (Buehner and Horgen, 2005) (see Chapter 5).

In a study comparing 225 women in substance abuse treatment with 222 women at a shelter for domestic violence, William Downs (2000) found that the overlap was considerable. While a majority of the substance abuse treatment participants reported a recent incident of partner violence, a majority of the women at the shelter reported problematic use of substances. In their review of the literature on domestic violence and substance use, Humphreys et al. (2005) found recognition of the considerable overlap between victimization and use of substances in both the United States and in the UK. Not only is the overlap found because of use of addictive substances as a coping mechanism but drug use itself makes women more vulnerable to abuse.

The correlation between substance use and partner violence is further revealed in the following research studies:

- In an examination of records of over 2,000 instances of domestic assault, Buzawa and Hirschel (2008) found that substance abuse in the male predicted a high likelihood of reoffending.
- In assessments done on over 400 women in domestic violence programs and substance abuse treatment, 67 percent in substance abuse treatment reported physical abuse and 60.5 percent in the domestic violence program had a problem with alcohol and/or other drugs (Downs, Rindels, and Atkinson, 2007).
- Cocaine, methamphetamine, and alcohol in high doses are all associated with hyperactivity and violence. Marijuana and heroin have not been proven to be associated with violence (van Wormer and Davis, 2008).
- A study of alcohol consumption in the army revealed that soldiers who drink heavily are likely to abuse their partners both when they drink and when they don't, compared to moderately drinking soldiers (Bell et al., 2004).
- A study of men in treatment for domestic violence showed that severe physical aggression was eleven times higher on days when the male partners were intoxicated than on other days (Fals-Stewart, 2003).
- Women in methadone treatment who reported frequent crack cocaine use or frequent marijuana use were likely to be victimized over the next six months; women who were physically assaulted were more likely than other women to indicate frequent heroin use over the next six months (El-Bassel et al., 2005).

The close correlation between substance abuse and relationship violence appears to be unquestionable. The only doubt is over the interpretation of this relationship. What all researchers and treatment personnel agree on is the crying need to put a stop to the violence and the high-risk substance abuse. Unfortunately, the relationship between the treatment providers at substance abuse and domestic violence programs is problematic (van Wormer and Davis, 2008). At the core of the problem is the tendency to dichotomize problems and to treat various components of antisocial behavior as separate entities. The differences arise not only from differing worldviews—disease model versus feminist approach—but also from a parallel tendency to view reality in terms of linear causation. Lack of knowledge and training by professionals at the different agencies is generally acknowledged as a major barrier to the development of more appropriate holistic responses by staff (Humphreys et al., 2005). A recent survey of domestic violence programs in North Carolina showed that substance abuse problems were common among the clients, but only half of the programs had policies in place concerning such clients

(Martin et al., 2008). The large majority of the programs had at least one staff member with training in substance abuse issues, however.

In the addictions treatment field, where many of the male clients have been enrolled for treatment for domestic violence offenses, the family is viewed as a system. This viewpoint tends to regard the violence as well as the substance abuse as closely linked and the victim in the family playing a role in enabling these bad behaviors to continue. Moreover, substance abuse counselors see addiction as the primary problem. The focus is therefore on sobriety: Get the chemicals out of the system and many of the other problems will subside.

The addictions focus in the substance abuse treatment field is matched by the male culture determinism of the domestic violence field. Workers in domestic violence programs have no less firm and sincere a commitment to their clients than do substance abuse counselors to theirs. And just as their counterparts in addictions work tend to be recovering addicts/alcoholics, many of those who counsel battered women have themselves been abused. Women's shelter counselors tend to stress individual/cultural responsibility for antisocial behavior. Drug usage is viewed by these workers as merely an excuse for deliberate acts of aggression. The tendency toward antisocial, risk-taking, and impulsive behavior may play a role in the development of both substance abuse and violence. Studies link low serotonin in the brain to both aggression and addiction as well as to a host of other behaviors.

Social factors link substance abuse and violence against women in regard to cultural expectations. In families in which men are expected to beat their wives when drunk, they will be inclined to do so. The effect of alcohol can be a disaster in a violence-prone individual in that it contributes to a misreading of social cues through cognitive impairment, and violence may provide some sense of immediate gratification (Dawson, Bunge, and Balde, 2009). A woman's substance abuse often parallels her partner's drug usage. "It takes being drunk to be married to a drunk," as one of van Wormer's clients once succinctly put it. Once the man was in recovery, accordingly, his wife's sobriety quickly followed.

Substance abuse treatment can be integrated into a harm reduction model so that women can work on reducing the harm that substance abuse is playing in their lives at the same time that they develop a safety plan to reduce the harm of violence to themselves and their loved ones. Mandated substance abuse treatment for the batterer is also indicated. To the extent that the violence is drug-induced, treatment can be beneficial in curbing it.

CHILDREN WITNESSING VIOLENCE

The harm done to children who witness horrendous scenes of violence cannot be underestimated. Abuse of the family pet, like abuse of their mother, is a form of psychological abuse that is especially distressing to a child (Ascione et al., 2007).Effects are both immediate and long-term. An extensive literature review by Kolbo, Blakely, and Engleman (1996) found that children who witness partner violence are more likely than other children to have problems in all major areas of functioning. Behaviorally, some children who have witnessed violence display aggression, cruelty to animals, and tantrums. Common emotional problems include anxiety, anger, and low self-esteem. Physical problems include sleeping and eating disturbances, bed-wetting, and other regressive behaviors; cognitive difficulties show up in learning and language lags.

In a large sample of predominantly Mexican American female students, the relationship between childhood exposure to parental violence and adult functioning was examined. Davies, DiLillo, and Martinez (2004) found that witnessing such violence was associated with depressive symptoms, low self-esteem, and trauma symptoms, even after controlling for child physical and sexual abuse.

Abused women do worry about their children and about their ability to protect them from experiencing or witnessing abuse. This is not surprising, since children of battered women are at risk for a variety of emotional, cognitive, and behavioral difficulties. Compared with the literature regarding child abuse and abuse of women, little has been published about the children of battered women. Children's protective services have focused on child abuse and neglect and on the mother's responsibilities in this regard, often overlooking the origin of the mother's helplessness. By the same token, the focus of women's shelters is on the battering of the woman with little attention to the long-term psychological consequences that family violence has had on the children. The result is that women's shelters and child welfare agencies are often seeing the same families. Some attention has been paid in recent years to the coexistence of wife abuse and child abuse in the same households.

Unless the child protective worker understands that a battered woman is often more afraid of her abusive partner than even of the loss of her children, he or she cannot be expected to obtain accurate information. Apart from interviewing the mother privately, key indicators are a child who is overprotective of his or her mother and a child who is abusive toward the mother.

Competition for funding, overwhelming child welfare caseloads, specialization of training and focus, and different philosophies and mandates have artificially separated the issues of wife and child abuse. The fact that both women and children may be simultaneously victimized and in terror, therefore, may not even be considered. And the fact that domestic violence against a child's mother is in itself a form of child abuse often escapes notice by child protection agencies.

The interrelationship between wife and child abuse is real. Although specialized training programs are being offered in the United States, evaluative research, even in progressive states such as Minnesota, continue to show that child welfare workers fail to investigate the coexistence of child abuse and wife abuse. A survey of child welfare cases and of domestic abuse cases conducted by Raschick and Shepard (1997) indicated that approximately one-third of each involved dual incidents of wife and child abuse. Battering men may slap their children around out of sense of jealousy, as a power play, or as a way of sadistically hurting the wife. In an examination of national survey data on victimization, medical researchers Zolotor et al. (2007) found much overlap between physical abuse of the mother and child abuse, neglect, and especially sexual abuse.

Casanueva, Foshee, and Barth (2004) in their investigation of emergency room visits by children found that when the caregiver was willing to disclose that their child's injury was related to domestic violence, mothers' reports of current, severe violence were positively associated with children's use of the hospital emergency room. The authors went on to find that maternal depression (a key factor associated with child neglect) and lack of supervision (an element of child neglect) were also associated with children's injuries. They concluded that the identification of current, severe family violence and depression among mothers would help prevent future injuries to children.

What is the impact on the child of witnessing relationship violence in the home? Research suggests that children who witness relationship violence, not to mention homicide, have many issues to work through. With small children, play therapy can be immensely helpful. Mental health professionals, by working with child witnesses to family violence, can play a key role in teaching children nonviolent methods of resolving conflict and thereby can help break the generational cycle of violence (Barnett, Miller-Perrin, and Perrin, 2005).

The paradox facing a battered mother is that if she reports domestic violence in her home, and especially if children are involved, her children may be removed. In order to get her children back, the mother has to demonstrate to the court and the social workers that she could provide a safe environment. The child's welfare understandably comes first.

Child welfare departments have a responsibility to respond to child maltreatment in situations of domestic violence even if the child was not directly attacked. Yet the choices facing social workers may present a dilemma. The twin goals of safety and permanence imply that caseworkers must consider both the safety and ultimate well-being of the child (Shlonsky and Wagner, 2005). Caseworkers must weigh the potential for harm if nothing is done (i.e., leaving the child in a potentially abusive home), with the risk that intrusive actions aimed at child protection will, ultimately, prove to be more traumatic than remaining in a violent home. The option of foster placement due to the risk of continuing violence in the home, in effect, is punishing to both the mother (through loss of her child) and the child. And these women, once the children are gone, typically lose whatever therapeutic supports they may have had, as the emphasis shifts to the children in the new milieu. There is no simple answer to the dilemma, but removal of the source of the violence might be the best place to start.

CRIMINAL JUSTICE PROCESS

Through the 1970s in most states, the police did not have the authority to make arrests in misdemeanor cases unless they personally had witnessed the offense. In general, police and criminal justice policy makers responded with ambivalence to complaints of wife battering (Dawson, Bunge, and Balde, 2009). In New York State, as in many states, domestic violence cases were heard in family court, a special nonpunitive court, the function of which was to stabilize the family. Married women thus had no legal protection from battery, and unmarried women beaten by their partners had less protection still. (Frisch and Caruso, 1996).

Over the next decades, however, drastic changes in the law occurred. The results from a large research study in the Minneapolis Police Department helped change the police perspective regarding the handling of domestic assault calls. In 1981, the Minneapolis Police Department participated in an experiment that assessed the effectiveness of three responses—mediate, separate, or arrest—in preventing future domestic abuse. Sherman and Berk (1984) concluded from this study that "The arrest treatment is clearly an improvement over sending the suspect away, which produced two and a half times as many repeat incidents as arrest" (p. 261). This finding held "regardless of the race, employment status, educational level, criminal history of the suspect, or how long the suspect was in jail when arrested" (p. 262). This landmark study which was to transform criminal justice policies all over the United States was seriously flawed.

Even though replication of this experiment has failed to achieve similar results, this early research seemed to silence many of those who doubted the wisdom of a law enforcement–centered approach to the problem of domestic violence (Chesney-Lind, 2006). In response to the Minneapolis domestic violence experiment and intense pressure from feminist groups, strict, mandatory arrest policies were instituted (Miller, 2003). In New York State, for example, the police were required to provide victims with information about their rights and community services available. Marital rape was criminalized in 1984; then in 1994 new legislation required that the police make arrests where there is probable cause to believe that a felony or misdemeanor was committed or if an order of protection was violated. Often this policy resulted in the arrest of both parties. A major impetus for this latter policy change from the police perspective was to prevent homicides, not necessarily to prevent domestic violence. Miller (2005) discovered this rationale in her extensive interviews with state troopers and city police. So it was a fear of lawsuits if the police did nothing and the victim was injured or killed that helped shape the mandatory arrest practice.

It is partly because of the policy changes nationwide that young women's arrest rates for assault have been on the rise. The arrest rate increase, in turn, fueled media reports of girls and women as increasingly violent, which in conjunction with the rising arrests, meant that the criminal justice system was more willing to sentence the women to jail and to batterer intervention programs. One can well imagine what a dampening effect the dual-arrest policy has on victims who want to call the police for help.

One group of women who are reluctant to call the police are the wives of police officers who suffer assault. Domestic violence among police officers, in fact, has gained recent recognition as a major problem (Lonsway, Wetendorf, and Conis, 2003). Although the research is limited, self-report surveys indicate that the domestic assault rate of male police officers is around two to three times that of men in the general public. Most police perpetrators do not have arrest records for this crime as they tend to plead guilty to a lesser charge. Because of the difficulty of sanctioning such officers, the International Association of Chiefs of Police, headed by Nancy Turner, has introduced new guidelines to address potentially problematic behavior. According to the guidelines, coworkers will be held responsible for withholding information about troubled officers. Supervisors will be trained to look for trouble signs, including increased controlling behavior, greater amount of alcohol or other drug use, and unwarranted verbal abuse. However, according to Lonsway et al., only a small percentage of departments are following these guidelines.

In 1996, the Lautenberg Amendment expanded the federal law barring gun ownership from those convicted of a felony domestic violence offense to include those who have been convicted of any (qualifying) misdemeanor domestic violence offense. However, the ban is removed if an individual gets the conviction expunged or pardoned. Research on the effects of the Lautenberg Amendment consistently shows that the use of the law has been rather limited and police officers have often been able to circumvent the ban and retain their weapons.

A major development that sprang out of Duluth, Minnesota ("the Duluth model"), is the "no-drop" policy of prosecutors. This policy is now in place in many jurisdictions in the United States and Canada. Instead of dropping charges of assault and battery, which the victim often requests under duress or a change of heart, prosecutors continue the case based on evidence produced by the police. Batterers are viewed as a menace to other potential victims, including their children, and as potential homicide/suicide risks. Victim-support units attached to the prosecutor's office assist with these cases. Requirements for the perpetrators to enter specialized treatment programs are generally a part of any probation plan. Noncompliance, ideally, results in a lengthy prison term. The use of restraining orders to keep offenders away from the survivors offers protection to women in cases of low-level abuse but offers no security in life-threatening situations. A man who is suicidal as well as violent has a high potential to kill his wife or partner.

Today, the mandatory arrest and no-drop policies are being reconsidered in a number of quarters. The replication studies have failed to demonstrate convincingly that arrest of batterers deters repeat offenses from occurring in sites other than Minneapolis; arrest may, in fact, as Miller (2003) suggests, make the situation worse. This is the escalation-of-violence effect related to antagonizing the perpetrator when the time served was relatively short. Another potential problem with mandatory arrest policies is with regard to the minority community. Such an arrest policy subjects minorities to what might seem like police harassment. For minorities who are poor and others of low socioeconomic class, other resources are lacking; they cannot simply move into a motel, for example. The economic consequences of arrest of a breadwinner in a low-income family may be devastating.

Chesney-Lind (2002, 2006) points to a major unintended consequence of pro-arrest policies for women and girls. This is the manner in which the law requiring an arrest has resulted in dual arrest—arrest of both parties to a "fight." If it is not clear who the aggressor is, if the man has a scratch or mark on him, or if both partners have been drinking, the police have taken to arresting both the man and woman. This change in policy is reflected in the arrest rate for assault, a fact that has fueled media reports of girls' and women's increasing violence. Studies on arrest rates from Wichita to Sacramento to Baltimore to Winnipeg, Canada, all found that the "zero tolerance" policy has had a dramatic effect on women's arrest patterns. Mothers who are arrested often see their children taken away to foster care; later loss of custody is a real risk. The arrest of girls, as Chesney-Lind documents, is a result most often of mother–daughter conflicts. Under the present circumstances, the reactions of victims to the treatment they receive from the criminal justice system are mixed (Weisz, Black, and Neva, 2008).

One solution, consistent with feminist practice, might be to simply listen to the victim of the assault. In their study of gender differences in police officers' perceptions about violence cases, Stalans and Finn (2000) found that women officers working in situations of marital abuse consulted with the wife and if she wished to settle the matter with the help of the police, the female officer gave consideration to the victim's preference and was more willing than male officers to make an arrest when the victim indicated an unwillingness to otherwise settle the matter.

Divorce court is another arena where a shift in practices is often at the expense of the woman. The shift from the need to prove a mother unfit for the father to get custody to an equality or gender-blind system for awarding custody for small children in those rare cases in which the father files a petition for custody. The father can more often afford to hire a lawyer than can the mother. The father more often having a job, and a new wife or mother who can care for the child, may appear to be in a better position to take responsibility. Battering, if involved, is often overlooked if the wife has flaws such as a drinking problem or a poor work history. It is common for courts to rule that the father's violence toward the mother has no effect on the children. Unfortunately, fathers with a history of battering are twice as likely to seek the sole physical custody of their children as are nonviolent fathers, and as a result of their financial advantages, fathers in contested cases are being awarded custody more often than their wives (Meir, 2003). In her survey of the case law in 2001, Meir identified thirty-eight appellate state court decisions concerning custody and domestic violence. To her astonishment, thirty-six of the thirty-eight trial courts had awarded joint or sole custody to alleged and adjudicated batterers. Two-thirds of these decisions, however, were reversed on appeal.

In Canada and the United States, fathers' rights organizations vehemently contest claims that fathers have the advantage in court as they aggressively fight for fathers' rights to joint custody and to sole custody of children in divorce cases (Miller, 2005). Thanks to the Internet, this movement of divorced men and their second wives for new laws favorable to the father is sweeping the United States and other countries. Because of a backlash in Canada against a rash of claims of father/child incest and the widespread belief that such claims may be false, some lawyers are advising the mothers in custody disputes to be silent about such abuse (S. Charlesworth, personal communication, March 16, 2000).

To prevent situations such as these, domestic violence education is a must for child welfare authorities and judicial magistrates. Morrill et al. (2005) evaluated hundreds of child custody and visitation orders in cases of father-perpetrated domestic violence. Judges were surveyed as well. Judges who had received specialized education on partner violence gave mothers sole physical custody more often than those without such education, yet few structured or restricted the fathers' visitation. The researchers recommend improvement in the education that is provided.

The Domestic Violence Home Visit Intervention program in New Haven, Connecticut, was developed with the well-being of children in mind (Stover et al., 2008). Families with a history of arrest for domestic assault engage in preventative strategies. Developing a relationship with the family, members of the team address continuing safety concerns and act as a liaison to community services. The focus of the program is to help couples deal with some of the underlying problems that led to the violent incident. Follow-up evaluations showed that of all ethnic groups served, Latina women benefited the most. The success was attributed to the fact that they were visited by Spanish-speaking advocate-officer teams from their own cultural background. A further bright spot is the entry of women in large numbers into the legal profession and therefore into the ranks of prosecutors and judges. This has helped reshape the justice meted out to wife abusers and, more important, the process itself.

EMPOWERMENT

Sometimes you can learn as much from a negative example as from a positive one. In an ethnographic analysis of services that battered women received, Baker (1996) found that the sixteen Iowa women interviewed encountered varying responses to their situations. On the whole, police encounters were conceived of as negative due to the slowness of response and lack of respect for the woman. Contacts with clergy did more harm than good because ministers tended to focus on the woman's behavior as a cause of the violence. Couples counseling was especially destructive in treating the partners as coacting equals and leading to assaults immediately afterward for something that was said in therapy. On the positive side, participation in women's support groups led to a heightened awareness and camaraderie that helped group members gain control over their own lives. Baker discovered from her interviews that being stronger, more aware, and knowledgeable about social and political aspects of domestic violence was among the ways battered women felt helped by the group therapy experience.

Victim satisfaction surveys indicate considerable variability in police response to calls of family violence. Russell and Light (2006) interviewed dozens of police officers and victims to determine which dimensions of police intervention enhanced victim empowerment. Police attitudes that the woman did not deserve the violence and proactive, gender integrated team were experienced as empowering by the women.

Crisis Intervention

Immediate care for a woman in a potentially harmful or already abusive situation involves the development of a safety plan (Boes, 2007). Through obtaining crisis intervention services, many women are able to regain control of their lives by identifying current options and goals and by working to attain those goals. Typically, the battered woman has been subject to psychological and physical abuse for a long period of time before calling for help. She may be mobilized to call a telephone hotline, the police, or a women's shelter or to go to a hospital emergency room. Effective treatment for battered women and their children includes thorough documentation for the possibility of a later legal complaint.

Roberts's Seven-Stage Crisis Intervention Model offers a framework that can be applied by hospital staff, social workers, or shelter workers. The stages of the crisis intervention model are:

1. Plan and conduct a thorough assessment (including a level-of-danger assessment); inquire about death threats, suicide threats, weapons present, and so forth and immediate psychosocial needs.
2. Establish rapport and rapidly establish a relationship based on genuineness and respect.

3. Identify the precipitating event that led the client to seek treatment; encourage the client to describe the immediate situation.
4. Deal with feelings and emotions. Open-ended questions are recommended. Some examples: *How are you feeling now? What are some of the options you're thinking about? What is the usual situation at home?* Use verbal counseling skills such as reflection of feelings, reassurance, paraphrasing, and attentive silence.
5. Generate and explore alternatives. Helping the client find a safe place is essential.
6. Develop and formulate an action plan. Help the client face her fears and gain control as a self-empowering act. Assistance in a shift from fatalistic thinking toward an attitude of hope and renewal is essential. A cognitive approach will help redirect destructive thought patterns, such as "I can't live without him" or "I must stay for the sake of the kids," and a redirection to empowering affirmations and beliefs, such as, "If other women have made it, so can I."
7. Follow up. Informal and formal agreements should be reached for another meeting to gauge the client's progress and daily functioning. It is hoped that future moves will be toward healing and growth. (van Wormer and Roberts, 2009, pp. 157–158)

Given the enormity and depth of the problems encountered, battered women need a continuity of supportive networks and helping services. Crisis intervention, as Roberts and Burman (2007) indicate, can be the starting point on a longer journey toward safety and renewal. For the majority of battered women, permanently leaving the batterer, regaining self-esteem, and finding safe housing and a job are all necessary.

Empowerment can come to a survivor of domestic abuse in working closely with a counselor or other helper as she becomes conscious of inner strengths of which she was unaware, even strengths paradoxically that emerged from her history of abuse. Like many other women who have survived trauma and called for help, she may come to recognize her strength in retrospect. Viewed in the context of the abusive situation and the structural oppression of women, all coping strategies can be recognized as valid resourcefulness and resistance in the face of severe stress.

A serious hindrance to adequate long-term treatment for survivors is the unavailability of affordable services. Sadly, mental health providers must compete with other human service agencies for scarce economic resources in a climate that defines nonemergency services as expendable whenever there is a budget crunch. The hope is that, with the current political focus on the needs of crime victims, advocates for prevention of domestic violence and for treatment of its survivors will be heard.

Shelters for Battered Women

Thanks to feminist activism starting in the 1970s, over 1,500 women's shelters have been established as safe havens for women and their children (Lyon and Lane, 2008). Shelters offer more than safety and a way out; living in close quarters with other battered women and participating in group counseling provides an opportunity for consciousness-raising. Unfortunately, due to serious underfunding, most shelters can take in only a minority of the women who need their help. The importance of domestic violence services and safe spaces in preventing further battering, in saving lives, and in revealing options other than returning to an abusive situation is widely acknowledged.

Before the establishment of safe houses and shelters (refuges in Britain), abused women were whispered about and generally regarded as a source of embarrassment. When women's shelters were opened to provide safety, they ended up providing a whole lot more. Generally run by feminist-oriented volunteers, domestic violence services offered the supportive framework through which thousands of women began to rid themselves of self-blame and develop an aware-ness of forces in society that deliberately keep women down. In virtually every community of any size, by the 1980s women were organizing to help each other and to fight the institutio-nalized sexism that left millions of women violently victimized.

Institutionalized racism or the kind of racism that is unintended has been a continuous problem with the shelters. Donnelly et al. (2005) made a study of white privilege in battered women's shelters in the Deep South. The sixty executive directors of the shelter who were interviewed were proud of being "color blind," and as the researchers argue, that is part of the problem. By not noticing race, they ignore cultural diversity and attitude differences in African Americans. For example, the feminist philosophy concerning the causes of male violence often doesn't coincide with black women's understandings. Battered women of color are less likely than whites to seek the services of the shelters. Greater outreach and culturally specific services are needed.

Although domestic violence services may not always live up to their ideology, the empower-ment philosophy characteristic of women's shelters centers on an awareness of oppression based on race, class, sexual orientation, and gender. Shelter life is woman-centered, chaotic with so much coming and going, emotionally charged, and guided by women who have an agenda and an aware-ness often different from that of their charges. Threat to life and bodily integrity overwhelms normal adaptive processes. In group sessions, the process of empowerment takes place as women fully acknowledge their vulnerability to male violence. The emphasis on self-protection, on finding one's voice, sharing, and listening to others frees up the mind to contemplate the forbidden and prepares the way for progression from fear to anger to self-expression.

Excellent results were obtained with a small sample of sheltered women when counselors adopted the Helping to Overcome PTSD with Empowerment (HOPE) model (Johnson and Zlonick, 2006). This approach helped women reframe their negative cognitive beliefs and to reduce their sense of self-blame while assuming responsibility for their own lives. Following treatment, the women reported a reduction in PTSD symptoms and depression.

A groundbreaking study based on a survey of thousands served by domestic violence shelters in eight states found that 92 percent of respondents rated the services they received positively. Not only did they get help in healing from the violence, but also they were pleased with the services received by their children. Produced by the National Institute of Justice (2009), the 145 report is available to download online.

One should not assume that women who receive counseling and decide to stay with their abuser have not benefited from the counseling. Based on their review of the literature and inter-views with battered women in Singapore, Khng and Ow (2009) indicate that even when a woman decides to stay with the batterer, turning points can still take place. In other words, women may choose to stay in the relationship but never again on the same terms as before. Such a turning point, as these authors suggest, is not sudden but the culmination of a lengthy process in which a woman gradually develops self-awareness and an awareness that the situation will never change. Concern for her children may be a key motivating factor.

That the general public has little awareness of this process was revealed in the recent furor following the widely publicized beating of Rihanna Fenty, age 21, by her rock star boyfriend, Chris Brown, age 19. This case, which was featured on a number of TV programs including the *Oprah Winfrey Show*, nevertheless provided a teaching moment (Brotman, 2009). Discussions on the programs included explanations for the complicated, manipulative nature of abuse, the psychological repercussions, and risks to the victim of being choked. Choking is not just a danger in itself but a harbinger of potential murder in the future.

A woman who decides to stay, despite the danger signs, needs a safety plan (Lindhorst, Macey, and Nurius, 2005). Such a plan should include acquiring job skills for personal independence; maintaining and reviving friendships; attending a support group on a regular basis; knowing the phone number of the women's shelter by heart; keeping money on hand for emergencies; working out a signal system with a neighbor; getting rid of all weapons and keeping sharp knives in hard-to-reach places; learning how to anticipate violence so as to slip away while it is still safe; preparing older children to call for help; and, finally, preparing to make an escape with the children rather than leaving them behind. The availability of community resources and the possibility of receiving financial aid without being forced onto the job market for the time being are vital for the safety of battered women who are trying to start a new life. See Box 9.4 to read of a typical helping effort at a women's shelter in Iowa.

BOX 9.4
Snapshot—A Social Worker's Daily Reality at a Domestic Violence Shelter

On this beautiful day I'm driving to the local hospital to pick up yet another woman and children affected by the crime of domestic violence. Looking out of my window at everyday people going about their business, I would have little awareness that a woman is assaulted and her children traumatized by this crime that happens every six seconds in this country.

I've been manager of this domestic violence shelter for battered women and children for four years. In that time we have had over a thousand women and children pass through our doors. The stories are all unique and yet all the same. We assist some in relocating out of state to hide and escape the violence; some move in with a mother or sister close to home; and others go back to their homes with promises that the abuser would change.

In my mind I'm making mental notes to prepare to meet the caller and her children. My backseat has three brand-new stuffed animals for the children and a car seat for the baby. There are extra diapers and a blanket in my trunk. I must be alert for anyone suspicious in the parking lot, just in case her abuser has followed her here. That must be her in the waiting room trying to juggle the baby in one arm and two more toddlers in the other. "Hi, I'm Janet from the shelter." She looks scared, but relieved that I'm finally here as I scoop up a toddler. Thus begins another journey that I will take alongside this woman and her babies.

I know that she will have many decisions to make and many obstacles to overcome. Later I find out that this mother is only nineteen years old, uneducated and with few job skills. Her income came totally from her abuser and now is no more. I marvel at her bravery and her desire for a better life.

Another factor complicating this battered woman's life is the fact that she is Caucasian and her children are biracial (African American). I've seen many women come through the shelter under such bicultural circumstances that pose their unique set of problems. In many cases the support systems for these women and, most of all, for the children are lacking. The white world does not embrace biracial children with white mothers. There is a negative stigma in our society attached to a Caucasian woman with biracial children, especially if she has personal problems. Oftentimes her own family has cut her off, disapproving of her choice of partners. The African American community seems more accepting of her and her children, but not when there are accusations of abuse toward one of its members. This leaves her in limbo. Where can she go for help? It is very difficult to find a safe, supportive, nurturing place for her and her children.

Now, we will sit down and begin the process. First come the pain and tears. Then, the harsh reality of figuring out what to do and where to go. I hope we can find some answers.

Critical Thinking Question: How does the intersection of class, race, and gender come into play in the case history described in this reading?

Source: Janet Wood, LBSW. Printed with permission of Janet Wood.

Treatment for Batterers and Prevention

Can batterers change their behavior? This is a major consideration because if all the treatment effort is directed toward rescuing the woman, sooner or later the batterer will find another family to victimize. If the partner's behavior can be changed, however, a far more effective form of crime prevention is available.

At the national level, the advocacy-oriented Violence Against Women Office of the U.S. Justice Department has been designed to bolster police and prosecutorial work on domestic and sexual violence cases. Funding is allocated for prevention and victim services programs as well. The Justice Department, however, has failed to provide sufficient funding for abuser programming; only about 5 percent of the total amount of money allotted for domestic violence prevention programs goes to courts for batterer intervention (Balestra, 2008). Victims' services tend to be funded at higher rates through grants and private donations. The fact that batterers have to pay for their own treatment is a drawback because, in many cases, this means a sacrifice for the families.

Given the fact that batterer education is completed for about half of the participants and the probability of re-assault is considerably reduced for these graduates, this programming should be a high priority for the prevention of violence against women (Stoops, 2008). According to some domestic violence experts, the success rate could even be higher if evidence-based strategies were used to engage the batterers in treatment, instead of the ineffective confrontational models that are currently favored (McPhail et al., 2007; van Wormer and Roberts, 2009). For maximum effectiveness, individualized programming is required that is tailored to the batterers' personality characteristics (e.g., whether they have character or mental disorders and whether substance use is involved). The dominant model explains the violence in terms of male entitlement and socialization in a patriarchal society. Batterer education programming for men is built around this narrow explanatory model. Psychologist Donald Dutton refers to the interventions that result as "shaming" programs (cited by Balestra, 2008).

With regard to violence intervention, much more programming is needed, especially at the high school level, to help youths develop healthy relationships. More culturally specific programming is needed as well. Anecdotal evidence from programs designed specifically for African American men suggest that such programs are more successful with African Americans than are other batterers' programs (National Research Council, 1996). For an example of the goals of a healthy relationship, see the equality wheel depicted in Figure 9.2 designed by battered women of Duluth, Minnesota.

One such program, the Duluth model, is based on the feminist theory that patriarchal ideology, which encourages men to control their partners, causes domestic violence (Jackson et al., 2003). The Duluth model helps men confront their attitudes about control and teaches them other strategies for dealing with their partners. This model is the most common form of batterer education in the nation; many states mandate that these programs conform to the Duluth model. The National Institute of Justice examined two studies in considerable depth, one from Florida and one from New York, both of which used control groups. Results showed that the one-size-fits-all model does not work; the best predictor of success was whether or not the individual was employed and lived under stable residential circumstances.

Ellen Pence (1999) fills us in on the history of the Duluth Abuse Intervention Program (DAIP) in an earlier review of the project's evolution. She described an ideological shift that moved professionals from their early emphasis on psychological explanations for violence towards the notion that power and control were the underlying motivation for battering. While staff persisted in explaining the underlying power motive, few men seemed to identify with the explanation. In addition, attempts to explain violence by women against men, lesbian violence,

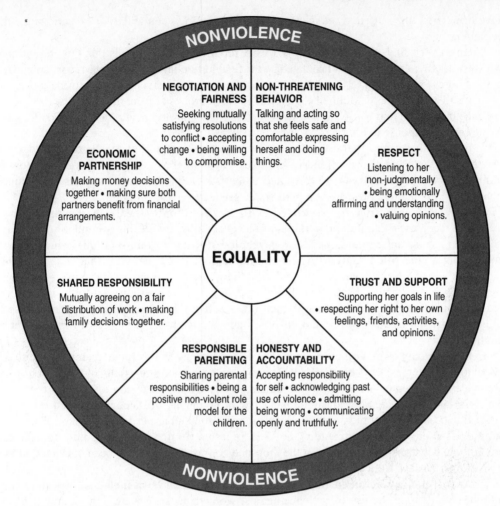

FIGURE 9.2 Equality Wheel *Source:* Domestic Abuse Violence Project, 202 E. Superior Street, Duluth, MN 55802. Printed with permission of the Domestic Abuse Intervention Project.

and the violence of men who were appalled by their own actions further undermined the theory that violence was solely a tool of control. Pence's expectation was that the DAIP was now coming to acknowledge that violence may come about in many ways. However, van Wormer (in private telephone conference with Michelle Johnson and her associate, training coordinator of DAIP, of February 21, 2006) was told that the sole reason for the violence was patriarchal. There was no evidence of a consideration of the development of a more holistic approach to batterer intervention here.

A recent article in the *Journal of the American Medical Association* (JAMA) by Stuart, Temple, and Moore (2007) on the research effectiveness of batterer education programming states that the treatment results are discouraging. Their recommendation is for further development of the model based on empirical research. Unlike other areas of counseling and therapy, which have developed and improved over time as new strategies and approaches have been tried, the batterers' educational programming has remained fairly static since the beginning.

Given such findings as these in the JAMA report, our prediction is that the present one-size-fits-all programming that is mandated by the federal funding is likely to be reconceptualized in the future. Feminists have a major interest in the batterer intervention effectiveness because women's lives are at stake. McPhail et al. found in focus groups of front line workers in domestic violence prevention that participants were receptive to the development of an expanded feminist framework in response to critiques of current practices.

In intensive group therapy sessions, such as those offered at the Batterer Education Program in Waterloo, Iowa offenders confront each other whenever they rationalize and minimize their behavior (van Wormer and Roberts, 2009). Anecdotal reports show much improvement in the treatment of their partners by graduates of the program.

Because aggression is associated with low serotonin levels in the brain, drug treatment, such as with antidepressant therapy, is becoming increasingly common. "I always tell abusers to try antidepressants," says psychologist Roland Maiuro (1998), who has been conducting a controlled study using the antidepressant Paxil. He adds that "anything that increases serotonin will reduce shame," and shame causes anger and aggression (p. 83). Bednar (2001) and Lee, Uken, and Sebold (2007) claim excellent results in their harm reduction program for abusive men, which utilizes feeling-regulation techniques and self-directed goal setting instead of a deficit-based perspective to keep them from getting out of control.

Because only a fraction of the men who batter actually will receive treatment, additional prevention strategies must be adopted. Because guns play an important role in many of the homicides, enforcement of laws forbidding the purchase and possession of guns by convicted batterers can be expected to reduce the incidence of homicide. In states where such laws were enacted and enforced, in fact, a decrease in overall intimate partner homicide has taken place (Campbell et al., 2007). Fortunately, the U.S. Supreme Court recently upheld a federal gun control law the strips gun rights from the thousands of people who have been convicted of any domestic violence-related crime (Savage, 2009).

Apart from law enforcement, prevention at the societal level includes work to change attitudes concerning the use of violence against women. Jackson Katz (2006), author of the bestseller *The Macho Paradox*, has introduced a model that actively recruits young males to be part of the solution rather than part of the problem. His program has been introduced in schools and sports institutions all across America to teach tactics of bystander intervention and male peer support to male youth leaders. Only in changing attitudes in this fashion, will behavior change.

Summary

Learning to believe in oneself as a woman is a lifelong process in a patriarchal society. Learning the functions that violence and the threat of violence serve for the abuser in quelling all criticism and dialogue is a part of that process. Partner abuse is pervasive and an unrecognized cause of chronic psychological and physical health problems. One of the most underreported crimes in the United States, family violence is the single most significant cause of injury to women. About 2 million women are victimized in this way each year. In whatever capacity we encounter these victim/survivors, whether we are police officers, court officials, child welfare workers, or shelter advocates, we must recognize and challenge the dominant ideology of victim-blaming, welfare "reform," and anti–affirmative action backlash. Moreover, we must do more to educate our children in nonviolent ways of resolving disputes and teach them how to deal with powerful feelings and about the danger signs of psychological abuse.

We began this chapter with a historical overview of domestic woman violence. During Colonial times and even before that, the man was "the lord and master" of the household; he could physically chastise his wife to correct her behavior. In the twentieth century, physical punishment of wives was outlawed. Nevertheless, one form of violence that was retained was marital rape, which is still legal in some states today. Wife beating was not defined as a significant social problem until the 1970s when, in the wake of the civil rights movement, feminists publicized this issue as one that affected all social classes.

Feminist perspectives on wife and partner abuse have encompassed both a challenge to the presumption that domestic violence is rare—demonstrating that on some levels and in some parts of society wife beating is normative—and a call to public action. Incredible strides have been made; the establishment of thousands of women's shelters across North America is the most obvious example. Despite these advances, much more needs to be done at the societal level to aid women on the road to independence. Welfare reforms are a priority. Public assistance programs need to be responsive to women at risk of being trapped in a situation of abuse and much more flexible regarding workfare requirements. Moreover, allowance must be made for the risks that battered women face in cooperating with child support enforcement efforts. Safe and affordable housing must be provided for families on the run. Finally, to be self-supporting women require access to an array of educational and vocational training opportunities.

Unfortunately, false claims that levels of abuse between men and women are equal and mutual have been used to cut funding for women's shelters. Such an argument of conjoint violence can also be used to reinforce those family systems therapists who perceive family violence as an outgrowth of faulty communication styles between husband and wife.

Repeated physical and sexual violations are assaults on the integrity and value of the self. Empowerment is critically important so that battered women can recover, heal, and lead lives free from fear and psychological cruelty. Economic and social empowerment is essential to personal survival. Equally essential are institutional and group support to help women subjected to violence to survive and thrive. Substance abuse treatment may be a necessary but not sufficient requirement to end male violence and threatening power plays. What is both necessary and sufficient is to sacrifice a sick relationship for personal wellness, perhaps even embracing a survivor mission as a part of the recovery process. Whichever path is chosen—life within a renewed relationship or apart from it—women released from rigid role stereotypes will be better able to manage their own lives and those of their children.

Key Terms

battered woman syndrome *252*	National Violence Against Women (NVAW) Survey *241*	traumatic bonding theory *251*
cobras and pit bulls *254*		Violence Against Women Act (VAWA) *232*
exposure reduction theory *245*	Stockholm syndrome *251*	
intimate partner violence *233*	suicide-murder systems theory *248*	
murder-suicide *245*		

Critical Thinking Questions

1. Why is the home the most dangerous place for women with regard to violence?
2. Discuss the significance of the Violence Against Women Act and the impact of "welfare reform" in protecting women.
3. Consider the plight of immigrant battered women.
4. Check out the controversy that women are as violent as men. Argue pro or con using recent data.
5. Should marital rape be treated the same as stranger or date rape? How is it different and the same?
6. How is suicide-murder different from murder-suicide, according to van Wormer? What are the psychological factors involved in cases of intimate partner murders that end in suicide of the murderer?

Check news sources in your state and analyze situations of this sort in terms of motives.

7. Argue that traumatic bonding or the Stockholm syndrome is not specific to the female gender.
8. Think about the conflict between women's shelters and substance abuse treatment centers in terms of factors in violence.
9. Study the Power and Control Wheel. Why do victims identify with this wheel? How might its use in batterer intervention programs fail to bring about the desired results?
10. Discuss the psychology of men who batter. How can interventions be individualized for men of various personality types?

Web Destinations

Bureau of Justice Statistics for victimization data: www.ojp.usdoj.gov/bjs

Centre for Children and Families in the Justice System (Canadian): http://www.lfcc.on.ca/

Family Violence Prevention Fund: http://endabuse.org

Family Violence Statistics: www.ojp.usdoj.gov/bjs/abstract/fvs.htm

Infoplease-information on domestic violence surveys: www.infoplease.com/ipa/A0875303.html

National Teen Dating Abuse Hotline: www.loveis respect.org

National Coalition against Domestic Violence: http://www.ncadv.org/

National Center for Injury Prevention and Control: www.cdc.gov/ncipc

Violence Policy Center: www.vpc.org

References

Adams, D. (2007). *Why do they kill? Men who murder their intimate partners*. Nashville, TN: Vanderbilt University Press.

Anderson, M. (1997, October 26). The family home is the most dangerous place for women. *Des Moines Register*, p. 4AA.

Ascione, F., Weber, C., Thompson, T., Heath, J., Maruyama, M., and Hayashi, K. (2007). Battered pets and domestic violence. *Violence Against Women* 13(4): 354–373.

Associated Press. (2008, December 28). Killer Santa lost his job, wife before gory attack. *The Courier*. Waterloo/Cedar Falls, IA, p. A3.

Associated Press. (2009, January 25). Stalker admits Iowa murder, but illness clouds case.*The Des Moines Register*, pp. 1A, 4A.

Baker, P. L. (1996). Doin' what it takes to survive: Battered women and the consequences of compliance to a cultural script. *Studies in Symbolic Interaction 20*: 73–90.

Balestra, K. (2008, September 23). Taking a new tack on domestic violence. *Washington Post*, p. HE08.

Banks, L., Crandall, C., Sklar, D., and Bauer, M. (2008). A comparison of intimate partner homicide to intimate partner homicide-suicide. *Violence Against Women 14*: 1065–1078.

Barnett, O., Miller-Perrin, C. L., and Perrin, R. D. (2005). *Family violence across the lifespan*, 2nd ed. Thousand Oaks, CA: Sage Publications.

Barrachlough, B., and Harris, E. (2002, May). Suicide preceded by murder: The epidemiology of homicide-suicide in England and Wales 1988–92. *Psychological Medicine 32*(2): 577–584.

Baum, K. (2005). Juvenile victimization and offending, 1993–2003, Washington, DC: Bureau of Justice Statistics.

Bednar, S. (2001). Recovering strengths in batterers. In Sidebar in K. van Wormer, *Counseling female offenders and victims: A strengths-restorative approach*. New York: Springer Publishing.

Bell, N., Hartford, T., McCarroll, J., and Senier, L. (2004). Drinking and spouse abuse among U.S. army soldiers. *Alcoholism: Clinical and Experimental Research 28*(12): 1890–1897.

Bergen, R. K. (1998). The reality of wife rape. In R. K. Beyen (ed.), *Issues in intimate violence*. Thousand Oaks, CA: Sage.

Bettleheim, B. (1943). Individual and mass behavior in extreme situations. *Journal of Abnormal and Social Psychology 38:* 417–452.

Black, B., and Weisz, A. (2005). Dating violence: A qualitative analysis of Mexican American youths' views.*Journal of Ethnic and Cultural Diversity in Social Work 13*(3): 69–90.

Blackstone, W. (1979). *Commentaries on the laws of England Volume3: Facsimile of the first edition of 1765–1769* (pp. 444–445). Chicago, IL: University of Chicago Press.

Block, C. R. (2003). How can practitioners help an abused woman lower her risk of death? In Intimate Partner Homicide. *NIJ Journal 250:* 4–7. Washington, DC: National Institute of Justice, U.S. Dept. of Justice.

Boes, M. (2007). Battered women in the emergency room: Emerging roles for the ER social worker and clinical nurse specialist. In A. Roberts (ed.), *Battered women and their families*, 3rd ed. (pp. 301–326). New York: Springer.

Bourke, J. (2007). *Rape, sex, violence history*. Berkeley, CA: Shoemaker and Hoard.

Brabeck, K., and Guzmán, M. (2008). Frequency and perceived effectiveness of strategies to survive abuse employed by battered Mexican-origin women. *Violence Against Women 14*(11): 1274–1294.

Breed, A. (2009, April 7). Loss, revenge drive wave of mass slayings. *The Seattle Times*, p. 4A.

Britt, R. (2009). Recession to fuel more family murder, suicide. *LiveScience*. Retrieved April 2009 from www.livescience.com/culture/090202-recession-suicide. html

Brotman, B. (2009, March 19). McClatchy News Service. Rihann, Chris Brown spotlight lessons on domestic violence. *The Courier*. Waterloo/Cedar Falls, Iowa, p. B3.

Brown, L., Chesney-Lind, M., and Stein, N. (2007). Patriarchy matters: Toward a gendered theory of teen violence and victimization. *Violence Against Women 13*: 1249–1273.

Browne, A. (2004). Fear and the perception of alternatives: Asking "why battered women don't leave" is the wrong question. In B. R. Price and N. Sokoloff (eds.), *The criminal justice system and women: Offenders, victims, and workers* (pp. 343–360). New York: McGraw-Hill.

Browning, M. (2003, March 14). Brainwashing agitates victims into submission. *Palm Beach Post*. Retrieved from www.rickross.com/brainwashing

Buehner, K., and Horgen, J. (2005, January 31). Abuse connected to methamphetamine use. Mason City (Iowa) *Globe Gazette*. Retrieved from www.globegazette.com

Bumiller, K. (2008). *In an abusive state: How neoliberalism appropriated the feminist movement against sexual violence*. Durham, NC: Duke University Press.

Bureau of Justice Statistics (BJS). (2007a). *Homicide trends in the U.S.: Intimate homicide*. Washington, DC: U.S. Department of Justice, Retrieved January 2009 from, http://ojp.usdoj.gov/bjs/homicide/intimates.htm

Bureau of Justice Statistics (BJS). (2007b, December 19). *Intimate partner violence*. Washington, DC: U.S. Department of Justice. Retrieved January 2009 from http://www.ojp.usdoj.gov/bjs/intimate/offender.htm

Buzawa, E., and Hirschel, D. (2008). Domestic violence: The beginning, continuation, or final act in a criminal career? *Victims and Offenders 3*: 391–411.

Campbell, J. C., Glass, N., Sharps, P., Laughon, K., and Bloom, T., (2007). Intimate partner homicide: Review and implications of research and policy. *Trauma, Violence, & Abuse 8*: 246–269.

Campbell, J. C., Webster, D., Koziol-McLain, J., Block, C. R., Campbell, D., Curry, M. A., et al. (2003). Assessing risk factors for intimate partner homicide. In Intimate Partner Homicide, *NIJ Journal 250:* 14–19. Washington, DC: National Institute of Justice, U.S. Dept. of Justice.

Casanueva, D., Foshee, V., and Barth, R. P. (2004). Intimate partner violence as a risk factor for children's use of the emergency room and injuries. *Children and Youth Services Review 27*: 1223–1242.

Cathcart, R., and Archibold, R. (2009, January 28). Man kills his wife and five children. *The New York Times*. Retrieved January 2009 from http://www.nytimes.com/2009/01/28/us/28family.html

Centers for Disease Control and Prevention (CDC). (2006). Dating Violence Fact Sheet. CDC. Retrieved January 2009 from http://www.cdc.gov/ncipc/dvp/dating_violence.htm

Centers for Disease Control and Prevention (CDC). (2008, June 6). Youth risk behavior surveillance. *Morbidity and mortality weekly report*. Retrieved January 2009 from http://www.cdc.gov/Healthy Youth/yrbs/pdf/yrbss07_mmwr.pdf

Chesney-Lind, M. (2002, November). Criminalizing victimization: The unintended cones quences of pro-arrest policies for girls and women. *Criminology and Public Policy 2*(1): 81–90.

Chesney-Lind, M. (2006). Patriarchy, crime, and justice: Feminist criminology in an era of back lash. *Feminist Criminology 1*: 6–26.

Davies, C., DiLillo, D., and Martinez, I. (2004, December). Isolating adult psychological correlates of witnessing parental violence: Findings from a predominantly Latina sample. *Journal of Family Violence 19*(6): 369–378.

Davis, A., (2008, September). Interpersonal and physical dating violence among teens. Views from the National Council on Crime and Delinquency (NCCD). Retrieved January 2009 from http://www.nccd-crc.org/nccd/pubs/Dating%20Violence%20Among%20Teens.pdf

Dawson, M., Bunge, V., and Balde, T. (2009). National trends in intimate partner homicides: Explaining declines in Canada, 1976 to 2001. *Violence Against Women 15*(3): 276–306.

Dearwater, S. R., Coben, J. H., Campbell, J. C., Nah, G., Glass, N., McLoughlin, E., et al. (1998). Prevalence of intimate partner abuse in women treated at community hospital emergency departments. *Journal of the American Medical Association 280*(5): 433–438.

Donnelly, D., Cook, K., Ausdale, D., and Foley, L. (2005, January). White privilege, color blindness, and services to battered women. *Violence Against Women 11*(1): 6–37.

Downs, W. (2000, February). *Paper presentation: Partner violence and substance abuse*. Cedar Falls, Iowa: University of Northern Iowa.

Downs, W. R., Rindels, B., and Atkinson, C. (2007). Women's use of physical and nonphysical self-defense strategies during incidents of partner violence. *Violence Against Women 13*: 28–46.

Dugan, L., and Apel, R. (2003). An exploratory study of the violent victimization of women: Race/ethnicity and situational context. *Criminology 41*(3): 959–979.

Dutton, D. 2007. *Rethinking domestic violence*. Vancouver, Canada: University of British Columbia Press.

Dutton, D. G., and Painter, S. (1993). Emotional attachments in abusive relationships: A test of traumatic bonding theory. *Violence and Victims 8*(2): 105–120.

Dyer, C. (2005, November 29). Men who kill partners face tougher sentences. *The Guardian*. Retrieved February 2009 from http://www.guardian.co.uk/uk/2005/nov/29/law.topstories3

Echeburua, E., and Fernandez-Montalvo, J. (2007). Male batterers with and without psychopathy: An exploratory study in Spanish prisons. *International Journal of Offender Therapy and Comparative Criminology 51*: 254–263.

El-Bassel, N., Gilbert, L., Wu, E., Go, H., and Hill, J. (2005, March). Relationship between drug abuse and intimate partner violence: A longitudinal study among women receiving methadone. *The American Journal of Public Health 95*(3): 465–471.

Fals-Stewart, W. (2003). The occurrence of partner physical aggression on days of alcohol consumption: A longitudinal diary study. *Journal of Consulting and Clinical Psychology 71:* 41–52.

Family Violence in Canada: A Statistical Profile. (2005, July 14). *The Daily*. Retrieved from http://www.statcan.ca/Daily/English/050714/d050714a.htm.

Family Violence Prevention Fund (FVPF). (2008). Immigrant women. Retrieved August 2008 from FVPF. http://endabuse.org/programs/display.php3?DocID=116

Family Violence Prevention Fund (FVPF). (2009). Action Center. Retrieved February 2009 from http://endabuse.org/content/action_center/detail/754

Farr, K. A. (2002). Battered women who were "being killed and survived it": Straight talk from survivors. *Violence and Victims 17*: 267–281.

Federal Bureau of Investigation (FBI). (2008, September). *Crime in the United States, 2007*. Washington, DC: U.S. Department of Justice.

Frisch, L. A., and Caruso, J. M. (1996). The criminalization of woman battering: Planned change experiences in New York State. In A. Roberts (ed.), *Helping battered women: New perspectives and remedies* (pp. 102–131). New York: Oxford University Press.

Garcia, L., Soria, C., and Hurwitz., E. (2007). Homicides and intimate partner violence: A literature review. Trauma. *Violence & Abuse 8*: 370–383.

Geddes, J. (1998, February 23). Victims who kill. *Maclean's*, p. 64.

Gillum, T. (2008). The benefits of a culturally specific intimate partner violence intervention for African American survivors. *Violence Against Women 14*: 917–943.

Graebner, W. (2008). *Patty's got a gun: Patricia Hearst in 1970s America*. Chicago, IL: University of Chicago Press.

Graham, D. L., with Rawlings, E., and Rigsby, R. K. (1994). *Loving to survive: Sexual terror, men's violence, and women's lives*. New York: University Press.

Halpern, C. T., Young, M. L., Waller, M. W., Martin, S. L., and Kupper, L. L. (2004). Prevalence of partner violence in same-sex romantic and sexual relationships in a national sample of adolescents. *Journal of Adolescent Health 35*(2): 124–131.

Harper, D. W., and Voigt, L. (2007). Homicide followed by suicide. *Homicide Studies 11*(4): 295–318.

Hernandez, A. (2008, November 13). North Las Vegas murder/suicide a result of economic Stress. Retrieved February 2009 from http://www.klastv.com/Global/story.asp?s=9340969

Humphreys, J., Regan, L., River, D., and Thiara, R. (2005). Domestic violence and substance use: Tackling complexity. *British Journal of Social Work 35*(8): 1303–1320.

Ingram, E. (2007). A comparison of help seeking between Latino and non-Latino victims of intimate partner violence. *Violence Against Women 13*(2): 159–171.

Ingrassia, M., and Beck, M. (1994, July 4). Patterns of abuse. *Newsweek*, pp. 26–33.

Jackson, S., Feder, L., Forde, D., Davis, R., Maxwell, C., and Taylor, B. (2003, June). *Batterer intervention programs: Where do we go from here?* Washington, DC: U.S. Department of Justice, National Institute of Justice.

Jacobson, N. S., and Gottman, J. M. (1998). *When men batter women: New insights into ending abusive relationships*. New York: Simon and Schuster.

Jentz, T. (2006). *Strange piece of paradise*. New York: Farrar, Straus, and Giroux. Justice. Retrieved February 2009 from http://www.ncjrs.gov/pdffiles/nij/195079.pdf

Jerin, R. A., and Moriarty, L. J. (1998). *Victims of crime*. Chicago, IL: Nelson-Hall.

Johnson, D. M., and Zlotnick, C. (2006). A cognitive-behavioral treatment for battered women with PTSD in shelters.*Journal of Traumatic Stress 19*(4): 559–564.

Katz, J. (2006). *The macho paradox: Why some men hurt women and how all men can help*. Naperville, IL: Sourcebooks.

Khng, J., and Ow, R. (2009). Getting out: Factors that influenced abused wives' decisions to leave their abusive spousal relationships in Singapore. *Families in Society 90*(2): 153–161.

Kohn, D. (2008, December 14). Hard times mean more abuse. *Baltimore Sun*. Retrieved January 2009 from http://www.baltimoresun.com/services/newspaper/|printedition/sunday/ideas/bal-id.violence14dec14,0,5078500.story

Kolbo, J. R., Blakely, E. H., and Engelman, D. (1996). Children who witness domestic violence: A review of empirical literature. *Journal of Interpersonal Violence 11:* 281–294.

Kulkin, H. S., Williams, J., Borne, H., Bretonne, D., and Laurendine, J. (2007). A review of research on violence in same-gender couples: A resource for clinicians.*Journal of Homosexuality 53*(4): 71–87.

Lauritsen, J., and White, N. (2001). Putting violence in its place: The influence of race, ethnicity, gender, and place on the risk for violence. *Criminology & Public Policy 1*(1): 37–59.

Lee, M.-Y., and Au, P. (2007). Chinese battered women in North America: Their experiences and treatment. In A. Roberts (ed.), *Battered women and their families,* 3rd ed. (pp. 529–562). New York: Springer.

Lee, M. Y., Uken, A., and Sebold, J. (2007). Role of self-determined goals in predicting recidivism in domestic violence offenders. *Research in Social Work Practice 17*(1): 30–41.

Lindhorst, T., Macey, R., and Nurius, P. (2005 Spring/Summer). Contextualized assessment with battered women: Strategic safety planning to cope with multiple harms. *Journal of Social Work Education 41*(2): 331–352.

Lonsway, K., Wetendorf, D., and Conis, P. (2003). Abuse of Power. Info. Lessons Learned from Tacoma: The Problem of Police Officer Domestic Violence. Retrieved January 2009 from http://www.abuse ofpower.info/Lonsway_TacomaLessonsPDV.pdf

Lyon, E., and Lane, S. (2008, October 31). The national domestic violence shelter study: Survivors' reports of their shelter experiences. Paper presentation at the annual program meeting of the Council on Social Work Education, Philadelphia.

Maiuro, R. (1998, March/April). Interviewed in "Can they stop?" *Psychology Today*, p. 83.

Mann, R. M. (2008). Men's rights and feminist advocacy in Canadian domestic violence policy arenas. *Feminist Criminology 3*: 44–75.

Marano, H. (1993, November/December). Inside the heart of marital violence. *Psychology Today*, pp. 50–53, 76–78, 91.

Martin, S., Moracco, K., Chang, J., and Dulli, L. (2008). Substance abuse issues among women in domestic violence programs. *Violence Against Women 14*(9): 985–997.

McPhail, B., Busch, N., Kulkarni, S., and Rice, G. (2007). An integrative feminist model: The evolving feminist perspective on intimate partner violence. *Violence Against Women 13*: 817–841.

Meir, J. (2003). Domestic violence, child custody, and child protection: Understanding judicial resistance and imagining the solutions. *Gender, Society, Policy & the Law 11*(2): 657–731.

Menard, K., Anderson, A., and Godboldt, S. (2009). Gender differences in intimate partner recidivism: A 5-year follow-up. *Criminal Justice and Behavior 36*(1): 61–77.

Miller, S. (2003). Arrest policies for domestic violence: Their implications for battered women. In R. Muraskin (ed.), *It's a crime: Women and justice*, 3rd ed. (pp. 307–329). Upper Saddle River, NJ: Prentice Hall.

Miller, S. (2005). *Victims as offenders: The paradox of women's violence in relationships*. New Brunswick, NJ: Rutgers University Press.

Miller, S. L., and Meloy, M. (2006). Women's use of force: Voices of women arrested for domestic violence. *Violence Against Women 12*(1): 89–115.

Miller, J., and White, N. (2003). Gender and adolescent relationship violence: A contextual examination. *Criminology 41*(4): 1207–1245.

Mills, L. G. (2008). *Violent partners: A breakthrough plan for ending the cycle of abuse*. New York: Basic Books.

Morrill, A., Dai, J., Dunor, S., Sung, I., and Smith, K. (2005). Child custody and visitation decisions when the father has perpetrated violence against the mother. *Violence Against Women 11*(8): 1076–1107.

Mulford, C., and Giaordano, P. (2008, October). Teen dating violence: A closer look at adolescent romantic relationships. *National Institute of Justice (NIJ) Journal*, no. 261, pp. 34–40.

Myhill, A., and Allen, J. (2002). *Rape and sexual assault of women: The extent and nature of the problem*. Home Office Research Study No. 237. London: Home Office.

National Institute of Justice (NIJ). (2004). *NIJ's violence against women research and evaluation program: Selected results*. Violence against women and family violence. Retrieved from www.ojp.usdoj.gov/nij/vawprog

National Institute of Justice (NIJ). (2007, October 24). *Measuring interpersonal partner violence*. Washington, DC: U.S. Department of Justice.

National Institute of Justice (NIJ). (2009). *Meeting survivors' needs: A multi-state study of domestic violence shelter experiences*. Washington, DC: Department of Justice Office of Justice Programs. Retrieved March 2009 from http://new.vawnet.org/Assoc_Files_VAWnet/MeetingSurvivorsNeeds-FullReport.pdf

National Research Council. (1996). *Understanding violence against women*. Washington, DC: National Academy Press.

Office on Violence Against Women. (2009). Facts about the Office on Violence Against Women. Retrieved January 2009 from http://www.ovw.usdoj.gov/ovw-fs.htm

Olson, E. (2009, January 4). A rise in efforts to spot abuse in teen dating. *New York Times*. Retrieved January 2009 from http://www.nytimes.com/2009/01/04/us/04abuse.html?_r=1&partner=rss&emc=rss

Palermo, G. B. (1994). Murder-suicide—An extended suicide. *International Journal of Offender Therapy and Comparative Criminology 8*(3): 205–216.

Pence, E. (1999). Some thoughts on philosophy. In M. Shepard and E. Pence (eds.), *Coordinating community responses to domestic violence: Lessons from Duluth and beyond* (pp. 25–40). Thousand Oaks, CA: Sage.

Pence, E., and Dasgupta, S. D. (2006, June 20). Re-Examining 'Battering': Are All Acts of Violence Against Intimate Partners the Same? Praxis International, Inc. Retrieved January 2009 from http://www.praxisinternational.org/pages/library/files/pdf/ReexaminingBattering.pdf

Presser, L., and Gaarder, E. (2004). Can restorative justice reduce battering? In B. R. Price and N. J. Solokoff (eds.), *The criminal justice system and women offenders, prisoners, mothers and workers*, 3rd ed. (pp. 403–418). New York: McGraw-Hill.

Ptacek, J. (1997). The tactics and strategies of men who batter: Testimony from women seeking restraining orders. *Violence between intimate partners: Patterns, causes, and effects* (pp. 104–123). Boston, MA: Allyn & Bacon.

Public Health Agency in Canada. (2009, March). Domestic Violence Courts in Canada. Retrieved April 2009 from http://www.phac-aspc.gc.ca/ncfv-cnivf/EB/eb-eng.php#article

Raquel, K., and Bukovec, P. (2006). Men and intimate partner rape: Characteristics of men who sexually abuse their partner. *Journal of Interpersonal violence 21*(10): 1375–1385.

Raschick, M., and Shephard, M. (1997, June 20). How child welfare workers assess and intervene around issues of domestic violence. A paper presented at the Fifth International Family Violence Research Conference, Durham, NH

Reed, E., Silverman, J., Raj, A., Rothman, E., Decker, M., Gottlieb, B., et al. (2008). The social and emotional contexts of adolescent and young adult male perpetrators of intimate partner violence: A qualitative study. *Journal of Men's Health 2*(3): 260–271.

Rennison, C. M. (2003). Intimate partner violence 1993–2001. Bureau of Justice Statistics (BJS). Washington, DC: U.S. Department of Justice.

Roberts, A. R. (2007). Domestic violence continuum, forensic assessment and crisis intervention. *Families in Society 88*(1): 42–54.

Roberts, A. R., and Burman, S. (2007). Crisis intervention and cognitive problem-solving therapy with battered women: A national survey and practice model. In A. Roberts (ed.), *Battered women and their families*, 3rd ed. (pp. 63–87). New York: Springer.

Rothenberg, B. (2003, October). "We don't have time for social change": Cultural compromise and the battered woman syndrome. *Gender and Society 17*(5): 771–787.

Russell, M., and Light, L. (2006). Police and victim perspectives on empowerment of domestic violence. *Police Quarterly 9*(4): 375–396.

Savage, D. (2009, February 25). Supreme Court upholds gun-control law. Los Angeles Times. Retrieved March 2009 from http://www.latimes.com/news/nationworld/nation/la-na-supreme-court-guns25-2009feb25,0,3038861.story

Schakowsky, J. (2005, September 3). Indian immigrant women in U.S. are trapped in abusive marriages. Retrieved from www.newmindpress.com

Sherman, L. W., and Berk, R. A. (1984). The specific deterrent effects of arrest for domestic as sault. *American Sociological Review 49:* 261–272.

Shlonsky, A, and Wagner, D. (2005). The next step: Integrating actuarial risk assessment and clinical judgment into an evidence-based practice framework in CPS case management. *Children and Youth Services Review 27*: 409–427.

Slatkin, A. (2008). The Stockholm syndrome revisited. *The Police Chief 65*(12). Retrieved January 2009 from http://www.policechiefmagazine.org

Smith, A. (2003). Battered women on mandatory arrest laws: A comparison across three states. In R. Muraskin (ed.), *It's a crime: Women and justice* (pp. 380–393). Upper Saddle River, NJ: Prentice Hall.

Staff Reporter. (2005, November 19). Ireland "still doesn't see marital rape as criminal."*The Irish News*. Retrieved February 2009 from http://www.irishnews.com/pageacc.asp%3Ftser1%3Dser%26par%3Dben%26sid%3D508396+uk+marital+rape&hl=en&ct=clnk&cd=36&gl=us&client=firefox-a

Stalans, L., and Finn, M. (2000). Gender differences in officers' perceptions and decisions about domestic violence cases. *Women & Criminal Justice 11*(3): 1–24.

Statistics Canada. (2005). *Family violence in Canada: A statistical profile 2005*. Ottawa: Statistics Canada.

Stoops, C. (2008, October 31). Research on men who batter: Implications for social work education. Paper Presentation. Council on Social Work Education. 54th Annual Meeting, Philadelphia.

Stover, C., Rainey, A., Berkman, M., and Marans, S. (2008). Factors associated with engagement in a police-advocacy hoje-visit intervention to prevent domestic violence.*Violence Against Women 14*(12); 1430–1450.

Straus, M. A. (2006). Future research on gender symmetry in physical assault on partners. *Violence Against Women 12*: 1086–1097.

Straus, M., and Gelles, R. (1986). Societal change and change in family violence from 1975 to 1985 as revealed by two national surveys. *Journal of Marriage and the Family 48:* 465–479.

Stuart, G., Moore, T., Ramsey, S., and Kahler, C. (2004, January). Hazardous drinking and relationship violence perpetration and victimization in women arrested for domestic violence. *Journal of Studies on Alcohol 65*(1): 46–54.

Stuart, G. L., Temple, J. R., and Moore, T. M. (2007). Improving batterer intervention programs through theory-based research. *Journal of the American Medical Association (JAMA) 298*(5): 560–562.

Tjaden, P., and Thoennes, N. (2000). *Full report of the prevalence, incidence, and consequences of violence against women: Findings from the national violence against women survey.* Bureau of Justice Statistics. Washington, DC: U.S. Department of Justice.

Turse, N. (2009, January 28). Desperate times, desperate measures. Tomdispatch.com. Retrieved January 2009 from http://www.tomdispatch.com/post/175027/ Tomgram%3A%20%20Nick%20Turse%2C%20 Desperate%20Times%20and%20Desperate%20 Measures

USA Today. (2005, February 7). Groups challenge Arizona spousal rape law. *USA Today.* Retrieved from www.usatoday.com/news

U.S. Department of Justice. (2009, January 13). Office on Violence Against Women highlights significant findings of stalking crimes report. Retrieved January 2009 from http://www.ovw.usdoj.gov/docs/stalking-crime-report.pdf

van Wormer, K., and Davis, D. R. (2008). *Addiction treatment: A strengths perspective*, 2nd ed. Belmont, CA: Cengage.

van Wormer, K., and Roberts, A. R. (2009). *Death by domestic violence: Preventing the murders and the murder-suicides.* Westport, CT: Praeger.

Violence Policy Center. (2008). *American roulette: Murder-suicide in the United States.* Washington, DC: VPC. Retrieved July 2008 from http://www. vpc.org/studies/amroul2008.pdf

Walker, L. (1979). *The battered woman.* New York: Harper and Row.

Walker, L. (2009). *The battered woman syndrome*, 3rd ed. New York: Springer Publishing Company.

Waltz, J., Babcock, J. C., Jacobson, N. S., and Gottman, J. M. (2000). Testing a typology of batterers. *Journal of Consulting and Clinical Psychology 68*: 658–669.

Washington Times. (2008, February 14). "Tweens" in sexual, abusive relationships. Retrieved August 2008 from www .washingtontimes.com/news/2008/ feb/14

Wells, W., and DeLeon-Granados, W. (2004, June). The intimate partner homicide decline: Disaggregated trends, theoretical explanations, and policy implications. *Criminal Justice Policy Review 15*(2): 229–246.

Weisz, A., Black, B., and Neva, N. (2008, October 31). Urban, under-served battered women: What they want from the criminal justice system. Paper presentation at the Council on Social Work Education annual program meeting, Philadelphia.

West, C. M. (1998). Lifting the political gag order: Breaking the silence around partner violence in ethnic minority families. In J. Jasinski and L. Williams (eds.), *Partner violence: A comprehensive review of 20 years of research* (pp. 184–209). Thousand Oaks, CA: Sage.

Zolotor, A., Theodore, A., Coyne-Beasley, T., and Ruyan, D. (2007). Intimate partner violence and child maltreatment: Overlapping risk. *Brief Treatment and Crisis Intervention 7*(4): 305–321.

10

Women's Victimization: Global Perspectives

The study of the victimization of women is incomplete without a consideration of the treatment of women worldwide. While we recognize that the offering of such a global view is a first in a book of this kind, we made the decision to write a chapter analyzing international perspectives for several reasons. The first consideration is the impact of **globalization**, the fact that due to the growth of the global economy and the revolution in communication technologies, the world is growing palpably smaller. The impact of this commercial "flattening" of the world (see Friedman, *The World Is Flat*, 2005; and Stiglitz, *Making Globalization Work*, 2007) is seen not only in the blurring of trade and political barriers but also in the nature of crime, the passage and enforcement of transnational laws, and the victimization of women. Feminist theory recognizes that economic factors stemming from global competition play a part in the international exploitation of women's labor and the trade in girls' and women's bodies. The ubiquity of organized crime, terrorism, drug abuse, and the sex trade industry graphically illustrates the interconnectedness of nations in this regard. Attention to such issues and to issues of human rights violations today has catapulted to the forefront of international media concerns.

The second reason for a chapter on global perspectives is to reflect on the increasing numbers of undocumented immigrants and refugees and the concomitant diversification of the U.S. population. The reality of global interdependence, in fact, extends to every profession in the criminal justice field. The case can easily be made, therefore, that to be a culturally competent correctional worker, a familiarity with the values and customs of diversified populations is required.

The third and perhaps most salient argument for including such a chapter in a criminal justice text is that we have so much to learn from other countries. All nations face more or less the same problems, yet the solutions are varied. At the policy-making level, acknowledgment of other nations' approaches to the prevention of crime, the resolution of domestic conflict, the enacting and enforcing of laws, and the protection of vulnerable women can contribute to the resolution of domestic problems. Such comparative study reveals the commonality of social problems across the world and the fact that solutions found to work in one country might be worth a try elsewhere. Comparative criminology, furthermore, introduces the student to creative options of proven feasibility and to ideas that might someday be the inspiration for grant-funded research or be incorporated in state legislation for improved correctional services. From a research standpoint, when a correlation (as between pregnancy and battering by the spouse) is found in one nation, and then the correlation holds in one or more other nations surveyed, this fact helps give credence to the original finding. From the broader perspective, global truths help resolve the issue of whether or not certain behaviors (e.g., rape) are culturally specific or whether they are universal in nature.

In summary, a multicultural worldview can direct our attention to new concepts, theoretical frameworks, and approaches that never would have been contemplated otherwise. This is what critical thinking is all about—developing a perspective based on a comprehensive, "no-holds-barred" knowledge base. Through learning about alternative attitudes and programming, for example, we can come to appreciate the uniqueness of American values. Relevant to women's issues is the belief in gender equality (relatively), individualism, the primacy of the nuclear family, and moralism played out as punitiveness (van Wormer, 2004). We can also, through a global view, come to appreciate how prevalent are certain negative cultural characteristics so closely associated in the public mind with the United States—classism, racism, and sexism, for example.

This chapter has as its starting point an examination of international law through relevant human rights documents; such documents provide a template for the study of the mistreatment of women worldwide as well as a universal standard according to which the treatment of women can be measured. The major part of the chapter is devoted to human rights violations that are gendered—for example, the sex trade in women, punishment of women for disobedience of sex-restrictive laws such as not wearing a veil, and femicide. **Femicide** is not just the act of killing a female. It is killing a female because she is a female. Femicide includes "honor killings" in places such as Jordan and Pakistan, "dowry deaths" (or killings related to dowry disputes), genital mutilation, rape in war, and the victimization of female refugees. A related issue is the harsh treatment of women prisoners worldwide and of immigrant women who are detained in U.S. detention centers and prisons. The plight of immigrant women married to abusive men is also explored.

The final portion of the chapter is devoted to positive developments across the world from which Americans have much to learn. These are initiatives of empowerment, ideas that have been tested in various parts of the world. In New Zealand, restorative justice conferencing reveals a potential for providing justice in cases of abuse and sexual assault; in Brazil, a women's police station supports female victims of family violence; and an all-women's village in Kenya opens its doors to escapees from male violence. In these and other countries, the role of international nongovernmental organizations (NGOs) has been prominent in opening the eyes of the world to antifemale abuses. NGOs have engaged in social action, for example, in reuniting abducted and sexually abused girls with their families. And more often, they have investigated crimes against humanity, such as the mass raping of women in wartime.

Feminist criminological theory is the underlying theoretical framework for this chapter. A focus on empowerment of women is integral to this perspective. Feminist criminological theory provides an important grounding for the understanding of the treatment of women worldwide in locating sources of women's oppression in social practices of the wider societal structure. This theoretical approach offers an alternative vision of crime in directing our attention to **gender-based violence**, or crimes committed against women because they are women. Feminist writers, increasingly, are turning their attention to events of global import. We start with a brief overview of women's victimization globally.

Statistics tell the story of a world where, on too many fronts, women are still struggling to gain equal rights. The following facts are drawn from the the Family Violence Prevention Fund (2008) and the United Nations Population Fund (2008).

- Every year, over half a million women die from pregnancy-related causes. This includes illegal abortions, which kill around 68,000 women per year, mainly in Africa and Asia.
- The risk of a woman dying as a result of pregnancy or childbirth during her lifetime is about 1 in 8 in Afghanistan and Sierra Leone compared with fewer than 1 in 17,400 in Sweden.
- Worldwide, AIDS infection rates are now higher for women than for men. In sub-Saharan Africa, where AIDS is spreading faster than anywhere else on the planet, women account for 55 percent of all new cases of HIV. Sadly, most of these women lack the sexual autonomy to refuse sex or demand that their "partner" use a condom.
- Twenty to 50 percent of all women have experienced violence from a so-called "loved one." Gender-based violence takes many forms and plagues girls and women throughout their lives. An estimated 60,000 girls are considered "missing" in China and India because of sex-selective abortions, female infanticide, and neglect. In 2000, more than 5,000 girls were murdered by their parents or other family members because they spoke to boys on the street or "dishonored" the family by becoming a rape victim. More than 2 million women undergo female genital mutilation each year, which leads to a lifetime of suffering.
- Each year, more than 2 million children are exploited in the global commercial sex trade, many of them trapped in prostitution.
- Eight million children are trapped in the worst forms of child labor, which include slavery, trafficking, debt bondage, forced recruitment for use in armed conflict, prostitution, pornography and illicit activities.
- The United Nations Development Fund for Women estimates that at least one in every three women globally will be beaten, raped, or otherwise abused during her lifetime. In most cases, the abuser is a member of her own family.
- Studies from Egypt, Ethiopia, India, Mexico and Nicaragua have found that 14–32 percent of women report having been physically or sexually abused during pregnancy—and the perpetrator is usually their partner.
- An estimated 100–140 million girls and women worldwide are currently living with the consequences of female genital mutilation or cutting, with the majority of these instances taking place in Africa and the Middle East.
- Throughout most of the world, women earn on average two-thirds to three-fourths as much as men for the same work. In addition, women perform most of the invisible work that keeps families going day to day. However, housekeeping, child care, water fetching, collection of firewood, and other activities mainly performed by women are rarely included in economic accounting, although their value is about one-third of the world's economic production.

According to the United Nations Girls' Education Initiative, girls' education plays a pivotal role in enhancing the social and economic welfare of societies, especially in the developing world (Faye, 2008). Providing the resources to keep girls in school can be more effective than improved sanitation, employment, or higher income in boosting child survival rates. Research has demonstrated that educating girls unlocks their potential and exerts a multiplier effect on their communities, even in nations experiencing a high rate of poverty. Educating girls has been found to be a key factor in preventing AIDS and reducing the rates of infant mortality in a society and in promoting safe health practices for the whole family. Ultimately, educating girls and promoting women's rights is the key to global health.

THE IMPACT OF GLOBALIZATION

Globalization can be looked at in a number of contexts, both positive and negative, that are relevant to the lives of women. First, as noted by Dominelli (2002), increasing global interconnectedness has resulted in social problems that transcend national boundaries. Among these problems are the plights of women refugees escaping the ravages of war, the mass emigration of immigrants escaping personal and political violence, sex trafficking, and women used as "mules" to transport illegal drugs across borders. The war on drugs is a war of global proportions, and its impact falls sharply on the shoulders of women. A second context, from an economic perspective, is the impact of market-driven measures of capitalism as evidenced in the reduction of social services through cutbacks, the privatization of services, and the deprofessionalization of workers. The loss of welfare benefits and services by the state, in conjunction with deinstitutionalization of mental patients, in turn, has increased the numbers of homeless young people roaming the streets; this fact has intensified the vulnerability of girls and women to sexual victimization, sexual exploitation, and drug use. Consider also the reduction in funding for victim assistance services and women's shelters. Third, global market forces pave the way for agency consolidation and corporate management techniques, with the result that men displace women managers (Dominelli, 2002). This fact is seen in connection with the masculinization of correctional services and standardization of treatment philosophies (see Chapter 6). The bulk of the funding here has gone to high-tech security systems and to surveillance rather than to educational and counseling services. The fourth aspect of globalization relates to the clash of civilizations through the communications revolution. The fear in certain quarters across the globe is that if women's consciousness is raised, they will demand their rights. A counterreaction, therefore, has taken place, a backlash by entrenched forces with a vested interest in the status quo. This backlash is especially pronounced in regions of the world where religious fundamentalism has been used to threaten women and suppress them. Economic competition undoubtedly plays a role in what has been termed the "world's war against women" as well.

Worldwide, as competition for well-paying and secure jobs in a global economy heats up, dangerous right-wing extremist movements are seizing political power. The mistreatment of women globally tends to be expressed in the guise of an attack on modernization, including the threatened liberation of women (van Wormer, 2004).

Economic globalization, or the macroeconomic policies associated with the global economy, has important human rights implications. Such policies require that the nonindustrialized nations reduce their indebtedness to the world banks by reducing social welfare spending of the kind that makes life livable. Relevant to economic inequities, women perform two-thirds of the world's work but earn only one-tenth of all income; women own less than one-tenth of the world's property (Human Rights Watch, 2002a). People in a position of economic servitude to others who have control over the resources are generally vulnerable to mistreatment, and they have little recourse for justice. Economic destitution makes a young woman ripe for sexual exploitation, including being tricked into prostitution with the promise of a lucrative job abroad.

It stands to reason that as the economy improves in a country, more girls are educated, birth control is practiced more widely, women move into the workforce, and the lives of women improve. The United Nations (2005) in a new report has reversed the proposition that ending poverty is key to ending violence against women by stating instead that stopping violence against women is the key to eliminating poverty. This is because women who are not terrorized by violence, and live in circumstances of gender equality, are free to make decisions concerning family size and to access health care for themselves and for their children, including girls, thereby reducing incidences of harmful traditional practices. Studies show that when women control the family spending, they are more likely than men to invest a higher percentage of their earnings in family needs (United Nations, 2005).

The adoption of a human rights framework is increasingly relevant today, given the realities of the global market. International law provides for freedom from domestic violence under the 1980 Convention for the Elimination of All Forms of Discrimination Against Women. Former President Jimmy Carter signed the document, which has never been ratified by the U.S. Senate. As of this writing, emboldened by the rise of Democrats to power, feminists are renewing the drive for the passage of this important agreement that all other industrialized nations have signed. The city of San Francisco passed a model version, which has been influential in helping preserve programs for girls and women in the face of state-wide budget cuts (Andronici, 2009). The European Convention for the Protection of Human Rights provides for the same protection against domestic violence.

This example of reliance on international law to link partner violence with human rights violations has important implications worldwide for women who are subjected to behaviors that could be described as torture, including the element of captivity. Were we to reclassify partner violence as a human rights violation, recognized as such by international organizations such as the United Nations, this move would aid in promoting international standards of humanity and equality.

Human rights violations of women take place at three levels—family (e.g., battering, family sexual abuse, honor killings), community (rape, forced early marriage, trafficking), and state (rape in war, sexual abuse by prison officials). Let us consider the factor of transnational crime related to global markets and mass migration and trafficking.

WOMEN'S RIGHTS ARE HUMAN RIGHTS

According to the modern human rights perspective, there are universal principles that transcend individual national practices and cultural norms when these principles are violated. International pressure then can be exerted on the nations involved, often first through NGOs, which report to the United Nations at the second and final level; intervention may take place to protect the individuals and groups whose rights are being violated. Over most of the course of human rights history (the starting point was in the 1940s with the passage of the Universal Declaration of Human Rights), issues of gender have been ignored. Much of the reason lay in the philosophy of cultural relativism, the belief that we must respect cultural tradition, even those that seem abhorrent to us because of our own cultural conditioning. This reluctance of social scientists, including feminists, to appear ethnocentric, to judge other people according to principles of Western society, is understandable. But this reluctance has meant that until relatively recently, such abuses as family murders for adultery ("honor killings") and mutilation of girls' genital organs were not investigated and rarely, if ever, mentioned in the literature. And it would have been thought that it is up to the women in the individual countries to bring about the changes they desired without outside interference.

This hands-off attitude has changed drastically in recent years as reformers—feminists and other social activists—in collaboration with indigenous women or women who have become refugees from violence—increasingly look to international law. The focus on human rights is, by definition, international—the belief in higher laws that transcend national laws. This broadening of focus is a legacy of the Nuremburg Trials that followed World War II when Nazi leaders were judged by a world body (albeit one organized by the victors) for crimes against humanity. Even more significant as a legacy was the United Nations Declaration of Human Rights that was adopted in 1948.

The Declaration's significance is that it gave the world, for the first time in history, international principles on the basis of which sovereign nations could be held accountable. This human rights document transcends social justice to civil and political customs, in consideration of the basic life-sustaining needs of all human beings, without distinction (National Association of Social Work, 2006).

The U.N. document consists of two covenants: one for political and civil rights; another for economic, social, and cultural rights. The civil and political rights against the arbitrary powers of the state are the ones that concern us here. The United Nations Declaration of Human Rights had included women as an at-risk population since it was written in 1948. Yet, just as with the Civil Rights Act of 1964, which forbade discrimination on grounds of sex, little heed was paid to gender issues until women organized to demand it. It was largely through their participation in the U.N. world conference that women's groups have brought attention to the United Nations as a key forum for advancing women's rights (Cole and Phillips, 2008). "Human rights are women's rights" became the motto of the international movement to protect women from abuse. In 1995, women linked up from Austria to Zambia at the United Nations Fourth World Conference on Women. The historic conference was held at Huaira and Beijing, China. Whereas at previous women's conferences, feminists from the Westernized nations were reluctant to even appear to criticize traditions from other parts of the world for fear of being accused of lacking cultural sensitivity, this time women's voices were united on behalf of the many who are unable to speak. At the 1995 conference, the debate on health and reproductive rights was led primarily by delegates who were neither Western nor white. In demanding that women's rights should supersede national traditions, the Beijing accord marked a historic breakthrough.

It was only after the Beijing conference that Amnesty International, the well-known NGO that has done so much to publicize human rights abuses worldwide, took up the call and listed trafficking in women along with torture, slavery, and jailing "prisoners of conscience" as a human rights violation. In its annual reports, Amnesty International continues to outline the mechanism by which hundreds of women a year are smuggled, imprisoned, exploited, raped continuously, blackmailed, and physically and sexually abused, and documents attempts made to combat this human rights violation. Some promising steps are being taken, according to Amnesty International (2007), in the founding of the Council of Europe Convention Against Trafficking. This organization has formed to offer a concerted effort to end sex and labor trafficking and to protect the victims of these international operations. Israel, which had been criticized earlier for its failure to protect women from the former Soviet Union and Eastern Europe who were brought in for purposes of sexual exploitation. Probably in reaction to the criticism, Israel has since passed laws outlawing human trafficking, punishing traffickers, and aiding victims of this human trade (Israel News, 2006).

Today, feminists and human rights activists unreservedly endorse the human rights of people as a universal value that takes precedence over cultural norms when cultural norms conflict with such values. However much rituals such as the genital mutilation of girls and women or the infanticide of females are integrated with cultural and religious beliefs, such practices are actively opposed and condemned as human rights violations.

The cultural origins of this violence are reflected in the historically low social and economic status of women; indeed this lack of independent resources can be both a cause and a consequence of violence against women. The bride burnings for dowry demands in India (an illegal practice in which a bride is set on fire by her in-laws if the demands for dowry payment from the bride's family are unmet), which number over five a day, illustrate crass materialism at its extreme. A report by the United Nations International Children's Fund (UNICEF, 2003) calls for international solidarity against antifemale homicides such as the honor killings in Pakistan (to "restore honor" to a family when an unmarried woman lost her virginity whether she had been raped or not), the acid attacks on women in Bangladesh who had displeased men, and the bride deaths in India. The phenomenon in India can be examined in terms of recent changes in women's roles and sources of female power. Bride burnings occur most often in cases of arranged marriages and among the urban middle class. Economic gain for the groom's family is a major factor in the practice of the dowry system in India today (Rastogi and Therly, 2006). Dissatisfaction with the dowry often leads to abuse of the wife by the husband and in-laws. As India has shifted to a market cash economy, the new consumerism has put more value on the size of the dowry itself than on the woman. Economic discrimination against women and their vulnerability to violence are thus intertwined (van Wormer, 2004).

The United Nations adopted the Convention on the Elimination of All Forms of Discrimination against Women in 1979. The United States stands alone among Western nations in its reluctance to ratify this document. (President Jimmy Carter signed it, but the U.S. Senate has never ratified it; the major concern is about the preservation of the traditional family.) If the United States would join other nations in endorsing this treaty, it would provide a tool for women fighting for their lives across the world; it would strengthen, not weaken, the family. Such human rights laws provide a valuable theoretical and practical base for assisting in social change. Because Canada was a signatory (unlike the United States) to the Covenant on Economic, Social and Political Rights, human rights activists in that country can turn to international law as a valuable tool for advocacy for social and economic justice within the era of globalization. Their counterparts in the United States are relatively limited in this regard.

Around the globe, death by stoning in Iran and Nigeria, genital mutilation in twenty-eight African nations, rape of young girls and even infants in South Africa, dowry deaths in India and Pakistan, sexual slavery in Thailand, and wife abuse in all countries have shocked the sensibilities of humanists. The savage suppression of women by the Taliban in Afghanistan received enormous media attention in the 1990s. It was only after September 11, however, that the American government, which had previously looked the other way, called for the liberation of these women (Vanden Heuvel, 2009). Today, under a new regime in Afghanistan, many women are still forced to cover their bodies in the burqa, and girls' schools are subject to burning.

The treatment of women in the United States, although strikingly better than their treatment in some parts of the world, is not exempt from international concern. According to an Amnesty International (2001) investigation, *Broken Bodies, Shattered Minds*, family violence against women is a common occurrence in the United States. Women in U.S. jails and prisons have been widely susceptible to sexual abuse by male officers (see Chapter 6). A Human Rights Watch (2007) report decries the locking of mentally ill inmates in solitary confinement for months for their erratic, disturbed behavior. And two years before the writing of *Broken Bodies*, the sexual abuse of women in U.S. prisons by male guards was the source of a major investigation (Amnesty International, 1999).

VIOLATIONS OF WOMEN DOMESTICALLY

Much of the family violence against girls and women that takes place across the globe is culturally sanctioned, a fact that makes it difficult to prevent and control. Under this category are included male-against-female partner violence, dowry-related violence, marital rape, genital mutilation, and honor killing. Ponder the following headlines:

- "Italy: 600 Girls at Risk of Female Genital Mutilation" (*Europe News*, 2009)
- "Man Accused of Killing Daughter for Family Honor" (Tarabay, *NPR*, 2009)
- "Too Young to Marry: Child Brides Are Stripped of Their Rights, Their Health, Their Lives" (Ford, *Ms Magazine*, 2009)

The **World Health Organization's (WHO)** (2002) comprehensive report, "World Report on Violence and Health," provides data on gender-based violence worldwide. In recognition of the difficulty of making international comparisons, they have developed guidelines to help improve the comparability of data for future use. In the meantime, WHO relies on data from a wide range of national sources; these data suggest that partner violence accounts for a significant number of deaths by murder of women. Studies from Australia, Canada, Israel, South Africa, and the United States, for example, collectively show that 40–70 percent of female murder victims were killed by their boyfriends and husbands, frequently in the context of an ongoing abusive relationship.

The United Nations (2008) includes the following facts concerning family violence against girls and women:

- Dowry murder is a brutal practice where a woman is killed by her husband or in-laws because her family cannot meet their demands for dowry—a payment made to a woman's in-laws upon her marriage as a gift to her new family. While dowries or similar payments are prevalent worldwide, dowry murder occurs predominantly in South Asia.
- The practice of early marriage is common worldwide, especially in Africa and South Asia. This is a form of sexual violence, for young girls are often forced into the marriage and into sexual relations, causing health risks, including exposure to HIV/AIDS, and limiting their attendance in school.

In contrast to the American pattern in which the weapon of choice was a gun, in India, a large number of deaths among women, as mentioned above, were "bride burnings" and officially recorded as accidental burns. Indian feminists use the term *femicide* to fit the reality of such female-killing in their country. This term also includes the common practice of elimination of female fetuses through abortion or of female infants through neglect. Such killing of females is considered femicide, according to the United Nations (2007) definition, inasmuch as it is the gender-based murder of women. In China, the number of "missing females" is the highest in the world. At birth, the sex ratio is 117 boys to 100 girls (Banister, 2004). The Chinese "one-child" policy, coupled with modern technology (ultrasound tests), favors the selection of male over female children because parents, for economic reasons and tradition, favor having sons over daughters.

An especially brutal form of child abuse, one that has involved millions of girls throughout the world is known as **genital mutilation**. Genital mutilation is closely related to femicide because of the high rate of fatalities due to poor sanitation of instruments used and its indirect association with AIDS. Unknown numbers of girls and women who are butchered in this way contract the AIDS virus, either in the short term due to the crude, unsanitary instruments used, or in early adulthood, due to the genital bleeding related to the mutilation when intercourse takes place. When the man is infected, the infection spreads.

As stated in the United Nations (1989) Convention on the Rights of the Child:

> Children have a right to protection from all forms of physical or mental violence, injury or abuse, negligent treatment, maltreatment, or exploitation, including sexual abuse, while in the care of parents, legal guardians, or any other person who has the care of the child. (Article 19)

International health authorities find the most extensive evidence of such customs in the African continent and parts of the Middle East. Like the now abandoned foot-binding in China and the practice of dowry and child marriage, female genital mutilation represents society's control over women. Such practices have the effect of perpetuating normative gender roles that are unequal and harm women (World Health Organization, 2008). A high rate of mortality is related to this mutilation. DeMause (2002), drawing on indigenous sources, graphically describes the procedure:

> The girl's sexuality is so hated that when she is five or so, the women grab her, pin her down, and chop off her clitoris and often her labia with a razor blade or piece of glass, ignoring her agony and screams for help, because, they say, her clitoris is "dirty," "ugly," "poisonous," "can cause a voracious appetite for promiscuous sex," and "might render men impotent." The area is then often sewn up to prevent intercourse, leaving only a tiny hole for urination. The genital mutilation is excruciatingly painful. (p. 341)

Such practices frequently are erroneously described as "female circumcision," a puberty ritual. Yet the degree of damage, psychological and physical, is not comparable to the African custom of male circumcision. Such male circumcision, although it may be considered abusive in its own right, is not performed for the purpose of destroying its victim's capacity for sexual pleasure.

Although some African countries such as Sudan, Egypt, Ghana, and Guinea have banned genital mutilation, in recognition of Western sensibilities, the laws, generally, are not enforced. Recently, ten international human rights organizations have banded together with the goal of ending genital mutilation altogether. Their approach is through community awareness campaigns rather than seeking legal remedies (WHO, 2008).

Sexual oppression, too, rears its ugly head in the statistical anomaly of the births of far more males than females in parts of Southeast Asia. Griswold (2003), a journalist reporting on life in the Taliban-controlled area of Pakistan, for example, provides this description of an interview he had with a young mother: "How many children does she have now? 'Two,' she says. 'Three if you count the girl' " (p. 62).

In China, as mentioned above, a serious sex ratio disparity exists. One result of this deliberate disparity is that, according to an article in the *International Herald Tribune*, Vietnamese women are being sold and trafficked to serve as brides to Chinese men (Subler, 2008). In India, there is a similar shortfall of women, despite a government ban on ultrasound. Estimates are that half a million females have "disappeared" per year for the past two decades as a result of prenatal sex selection and infanticide (United Nations, 2007). Young Indian men have difficulty finding wives (the girl/boy ratio has dropped to 927 per 1,000 and far less in certain regions), so prosperous men are buying girls from poor villagers (Kennedy, 2004). Such children become part of a mass trafficking trade to meet the demand for brides, often to provide sexual favors to the men in an entire family.

Wife Beating

From the World Bank Research Observer Advance Access (2007), we learn about comparable estimates of the prevalence of violence by intimate partners across 15 sites in 11 countries:

- In urban areas between 12.9 percent (Japan) and 48.6 percent (Peru) of women have suffered physical violence at some point in their lives.
- In rural areas, the lifetime prevalence rates for physical violence range from 33.8 percent (Brazil and Thailand) to 61 percent (Peru). For sexual violence by an intimate partner, the rates range from a low of 6.1 percent in urban Japan to a high of 58.6 percent in rural Ethiopia (p. 2).

From the WHO (2005) Multi-Country Study on Womens' Health and Domestic Violence Against Women, we are informed that:

- Between 15 and 71 percent of women reported physical or sexual violence by a husband or partner.
- Between 4 and 12 percent of women reported being physically abused during pregnancy.
- Forced marriages and child marriages violate the human rights of women and girls, but they are widely practiced in many countries in Asia, the Middle East, and sub-Saharan Africa.

Over 100 states have no specific legal provisions against domestic violence (United Nations, 2008). Unlike in the United States and northern Europe, where domestic violence has been recognized as a public health problem for several decades, this awareness among health care workers in even some industrialized nations such as Japan and South Korea has only developed in recent years. A nationwide government survey showed that 27.5 percent of Japanese wives said they had been beaten by their husbands and 4.6 percent of women in another study said spousal abuse had put them in a life-threatening situation (Kambayashi, 2004). Most perpetrators were habitual drinkers. (Comparable U.S. rates are estimated to be between 1 and 3 percent.) In 2001, because of the work of grassroots efforts, publicly funded shelters were mandated by Japanese law.

In Britain, as elsewhere, a woman is more vulnerable to violence in her home than in public. The latest available figures from the government Home Office (2008) reveal that:

- Domestic violence accounts for 15 percent of all violent incidents.
- One in four women and one in six men will be a victim of domestic violence in their lifetime, with women at greater risk of repeat victimization and serious injury.
- Eighty-nine percent of those suffering four or more such incidents are women.
- One incident of domestic violence is reported to the police every minute.
- On average, two women a week are killed by a current or former male partner.

Until the past few years, the handling of domestic violence cases in Britain showed little concern for the victims' welfare, with the result that most of the perpetrators who were brought to trial escaped punishment. Recently, according to a BBC report (McFarlane, 2008), a promising development has taken place in the form of specialist domestic violence courts that provide training for all court personnel in victim sensitivity. Victim-witnesses are now nurtured through the process by advocates; care is taken to reduce their stress in giving testimony and to ensure their personal safety. The changes are being credited with helping increase the conviction rate for domestic violence offenses in England and Wales.

The Canadian Centre for Justice Statistics (2008) provides a thorough portrait of violence against women in the annual report "Family Violence in Canada." Based on a national telephone survey, researchers found that the rate of partner physical assault over the past five years has remained relatively unchanged from previous reports of 7 percent of women and 6 percent of men. In 83 percent of the cases of spousal violence reported to the police, the victim is a female. From 1977 to 2006, the rate of female deaths from spousal homicide is three to five times the male rate. Most of the victims were stabbed, strangled, or beaten to death. When women were the perpetrators, the weapon was usually a knife or gun. An earlier report from Statistics Canada (2005) revealed that, in their lifetimes, 21 percent of females and 16 percent of males had experienced partner violence. Female victims were more than twice as likely as male victims to be injured, also twice as likely to be stalked by a previous partner. Among aboriginal people, 24 percent of the women and 18 percent of the men said they had suffered violence from a current or previous partner. Similar to studies in Mexico, the strongest predictors of wife assault are the young age of the couple, chronic unemployment by male partners, women and men who witnessed parental abuse as children, and the presence of emotional abuse in the relationship. Just over half the violent partners usually drank at the time of the assaults.

Many women face multiple forms of discrimination and increased risk of violence. According to the United Nations (2008), indigenous women in Canada are five times more likely than other women of the same age to die as the result of violence. In Europe, North America, and Australia, over half of women with disabilities have experienced physical abuse, compared with one-third of nondisabled women.

According to a WHO (2002) report based on forty-eight surveys from around the world, between 10 and 69 percent of women report having been physically assaulted by a partner. As we learned in Chapter 9, in the United States, approximately 22 percent or women report victimization by domestic violence.

To generalize from an overview of women's status and treatment worldwide, research shows that in countries where women's status is high and where they are well educated, their level of lethal victimization is low, regardless of their occupational involvement (Dawson, Bunge, and Balde, 2009). In contrast, where women's status is low, they are vulnerable to domestic homicide.

In traditional societies, wife beating is largely regarded as a consequence of a man's right to inflict physical punishment on his wife—something indicated by studies from Bangladesh, Cambodia, India, Mexico, Nigeria, Pakistan, Papua New Guinea, and Zimbabwe (WHO, 2002). Research from industrialized and nonindustrialized nations alike shows that partner violence is justified by the perpetrator on the following grounds: the woman's arguing back, refusing sex, not having the meal ready, suspected infidelity, and disobedience. In many nations, women who were interviewed agreed that beatings were justified under certain circumstances. According to a *New York Times* report, about half of the women interviewed in a Zambian survey said husbands had a right to beat wives for cause—burning the dinner, for example, or refusing sex. But even where the culture grants men the right to beat their wives, there are limits. Studies reviewed by WHO suggest that women stay in abusive situations because of fear of retribution, lack of means of economic support, concern for the children, and the stigma attached to being unmarried. Research also showed that leaving such a relationship was not a one-time thing, that most women leave and return several times before making the final break (LaFraniere, 2005).

International research has shown that societies with community sanctions against partner violence and support for abused women had the lowest levels of partner violence (WHO, 2005). Because maintaining shelters is expensive, many poor nations have set up an informal network of "safe houses" to deal with the emergency of domestic abuse. NGOs often offer specialized services for victims of abuse in countries in which they are active. A growing body of evidence documents the consequences of gender-based violence for women's health and well-being, ranging from fatal outcomes such as homicide, suicide, and AIDS-related deaths to nonfatal outcomes such as physical injuries, chronic pain syndrome, gastrointestinal disorders, unintended pregnancies, and sexually transmitted infections (Morrison, Ellsburg, and Bott, 2007).

When a woman is pregnant she is at a high risk for physical abuse and loss of the developing fetus as well. Estimates of abuse during pregnancy range from 3 to 15 percent in population-based studies in Canada, Egypt, Nicaragua, Chile, and the United States (WHO, 2002). Sexual abuse is a common co-occurring component of partner violence. In many countries, marital rape is considered an oxymoron. Marital rape is not, in fact, a prosecutable offense in at least fifty-three states (United Nations, 2008). In Ethiopia, until recently, a man who wanted to marry a girl or women could kidnap and rape her, then agree to marry her and escape punishment (Women's Action, 2005). Since the girl or woman was defiled, the family had to agree to the arrangement. Recent legal reform removed the exemption for forced marriage from the crime of rape as abduction. So far, the new antirape law has not been enforced.

The prevalence of partner sexual violence and of HIV/AIDS are interlinked. Women's inability to negotiate safe sex and refuse unwanted sex is closely linked to the high prevalence of HIV/AIDS. Unwanted sex results in a higher risk of abrasion and bleeding and easier transmission of the virus. Women who are beaten by their partners are 48 percent more likely to be infected with HIV/AIDS (United Nations, 2008).

As in parts of the world where gender equality is more of a norm, some battered women resort to killing their battering partners. Kim and Titterington (2009) provide insights on intimate partner homicide by women in South Korea, a nation with strong traditional norms that emphasize male dominance. A strong emphasis on Confucianism means that interests of the family take precedence over individual interests. Their investigation parallels research in the United States comparing samples of battered women who killed their abusers with those who did not do so. The investigator's purpose was to see if, as in the United States, access to domestic violence services is associated with a decline in women's partner homicide. A sample of ninety-seven women in the South Korean prison for women and forty-three women from battered women's shelters were interviewed. The inmates who had killed their partners were found to hold stronger patriarchal attitudes than women in shelters and to be far less educated. (In private correspondence of February 10, the first author, Bitna Kim, revealed that these women had used knives or relied on third parties to do the killings; their pleas of self-defense were not accepted by the court.) Compared to the sample of shelter women, the incarcerated women had experienced more severe forms of violence, and they had believed themselves in danger from further harm. The results indicated, as in research in the West, that the socioeconomically disadvantaged apparently were less aware of other forms of escape other than resorting to homicide.

Honor Killing

In Pakistan, especially in southern Punjab province, women who are raped typically experience rejection by their family and society. Tribal traditions dictate that a raped woman is dishonored, cannot marry, and should be discarded, if not killed, by her family (Rupert, 2005). Suicide is common. This brings us to the tragic story of Dr. Shazia, a 32-year-old Pakistani physician (Equality Now, 2005). Her story began with rape in her home by an intruder. When she reported the crime to the police, her employers and the government pressured her to keep silent. Her husband was supportive, but her father-in-law declared that she was a stain on the family honor. When she pursued the case, the president announced on television that her life was in danger. Shazia contemplated suicide but then decided to emigrate instead in hopes of getting political asylum somewhere. To date, she has not been granted asylum in any country. Although in this case it was probably not her family members who threatened her life, women in Pakistan who have been raped are at risk of honor killing by a male relative for a perceived violation to the family honor. An estimated 1,000 honor killings take place each year in Pakistan.

Honor killing is the ancient practice in which men, often brothers, kill female relatives who have disgraced the family through sexual activity, even rape victimization. According to the World Health Organization (WHO), about 5,000 women are murdered by family members in the name of honor each year worldwide.

In Jordan, according to the Middle East Online (2008), between 15 and 20 women are murdered annually in the name of honor and at least eight such killings have been reported so far this year, according to Jordanian authorities. Last year, seventeen such murders were recorded. The United Nations has reported such crimes in Brazil, Britain, Ecuador, India, Israel, Italy, Sweden, and Uganda as well as in nations such as Morocco, Pakistan, and Turkey.

According to the news report, the label "honor killings" can be misleading in Jordan's male-dominated society. Judges, lawyers, activists, and experts agree that in many cases men exploit lenient laws to murder women for inheritance, settling family feuds, or to hide other crimes.

Amnesty International's (2001) report *Broken Bodies, Shattered Minds* was a complement to earlier reports of sexual abuse of women in custody and the use of sexual violence as a weapon of war. In providing the results of investigations of abuses committed by private individuals, of acts of torture against women in the home, this report shows that women at risk of violence require protection, whether through refugee services that grant them the right of political asylum or safe places such as women's shelters in their own countries. Escape through emigration may be the only recourse. This brings us to the topic of immigration and the kind of domestic violence to which immigrants are uniquely subject.

Immigration and Domestic Violence

Many factors, notes Hochschild (2003), contribute to what she calls "the growing feminization of migration" (p. 17). Economic opportunity is one such factor; romantic attachments and the promise of happiness in a land where women have more freedom undoubtedly are others. In her discussion of battered immigrant women, Gilfus (2002) describes how immigration status can be used as a weapon of abuse by husbands who threaten to destroy vital documents and by threats to turn their wives over to the Immigration and Naturalization Service for deportation. A power imbalance takes place here because immigration laws allow men to sponsor their wives and thus to control their wives' immigration status. Many women also fear that the batterer himself, due to his violent behavior, might be deported or leave the country, taking the children with him. In addition to difficulties encountered by all abused women, such as cultural attitudes that minimize or excuse victimization, immigrant women experience unique barriers that include language and communication problems, a lack of information about the legal process or availability of support and assistance, perceived or anticipated racism if they should venture out into the community on their own, and discrimination by the justice system.

A study of the experience of domestic violence among Cambodian refugees (who met in focus groups) revealed that, according to these women, such violence was often viewed as the woman's fault (Bhuyan et al., 2005). Divorced women faced disapproval within the community. The participants in the focus groups described extensive verbal abuse within their marriages. Some of the women described their husband's affairs with other women as a form of abuse. The women's wish for the future was for support from the community, not to end the marriage.

In her study of Vietnam, Bui (2003) stressed the impact of resettlement on the man's sense of control and the impact of exposure to racism and classism in the new society. Downward mobility, changes in gender-role practices, and role reversals may cause family conflict and lead to aggression in immigrant families. Data drawn from interviews with the women in Bui's study showed that wife abuse occurred within the context of adjustment to life in a new and frustrating environment. Loss of status emerged as a key aspect in the men's personal adjustment. Moreover, when Vietnamese American women changed their attitudes toward gender equality while their husbands did not, the men sometimes tried to assert their control through violence.

An interesting study from the Yale School of Public Health surveyed immigrant men from the Caribbean and Latin America (Yale University, 2008). Men who had experienced political violence in their homelands were found to be more than twice as likely as other men to report that they had abused their wives, physically or sexually, in the past year. Untreated mental or posttraumatic stress disorder (PTSD) was considered a likely factor.

Surveys of the general population suggest that victimization among recent immigrants and visible minorities is lower than other populations, although factors such as language spoken and a reluctance to participate in telephone surveys can impact the accuracy of victimization data (Statistics Canada, 2004). Reports of problems within the immigrant community, however, come from other sources. Cases of spousal abuse within the Punjabi community have been regularly reported in the Toronto newspapers. One such incident involved a woman from the East Indian community who was thrown off a balcony by her husband. Reading of such attacks on immigrant women, in fact, inspired Deepa Mehta, a writer and film producer, to make a movie, *Heaven on Earth* (Khorana, 2009). *Heaven on Earth* is the story of a young Punjabi woman who finds herself reduced to a despised servant and punching bag when she marries into an Indo-Canadian Indian family. Many of the abused women in this community were part of arranged marriages and cut all family ties when they left India, according to the article. In one's home country, if a man hurts a woman, there may be some sanction from the woman's family or community. But in Canada, such abuse of immigrant women who are culturally isolated and unable to speak the language of the country often goes undetected. Abusive men in all immigrant groups, in fact, can isolate their women by keeping them from learning the language of the adopted country (Smith, 2004). A major need in domestic violence services is for professionals who are fluent in the languages of the women seeking help. The present arrangements of using family members to translate violates confidentiality standards and sometimes leads to purposeful mistranslation. To enhance services to the East Indian women, several volunteers at a new shelter in the East Indian community of Toronto, described by Khorana, will speak Punjabi.

Erez, Adelman, and Gregory (2009) conducted research through bilingual interviewers of 137 immigrant women who sought help with immigration and/or domestic violence problems. Most had no access to a car and had worked in the home. Some had wed to escape a bad situation in the home country. Because of the dislocation, their risk of abuse was compounded; members of the husband's family often participated in the abuse. These women were both legally and economically dependent on their husbands. Some of the women attributed the abuse to the spouse's employment difficulties in the United States and also to conflict concerning sending money to relatives back home. The women, most of whom came from countries in which wife beating was not considered a crime, reported that they were grateful for the help they received through the U.S. justice system. The situation concerning undocumented immigrants is precarious, however, due to new laws and practices putting these women at risk of deportation.

Foreign wives of military men often have difficulties as well; one-eighth of the battered women in the study by Erez et al. were married to U.S. citizens, most of whom were in the military. In an earlier paper, Erez and Bach (2003) confirmed, based on in-depth interviews of ten immigrant women who were intimate partners of U.S. servicemen, that abuse of these "military brides" was a common occurrence. Here too, the women's immigrant status and the military context compounded the abuse. While we know that military men, especially those returning from war, often have problems with violence at home (Zamichow and Perry, 2003), foreign women are especially vulnerable. They may not speak the language, lack familiarity with American cultural norms and the law, and tend to be socially isolated and dependent for their immigration status on the man. Military men who choose to marry foreign women may be atypical Americans in the sense that they may expect that a foreign woman would be submissive as well as extremely grateful for the opportunity to have material comforts not available at home. Such men may be personally insecure, in other words, and therefore prone to overreact when they feel threatened through interpersonal conflicts. Some of the men, if war veterans, may also be suffering the after-effects of warfare, including war trauma. Let us now look more closely at what the experience of combat does to a relationship.

The Legacy of the Iraq War

Unique to the military is the training of men (and women) to kill. In warfare, the soldier kills almost as a reflex in a situation of danger. **Military socialization** "to make a man out of the boy" not only attempts to obliterate all that is feminine but also breeds misogynous heterosexuality in the soldier as well (Farr, 2005). The degradation of traits associated with femininity such as weakness in battle, squeamishness, and compassion—traditionally associated with femininity— helps create or preserve masculine detachment and aggression desirable for battle. Such conditioning can be devastating for later family functioning.

On the home front, a condition such as PTSD or a state of intoxication (even being suddenly aroused from sleep) can trigger violence. Depression related to PTSD can lead to suicide. Anderson (2005) studied the seven homicides and three suicides that have taken place in western Washington State by soldiers returning from the war in Iraq. Five wives, one girlfriend, and a child have all been killed. Two of the suicides were committed after murder.

In a recent *New York Times* article, Alvarez and Sontag (2008) discuss the spate of murders and murder suicides that have been committed by soldiers returning from combat. They describe, for example, the murder of Erin Edwards, herself a soldier who like her husband had served in Iraq. After being severely beaten by her husband, she left town and obtained a restraining order:

> On the morning of July 22, 2004, William Edwards easily slipped off base, skipping his anger-management class, and drove to his wife's house in the Texas town of Killeen. He waited for her to step outside and then, after a struggle, shot her point-blank in the head before turning the gun on himself. (p. A1)

This case was reminiscent of several murder suicides that took place within a six-week period in 2002 when three Special Forces sergeants returned from Afghanistan and murdered their wives at Fort Bragg in North Carolina. Two immediately turned their guns on themselves; the third hanged himself in a jail cell. A fourth soldier at the same Army base also killed his wife during those six weeks (Alverez and Sontag). There was a barrage of media attention to these homicides and much speculation about the link between combat duty and domestic violence when the men came home. But as Alverez and Sontag suggest, the war effort generally takes precedence over the welfare of the families involved.

These cases and others like them reported across the United States seem to suggest that as an antiwar slogan popular in the 1960s said, "War is not good for people or other living things."

COMMUNITY-LEVEL VICTIMIZATION: SEXUAL ASSAULT AND SEX TRAFFICKING

The crime of sexual abuse by a member or members of the community is an offense that exists along a continuum ranging from sexual harassment or the "little rapes" to full-blown sexual assault including gang rape. Both in the frequency of its occurrence and in the treatment accorded the victims, the facts (as provided by the United Nations [2008]) are disturbing:

- Women experience sexual harassment throughout their lives. Between 40 and 50 percent of women in the European Union reported some form of sexual harassment in the workplace. In Malawi, 50 percent of schoolgirls surveyed reported sexual harassment at school.
- In many places, laws contain loopholes that allow perpetrators to act with impunity. In a number of countries, a rapist can go free under the penal code if he marries the victim.
- In many societies, rape victims, women suspected of engaging in premarital sex, and women accused of adultery have been murdered by their relatives because the violation of a woman's chastity is viewed as an affront to the family's honor.
- Young women are particularly vulnerable to coerced sex and are increasingly being infected with HIV/AIDS. Over half of new HIV infections worldwide are occurring among young people between the ages of 15 and 24, and more than 60 percent of HIV-positive youth in this age bracket are female.

And from WHO (2005), we learn that many women said that their first sexual experience was not consensual. Surveys showed, for example, that 24 percent in rural Peru, 28 percent in Tanzania, 30 percent in rural Bangladesh, and 40 percent in South Africa reported sexual victimization of some sort.

Sex Trafficking

One of the tragedies of globalization and the free market economy is trade in human bodies and labor, from which huge profits are made by transnational criminals. In her paper presentation "Women as Victims and Survivors in the Context of Transnational Crime," Edna Erez (2000) argues that current global economic strategies and the power divide between first- and third-world countries reinforce the vulnerability of women through the introduction of so-called "structural adjustment" policies that remove social benefits at the social, economic, and political levels. In the former communist nations, for example, the adjustments are played out in women's higher unemployment rates and the elimination of child care options due to the breakdown of socialist infrastructures.

Sex trafficking is defined simply by Kathryn Farr (2005), the author of a book by that title, as "a business venture in which traffickers trade the sexualized bodies of others for money" (p. 2). As defined by WHO (2002), sexual trafficking "encompasses the organized movement of people, usually women, between countries and within countries for sex work" (p. 150). Between 500,000 and 2 million people, the majority of them women and children, are trafficked annually into situations including prostitution, forced labor, slavery or servitude, according to estimates provided by the United Nations (2008).

Girls and women are bought or kidnapped from poor countries such as Thailand, Nepal, or countries of the former Soviet Union to richer countries such as China, Germany, Japan, or the Netherlands. Israel is a major destination site for Russian and Ukrainian women. The women work for little or no pay, while the pimps earn thousands of dollars each week per prostitute. In *Global Woman: Nannies, Maids, and Sex Workers in the New Economy*, Ehrenreich and Hochschild (2003) write graphically of girls from rural areas of Thailand sold into sexual slavery. The girls are not allowed to use condoms; eventually most will die of AIDS.

Farr (2005) describes the various roles in the trafficking industry that range from recruiter to travel agent to transporter to employer (the employer sells the service to the customer and provides the women with a place to live and work). The recruiter typically puts together the book of photographs and other promotional material for mass distribution. The girls and women generally are recruited for prostitution through coercion or deception (usually regarding the nature of the work). Most of the women are controlled through threats and often severe violence. The majority live under a debt bondage system in which they are held in debt for their transportation and expenses. As Farr describes it, beatings take place because of rule violations, failure to please customers, indebtedness, or failure to report to the pimp on time.

The recently established Human Trafficking Reporting System recorded information on more than 1,200 alleged incidents of human trafficking. As reported by this system and announced in a press release by the Bureau of Justice Statistics (2009), from 2007 to 2008, for a period of eight months:

- Most (83 percent) of the reported human trafficking incidents involved allegations of sex trafficking. Labor trafficking accounted for 12 percent of incidents, and other or unknown forms of human trafficking made up the remaining 5 percent. About a third (32 percent) of the 1,229 alleged human trafficking incidents involved sex trafficking of children.
- More than a quarter of alleged sex trafficking incidents contained multiple victims. Over 90 percent of victims in both alleged and confirmed human trafficking incidents were female.
- Hispanic victims comprised the largest share (37 percent) of alleged sex trafficking victims. Asians made up 10 percent of alleged sex trafficking victims.

Other documentation of routine abuse of women trafficked in the United States shows that over 70 percent had been abused by their traffickers and/or pimps, often sexually. As Johnson (2009), reminds us, the horror of teen sex slavery is happening right here in the United States. As stated in the article that described a press conference in Columbus, Ohio:

Worldwide, human trafficking generates $9.5 billion, ahead of the arms trade and second among illegal trading only to drugs, said Kathleen Davis, a human-trafficking expert from Cincinnati. It might involve 300,000 children in the United States, some as young as 12. She said the FBI considers northwestern Ohio one of the "top recruiting locations" in the U.S. for underage prostitution. (p. B1)

Logan, Walker, and Hunt (2009) describe the extreme fear and sense of helplessness that keep the victims from breaking loose. Many are forced to engage in illegal activities such as drug use and prostitution so they dare not become visible to the authorities. Violence against the trafficked girls and women serves the purpose first of breaking them in, then of maintaining their submission and obedience (Farr, 2005). Examples from Nepal and India are especially horrific because they involve children sold to brothels such as one in Mumbai, India, where "tens of thousands of young women are displayed in row after row of zoo-like animal cages" (Farr, p. 39).

The very same forces that lead to the organization of the sex trade and to the male demand for it, as Farr indicates, are rooted in patriarchal constructs about women and men and the relations between them. Wartime prostitution and rape in war occur within the patriarchal structure of the military. This topic that Farr terms "the militarized view of women as both male property and inferior to men" (2005, p. 164) brings us to the third dimension of global victimization of women (the first two of which were victimization within the family and community-level victimization of sex trafficking). This is the level of violence by the state. Although much is being done globally by NGOs, to date only ninety-three states (of 191 reviewed) have some legislative provision prohibiting trafficking in human beings (United Nations, 2008).

VICTIMIZATION OF WOMEN AT THE STATE LEVEL

Under the category of **state violence**, Erez (2000) includes violence that is perpetrated or condoned by the state. Included under this rubric is rape committed during armed conflict or cultural wars, forced abortion or sterilization, and custodial rape and sexual harassment by police and prison officers. We start with the sexual defilement of women under the auspices of military structures. To the victors of military conquest, the enemy's property, including women, are seen as legitimate spoils of war, ripe for the taking (Farr, 2005). Sometimes, too, rape of the enemy's women is a deliberate strategy for winning the war.

Rape in War

Rape has long been used as a weapon of war. Women as old as grandmothers and as young as toddlers have routinely suffered violent sexual abuse at the hands of military and rebel forces (United Nations, 2008). An important but belated development in recent years was the recognition of rape of the enemy's women—a common occurrence during and after a war—as a war crime. The International War Crimes Tribunal in The Hague took a revolutionary step when three Bosnian soldiers were convicted of rape and sexual enslavement as crimes against humanity. The judgment followed years of lobbying by women's rights groups. Thanks to women's rights activists who have actively been involved in the establishment of the new International Criminal Court (ICC), the ICC prosecutor has appointed a special advisor on women's crimes to ensure that the rights of women survivors are represented (International Law Observer, 2008).

The advantage of an international tribunal is in sending a message worldwide that such violence is widely condemned and in the tribunal's image of impartiality. The "power of shame" can play a role both as an enforcement tool and in helping to impart justice to the victim population. An exciting development today is the establishment of a permanent world criminal tribunal, the ICC, based in The Hague, which now has jurisdiction over crimes against humanity committed by ratifying states and nationals of those states. As of March 2008, 106 nations are parties to the statute that established the international court (International Center for Criminal Law Reform and Criminal Justice Policy [ICCLR], (2008). Article 68(2) provides for measures to facilitate the testimony of victims of sexual violence. The Court is staffed with people knowledgeable in issues relating to violence against women, and there is to be a fair representation of both female and male judges at the Court. Unfortunately, the United States under the Bush administration expressed strong opposition to the existence of the world court and withdrew the U.S. signature on the treaty (Human Rights Watch, 2008). Recently, however, the Secretary of State Hillary Clinton expressed "great regret" that the United States is not a member of the international court (MacAskill, 2009). Whether or not membership will be enacted under the present administration remains to be seen. Despite the reluctance of the United States to join, the establishment of such a world court of justice, a dream ever since the United Nations was established, is a major victory for world peace and human rights.

The ICC, which has replaced the U.N. tribunals that have been convened on strictly an ad-hoc basis, has officially (in statutes seven and eight) declared rape, sexual slavery, enforced prostitution, forced pregnancy, enforced sterilization, or any other form of sexual violence as crimes against humanity and war crimes. The statute also provides a voice to victims to testify, to participate at all stages of the Court proceedings and to protect their safety and interests (ICCLR, 2008).

War rape of the enemy's women is so much a part of war and its aftermath that, under conditions of military occupation, it is more remarkable in its absence than in its presence. The rape that accompanies war involves both a tremendous act of aggression and humiliation against a conquered people and a reward to soldiers who are encouraged by their officers to loot a village and rape the women at will. Rape is the act of patriotism, misogyny, and lust combined. In the name of victory, war provides men with a tacit license to rape. In her analysis of rape in warfare, Brownmiller (1993) forcefully concludes:

> Rape of a doubly dehumanized object—as woman, as enemy—carries its own terrible logic. In one act of aggression, the collective spirit of women and of the nation is broken, leaving a reminder long after the troops depart. And if she survives the assault, what does the victim of wartime rape become to her people? Evidence of the enemy's bestiality. Symbol of her nation's defeat. A pariah. Damaged property. A pawn in the subtle wars of international propaganda. (p. 37)

Notably, in the battles of ancient Greece, the Crusades, the U.S. Civil War, World Wars I and II, and the Vietnam war, rape was utilized as a physical and psychological weapon of war. Within this context, it is not surprising to hear of mass rapes by all factions in the Bosnian and Rwandan conflicts. In Haiti, too, military rapists targeted women in terrorism preceding the recent government overthrow. Compounding the injury to the victims, the husbands often transfer their feelings of revulsion from the enemy to their victimized wives. Such rejection of women as defiled beings is consistent with traditional patriarchal ideology that universally demands that women should not allow more than one man to have access to their bodies.

Wing and Merchan (1993) drew a gripping parallel between the ethnic cleansing and forced impregnation in Bosnia and the history of rape and miscegenation in the American South. On six key attributes related to what Wing and Merchan call "spirit injury" or "the slow death of the psyche, of the soul, and of the identity of the individual" (p. 2) and of the group, the early American South and Bosnia share a common ground. These traits are rape as defilement not only of the individual woman but of a whole culture; rape as silence as the women internalize their experience of oppression, rendering them more vulnerable to males within their own group; rape as sexuality, with raped women seen as promiscuous and impure; rape as emasculation of men due to their sense of helplessness to protect their wives and daughters; rape as trespass on the "property" rights of men most pronounced under slavery where the women were the property of their white masters as were the racially mixed offspring; and rape as pollution of the victim and of her children born as a result of nonconsensual sex.

Rape as an instrument of war is clearly a violation of international law and its proscriptions against war crimes, taking of hostages, torture, and violation of human dignity. Deplorably, although torture has been prosecuted as a war crime, only recently has war rape been considered anything more than an inevitable byproduct of war. Now, at last, women's rights are seen as human rights. And justice and accountability for past abuses increasingly are seen as bedrock issues for human rights organizations everywhere and a vital protection against future abuses. That the ICC has come into force today as a potentially powerful instrument for protecting women's rights is a testament to the mass networking and courage of women's rights activists throughout the world (Human Rights Watch, 2002b).

In their investigation of the extent of rape in recent wars, the United Nations Office for the Coordination of Humanitarian Affairs (2004) relied on data that women's groups have managed painstakingly to piece together. As summarized by the U.N. office:

> An estimated half a million women were raped during the 1994 genocide in Rwanda. A staggering 50 percent of all women in Sierra Leone were subjected to sexual violence, including rape, torture and sexual slavery, according to a 2002 report by Physicians for Human Rights. In Liberia, an estimated 40 percent of all girls and women have fallen victim to abuse. During the war in Bosnia-Herzegovina in the 1990s, between 20,000 and 50,000 women were raped.
>
> Many researchers feel this is not just the result of violent male opportunism, but rather a weapon of war. This is particularly true of ethnic conflicts, during which systematic rape is commonly used to destabilize populations and destroy community and family bonds. Amnesty International now considers rape a commonly used tool for "ethnic cleansing," including the forced impregnation of girls.
>
> Rape is also used to humiliate and demoralize families and communities. In many cases, men are forced to watch the rape of their wives or daughters. In Bosnia-Herzegovina sons and fathers were forced to commit sexual atrocities against each other. (p. 1)

A contemporary interest in the social and cultural side of war has brought *A Woman in Berlin: Eight Weeks in the Conquered City* (Anonymous, 2005/1945) to the forefront of world consciousness. The anonymous author, a journalist, recorded the horrors of mass rape imposed on German women by Russian "liberators" during World War II. At the time of its original publication, the book was condemned for its shameless immorality in discussing what could not be discussed, not by Germans, and not by people who hated Germans (Dotinga, 2005). Written as an eight-week diary, *A Woman in Berlin* recorded stories of some of the 100,000 women in Berlin who were raped by drunken Russian soldiers. The author herself was raped by two Russians on the first day of the occupation. Later that day she offered to submit to a high-ranking Russian officer to get protection from multiple assailants. He took her up on the offer. The book was ahead of its time when it was first published and has only now with its reissue received the recognition it was due.

The story of the conquered Berlin women is echoed in more recent times in the Democratic Republic of Congo, in Darfur, in Sierra Leone, and in Liberia; whenever there is armed conflict women's bodies become targets of war. So widespread are such attacks on women that gender-based violence accounts for more death and disability worldwide among women aged fifteen to forty years old than cancer, malaria, traffic injuries, and war combined, according to the World Health Organization (United Nations Office for the Coordination of Humanitarian Affairs, 2004).

An academic study of mass war rape in Bosnia-Herzegovina is offered by Snyder et al. (2006). This study traces the history of the rise of ethnic nationalism that accompanied a complete rejection of state socialism in what used to be Yugoslavia. Gender equality that had been a hallmark of the communist government then took a backseat as well. The new task of womanhood was now to regenerate the nation through motherhood, not through careers. A strong antiabortion movement was mobilized as well in Croatia, Slovenia, and Serbia. Meanwhile, the feminist movement fractured along ethnic lines. Serbia's plan to establish a Greater Serbia and drive out the Muslims was thwarted in 1992 when Bosnia declared its independence from Yugoslavia. Within this context then, Serb nationalists launched a war that produced a campaign of killing and mass rape. While rapes were committed by men from all ethnicities, the vast majority were initiated by Serbs who attacked Muslim women during the Bosnian conflict. The Serbs' strategy included rape of women in front of their husbands and fathers, and confinement of women in rape camps for the purpose of impregnation with rape babies. From an ethnic cleansing perspective, the child assumes the nationality of the rapist. Snyder et al. put these events in perspective:

> The Bosnian conflict signaled the end of invisibility of women raped in war. No longer could war rape be viewed as an unfortunate by-product of war. It was now clear that it was being used as an intentional strategy to achieve genocide. (p. 191)

An especially odious development took place in the rape and genocide campaign during the civil war in Rwanda. Within the span of 100 days over 1 million people were killed (Hentz, 2005). The calculation of 1 million, however, does not include those women who were intentionally infected with HIV as a part of a calculated campaign to destroy Tutsi culture. Significantly, before the genocide took place, cartoons were printed depicting Tutsi women as sexual creatures who used their sexuality for political purposes. Testimony before the international tribunal, which in a landmark decision in 1998 declared rape an independent crime under international law, established that virtually every woman who survived the genocide was raped and that the crimes of gang rape, sexual torture and humiliation, and sexual slavery took place. Men who were HIV positive were paid by the Hutu government to rape Tutsi women.

The conflict raging in the eastern provinces of the Democratic Republic of the Congo is one of the most brutal wars in the world today. "Hundreds of Thousands of Women Raped for Being on the Wrong Side," proclaims a headline from *The Guardian* (McGreal, 2007). Four million people are thought to have perished in a civil war that raged throughout Congo from 1998 to 2002 and that continues today. As described by McGreal (2007):

> Rape has been used to terrorize and punish civilians in Congo who support the "wrong side," and it is perhaps no coincidence that it was also a tool of genocide in the mass murder of the Tutsis. Sexual violence is now so widespread that the medical aid charity, Medecins sans Frontieres, says that 75 percent of all the rape cases it deals with worldwide are in eastern Congo. Darfur is a distant second.

It is believed, according to the United Nations (2008), that tens of thousands of women have suffered from sexual violence in the Democratic Republic of the Congo since armed conflict began. The health consequences that can afflict those who survive mass rape in war are dire. One effect of sexual abuse is traumatic gynecologic fistula: an injury resulting from severe tearing of the vaginal tissues, rendering the woman incontinent and socially undesirable.

One of the long-term effects of war is the militarization of society. A militarizing society calls on patriarchal values and mechanisms of domination and control that heighten hierarchical relations between men and women. And sexual violence by marauding armies or militias can wreck or uproot communities with shame, turning the victims into outcasts (Economist, 2009).

Women, War, and Peace

The title for this section is taken from a book by Elisabeth Rehn of Finland and Ellen Johnson Sirleaf of Liberia. Commissioned by the United Nations Development Fund for Women (UNIFEM), Rehn and Sirleaf (2002) conducted an independent expert assessment on the gender dimensions of conflict. This effort parallels a new impetus by the U.N. Security Council to attend to the needs of war-affected women. *Women, War and Peace* documents in graphic detail the injustices inflicted on the bodies and lives of women stemming from the horrors of war and its aftermath. Women in war zones throughout the world shared the impact of armed conflict on their families. They told how militarization affected their sons, their husbands, and brothers—turning them into different, often explosive, and violent people. They described the unaccustomed roles they were required to fill as the peacetime infrastructure was destroyed. In the upheaval that follows war, women become especially vulnerable as the social and legal institutions are weakened.

Kavita Ramdas, President and CEO of the Global Fund for Women, who works with women's groups in Afghanistan, describes (in an interview with Vanden Heuvel, 2009) what war and the NATO occupation have done to women's lives in that country.

It's doubtful whether America's foreign policy has ever had the welfare of Afghan women at heart. As many Afghani women have said to us, "You know, you didn't even think about us 25 years ago," and then all of a sudden post 9-11, we're sending troops to Afghanistan and ostensibly we're very concerned about women. But there's very little willingness to really look at the implications of a military strategy on women's security. . . .

In most parts of the world, highly militarized societies in almost every instance lead to bad results for women. The security of women is not improved and in many instances it actually becomes worse.

What do I mean by that? Take, for example, Afghanistan. In 2003, almost every woman's group I met with in Afghanistan, which was already a few years after the initial invasion, said that although they were very grateful for the fact that the Taliban was gone, the presence of foreign troops in Afghanistan in general and in Kabul in particular had highly increased the incidence of both prostitution as well as trafficking. . . . I talked to so many women and women's organizations who've said, young girls sleep with a soldier in Kabul for $40, $50, which is more than their mothers could make as a teacher in a full month. That's the incidence of prostitution as a function of—people call it in the women's movement "survival sex." The trading of sex for food on a survival basis.

Then there is also trafficking which actually also increases because when there are military settlements, camps, barracks . . . criminal elements start bringing in women—forcibly or coercing them under other guises. Girls—in this case mainly from the Uzbek and Hazara tribes, as well as a number of Chinese girls in Kabul— are actually trafficked in to fill the "needs" of foreign troops. Very few Afghans can afford to actually pay for these kinds of services, so you have a situation where the main customers are the military troops.

The injury to women and their families can be seen as well in uprootedness; mental trauma; lack of food, potable water, and electricity; health problems stemming from exposure to chemicals such as uranium; violence and sexual assault in refugee camps; and the numbers of women resorting to sex work to feed their children. Eighty percent of the world's refugees are women and children.

Refugees from war in one land become immigrants in another land, often in Europe, the United States, and Canada. Refugee women are especially vulnerable to abuse, both in their travels across the world and in their detention as they seek asylum in circumstances that inevitably are less than hospitable.

Treatment of Immigrants in U.S. Detention

Female immigrants, including refugees in detention, are another group of women who have suffered serious human rights violations. Even before the war on terrorism was declared, brutal treatment of detained political refugees was the norm. Yet because the detainees are not U.S. citizens, they are considered to be outside the jurisdiction of the protections of the U.S. Constitution. They are not, however, outside the scope of international law.

Amnesty International, in its 1999 report *"Not Part of My Sentence": Violations of the Human Rights of Women in Custody*, expressed the following concern with reference to immigrants in detention:

> Women asylum seekers are often subjected to harsh treatment. While awaiting action
> on the INS claims, they often languish in penal institutions facing the same human
> rights violations all women prisoners face. Many times they are placed in cells with
> hardened criminals. (pp. 8, 9)

That conditions are no better today is revealed in a report in the *New York Times*. It describes the situation facing female immigrants who are detained at immigration centers in Arizona (Frosch, 2009). Mistreatment of the 3,000 or so women who are detained in this manner is not unusual. Researchers who examined the conditions facing the women found a lack of prenatal care, treatment for cancer and other serious diseases; one woman, for example, was denied treatment following abdominal pain for months that resulted from her having been forced to undergo genital mutilation in West Africa.

New harsh sentencing laws have created a special population of prisoners—immigrant prisoners—whom the federal government segregates from the rest of the prison population and turns over to private companies (Dow, 2004). (Advantages of privatization of prisons include cost savings and exemption of the government from lawsuits.) Since September 11, when U.S. national security became the top priority of the nation, the numbers of immigrants in detention have increased in conjunction with new antiterrorism laws. A search of the Web reveals numerous reports on the human rights violations, some in connection with facts that have come out in lawsuits. The American Civil Liberties Union (ACLU) (2008), in a first-of-its-kind study, has documented jail conditions and due process issues for immigrants contained in Massachusetts. Conditions at the jails violate rights as provided in the U.S. Constitution against cruel and unusual punishment. The report, "Detention and Deportation in the Age of ICE: Immigrants and Human Rights in Massachusetts," released on the 60th anniversary of the Universal Declaration of Human Rights, reveals the following violations of human rights at the jails:

- Locking up people for indefinite periods in overcrowded conditions, lack of access to bathrooms, and lack of access to private rooms to meet with attorneys;
- Abuse including threats, coercion, physical force, and use of racial and ethnic epithets;
- Denial of access to needed medical care;
- The housing of immigration detainees who have not been accused of a crime with convicted, violent criminal offenders.

GLOBAL INITIATIVES FOR RIGHTS AND JUSTICE

Although very little is being done to improve conditions for immigrants in detention in the United States by public officials, the United Nations and other international organizations are mounting campaigns to prevent further victimization of girls and women from the type of gender-based violence described in this chapter. The Coalition Against Trafficking in Women (CATW) (2008), for example, gathers information on trafficking in countries all over the world and organizes campaigns to combat trafficking. In a project in conjunction with the European Women's Lobby, the CATW is investigating the gaps in current anti-trafficking programs and policies that avoid focusing on gender equality, the demand for trafficked women, and the links between trafficking and prostitution. The project, as described by the United Nations (2008), will support NGOs working on these issues in 13 countries in Eastern Europe. The project aims to raise awareness about the root causes of prostitution and trafficking in women and children, and propose measures to discourage the *demand* for sexual exploitation such as the Swedish model of focusing on the men who engage in trafficking and the customers who make this trade profitable.

Political empowerment is seen in the transformation from individual and collective powerlessness to personal, political, and cultural power. Of special relevance to addressing victimization is the gaining of a sense of personal power, assuming responsibility for recovery, and change, which may entail carrying the message to others. Of special relevance to addressing criminal behavior, and without which change is unlikely, is the taking of personal responsibility for one's actions and one's life.

One model program that could be emulated elsewhere is offered by the International Rescue Committee (IRC) in Sierra Leone to aid the victims of war. Susan Koch (2003), a global health expert, describes the remarkable work performed by this organization. Originally founded by Albert Einstein, the IRC conducts a reunification project in war-torn Sierra Leone to reunite abducted girls and their families or help the girls receive education for a new life if family members can't be found. The matter of reunification is problematic because typically the girls who were kidnapped were sexually abused and used as sex slaves. Some families might refuse to take them back, seeing them as tainted or as changed. IRC works to locate the families. Videotapes are made of the girl talking about how much she wants to come home. The family sees this. Then if they are receptive, family members are videotaped saying how much they miss their daughter. To date, there have been sixty successful reunifications.

Other approaches to empowerment for survivors of war rape are described by Farwell (2004). A Rwandan women's NGO, the Association of Widows of Genocide, includes in its membership survivors who are taking care of orphans of extended family members. In Bosnia-Herzegovina, a center for traumatized displaced women staffed by women physicians and other professionals has treated tens of thousands of women. The team has offered treatment to Kosovan refugees as well.

Rehn and Sirleaf (2002) credit the United Nations for its expression of political commitment to women's special needs in war-torn societies. But, as the authors point out, the resources allocated to the relief efforts are entirely inadequate, and greater high-level support to effectively address the gender dimensions of war and peace are required. And women need to be at the forefront of any peacemaking and humanitarian relief efforts. In fact, the efforts of women's grass-roots movements, most notably women from countries of the Global South, are quite amazing.

The new feminist alliances, such as those that are conducting anti–violence-against-women campaigns throughout Latin America have helped to break the silence concerning gender violence as practiced at the state level and behind closed doors (Cole and Phillips, 2008). The discourse of women's rights as human rights has a powerful resonance in the new global era; it is thanks to women's collective militancy that the United Nations took as extensive a role as it did against gender violence across the globe. The mobilization of feminists working for gender equality and popular education teaches the impact of free trade mandates on women. Cole and Phillips single out Brazil and Ecuador as two countries where the impact of the women's movement has been especially pronounced.

Women's organizations, as Farwell argues, must go beyond therapy; they need to engage in a range of strategies to combat war rape and address its cause and consequences. One such strategy, which the Women's Rights International uses, is the collection of extensive documentation of human rights violations against women to focus attention on the pervasiveness of sexual crimes in wartime. As feminists with a global perspective, Farwell further suggests we need to examine the causal connections between burgeoning militarism and all forms of violence against women.

Two innovative models from abroad are the all-women police stations in Brazil and an all-female village in Kenya. In Brazil, more than 300 **women's police stations** have opened. Women who have been attacked go to these stations, where they know they will be heard (Downie, 2005). In the past, such crimes long went unreported largely because of Brazil's macho culture and the legal system's leniency for male offenders. This innovation has been modeled now in at least ten nations in Latin America and Asia. The women go to these stations, not to end the relationship but to stop the violence. This process empowers the woman and holds the man accountable. The all-female village of thirty-six women at Umoja, Kenya, was formed ten years ago by a group of homeless women who were abandoned by their husbands after they were raped (Feminist Majority Foundation, 2005). This village continues to serve as a safe haven for women escaping violence, including genital mutilation.

The United Nations (2008) brings our attention to active NGO units in Egypt mobilized against genital mutilation and the "One-Stop Crisis Centre" of integrated health services for rape victims in Malaysian hospitals. In Upper Egypt, NGOs used community mobilization to inform local and religious leaders of the adverse effects of female genital mutilation/cutting and to call for an end to the practice. First developed in Malaysia, the One-Stop Crisis Centre model is currently being replicated in much of Asia as well as in other countries, including South Africa.

An increasing number of education initiatives focus on masculinity and working with men and boys. For example, a program in Nicaragua for fifteen- to twenty-five-year-old youths sought to change their attitudes to gender relations (United Nations Interregional Crime and Justice Research [UNICRI, 2008]). Run by a Nicaraguan NGO specializing in communication between the sexes using popular education, the program offered courses on masculinity for young men. An evaluation found considerable changes in attitudes among participants. The United Nations has highlighted the need to work with men to address violence against women, and the UN International Research and Training Institute for the Advancement of Women (UNICRI, 2008) provides guidelines.

Restorative Justice

In an aboriginal peacekeeping circle, members of the community open the session with a prayer and reminder that the circle has been convened to discuss the behavior of a young man who assaulted his sister in a drunken rage; an eagle feather is passed around the circle, held by each speaker as he or she expresses feelings about the harmful behavior. This process is about reconciliation and the healing of wounds. It is about restoring the balance or the sense of justice that was lost.

Restorative justice, as we learned in Chapter 7, is a broad term that refers to various strategies to find solutions to criminal and human rights violations. Both an ideal principle—providing justice to the offender, victim, and community—and a method of dispensing justice when a violation has been committed, restorative justice can be considered a form of social justice because of its fairness to all parties.

Where there has been victimization and possible trauma, rituals are needed to "heal the damaged souls of the people, to help them find ways to transform hatred into sorrow or forgiveness, to be able to move forward with hope rather than wallow in the evil of the past" (Braithwaite, 2002, p. 207). When the state is the culprit, restorative justice means reparations for the human rights violations that occurred. Reparations may take the form of governmental acceptance of responsibility for the wrongs done, often following a national inquiry. The victims may even be later generations; the descendants of the original injured parties may be the actual complainants. The complaint is often filed in court through an attorney. The connection to restorative justice is in the aim of reparation or restoring what is due to victims. Moreover, as with other forms of restorative justice, the movement for reparations is a grassroots movement for social justice.

A key theme with respect to ending conflict and healing wounds is forgiveness in communities and societies. Russell Daye (2004) introduces the notion of **political forgiveness**, which he describes as a form of deep reconciliation, a kind of social healing. South Africa set the stage for such a process of social healing in the post-apartheid era, especially through the principles and practice of the Truth and Reconciliation Commission. Truth commissions investigate situations of gross human rights violations and serve to validate the experiences of victims and propose ways to repair the harm.

Modeled on the truth-seeking efforts in South Africa, the Peruvian Truth and Reconciliation Commission specifically addressed sexual violence against women that had been inflicted on them by warring factions. This commission issued its final report in 2003. The report, following those investigating war rape in Rwanda and Bosnia, documented that rape was used as a deliberate tactic of war to degrade the population and punish women who were members of subversive groups (Falcón, 2005). These special courts were the first to investigate the use of rape as an instrument of war. A similar body for Sierra Leone won the first conviction ever for sex slavery (Economist, 2009). In the future, the ICC at The Hague will handle such matters. Another positive development took place in 2008 when the UN Security Council adopted a resolution affirming that sexual violence as a weapon of war affects international peace and security and can trigger sanctions.

All of these initiatives (including the women's police stations and women's village) meet the criteria recommended by Erez (2000) of indigenous solutions to women's victimization. At the macro level, establishing gender equality and economically viable options for women is an essential step in reducing victimization, particularly regarding sex trafficking. As Erez suggests:

> The extent of women's victimization should serve as a barometer for the country's compliance with human rights laws, or conversely, as its record of human rights violations. Visions for international cooperation on ways to reduce women's victimization, empower women and girls, increase their independence and autonomy, and preserve their integrity and dignity, should be top priorities of the international community. (p. 5)

Summary

This chapter, following Erez's organizational scheme for examining women's victimization globally (what we might term "the world's war against women"), has discussed family, community, and state victimization, respectively. The starting point was globalization, a force that enters into the equation in terms of economically restricting poor women's progress as they live at the bottom end of the market economy, while also making mass organization on their behalf possible through the communications revolution.

Under family violence, we looked at such violations as genital mutilation in Egypt, wife beating among ethnic groups in Canada, honor killing in Pakistan, and the plight of battered immigrant women married to American soldiers. Sex trafficking was the example of community-level victimization, a phenomenon closely tied to global markets, a transportation of women from struggling nations to richer ones. At the state level, we focused on rape as an act of war, militarization in general, and the mistreatment of female immigrants in U.S. detentions.

This chapter discussed innovative programming to protect women with an emphasis on global restorative justice processes at the societal level. It highlighted restorative justice because of its truth-telling and healing attributes. The South African Truth and Reconciliation Commission served as the model. The chapter also described empowerment strategies from Africa and Latin America.

Central to this chapter was the theme of human rights: rights inscribed in international laws to protect women and other marginalized populations from abuse. The Beijing Fourth World Conference in 1995 marked a milestone in women's rights history as women of the world let go of their cultural differences and stood united against antiwoman violence, whether in the home or community. Still the horror stories persist—the infanticides in China of unwanted girls, the public stoning of rape victims in Pakistan, and so on. A promising development is the founding of the ICC, which will investigate war rape as a war crime and crime against humanity. Meanwhile, NGOs such as Human Rights Watch and Amnesty International inform the media and report to the United Nations on human rights violations across the globe that they have investigated. The days of looking the other way out of respect for cultural practices in the interests of cultural autonomy are over. Change will only come through international unity against the forces of oppression.

United under the banner of a human rights framework, feminists in collaboration with oppressed minorities and other allies are challenging governments to honor the rights of their citizens. Such a global, human rights perspective provides for justification for demands of social justice by drawing on principles from a higher authority. Just as the demands of social justice are new, so we must think anew. And such new thinking is enhanced through the globalization of information through the new communications technologies.

Key Terms

economic globalization *282*
femicide *280*
gender-based violence *281*
genital mutilation *287*
globalization *279*

honor killing *291*
military socialization *293*
political forgiveness *304*
restorative justice *304*
sex trafficking *295*

state violence *296*
war rape *297*
women's police stations *303*
World Health Organization
    (WHO) *286*

Critical Thinking Questions

1. What is the nature of female victimization worldwide? What are some of the barriers to women's reporting such victimization?
2. How can crime be gender based? How about male victimization?
3. Argue either for cultural relativism or a modern human rights perspective concerning some practices in nonindustrialized parts of the world.
4. Consider the jurisdiction of the International Criminal Court and the reluctance of the United States to join this body. Consider also the unofficial role of the United States as the world's primary policing structure. Is this arrogance or altruism?
5. What are some parallels of mistreatment of women globally discussed in this chapter and within the United States as revealed in early chapters?

6. Research rape in one war of interest. Is war rape simply collateral damage of war or a deliberate use of women for dehumanization or both?
7. Discuss marriages of immigrant women with U.S. soldiers and to what extent these arrangements are successful or problematic.
8. Check out the Universal Declaration of Human Rights on the Internet and its civil and social provisions. Are there some rights spelled out in this document that Americans lack?
9. What lessons can be learned from abroad that are relevant to empowerment of women?

Web Destinations

Amnesty International: www.amnesty.org

Captive Women Rescue: www.captivedaughters.org

Coalition Against Women in Trafficking: http://www.catwinternational.org

Demanding human rights for women and families around the world: www.madre.org

Equality Now: www.equalitynow.org

Feminist Majority Foundation: www.feminist.org

Human Rights Watch: www.hrw.org

International Victimology Web site: www.victimology.nl

Minnesota Restorative Justice: www.doc.state.mn.us

Restorative Justice Resources: www.restorativejustice.org

UN Universal Declaration of Human Rights: www.un.org

Women's Human Rights: www.whrnet.org

World Health Organization: www.who.org

References

Alvarez, L., and Sontag, D. (2008, February 15). When strains on military families turn deadly. *The New York Times*, pp. A1, A14, A15.

American Civil Liberties Union (ACLU). (2008, December 10). ACLU report blasts violations of basic rights for hundreds of immigrants detained in

Massachusetts. Retrieved February 2009 *from* http://www.aclum.org/ice/documents/20081210_aclu_ice_report_news_release.pdf

Amnesty International. (1999). *Not part of my sentence: Violations of human rights of women in custody.* New York: Amnesty International.

Amnesty International. (2001). *Broken bodies, shattered minds: Torture and ill treatment of women*. New York: Amnesty International.

Amnesty International. (2007). *Council of Europe convention against trafficking*. New York: Amnesty International.

Anderson, R. (2005, September 6). Home front casualties. *Seattle Weekly*. Retrieved August 2009 from http://www.seattleweekly.com/2005-08-31/news/home-front-casualties

Andronici, J. (2009, winter). A women's bill of rights. *Ms Magazine*, pp. 12–13.

Anonymous. (2005/1945). *A woman in Berlin: Eight weeks in the conquered city*. New York: Metropolitan Books.

Banister, J. (2004). Shortage of girls in China today. *Journal of Population Research 21*(1): 19–45.

Bhuyan, R., Mell, M., Senturia, K., Sullivan, M., and Shiu-Thornton, S. (2005, August). "Women must endure according to their karma." *Journal of Interpersonal Violence 20*(8): 902–921.

Braithwaite, J. (2002). *Restorative justice and responsive regulation*. Oxford, U.K.: Oxford University Press.

Brownmiller, S. (1993). Making female bodies the battlefield. *Newsweek*, p. 37.

Bui, H. (2003). Immigration context of wife abuse: A case of Vietnamese immigrants in the United States. In R. Muraskin (ed.), *It's a crime: Women and justice* (pp. 394–410). Upper Saddle River, NJ: Prentice Hall.

Bureau of Justice Statistics (BJS). (2009, January 15). More than 1,200 incidents of human trafficking reported in the U.S. Press Release. Washington, DC: U.S. Department of Justice. Retrieved February 2009 from http://www.ojp.usdoj.gov/bjs/pub/press/cshti08pr.htm

Canadian Centre for Justice Statistics. (2008). *Family violence in Canada: A statistical profile 2008*. Ottawa: Minister of Industry.

Center for Criminal Law Reform and Criminal Justice Policy (ICCLR). (2008, March). *International criminal court manual for the ratification and implementation of the Rome statute*, 3rd ed. Retrieved August 2009 from http://www.icclr.law.ubc.ca/Publications/Reports/ICC%203rd%20Ed%20Manual%20for%20Website.pdf

Coalition Against Trafficking in Women (CATW). (2008). Measures to combat trafficking in human beings for sexual exploitation. CATW. Retrieved February 2009 from http://www.catwinternational.org/campaigns.php#prevent

Cole, S., and Phillips, L. (2008). The violence against women campaigns in Latin America. *Feminist Criminology 3*: 145–168.

Dawson, M., Bunge, V., and Balde, T. (2009). National trends in intimate partner homicides: Explaining declines in Canada, 1976 to 2001. *Violence Against Women 15*(3): 276–306.

Daye, R. (2004). *Political forgiveness: Lessons from South Africa*. Maryknoll, NY: Orbis Books.

DeMause, L. (2002, Spring). The childhood origins of terrorism. *Journal of Psychohistory 29*(4): 340–348.

Dominelli, L. (2002). *Feminist social work theory and practice*. Hampshire, U.K.: Palgrave.

Dotinga, R. (2005, September 14). Wartime memoirs by women in vogue. *Christian Science Monitor*, p. 15.

Dow, M. (2004). *American gulag: Inside U.S. immigrant prisons*. Berkeley, CA: University of California Press.

Downie, A. (2005, July 20). A police station of their own. *Christian Science Monitor*, p. 15.

Economist. (2009, February 21). Women and children worst. *The Economist*, p. 61.

Ehrenreich, B., and Hochschild, A. (eds.). (2003). *Global woman: Nannies, maids, and sex workers in the new economy*. New York: Metropolitan Books.

Equality Now. (2005, August). Pakistan: The Hudood ordinances—Denial of justice for rape. Equality Now. Retrieved August from http://www.equalitynow.org/reports/annualreport_2005.pdf

Erez, E. (2000, April 10–17). Women as victims and survivors in the context of transnational crime. Paper presented at the 10th U.N. Congress on Crime Prevention and the Treatment of Offenders, Vienna, Austria.

Erez, E., Adelman, M., and Gregory, C. (2009). Intersections of immigration and domestic violence: Voices of battered immigrant women. *Feminist Criminology 4*: 32–56.

Erez, E., and Bach, S. (2003). Immigration, domestic violence, and the military: The case of "military brides." *Violence Against Women 9*(9): 1093–1117.

Europe News. (2009, January 28). Italy: 600 girls at risk of FGM (Female Genital Mutilation). *Europe News*. Retrieved February 2009 from http://europenews.dk/en/node/18972

Falcón, J. (2005). The Peruvian truth and reconciliation commission's treatment of sexual violence against women. *Human Rights Brief 12*(2): 1–4.

Farr, K. (2005). *Sex trafficking: The global market in women and children*. New York: Worth.

Farwell, N. (2004). War rape: New conceptualizations and responses. *Affilia 19*(4): 389–403.

Faye, C. G. (2008). The real girl power. United Nations Girls' Education Initiative. Retrieved April 2009 from http://www.ungei.org/infobycountry/usa_2093.html

Feminist Majority Foundation. (2005, July 14). All-female African village thriving after 10 years. *Feminist Daily News Wire*. Retrieved August 2009 from http://www.msmagazine.com/news/uswirestory.asp?id=9160

Ford, A. (2009, winter). Too young to marry: Child brides are stripped of their rights, their health, their lives. *Ms Magazine*, pp. 30–31.

Friedman, T. (2005). *The world is flat: A brief history of the 21st century*. New York: Farrar, Straus and Giroux.

Frosch, D. (2009, January 20). Report faults treatment of women held at immigration centers. *New York Times*. Retrieved August 2009 from http://www.nytimes.com/2009/01/21/us/21immig.html?_r=1

Gilfus, M. (2002). Women's experiences of abuse as a risk factor for incarceration. *National Electronic Network on Violence against Women*. Retrieved August 2009 from http://new.vawnet.org/category/Main_Doc.php?docid=412

Griswold, E. (2003, September). Where the Taliban roam. *Harpers*, pp. 57–65.

Hentz, J. (2005). The impact of HIV on the rape crisis in the African Great Lakes region. *Human Rights Brief 12*(2): 12–15.

Hochschild, A. (2003). Love and gold. In B. Ehrenreich and A. Hochschild (eds.), *Global woman: Nannies, maids, and sex workers in the new economy* (pp. 15–30). New York: Metropolitan Books.

Home Office (UK). (2008, November). Domestic Violence Mini-Site. Retrieved February 2009 from http://www.crimereduction.homeoffice.gov.uk/dv/dv01.htm

Human Rights Watch. (2002a). Human Rights Watch world report: United States. Retrieved August 2009 from http://www.hrw.org/legacy/wr2k2/

Human Rights Watch. (2002b, July 1). International justice for women: The ICC marks a new era. Retrieved August 2009 from http://www.hrw.org/en/reports/2002/07/01/international-justice-women-icc-marks-new-era

Human Rights Watch. (2007). *Keep mentally ill out of solitary confinement*. Human Rights Watch. Retrieved February 2009 from http://www.hrw.org/en/news/2007/07/19/keep-mentally-ill-out-solitary-confinement

Human Rights Watch. (2008, July 10). ICC: Good progress amid missteps in first five years. Retrieved August 2009 from http://www.hrw.org/en/news/2008/07/10/icc-good-progress-amid-missteps-first-five-yearsInternational

International Law Observer. (2008, December 5). The ICC prosecutor's appointment of a special advisor on women's crimes. Retrieved August 2009 from http://internationallawobserver.eu/2008/12/05/the-icc-prosecutors-appointment-of-a-special-advisor-on-gender-crimes/

Israel News. (2006, October, 17). Knesset approves harsh punishments for human trade. YNet News. Retrieved February 2009 from http://www.ynetnews.com/articles/0,7340,L-3316286,00.html

Johnson, A. (2009, January 25). Horror of teen sex slavery not foreign woe; It's here. *The Columbus Dispatch* (Ohio), p. B1.

Kambayashi, T. (2004, February 24). A defender for Japan's battered women. *Christian Science Monitor*. Retrieved August 2009 from http://www.csmonitor.com/2004/0204/p11s01-lifp.html

Kennedy, M. (2004, Spring). Cheaper than a cow. *Ms*, pp. 50–53.

Khorana, S. (2009, February). Maps and moves: Talking with Deepa Mehta. *Bright Lights Film Journal, issue 63*. Retrieved February 2009 from http://www.brightlightsfilm.com/63/63mehtaiv.htmlimmigrant

Kim, B., and Titterington, V. (2009). Abused South Korean women: A comparison of those who do and those who do not resort to lethal violence. *International Journal of Offender Therapy and Comparative Criminology 53*: 93–112.

Koch, S. (2003, May 15). Women, war, and peace. Paper presented at the May Institute, University of Northern Iowa, on Peace, Human Rights and U.S. Foreign Policy.

LaFraniere, S. (2005, August 11). Entrenched epidemic: Wife-beatings in Africa. *New York Times*, p. A1.

Landsberg, M. (2002, September 8). Afghan women remain victims of hope unfulfilled. *Toronto Star*, p. A2.

Logan, T., Walker, R., and Hunt, G. (2009). Understanding human trafficking in the United States. *Trauma, Violence, & Abuse 10*: 3–30.

MacAskill. (2009, August 6). Clinton: It is a "great regret" the U.S. is not in international criminal court. The Guardian. Retrieved August 2009 from http://www.guardian.co.uk/world/2009/aug/06/us-international-criminal-court

McFarlane, A. (2008, November 7). Special courts target domestic violence. *BBC News*. Retrieved February 2009 from http://news.bbc.co.uk/2/hi/uk_news/7713821.stm

McGreal, C. (2007, November 12). Hundreds of thousands of women raped for being on the wrong side: Sexual violence in the Democratic Republic of Congo. *The Guardian*. Retrieved February 2009 from http://www.guardian.co.uk/world/2007/nov/12/congo.international

Middle East Online. (2008, September 3). Jordan "honour killings" cover for other crimes. Retrieved February 2009 from http://www.middle-east-online.com/english/?id=27668

Morrison, A., Ellsburg, M., and Bott, S. (2007, May 7). *Addressing gender-based violence: A critical review of interventions*. The World Bank Research Observer. Retrieved February 2009 from http://wbro.oxfordjournals.org/cgi/reprint/lkm003v1

National Association of Social Workers (NASW). (2006). International policy on human rights. In *Social work speaks: National Association of Social Workers policy statements 2006–2009* (pp. 230–238). Washington, DC: NASW Press.

Rastogi, M., and Therly, P. (2006). Dowry and its link to violence against women in India. *Trauma, Violence & Abuse 7*(1): 66–77.

Rehn, E., and Sirleaf, E. J. (2002). *Women, war and peace: The independent expert's assessment on the impact of armed conflict on women and women's role in peace-building*. New York: United Nations Development Fund for Women.

Rupert, J. (2005, March 29). Report from Pakistan. Pakistani women: A cruel repression. Newsday. Retrieved from http://web.lexis-nexis.com

Smith, E. (2004). *Nowhere to turn? Responding to partner violence against immigrant and visible minority women*. Ottawa: Canadian Council on Social Development. Retrieved February from http://www.ccsd.ca/pubs/2004/nowhere/voices.pdf

Snyder, C. S., Gabbard, W. J., May, D., and Zulic, N. (2006). On the battleground of women's bodies: Mass rape in Bosnia-Herzegovina. *Affilia 21*(2): 184–195.

Statistics Canada. (2004). Juristat: Victim services in Canada by Rebecca Kong Catalogue no. 85-002, Vol. 24, no. 11. Retrieved February 2009 from http://www.statcan.gc.ca/pub/85-002-x/85-002-x2004011-eng.pdf

Statistics Canada. (2005). *Family violence in Canada: A statistical profile 2005*. Ottawa: Statistics Canada.

Stiglitz, J. (2007). *Making globalization work*. New York: W.W. Norton.

Subler, J. (2008, November 27). Trafficked Vietnamese women rescued in China. *International Herald Tribune-Asia-Pacific*. Retrieved from http://www.iht.com/articles/reuters/2008/11/27/asia/OUKWD-UK-CHINA-VIETNAM-KIDNAPPINGS.php

Tarabay, J. (2009, January 28). Man accused of killing daughter for family honor. National Public Radio (NPR).

The Family Violence Prevention Fund. (2008, January). Facts about safe motherhood. Retrieved April 2009 from http://www.unfpa.org/mothers/facts.htm

United Nations. (1948). *Universal declaration of human rights*. Resolution 217A (III). New York: United Nations.

United Nations. (1989). *Convention on the rights of the child* (U.N. Document A/res/44/23). New York: United Nations.

United Nations. (2005, October 12). The promise of equality: Gender equity, reproductive health and the millennium development goals. *The State of World Population 2005*. New York: United Nations Population Fund.

United Nations. (2007, January). *Ending violence against women: From words to action*. Geneva: United Nations Press.

United Nations. (2008, February). *Unite to end violence against women*. Fact Sheet. Retrieved February 2009 from http://www.un.org/women/endviolence/docs/VAW.pdf

United Nations Children's Fund (UNICEF). (2003). *The state of the world's children 2003*. New York: UNICEF.

United Nations Interregional Crime and Justice Research (UNICRI). (2008). *Eliminating vioence against women: Forms, strategies, and tools*. UNICRI. Retrieved February 2009 from http://www.unicri.it/wwk/publications/books/docs/eliminating_violence.pdf

United Nations Office for the Coordination of Humanitarian Affairs. (2004). Our bodies—Their battle ground: Gender-based violence in conflict zones. *Integrated Regional Information Networks*. Retrieved from www.irinnews.org/webspecials

United Nations Population Fund (UNFPA). (2008, January). Facts about safe motherhood. UNFPA. Retrieved April 2009 from http://www.unfpa.org/mothers/facts.htm

Vanden Heuvel, K. (2009, February 2). Helping Afghan women and girls. *The Nation*. Retrieved February 2009 from http://www.thenation.com/blogs/edcut/404388/helping_afghan_women_and_girls

van Wormer, K. (2004). *Confronting oppression, restoring justice: From policy analysis to social action*. Alexandria, VA: Council on Social Work Education.

Wing, A., and Merchan, S. (1993). Rape, ethnicity, and culture: Spirit injury from Bosnia to Black America. *Columbia Human Rights Law Review 25*(1): 1–46.

Women's Action. (2005, June). Ethiopia: Abduction and rape. *Equality Now*. Retrieved August 2009 from http://www.equalitynow.org/english/actions/action_2204_en.html

World Health Organization (WHO). (2002). *World report on violence and health*. Geneva: WHO.

World Health Organization (WHO). (2005). WHO multi-county study on women's health and domestic violence against women. Geneva: WHO. Retrieved February 2009 from http://www.who.int/gender/violence/who_multicountry_study

World Health Organization (WHO). (2008). *Eliminating female genital mutilation: An interagency statement*. Geneva: WHO.

Yale University. (2008, November 6). Office of Public Affairs. Political violence may predict intimate partner abuse among immigrants. Retrieved February 2009 from http://opa.yale.edu/news/article.aspx?id=6195

Zamichow, N., and Perry, T. (2003, June 25). Home is where the hurt is. *The Los Angeles Times*, p. A1.

PART

V

Women as Professionals

The three chapters of this part—on the woman police officer, the woman lawyer, and the woman who works in corrections—have many similarities. They examine the role behavior of women who are attempting to break into a male subculture, one that sees itself as reserved for males. Women lawyers appear to have had the greatest success in breaking into this man's world, but women probation and parole officers have also been widely accepted, both by fellow workers and by clients. Women police officers have had the most difficulty in breaking into the men's club of policing, but women correctional officers in men's prisons are not far behind in encountering barriers and obstacles created by male corrections staff. In addition to the lack of acceptance that women have experienced, sexual harassment, especially in policing and in men's prisons, has posed a real problem for women who are employed in these fields.

Racial discrimination has joined with gender and culture in revealing the oppression that women professionals experience. The African American woman who is a police officer experiences even less acceptance in police agencies than does the white woman who is a police officer. She frequently feels alienated from white male and female officers and often even from African American male officers. In law school, the African American woman may experience discrimination in areas ranging from acceptance to admittance to student study groups. Subsequent to law school, this pattern of racial discrimination extends to limited opportunities for African American women attorneys to practice in high-status, financially remunerative, and powerful positions.

11

Women in Law Enforcement

There are important tasks in understanding the role of the police in the United States. Policing in this nation must be examined within the context of a free and democratic society. It was decided early in the history of this nation that the prevention of crime was the proper role of government. If that could not be accomplished, then moderate rather than severe punishment was more fitting for a free and democratic society. Another early belief was that government is best that governs the least (Law Enforcement Ethics Center, 1997). A further belief was that the authority of the state should be limited and, until suspects of crime were convicted in a court of law, the freedoms guaranteed them in the Constitution were to be zealously protected. Finally, it was held that police power must be regarded with grave suspicion in democratic societies. This is particularly true because of the enormous political power given to police officers. They are granted the authority to detain and arrest, to search for and seize evidence, and to use deadly force. See Box 11.1 for what one police officer says about the challenges and satisfactions of his job.

This veteran police officer is making several important statements about becoming a police officer. He is contending that policing "gets into the blood and possesses the spirit," and that once you become a police officer, you become the job and the job becomes you. In the words of this interviewee, policing is "not a job but a vocation." It becomes a calling, rather than a set of bureaucratically defined duties. Indeed, it is a calling remaining with officers until the day they die. Like a mental patient and a criminal, who always take the labels of *ex-patient* and *ex-offender* with the cop who leaves policing is still the ex-cop.

BOX 11.1

Excitement about Being a Cop

"How does one explain the raw excitement of being a cop? This is an excitement so powerful that it consumes and changes the officer's personality. For the officer, all five senses are involved, especially in dangerous situations. They are stirred in a soup of emotions and adrenaline and provide an adrenaline rush that surpasses anything felt before. You are stronger and more agile; your mind functions on a higher level of quickness and alertness. Afterwards, the grass seems greener, the air fresher, food tastes better, and the spouse and children are even more precious. It is an addictive feeling that makes the runner's high in comparison feel like a hangover. Police work gets into the blood and possesses the spirit. You become the job and the job becomes you, until the day you die."

Source: Anonymous line police officer, personal interview, 1997.

It is not surprising then that becoming a police officer is looked upon as a promising career for increasing number of women. Beyond the excitement of policing, there are others reasons why this is an attractive career for women. The first and obvious answer is the freedom to have the same privileges, rights, and responsibilities that men have (Schaper, 1997, p. 32). Pure economics is a second reason. The pay is good in most agencies, benefits are usually excellent, and it is a secure job once you have passed probation (Harrington, 2004, p. 2). A third, and perhaps even more important, reason many women enter policing is that they have a lot of enthusiasm for and commitment to becoming police officers. They see policing as a career in which they can make a difference, or they may anticipate that policing is an exciting job. Similar to men entering policing, women want to put the uniform on and feel that adrenaline rush when the action goes down. Or they may be attempting to prove something, for example, that they can do this job just as well as men can.

However, entry into the men's club of policing is difficult for a woman. The resistance to entering this male-dominated world seems to continue throughout a woman's career. The difficulty of finding acceptance may start on the first day in the academy and not end until retirement. The problematic nature of policing as a career for women further expresses itself in the appraisal process of new recruits, in supervisory attitudes and treatment, in attitudes of male line police officers, and in promotional opportunities and career advancement. Reluctance to accept a woman police officer extends also to citizens in the community.

Another expression of the problematic nature of policing for women involves the career adjustments women face to make it as police officers. Even though a number of studies reveal that female police officers are equally as competent as male police officers, policewomen typically feel that they must prove themselves over and over. Women police officers often feel that they must display and identify with a "masculine" role (competency, intelligence, and independence), but the danger is that this may result in their being typecast as pushy, unfeminine, and aggressive (Lord, 1995, p. 631). Women police officers also must decide whether they want to be respected as crime fighters and work with the men or become specialists in community-oriented policing, in juveniles, or in vice. Policewomen must further find ways to establish their own networks and support groups, because they have been excluded from the male-dominated police culture.

In addition, the majority of women acknowledge that they have experienced abuse and sexual harassment and that each woman police officer must decide how much is too much. Susan L. Webb (1994) defines **sexual harassment** as:

1. The behavior in question is sexual in nature.
2. The behavior is deliberate and/or repeated.
3. The behavior is not welcome or asked for and is not returned.
4. The more severe the behavior is, the fewer times it needs to be repeated before it can be reasonably defined as harassment, and the less responsibility the receiver has to speak up.
5. The less severe the behavior is, the more times it needs to be repeated, and the more responsibility the receiver has to speak up (pp. 26–29).

A HISTORY OF WOMEN IN POLICING

The policewomen's movement can be traced to demands of benevolent groups for prison, jail, and police matrons. In the 1820s volunteer Quaker women, along with upper-middle-class women, blamed the poor living conditions of female inmates on "neglect and sexual exploitation by male keepers." For example, "Rachel Welch, one of a small number of women in Auburn Prison in New York, became pregnant while serving a punishment sentence in a solitary cell. As a result of a flogging by a male prison official, Welch died after childbirth" (Schulz, 1995, p. 10).

The pressure for reform that followed this scandalous event resulted in Auburn creating the position of prison matron to oversee women's quarters in 1832 and influenced the passing of the 1928 law requiring the separation of males and females in county prisons. New York City officials followed the Auburn example by responding to pressure from the American Female Moral Reform Society to hire six matrons for its two jails in 1845 (Schulz, 1995, pp. 10–11).

During the post–Civil War period, women again became concerned about the welfare of female prisoners, noting "overcrowding, harsh treatment, and sexual abuse by their male keepers" (Schulz, 1995, p. 11). The Women's Christian Temperance Union and the General Federation of Women's Clubs demanded an increased role for women in caring for women and children in police custody. These organizations helped create and finance the position of police matron in the 1880s, which was women's first entry into police departments, albeit as social workers.

New York was the first city to hire full-time police matrons in 1845 (Berg and Budnick, 1986). But in 1887, the Men's Prison Association expressed opposition to placing matrons in each station house in New York City. At this time, the "city detained 14,000 women prisoners and received 42,000 female lodgers for overnight shelter." The association based its objection "on lack of space for a matron, on the violent state of the women, and on their fear of a matron's physical inability to handle the women" (p. 314).

In the late nineteenth and early twentieth centuries, a number of social forces contributed to the appearance of women police officers outside correctional settings. The most significant of these social forces were the expansion of the frontier, the surge toward industrialization, the development of the steam engine, the extension of political democracy, and the development of new economic institutions. This was also an era of religious revivalism, utopian experiments, and increased social consciousness. People joined together to sponsor the temperance movement, to institute public education, and to establish humane management systems for the insane, deviant, and delinquent.

The experience of the female abolitionists, as well as such social problems as widespread poverty, breakdown of the family, child labor, and increases in juvenile delinquency and female-related crime, provided the catalyst for the appearance of a women's movement called the suffragettes. The primary goal of this movement was to eliminate some of the social ills besetting children and women. This movement also gave birth to what is called the "child-saving movement" and the development of the juvenile court and its *parens patriae* philosophy (Platt, 1969, p. 76). The entry of women into law enforcement in a social worker mode during this era was "due to the reformist zeal of the period, an acceptance of a limited and special role for women in law enforcement, and the efforts of a few dedicated progressive reformers" (Lord, 1995, p. 628).

Reformers began to push for the appointment of women with the skills to work in the streets with prostitutes, runaways, and juvenile delinquents (Feinman, 1986, p. 81). In 1905, Lola Baldwin, secretary to the protective group Travelers' Aid Society, was hired as a "safety worker" as part of the Lewis and Clark Exposition in Portland, Oregon. Hers was the first documented appointment of a woman with police power, and her duties were to protect girls and women from harassment as well as to stop men from pursuing girls and women from pursuing men. The city government decided to retain Baldwin as director of the Department of Public Safety for the Protection of Young Girls and Women after the exhibition ended (Heidensohn, 1992, p. 43).

> Neither she nor the police department wanted women to be called "policewomen," because neither wished to associate women with the concept or job of policemen. The women, called "operatives" or "safety workers," considered themselves social service workers. (Feinman, 1986, pp. 81–82)

In 1910, Alice Stebbins Wells was officially classified as a "policewoman" in Los Angeles, California. Her contributions to women in police were significant. She was hired at the rank of detective after she convinced the city that a sworn woman police officer could be effective. The publicity about her hiring caused other cities to hire women, and in 1915, she founded the International Association of Policewomen.

Although Alice Wells was pictured in newspapers as "a masculine individual, grasping a revolver, and dressed in unfeminine clothing," policewomen of her era did not consider themselves female versions of policemen, a concept they derogatorily termed "little men" (Schulz, 1995, p. 4). They perceived themselves to be superior to policemen in social class, education, and professionalism. They "embodied the concept of the policewoman-as-social worker . . . seeking to bring social services and order into the lives of women and children. . . . " At the same time they avoided "the trappings of police, opposing uniforms for themselves and choosing not to carry firearms even if permitted to do so" (p. 4). Despite this limited role, their acceptance was only marginal, and the demands for policewomen were almost always imposed on police executives from outside sources (pp. 2–5).

Frances Heidensohn's (1992) examination of this period concluded that a number of factors shaped the development of women policing in both the United States and Britain. First, this movement had a moral basis: The entrance of women in policing was "vigorously promoted by groups formed for moral protection, and sometimes feminist causes who did so to attain social purity, rescue, and welfare goals" (p. 52). Second, volunteers had an important role in the origins of women police officers. A group of women who sought to be police officers were willing to volunteer their services on patrol. Third, considerable proselytizing for women took place in policing; supporters of this movement, as well as the pioneers themselves, pursued their cause with missionary zeal. Fourth, policewomen's strongest opposition came from both rank-and-file and senior police officers. Fifth, the women's movement in policing advocated specialist work because it sought the right of women to work with women and children. Finally, women sought gender control, in that they wanted to protect their own sex and did not seek a mandate to policemen (pp. 52–54).

Women's place in policing became more secure after the First World War. In 1922, there were 500 women officers; by 1932, there were more than 1,500. Then, partly due to the Great

Depression, the number leveled off. In 1950, there were 2,600 policewomen and in 1960, there were 5,617 (Heidensohn, 1992, pp. 52–54). The number of women police officers was to nearly double in the decade of the 1960s due in part to the social experimentation of that period. Both the civil rights movement and the women's movement benefited from the spirit of the times, but it was the women's movement that fueled the demands of women to have equal opportunity and career advancements in police departments (Lord, 1995, p. 628).

The 1950s brought a different type of woman into policing (Schulz, 1993). These "second-generation" policewomen, who were often military veterans, were middle-class careerists. Having more education (most had at least some college education) and higher in social-class orientation than their male peers, these women had more similarity with male police officers than did their predecessors. According to Schulz, "they formed a bridge between the upper-middle class, college-educated, feminist, progressive women who had served as policewomen before them and today's women officers, most of whom are comparable to the overwhelmingly working-class, high school educated men with whom they serve" (p. 7).

The demand for expanded roles in policing for women greatly increased after a 1961 lawsuit that allowed women police officers to compete in promotional examinations. The New York Police Department promoted its first female sergeant in 1964 (Schulz, 1995, pp. 2–5). In 1968, Indianapolis police officers Betty Blankenship and Elizabeth Coffal were the first women to put on a uniform, strap on a gun belt, and drive a marked police vehicle, answering police calls like their male counterparts (pp. 2–5).

The 1964 Civil Rights Act and the 1972 Equal Employment Opportunity Commission (EEOC) expanded the rules of state and civil service bodies and made it illegal to discriminate in employment. The EEOC rules, which pressured police agencies to change hiring practices and show why a woman or minority person is not qualified to become a police officer, had a major impact on the presence of women on the police employment lists.

On September 20, 1974, while attempting to arrest a bank robber, 24-year-old Gail Cobb became the first African American policewoman to die of gunshot wounds (Schulz, 1995, p. 140). Currently, the National Law Enforcement Officers Memorial has 111 female officers' names engraved on its wall, only seven of whom were killed before 1970 (National Law Enforcement Officers Memorial Fund, 1997). Box 11.2 reveals the evolving role of women in policing during the twentieth century.

BOX 11.2
Women in Law Enforcement

Gloria E. Myers's *Municipal Mother: Portland's Lola Greene Baldwin, America's First Policewoman* takes a detailed look at Baldwin's 17-year career. What makes this book so valuable is that Myers analyzes the social and historical factors that led to the appointment of policewomen in a number of cities in the United States and Canada in the early decades of the twentieth century. Baldwin's initial success, as well as her longevity (she remained in her position through the incumbency of six chiefs of police and five mayors), was not so much a story of police reform as the story of Progressive Reformers' concern about morality and sexual activity among girls and women.

Myers's book describes how issues of class, crime, and social control merged with concerns about leisure-time activities to create a climate leading to a new career for women—that of policewoman. She explains how Portland's upper-middle-class activist women used concerns about immorality among both women and men to forge alliances with social hygiene and temperance activists to alter societal expectations of police enforcement. It was this combination of interests in Portland and around the nation that led to positions for women in police departments.

Gayleen Hays, with Kathleen Moloney's autobiography *Policewoman One: My Twenty Years on the LAPD*, offers a candid streetwise autobiography that explores all aspects of Hays's professional and personal life. It traces her career from its beginnings in 1967 as a "policewoman" (not a police officer) to her retirement in October 1989. In 1972, when the department was forced to sexually integrate its workforce and eliminate separate and discriminatory job categories, Hays made the decision not to become a police officer. Thus, she chose to forgo the possibility of promotion and assignments to regular patrol or traffic duty. She felt that the image of a policewoman is different from that of a policeman. She comments that there are many situations "where it's better to have a nurturing female persona than that of a confrontational male."

During her career, Hays worked in bureaus dealing with prostitution as well as rape and child abuse and in almost every bureau of the Los Angeles Police Department. She even worked in an elite plainclothes unit whose duty was to pursue hard-core criminals. Hays frankly discusses her personal life throughout the book, including her three marriages, her atypical childhood, being sexually molested, and how these personal experiences affected her on the job. Nicknamed as a dinosaur, Hays was the last of a dying breed. When she left the force, her badge, "Policewoman #1," was retired. Today, only police officers are on the LAPD.

Hosansky and Sparling's *Working Vice* chronicles the career of Lieutenant Lucie J. Duvall in the Cleveland Police Department. In her current position, she is head of the department's sex crime and child abuse unit. She was still working when the book was published. In the beginning of the book, we find a confident police lieutenant as she is put through a yearly firearms qualification exercise. She is comfortable with her work, the mechanics of her job, and the decisions she must make because of the responsible position she holds. Using "flashback" sequences, the reader is taken through her career. When Lieutenant Duvall began her career in law enforcement during the early 1970s, she was part of a monumental time in the history of women in policing, because women were first hired to do the same job as male police officers. The book explores fully her devotion to her life's work. It follows her personal triumphs as well as hardships; it reveals other officers' positive and negative opinions of her police work.

Critical Thinking Questions: What is the value of looking at biographical sketches of the early women police officers? What can they teach us about the development of policing in the United States?

Sources: Gloria E. Myers, *A Municipal Mother: Portland's Lola Greene Baldwin, America's First Policewoman* (Corvallis, OR: Oregon State University Press, 1995); Gayleen Hays with Kathleen Moloney, *Policewoman One: My Twenty Years on the LAPD* (New York: Vilard Books, 1992); Tamar Hosansky and Pat Sparling, *Working Vice: The Gritty True Story of Lt. Lucie J. Duvall* (New York: HarperCollins, 1992).

BARRIERS TO WOMEN IN POLICING

Penny Harrington and Kimberly A. Lonsway (2004), in examining the status of women in policing, list a number of barriers that women face in becoming a police officer.

- Women face damaging stereotypes, especially the one that women are not strong enough or aggressive enough for police work.
- Women also face discrimination in the hiring process; both the written examination and oral interview process can be used to keep women out of policing.
- Women are vulnerable to sexual harassment during both academy training and field training.
- Women police officers experience isolation, as they learn that they are not accepted as equally valued members of the organization.

- Women sometimes face a double standard in performance evaluations, in which they feel that they must outperform the men officers to be considered "as good" as they are. The double standard can operate to the particular detriment of women of color, who are often viewed as "tokens" even more than white women are.
- Male officers usually receive the most highly valued assignments, which are dangerous or otherwise require a great deal of physical endurance. In contrast, women are assigned to less desirable assignments, including child abuse investigations, domestic violence units, and community relations, generally defined as "women work" within policing.
- Promotions have been more difficult for women to attain, because of the cumulative bias against women police officers. Only about 125 women serve as police chiefs.
- Women also face in policing the lack of family-friendly policies and programs, such as child care, pregnancy leave, and elder care.
- Sexual harassment and retaliation, as will be discussed later in this chapter, constitute one of the major barriers to women in policing (pp. 499–507).

COMPARISON OF MALE AND FEMALE OFFICERS' JOB PERFORMANCE

As you read this section, consider some of the advantages that women officers have on the basis of their gender. This fact was brought to light recently in the cracking of the Jaycee Dugard kidnap-ping case, a case that had gone unsolved for 18 years. A day officers Allison Jacobs and Lisa Campbell say they will never forget began as they met with a man to discuss an upcoming event on the University of California campus in Berkeley. The man, Phillip Garrido, had his two children with him. Something about his relationship with the girls struck the officers as strange as did facts revealed in conversations the officers initiated with the girls. Later, when they conducted a back-ground search of Garrido, they discovered he was a convicted child molester who was on parole. Further investigation eventually led to the girls' mother, who had been kidnapped 18 years before by Garrido. Jacobs, in an interview on CNN (2009), explained how she was able to pick up on the clues:

> My police intuition was kicking in, but I would say it's more of a mother's intuition. I was worried about these little girls. I knew something wasn't right. I could kind of see it in their eyes, although I really didn't know what it was. And just being the protective mom that I am, my reaction was to try and do what I could to help them.
>
> Now, thanks to these women, who have received praise as heroes in news reports worldwide, there has been a breakthrough in a kidnapping case that had stumped authorities for almost two decades. And two children and their mother can start a new life. These women got where they are today because of the pioneers who blazed the trail before them in the face of continuous resistance to the idea of women on patrol.

One of the criticisms of women who want to enter policing is that they lack skills to per-form well as police officers. In the 1970s, a large amount of research was done to evaluate the performance of women police officers. These studies were conducted in Washington, DC; New York City; Denver, Colorado; Newton, Massachusetts; Philadelphia, Pennsylvania; the California State Highway Patrol; and St. Louis County, Missouri (Lord, 1995, p. 632).

In those studies, as well as more recent ones, researchers consistently demonstrated that women can handle the crime-fighting, rescue, combat, peacekeeping, and social service aspects of police work as well as men, regardless of differences in biological constitution and socialization practices (Horne, 1980). A lingering question in the minds of many male officers is whether female officers can handle patrol duties as well as male officers. Although some gender differences were found, all but the second phase of the Philadelphia study found that men and women were equally capable of patrol work (Martin and Jurik, 1995, p. 55). These studies also generally indicate that "men are in no more danger with women as partners than with men as partners" (Feinman, 1986, p. 95).

Differences occurred between male and female police officers in how they performed on the job. Policewomen were typically seen as showing more restraint in using their firearms and in managing family disturbances; as being more sensitive to citizens' needs and using a more community-oriented policing style; and as using less sick time. Moreover, women were significantly less likely to be involved in employing excessive force and deadly force and in acts of corruption than were men officers (Harrington and Lonsway, 2004, pp. 499–507). Policemen generally had better shooting ability, had superior strength and agility, and required less assistance in making arrests (Lord, 1995, p. 632). The findings from the Philadelphia study also reported that women officers were assaulted more often, had more vehicle collisions, and sustained more injuries. Furthermore, some evidence exists that women have higher turnover rates than men in policing (Doerner, 1995, p. 205).

Gender and Culture: Women Are Not Wanted—This Is a Man's Job

Policing has been one of the most resistant occupations to accept women (Belknap and Shelley, 1992, p. 47). Susan E. Martin described the initial resistance as "strong, organized, and sometimes life-threatening" (Martin, 1994, p. 389). Catherine Milton's 1992 study reported that policewomen were being used almost exclusively in clerical or juvenile functions, that they were required to have more education than men, that they were regulated by hiring quotas, and that they were allowed to compete for promotions or openings only in the women's bureau. Donna Schaper (1997) writes about her experience:

> For me, the myth that women are physically less able than men found a remarkable rebuff one day in San Francisco 20 years ago. The San Francisco police department was in the throes of a lawsuit that would allow women to become police officers. I as taking a group of teenagers on a tour of the police department when the officer guiding us said that the real reason women couldn't be on the force was that they could never pass basic training, which required carrying a 100-pound bag of sand in a straight line for 100 feet. Then, an 18-year-old horsewoman in our group spotted the sandbag in the weight-training room, hoisted it on her shoulders and carried it for the rest of the tour. (p. 32)

Women have made gains in policing, which Susan Martin (1989, p. 162) claims are related in large part to the "development of a substantial body of law requiring nondiscrimination on the basis of sex in terms and conditions of employment" (p. 315). As of 2001, women comprised only 12.7 percent of all sworn law enforcement positions in the United States (National Center for Women & Policing, 2002). For other key findings of this report, see Box 11.3.

In appraising the progress of women in law enforcement, Lonsway contends that while women gained an average of approximately half a percentage point per year within large law enforcement departments from 1972 to 1999, mounting evidence now exists that this trend has stalled or even reversed (Lonsway, 2006). For example, women's representation in large law

BOX 11.3
The Percentage of Sworn Women Police Officers, 2001

- Over the last ten years, the representation of women in large police agencies has slowly increased from 9 percent in 1990 to 12.7 percent in 2001—a gain of less than 4 percent.
- There is mounting evidence that the slow pace of increase in the representation of women in large police agencies has stalled or even possibly reversed. For example, the percentage of women in large police agencies was 14.3 percent in 1999, 13.0 percent in 2000, and 12.7 percent in 2001.
- Women currently hold only 7.3 percent of top command positions, 9.6 percent of supervisory positions, and 13.5 percent of line operation positions. Sworn women of color hold 1.6 percent of top command positions, 3.1 percent of supervisory positions, and 5.3 percent of line operations positions.
- More than half (55.9 percent) of the large police agencies surveyed reported no women in top command positions, and the vast majority (87.9 percent) reported no women of color in their highest ranks. For small and rural

agencies, 97.4 percent have no women in top command positions, and only 1 of the 235 agencies has a woman of color in their highest ranks.

- The percentage of women serving in corrections facilities is more than twice as high as the percentage of sworn women police personnel, 26.3 percent in corrections compared with 12.7 percent in sworn law enforcement positions.

Critical Thinking Questions: What is the significance of the statistic that the representation of women in large police departments has stalled or even perhaps reversed? Why do you think the percentage of women serving in corrections is more than twice as high as the percentage of sworn women police personnel?

Source: National Center for Women and Policing, *Equality Denied: The Status of Women in Policing: 2001* (Washington, DC: U.S. Government Printing Office, 2002), pp. 4, 9.

enforcement departments actually declined, from 14.3 percent in 1999 and 13.0 percent in 2000 to 12.7 percent in 2001 (National Center for Women & Policing, 2001).

Larger police departments tend to hire more women than smaller departments. The Madison, Wisconsin, police department is an exception. This small university town boasts 31.9 percent women officers, the highest percentage of any department in the nation. For the top ten agencies with the largest percentage of sworn women officers, see Table 11.1.

The resistance toward women in policing must ultimately be viewed in terms of the patriarchal society. For the past 3,000 years, society has been based on social, philosophical, and political systems in which men have controlled women. Men have used force, direct pressure, tradition, ritual, customs, law, and language to determine what roles women shall or shall not play. In this male-dominated social role, the female is everywhere subordinated to the male. In policing, women had the "audacity" to desire entrance to an all-male occupation, one that male officers perceived to demand dominance, aggressiveness, superiority, and power.

In addition to the cultural barrier of the wider society, it is thought that certain aspects of police work are unsuitable for women. First, it is believed that women are unsuitable for police work because "they cannot cope with danger, do not command authority, and should not be exposed to degradation." Second, there is the fear that the introduction of women "will undermine male solidarity, threaten their security, and their self-image" (Heidensohn, 1992, p. 200). This could be regarded as the "porcelain policeman" argument; that is, male police officers "are

TABLE 11.1 Top Ten Agencies with the Largest Percentage of Sworn Women Officers, 2001

Agency	Total Sworn Officers	Total Sworn Women Officers	Percentage Sworn Women Officers	Percentage Sworn Women Top Command	Percentage Sworn Women Supervisory	Percentage Sworn Women of Color
Terrebonne Parish, Sheriff, La.	187	78	41.71	9.09	3.33	2.14
Madison Police, Wisc.	347	111	31.99	16.67	22.22	4.03
Lafayette Parish Sheriff, La.	251	71	28.29	9.09	20.00	4.38
Cook County Sheriff, Ill.	2,587	699	27.02	17.24	24.64	10.32
Detroit Police, Mich.	4,195	1,085	25.86	17.39	27.28	20.07
Boulder Police, Col.	176	45	25.57	12.50	4.55	0.57
Philadelphia Police, Penn.	6,990	1,682	24.06	7.74	9.60	15.64
Spartanburg Police, SC	139	31	22.30	0.00	21.43	7.91
Miami-Dade Police, Fla.	3,078	676	21.96	17.98	18.46	13.55
Douglas County Sheriff, Ga.	116	256	21.55	0.00	23.55	0.00

Source: National Center for Women and Policing, *Equality Denied: The Status of Women in Policing: 2001* (Washington, DC: U.S. Government Printing Office, 2002), p. 21 (Appendix B).

so fragile and delicate that they will feel threatened and undermined, their solidarity shattered, and their loyalty over-stretched by the presence of women" (Heidensohn, 1992, p. 216). Third, women officers must cope with norms that create a disadvantage in interacting with male officers. Swearing and sexual jokes, it is charged, are an inevitable part of police culture and women should not have to deal with this "seamy" aspect. Finally, the argument for the exclusion of women is made that their lower status (in comparison with male officers) creates problems in arrest situations with both male and female citizens (Martin, 1989, pp. 321–322).

The issue of women as tokenism in policing has received some attention. Rosabeth Moss Kanter (1976) claims that token women (whose numbers fall below 15 percent of the total population) perceive themselves to be highly visible, attracting disproportionate attention to themselves. This often results, asserts Kanter, in dysfunctional performance pressures (pp. 415–430). Joanne Belknap and Jill Shelley's (1992) research supported Kanter's theory regarding one aspect of tokenism—visibility—because they found that "the most consistent characteristic significantly related to policewomen's perceptions and experiences was the percentage of women in the department" (p. 47).

Martin's examination of women in policing (1979) found that women are considered only tokens for male police officers and "they face performance pressure, isolation from coworkers, entrapment in stereotypic roles, and tests of loyalty" (p. 314). She concluded that the future is not bright: "It is likely that the dynamics of tokenism will continue to operate, leaving policewomen with a number of difficult choices in the face of the expectation that they think like men, work like dogs, and act like ladies" (pp. 314–323).

Teresa Lynn Wertsch (1998) also examined the issue of women police officers and tokenism among one group of female police officers employed in a medium-sized Pacific Northwest city. Of the twenty-four female officers in that department, sixteen agreed to be interviewed. Wertsch found that tokenism, when combined with such factors as family commitments and organizational structures, plays a major role in determining upward mobility and in serving to reduce the frequency of women's promotion to supervisory positions in police departments (pp. 25–26). According to this study, stereotypical categorization of the token into specific roles also created dissatisfaction and frustration. Two women officers reveal this dissatisfaction in the following statements:

> The guys can view you as a sex object instead of a professional. It makes me try harder to put up more fronts and play more of the macho, boy role rather than accept that I am a female. It makes me nervous and uncomfortable. You can't be meek or mild, too quiet. You can't be too loud or boisterous because then you would be a dike, too masculine. "That's why she can do the job because she's a dike," so the men automatically put you in a male role. If you're not good looking and act very masculine, they'll give you the job because you're a dike.
>
> I wish it didn't have to be this way, but you're either a bitch, a dike, or a slut. It makes me frustrated because I don't know which I am. I'm not gay. I'm not a slut. I would probably fall more into the bitch category, which is the one that I have decided I would rather be in. (pp. 35–36)

Lesbian police officers report experiencing greater barriers as a result of their gender (because men officers see policing as such a "macho" job) rather than their sexual orientation. Using data collected from two Midwestern police departments, one emphasizing traditional crime control and the other community policing, Martin, Forest, and Jurif (2004) examined how the lesbians' sexual orientation affects their police performance in a culture in which gender, sexuality, and race are all important components. Whether they come out or hide their identity, it is necessary for lesbian officers to negotiate their identities while doing their jobs. In the department emphasizing traditional crime control, lesbians believed that sexism as well as homophobia created barriers to their success in policing. Officers in this department who chose to hide their identity found this to be a stressful experience, because they were especially fearful of losing the respect of coworkers once their sexual orientation became known. In the department emphasizing community policing, lesbian officers perceived that their greatest barriers related to gender rather than sexual orientation. Martin and colleagues found that lesbians of color in both departments had the most concern about disclosing their sexual identity (pp. 511, 519, 521, 523).

Colvin's 2009 study survey of sixty-six lesbian and gay police officers revealed that not only did these officers face barriers to equal employment opportunities similar to those faced by women and other minorities in law enforcement, but they also perceived some workplace benefits as lesbian or gay officers. Law enforcement, they found, has made good strides in opening the law enforcement workforce for lesbian or gay officers but continue to face ongoing challenges in creating diverse, fair, and representative work environments for lesbian and gay officers (Colvin, 2009).

Community to Community: Changing Roles for Police Officers

The nationwide movement toward community policing, the newest trend in policing today, aims to build closer ties between police and residents through frequent and informal noncriminal contact. This approach emphasizes a spirit of cooperation, familiarity, trust, and appreciation between police and community residents. These traits have traditionally been associated with female gender roles and attributes (Martin, 2000, p. 260).

Yet as a masculine occupation, policing has overwhelmingly rejected "feminine" voices and virtues; indeed, the criminal justice and legal system has been traditionally viewed as operating with a uniquely masculine voice—a detached and impersonal one emphasizing the traditional over the relational (Martin, 1990). Accordingly, when the ideological preoccupation with masculinity in policing is considered, any behavior that suggests femininity, subjectivity, or weakness is suspect and questioned in police subcultures (Martin, 2000, p. 260).

Martin suggests that this movement in many departments toward community policing raised some interesting questions:

> . . . How can this alternative style [community policing] be accepted by the police, since for it to be adopted, "feminine" traits must be appropriated as masculine traits and reshaped to appear as powerful and desirable? What happens if some men only "pretend" to personify this new breed of officer, particularly if they think doing so is tied to promotion? Do women police officers bring a "different voice" to policing than their male counterparts? Can a more feminine style of policing be introduced in a way that both men and women will embrace this approach and not fear the consequences of "doing policing" in this transformed style? (Martin, 2000, p. 260)

Community policing has varying levels of commitment in those departments that claim to be focused toward the mission of community policing. It is not unusual for top command of departments to have much more commitment toward community policing than is true among line officers. Nevertheless, Martin's questions are a reminder that, at least in some community-oriented policing departments, negotiated role identities must take place with male officers, and it would appear that "feminine" traits will need to be more valued in policing than they have been in the past. What this means is that at least some departments will need to redefine what constitutes a "good" police officer and hence a "good" candidate for a position (Harrington and Lonsway, 2004, p. 507).

Sexual Harassment in the Police Culture

One of the most unbelievable accounts of sexual harassment is what Romona Arnold, the first female officer in the City of Seminole, Oklahoma, police department, experienced. This case, which was decided on July 10, 1985, documented that in 1977 Arnold's problems began when she was transferred to the midnight shift under the supervision of Lt. Herdlitchka. He informed her that "he did not believe in women officers." He not only refused to speak with her and was hostile toward her, but "he told her that he would harass her until she quit or was fired" (*Arnold v. City of Seminole*, 1985).

The sexual harassment became stationwide when "demeaning cartoons and pictures were posted for public view within the police station with the plaintiff's name written thereon." Her son was arrested and taken to jail in June 1979. The charges against him were eventually dropped "because it was determined that the arrest and detention of plaintiff's son were totally unjustified.

Lt. Downing advised plaintiff that the arrest of plaintiff's son was pure harassment." Officers with less service and seniority were promoted over her. When the department obtained new vehicles, male officers got them. She was informed that "as a woman, she didn't know how to take care of it." The windows of her car were rolled down when it was raining so that her seats would become wet. Her name was removed from her mail shelf, and the shelf was eventually removed altogether. Her husband, "a fireman for the City of Seminole, was told that if his wife filed a discrimination complaint, both husband and plaintiff would be fired" (*Arnold v. City of Seminole*, 1985).

On February 25, 1983, perhaps the most serious of all events in this sad account of police deviancy took place. Arnold received a call from Tommy Gaines, a known drug and alcohol addict, who wanted to see her. "He said it would only take five minutes and that it was urgent. When she arrived, Gaines told her that 'the County' had tapped his phone and was taping conversations." He also said, "In exchange for a reduced sentence," he "was to try to set plaintiff up in an illegal drug transaction." He assured her "that the Seminole Sheriff's office and the city police were involved" (*Arnold v. City of Seminole*, 1985).

The court decision concluded that "the plaintiff suffers from sexual assault stress syndrome caused by the sexual harassment and discrimination detailed herein; in addition, she suffers from physiological problems induced by stress and anxiety." As a result, she "has been unable to return to work at the Seminole Police Department essentially since January 1, 1984, due to the deterioration of her physical and mental health as outlined above."

Eighty plaintiffs have joined the growing class-action sexual harassment and discrimination lawsuit of *Tipton-Whittingham v. Los Angeles*. According to the *Los Angeles Times*, many of the Los Angeles Police Department's female officers felt that the 1994 inquiry into sexual harassment at the West Los Angeles Division was a failure of department leadership, because it did not follow through on this inquiry's recommendations. The inquiry reported sexist and racist remarks, male police officers who failed to back up female officers needing help, and so deeply ingrained mistreatment that policewomen had come to accept it as a part of life. The true scope of the problem will never be known because many female officers were reluctant to complain for fear of retaliation. As expressed by officer May Elizabeth Hatter, who has joined the *Tipton-Whittingham* case, "Management has thumbed its nose at this problem. . . . I had to prove myself every single day as a police officer. How can management just turn its back on me?" (Daum and Johns, 1994, p. 49).

There are a number of other tragic examples of sexual harassment. A two-week academy cadet was victimized when a firearms instructor approached her from behind, reached around, and grabbed her left breast as she was practicing. In repulsing the advance, she made it very clear that it was unwelcome and offensive. As a result, she failed her marksmanship test. This same instructor refused to send the cadet's broken firearm in for repair, claiming she could not shoot. He told the cadet the next day that she had "better learn to shoot" and called her "stupid" and "a dumb broad." Moreover, this same cadet was assaulted twice by a classmate who "pulled her against his body, and told her that he wanted to feel her body and that her body felt good" (*Watts v. New York City Police Dept.*, 1989).

A policewoman of color was working in the traffic division when she returned to her desk to find seven of her case files ripped and soda poured into her typewriter. She was harassed on other occasions when her personal vehicle was vandalized, including tires slashed, windshield wipers removed, and paint scratched. Furthermore, pornographic pictures were placed in her personal desk drawer and her male coworkers addressed her in sexist terms. Another disturbing incident involved items of her clothing, located in the officer's locker, which had a lime substance placed on them that caused severe burns to her back (*Andrews v. City of Philadelphia*, 1990).

A Caucasian policewoman in the same division was harassed in sexually foul and lascivious language. When she found sexual devices and pornographic magazines in her desk drawer, the males in the unit laughed at her. Officers also removed files from her desk, coworkers refused to help her with work, and she received obscene phone calls at her unlisted home phone number. After complaining to her supervisor about a case file removed from her desk, he warned her, "You know, you're no spring chicken. You have to expect this working with the guys" (*Andrews v. City of Philadelphia*, 1990).

A study done by R. Max Mendel and Elizabeth Shoenfelt (1991) demonstrates bias even in the appraisal process for new recruits. They surveyed a random sample of 226 police chiefs, serving populations over 80,000, to determine what administrative action they would use based on an actual arrest during which a male training officer was shot and after which his female trainee-partner was fired for cowardice. Mendel and Shoenfelt concluded that female trainees were significantly more likely than male trainees to be terminated for the same actions. This predisposition toward biased judgments of policewomen's performance not only questions disciplinary actions against female officers but also contributes to female officers' reluctance to report harassment.

Many of the harassment problems endured by female officers in large departments are likewise experienced by policewomen in small-town law enforcement, which makes up 85 percent of municipal departments in the United States. Curt R. Bartol and colleagues' (1992) study on stressors and problems in small-town police departments reported that 53 percent of female officers had been sexually harassed, predominantly by male supervisors; two respondents reported they had been sexually assaulted by male supervisors. Eighty-three percent felt that male supervisors frequently communicated negative attitudes about women in policing. One female officer wrote, "The most stressful factor is the belief that the attitude of male supervisors toward female police officers is not likely to change anytime in the near future or during my career as a law enforcement officer" (p. 240).

Lonsway and Alipio's 2007 article examined the experiences of thirteen women who sued their law enforcement agencies for sexual harassment or another form of sex discrimination. When the women reported the behaviors, they received a variety of forms of retaliation. Only five of the thirteen women stated that changes were implemented in their agencies as a result of the lawsuit. Nevertheless, most of the women indicated that they were glad that they had sued the agency in a lawsuit (Lonsway and Alipio, 2007).

African American Women in Policing

Some evidence exists that African American women entering policing have to face a much different reception from African American males. The combination of the effects of race and gender expose African American women to multiple disadvantages, known as "double jeopardy" (Martin, 1994, pp. 383–384). According to some analysts, the African American's "unique social location at the intersection of different hierarchies has produced a distinct feminist consciousness different from that of white women." Martin continues, "White women have ample contact with white men and the potential for increased power by association with one of them. But they have limited their influence by internalizing an image of helplessness and allowing themselves to be 'put on a pedestal'" (p. 384). She concludes that "due to racism, black women have experienced far less protection and a far greater element of fear based on white hostility, physical separation, and intimidation" (p. 384).

Felkenes and Schroeder (1993) found that, during the police training academy experience, the dominant group of white male officers created and supported a culture that both implicitly and explicitly encouraged a wide range of discriminatory behaviors directed against minority women. It is no wonder, then, that minority women officers had higher rates of attrition and lower levels of satisfaction with the training. Subsequent to graduating from the academy, minority women officers continued to experience social discrimination, to face racist and sexist comments sent as computer messages from one patrol car to another, and to have to deal with the existence of openly racist and sexist cliques operating out of several bureaus in the Los Angeles Police Department.

Martin, in examining the interactive effects of race and gender in five large municipal police agencies, conducted in-depth interviews with 106 African American and European American officers and supervisors. One African American woman recounted:

> Males didn't want to work with females, and at times I was the only female or black on the shift so I had to do a lot to prove myself. I was at the precinct 10 days before I knew I had a partner 'cause . . . (the men) called in sick and I was put in the station. The other white guys called the man who was assigned to work with me the 11th day and told him to call in sick . . . he came anyway. (p. 390)

Martin's study also found that several African American women "observed differences in their treatment that reflect differences in the cultural images and employment experiences of black and white women" (p. 394). European American women, especially those who were physically attractive or attached to influential European American men, were more likely than African American women to be protected from street patrol by being given station house duty. When European American women were assigned to the streets, they were more likely than African American women to receive protection from both European American and African American males (p. 394).

This study also found that African American women's relationships to African American males were "strained by tensions and dilemmas associated with sexuality and competition for desirable assignments and promotions." Part of the explanation for these strained relationships was the competition "for position and promotions earmarked 'black' by affirmative action programs." Thus, within these five departments, African American women were, in a number of ways, the victims of "widespread racial stereotypes as well as outright racial harassment" (p. 394).

SUCCESS IN A DIFFICULT CAREER PATH

Women must decide how they will cope with their jobs because they are, at best, accepted at the fringes of the male's culture of policing. At the extremes of adaptation, women can decide to become either defeminized or deprofessionalized. "Defeminized" women become superefficient and see themselves as as good as or better than their male colleagues. Their competence, then, serves to mask their femininity. In contrast to competing with male colleagues, "deprofessionalized" women accept subordinate status and concessions granted to them (Hochschild, 1973, pp. 79–82).

Martin, in applying these extremes of adaptation to twenty-eight women patrol officers in Washington, DC, renamed the two polar positions calling them **"policeWOMEN"** and **"POLICEwomen."** POLICEwomen focus on law enforcement, rather than service. They show a high commitment to the job and even criticize fellow female officers. Similar to male police officers, they wish to do specialist work and be promoted. PoliceWOMEN, on the other hand, emphasize the feminine. By accepting the male's invitation to function as a nominal equal, they are actually functioning as assistants or junior partners. They usually receive treatment and exemptions from work tasks that are inappropriate for a "lady" (Martin, 1980, p. 315).

More recently, Brewer (1991) observed two primary groups of women police officers in the Royal Ulster Constabulary in Northern Ireland. The first he labeled "Hippolytes." These women "interactionally manage the question of gender identity by retaining for themselves as much of their femininity as the bureaucratic regimen and the situation allows, and they resist the adoption and performance of occupational traits that are masculine" (p. 241). Described as loners, they avoided participation in the police occupational culture and were not looked on as effective as police officers. The "Amazons" were the polar opposites of the Hippolytes. Brewer reported that these officers used "aggressive humour and all the interactional and conversational devices associated with being 'one of the boys.' Being one of the boys is the defining charac-teristic of the way the Amazon type handle the problem of their female gender in the masculine occupational culture of the police station" (p. 242).

Regardless of what roles they pursue, women who survive in policing usually develop a thick skin. Men officers frequently pick on female officers, and if they discover their tender points, then they intensify their ribbing. One woman officer, in acknowledging that those sensitive to abuse could not survive an eight-hour shift, revealed her means of adaptation: "I've got a skin like a table. Nothing bothers me. I just made up my mind that I had to take it and live with it and just move on from there and that's what I did. Truly, truly nothing bothers me jobwise" (Fletcher, 1995, p. 162).

Another successful coping technique that women officers use is the talents they have on the job. Many women use their verbal skills to deescalate confrontative or potentially violent situations. Jeanne McDowell (1992) puts it this way, "cool, calm and communicative, they [women officers] help put a lid on violence before it erupts" (p. 70). Another woman officer expressed the importance of verbal skills a little differently:

> So my theory is, you have to go in with your brain. I talk to people. And I talk to big guys and I talk to little guys and I talk to big women and I talk to little women. I talk to everybody. I think it comes in with this basic amount of respect for others as human beings. I don't take things personally. You can't. But a lot of people take things personally. As far as I'm concerned, the uniform walks into a situation all by itself. But it's not me. (Fletcher, 1995, p. 24)

Women, who are normally excluded from the culture of policing, must establish their own supportive and nourishing network if they intend to survive on the job. These networks may be in the departments in which they are employed or they may be statewide or national networks of associations of policewomen (Heidensohn, 1992, p. 197).

Because of their superior interpersonal relationship skills, policewomen appear to handle stress better than their male counterparts. According to Patricia Lunneborg (1989), 90 percent of the policewomen talked out their sources of stress, versus 45 percent of the policemen she surveyed (p. 99). Beermann and colleagues (cited in Blumenthal, 1994) also found that the "double burden" of the unequal division of domestic duties, particularly for those with children, did not result in more severe psychosocial or subjective health impairments. This extra burden, in fact, may be a source of stress relief as policewomen are forced to change roles from cop to mom. This allows them to leave the job behind, avoiding the "live to work" mentality that traps male officers as they become couch potatoes (resulting in withdrawal and numbing of emotions) or associate with other officers after work. Accordingly, "being married and having children is a protective factor against completed suicide for women—but not for men" (p. 3).

Cara Rabe-Hemp found that female officers usually define their acceptance into the police culture in one of three ways:

- through achieving rank;
- through completing some tough and manful act;
- through being different or unique to the typical male police role (Rabe-Hemp, 2008b).

The first two solutions required female officers to adopt the norms and values of aggression, violence, danger, courageousness, and solidarity, which are typical of the masculine police culture. The last mechanism to gain acceptance, according to Rabe-Hemp could be risky, because it encouraged women to highlight their token status in the department in order to exaggerate their skills as being polarized to their male counterparts, and to become highly visible in the process. (Rabe-Hemp, 2008a).

Women officers do experience the stressors of both low acceptance in the police agency and lack of access to the peer-group support structure of male officers. The importance of access to this peer-group support structure or police culture is that it helps to mitigate the strain of occupation-related stress by providing a forum within which individual officers can safely ventilate (Lord, 1995, p. 631). J. G. Wexler and V. Quinn's (1985) examination of the occupation-related stress experiences of women officers in a major metropolitan department in California found that women experienced a major stressor in attempting to demonstrate that they could be effective officers without compromising their femininity (pp. 98–105).

Many women police officers report that their jobs contribute to social and marriage problems. They claim that some men are too intimidated to date or marry a female cop (Kirschman, 1997, p. 203). They appear to be intimidated by assertive and self-confident women, whose work is a driving force in their lives, who sometimes are tougher and stronger than they are, and who are authority figures who strap on a gun to protect society and them. An officer reflects on her dating experiences:

> If you're a single woman cop and you meet a guy, it's a three-month thing. That's it. Three months. At first, they love the fact that you're a cop. Then you notice a change. What's the matter? They're intimidated, they're disturbed that you're capable and intelligent.
>
> Well, try to understand. They work nine to five. They go home. You go out on midnights. You put on a gun so you can protect people. That's intimidating. They think they can handle it. But that's bullshit. They can't handle it. They're gone after three months.
>
> Now I don't tell people what I do. (Fletcher, 1995, p. 187)

It is not surprising that policewomen have higher attrition rates than do men officers. They often leave for reasons very different from that faced by their male counterparts. Among these problems are coworker gossip, lack of promotional opportunity, inflexible working patterns, gender discrimination, sexual harassment, and administrative policies that disadvantage sworn female officers (Lonsway, 2006: p. 3). Kurtz adds that for women officers, stress and burnout are embedded in the gender structure and process of policing and is not simply a response to highly stressful events (Kurtz, 2008).

An Arizona State University study found the divorce rate of female officers to be twice that of the national average and three times that of male officers. In addition, female officers were almost twice as likely to be separated. Twenty-one percent felt that police work was definitely a factor in their divorce, and another 20 percent were undecided (testimony of Leanor Boulin Johnson, 1991).

Women officers also have a lower suicide rate than male officers. Explanations for this are that women are more likely than men to have stronger social supports; women seem to be more willing to seek professional help; and men are more humiliated by job-related life events, job loss, or problems. According to Susan Blumenthal (1994), former head of the Suicide Research Unit at the National Institute of Mental Health, "being married and having children is a protective factor against completed suicide for women but not men" (p. 3).

Policewomen generally are much less involved in deviancy than are policemen. For example, the Christopher Commission found that women officers handled suspects more successfully than men did as they are "less personally challenged by defiant suspects and feel less need to deal with immediate force or confrontational language" (Morrison, 1991, p. 84). Little evidence also exists that women officers are frequently involved in corruption. As Hunt (1990) suggests, an explanation for this might be that male officers tend to fear that "the moral woman would expose police involvement in corruption" (p. 14). Female officers, then, are likely to be excluded from both socializing events with male officers and from whatever corruption is taking place in the department.

LEGAL PROTECTIONS

In terms of having a successful and satisfying police career, women police officers need protection from the sexual harassment that traditionally has been present in most police departments.

Four categories of law cover sexual harassment in the workplace: (1) the United States Civil Rights Act of 1964 and 1991; (2) state statutes on fair employment practices; (3) common tort and criminal law; and (4) Statute 42 United States Code Section 1983 (Civil Rights Act of 1871).

United States Civil Rights Act

The **Civil Rights Act of 1964** makes discrimination on the basis of race, color, religion, sex, or national origin illegal. Title VII of this act "prohibits employers from, among other things, discriminating on the basis of sex with respect to compensation, terms, conditions, or privileges of employment" (Rubin, 1995, p. 1).

Congress established the **Equal Employment Opportunity Commission** (EEOC) as the enforcing agency, but restricted its oversight to employers with fifteen employees or more and placed a back pay liability limitation of two years before the filing of charges (O'Linn, 1995, p. 2). In addition, Title VII did not apply to local governments, including police departments, until almost a decade later when Congress passed the Equal Opportunity Act of 1972 (Berg and Budnick, 1986, p. 314). Until then it was rare to see policewomen in a patrol function (Charles, 1982, p. 194).

By 1980, as a result of pressure from women's groups, the Equal Employment Opportunity Commission ruled that sexual harassment was a form of sex discrimination covered under Title VII and issued guidelines on discrimination because of gender (Petrocelli and Repa, 1994, pp. 1, 19). These guidelines did not have the force of law, but were acknowledged by the United States Supreme Court in its first ruling on sexual harassment, *Meritor Savings Bank, FSB v. Vinson et al.* Sixteen years after the *Meritor* decision, Congress passed the Civil Rights Act of 1991 to correct some inadequacies in the Civil Rights Act of 1964.

The new law made possible a jury trial if punitive damages are alleged. Punitive damages are available under Title VII, providing the employer acted with reckless indifference or malice to federally protected rights. The limits on punitives range from $50,000 to $300,000 depending on the size of the workforce. If an employee is successful, the Civil Rights Act provides redress of reinstatement and promotion, back pay and benefits, a limited amount of money damages, injunctive relief to prevent similar harassment from taking place in the future, and a portion of or all of attorney's fees.

Fair Employment Practices (FEP)

Legal definitions of sexual harassment, as well as laws governing the enforcement of sexual harassment laws, vary from state to state. Although some states have no laws at all, most state **Fair Employment Practices (FEP) agencies** have powers similar to the EEOC's to seek remedies. In addition, various states' FEP laws provide remedies for recovering substantial monetary damages for personal injuries without limitations; other states have no remedy. Moreover, states vary widely on the amount of compensation they allow for damages. Only about half the states allow for punitive damages. Several states require that an administrative claim be filed with the enforcing agency before relief can be pursued under the FEP laws in court. Finally, counties and cities often have their own laws prohibiting sexual harassment and administrative agencies (Petrocelli and Repa, 1994). A complainant may find better relief filing with a state agency, but research and possibly legal advice is required to seek the best avenue for a remedy.

Tort Laws and Criminal Charges

A tort claim in state court may be the best solution for some victims; indeed, it may be the only remedy for victims who work for a small agency, whose governing entity's aggregate employment is fewer than fifteen employees (O'Linn, 1995). A tort is a "breach of duty, other than a breach of contract, for which the offender will be subject to legal responsibility" (*The New Lexicon Webster's Encyclopedic Dictionary of the English Language*, 1992, p. 1402). Common law torts include assault, battery, intentional infliction of emotional distress, wrongful discharge, and defamation (O'Linn, 1995, p. 5).

Providing a wider range of remedies than those available under the Civil Rights Act and most states' FEP laws, torts include both compensatory damages for the emotional and physical distress suffered from the workplace harassment and the possibility of large punitive damages aimed at punishing the wrongdoer (Petrocelli and Repa, 1994, pp. 2, 8). Unlike the Civil Rights Act, which pertains only to the employer, common tort actions can penalize the predator with punitive damages. The following are two examples of common tort claims based on sexual harassment: A woman who quit her job because of sexual harassment was entitled to unemployment benefits even though she voluntarily resigned. The court found that she had been subjected to severe sexual harassment and that any prudent person would have quit. She was awarded unemployment benefits and attorney's fees. The Court of Appeals in Atlanta ruled that a female who brought suit under Title VII against an employer for sexual harassment was properly permitted to bring state law tort claims. This woman was awarded $3,000 in back wages under Title VII, and a jury awarded her $10,000 for common law battery and $25,000 in compensatory damages for invasion of privacy under state law.

In addition to tort claims, criminal charges can be filed against the perpetrator for such actions as assault, battery, and sexual assault. As witnessed in the O. J. Simpson trials, filing criminal charges does not preclude taking civil action. In fact, the criminal action often precedes the civil one for the purpose of solidifying a claim or as a fact-finding measure.

Statute 42 United States Code Section 1983

Until the Civil Rights Act of 1991, there was more incentive to file under United States Code Section 1983 to obtain punitive damages and a jury trial. Unlike the Civil Rights Act of 1991, Section 1983 provides the opportunity to file for punitive damages against the offending party by establishing personal liability. Punitive damages allowed by Title VII are against the employer; Section 1983 can be against the predator (O'Linn, 1995). Section 1983 states:

> Every person who, under color of any statute, ordinance, regulation, custom or usage, of any State . . . subjects, or causes to be subjected, any citizen of the United States . . . to the deprivation of any rights, privileges, or immunities secured by the constitution and laws, shall be liable to the party injured in an action at law." (42 United States Code Section 1983; *O'Neal v. DeKalb County*, 1988)

Mildred K. O'Linn, an attorney who specializes in the representation of law enforcement personnel and agencies in civil litigation, reminds law enforcement officers that "Statute 42 of the United States Code Section 1983 provides for civil remedies if an individual acting under color of law violates the civil rights of another individual." She adds that "if you are a peace officer, you are acting under color of law whenever you are on duty or off duty if there is a strong enough nexus or connection made between whatever your actions were and the fact that you are a police officer. Simply put," she says, "you are still acting under color of law if you are using the powers of your office. Under that statute, if you violate an individual's civil rights as a police officer in the form of sexual harassment, you can be sued under Section 1983" (interviewed in 1997).

In *Monell v. New York City Department of Social Services*, the court concluded that "sexual harassment can violate the equal protection provisions of the Fourteenth Amendment, thus creating a basis for an award of damages under Section 1983" (*Carrero v. New York City Housing Authority*, 1989). In addition, Section 1983 offers incentives for attorneys because employers can also be sued as persons (deep-pocket theory), and attorney's fees are recoverable pursuant to 42 U.S.C. §1988 (*Monell v. New York City Department of Social Services*).

THE COURTS AND FINDINGS OF SEXUAL HARASSMENT

Harassment violations were first considered by the court in 1972 in *Anderson v. Methodist Evangelical Hospital*, which required employers to maintain a work atmosphere free from racial and ethnic intimidation and insult (O'Linn, 1993, pp. 4, 14). Since that time, sexual harassment law has been rapidly evolving as courts interpret federal, state, and local antidiscrimination statutes.

According to Sarah E. Burns (1995), the most important unresolved issues concern the amount and kind of proof required to establish certain elements of sexual harassment claims and the employer's liability for harassment by nonsupervisory personnel (p. 193). Other important aspects concern the application of the law to the factual circumstances of a specific case, the evaluation of the parties' claims and proof, and the determination of proper damages. Nonetheless, courts have shown their disdain for sexual harassment practices:

> Sexual harassment which creates a hostile or offensive environment for members of one sex is every bit the arbitrary barrier to sexual equality at the work place that racial harassment is to racial equality. Surely, a requirement that a man or woman run a gauntlet of sexual abuse in return for the privilege of being allowed to work and make a living can be as demeaning and disconcerting as the harshest of racial epithets. (*Henson v. Dundee*, 1982)

Sexual harassment has been categorized in two forms: (1) "quid pro quo" (something for something) harassment—sexual favors as a condition for receiving a tangible benefit, and (2) as a hostile work environment—an offensive environment that unreasonably interferes with the employee's job performance. The first two sections of the Equal Employment Opportunity Commission's definition of sexual harassment pertain to quid pro quo harassment; the last refers to hostile work environment.

Until the United States Supreme Court's ruling in *Meritor Savings Bank v. Vinson*, there was considerable debate in the lower courts as to whether harassment fell into the legal definitions of sexual discrimination (O'Linn, 1995). The Supreme Court concluded:

> The EEOC Guidelines fully support the view that harassment leading to noneconomic injury can violate Title VII. . . . Since the Guidelines were issued, courts have uniformly held, and we agree, that a plaintiff may establish a violation of Title VII by proving that discrimination based on sex has created a hostile or abusive work environment. (Meritor Savings Bank, *FSB v. Vinson*, 1986)

In addition the Supreme Court held that: " . . . The correct inquiry is whether respondent by her conduct indicated that the alleged sexual advances were unwelcome . . . " (*Henson v. Dundee*, 1982).

According to some critics, the unwelcome standard places the plaintiff on trial similar to a rape victim. A plaintiff is "routinely required to explain why, if she was being subjected to sexual harassment, consistent with her claim of unwelcomeness, she failed to complain, remained politely silent, appeared flattered, joked, or even affirmatively participated in reciprocal slurs" (Burns, 1995, p. 194). In essence, she becomes the accused having to defend her actions. The proof of unwelcomeness "is usually determined by the sufferer's testimony corroborated by evidence that either she behaved as if the conduct were 'unwelcome' to her or the conduct was the kind likely to be obviously unwelcome or both" (Burns, 1995, p. 195). Proving or refuting a claim of sexual harassment can be very difficult, a he said/she said paradox centering on who is the most creditable person.

The Reasonable Woman Standard

The Ninth Circuit in *Ellison v. Brady* in 1991 focused the severity and persuasiveness of sexual harassment on the perspective of the victim, applying the **"reasonable woman" standard:**

> We hold that a female plaintiff states a prima facie case of hostile environment sexual harassment when she alleges conduct which a reasonable woman would consider sufficiently severe or pervasive to alter the conditions of employment and create an abusive working environment. (*Ellison v. Brady*, 1991)

The circuit court felt that the "reasonable man" or "reasonable person" did not take into account the concerns women share. "For example, because women are disproportionately victims of rape and sexual assault, women have a stronger incentive to be concerned with sexual behavior than men" (*Ellison v. Brady*, 1991).

The decision of the Supreme Court in *Harris v. Forklift Systems, Inc.* two years later was its second on sexual harassment. The Court took the middle ground to resolve a conflict among the circuit courts, holding "that to be actionable under Title VII 'abusive work environment' harassment, the conduct need not seriously affect an employee's psychological well-being or lead to the employee to suffer injury" (O'Linn, 1995, p. 18). The Court did leave vague what standard the plaintiff needed to meet to prevail in such a claim (reasonable woman, reasonable victim, reasonable person standard). In using the test of an objectively reasonable employee, the Court did provide guidance, saying that the totality of the circumstances needed to be considered:

1. How often the conduct occurs;
2. How serious the conduct is;
3. Whether the behavior physically threatens the victim, or stops at offensive comments; and
4. Whether the behavior unreasonably interferes with work performance; and
5. The victims must perceive the environment to be abrasive in order for the conduct to be considered illegal. (*Harris v. Forklift Systems, Inc.,* 1993)

Anita Bernstein (1997) argues in an article in *Harvard Law Review* that sexual harassment can be better explained using the concept of respect. She defended the legal virtues of a legal rule that affirms respect, saying that these virtues

> include the resonance of respect as a value among ordinary people, the history of inclusion based on human dignity that informs respect, the orientation of respect around the conduct of an agent (rather than the reaction of a complainant, the focus of current rules) and congruence with a tradition, found in many other areas of American law, of calling on citizens to render respect. (Bernstein, 1997, p. 446)

This standard of respect is actually being used to guide behavior in many businesses. For example, the 3M Corporation's "Appropriateness Test" raises the following questions: "Would I be embarrassed to discuss my language and behavior at work with my family? Would a newspaper account of my language and behavior at work embarrass me or my family? Would I be embarrassed to discuss my language and behavior at work with my supervisors and members of management?" ("The Appropriateness Test").

Rosemarie Skaine (1996) provides more in-depth questions for men to ask themselves to aid in assessing their behaviors:

> Would I mind if someone treated my wife, partner, girlfriend, mother, sister, or daughter this way? Would I mind if this person told my wife, partner, girlfriend, mother, sister, or daughter about what I was saying or doing? Would I do this if my wife, partner, girlfriend, mother, sister, or daughter were present? Would I mind if a reporter wanted to write about what I was doing? If I ask someone for a date and the answer is "no," do I keep asking? If someone asks me to stop a particular behavior, do I get angry and do more of the same instead of apologizing and stopping? Do I tell jokes or make "funny" remarks involving women and/or sexuality? (p. 401)

Issues of Women Working as Police Officers

The good news for women in policing is that they have made considerable progress. The bad news, as documented by the *2001 Status of Women in Policing Survey*, is that the number of sworn women police officers remains small and the pace of increase has stalled or even reversed in large agencies.

It is also discouraging that so few women are in command positions in police departments. As previously noted, over half of the large police agencies reported in the *2001 Status of Women in Policing Survey* (2002) that only 7.3 percent of sworn women officers hold top command positions. In small and rural agencies, fewer sworn women officers (3.4 percent) hold top command positions (p. 4).

In addition, the various studies have revealed how embedded sexism and racism are in policing. Martin found that racism divides white women from African American women and sexism divides African men officers from African women officers. Women of color, then, have the interactive effects of racism and sexism (Martin, 2004, p. 527). African American women continue to enter policing at higher rates than in the past, but few women of color have been hired in the majority of departments, and even in urban departments that have employed more women of color, few are promoted to supervisory status, with even fewer promoted to top command positions (p. 21).

The advent of community policing, especially in those departments that give more than lip service to community-oriented policing, has ushered in a new perspective on the police role that emphasizes cooperation and maintenance of connection with the community. The ideal community officer needs such "feminine" skills as caring, empathy, and connection that historically were unacceptable to male officers and continue to be challenged by many male officers. Yet as Martin has noted, for community policing to succeed, it will need to be repackaged so that adherents of traditional policing do not sabotage its potential for success. Thus, the success of community policing may greatly depend on reshaping unacceptable traits associated with femininity into acceptable traits associated with masculinity and "real police work" so that both men and women are able to deploy talents and skills in the gender-neutral realm of community policing (Martin, 1990, p. 95).

Summary

Policing has been reluctant to accept women police officers for several reasons. Law enforcement is perceived to be a man's job, and it is feared that its image of masculinity can be tarnished by the presence of women wearing police uniforms and carrying guns. The vulnerability of male police officers, so its defenders claim, is increased when men must depend on women for backup and support. There is also the concern that male camaraderie would be immeasurably harmed if a woman's presence interferes with men's talk in the locker room. In this age of sexual scandal, police supervisors are, of course, greatly concerned about the presence of women in the station house and on the street, resulting in sexual alliances with married officers and contributing to the breakup of marriages of male officers.

Despite these concocted explanations for rejecting women as police officers, the most viable consideration is whether women can do the job. Research studies continue to indicate that female police officers have somewhat different skills from male police officers but that their competence is equal to that of male officers. These studies have specifically found that women can handle the crime-fighting, combat, rescue, peacekeeping, and social service aspects of police work as well as men. Studies have also found that men and women are equally capable of patrol work. In addition, there is strong evidence that men are in no greater danger with women as partners than they are with men as partners.

Yet the initial resistance to women entering this male-dominated world continues in too many departments. It is found in the appraisal process of new recruits, in supervisory attitudes and treatment, in attitudes of male line officers, and in promotional opportunities and career advancements. Policing may be gender resistant to women, but it is more resistant to an African American police officer. The effects of race and gender expose African American women police officers to "double jeopardy" (Martin, 1994, pp. 383–384). Particularly unfortunate is that African American policewomen not only experience the effects of race from white women and men, but their relationships with

African American males on the police force are also often strained (p. 394).

The issue of sexual harassment affects women who work in the criminal justice system. It is a particular concern for women police officers, most of whom have experienced some form of sexual harassment at some point in their careers. The examination of sexual harassment in this chapter reveals that the term *sexual harassment* itself is multidimensional and has been expressed in various ways in law enforcement.

There is much that we do not know about sexual harassment in law enforcement. We do not know what the backgrounds of the offenders are. Are race and ethnicity factors? Are males from some groups more likely to harass women sexually than are males from other groups? Is education a factor? Are college-educated male

officers more or less likely to victimize female officers? Is satisfaction in police work a factor? What is the relationship between job satisfaction and sexual harassment? Is emotional maturity a factor? How well adjusted are those who sexually victimize others?

Women police officers who have been pleased with their careers have generally pursued three adaptive strategies to the men's club they must deal with on a daily basis: First, they have attempted to be competent and do the best job possible. Second, on a departmental, state, or national level (and sometimes on all three), they have developed a supportive network with other women officers. Third, they have found positive reinforcements outside the job, such as family, friends, and hobbies, that permit them to balance the difficult experiences they often face on a daily basis.

Key terms

Civil Rights Act of
 1964 *329*
Equal Employment Opportunity
 Commission *329*

Fair Employment Practices
 (FEP) agencies *330*
lesbian police officers *329*
policeWOMEN *326*

POLICEwomen *326*
"reasonable woman"
 standard *332*
sexual harassment *314*

Critical Thinking Questions

1. You're a sergeant. A female officer takes you into her confidence to talk to you about male officers who are making vulgar comments about women. She tells you that she does not want to get anyone in trouble or to have the complaint followed up on. What should you do?
2. While attending a briefing, some officers start complaining about a female dispatcher. The male lieutenant responds, "That big-titted bitch is not going to dispatch on my shift." As a patrol officer, what would you do next?
3. You're an officer on the Special Weapons and Tractical Team (SWAT) when a female officer joins the team. She is only allowed to participate in

drug raids by driving the support vehicle. The team leader will not help her with her gear and yells at her in front of the team for the smallest mistakes. After she endures a particularly vicious encounter with the team leader, you notice her vomiting behind the van, apparently traumatized by her harsh treatment. What should you do?
4. In your role of lieutenant, several female officers complain to you about three other female officers watching them in the locker room. They are very uncomfortable about this, and if you do not do something about it, they will start reporting for work late to avoid these officers. What would you recommend?

Web Destinations

Statistics on women and men personnel in the criminal justice system can be found in: www.albany.edu/sourcebook.

The International Association of Women Police can be found at: http://www.iawp.org/

For the National Center for Women and Policing, *Equity Denied: the Status of Women in Policing 2001*, see: www.womenandpolicing.org

National Criminal Justice Reference Service, Policing in Europe: www.ncjrs.org/policing/fem635.htm

References

3M Corporation. The Appropriateness Test.

42 United States Code Section 1983.

Andrews v. City of Philadelphia, 895 F.2d 1469 (3rd Cir. 1990).

Arnold v. City of Seminole, Okl. 614 F.Supp. 853 (D.C.Okl. 1985).

Bartol, C. R., Bergen, G. T., Seager Volckens, J., and Knoras, K. M. (1992, September 1). Women in small-town policing. *Criminal Justice and Behavior 19*: 240.

Belknap, J., and Shelly, J. K. (1992). The new lone ranger: Policewomen on patrol. *American Journal of Police 12*(2): 47–75.

Berg, B. L., and Budnick, K. J. (1986). Defeminization of women in law enforcement: A new twist in the traditional police personality. *Journal of Police Science and Administration 14:* 314.

Bernstein, A. (1997). Treating sexual harassment with respect. *Harvard Law Review 111:* 446.

Blumenthal, S. J. (1994). Cited in suicide and gender. *American Foundation for Suicide Prevention.*

Brewer, J. D. (1991). Hercules, Hippolyte and the Amazons—or policemen in the RUC. *British Journal of Sociology 42*(2): 231–248.

Burns, S. E. (1995). Issues in workplace sexual harassment law and related social science research. *Author's Abstract Journal of Social Issues 51*(1): 193.

Carrero v. New York City Housing Authority, 890 F.2d 569 (2nd Cir. 1989).

Charles, M. T. (1982). Women in policing: The physical aspect. *Journal of Police Science and Administration 10:* 194.

Cable News Network (CNN) (2009, August 31). Officers who cracked missing girl case: Something wasn't right. CNN.com. Retrieved August 31 from http://www.cnn.com/2009/CRIME/08/31/missing.girl.officers/index.html

Colvin, R. (2009). Shared perceptions among lesbian and gay police officers: Barriers and opportunities in the Law Enforcement Work Environment. *Police Quarterly 12*: 86–101.

Daum, J. M., and Johns, C. M. (1994, September). Police work from a woman's perspective. *The Police Chief*, p. 49.

Doerner, W. G. (1995). Officer retention patterns: An affirmative action concern for police agencies. *American Journal of Police 14:* 205.

Ellison v. Brady, 924 F.2d 872 (9th Cir. 1991): 878–879.

Feinman, C. (1986). *Women in the criminal justice system*, 2nd ed. (pp. 81–82, 95). New York: Praeger.

Felkenes, G. T., and Schroeder, J. R. (1993). A case study of minority women in policing. *Women and Criminal Justice 4:* 65–89.

Fletcher, C. (1995). *Breaking and entering: Women cops talk about life in the ultimate men's club* (pp. xi, 24, 162, 187). New York: HarperCollins.

Harrington, P. E. (2000). Advice to women beginning a career in policing. *Women and Criminal Justice 14:* 1–13.

Harrington, P. E., and Lonsway, K. A. (2004). Current barriers and future prospects for women in policing. In B. R. Price and N. J. Sokoloff (eds.), *The criminal justice system and women: Offenders, prisoners, victims, and workers*, 3rd ed. (pp. 495–510). New York: McGraw-Hill.

Harris v. Forklift Systems, Inc., 114 S.Ct. 367 (1993).

Heidensohn, F. (1992). *Women in control? The role of women in law enforcement.* Oxford: Clarendon Press.

Henson v. Dundee, 682 F.2d 897 (1982), p. 902, as cited in *Meritor Savings Bank, FSB v. Vinson, et al.*, 477 U.S. 57 (1986), p. 67.

Hochschild, A. P. (1973). Making it: Marginality and obstacles to minority consciousness. *Annals of the New York Academy of Science 208:* 79–82.

Horne, P. (1980). *Women in Law Enforcement*, 2nd ed. (pp. xix–xx, 2–5, 10–11, 15–17, 23, 35–36, 52–55,

114, 140, 151, 192, 216). Springfield, IL: Charles C. Thomas.

Hunt, J. C. (1990). The logic of sexism among police. *Women and Criminal Justice 1:* 3–30.

Johnson, L. B. (1991, May 20). Testimony in hearing before the Select Committee on Children, Youth, and Families, House of Representives (pp. 41–42). Washington, DC: U.S. Government Printing Office.

Kanter, R. M. (1976). The impact of hierarchical structures on the work behavior of women and men. *Social Problems 23:* 415–430.

Kirschman, Ellen. (1997). *I love a cop: What police families need to know* (p. 203). New York: Guilford.

Kurtz, Don L. (2008). Controlled Burn. The Gendering of stress and burnout in modern policing. *Feminist Criminology 3*: 216–238.

Law Enforcement Ethics Center. (1997). *The Ethics Roll Call.*

Lonsway, K. A. (2006). Are we there yet? The progress of women in one large Law Enforcement Agency. *Women & Criminal Justice 18*: 1–48.

Lonsway, K. A., and Alipio, A. M. (2007). Sex discrimination lawsuits in Law Enforcement: A case study of thirteen Female officers who Sued their Agencies, *Women & criminal Justice 18*: 63–103.

Lord, L. K. (1995). Policewomen. In William G. Bailey (ed.), *The encyclopedia of police science*, 2nd ed. (pp. 627–636). New York: Garland Press. See also P. Horne (1980). *Women in law enforcement.* Springfield, IL: Charles C. Thomas.

Lunneborg, P. W. (1989). *Women police officers current career profile* (p. 99). Springfield, IL: Charles C. Thomas.

Martin, S. E. (1979). Policewomen and police*women:* Occupational role dilemmas and choices of female officers. *Journal of Police Science and Administration 7*: 314–323.

Martin, S. E. (1980). *Breaking and entering* (p. 315). Berkeley, CA: University of California Press.

Martin, S. E. (1989). Female officers on the move? A status report on women in policing. In R. Dunham and G. Alpert (eds.), *Critical issues in policing: Contemporary readings* (pp. 313, 315, 321–322). Prospect Heights, IL: Waveland Press.

Martin, S. L. (1990). *Gender and community policing: Walking the talk.* Boston, MA: Northeastern University Press.

Martin, S. E. (1994, August). "Outsider within" the station house: The impact of race and gender on black women police. *Social Problems 41*: 383–384, 389.

Martin, S. L. (2000). Gender and policing. In C. Renzetti and L. Goodstein (eds.), *Women, crime, and criminal justice: Original feminist readings.* Los Angeles: Roxbury Publishing Company.

Martin, S. L. (2004). The interactive effects of race and sex on women police officers. In B. R. Price and N. J. Sokoloff (eds.), *The criminal justice system and women: Offenders, prisoners, victims, and workers*, 3rd ed. (pp. 527–541). New York: McGraw-Hill.

Martin, S. L., Forest, K. B., and Jurik, N. C. (2004). Lesbians in policing: Perceptions and work experiences within the macho cop culture. In B. R. Price and N. J. Sokoloff (eds.), *The criminal justice system and women: Offenders, prisoners, victims, and workers*, 3rd ed. (pp. 511–525). New York: McGraw-Hill.

Martin, S. E., and Jurik, N. C. (1995). *Doing justice, doing gender* (p. 55). Thousand Oaks, CA: Sage Publications.

McDowell, J. (1992, February 17). Are women better cops? *Time*, pp. 70, 72.

Mendel, R. M., and Shoenfelt, E. (1991, March 21). Gender bias in the evaluation of male and female police officer performance. Paper presented at the Annual Convention of the Southeastern Psychological Association, New Orleans.

Meritor Savings Bank, FSB v. Vinson, et al., 477 U.S. 57 (1986), p. 66.

Morrison, P. (1991, July 14). Women make better cops L.A. probers find. *Los Angeles Times.*

National Center for Women & Policing. (2002). *Equality denied: The status of women in policing: 2001.* Washington, DC: U.S. Government Printing Office.

National Law Enforcement Officers Memorial Fund, Inc. (1997). *Law enforcement facts.*

O'Linn, M. K. (1993). Sexual harassment in *Supervisory Survival.* Ed. Nowicki (ed.). Lake Performance dimensions.

O'Linn, M. K. (1995, January). Sexual harassment, handout prepared for the American Society of Law Enforcement Trainers Convention. Anchorage, Alaska, pp. 2, 4, 5, 14, 18.

Petrocelli, W., and Repa, B. K. (1994). *Sexual harassment on the job*, 2nd ed. (pp. 1, 2, 8, 19). Berkeley, CA: Nolo Press.

Platt, A. (1969). *The child savers* (p. 76). Chicago, IL: University of Chicago Press.

Rabe-Hemp, C. (2008a), Survival in an "all-boys club": Policewomen and their fight for acceptance. *Policing: American International Journal of Police Strategies and Management 31*(2): 251–270.

Rabe-Hemp, C. (2008b). Female officers and the ethic of care: Does officer gender impact police behavior? *Journal of Criminal Justice 36*: 426–434.

Rubin, P. N. (1995, October). Civil rights and criminal justice: Primer on sexual harassment. *National Institute of Justice: Research in action.* Washington, DC: U.S. Government Printing Office, p. 1.

Schaper, D. (1997, January 28). More women in uniform could be a force for peace. *Newsday,* p. 32.

Schulz, D. M. (1993). Policewomen in the 1950s: Paving the way for patrol. *Women and Criminal Justice 4*: 5–30.

Schulz, D. M. (1995). *From social worker to crimefighter: Women in United States municipal policing* (pp. 4, 10, 134, 135). Westport, CT: Praeger Publishers.

Skaine, R. (1996). *Power and gender: Issues in sexual dominance and harassment* (p. 401). Jefferson, NC: McFarland.

*Status of women in policing:*2001. (2002). Washington, DC: National Center for Women & Policing.

The new Lexicon Webster's encyclopedic dictionary of the English language (p. 1042), Deluxe ed. (1992). Danbury, CT: Lexicon Publications.

Watts v. New York City Police Dept., 724 F.Supp. 99 (S.D.N.Y., 1989).

Webb, S. L. (1994). *The global impact of sexual harassment.* New York: Master Media Limited.

Wertsch, T. L. (1998). Walking the thin blue line: Policewomen and tokenism today. *Women and Criminal Justice 9*: 25–26.

Wexler, J. G., and Quinn, V. (1985). Considerations on the training and development of women sergeants. *Journal of Police Science and Administration 13*: 98–105.

12

Women in the Legal Profession

Women have made far more significant advances in the legal profession than in law enforcement or in any branch of the criminal justice system. Women now make up almost a third of the profession, and most law schools have an almost equal enrollment of both sexes. According to a report from the American Bar Association (ABA) Goal IX Commission, between 1991 and 2008, the percentage of women members of the bar association rose from 25 to 31.4 percent (Rhode and Yu, 2008). The percentage of women involved in ABA leadership has increased as well.

Women have gravitated toward law in record numbers. Their rapid movement into the profession, in turn, has laid the groundwork for further possibilities. From the famous former federal prosecutor Janet Napolitano, who went on to become the governor of Arizona and then the Secretary of Homeland Security, to Secretary of State Hillary Rodham Clinton, to First Lady Michelle Obama, to Supreme Court Justices Sandra Day O'Connor (retired) and Ruth Ginsburg, to law professors Lani Guinier and Anita Hill, to TV host Nancy Grace, women lawyers are in the limelight. And for every one who has achieved national prominence, many more across the country are quietly making a contribution to law and, through law, to the whole society.

When a Supreme Court vacancy recently provided President Obama with the opportunity to choose a woman, he found a vastly altered scene, according to an article in the *New York Times*, "with women holding dozens of seats on the nation's appellate courts, occupying dean's offices at prestigious law schools, and serving in some of the highest political offices in the nation" (Savage, 2009, p. A1). The legal landscape has been transformed since previous administrations searched for applicants for the highest judicial office from women with experience at the federal appellate level or comparable experience in political office. The Senate's confirmation of Sonia Sotomayor to the Supreme Court marked an important milestone in U.S. history for many Latinos—an affirmation of their struggles and hard work, an inspiration for them and their children (Keen, 2009). The celebration was especially pronounced for Latina law students who now would have a role model on the bench. If a student on scholarship who was brought up by a single mother in the Bronxdale projects inspired by watching the *Perry Mason* show could achieve such success, then perhaps doors will open for others as well. As stated in the *USA Today* article,

- When law student Anna Lozoya looks at Sotomayor, she sees herself: a Latina who overcame the limits her culture sometimes places on women.
- Lozoya sees her own stubborn nature in the new U.S. Supreme Court justice, and both are diabetic.
- When Sotomayor was nominated, Lozoya had not heard of her. Now the justice is a role model as Lozoya, 28, a nurse, studies to be a lawyer (Keen, p. 4A).

Because in the Anglo-Saxon tradition, the judiciary plays a recognizably powerful role, women's success here is of no small consequence. The "feminization of the legal profession," as Chen (2003) optimistically terms it, is occurring not only in the United States but in several Anglo-Saxon and European nations as well. In Canada, for example, women are entering law school in around equal numbers to men, and according to Kay (2008), women "appear to be slipping through the 'glass ceiling'" (p. 188). In the United Kingdom, 30 percent of all barristers (those who argue cases in court) and 40 percent of all solicitors are women (UK Department for Constitutional Affairs, 2005). This year about half of those called to the bar in the UK are women.

The first-ever report on women lawyers in Ireland, conducted by legal researchers at Trinity College, Dublin, remarked on the dramatic increase in the numbers of women entering the legal profession in recent years; two-thirds of law students in Ireland, in fact, are women. Solicitors are 41 percent women, while one-third of barristers (courtroom lawyers) are women and one-fifth of judges are women (Finnigan, 2007). The latter figure, as the report indicates, compares favorably with the number of judges in the United Kingdom, but not with France and Finland, where the sex ratios for judges are about even.

A United Nations Educational, Scientific and Cultural Organization (UNESCO) (2006) report on women in the legal profession in the Middle East found that women's participation as lawyers and judges is similarly mixed across the region. Some Middle Eastern countries report respectable percentages of women judges (e.g., Algeria and Tunisia), while elsewhere in the region women are banned from the profession of judge (e.g., Iran, Saudi Arabia). This reflects cultural biases against gender equality. In egalitarian Norway, which in 2003 became the first country in the world to introduce legislation stipulating balanced gender representation on company boards, over half of law students are female (Norwegian Ministry of Children and Equality, 2007). Still, only 26 percent of lawyers are women, and, as elsewhere, they are rarely involved in litigation.

Women are well represented in the legal profession in Russia, where the practice of law is highly bureaucratized, and in China, where they are likely to work in public service. The situation in China is typical of that in a newly industrializing nation. Although employment opportunities for women lawyers have greatly expanded, their careers are less successful than those of their male counterparts in terms of both income and partnership status (Michelson, 2009).

The proportion of women lawyers is smallest in Japan and India, where traditional sex roles remain very strong. In Japan, however, this may be turning around thanks to a popular TV show called *Seven Women Lawyers*. The escapades of the seven attractive female attorneys take place at a law firm that is specially designed to rescue helpless women involved in crimes, sexual harassments, and marital problems. In Germany, legal education is the ticket to entry into the highest positions in public service and industry. Only recently have women lawyers begun to infiltrate the all-male club of law school faculties (Schultz and Shaw, 2003). German women flock into civil service jobs because family and maternity leaves are substantial; approximately half of the judges in lower courts are women.

Felstiner (2005) examines the evolution of women's entry in the legal professions throughout the world, with an emphasis on industrialized nations. Everywhere, Felstiner finds an increase in the numbers of women law students and practitioners that is encouraging. Women now constitute over a quarter of the practicing profession in Australia, Canada, Germany, Mexico and over a third in the Netherlands and nearly half of the profession in France. The data presented from Canada and Germany, however, indicate that the attrition rate in private practice is higher for women than men. And a glass ceiling remains firmly in place virtually everywhere, but most strikingly in France, the Netherlands, Australia, Mexico, and Canada. Discrimination is manifested in pay, promotion into partnerships at elite corporate law firms, and limited access to positions of power and responsibility relative to their experience. In the United States, significantly, almost all paralegals are women. Women's recent progress notwithstanding, the fact is that women are concentrated in the lowest echelons of the profession. The consistent pattern is that women are "pulled" into work for which they are thought to have special talent, such as domestic relations, and "pushed" or kept out of high-status work, such as private commercial matters.

Women's advances in the legal profession, in short, are cause for celebration but not complacency. In the law, as elsewhere, status and income disparities still exist. Significant differentials between male and female are reflected in statistics released in the national Survey on Retention and Promotion of Women in Law Firms conducted by the National Association of Women Lawyers (NAWL) (2008). This survey tracks the progress of women lawyers at all levels of private practice. A major conclusion of the study is that women, although they enter into law firms at about the same level as men, fail to advance beyond the associate level comparable to men. In short, law firm governance is overwhelmingly male, with fully 15 percent of the surveyed firms lacking a female on its top committee.

Income disparities between male and female lawyers are pronounced. Women lawyers' median weekly salary for full-time work is 77.5 percent of men's (ABA, 2008). The disparities in pay are the most extreme in private practice, even when years of practice are accounted for. Also reported in an ABA survey was the lack of credibility women felt they had; about half reported being mistaken for an assistant (Compensation and Benefits for Law Offices, 2003).

What is true for women is true for minorities as well. Women of color are often isolated in law firms, and most leave before their seventh year. African American women gravitate toward work in the public sector and in small firms in big cities with a large African American clientele. Women of color are much less likely to be in partnership positions than white lawyers of either gender or men of color. Minority women are about 11 percent of associates but only 4 percent of partners.

This does not mean their contribution is to be discounted, however. Take, for example, the work of Yeshimebet Abebe. The granddaughter of a well-known African American and the daughter of a native of Ethiopia, Abebe exemplifies the adage, "Think globally, act locally." In 2003, Abebe's strong showing in a Waterloo, Iowa, mayoral election ultimately threw the election to a third candidate. Her education has been strikingly global (Jamison, 2003). After finishing law school, Abebe, who holds a master's degree in international law as well as a law degree, was the first American to receive full funding to study at the United Nations' University for Peace in Costa Rica. She has worked on the settlement of disputes through international tribunals and has spoken out internationally against human rights violations, including the racism of her U.S. milieu at home. Today Abebe continues her international work in human rights from her law office in Atlanta, Georgia (interviewed by van Wormer, October 7, 2005). See also the boxed readings to follow about the contributions of immigration lawyer Miryam Antunez de Mayolo (Box 12.1) and African American legal aid director Jessie Nicholson (Box 12.2).

BOX 12.1
Lawyer Juggles Motherhood, Cases

Miryam Antunez de Mayolo is a living proof of the American dream both in her profession and her personal life.

The immigration attorney and mother of seven-year-old triplets says that her story is very different from those of the immigrants she represents, but her reasons for coming to this country fourteen years ago were just as compelling.

Miryam left her native Peru to follow her husband, Philip Mauceri, a professor of political science at the University of Northern Iowa, to the U.S.

In the past seven years, Miryam has heard hundreds of immigrants stories, much less fortunate than hers. The 1998 University of Iowa Law School graduate believes that being an immigration lawyer in the heart of the country is a noble calling.

"When you take into account that there are very few Spanish-speaking immigration attorneys in the state of Iowa, and there is such a need for representation, practicing immigration law is tantamount to missionary work," she says over coffee and a cone at Cup of Joe's on a recent Tuesday morning. "I have to drive four and a half hours to get to immigration court."

Last month, Miryam moved her office to 315 West Second St., across the street from the premises she shared with attorney Ronnie Podolefsky. The transition has inspired Miryam to paint the house in colors reminiscent of paintings by Latin American artists. The ocean blue in her office reminds her of the Pacific Ocean where she used to surf while growing up in Lima. Surrounded by the pictures of her mother, Mari Teresa, and her father, Santiago, Miryam feels that she is continuing the family tradition while at the same time blazing her own path on American soil.

The cases she has worked on have enriched her life, Miryam says.

Her cases have caught the attention of local and statewide newspapers. The case of William Keleture, an assistant track coach in the Quad Cities, originally from the Sudan, is her most recent victory.

"He was almost on the plane, being deported to the Sudan, when I took the case," she says. "An attorney he had hired previously failed to do his job and did not file a brief in a timely fashion, so William was apprehended and taken into custody, regardless of the fact that he is married to an American citizen with whom he has a girl almost the same age as my children."

Last week, when the judge granted Keleture permanent residence, the emotion in the courtroom overwhelmed William and his wife.

"They were just in tears," says Miryam. "Even the journalist from the Quad-City Times who was there to cover the story was crying."

Immigration law is rather complex, says Miryam, because of the way it is drafted. "The power that the Department of Homeland Security has is unparalleled. After 9/11, things changed dramatically for the worst. People are so accustomed to their freedoms here that they don't really know or can't imagine

(continued)

(continued)

that some of those freedoms are not enjoyed by immigrants who are placed in the removal proceedings. Sometimes, they are not even bondable, which I believe is unconstitutional because everybody should have the right to be bonded out. We are not talking about criminal proceedings here since immigration court is an administrative body."

With all the hurdles immigrants face, coming to the U.S. continues to be a magnet for many.

"Most of the people I have represented throughout the years want to play by the rules and they just want what everybody else wants—a better future for their families and that's why they are here."

Motherhood has made Miryam a better lawyer, she admits. "When I represent someone who is going to be separated from his or her children, I know what is at stake," she adds.

Critical Thinking Questions: What is the nature of de Mayolo's contribution? How does this attorney's personal story impact her law practice?

Source: By Anelia Dimitrova, Cedar Falls Times (July 23, 2005), p. 1. Reprinted with permission of Anelia Dimitrova, editor.

In private correspondence to van Wormer (of August 18, 2005), de Mayolo described how her work relates to criminal law: "Criminal law intersects with immigration law quite often, since immigrants, even those who have been legally here for many years, and have spouses and children who are U.S. citizens, can be deported for committing even minor crimes. For instance, someone with a conviction for possession of cocaine will be deported, even if it's for personal use, even it's a first-time offense, regardless of the time he has spent in the U.S., regardless of the ties he has to this country, and regardless of the hardship that his deportation would pose to his family members. It is quite draconian." Then in a final paragraph she expresses her gratitude to the earlier generation of lawyers such as Flora Stuart, who blazed the trail before her. "Every time I enter a courtroom, I am keenly aware that I have the privilege, because women like her [Stuart] had the guts to pave the path for me; and I am oh so thankful!"

HISTORY OF WOMEN IN LAW

Women lawyers have come a long way, and most of the growth has occurred in the last ten to fifteen years. Besides Shakespeare's Portia who, disguised as a young man, brought a soft touch to the law in her famous "the quality of mercy is not strained" exhortation (Shakespeare, 1600/1952 4.1.182), few literary or historical examples of women advocates in court exist. The first practicing lawyer in North America was Margaret Brent, who was asked by the governor of Maryland to be the executor of his estate. Brent became officially empowered by the Maryland legislature to serve as the governor's executor and lawyer and to settle claims by soldiers against his estate (Encyclopaedia Britannica, 2009). So powerful was she in her day that colonists called her "Gentleman Brent" (Belknap, 2007). After litigating 124 court cases on behalf of the governor's estate, Brent moved out of Maryland because she was denied the right to vote. In 1991, Sen. Hillary Clinton, then Chair of the ABA's Commission on Women in the Profession, established the Margaret Brent Women Lawyers of Achievement Award.

Not much was heard from women again on the issue for a long time, until the mid-1800s. Before that time, women were prohibited from attending law school or otherwise qualifying to take the bar exam. Some evidence does exist that some women appeared before the local courts, especially out West to defend land claims. One such woman, an African American named Lucy Terry Prince, successfully defended a land claim before the U.S. Supreme Court before the Civil War (Morello, 1986).

During the 1830s and 1840s, women began to struggle for the right to own property and to work (Drachman, 2001). In Britain, women worked hard to reform marriage and divorce law and property rights. Under the principle of coverture, women could not own property in their own names or enter the legal profession. The professions were considered improper avenues for women because of their unique biological characteristics, which suited them to the home.

BOX 12.2

Giving a Hand Up: Providing Leadership for Today's Generation

Leadership means knowing who I am. Not here (pointing to her head) but here (pointing to her heart). Where did I come from? I was raised in Waterloo, Iowa, and in 1970 graduated from the University of Northern Iowa with a master's degree in sociology. This is my background: In the 1940s, a lot of African Americans were coming to Iowa from Mississippi so my Dad came to Iowa to give us kids a better opportunity. We would go back to south in the summer to visit my grandparents. We traveled in the dark so we would not be pulled over. One of the most fun parts was that we would bring fried chicken and a loaf of special bread which we would eat along the way. We would eat and drink; the trip was around twelve hours long so we would have to stop to go to the bathroom. When it came time that we had to go to the bathroom we would go in the back door of a gas station, or we would stop on the side of the road. I remember when I was around seven years old asking myself, Why is that? Why are people like that? Later I figured out that by traveling at night, we could preserve our modesty when we stopped. So, asking these questions later brought me to sociology.

I was raised in the Antioch Baptist Church, singing in the choir. Judge Parker was the preacher and also the first African American judge in Waterloo. From this upbringing and my faith life I learned that we need to remember that we come from something, and we have to give back. Always remember that it doesn't stop with you.

At some point I moved to Minnesota, and in 1978 I attended William Mitchell College of Law at night and worked in social services in the daytime. Today, I am where I need to be; I am working on behalf of low income children, a non-profit law firm in St. Paul, working with domestic violence issues, immigration, social benefits, not criminal law. In my office, all you see is women and children—that's who we serve, people who don't have access to lawyers. These people deserve dignity and respect something different from what I experienced at the back of the gas station.

After I had worked as a legal aid lawyer for some time, the Board of Directors interviewed me for the position of chief legal aid officer. I want to say to you that as an African American woman when I had this interview before seven or eight board members, I got asked this question: "You're a black woman; can you run this thing? I just wanted to ask. What if both or if most of your staff would leave because they couldn't work for a black woman?"

But I was offered the job and I accepted. Now in my position I can influence who we hire. We employ sixty-one lawyers and serve ten offices. In 2008, we served 10,800 clients; we have a $10 million budget. This responsibility says that I as a black woman dare to dream high. My leadership style is to be able to value the perspective of everyone I come into contact with—to listen, to recognize I can be a consensus builder, be able to say no when I need to say no and say yes when I need to say yes. That's who I am.

I keep a baby picture of myself in my office, of me as a baby on a bear rug. This keeps me humble. Are there any questions?

[In response to a question concerning immigration cases] There is a lot of trafficking in this country; women are brought to southern Minnesota from South East Asia or Mexico as brides or fiancées. We see two or three a week. One example would be a woman we had from Ukraine who was brought to America by the Russian Jewish Community Center. She was married to someone here and suffered physical abuse. She went back to Russia; then someone else brought her back. This time she was sexually exploited, and her immigration status threatened. She was forced into prostitution. Fortunately, there is a federal law to protect such women and help them get legal status. So we got that for her. The Russian community is very close knit and told her about us. Some of the trafficked women come from the Philippines and Thailand; they may not speak any English. Often the women are scared to death, and they don't want to go home. We refer them to the services they need and housing.

Source: By Jessie R. Nicholson, Chief Executive Officer, Southern Minnesota Regional Legal Services, Invitational speech given at the University of Northern Iowa, Cedar Falls (March 27, 2009).

Working-class women and the servant classes, of course, were under no such requirements to stay home. In both Britain and the United States, women's involvement in the abolitionist, suffrage, and temperance movements galvanized them to further ambitions.

The usual method of becoming a lawyer in the early days was through a clerkship under the auspices of a practicing attorney. Women who did study the law under this arrangement clerked with their husbands and fathers. The reasons that impelled women to enter law were somewhat different from those that drew women to corrections and law enforcement; pioneers in legal practice were not primarily reformers but were motivated more by practical and intellectual considerations (Feinman, 1994).

The first woman to be officially recognized as a lawyer in the United States was Arabella Babb Mansfield, who was admitted to the Iowa State bar in 1869. The first female to graduate from a law school in the United States was Ada Kepley, who graduated from the University of Chicago law school in 1870. In 1872, Charlotte E. Ray became the first black woman to formally enter the practice of law (Drachman, 2001). She was admitted to the District of Columbia bar the same year she graduated from Howard Law School.

An ardent suffragist, Ada Kepley urged women to support temperance and seize political power. As long as discriminatory admissions policies continued, however, women could not get their hands on power. In eastern urban schools and at Ivy League colleges, women were denied admission well into the twentieth century (Drachman). The state laws were gradually changing, but in Britain, it was not until 1919 when the Sex Disqualification Removal Act was passed that the official barriers to women lawyers were lifted. Moreover, the legal profession continued to be exclusionary on the basis of class, race, ethnicity, and gender. The proliferation of the apprenticeship system kept "unsuitable" aspirants out. On the Continent, where the university was the entry route, women entered the legal profession earlier than they did in England, which relied on legal apprenticeship.

Admission to the bar presented a barrier to women in the United States. Before the summer of 1869, there was little hope that a woman would be permitted to practice law anywhere in the country. One fear was that if women were permitted to practice law, this might qualify them to vote. Then, surprisingly, thanks to a progressive Iowa judge who was dedicated to women's equality, Arabella Mansfield was quietly admitted to the bar in Iowa (Sarver, Keheny, and Szmer, 2008). She never did practice law, however. One state away, in Illinois, Myra Bradwell (who studied law in her husband's law office) was seriously committed to a legal career. After performing brilliantly on the bar exam, Bradwell was still denied admission to the Illinois bar. Her appeal to the U.S. Supreme Court was denied not solely on the basis of gender, but also because as a married woman she could not sign contracts on behalf of her clients, a requirement for any lawyer. The Court's refusal to overturn Illinois's prohibition against women practicing law meant that women, by necessity, would be engaged in a state-by-state struggle for admission to the bar. Bradwell was to achieve her major impact on the legal field not through the practice of law but as editor of the highly influential *Chicago Legal Notes*.

It was not until 1918 that the ABA began to accept women. Ultimately, it was the state legislatures, not the courts, that struck down the barriers to female practice. Women made up 1.1 percent of all lawyers in 1920, and one century following the granting of an Iowa law license to Arabella Mansfield, women were still only 4.7 percent of all practicing attorneys in the United States (Sarver, Keheny, and Szmer, 2008).

Special mention should be made of the civil rights pioneer Constance Baker Motley, who as a young attorney represented Martin Luther King, Jr. and played a pivotal role in the civil rights movement (Neumeister, 2005). Earlier she had been a law clerk to Thurgood Marshall and through this connection she helped prepare some of the nation's most important civil rights cases, including the 1954 landmark case *Brown v. Board of Education* of Topeka, Kansas, in which the Supreme Court ruled that segregation in the public schools was unconstitutional. Motley died recently at the age of eighty-four.

This limited historical overview reveals a firm resistance to women's entry into the legal profession, as compared with their acceptance into social work, teaching, nursing, and even medicine. Most of the opposition to women practicing law came from males in the profession (Belknap, 2007). Women had more success in medicine than they did in law. Although law is construed as masculine, perhaps thanks to its legacy of trial by combat, women could argue that their special qualities render them especially suited to caring for the sick.

The passage of **Title IX** of the Higher Education Act in 1972, which prohibited discrimination based on sex in the enrollment of students and hiring of faculty, was a landmark decision in terms of opening the doors to budding female attorneys (Jackson, 2007). Facing denial of federal funds if they continued to discriminate, law schools began admitting women applicants in unprecedented numbers and still do so today.

As women gained entry into law school in the 1970s, they continued to find many unexpected obstacles in their path. The reasons for the resistance to women in law can never be fully explained, but it is likely that it has to do with the law's close relationship to power in society. As in other male-dominated fields, such as the police or firefighting, many men felt that their masculinity and stature would be threatened if women were admitted to their ranks. The story of Flora Stuart (author van Wormer's sister), the first woman attorney to practice trial law in Bowling Green, Kentucky, typifies some of the difficulties women faced breaking into the profession in the 1970s. One of few women in her northern Kentucky Law School class, Stuart met tremendous resentment from professors (Hurst, 1977). Because of this coupled with the fact that some of the male law students refused to have anything to do with the women, Stuart helped found the Women Lawyer's Club, which was to grow dramatically over the following decade. How to dress professionally for court, to be confident and assertive without seeming aggressive or whiny, to be feminine without appearing flirtatious, and to persuade the members of a jury used to heeding male authority—all were dilemmas the women law students confronted that had to be resolved in the absence of role models or mentors.

Shortly after passing the bar exam, Stuart, as a young public defender, was catapulted to early prominence with a case that was any feminist's dream: a young woman, Marla Pitchford, charged with manslaughter for performing an abortion on herself with a knitting needle.

"Miss Flora," as the judge called her, argued for her beautiful young client, the defendant, before a packed courtroom. Reporters from *Time* magazine and *Newsweek* were among those in attendance. Following a not-guilty verdict, the lawyer and her client received invitations for guest appearances on *Good Morning, America* and the *Phil Donahue Show*.

Recently, a lawyer from New York who specializes in researching cases involving abortion and pregnancy contacted van Wormer concerning the Marla Pitchford case. Kathrine Jack (in private correspondence of January 2009) explains her interest in this earlier case and links this now historic case with the treatment of some women today:

> In the work I do, I see women discriminated against in exactly the same manner that occurred in the 1970s. The discrimination is one layer below the surface now, whereas it was much more open in the 1970s. There have been a lot of victories for women since the 1970s, but these victories only went so far. Our purpose in looking at these old cases is to figure out what strategies worked, what arguments were made by prosecutors, and

how these arguments were addressed. The goal is to raise awareness about the cases, which few people, even within organizations that we work closely with, are aware of today, and to provide ammunition to fight the next prosecution.

For many complicated reasons, cases just like Marla Pitchford are still occurring today. In 2007, a woman in Virginia shot herself in the stomach in her ninth month of pregnancy. Like Marla, the woman was desperate and in an emotional/mental health crisis. Because the fetus died, the prosecutors wanted to charge her with homicide, but eventually charged her with performing an illegal abortion. That charge was also eventually dismissed after her attorney vigorously defended her. (p. 2)

Today, in Kentucky, Flora Stuart concentrates on personal injury cases; several years ago she reached settlements in dozens of silicone breast implant lawsuits. She has what must be one of the few mother–daughter law firms in the country. In her words:

A second glance at the major law firms would immediately reveal the fact that the lead partners are mostly male. Women who join the firms now rarely move to the top. Finding a mother and daughter as a legal team is still rare, but it is not unusual to find a father and son duo practicing law together. Some attorneys (particularly from the earlier generation) still find it difficult to accept a female attorney as their full equal. Time will eventually melt away these extreme prejudices against our gender, but the battle is far from being won.

Twenty-two years after I started my journey down the legal road, my daughter now practices law by my side. It is a different world from when I began. (Stuart, 2005, p. 1)

The contrast between the professional challenges that mother and daughter have known symbolizes the differences in the world a woman lawyer faced in the 1970s and the world of today. Unlike her mother, Natalie Stuart attended a law school in which almost half the students were female and was taught by female as well as male professors. On graduation, a place in an established law firm was ready for her. In her hometown, her mother had already blazed the trail. Not only is there no shock on people's faces today as the younger Stuart begins her opening statement before the "ladies and gentlemen of the jury," but the judge is likely to be a female, as is the opposing counsel.

A historical perspective is provided as well by the host of CNN *Headline News*' legal analysis show, Nancy Grace (2005) who recalls in her autobiography, *Objection!*, her early days as a prosecutor. In her words:

Sexism is alive and well in the courtroom. . . . One of the reasons I am writing this book is to propose remedies for the existing problems in our justice systems. Sexism is still an issue. It's the same way in the courtroom as it is in every other profession in this country: Women have to work twice as hard to be taken seriously and get the same job done as their male counterparts do. Lawyering is no different from any other profession in that way. There is one big difference in how it affects female lawyers, though. The prejudice against female lawyers has an impact on more than the individual—it affects her clients, her cases, and her causes. A case could be won or lost because of a sexual bias. Traditionally, juries love judges, because they look up to them and respect them. Whether that bias originates with the judge or the defense, the jury picks up on it.

When I first came to the district attorney's office, there were very few female cops and lawyers—female judges were even harder to find. At the time, women were usually assigned to work juvenile cases, which are not jury trials and do not apply many of the standard rules of evidence. We were usually going after deadbeat dads, writing appeals, or acting as assistants to trial lawyers. Practically everybody involved in the actual trial of cases was a man—except the jury and, in many cases, the victim.

I've been called "little lady," "young lady," "lady lawyer," and other not-so-nice names, right in front of juries by defense lawyers, experts, and judges—pretty much by everybody but the jury. (p. 163)

Grace goes on to say that if a lawyer files a sexual harassment complaint or a motion for a hostile judge to recuse himself, it could seriously harm the case and all future cases before that judge or his cronies.

LAW SCHOOL SOCIALIZATION

Given what law professor Patricia Williams terms the "clearly stated authority" of the law, that body of "hypnotically powerful rhetorical truths," as a female African American teacher of law she had to wrestle with the appropriate introduction of race, gender, class, and social policy into the law school curriculum (Williams, 1991, p. 10). She also had to confront the legacy of the institutional racism, sexism, and classism at her university. Williams's iconoclastic book, *The Alchemy of Race and Rights*, is the product of that struggle. Law school's mask of impersonality and "hyperauthenticity," as Williams suggests, is a cover for rigidity and prejudice. Being in law school is described by Williams as being on another planet, and being a law professor as being in another galaxy.

A second study of female law students in the 1990s by Guinier et al. (1994) presented a wealth of data on students, male and female, enrolled in law school. Entitled "Becoming Gentlemen: Women's Experience at One Ivy League Law School," these researchers found that one of the most pervasive values of legal culture inculcated in law school is the belief in individuation through hierarchical stratification. Such practices as rigidly ranking students against each other and ranking faculty and deans as well as upper-level students above lower-level students within the law school trains students for later hierarchical relationships and a winner-take-all mentality. For female law school recruits, learning to think like a lawyer, as Guinier and her associates suggest, means learning to think and act like a man.

The narrative data collected by these authors add poignancy to the findings. In interviews, women law students told of eating disorders, sleeping difficulties, crying (35 percent reported crying from stress compared with none of the men), and failure to learn in the intimidating environment of hostile questioning. As one third-year law student described her experience,

Just look at the way many professors here conduct their classes. They call on men predominantly. . . . I think if you look at the people in our class who have formed relationships with professors, they are very much the same men who all of us despise in class. The ones who feel they can monopolize the class time. (p. 51)

Another woman concurs, "Women's sexuality becomes the focus for keeping us in place. If someone was rumored to be a woman who speaks too much, she was a lesbian" (p. 14). All the female students seem to echo the sentiment that human compassion is a negative trait in budding lawyers.

The traditional law school experience is sufficiently rigorous and formidable to be the subject of numerous films, novels, and nonfiction books. Because the dictates of the bar exam in each state to a large extent decree the nature of the education that law schools must offer, the law school experience is relatively comparable across the states.

In her research on current experiences of women in law and law school, Jackson (2007) echoes the sentiments of Guinier and her associates that U.S. law students generally succumb to peer pressure to abandon dreams of public interest work in favor of more lucrative and less altruistic forms of practice. Women still are found to volunteer less in class than men, and unlike men, to believe that they are at the lower end of the class academically. The uncertainty and loss of confidence that women suffer in law school no doubt crushes their resistance and leads to a turnabout in attitude.

But in some law schools, thanks to the influence of the influx of female students and women in positions of prominence on the faculty, the academic climate is changing. Law professors Lani Guinier, who now teaches at Harvard Law School, have been instrumental in introducing more women-friendly approaches to teaching law (Zhao, 2004). Guinier's mission is to end the dominance of the Socratic Method, which demands quick responses and invites caustic treatment. Men are often better at giving quick, definitive answers under the intense pressure that this method creates. Guinier likens the Socratic Method to ritualized combat. The new teaching approach is built on teamwork and role-playing; the purpose is to redesign the classroom experience so that people with different learning styles can all thrive.

In private correspondence with van Wormer, Kathrine Jack (2009) recalls her experience as a law student:

> In law school, it is true that you learn to think like a lawyer, not the law itself. What this means is that you are taught to divorce your personal views from the logic of the law. Regarding whether people lose their idealism in law school, I think it is a highly individualized process. Some people do, but some people, like myself, become more idealistic. Being in a conservative and/or business environment most of my life, I found a practical application for my more progressive ideas while in law school.
>
> I think female law professors help in getting women's issues into law school and providing context. But those professors who teach feminist jurisprudence or reproductive rights (if they are allowed to) risk getting pigeonholed into these issues. Women's perspectives and the impact of laws on women are definitely not a mainstream focus of law school. Unless you are in a class specifically called "feminist jurisprudence" or similar, women's issues will probably not be mentioned. There are exceptions. My evidence law professor (Aviva Orenstein) presented many of the feminist perspectives regarding evidence in rape cases. I also remember her talking about the struggle of women activists in reforming evidence law in rape cases. (p. 2)

PATRIARCHAL NATURE OF THE WORLD OF LAW

The world of law is decidedly and unequivocally masculine. It is not masculine in a physical sense but in a psychological sense. To have a "legal mind" is to be logical, or left-brain dominant. The law, in its Anglo-American format, is necessarily a site of conflict. It provides a means of dispute, notes DeBarba, (2002), but the means are combative.

A brief overview of the Anglo-Saxon **adversary system** will put the masculine, winner-take-all ethos of today's courtroom into historical perspective. "We are what we were," as the John Quincy Adams character in the 1998 movie *Amistad* so eloquently informed us. The origins of the adversary system hark back to trial by combat and before that and even more primitive, to trial by ordeal. Today the trial is the ordeal.

The rationale for our Anglo-American adversarial legal approach is found in its history. The history is one of ancient customs of judicial ordeal based on magical dogma. In the Middle Ages in England, the ordeals of fire, food, and poison required the accused to demonstrate the solicitude of some all-powerful spirit. With William the Conqueror, trial by battle was brought to the island. Eventually, no dispute existed that might not be submitted to the decision of the sword or club. Hired champions represented the interests of involved parties. According to Anne Strick (1977), trial by ordeal is alive and functioning in the United States; the judicial ordeal is now called the "adversary system" (p. 37).

The adversary model attempts to resolve differences through the opposition of two parties; the ultimate aim of cross-examination is to arrive at the truth (DeBarba, 2002). Whether this gladiatorial process is properly suited to the resolution of most family relations problems, such as divorce, or to provide justice to crime victims is another matter (Bazemore and Schiff, 2001).

The "hired champions" who fought in combat on behalf of the accused or accusing party were all men. Victory depended on physical strength and quickness. Law schools today are the training ground for success in the juridical ring. Through the harsh discipline of law school, the minds of the students are molded into marvelous instruments of control, or such is the aim. Law students are trained in verbal argumentation "to make the worse appear the better cause" (see Aristophanes, 423 B.C.). Strategies that are compelling and victorious in the courtroom may one day suffice in the political arena as well. Lau (1983) viewed the patterns of legal thinking—the dichotomizing and aggressive argumentation—as having started far earlier than law school. In a comparison between the stereotypical masculine lawyer and the feminine social worker, Lau suggested that the characteristics might have a basis in dominant thought processes. The distinction may be biological, she contended, in that certain types of personalities are more attracted to certain types of professions. The qualities that make for a good lawyer are competitiveness; the ability to find creative solutions to problems and to persuade clients to take them; a willingness to take risks but knowing when to pull back and compromise; acting talent for convincing juries that the implausible is plausible; excellent short-term memory for quick mastery of the facts in a complicated case; sharp attention to detail while never losing sight of the big picture; and, above all, the versatility to work with people of diverse class and ethnic backgrounds. That these traits are not gender specific is revealed in the success of women attorneys in this competitive field today.

LEGAL PRACTICE: STRUGGLES IN A MAN'S WORLD

At the law office, women are torn between requirements of "the mind" and of "the body" and between the need to dress professionally and to be considered feminine at the same time. How to wear their hair is a minor crisis in itself. Several basic themes emerge in the essays contributed by practicing attorneys writing in *It's Harder in Heels* (Slotker and Goodman, 2007). These are: "the blue suit, women supporting women; inappropriate questions during job interviews and in court . . . discrimination against women with children; the perfect job and the less than perfect work environment" (p. 3).

Because modern legal practice has evolved into big business, the pressures to make a profit are primary. For mothers, in particular, the legal landscape can easily become a hostile work environment (Naimi, 2009). A fascinating biography of Hillary Clinton by Brock (1996), appropriately entitled *The Seduction of Hillary Rodham*, gives some idea of the pressures facing a young radical feminist trying to break into an established southern law firm:

> The firm's secretaries, who resented having to work for a woman in the first place, made cruel comments about Hillary's appearance behind her back, to which she could not have been oblivious. The comments likely amplified her sense of alienation and rejection by the locals, whom she may accordingly have judged in her own mind all the more harshly as country bumpkins.
>
> "At first, she didn't wear stockings and the old ladies at the firm were horrified," said Hillary's former Rose secretary from the late 1970s. "She was a comic figure as a lady lawyer. Her hair was fried into an orphan Annie perm. She had one large eyebrow across her forehead that looked like a giant caterpillar. We laughed until we cried. She tried to look good when she went to court, and she would put on some awful plastic jewelry. She'd be wearing high heels she couldn't walk in. There wasn't one stereotypically womanly or feminine thing about her." The office staff considered Hillary's weight problem an endless source of amusement as well. "She was on a perpetual diet," the secretary said. "She would show up for work with a big bag of lettuce and eat out of it all day." (p. 81)

Even when women achieve conformity to the standardized legal norms, their patterns of interaction separate them from their male colleagues. In a content analysis of conversations between male lawyers and male clients, female lawyers and female clients, male lawyers and female clients, female lawyers and male clients, and same sex and mixed dyads of lawyer and lawyer, Bogoch (1997) was able to systematically measure gender differences in interaction. The setting was a legal aid office in Israel. What Bogoch found is that when clients related to female lawyers as women rather than as professionals, the women felt compelled to emphasize their legal role to the client. For example:

> Lawyer to client: Look Madam, I am not a social worker. I'm a lawyer and I can't, I don't have time to hear this whole story from the beginning. (p. 10)

Male lawyers in similar situations did not feel the need to define their professional roles; they simply deemed the client's remarks as irrelevant and returned to the task at hand. Occasionally, female attorneys did step out of their professional conception of themselves to relate to the life world of the clients; women lawyers especially granted legitimacy to the emotions of male clients.

A major stumbling block for women is the relentless work ethic and resistance to reduced or flexible schedules. Salaried legal associates and partners are expected to work sixty- to seventy-hour weeks. Many of the large law firms in the East have an annual 2,000 **billable-hour quota** (Jackson, 2007). This leaves no time for social life, family, or to "have a life." Twelve-hour days and weekend work are typical. Unpredictable deadlines, uneven workloads, and frequent travel pose further difficulties for those with family obligations. Although many of the largest law firms allow for flexible schedules, the message is, if you take that path you are not serious about your career (Naimi, 2009). Part of the reason women can't take advantage of part-time schedules is that men are socialized not to take them. Due to the excessive demands of the work structure, there is a continual outmigration of women from the big firms, the "warrior-lawyer's habitat," and into routine, in-house positions, such as in the realty department of an investment firm. The cloistered aspect of the in-house position works to remove women from the power structure. Other possibilities, however, such as joining a small law firm with a civil rights focus or teaching on the faculty of a law school, do give women a voice and provide a network of lawyers who can recognize themselves as a class.

Kathrine Jack chose to pursue a public interest job in a nonprofit organization in New York City. She describes (in private correspondence, 2009) the difficulty in pursuing this path:

> Money is one of the biggest issues for young lawyers who want to work for public interest. With the level of student loans that most law students take, one can barely survive on the salary of a public interest lawyer. I graduated from law school with over $100,000 in loans, including law school and undergraduate. Of course, working for a big law firm offers a larger salary and is the ONLY way to pay bills (p. 1). . . .
>
> For women, especially those who have family responsibilities, the big law firm is often not always a realistic option, and a lower paying job (usually non-profit or government) is where they go. One law firm partner who I sought career advice from explicitly told me that if I was planning to have a family, I should not work for a law firm. He urged me to apply for a government job because that would offer better hours and stress level for a mother. (sidenote—I was shocked when he told me this. I did not know how to respond so I just listened. I thought about his comments for a long time. . . . This partner himself has three children, and I believe his wife stays at home.) I should caveat this section by saying that there are some smaller or medium sized firms that do not follow the trends I've just mentioned. (p. 2)

Women such as Jack are using their legal education to pursue altruistic goals related to social justice. Read Box 12.1 to see how another lawyer has managed to juggle motherhood while taking on cases on behalf of some of the most vulnerable people in the population—undocumented immigrants.

WOMEN ON THE BENCH

The number of women on the bench in any generation is the product of the opportunities and experiences of women in law school and practice in earlier periods (Miller and Meloy, 2007). When women are restricted to law specialties handled in the back room rather than the courtroom, to legal research rather than litigation, they are effectively kept out of the eligibility pool for judgeships. They are also prevented from establishing the kind of reputation that could lead to judicial appointment.

Because many women today, trying to balance their personal and professional lives, are not attracted to the partnership track in large law firms, judgeships offer attractive options. When it comes to judges elected to the bench through a political process, the prospects are excellent for well-qualified women (Jackson, 2007). Judicial appointments, however, are another story, for one reason—that women are not always willing to move to a new location. Then, because they are women, potential candidates may experience a different kind of scrutiny because of their gender.

In the UK, until recently, there was a virtual absence of women judges. Traditionally, judges were chosen from a very narrow and selective pool by gatekeepers who did not prioritize a gender-diverse bench (Kenney, 2008). Feminists did not campaign for female representation on the bench in the UK, and possibly as a result, on the other side of the Atlantic, the participation of female judges was twenty-five years behind that in the United States and Canada. Then the appointment of a new Lord Chancellor who was bent on modernization of the judiciary led to major policy change. This change, in turn, as Kenney suggests, led to a consensus in favor of women judges which had not existed before.

At a conference in St. Louis, the National Association of Women Judges (NAWJ), an organization that has grown from 100 members in 1979 to more than 1,300 members over the next two decades, current and former chief judges shared their stories. The stories typically concerned opposition to women in such positions of leadership by "in-your-face" male colleagues. Resistance to the female judges took many forms, ranging from locking one woman in her chamber room to inflicting verbal abuse on others (Lhotka, 1998). Not too many years ago, according to Janz (1998), the only robes women were permitted to wear were bathrobes.

According to its Web site, NAWJ (2006) has been at the forefront in the establishment and implementation of gender bias task forces in both federal and state courts. This organization has greatly advanced the administration of justice in areas of domestic violence, the sentencing of women offenders with substance abuse problems, conditions for women in prison, child support and child custody, and the treatment of women in the courts.

Today, about 25 percent of federal district court judges and U.S. court of appeal judges are women (ABA, 2008). At the state level, women's numbers have risen to 28 percent. The number of judges seated as state supreme court judges has increased in recent years to around 30 percent. Women are often assigned to jurisdictions that are traditionally considered the specialty of women, such as municipal or domestic courts, in which women judges have little status and are provided few contacts so essential for those seeking a political career. Judges in domestic relations court (where many women judges work) do have wide discretion, but these courts—which handle matters such as divorce, child custody, and adoption arrangements—are at the lowest end of the judicial status totem pole. Although severely limited by court procedures and case law, not to mention mandatory sentencing laws, trial judges still possess an influence that extends beyond what they do on the bench. In the words of one Kentucky female circuit judge, "What you all do in the back halls and your informal conversations with male judges really has an influence on how they treat women in the courtroom" (Cross, 1999, p. 1B). Through such influence at equal status levels, women judges can help their male colleagues have greater sensitivity both for the kinds of pressure female attorneys face in the courtroom and for female victims and offenders who appear before the court. They also can help male judges have greater awareness when it comes to such matters as sexual harassment and job discrimination.

An empirically based analysis of over 500 federal appellate cases published in *The Yale Law Journal* reveals that judges' gender matters in case outcomes involving claims of sexual harassment (Peresie, 2005). Though plaintiffs lost in the vast majority of cases, they were twice as likely to prevail when a female judge was present on the panel of judges in Title VII sexual harassment and sex discrimination cases.

It is the multijudge appellate courts, including state and federal supreme courts, however, where women can have the most impact. Here, as Feinman suggests, a woman can ask questions, raise issues, present data, and influence the progress of the discussion or debate. Therefore, it is significant that women are now being appointed to state and federal appellate courts in unprecedented numbers. One might expect that those women will help move public policy in the direction of greater sex equality. The need for adequate representation of women on the U.S. Supreme Court is, of course, essential.

But do women on the bench bring a different touch to justice? Does gender affect judicial decision making at all? Studies of judges' attitudes and observations seem to indicate that they do, and not only in the United States.

In their review of recent surveys on female judges, Noblitt and Zeigler (2009) found that even those women who reach the position of judge report consistent discrimination that induces them to change their bench manner. One survey of federal judges found that 81 percent of female judges surveyed identified sex discrimination as a major problem in the legal profession. Female judges have commented that male attorneys often do not take them seriously and argue back contemptuously. As women, they must "work harder" to command the respect of attorneys in their courtrooms.

In-depth interviews with five female judges in an eastern state revealed that the women judges believe they are able to empathize more with victims than their male counterparts (Miller and Meloy, 2007). As more women take their place beside men in "courts of last resort," a new dynamic is emerging, according to an article in *The Christian Science Monitor* by Ryback (1998). "We do not feminize the bench, we humanize it," the California superior court judge is quoted as saying in this article (p. 1). Often focused on different issues from their male counterparts, women are subtly changing courthouse culture and the tenor of American jurisprudence. This fact is confirmed by Minnesota female supreme court justice Chief Justice Kathleen Blatz. A longtime supporter of children's issues, Blatz has a master's degree in social work as well as a law degree. Her self-description includes this accomplishment: "Loves to bake and is renowned for her peach cobbler" (p. 1).

Judy Sheindlin has been a matriarch of the family courts since 1972, working first as a prosecutor of juvenile delinquents and then as a judge (Fessier, 2009). Foust (2004) closely examined the personal style of women in public life in relation to their fulfillment of the cultural gender myth. Her discussion centers on the career and persona of Judge Judy Sheindlin, a TV judge who tries real cases and has been able to hold the attention of a wide audience. On the surface, Judge Judy's success is a paradox in that she is personally aggressive and sharp-spoken, yet popular with the American public and seen as a non-threatening. Foust explains Sheindlin's acceptability in terms of her role as **Tough Mother**. Like women of the early American Temperance Movement, Sheindlin may publicly speak in an aggressive way because society respects her moral authority. The Tough Mother emerges, as Foust explains, as an ideologically conservative, virtuous agent who employs practical advice to rescue a scene corrupted by morally lax citizens. Moreover, her persona plays into some of the public's worst victim blaming tendencies as she verbally assaults the people, usually poor and uneducated, who come before her. She scolds litigants for disrespect as well if they interrupt her or speak out of turn. Moreover, she often tells them they are lying and relies on intuition rather than the law in her rulings. Sheindlin's "take-no-prisoners" style taps into the public's growing resentment of people who are out to cheat the system or otherwise behave immorally. Foust's analysis draws our attention to the fact that a woman in law or politics who adopts a conservative, aggressive style may be less prone to criticism than her counterpart from the left wing who may invite the wrath of neoconservative elements and seem threatening to men (of a certain type).

GENDER, RACE, CLASS

To review one of the major assumptions of this book, the oppressions found in gender, class, and race are very much related to the careers of women lawyers.

Gender and Discrimination

Despite the generally favorable climate and the unprecedented opportunities for women in the law today, a legacy of discrimination remains. Although more women now hold faculty and administrative positions in law schools than in earlier decades, they are still accorded relatively low prestige if, as teachers, their main focus is on "women's issues" as opposed to business and corporation law (Jack, 2009, in private correspondence with van Wormer). Furthermore, as Jack informs us, law students study case law from the male point of view; only men's opinions are cited. Legal issues that are important to women, such as marital rape, wife beating, and family law may be dealt with only superficially.

As in other professions, women who are naturally aggressive and competitive may be considered bossy and unpleasant (Jackson, 2007). Yet successful lawyers are expected to possess these very same characteristics which are usually found acceptable in a man. Women who seek out their male boss for a chat may be seen as overly aggressive or even flirtatious. Another phenomenon that often holds women back is their reluctance to promote themselves or even in asking for what they need professionally.

Rainmaking is a term that refers to the amount of business a member of a law firm can generate. More than anything else, rainmaking is the barometer of success in the legal world today. Critics complain that law is less driven by altruism and more driven by profit than it formerly was. Lawyers interviewed by Jackson (2007) recommended learning to play golf and even joining hunting and fishing trips, because it is here where major contacts are made. Serving on community boards and volunteering at community events are also excellent ways to promote the development of a law practice.

To help compensate for their lack of connections, some female lawyers are forming clubs and their own bar associations. The National Conference of Women's Bar Associations promotes the development of networking of female lawyers across the United States and to promote advocacy among women in the profession. In California, the California Women Lawyers (CWL) (2009) is a strong voice in the public policy debate, shaping standards for women's rights in the workplace and society. While women and Cuban Americans have had success in being elected and appointed to the bench, African Americans and Caribbean Americans have been under-represented, and therefore the focus of the Miami-Dade County chapter of women lawyers is on this group. This chapter monitors the hiring and promotion of women and minority attorneys within the ranks which has been especially slow in the recession (Roberts, 2009). And in Chicago, women lawyers network over breakfast or lunch (Murphy, 2004). There is a bit of a sorority feeling at such events as women talk about things they don't discuss around men. At the national level, the NAWL holds annual conferences that focus on issues relevant to career goals. Masters (2004) described a panel presentation at the Washington, DC, gathering on the importance to women's success of an effective mentoring program and balanced working hours. Similar conferences are planned in major cities across the United States.

Also at the national level women are taking a very active role in annual meetings of the ABA. They also have been instrumental collectively in establishing state and federal task forces on women and gender bias in the courts. Sexual harassment is a part of this bias, which is being thoroughly investigated.

Sexual Harassment

Following the Clarence Thomas–Anita Hill hearings, **sexual harassment** and discrimination claims filed with the Equal Employment Opportunities Commission increased 71 percent. Among the litigants were partners and associates in major law firms. Unwanted touching and other forms of sexual harassment were among the charges.

Like sexual demands on an unwilling wife, sexual harassment of women by male colleagues expresses the ancient rule that women should be sexually available to men. The existence of sexual harassment means that the woman who objects may put her career at risk; this form of activity reminds the professional woman that she is not really an equal (Martin and Jurik, 2007). Above all, sexual harassment is an abuse of power, sometimes by an older man inflicting unwanted attention on a younger, often unmarried woman. Typically, the harasser flatters himself that the woman enjoys his attentions. Most women are familiar with such examples of abuse of power in the form of sexual games and innuendos. Another form of harassment, *gender harassment*, is less obvious and less related to the perceived sexual attractiveness of a woman. Gender harassment entails *belittling* a woman as a woman, as a means of putting her down and preserving the status quo. Although prohibited under federal law by 1980, and by the Civil Rights Act before that, tradition decreed that sexual bantering and teasing were natural to relations between the sexes and that only male-bashing, prudish women would raise a fuss over teasing or "sweet talk."

The **Equal Employment Opportunity Commission (EEOC)** regulations passed in 1980 to protect the rights of minorities and women followed a survey that produced hard data on the extent of sexual harassment within the federal government. The two aspects of sexual harassment that were discussed in the previous chapter are *quid pro quo*, which implies a trade-off of sexual favors for job benefits, and the creation of a hostile work environment through offensive sexual conduct. These categories are the basis for sexual harassment suits (The Commission on Women in the Profession, 2008). The law, however, tends to equate workplace harassment with sexual pursuits to the utter disregard of nonsexual forms of harassment that are structural in nature in organizations in which both sexual and not-so-sexual forms of harassment flourish.

Surveys show that between almost half to two-thirds of female lawyers and somewhat fewer court personnel report experiencing or observing sexual harassment (The Commission on Women in the Professions, 2008). Sexual propositions, physical groping, and abusive comments remain a problem. Women lawyers encounter inappropriate terms of address, touching, exposure to sexist jokes, derogatory remarks about pregnancy, and *quid pro quo* sexual harassment (Martin and Jurik). As Martin and Jurik conclude in study of women's roles in the legal profession, a lot of progress has been made over the last decade. Most law firms have adopted sexual harassment policies today which typically follow federal regulations prohibiting unwelcome sexual advances and conduct creating an intimidating, hostile, or offensive working environment. This very advance, however, means that some established male lawyers are reluctant to mentor younger attorneys for fear of possible law suits. When harassment is reported, retaliation in the form of discharge, demotion, or other adverse action taken by employers remains a serious problem in the workplace (The Commission on Women in the Professions). More could be done in the future through training of supervisors and ensuring protection against retaliation. Stereotypical assumptions about gender, race, ethnicity, and sexual orientation are equally in need of attention.

Synergistic Nature of Race, Class, Gender, and Sexual Orientation

Race, class, and gender, as previously noted, are not simply additive forces; the effect of membership in more than one of these categories is **synergistic**. A woman, for example, who is both African American and belongs to the working class inhabits a world in which the forces of gender, race, and class intersect with each other through the social and economic structure.

The fact that approximately half of all African Americans grow up in poverty restricts their life chances; it also stigmatizes the members of that race as lazy and uneducated. We need to recognize that the intersection of race, class, and gender is not limited to those at the bottom of the social ladder. In the professions, especially prestigious professions such as law, one is expected to have the bearings of gentry. This includes a polished manner of speech, and dressing like a lawyer in a subdued, not flashy, style of dress (Binkley, 2008). A desirable attribute of a lawyer is the ability to bring business into the law firm. Bringing in poor clients charged with petty crimes may be considered a minus more than a plus.

In the legal profession, to be a person of color, lower class, and a woman is to have three strikes against you before you start. The path to law school is extremely difficult for persons without educational and financial advantages. The low-income college student must obtain loans and work his or her way through college. This ordinarily means less study time and a lower grade point average. The privileged student, on the other hand, has the luxury of study time and the lack of heavy financial debt. Then come the expensive crash courses in LSAT (Law Scholastic Aptitude Test), an exam that appears to be culturally and gender biased. Affirmative action programs help compensate for gender and racial discrimination in our society but not for class.

In her study, "The Plexiglass Ceiling: The Careers of Black Women Lawyers," Simpson (1996) examined the ways in which race and gender intersected to shape the career transitions of 238 African American women lawyers. Respondents worked in municipal and federal government predominantly, but also in private practice and law firms. Fifty-four percent had college-educated parents. Racism and sexism in law were first evidenced in law school. Of the respondents, 87 percent said discrimination was rampant. Alumni from a prestigious northeastern school recalled that the dean of students said that admitting blacks had lowered their academic standards. Ninety percent of respondents stated that they had been excluded from student study groups. This pattern of discrimination was further evidenced at the job entry level. Opportunities to practice in high status, powerful, and financially remunerative sectors of the profession were found to be few and far between for these African American attorneys.

In the University of Pennsylvania study described earlier (Guinier et al., 1994), attrition rates, or movement from job to job, were studied as an indirect gauge of career satisfaction. Almost 90 percent of the respondents moved from their first job to another entry-level position. Government lawyers showed the most stability. Respondents felt that "not being a white male" limited their chances of promotion tremendously. Questionnaire and interview results revealed that although affirmative action policies and programs dramatically increased the number of African American women lawyers, a "Plexiglass ceiling" limited their career choices.

A major economic obstacle confronts most law school graduates. Following law school, these graduates, like others, must pay for an expensive crash course to prepare for the bar exam and take a legal assistant job while awaiting bar exam results. Assuming favorable results, the newly admitted member of the bar may bear a debt of easily well over $100,000.

A major difference in the kind of specialty that women and minorities tend to choose occurs in the public interest arena (in which 4 percent of women compared with 1.7 percent of men choose to work). This arena includes legal aid and public defender work and, in general, work with the poor. Within the other branches of law, women are more likely than men to be willing to engage in pro bono legal work. The law firms do not reward their lawyers for performing work for the needy as a public service, but only for billable hours.

Women of color are especially likely to work in government positions, and in public defender and legal aid settings. Work in these areas is especially attractive because of job security and regular working hours, and also the opportunity to work with other women. Studies of African American female lawyers, however, indicate that many of these women originally planned to find employment with a law firm (Martin and Jurik, 2007). While there has been significant growth in the absolute numbers of black lawyers in corporate firms, the percentages remain "microscopically" small.

Resentment against women and minority women sometimes comes through in unexpected ways. A news story carried in the *ABA Journal* carries the headline: "Judge reprimanded for calling three black female public defenders 'The Supremes'" (Weiss, 2008). The Maryland judge, according to the article, made his comments during a hearing for a defendant who wanted to replace his public defender. The judge later apologized to the women and offered to recuse himself from their future cases. After he was reprimanded by the Maryland Commission, he acknowledged his comments were suggestive of racial and sexual bias.

In summary, given the structural conditions of the legal profession, it is very difficult for women of any ethnicity or background to assume positions of leadership or power within the profession. And yet, entering into the ranks of the powerful (whether through marriage or career) is the only way to have an impact. This is what is happening today, slowly and surely, as women acquire the language and tools of their successful brothers.

MASS MEDIA IMAGES

"The first thing we do, let's kill all the lawyers" (Shakespeare, 1590/1952 *King Henry VI, Part II*, 4.2.86). This sentiment from the sixteenth century is echoed today in newspaper articles, joke books, and comments by the general public concerning the alleged greed of attorneys. Whether or not everybody is suing everybody, this is often the public image. And it is true that the United States has the highest number of lawyers per capita of any country (the count surpassed one million in 2000) and the greatest number of legal cases.

The low public image of lawyers is pervasive (Foust, 2004). Newspaper articles and magazine accounts decry (or proclaim) the unprecedented number of attorneys opting out of the profession. In Canada, too, many lawyers are dissatisfied with their work because of the long hours and the "tyranny of billable hours." The attrition rate for women who have left the profession fifteen years after qualifying to practice is almost double that of men (Macaulay, 2009).

For the public ambivalence toward the legal profession, Haltom and McCann (2004) fault the much publicized antics of lawyers in high profile cases, the system which allows lawyers to collect huge fees in a single winning case, some of the obviously deceptive television and billboard advertising that is now commonplace, and the power of the profession in American political life. The pervasive practice of telling lawyer jokes at once reflects and reinforces the profound distrust citizens have for lawyers, especially for personal injury lawyers. Surveys consistently show that while attorneys are respected for their intelligence and competence, they also are considered greedy and dishonest. This paradox, according to Haltom and McCann, in the core image of the legal professional as a value-neutral "hired gun" is just the sort of advocate the individual client wants to fight his or her case.

"No fee unless you win." This phrase, used in legal advertising to entice winning personal injury cases, sums up the contingency fee arrangement in a nutshell. Lawyers sue on behalf of injured clients when the claim is against a company or individual with assets. Lawyers collect 33–40 percent of the damages; usually such cases are settled out of court. If the case comes to court, as a civil case, the level of proof required is lower than that in a criminal case. The winning civil case against O. J. Simpson in the death of his wife illustrates how civil justice can be achieved monetarily, while it is not so for criminal justice. Consumers' rights have been greatly enhanced by the fear of lawsuits. The flaw in this system as it operates in the United States is that innocent people can be sued for damages and win, but then to have to pay exorbitant legal expenses. This causes many companies and some individuals to settle cases quickly out of court even for claims that are fraudulent.

In the past, female attorneys concentrated on the divorce and family law, legal aid work, writing wills, and taking criminal law cases that nobody wanted. Personal injury settlements were handled by men. Today, in states where lawyers advertise without restriction, assertive women can market their services through ads in telephone books, on the radio, and on television. Whether from reticence or complacency, however, few women have taken advantage of the possibilities for acquiring business through the use of the media.

In personal correspondence, Stuart (2005) recalls her success in marketing her services in the state of Kentucky:

> Being somewhat of an anomaly and minority has had its advantages. My own firm, consisting of predominantly female attorneys, started many years ago and now includes my daughter. We describe ourselves as being the "family law firm that cares about people." What better way for an office of all females to express the compassion we have for our clients? I have even been known to shed a few tears with my clients (imagine a male attorney shedding tears). Our clients love it! (p. 2)

Television and Film Portrayals

We have been talking about the mass media. One of the main ways the general public forms impressions of a particular profession is through fictional accounts, especially through television portrayals. The first point that should be made about such portrayals is that they are far removed from legal reality. Typically these fictional accounts center on courtroom drama; never mind that the drama of trial is only an infinitesimal part of what lawyers do (Goldfarb, 2004). Even in criminal and civil law, most cases are settled out of court. And sensational cases are few.

On the whole, as Bergman and Asinow (2006) argue in *Reel Justice: The Courtroom Goes to the Movies*, the roles of female lawyers in the movies have been uncomplimentary to women and to lawyers. This was especially true from after 1980. After that time, women lawyers were portrayed as tough and aggressive, as well as overly emotional and exercising poor judgment such as getting romantically involved with clients. It didn't start out that way, however, as Katharine Hepburn successfully defended a woman who had shot her husband in the 1949 romantic comedy, *Adam's Rib*. The humor was directed at her relationship with her husband, played by Spencer Tracy, who was the prosecutor in the case, and not at Hepburn's bungling as an attorney. In fact, as Bergman and Asinow assert, Hepburn's character of Amanda "remains the most positive movie lawyer role model of all time" (p. 94). Bergman and Asinow contrast this positive portrayal of professional competence with the stereotypical image of women lawyers represented in later films such as the 1985 production *Jagged Edge*, a courtroom thriller in which the female attorney is guilty of some highly unethical practices including having an affair with her client and *Presumed Innocent*, made in 1990, which tells of a woman prosecutor who climbs up the professional ladder through sleeping with powerful men. *I Am Sam* (produced in 2001) presents Michelle Pfeiffer's character as rude, disorganized, and unprofessional in her representation of a retarded man who is fighting to retain custody of his daughter. Surely the most despicable woman in the Hollywood courtroom is the defense attorney in *Philadelphia* (1993). Her anti-gay cross-examination of the hero who is dying of AIDS is unnecessarily cruel.

Other images of women lawyers during this period, however, were more positive, involving women who successfully fought for justice through their clients, such as in *The Accused* (1988) and *The Client* (1994). Similarly, lawyer heroines exposed corruption in *Class Action* (1991) and *Music Box* (1989), although at considerable personal cost.

These fictional heroines, if you can call them that, do not include a cadre of idealistic lawyers. Goldberg (2005) refers to these as the backlash movies of the 1980s, which were cautionary tales to would-be professional women. You can win a victory in the courtroom, but your personal life will be empty—this is the message that was conveyed.

In contrast to Hollywood's treatment of female lawyers, television productions have done for the female lawyer image what *Cagney and Lacey*, a popular TV series of the 1980s did to boost the professional image of women police officers. Women lawyers now are coming into their own in dozens of shows on the major networks; the characterizations are well rounded and convincing (Goldberg, 2005). In 1998, ABC's *The Practice* premiered to great reviews. Working beside men as equal partners, strong women were cast as the district attorney and defense attorneys. Many plus-sized women had an excellent role model in Camryn Manheim, who fought for the underdog with great conviction. Although it degenerated into "gimmicky sideshows" (Goldfarb, p. 5) before it came to an end, *The Practice* revealed some realistic attorney disagreements about the handling of tricky cases and portrayed women lawyers and judges intelligently during most of its protracted run. A later CBS production, *Close to Home,* presented Annabeth Chase as a young, attractive prosecutor of high ethical commitment, and an advocate of victimized women. Goldberg (2005) singles out *Judging Amy* and *Boston Legal* for their positive portrayals of a judge and lawyer respectively. One scene, in which the lawyer is played by Candace Bergen, is illustrative of a typical exchange between a mature attorney and her protégé: "She says to the woman who is wearing a low-cut top and a miniskirt, 'Are you a lawyer? Go home and change your clothes and dress the part. We need women who appear the way a jury expects them to appear'" (p. 1 of 3).

These shows have now come and gone and been replaced with *Damages*, starring Glenn Close. In preparation for the role, Close consulted women lawyers at a top law firm. Critics have been very complimentary of the series (Bellafonte, 2009). Another positive development is that viewers can now find real courtroom drama and gain insight into legal practices through the popular program, *Court TV.* In the real situations presented, the competence of women as defense attorneys and prosecutors shines through.

STRENGTHS OF WOMEN ATTORNEYS

How are women lawyers using their authority to help individual women? How are they advancing the equality of women generally?

To answer the first question, we can consider the work of the lawyers who described their careers for this chapter. Jones (2004) describes two law firms, one in New York and one in Philadelphia, devoted exclusively to female clients and women's issues such as hormone-replacement and breast and uterine cancer diagnosis litigation. The clients, as Jones notes, find their women lawyers more understanding and empathic for such medical work. A New Orleans attorney sees much potential in marketing her business as a woman's firm; this firm offers a "grandmotherly" image and specializes in child custody cases.

In one type of criminal defense work, a woman has an advantage that raises serious ethical issues for feminists, and that is in representation of accused rapists, child molesters, and male batterers. Sociologist Cynthia Siemsen (2004) sought to discover how female defense attorneys balance feminist ideology against the defense of men accused of rape and similar antiwoman crimes. Most of the lawyers she interviewed who took such cases put the higher value on seeing that everyone gets a fair trial. The reason this is an ethical problem for women is that women are asked to use their gender as a strategy to strengthen the defense. When the defense attorney cross-examines the victim, members of the jury see one woman attacking another, and often blame the victim. Fortunately, women in private practice can usually decline to represent clients accused of rape, domestic violence, and the like, and many undoubtedly do so. But others, as Siemsen suggests, focus their attention on constitutional rights and manage their emotions accordingly.

Now to the second question: How are women lawyers advancing the equality of women generally? Whether the influx of women into the legal profession will transform the profession—feminize it—or whether the legal profession will transform women into clones of men who "think like a lawyer" is a hotly debated issue. Some theorists argue that women bring to the law a "different voice" that will enable such values as caring, empathy, and mediation to become more central to legal practice (see Anleu, 1992; Jones, 2004; Scales, 2006). Others proclaim that the bastion of the law is so imbued with male values such as value-free objectivity, abstract rights, and adversarial know-how that there is little scope for women to make a difference. Anleu refers to the former arguments as the "cultural feminist approach" and the latter as the "radical theorist approach." Both approaches offer a one-dimensional view of women, according to Anleu; women's differential locations within the settings need to be taken into account. Established female attorneys may thrive in their own law firms. Stuart (2005), in a semihumorous vein, provides the following account:

> My practice blossomed because women wanted a female attorney who could empathize with their plight—especially in divorce cases. Much to my surprise, men also began hiring me so they could have "a woman on their side." I later began handling bankruptcy cases in Federal Court and the creditors called me the "Bankruptcy Queen."
>
> Presently, we have established the only female law firm in our community. Through the years, some of my male clients have come up with such endearing names for me as "country child" (he wrote a poem for me). My favorite name was "pretty whipper snapper." Just this year, an opposing attorney with whom I was reviewing a case addressed me as "Listen Lady." (p. 2)

Let us now return to the question of whether women who enter law school lose their ideals through rigorous socialization or whether they emerge from their education with their principles unscathed. In truth, this is not an either–or proposition. As women or other minorities or working-class people enter the power structure, they can still hold onto their original values and goals. True, legal training socializes women to be advocates, to engage in gladiatorial-type contests for hire, and to be tough in negotiation. On the other hand, to paraphrase Audre Lorde (1984), acquiring the master's tools alone will never dismantle the master's house (p. 123). In other words, acquiring the legal knowledge and credentials may be a necessary but not sufficient condition for effecting social change. Real power and change, as Lorde argues, come with bonding (on the basis of race, class, and gender) and a militance in acknowledging rather than denying our differences. If we merge with the power structure, on the other hand, we will suffer a loss of identity. Borrowing Lorde's metaphor, we can conclude that only through acquiring the master's tools and gaining access to the power structure will we be able to dismantle the master's house. The risk is that in joining the rich and powerful, lawyers who set out to change the world will lose sight of their original goals.

Ronnie Podolefsky, a feminist activist turned lawyer, has seen how economic pressures and materialism can divert even the most idealistic law students from their original course. A specialist in employment discrimination and former member of the National Organization for Women board of directors, Podolefsky is also married to a university president. This fact that has created a conflict as this feminist attorney fights for justice in sexual harassment cases. An associated press story (Zagier, 2008) carried throughout the United States describes a dilemma for any attorney who takes on unpopular causes:

> The bad feeling has gone well beyond a spirited defense of Hough, who also serves as the softball coach and insists he's innocent.
>
> The teens have been called liars, bullies and even white trash (three of the players who have sued the white coach also are white, three are black). They've been insulted to their faces and on Facebook and MySpace pages. Their parents' jobs have been threatened. And the involvement of their attorney, who also happens to be the wife of the University of Central Missouri's president, has sparked a backlash that includes efforts to oust the college leader. . . . (p. 1 of 2)
>
> The youths' attorney, Ronnie Podolefsky, has been a particular target in a town long-accustomed to cordial relations with the Central Missouri campus.
>
> "She's the first lady of education," said Greg Hassler, a local radio station owner and sportscaster whose on-air broadsides against Podolefsky have fueled the criticism. "She's supposed to be a community leader."
>
> By the estimation of Hough's supporters, the college president's wife is out of line. They want her to stop representing the players, and if that means firing her husband—Aaron Podolefsky—then so be it. (p. 2 of 2)

SIGNIFICANCE OF WOMEN'S ENTRANCE INTO THE LAW

When women make their presence felt in a formerly all-male preserve, whether in the military, in prison, or in substance abuse treatment, the social climate changes: The effect is humanizing and even salutary (see Champion, 1998, p. 325). In an article entitled "Jurisprudence and Gender," Robin West (1998) argues that women bring to the legal culture a sense of literal connectedness with others and a linking between family and work that permeates the atmosphere. Jack and Jack (1989), in their study of the changing values of men and women lawyers, found the traditional male-female divide: men focusing on competition and winning, and women favoring cooperation and compromise; men reasoning formally and abstractly, and women reasoning contextually and holistically. As women intrude on an all-male preserve, such as a traditional law firm, the social climate changes. Conversations among colleagues are more personal than in male-only establishments. Personal experience and personal values relevant to legal work become integrated; the social norms shift to allow for ongoing conversations about one's family and recreational life. The level of friendliness and intimacy at a cogender law office is palpable.

Politically, women's presence in law has had an impact, even beyond their numbers. The impact of female activist lawyers has been pronounced. Consider the impact of Washington, DC, attorney Brigida Benitez, who worked for six years on affirmative action cases for the University of Michigan. When the Supreme Court finally settled the matter in June 2003, it marked the most important statement on affirmative action in a quarter of a century (Russell, 2005). The case involved a lawsuit by three white college applicants who claimed discrimination because race was considered in the application process. The Supreme Court upheld the university's policy to ensure diversity in the student body for the advantage of all students. *Hispanic Business* magazine singled out Benitez for her work on this once-in-a-lifetime case. Benitez was selected as Woman of the

Year not only for her groundbreaking work but also her community pro bono service. As a Latina lawyer, Benitez is a part of the minority of 3 percent of male and female lawyers who are Hispanic.

Law school is a powerful, transformative experience. Widely regarded as an ideological training ground, law school historically has been the domain of aggressive white males. Today, change is under way. Tightly enforced affirmative action programs at universities have resulted in an influx of minorities and women into the teaching arena. It is in this arena of law school that the feminist voice is increasingly heard.

Ann Scales (2006) describes feminist legal theory as a transformative potential that derives from women's unique experiences. These experiences create an outsider's critical perception, which engenders empathy for other subordinated and oppressed groups. In contrast to traditional legal theory, which stresses value neutrality, feminist theorists promote consciousness-raising as a central element in empowering the client. Through consciousness-raising, students are made aware of sexism, racism, and classism and of how some inequalities can be rectified through resourceful use of the law and courts. Feminist litigation is taught as one means of addressing human rights violations against women. Consistent with this perspective, law school professors and lawyers tend to recommend alternative, dispute resolution procedures, especially in family law and child welfare where the avoidance of adversarial conflict is an advantage to all parties. In regard to wife battering and rape, on the other hand, women's groups tend to be adamant about the use of criminal penalties; they see little scope for mediation in light of inequalities in bargaining power between men and women.

One hope for the future is that the active involvement of women in the law and their keen interest in human rights issues based on gender and race will help galvanize the United States in the international arena. We are referring to international treaties, signed and unsigned, and to earlier statements by retired Supreme Court Justice Sandra Day O'Connor and current Justice Ruth Ginsburg that international law should be taken into consideration on issues such as the execution of mentally retarded persons and juveniles (*The Economist*, 2005). Furthermore, in this increasingly globalized century, input from women lawyers and judges who collectively have been subject to human rights violations may make their mark in helping to shape legislation to protect the rights of vulnerable populations. Box 12.2 provides a portrait of a remarkable woman, Jessie Nicholson, who worked her way through law school because she wanted to make a difference. The information provided in this boxed reading came from an invitational speech that was made at the University of Northern Iowa during Women's History Month.

Summary

The members of the first generation of women lawyers tended to be white, upper-middle to upper-class, and the daughters or wives of lawyers, and they devoted all their energy to gaining the right to practice. They won tolerance rather than acceptance by playing conventional female roles and by being nonthreatening. Myra Bradwell, who worked toward legislative reform crucial to women, was an exception. The suffrage movement from the 1890s to 1920 and the postsuffrage era saw a little more legislative activity, but compared to other professions such as medicine or correctional administration, women have been largely excluded from the male legal power structure.

Thanks to federal laws from the 1960s, many of the traditional barriers against women's entry into the legal field, including law professorships, have been broken. Today, we are seeing a rise in a new class of professionals, women trained in knowledge of the law, who refuse to be treated as second-class citizens. The creation of specialized women's groups such as the Commission on Women in the Profession of the ABA, the National Women's Lawyers Association, the NAWJ, and regional networking groups helps compensate for the reluctance of established attorneys to mentor new female recruits. Professional networking among women has helped to catapult some among their ranks to positions of national prominence and provide other women with the psychological support they need for professional growth. For all women in society, the gain is tremendous. For victims of crime, especially of sexual and physical abuse, for women seeking a divorce or needing to write a will, and for female offenders, female advocacy can provide a rare sense of protection. Male clients, similarly, can benefit from a warm, personal touch.

Discrimination against women in the legal profession persists nevertheless. In this chapter, we reviewed evidence that continues to show that our judicial arena retains its status as a battleground between opposing forces and still tends to

be stratified by gender, race, and class and that women in law firms are less likely to become full partners during their careers, to earn as much money as their male peers, or to thrive in the highest-paid legal specialties. Moreover women, compared to men, express more dissatisfaction about their treatment in the courtroom and by other lawyers. Sexual harassment is the norm, especially for younger attorneys.

Despite the barriers erected to keep women out of the practice of law and, ultimately, lawmaking, many women have found a niche for themselves in this August and challenging field. Although only a small percentage of the female attorneys see themselves as social activists, those who do are developing new models for the practice of law and new arguments to guide their legal briefs. In short, in the practice of law, many women are finding fulfillment as they adopt the **tools of the master** for their clients' ends, perhaps not to "dismantle the master's house" as Lorde (1984) envisioned but, less drastically, to remodel and renovate it—and then to add some personal, finishing touches.

Key Terms

adversary system *350*
billable-hour quota *351*
Equal Employment Opportunity
  Commission (EEOC) *356*

sexual harassment *354*
synergistic Title IX *355*

tools of the master *364*
Tough Mother *354*

Critical Thinking Questions

1. Consider the career path for women in the legal profession; to what extent have women been able to get their hands on power through the law?
2. Discuss male resistance to women's entry into this profession and the reasons for it.
3. Consider the title of Lani Guinier and colleagues' book, *Becoming Gentlemen*. What is the meaning of this title with regard to law students?
4. What does having a "legal mind" entail?
5. Is it accurate to portray the adversary system as trial by combat?
6. How does the quality of competitiveness make for a good lawyer given the present system?

7. What are some of the stumbling blocks that women lawyers face? How can these be overcome?
8. Explain how race, class, and gender are synergistic forces.
9. Discuss positive and negative media images of lawyers.
10. What are some major advantages that women lawyers have by virtue of their gender? And what are some liabilities?
11. One theme of the chapter relates to Audre Lorde's notion that adopting the "tools of the master" is not sufficient. What is the relevance here regarding receiving a law school education?

Web Destinations

American Bar Association (ABA): www.abanet.org

Canadian Bar Association: www.cba.org

Legal information: http://www.law.com/jsp/law/index.jsp

National Association of Women Judges: http://www.nawj.org/index.asp

National Association of Women Lawyers: www.nawl.org

ABA Commission on Women: www.abanet.org/women

Australian Women Lawyers: http://www.womenlawyers.org.au/

British Bar Council: www.barcouncil.org

References

American Bar Association (ABA) (2008). A current glance at women in the law, 2008. Retrieved April 2009 from http://www.abanet.org/women/CurrentGlanceStatistics2008.pdf

Anleu, S. L. (1992). Women in law: Theory, research, and practice. *The Australian and New Zealand Journal of Sociology 28:* 391–410.

Bazemore, G., and Schiff, M. (2001). Understanding restorative community justice: What and why now? In G. Bazemore and M. Schiff (eds.), *Restoring Community Justice* (pp. 21–46). Cincinnati, OH: Anderson.

Belknap, J. (2007). *The invisible woman: Gender, crime, and justice*, 3rd ed. Belmont, CA: Wadsworth.

Bellafonte, G. (2009, April 1). A litigator's venomous veneer begins to crack. *New York Times*, p. C2.

Bergman, P., and Asinow, M. (2006). *Reel justice: The courtroom goes to the movies*. Kansas City: Andrews McMeel publishers.

Binkley, C. (2008, January 31). Law without suits: New hires flout tradition. *The Wall Street Journal*. Retrieved April 2009 from http://online.wsj.com/article/SB120175142140831193.html

Bogoch, B. (1997). Gendered lawyering: Difference and dominance in lawyer-client interaction. *Law and Society Review 31*(4): 677–712.

Brock, D. (1996). *The seduction of Hillary Rodham*. New York: Free Press.

California Women Rights (2009). Women's rights in the legislature. Retrieved August 2009 from http://www.cwl.org/advocacy/womens-rights

Champion, D. (1998). *Criminal justice in the United States*, 2nd ed. Chicago, IL: Nelson-Hall.

Chen, V. (2003, September 29). Women lawyers see cracks in the ceiling. *The American Lawyer 29*(39): 4.

Commission on Women in the Profession. (2008). *Sex-based harassment: Workplace policies for the legal profession*, 2nd ed. Chicago, IL: American Bar Association.

Compensation and Benefits for Law Offices (CBLO). (2003). Are women lawyers now faring better? *LexisNexis Academic*. Retrieved August 2009 from http://www.ioma.com/issues/CBLO/2003_10/563121-1.html

Cross, A. (1999, March 31). Women of the bench convene. *The Courier-Journal*. Louisville, Ken., p. 1B.

DeBarba, K. (2002). Maintaining the adversary system: The practice of allowing jurors to question witnesses during trial. *Vanderbilt Law Review 55*(5): 1521–1548.

Drachman, V. (2001). *Sisters in law: Women lawyers in modern American history*. Cambridge, MA: Harvard University Press.

Economist. (2005, June 11). The insidious wiles of foreign influence. *Economist*, pp. 25–26.

Encyclopaedia Britannica. (2009). Margaret Brent. In *Encyclopaedia Britannica*. Retrieved April 2009, from Encyclopaedia Britannica Online: http://www.britannica.com/EBchecked/topic/78821/Margaret-Brent

Feinman, C. (1994). *Women in the criminal justice system*, 3rd ed. Westport, CT: Praeger.

Felstiner, W. (ed.). (2005). *Reorganisation and resistance: Legal professions confront a changing world*. Oxford, UK: Hart Publishing.

Fessier, B. (2009, April 23). Judge Judy puts parenting at the top of priorities list. *The Desert Sun*. Retrieved April 2009 from http://www.mydesert.com/article/20090423/LIFESTYLES12/904220400/1026/news12

Finnigan, C. (2007, September 23). Report findings. Women in law: Trinity College Dublin. Retrieved August 2009 from http://www.tcd.ie/Law/WomeninLaw/index.php

Foust, C. (2004, Fall). A return to feminine public virtue: Judge Judy and the myth of the Tough Mother. *Women's Studies in Communication 27*(3): 269–294.

Goldberg, S. (2005, Fall). Women lawyers on TV moving closer to reality. *Perspectives Magazine 14*(2). Retrieved April 2009 from http://www.abanet.org/women/perspectives/WomenLawyersTVFall2005.pdf

Goldfarb, R. (2004). Lawyers on television. *Washington Lawyer.* Retrieved August 2009 from http://www.dcbar.org/for_lawyers/resources/publications/washington_lawyer/june_2004/tvlawyer.cfm

Grace, N. (2005). *Objection!: How high-priced defense attorneys, celebrity defendants and a 24/7 media have hijacked our criminal justice system.* New York: Hyperion.

Guinier, L., Fine, M., Balin, J., Bartow, A., and Stachel, D. L. (1994). Becoming gentlemen: Women's experiences at one Ivy League law school. *University of Pennsylvania Law Review 143*(1): 1–110.

Haltom, W., and McCann, M. (2004). *Distorting the law: Politics, media, and the litigation crisis.* Chicago, IL: University of Chicago Press.

Hurst, T. (1977, March 20). Bowling Green's only woman trial lawyer: "I wanted to change things." *Bowling Green Daily News*, p. 30.

Jack, K. (2009, January 21). Working in public interest. Unpublished essay shared in private correspondence with Katherine van Wormer.

Jack, R., and Jack, D. C. (1989). *Moral vision and professional decisions: The changing values of women and men lawyers.* New York: Cambridge University Press.

Jackson, L. W. (2007, Summer). Women in leadership positions in the legal profession: Do they face a glass ceiling or clogged pipeline, or is it now a ceiling of lifestyle bubbles. *Forum on Public Policy Online.* Retrieved August 2009 from http://www.forumonpublicpolicy.com/papersum07.html

Jamison, T. (2003, October 14). Waterloo mayoral hopefuls tout qualifications at forum. *Waterloo-Cedar Falls Courier.* Retrieved August 2009 from http://www.wcfcourier.com/articles/2003/10/14/news/metro/bd509e57b44113f086256dbf0045e8b6.txt

Janz, W. (1998, October 28). Women lawyers had to overcome society's verdict. *Milwaukee Journal Sentinel*, p. 1.

Jones, L. (2004, July 20). Women to women. *National Law Journal.* Retrieved August 2009 from http://www.law.com/jsp/article.jsp?id=1089315028316

Kay, F. (2008). Professional monopolies and divisive practices in law: "Les femmes juridiques" in civil law, Canada. *International Journal of Law in Context 4*: 187–215.

Keen, J. (2009, August 7). On sidelines, Hispanics cheer Sotomayor. *USA Today*, p. 4A.

Kenney, S. (2008). Gender on the agenda: How the paucity of women judges became an issue. *The Journal of Politics 70*: 717–735.

Lau, J. A. (1983). Lawyers vs. social workers: Is cerebral hemisphericity the culprit? *Child Welfare 62*: 21–29.

Lhotka, W. C. (1998, October 10). Women jurists discuss challenges from male colleagues. *St. Louis Post-Dispatch*, p. 8.

Lorde, A. (1984). *Sister outsider: Essays and speeches.* Trumansburg, NY: Crossing Press.

Macaulay, A. (2009). How to retain top female talent, and what women should look for in a law firm. Canadian Bar Association. Retrieved August 2009 from http://www.cba.org/CBA/practicelink/wwp/women.aspx

Martin, S. E., and Jurik, N. C. (2007). *Doing justice, doing gender: Women in law and criminal practice occupations*, 2nd ed. Thousand Oaks, CA: Sage.

Masters, L. (2004, April 26). What women [lawyers] want—and need. *Legal Times*, p. 18.

Michelson, E. (2009). Gender inequality in the Chinese legal profession. *Social Science Research Network.* Retrieved April 2009 from http://papers.ssrn.com/sol3/papers.cfm?abstract_id=1328500

Miller, S., and Meloy, M. (2007). Women on the bench: Mavericks, peacemakers, or something else? In R. Muraskin (ed.), *It's a crime: women and justice*, 4th ed. (pp. 679–722). Upper Saddle River, NJ: Prentice Hall.

Morello, K. B. (1986). *The invisible bar: The woman lawyer in America 1968 to the present.* New York: Random House.

Murphy, L. (2004, March 29). Female general counsel give women the biz; Sisterhood kicks in when projects are doled out. *Crain Chicago Business.* Retrieved August 2009 from http://www.highbeam.com/doc/1G1-114874486.html

Naimi, S. (2009, March 30). Balancing law, children. *Yale Daily News.* Retrieved April 2009 from http://www.yaledailynews.com/articles/view/28343

The National Association of Women Judges (NAWJ). (2006). Welcome to the NAWJ. Retrieved April 2009 from http://www.nawj.org/index.asp

The National Association of Women Lawyers (NAWL). (2008, November). Report of the third annual national survey on retention and promotion of women in law firms. Retrieved April 2009 from http://www.nawl.org/Assets/Documents/2008+Survey.pdf

Neumeister, L. (2005, September, 29). Civil rights pioneer Constance Baker Motley dies. *USA Today*, p. 3A.

Noblitt, L., and Zeigler, S. (2009). Bias on the bench? Sex, judges and mock trial simulations. *Paper presented at the annual meeting of the Southern Political Science Association, Hotel Intercontinental, New Orleans, LA.*

Norwegian Center of Children and Equality. (2007). Gender distribution in education and the workforce. Retrieved April 2009 from http://www.norway.si/policy/gender/workforce/workforce.htm

Peresie, J. (2005). Female judges matter: Gender and collegial decision making in the federal appeallate courts. *The Yale Law Journal 114*(7): 1759–1790.

Rhode, D. L., and Yu, D. (2008). The ABA goal IX commission reports tracking progress and trends. *Perspectives 17*(1): 16–22.

Roberts, A. (2009, April 22). Elevation of lawyers even slower in the recession. *Daily Business Review*, p. 1.

Russell, J. (2005, April). The case of a lifetime: A victory for affirmative action puts attorney Brigida Benitez in the winner's circle. *Hispanic Business*, pp. 22–25.

Ryback, D. (1998, March 12). Minnesota gets a new benchmark. *Christian Science Monitor*, p. 1.

Sarver, T., Kaheny, E., and Azmer, J. (2008). The attorney gender gap in U.S. Supreme Court litigation. *Judicature 91*(5): 238–250.

Savage, C. (2009, May 2). Wider world of choices to fill Souter's vacancy. *New York Times*, pp. A1, A10.

Scales, A. (2006). *Legal feminism, activism, lawyering and legal theory.* New York: New York University Press.

Schultz, U., and Shaw, G. (2003). *Women in the world's legal professions.* Oxford, UK: Hart Publishing.

Shakespeare, W. (1590/1952). King Henry IV, Part II. In *The complete works of William Shakespeare* (pp. 623–661). New York: Random House.

Shakespeare, W. (1600/1952). The merchant of Venice. In *The complete works of William Shakespeare* (pp. 223–253). New York: Random House.

Siemsen, C. (2004). *Emotional trials: The moral dilemmas of women criminal defense attorneys.* Hanover, NH: Northeastern University Press.

Simpson, G. (1996). The Plexiglass ceiling: The careers of black women lawyers. *Career Development Quarterly 45*(2): 173–188.

Slotker, J., and Goodman, S. S. (2007). *It's harder in heels: Essays by women lawyers achieving work-life balance.* Lake Mary, FL: Vandeplas Publishing.

Strick, A. (1977). *Injustice for all: How our adversary system of law victimizes us and subverts true justice.* London: Penguin.

Stuart, F. (2005, December). Personal reminiscence, unpublished communication with van Wormer.

UK Department for Constitutional Affairs. (2005, May). *The legal profession: Entry, retention, and competition.* UK government report. Retrieved from www.dca.gov.uk

United Nations Educational, Scientific and Cultural Organization (UNESCO). (2006). Women, law, and judicial decision-making in the Middle East and North Africa. UNESCO. Retrieved April 2009 from http://portal.unesco.org/shs/fr/files/10415/11647960621gender_justice.pdf/gender_justice.pdf

Weiss, D. (2008, February 1). Judge reprimanded for calling three black female public defenders "The Supremes". *ABA Journal.* Retrieved April 2009 from http://www.google.com/search?client=firefox-a&rls=org.mozilla%3Aen-US%3Aofficial&channel=s&hl=en&q=judge+reprimanded+for+calling+three+black&btnG=Google+Search

Williams, P. J. (1991). *The alchemy of race and rights.* Cambridge, MA: Harvard University Press.

Zhao, Y. (2004, November 7). Beyond "sweetie": Women's place in professional schools is merrier. *New York Times Ed. Life*, pp. 20–22.

Zagier, A. (2008, January 18). Abuse claims divide small town. Associated press. *Boston Globe.* Retrieved April 2009 from http://www.boston.com/news/education/higher/articles/2008/01/18/abuse_claims_divide_small_town/

13

Women in Corrections

It is the government's responsibility, established both by law and practice, to protect us from evil doers and reduce their potential for social harm irrespective of the severity of their offenses. A key part of this mission is to prevent those convicted of crime from repeating their criminal activities. To accomplish this goal, a correctional system has developed to confine, manage, and provide rehabilitative programs for those convicted of crime in a safe, secure, and humane environment. To carry out this task, the corrections systems utilizes the services of trained professionals who are committed to public safety, the rehabilitation of inmates, and, after completion of their sentence, the reentry of offenders into society.

For those who have been in a maximum-security prison or a super-max prison, with their tall walls or razor-wire fences, tiny cells, foreboding segregation units, and ever-present dangers, concepts as valued career or **professionalism** seem to be totally foreign, unrealistic, and idealistic. Certainly, corrections is not an easy job. Corrections is a complex field riddled with critical issues and deeply disturbing realities and focuses on human tragedy and failure. It is a field so shaped by its social context that political and economic realities at times make it seem ever impossible either to maintain or to change.

A major theme of this chapter is that in spite of its challenges and obstacles, individuals can feel good about working in this field. In corrections there are opportunities to make a positive difference in people's lives in community-based settings and in correctional institutions at different levels of the system, in ways ranging from common decency and kindness to penal reform. And, at the same time, you can be well paid and receive excellent benefits. The following recent interview of a correctional supervisor in Box 13.1 describes the satisfaction inherent in this line of work.

In the past, corrections was considered anything but a profession. In states' department of corrections, there were too many horror stories—the inmate trusties in Arkansas who carried weapons and brutalized inmates, the backbreaking work of scoop labor in the fields of Texas, and the staff brutality that was an ever-present feature in American corrections. Even in the federal system, there were incidents of staff brutality.

BOX 13.1
Employment in the Department of Corrections

How did you get involved in corrections?

I graduated from the University of Iowa in 1975 with a degree in social work. I wanted to stay in this area, near Cedar Rapids. I interviewed a lot with the Department of Human Services, and also with the Iowa Security and Medical Facility, which is now IMCC. And that's where I was hired. I was hired in 1976 as a correctional officer. Today I specialize in working with offenders arrested for domestic assault.

How do you feel you're able to help men and women you work with?

Right now the emphasis with our department is through motivational interviewing, so rather than me telling my clients that this is what you need to do, we assist them in coming up with their own vision for themselves, their own goals and then help them network, get the resources refer, them places so they can realize those goals for themselves.

Some of the literature indicates there is a tremendous amount of prejudice against females in the criminal justice system and it leads to burnout. Can you comment on that?

I don't think that I have experienced that. I don't think I've ever felt that way. I've worked in corrections for thirty-two years. One of the things I have liked about the job is that I have had the flexibility to work in different departments. I've worked in pretrial release; I've worked in presentence investigation; I've been a batterers' education facilitator. I'm currently now doing the Moving On curriculum for women referred to the batterers' education program. I'm now in a supervisory position so I've never felt burnout and I've always felt that working as female in corrections I've been given the utmost respect and have not had problems with that.

Could you tell us some of the things that you have done to get yourself away when you know that times are getting kind of rough or you know to take a time out or need to take a couple of days vacation?

Yes, we have flex time, so if you're having a particularly frustrating day you can take off if your supervisor says it's ok. We have a good vacation policy here with the department so I do take vacations every year. I work out at the Y three mornings a week before I come in to work. I find this tremendously beneficial. I like to walk, to swim so I keep active that way. I have a good network of friends who have worked here for years. We do things together after work, sometimes we just have some venting sessions about things going on at work.

What are some of the advantages or disadvantages that women have as correctional officers over men in this field?

When I first started working in my career, I was working in an institution. I do feel that there were some male correctional officers at that time—of course we're talking about 1976—who probably did not feel that women should be in those positions. So I guess I did feel a little bit of resistance there.

What have those advantages since that time have been?

In my particular unit, I have a female supervisor, we really co-supervise now. There's a lot of women working in our unit. We've all worked together well for a long time.

What about the disadvantages?

Working with clients, I can see some disadvantages, particularly working with the batterers' education program. Women who are working

(continued)

(continued)

with that clientele are up against some rather rigid beliefs about what women should do so it makes it difficult sometimes to work with those clients. I just see that as a challenge.

What kind of training was relevant to prepare you for this type of work; what other trainings did you have?

I got my start as a social worker. Through the years in the department I've had training in motivational interviewing, I've had training in the Duluth curriculum for the batterers' education program, recently completed the facilitators training to do the Moving On group for women for women referred to the batterers' education group. We have substance abuse training, safety issues. We are all required to do some training each year.

Is it easier to work with male or female offenders?

I think it might be easier working with men because by the time women are in the correctional system they have pretty chaotic lives and multiple problems going on, so looking at that this is a difficult population to work with.

What personal qualities should an officer working in corrections have?

I think you need to be flexible, patient, a good listener, a good interviewer. Probably the biggest thing, no matter who you're working with, you have to treat everybody with respect, either co-workers or clients.

Were there ever gender specific programs such as nurseries for inmates?

Our department was never able to provide child care for our clients because of licensure problems.

Are there some changes that could be made to help rehabilitate female offenders?

We are just doing a new women's program called WOMMC (Women Offenders Case Management Model), which is a gender specific way to work with women. With our Moving On curriculum that we're using for the women clients in the batterers' intervention program, it really is all about not dwelling on the past, to look toward the future. It's empowering women to see a vision for themselves and then set the goals and again learn the networking, learn the resources, where they can get assistance to meet those goals and really just empowering women to be healthier and happier.

Critical Thinking Questions. What kind of personal characteristics does this correctional supervisor bring to her work that perhaps account for her ability to overcome the challenges? Based on what you can learn from this brief interview, would you be suited to this line of work? Why or why not?

Source: Interview with Carolyn Scheer, Supervisor, Sixth Judicial District Department of Correctional Services, Cedar Rapids, Iowa; Interview conducted by Dan Pledge Johnson on March 11, 2009. Printed with permission of Dan Pledge Johnson, interviewer, and Carolyn Scheer.

It was not long before these signs of professionalism began to appear in correctional systems. State corrections training academies were established across the nation. Accreditation, spearheaded by the American Correctional Association, was developed and spread across community-based agencies and correctional institutions throughout the nation. Affirmative action policies were developed and implemented throughout corrections. The abuse of inmates began to be replaced with the belief that inmates are to be treated with dignity and respect. Some states moved more quickly than others, but this spirit of professionalism is now found throughout the nation. The characteristics and attitudes of what it means to be a corrections professional can be summarized, as follows:

- To see oneself as a person of integrity and to live at integrity level. A definition of integrity is to do the right thing when no one else is around.
- To treat offenders with dignity and respect. As one corrections professional puts it, to treat inmates as you would want your father or brother to be treated in a correctional setting (Bartollas, 2004).

- To model positive behaviors. One way this can be done is to adhere to the ethical principles principles set forth in the American Correctional Association.
- To be a person committed to a learning model and to be open to new ways of doing things. This person seeks to learn throughout his career and is always willing to pursue all the training opportunities that are available.
- To believe that it is possible to make a difference. This person believes that he or she can have an impact and, as a result, is not limited by what others have done.
- To keep your personal stuff from getting in the way. What this means is not to permit personal problems or issues from interfering our doing an effective job.
- To refuse to accept unethical behavior from fellow staff members.
- To stay positive and to do what is possible to create a workplace that is safe, healthy, and free of harassment in any form.

The reasonable person might ask: Why would women ever want to subject themselves to working in such a toxic environment as a prison? Women work in prisons for the same reasons that women become police officers. The pay is reasonably good, particularly with overtime; the job provides security; jobs are available; and they feel that they can do some good. But the fact is that when the definition of what it means to be a professional is examined, it is clear that women as a group bring attributes to the job that are particularly congruent with what it means to be a professional.

Women currently work in corrections in many capacities. They are employed as probation and parole officers and supervisors; residential counselors and supervisors in community-based corrections; correctional counselors; jail officers; correctional officers; and correctional administrators, including wardens and superintendents. As women have received resistance in policing and law practice, so has the world of corrections, especially institutional corrections, been reluctant to receive women within the walls of male prisons.

One of the problems of examining the careers of women who work in corrections is that so little research has been done in this area, with the exception of the female correctional officer who is working in a prison for male inmates. Accordingly, a major emphasis of this chapter is women who are correctional officers in men's prisons, but attention is also given to other positions in corrections that are employing increasing numbers of women.

HISTORY OF WOMEN IN CORRECTIONS

The history of women in probation and parole goes back to the early part of the twentieth century when there was an ever-increasing demand in juvenile probation for trained social workers to serve as probation officers. These social workers, trained under the medical model, began to treat juvenile probationers as disturbed children who needed psychiatric therapy. The philosophy and administration of probation thus retained the older concern with helping children adjust to their environment and added a new concern with helping them resolve their emotional problems. In addition to a greater interest in treating children's problems, twentieth-century probation theory also included the idea of more responsibility for the delivery of services to probationers, a greater consciousness of standards, and a desire to upgrade the probation officer and restore the volunteer to probation services.

This history of providing rehabilitative services was part of the rising *parens patriae* movement in juvenile justice and was also influenced by the Progressive Reformers who were committed to the "child-saving" crusade (Platt, 1976). It sought out those who could provide treatment services to children and, not surprisingly, were willing to turn to women who had been trained as social workers. Aftercare in juvenile justice took longer to develop than juvenile probation, but, it too was treatment oriented and remained so until the 1980s. As a result, women were also welcomed in aftercare services. Thus, although women in policing and law careers encountered opposition and resistance, women interested in juvenile probation experienced far more receptivity.

With their greater acceptance in juvenile probation, the way was paved for the receptivity of women in adult probation and parole as well. Indeed, as revealed later in this chapter, it was only in the late 1970s and 1980s that the rehabilitative emphasis in adult probation and parole changed to a "get-tough" approach in which individuals were held accountable for their actions.

Women in community-based residential corrections programs also benefited from the reintegrative philosophy developed in the late 1960s and early 1970s. At that time, the spirit was one of reform. The area of mental health had undergone a period of deinstitutionalization in the 1960s, during which greater numbers of mental patients were kept in the community rather than placed in large institutions. The turbulence brought on by the Vietnam War, urban riots, and disturbances on college campuses as well as the widespread questioning of tradition-al values by youth countercultures fostered receptivity to new solutions. The bloody prison riots that erupted between 1971 and 1973 also helped support the conclusion that there must be a better way.

Federal funding, finally, provided the catalyst that linked correctional reform with social and political realities, thereby creating a huge array of community-based programs throughout the United States. For example, from the inception of the Law Enforcement Assistance Administration (LEAA) in 1967 through July 1975, $23,837,512 of the Safe Street Act federal monies was matched with $12,300,710 from state and local funds for grants devoted solely to residential aftercare programs for adults. Thus, guided by reintegrative philosophy, advocated by a number of blue-ribbon commissions, and supported by federal dollars, community-based programs sprouted in nearly every state. Jobs were available in these programs. Ex-offenders were hired in some programs, and women also received an acceptance that was denied them in more security-oriented institutional contexts.

Community-based corrections began to decline in popularity even more than it had gained public approval. In the mid-1970s, as the mood of the nation suddenly changed to a "get-tough-with-criminals" approach, publication of official statistics and media coverage of street crime convinced the public that the crime problem had gotten out of hand. By then, women were firmly entrenched as part of the landscape of community-based corrections.

Some women in residential programs worked in programs for women, as either line staff or counselors. Others were employed in facilities that were co-correctional, serving both a male and a female population, and some were able to attain jobs as counselors for male-only residential programs. By the late 1970s, it was not unusual, especially in privately administered facilities, to find women who were directors of residential facilities. Debby Lidster (1979), director of the Talbert Halfway House of Women, in discussing her career in community-based programming, gives some good advice to new counselors (quoted in Bartollas, 1981):

> To work with these women, you need to know where they're coming from—where they dope out and where they're picking up their tricks. You also have to know what they're talking about. If someone comes to you and says "I'm using half a tea a day or eight and two shot," you better know about it. Unless you take the time to learn, you'll show your ignorance, and if you show your ignorance, you won't communicate. (p. 119)

Despite the greater receptivity of women in probation and parole and residential programs, the path of acceptance in jails and prisons was certainly different. The history of women in institutions, as previously stated, can be traced to demands by benevolent groups outside the criminal justice system for prison, jail, and police matrons. In the 1820s, volunteer Quaker women, joined by upper-middle-class women, were motivated to reform female inmates and blamed their poor living conditions on neglect and sexual exploitation by male keepers.

From 1825 to 1873, reformers achieved occasional success in acquiring matrons for women. Eliza Farnham, a feminist and head matron of the women's section of Sing Sing from 1844 to 1848, was one such success. She adopted the reform program of Elizabeth Gurney Fry, which was to make the environment of the prison more like a home and interaction between staff and inmates more like a family. Farnham upheld the conviction that environmental conditions caused criminal behavior and, therefore, that a change in the environment would change behavior. She ended the silence system, as she grouped the women together for the purpose of educational instruction. She also established a library of secular books. In teaching the women to read and write, she instructed them in U.S. history, geography, astronomy, physiology, and personal hygiene. She expected the women to work and encouraged them to become involved with handicrafts. She had the women's wing of the prison decorated with maps, pictures, flowers, and lamps, and she had a piano brought in to provide music. Yet Farnham was not reluctant to employ discipline if it was needed, and solitary confinement was applied for recalcitrant inmates (Feinman, 1994, pp. 43–44).

Farnham was replaced in 1848 for being too liberal, but this did not stop reformers from lobbying for the better treatment of women in corrections. Eventually, reformers were able to convince a male legislature to establish a separate women's prison and to hire women superintendents and matrons. The first prison for women staffed by women opened in Indiana in 1873. By 1913, other reformatories had opened in Framingham, Massachusetts; Bedford Hill, New York; and Clinton, New Jersey. In 1932, the House of Detention for Women opened in New York City, representing the first separate jail for women (Feinman, 1994, p. 44).

Until the 1970s, women were hired strictly to work in prisons for women. Working in male prisons was not viewed as a job for a woman. Still, there were several positions of responsibility for women in male and female corrections. For example, Kate Barnard was the Commissioner of Corrections for Oklahoma from 1907 to 1915, Katherine B. Davis was the Commissioner of Corrections for New York City between 1914 and 1918, and Clara Waters served as the warden of Oklahoma State Reformatory in 1927 (Merlo and Pollock, 1995, p. 98). See Box 13.2 for the career of Mary Belle Harris, one of the most distinguished figures in twentieth-century corrections.

WOMEN PROBATION OFFICERS

Probation is the most widely used judicial disposition for dealing with juvenile and adult offenders. Persons sentenced to probation are subject to conditions imposed by the court and are permitted to remain in the community under the supervision of a probation officer. Conditions of probation vary from jurisdiction to jurisdiction and from individual to individual, but they include some elements of payment of fines, restitution to victims, community service, periodic imprisonment, enrollment in drug or alcohol abuse programs, gainful employment, and cooperation with a citizen volunteer.

BOX 13.2
Mary Belle Harris: A Pioneer in Corrections

By her mid-twenties, Mary Belle Harris had gained a bachelor's degree in music, a master's degree in Latin and classics, and a Ph.D. in Sanskrit and Indo-European linguistics at the University of Chicago. In a journey that encompassed teaching Latin in schools in Kentucky and Chicago, working at the famous Hull House, playing the organ in various locales, and even publishing her musical compositions, her corrections career began in 1914 as a superintendent at the Workhouse in New York City. She then held positions as superintendent, State Reformatory for Women at Clinton, New Jersey; assistant director of the section on reformatories and detention homes for the U.S. War Department, and superintentent at/of the State Home for Girls in Trenton, New Jersey. In 1925, she was appointed the superintendent at the recently authorized Federal Institution for Women planned for Alderson, West Virginia.

In the period from 1925 to 1941, Harris championed rehabilitation at Alderson in a way that few had before or have since her time. Instead of the traditional prison structures, she insisted that this new federal facility be built with attractive red-brick Georgian Colonial buildings arranged around quadrangles, and that the women inmates be housed in cottages. She emphasized innovations, opportunity, and program options. Inmates were offered varied educational and vocational programs, extensive physical activities, a system of inmate self-government, exposure to music and other arts, a library, and typing equipment. They were even permitted to engage in charity affairs to benefit needy persons outside the prison.

There are shadows on the Harris legend for her implementation of racial segregation at Alderson and elsewhere, her fostering of sex-role stereotypes of her day, her tendency to exaggerate in her observations, and her frequent use and perhaps abuse of power. Nevertheless, beyond these shadows, she traveled where few women in corrections had gone before.

Critical Thinking Questions: How can an individual champion rehabilitation on the one hand and favor segregation on the other? Did the changes she made in corrections work accomplish her goal of better relating the prison as an institution to outside society?

Source: Joseph W. Rogers, "Mary Belle Harris: Warden and Rehabilitation Pioneer," *Women & Criminal Justice* (2000): 5–27.

Probation emerged from a treatment model in the early part of the twentieth century. It was spearheaded by white, women **probation officers** who had been trained as social workers. This emphasis on rehabilitative services was altered somewhat in the late 1960s and early 1970s, as a reintegrative philosophy became widely accepted in probation services across the United States. Many women probation officers became deeply involved in providing services to probationers to help them adjust to community living.

In the 1980s and 1990s, the goals of probation swung to risk assessment and increased surveillance models. In an attempt to convince the public, as well as policy makers, that probation could be "tougher" on criminals, probation administrators began to emphasize a number of strategies that would better ensure public acceptance of probation. The most widely used of these strategies have been the combination of probation and incarceration, financial restitution and community service programs, classification systems, intensive probation, and electronic monitoring and house arrest.

This change in goals in adult probation has adversely affected job morale and involvement. The demise of ideology contributed in large measure to the increased rates of burnout for both women and men adult probation officers. Yet, beyond dealing with the demise of ideology and the increased burnout rates, there are probably at least three reasons that women probation officers do not usually experience the rejection and harassment that they have faced in policing jobs and, to a lesser degree, in law careers. First, male probation and parole officers have not developed a culture, which is found in the men's club of policing and the "good old boys' network" in large law firms. Second, there is a long history of treatment in probation and even parole, and professionally trained social workers, including both women and men, have been welcomed with open arms to be line probation officers and supervisors. Third, probation, especially, has never been known as a male occupation and, accordingly, male probation officers do not usually see a problem with women being hired in the office.

G. Wunder's (1969) survey of West German male and female probation officers revealed that female officers believed that their work with male clients was successful because they were able "to establish contact rapidly and to communicate effectively." Both male and female officers in this study acknowledged that female offenders were substantially more difficult to work with than male offenders. Younger female officers also believed that younger male clients had difficulty in accepting the authority of a woman, and the majority of female officers agreed that male sex offenders were inappropriate clients for supervision by a woman (pp. 91–107).

Another study of female probation officers to sexual assault felons in a metropolitan Ohio county in the years 1978–1981 found that male probation officers made more serious sentencing recommendations for sexual assault offenders than did female officers (Walsh, 1984a). When given thirteen different criminal acts to consider, male officers ranked rape as the most serious and female officers ranked it eighth. Equally as surprising, female officers tended to view rape as a victim-precipitated crime, but male officers did not. Perhaps even more noteworthy, the average sex offender processed by male officers received about six more months of imprisonment than those offenders processed by female officers (Walsh 1984b, pp. 371–388).

Anderson and Spanier's (1980) study of juvenile probation officers in Pennsylvania found that officers with a higher level of education were less likely to label acts as delinquent than were officers with less education and that officers who were treatment and service oriented were less likely to label juvenile acts as delinquent than were those officers who responded to lawyer role models. Consistent with the first two findings, those officers who made rehabilitative recommendations were less likely to label acts as delinquent than were those officers who did not (pp. 505–514).

A 1995 study examined the role of gender in determining the offense seriousness by male and female probation officers in England and Wales. In a review of 169 presentence reports, it was found that the officers' gender was an insignificant factor in terms of the degree to which officers considered aggravating and mitigating circumstances in determining the seriousness of the offense (Nash, 1995, pp. 250–258).

Michelle Hayes (1989) examined whether female probation officers in England and Wales were held back as a consequence of their socially ascribed gender roles or because of indirect discrimination by the probation services. They concluded that what restricted promotion and management as choices for women were the women's philosophical disagreements about the present style of probation service management (pp. 12–17).

Slate, Wells, and Johnson's study (2003) measured the effects of stress on probation officers in a southern state, especially in the deterioration of the probation officer's physical health. The sample population (635 officers) was made up of 52 percent women and 48 percent male officers, with 61 percent married. Respondents identified the most influential stressors to be inadequate salary, lack of promotional opportunities, belief that courts are too lenient on offenders, excessive paperwork, frustration with the criminal justice system, its ineffectiveness, expectations to do too much in too little time, lack of recognition, inadequate support from the agency, and lack of community resources.

In sum, some preliminary understanding has been developed concerning the female probation and parole officer's role expectation and performance and gender inequality in probation and parole services. Yet this understanding only scratches the surface of perceiving the challenges and obstacles of probation and parole for women officers, the comparison of rates of burnout between men and women officers, the effect of the "get-tough" crusade on work attitudes of women officers, the similarities and differences between how women and men officers handle clients and the sentences they recommend, and the actual dynamics of gender equality or inequality in probation and parole services.

WOMEN IN PAROLE

Parole is one of the most controversial aspects of the criminal justice process and has received reduced use in recent years. What makes parole so controversial is that there are offenders who, in the public's mind, should never be paroled. And it is an offense to have them come up for parole at certain intervals. Then there are other ex-offenders who commit violent offenses, and the question is raised why they were paroled in the first place.

Today, at the expiration of their prison term, most inmates return to society and try to resume their lives there. For these inmates, their reintegration into society comes by way of parole—the planned community release and supervision of incarcerated offenders before the expiration of their full prison sentences. Today, there are nearly 825,000 people on parole, a number that has increased for the past decade. Each year about 480,000 inmates are released on parole, so that the total population continues to tread upward (Glaze and Bonczar, 2008).

State parole agencies employed nearly 65,000 full-time and 2,900 part-time workers on June 30, 2006. The average caseload was thirty-eight active parolees for each full-time position devoted to parole supervision. Males outnumbered female full-time parole officers (51–49 percent) (Bonczar, 2008). There are some communities in which parole officers continue to see service as an important part of the job. But, for the most part, parole officers are seen and view themselves as control agents (Byrne, 2008).

Parole officers have much in common with probation officers. Both perform duties that are investigatory and regulatory. They face similar role conflicts and frustrations. Both cope with excessive caseloads, both lack community resources, and both may be inadequately trained. In fact, in many states the same officer provides both probation and parole services. In separated departments, state-administered parole services usually pay officers somewhat better than do county-funded probation services. Parole officers also tend to be older and more experienced in the criminal justice system than are probation officers.

Up until recently, scant research has been done on women parole officers. What has been done has found that female parole agents report marginalization, harassment, and gendered adaptations similar to their policing counterparts (Ireland and Berg, 2006; Palacios and Ireland, 2005). In a more recent paper, Ireland and Berg used in-depth interviews with a small sample of female parole agents in California and participants relayed their experiences as parole agents from a women's perspective in a predominantly male occupation. They said that they used female traits of intuition, verbal communication, and relationships over physical tactics. They emphasized the importance of building respect and rapport with parolees in multiple contexts, including parolees' homes, with their families, and places of employment

(Ireland and Berg, 2008). One agent recently appointed to the parole board stated the following as her approach with parolees:

> If you treat them with dignity and respect, then you'll get that in return, for the most part. You really need to treat people with respect, give them some dignity. Parolees, if you treat them well and you do your job, even you have to lock them up, they will respect you and understand that you are just doing your job. If you treat them like a piece of crap, that's what you're going to get back. (Ireland and Berg, 2008)

Being in a traditional male-dominated profession, women parole officers always have the issue of gaining respect and acceptance from male officers. As a result, participants in this study carried weapons, so they said, for two reasons: (1) It was required for those hired after 1986; and (2) it gained respect from male parole agents. Respect was further earned from male officers if they saw that the women officers could handle themselves. (Ireland and Berg, 2008)

WOMEN JAIL OFFICERS

During the 1980s and 1990s, there was a dramatic increase in the number of women correctional officers working in U.S. jails (Pogrebin and Poole, 1997). In 1995, women constituted a larger percentage of correctional officers in jails (24.2 percent) than they did in either state (18 percent) or federal (11 percent) correctional institutions (Maguire and Pastore, 1996, pp. 91, 94). This number increased by 2003 to that women constituted 34 percent of correctional officers in government-run jails and 40.8 percent of officers in privately operated jails (U.S. Bureau of Justice Statistics, 2005).

Unfortunately, what is not identified by the available statistics is the rank or race of the staff at jails or prisons across the United States. Nor do these national statistics distinguish between male' and females' correctional institutions concerning the representation of women staff (Belknap, 2007). What we do know is that women constitute the highest percentage of staff in women's prisons (nearly half in one study of a Western state) and the lowest percentage in men's maximum security prisons (about 10 percent in the same state) (Hemmens et al., 2002).

Difficulty of Gaining Acceptance in Jails

Despite recent advances in employment in this nation's jails, women have had difficulty gaining acceptance in the jail setting. As Pogrebin and Poole (1997, p. 41) expressed it, the jail job "is perceived to be a highly sex-typed male job requiring qualities of dominance, authoritativeness, and aggressiveness. Female qualities of nurturing, sensitivity, and understanding are thought by many male jail officers to be unnecessary and even problematic." It is not surprising, then, that Pogrebin and Poole found from their semistructured interviews with 108 women deputies that women experience problems stemming from sexism and sexual harassment by their male coworkers.

Belknap's (1991) study of thirty-five **women correctional officers** working in a large metropolitan jail also revealed that women experienced discrimination and sexual harassment. Of this sample, 40 percent indicated that they chose a career in corrections because they wanted to become police officers; 40 percent responded that they were attracted to the money and benefits. In their support for gender equality, 94 percent of the respondents further indicated that they believed that men and women were equal and that they should receive more opportunities.

But when asked about their advancement opportunities, 89 percent of these officers believed that they fared poorly compared with male officers. In this study, 31 percent of the women reported that sexual harassment had been an issue for them while working in the jail. White women (45 percent) were more likely than African American women (13 percent) to report sexual harassment, and younger women (47 percent) were more likely to report sexual harassment than older women (13 percent). In addition, these women correctional officers believed that their behavior toward inmates was more respectful than that of men but that their actions were devalued in comparison to the men's more aggressive approaches.

M. I. Cadwaladr's study (1993) of all conditions took place in a modern urban Canadian jail that housed 150 men awaiting trial or bail. This institution was designed to accommodate women correctional officers—inmates' shower stalls and toilets were enclosed and separate change facilities existed for female correctional officers. In-depth interviews were conducted with twenty-one female officers, who reported that they performed the job with a less aggressive style than male officers. They said that they were more likely than the men to rely on verbal skills and intuition to get the inmates to cooperate and to talk out problems. Male officers relied more heavily on internal disciplinary procedures. The female respondents did indicate that male officers believed female officers performed the day to day tasks of the job, but at the same time the male officers expressed the concern that female officers would not be able to back them up in a crisis situation. Most of the women officers reported that they did not personally experience unwanted touching or suggestions. They did go on to describe other forms of harassment from male peers, such as threats, unfounded graphic sexual rumor about individual women, and daily doses of demeaning remarks from peers, supervisors, and inmates. But these women officers decided not to complain because in their view the costs of complaining would outweigh the benefits.

Stohr et al.'s (1998) study of sexual harassment incidents in seven women's jails revealed that 22 percent reported that they had been victims of sexual harassment. In explaining the low level of harassment victimization compared with that in other correctional settings, these researchers concluded that it was probably significant that women were in a majority and occupied some of the midlevel management positions. This is so because it provides "support for the hypothesis that harassment will be reduced as women achieved more situational and achieved power in the criminal justice workplace" (pp. 147–148).

Jails of the Twenty-First Century

Jails of the twenty-first century have a number of characteristics:

- Jails continue to touch the lives of more people than does any other penal institution because each year millions of people enter local institutions, stay there for short periods of time, and then are replaced by more people who commit petty crimes and misdemeanors.
- Jails hold large number of inmates. More than 780,000 inmates are held in jails today, a number that has been increasing despite both a failing crime rate and also bail reform efforts designed to keep people out of jail. From 1995 to 2007, the number of jail inmates per 100,000 U.S. residents rose form 193 to 259 (Bureau of Justice Statistics, 2008).
- Male inmates far outnumber females; almost nine out of every ten jail inmates are adult males. Women do account for a larger percentage of inmates in jail than they did in the past. Similar to males, African American and Hispanic females are more likely to receive jail sentences than are white female inmates (Bureau of Justice Statistics, 2007).

- The jail has developed into a complex correctional institution that has a number of functions, including various kinds of inmate populations.
- The New Generation jail, which now has increased to number over 300 in the United States, allows direct supervision of inmates (Harding et al., 2001). Nearly half of the recently constructed jails use this form of jail management. New Generation jails have five components: they create a new understanding of the role of the officer; they take officers out of control rooms and place them in living areas where they can interact directly with inmates; they implement decentralized, small living units (functional unit management); they promote the use of noninstitutional environments; and they focus on proactive management philosophy (Werner, 2005).

Jails are usually still part of the sheriff's departments, and officers are sheriff's deputies. The problems of crowding, violence, and inmates with mental health issues remain, but the spirit of professionalism has fused a new vision and vitality in many of this nation's jails. In this environment, in which one-third of the officers are women in government jails and over 40 percent are women in private jails, it is a good job for women. And it promises to become an increasingly better job in the years to come, especially for college-educated women.

WOMEN WARDENS

Women have been **superintendents of women's correctional institutions** since late in the nineteenth century, but today increasing numbers of women are seeking for and being appointed wardens of men's prisons.

Early in the chapter, we discussed Eliza W. B. Farnham, head matron at New York's Sing Sing Prison, and the reforms that she instituted between 1844 and 1848. The first woman administrator in U.S. corrections actually preceded Farnham, for Mary Weed was named principal keeper of the Walnut Street Jail in Philadelphia in 1793.

Other early leaders in women's corrections were Clara Barton, who served as superintendent of the Massachusetts Reformatory Prison for Women at Framingham in 1882; Kate Barnard, who was elected to be the first Commissioner of Charities and Corrections in Oklahoma in 1907 and served for two terms; Katherine Davis, who was superintendent of the Bedford Hills prison from 1901 to 1914; Kate Richards O'Hare, who was first an inmate sentenced for violation of the Federal Espionage Act and then, following her pardon, eventually became assistant director of the California Department of Penology; Mable Walker Willebrandt, who oversaw the administration of federal prisons from 1921 to 1929; and Dr. Miriam Van Waters, superintendent of the Massachusetts Reformatory for Women from 1932 to 1957 (Morton, 1992, pp. 76–82).

More recently, Elaine Hunt was appointed Louisiana corrections commissioner in 1972, but she died four years later before she could implement many of her reforms. In the 1980s, Ward Murphy in Maine, Ali Klein in New Jersey, and Ruth L. Rushen in California became directors of state systems. In 1990, Alaska, North Dakota, South Dakota, and Puerto Rico had women commissioners of adult corrections, a record number. In 1992, Kathleen M. Hawk was appointed director of the Federal Bureau of Prisons and became the sixth director of the Bureau of Prisons since its establishment in 1930. Women have also made some inroads in terms of administrators of male institutions, but the road has not been easy. By 1997, women represented about 10 percent of wardens and superintendents of the 900 statewide correctional facilities for men (Marks, 1997, p. 1). Camille Graham Camp was one groundbreaker who in 1977 became warden of the Maximum Security Center in South Carolina. She was responsible for the state's most violent inmates and was the first woman to head such a facility (Morton, 1992, p. 86).

Women have found an early and still present reception as superintendents of women's prisons, and a number of women have been appointed as chief administrators of aspects of or even total correctional systems. But to be appointed as warden of a prison for men has been a much more inaccessible career goal. Part of the difficulty is that women's acceptance in men's institutions has been extremely problematic. It is still believed, particularly by the old-timers, that women do not belong in a men's prison. On a different level, promotions to warden generally require a stint as assistant warden of operations of a men's prison. It is no simple matter for a woman correctional officer or woman correctional counselor to overcome the barriers to gender equality and to receive the promotion to head of security or assistant warden of operations of a men's prison. Old-timers, especially, charge that women may be there because the courts insist on it, but that does not mean that we have to trust institutional security to a *woman*.

Pamela K. Withrow (1992), who has served as warden in more than one men's prison, talks about her journey up the career ladder of corrections. In the midst of optimism in Michigan concerning the hiring of women in corrections, she notes that this movement took a backward step in 1987, when an inmate raped and murdered a female officer at the State Prison of Southern Michigan. In the early 1990s, she states that optimism was much less for women in the corrections profession. Women, she adds, continue to experience resistance from male coworkers, and the perception is still alive that prisons are too dangerous for women to work in. She contends, based on her conversations with a number of women corrections workers in Michigan, that women stay in corrections for a number of reasons. They like the interaction with others, especially the opportunity to work as a team; the wages and benefits; the opportunity to test their physical and mental abilities; the challenge of working with staff and inmates; and the fact that the job is fun and never monotonous (p. 90). Women also feel that they bring certain advantages to correctional institutions:

- A women's body language is nonthreatening.
- Being a woman reduces the number of critical incidents because women have to stop and think before getting physical. A low-key approach sometimes best controls a situation.
- Women can calm down hot situations. Male staff sometimes can't or won't back down.
- Women often hear things others present do not because they have good listening skills. Sharing these perceptions may help improve operations.
- Women can benefit from affirmative action, where available.
- Women receive a certain amount of respect simply because of their gender.
- Women are not as concerned with dominance and destructive power games.
- When a woman supervisor does make herself heard, staff really hear.
- Women more often are able to see inmates as people (pp. 91–92).

Kathleen M. Hawk (1992), former director of the U.S. Bureau of Prisons, adds, "I recognize that many women have suffered trials in the field of corrections over the years and that their perseverance certainly opened many doors for my generation." But she claims that in her years in the profession, being a woman "has been nothing but a plus" (p. 132).

Tekla Dennison Miller (1996), a former warden and author of *The Warden Wore Pink*, gives another twist to women's acceptance: "You have to be terribly strong, not just to deal with the offender population, but also to deal with the negative attitudes of the employees. Many people say it's changed, but it's still there."

The Reverend Jannie Poullard, the first woman warden of New York City's Brooklyn House of Detention and the J. A. Thomas Center on Riker's Island, claims that women are still held to a higher standard and still must work harder to gain equal recognition. She says, "If they're males, it's automatically assumed they're responsible, in charge, and can manage males or females." But "a woman, on the other hand, no matter how qualified she is, always has to prove she can do the job equally as well" (Marks, 1997, p. 1).

A sexual harassment suit settled on November 30, 1997, revealed that the sexual harassment present so widely in law enforcement and in men's prisons with women's correctional officers can also affect women who are wardens. In this suit filed by Linda George, a former associate warden, she charged chief deputy warden Augustine Infante with touching her breasts in front of a prison Equal Employment Opportunity investigator, grabbing her by an ankle, following her off prison grounds in a manner "somewhat like stalking" and telling her she had "the hottest seat in the prison." The settlement on this suit was $6.57 million; including $2 million in damages, $1.8 million paid to private defense attorneys, $1.7 million in fees and expenses to plaintiff attorney, and $353,955 already awarded to Linda George (Wisely, 1998, p. 15).

In sum, there has been a long line of distinguished superintendents of women's correctional institutions since late in the nineteenth century, but today increasing numbers of women superintendents and wardens are developing professionalism, within both male and female's prisons. A convincing argument can be made that both prisons for men and women need the talents and skills that women bring to institutional leadership. Their leadership includes the following characteristics:

- A commitment to develop programming for inmates that deals with their present and helps them plan for the future;
- A desire to treat inmates with dignity and respect;
- A wide commitment to engage staff in prison management and operations;
- A refusal to accept abusive treatment from staff toward inmates;
- A determination to provide a safe environment for both inmates and staff;
- A realization that staff training is a necessary aspect of a humane prison;
- A desire to model positive behavior, both within and outside of the prison; and
- A willingness to pursue accreditation of their facility.

Morton, who has recently completed a national study of women wardens, adds: "They tend to be reform oriented. They all talk about changes they've made to make things better for their staff and to find additional programming for the inmates. Morton also contributes that this has been the traditional role women have played in the criminal justice system, but they rarely had the authority to implement their ideas (Marks, 1997, p. 1).

Nevertheless, the number of women wardens will be limited until women gain greater acceptance as correctional officers and correctional counselors in men's prisons and are promoted to supervisory and administrative positions in greater numbers. It is this career path from which wardens are chosen by central offices.

THE CORRECTIONAL COUNSELOR

The **correctional counselor** is the basic treatment officer in many adult correctional institutions. Female correctional counselor serves several functions in women's and men's prisons. They are treatment agents who are responsible for providing casework cases to inmates, including interviewing inmates and providing the necessary paperwork that will process them through the institution, as well as providing for their particular concerns, such as phone calls and welfare of family and children. They have the responsibility to be advocates who make certain that inmates receive proper medical care and are assigned to desired programs upon availability. They further are resource developers who provide the link between the prisoner and the community, as they help inmates plan for their return to the community. Furthermore, they are advocates who ensure to the greatest possible extent that inmates are not deprived of their constitutional rights.

In performing these functions in state systems, counselors interview prisoners, their families, and other interested individuals or agencies to obtain personal history data; confer with administrative and medical personnel in formulating plans for work assignments, training, and other aids in institution adjustment; participate in disciplinary hearings; provide assistance in structuring the total institutional program for the individual prisoner; prepare reports and progress information for submission to the Parole Board; and develop case histories for use by psychiatrists and administrators for evaluation use in parole planning

In the federal system, the correctional counselor is part of a unit team in a cell house. There are actually three individuals who have job responsibilities in the functional unit, or unit management, of the federal system that are similar to the role expectations of correctional counselors in state correctional systems.

1. The unit supervisor provides overall direction of the treatment that takes place in the unit; the unit committee supervisor is also responsible for maintaining open communication with staff outside the unit.
2. The assistant unit supervisor has his or her caseload and also supervises counselors and other correctional counselors assigned to the unit.
3. The correctional counselor is expected to use personal relationships, planned experiences, and peer-group interactions to meet the program objectives developed for each inmate

This position generally requires a college education, and supervisory counseling positions sometimes require an M.A. degree. Counselors are expected to have knowledge of individual and group counseling techniques; to have knowledge of the goals and objectives of correctional treatment services; to have knowledge of the operations of a correctional facility; to possess knowledge of the goals and objectives of correctional treatment services; to have the ability to deal with persons having antisocial attitudes and to win their confidence; to have the ability to communicate effectively with others; and to have the ability to maintain records, prepare reports, and compose correspondence related to their jobs. The median salary for counselors with one to four years experience is $33,000; for those with five to nine years experience is $41,430, and for those with ten to nineteen years experience is $45,130, and for those with twenty years or more experience is $78,000 (Federal Bureau of Prisons, 2007).

Expectations of counselors range from the professional role they studied in college to the formal job description of the federal and state correctional systems to the role that institutional staff and inmates expect them to assume. The expectations of security staff and inmates are well documented in *Voices of Women from the Criminal Justice System* by van Wormer and Bartollas (2007) that "tell it like it is." The personal narratives reflect the lack of authority and status that both male and female corrections counselors have in correctional settings. Counselors may bring the concept that they are professionals to the prison, but it does not take them long in a maximum-security facility to realize that they have no formal authority at all and little informal power or status. Because they have no formal authority to deal with institutional problems, they can only make inquiries or recommendations to those in line positions. For example, if a resident has no sheets, a counselor cannot order the appropriate correctional officer to distribute them. If a resident wants to enter an educational program, a counselor often does not have the power to authorize his enrollment.

The low status of the counselor is directly related to his or her marginal position in the prison environment. Security is the number one priority of every prison. When security breaks down, everything stops, including treatment programs; nor do counselors meet with inmates during a period of lockdown, or deadlock. Although a counselor may be given information in confidence, he or she is expected by the authorities to immediately report any breach of security to a custody officer. The counselor who is informed by an inmate that he smoked a joint the previous night is expected to find the source of the marijuana, to ascertain whether there is any more in the institution, and to pass this information on to one of the custody staff.

The role of the counselor very much depends on the security level of the institution. In maximum-security institutions, counselors work in a violent atmosphere. Inmates generally assault only other inmates, but sometimes they strike out against staff. Many counselors now have their offices in a cellhouse rather than in the administration building, and those who still do have an office "up front" must usually spend most of their workweek in the cellhouse. Thus, counselors are placed in a vulnerable position, and they know that if a riot occurs, they may be taken hostage, injured, raped, or killed.

In sum, how the counselor feels about her job depends on the prison in which she works. In a federal prison, a minimum- or even medium-security facility, or a woman's prison, counselors generally feel positive about their jobs. However, in a state maximum-security prison, the double marginality of the environment for the female correctional counselor makes it difficult for her to feel overly positive about her job. It is even more difficult for her to gain the respect of staff and inmates so that she would be considered for higher administrative responsibilities.

THE FEMALE CORRECTIONAL OFFICER

The basic role expectation of the correctional officer is that he or she is to prevent escapes, riots, and disruptive inmate behavior. But this function is accomplished in various ways, depending on whether the correctional officer is assigned to a maximum-, medium-, or minimum-security institution.

In maximum-security and most medium-security cellhouses, the correctional officer is required to open and close the steel-barred door allowing entrance and exit; to conduct an inmate count several times a day; to distribute medicine, mail, and laundry; to supervise maintenance activities; and to answer the telephone. The guard must see that inmates are fed, either in the cellhouse or in the central dining facility, to which they must be escorted. The inmates' daily showers must also be supervised. If violations of rules occur, the cellhouse guard must write disciplinary tickets. During the day shift, the majority of the correctional officers are assigned to guard work areas, such as the metal factory, the furniture factory, the yard gang, the canteen, or another prison industry.

Correctional officers in maximum-security institutions also guard the towers and gates. Although faced with loneliness, often uncomfortable temperatures, and boredom, the guard in the tower must nevertheless keep inmates under constant surveillance. If a problem arises in the yard, the guard on the tower must resolve it. If an inmate attacks another prisoner or a correctional officer or dashes for the wall, the use of deadly force may be necessary.

The correctional officer at the gate is expected to search, check, and stamp the hands of all outsiders as they come into the prison. There are several gates in most maximum-security prisons, and a guard is assigned to each. Inmates are required to have a pass and to be "patted down" at each gate. Protected from the violence of prison life, the gate guard is also in the advantageous position of being highly visible to administrators and to outsiders. Thus, when promotions are made, the gate guard often has an advantage over those in the cellhouse and on the tower.

Officers in segregation units have many of the same responsibilities as officers in cellhouses, but they have the additional task of guarding inmates considered more disruptive than those in the general prison population. The job of these officers is more difficult today than ever before, for disruptive inmates no longer can be denied their constitutional rights. Nor is it wise to use brutality against inmates, because they can be awarded damages in a civil suit against their keepers. Thus, in view of the limitations placed on correctional officers, the pandemonium that exists in many of these units is not surprising.

Toxic Environment

The prison environment for both male and female correctional officers is toxic. Several studies have revealed that the arrival of female correctional officers has met with considerable resistance from male correctional officers (Owen, 1985; Peterson, 1982; Zimmer, 1986, pp. 156–159). Horne (1985) has stated this very strongly:

> Negative male attitudes towards women in corrections have been the most significant factor in hindering the advancement of female CO's. No solid proof supports this male bias against female CO's, but none is needed, since males run the corrections agencies. The feeling was, and still is, among the majority of male officers, that "prison work is a man's work." (p. 51)

However, Lawrence and Mahan's (1998) study of men and women officers working in men's prisons in a Midwestern state found that women officers did not face the resistance suggested by previous studies, but the resistance came chiefly from more experienced men officers. These researchers did note that this continued resistance is likely to provide an obstacle to the advancement and promotion of women officers in men's prisons.

Warden Pamela K. Withrow's (1992) conversation with women's correctional officers revealed a number of disadvantages women saw in working in men's prisons:

- Women often are not taken seriously. They have to work harder and do more before being able to increase staff respect for their abilities. This means having to prove themselves over and over every day—not only their abilities, but personal worth.
- If a woman is seen as an affirmative action appointment and makes a statement or gives an order, eyes may shift to supervisory men present for confirmation, even if the woman outranks them.
- Women are always on display. This visibility is not an advantage when a woman makes an error.
- Stereotypes live. Women get asked to type, take notes, or check punctuation and grammar even when they are custody staff.
- Informal networking—golf outings, fishing, hunting, and other traditionally male pursuits—excludes women.

- Tokenism is aggravating. Women may be assigned to the control center or the front desk so they will be visible to important visitors.
- In a tense, noisy situation, a woman's voice may not be audible or may lack the power to command.
- Sexual harassment and abuse of gender is widespread and difficult to combat, especially if the victim does not want to be seen as a snitch.
- Instead of sharing information, male coworkers let women figure things out for themselves and seem to hope they won't.
- When women want to be included, it seems they have to choose between using profanity or professional language. They also have to choose between conduct that may violate personal standards (such as barhopping) or seeming to be aloof. . . .
- There is pressure for women to seek advancement whether that is their goal or not. Also there is pressure to attend social functions that sometimes verges on sexual harassment.
- Women sometimes must develop multiple personae. A woman feels like an actress as the day progresses.
- Women and men have communication styles that often do not mesh, making the work harder than it already is.
- Male staff sometimes use "PMS" as an explanation for any action by a woman they don't like or agree with.
- Less-qualified male staff will sometimes complain that women get promoted over them because of their gender. (p. 92)

Jurik (1985), in an examination of barriers confronting women employed as correctional officers in a state department of corrections in the western United States, found that several organizational barriers have prevented greater acceptance of women correctional officers. One organizational problem is that the reforms initiated by the department created the perception of increased danger in the prison environment. This perception has contributed to the feeling that women are unreliable in such a violent setting. These fears about women's unreliability seem to be rooted in three popular beliefs about women: (1) the "greater physical weaknesses" of women make them incapable of functioning in dangerous situations; (2) the "mental weaknesses" of women prevents them from handling the strain of working in the prison; and (3) the sexual identity and behavior of female officers cast the fear that they will become emotionally involved with inmates (pp. 378–379).

Walters (1993) surveyed correctional officers at four facilities concerning their attitudes toward their jobs. As part of this study, male correctional officers were asked about their attitudes toward working with women correctional officers. The variables that were found to be significantly related to a "pro-woman" correctional officer attitude were the quality of the working relationship with women officers, custody orientation, job satisfaction, educational level, and prison type. But no significant relationships were found between a pro-woman correctional officer attitude and race, length of service, security level, rank, marital status, stress, or age of male respondents.

Crouch and Alpert (1982) studied occupational socialization among prison guards in three recruit classes trained at the Texas Department of Corrections between mid-June and the end of July 1979. They point out that research generally indicates that guards have an increased aggressive or punitive attitude toward inmates over time. However, when the variable of sex was examined, it was found that "women guards become much more tolerant and nonpunitive over time, while their male counterparts become increasingly punitive and aggressive" (pp. 169–170).

Gross et al. (1994), in a study comparing work-related stress in male and female correctional officers, found that there were statistically significant differences between gender and stress outcomes for male and female correctional officers. Women were more likely to be absent more frequently and to have taken sick leave more often than men, but the latter finding, especially, may be due in part to greater family responsibilities.

Carlson, Anson, and George (2003) administered the Maslach Burnout Inventory to 277 correctional officers within a maximum security prison for men. Women correctional officers revealed a greater sense of job-related personal achievement and accomplishment than men officers did. But both groups were found to have similar degrees of emotional exhaustion and depersonalization.

A female correctional officer in a men's prison usually finds that the stress of working in a violent environment is coupled with conflict with male coworkers. But even assuming that problems with male coworkers can be resolved, the role confusion or uncertainty of the job may cause her to seek out or be assigned to low-contact positions (Zimmer, 1986). This, in turn, results in dead-end work assignments or limited promotional possibilities (Jurik, 1985).

Jenne and Kersting (1996) compared how male and female correctional officers deal with volatile inmate situations with male inmates. They found that female officers usually respond to aggressive incidents in the same manner as do male correctional officers. Indeed, in some cases, female correctional officers even handle some encounters more aggressively than male correctional officers do. Jenne and Kersting claim that these results debunk the assumption or notion that women are incapable of handling situations that require an aggressive response.

Jurik and Halemba (1984) compared the job satisfaction of male and female correctional officers working at the same prison facility in a western state. They found that female correctional officers tended to be more highly educated than male correctional officers, come from more professional backgrounds, and have a much greater likelihood to be divorced or separated. In contrast, the majority of male correctional officers had previous law enforcement or military experience, but none of the female correctional officers had military experience and only about a third had previous police experience. But despite such demographic differences, Jurik and Halemba discovered that "women exhibited largely the same attitudes toward their work as did male officers," but that "female respondents, more often than men, cited intrinsic reasons for employment in corrections" (p. 564).

Britton (1997) examined the relationship between race and sex and perceptions of the work environment among correctional officers. Using data collected from the correctional officer subsample ($N = 2,979$) of the 1992 administration of the Prison Social Climate Survey, she found that sex and race played a role in shaping officers' perceptions of the work environment, that these differences between groups were not necessarily accounted for by job or institutional characteristics and did not reduce over time, and that there were factors that mediated this relationship between race and sex and workplace perceptions. With minority male officers, their greater efficacy in working with inmates seemed to be an important factor in creating lower levels of job stress, while white female officers' higher levels of overall job satisfaction were accounted for largely because of a more positive evaluation of the quality of supervision.

Privacy–Equal Employment Dilemma

Affirmative action measures have resulted in more minority officers, with the result that the percentage of racial minorities among officers is now equal in many states to that of the minority population of the state. But it was not until the enactment of equal employment legislation—specifically Title VII, which prohibited sex discrimination in hiring by state and local governments—that doors began to open for women in men's prisons.

Three criticisms have been directed toward women working as correctional officers in men's prisons: First, women are not fit for the job; for example, they are not strong enough, are too easily corrupted by inmates, or are poor backup for other officers in trouble. Second, women are a disruptive influence; that is, inmates will not follow their orders or will fight for their attention. Third, the presence of women violates inmate privacy, especially when women are working in shower areas or conducting strip searches of inmates (Hawkins and Alpert, 1989, p. 359).

Dothard v. Rawlinson (1977) and *Gunther v. Iowa State Men's Reformatory* (1979) have been the most important U.S. Supreme Court cases examining whether women are qualified to work in men's prisons. The former was an Alabama lawsuit filed by Diane Rawlinson, a recent college graduate in correctional psychology who was denied a job as a correctional officer because she was five pounds below the minimum weight requirement. Her class-action suit challenged the state's height and weight requirement; the suit also charged that a department of corrections' regulation preventing female officers from "continual close proximity" to prisoners in maximum-security prisons for men (known as the no-contact rule) was discriminatory. The Supreme Court, in a 5–4 decision, overturned a lower court decision that had invalidated the no-contact rule. The Court was unwilling to let women work in maximum-security prisons for men in Alabama because of the danger of sexual attack and because the extra vulnerability of women to attack would weaken security and endanger other prison employees.

However, in *Gunther v. Iowa*, the Court dismissed security issues as a reason for limiting women's employment as guards in that state. The *Gunther* decision defined that job requirements to strip search male inmates or witness them in showers constituted an attempt to prevent women from working as correctional officers.

These and other cases demonstrate that the courts have generally established procedures that both guarantee women the right to employment and protect inmate privacy as much as possible. In the *Forts v. Ward* decision (1978), the circuit court held that "equal job opportunity must in some measure give way to the right of privacy" (p. 1099). The background of this case was that female inmates at the Bedford Hills Correctional Facility in New York contended that their right to privacy was violated because male correctional officers were assigned to duties in hospital and housing units. As a result, the women inmates argued, male correctional officers were able to observe them while they were sleeping, showering, dressing, undressing, and using the toilet facilities. In the *Torres v. Wisconsin* decision (1988), prison officials used the bona fide occupational qualification (BFOQ) defense for restricting male correctional officers from working in the living units of a women's prison. The case went through two appeals processes, but eventually the rights of female inmates were determined to take precedence over the equal employment rights of male correctional officers (Maschke, 1996, p. 32).

Departments of corrections can maintain inmates' right to privacy by administrative policies preventing women from doing some types of searches, such as strip searches. The installation of modesty half-screens, fogged windows that permit figures to be seen, or privacy doors on toilet stalls offer another solution to privacy issues. Security does not have to be sacrificed, and these modifications can be made to the physical environment at little cost.

Comparison of How Female and Male Correctional Officers Do Their Jobs

Several studies have compared male and female correctional officers (Alpert, 1984, pp. 441–455; Peterson, 1982). They have generally found that men and women do not differ in the quality of their job performance. This does not mean that they are equal in all tasks. Although men may be able to handle physical assault better than women, women may more effectively defuse an incident before violence erupts (Peterson, 1982). Leo L. Meyer, a former warden in the Illinois correctional system, describes the role of women officers in a male medium-security institution (quoted in Bartollas, 1981):

> We probably have more female officers than any other correctional center because of the transfers from mental health. Two are lieutenants, and one of them just passed the NRA [National Rifle Association] test for instructor in firearms. I think she is the first woman in history to do this. A female who wants to be a warden has a real good opportunity. I say one thing about females, they're dependable and they seem to try harder. In terms of qualifying for their firearms test: Their scores are better than some men, and many have never shot a gun before. (p. 300)

Various studies have found that women correctional officers are more treatment oriented than are their male counterparts (Crouch and Alpert 1982; Jurik and Halemba, 1984). Women also tend to supervise inmates with a more personal interaction style than do men officers. For example, women will frequently ask inmates to perform certain tasks, rather than commanding them to do so (Pollock, 1995, p. 107). Zimmer (1986) adds that inmates claim that women officers explain orders more fully, while male officers tend to bark orders and resent any attempt by inmates to get a fuller explanation.

Issues of Women Working as Correctional Officers

Women correctional officers face the same issue as discussed previously that women police officers do: whether the better strategy in this male-dominated area is to adopt a gender-neutral approach (same behavior by women and men) or gendered approach to policing (different behavior by women and by men—each having value). The debate among feminists in correctional work is similar to that in police work. Gender-neutral guarding of inmates appears to be favored among the majority of women corrections officers because "equal" should mean the "the same as" rather than "different but just as good as" (Schulz, 2004, p. 491).

Another issue quite different from those that women police officers confront is the widely prevalent sexual abuse of female inmates that women correctional officers in women's prisons must address. As reported in an earlier chapter, this is a serious issue for correctional administrators, but on a much more personal level some women correctional officers certainly would have awareness of and possibly have witnessed this sexual exploitation. No study has been done on women correctional officers' responses to what must be an extremely disturbing experience, but the continued denial of or acceptance of such exploitation has serious ethical and moral issues for women officers.

Women correctional officers, especially in men's prisons, must deal with many levels of sexual and gender harassment. F. J. Till (1980) identified five levels of gender and sexual harassment that she reported from least to most severe. *Gender harassment*, the first level, involves putting down one's sex (usually women). Examples would be informing new officers or seasoned officers that "women aren't strong enough to control male prisoners" or that "women are too emotional to work with male offenders." *Seductive behavior* involves sexual advances or requests by the harasser to discuss the victim's dating or sexual life. This also takes place on a regular basis, but the more likely occurrences are sexual rumors circulated by male correctional officers. *Sexual bribery*, Till's third level of sexual harassment, involves the victims being promised some type of reward, such as a job or a promotion, if she complies with the harasser's sexual request. This probably takes place with women correctional officers to a lesser degree than in the private sector because promotions and desirable job opportunities are more limited.

All the evidence further suggests that *sexual coercion* and *outright sexual assaults and sexual abuse*, Till's fourth and fifth levels, infrequently take place in adult corrections facilities with women correctional officers.

Britton's 2003 book, *At Work in the Iron Cage*, proposes that the prison is a gendered organization:

> . . . By arguing that the prison qua organization is gendered, I mean that rather than existing as a neutral bureaucratic entity, the prison was formed in and through a matrix of gender, race, class, and sexuality, and that it reproduces individuals, ideas, and inequalities along all these dimensions. As it is gendered, the prison is also raced and classed and sexualized. Though one may choose to emphasize a single dimension for analytical purposes, they never operate in exclusion from one another. Individuals possess these characteristics, of course, and they shape and confirm notions about their own "essential self," as well as the selves of others, through their work. Jobs are not generic slots in the organizational hierarchy but instead contain embedded assumptions about who the ideal worker is. The veracity of these assumptions is confirmed through policies and practices that privilege and reproduce this ideal. (p. 216)

Summary

This chapter examined the role of women working in corrections. Although the empirical examination of women probation and parole officers, women jailers, correctional counselors, and even wardens of men's prisons is thin, every indication is that women continue to experience the problems faced throughout policing careers and legal professions. These problems are particularly highlighted with women who attempt to become correctional officers in men's prisons. Consistent with the men's club in policing, women correctional officers face the time-worn "truth" that women do not belong in a men's prison. Women correctional officers have faced stiff resistance and, at times, physical intimidation and sexual harassment. But some women correctional officers, as with women correctional counselors and correctional administrators, have survived and even thrived in men's prisons.

What is fortunate about women's survival in corrections is the impact that they can bring to the toxicity of correctional environments. The early entrance of women in probation and parole had a considerable impact on humanizing the profession. It can be argued that much of the ideology of probation and parole throughout most of the twentieth century is attributable to the influence of its early women leaders. In some sense, this same tendency seems to be occurring in correctional systems that employ women wardens. There seems to be a consistent difference in how women and men correctional staff approach inmates, handle problems, defuse violence, and respond to crises. These disparities, over time, can make major differences in the quality of institutional life.

Key Terms

correctional counselor *381*

parole *376*

probation *373*

probation officer *374*

professionalism *368*

women correctional officers *377*

superintendent of women's correctional institutions *379*

Critical Thinking Questions

1. How would the roles of the female probation officer, the female working in a jail, the female correctional officer, and the female warden or superintendent differ from males working in these positions?
2. Which position in corrections would be most difficult for women? Why?

3. Which position do you believe would be most fulfilling? Why?
4. Why do women choose to work in maximum-security prisons for men? Why not work only in women's prisons?

Web Destinations

This site gives details on the career of a correctional officer: http://www.jobbankusa.com/ohb/ohb156.html

This California Correctional Officers Association site is for anyone considering a career as a correctional officer: http://www.susanvillenews.com/co.html

This article surveys recent innovations in definitions of the attitudes and role behavior of prison guards: http://www.oicj.org/public/story.cfm?story=9FD2986A-F6AC-11D3-AA9E-00CO4F4309AD4

References

Alpert, G. P. (1984). The needs of the judiciary and mis-applications of social research: The case of female guards in men's prisons. *Criminology 22*: 441–455.

Anderson, E., and Spanier, G. (1980). Treatment of delinquent youth: The influence of the juvenile probation officer's perceptions of self and work. *Criminology 17*: 505–514.

Bartollas, C. (2004). *Becoming a model warden: Striving for excellence.* Landham, MD: American Correctional Association.

Belknap, J. (1991). Women in conflict: An analysis of women correctional officers. *Women and Criminal Justice 2*: 89–115.

Belknap, J. (2007). *The invisible women: Gender, crime and justice*, 3rd ed. Belmont, CA: Thompson.

Bonczar, Thomas P. (2008). *Characteristics of State Parole Supervising agenies, 2006*. Washington, DC: Bureau of Justice Statistics Special Report.

Bureau of Justice Statistics. (2005). *Jail Statistics.* Washington, DC: U.S. Department of Justice.

Bureau of Justice Statistics. (2007). *Jail Statistics.* Washington, DC: U.S. Department of Justice.

Bureau of Justice Statistics. (2008). *Jail Statistics.* Washington, DC: U.S. Department of Justice.

Britton, D. M. (1997). Perceptions of the work environment among correctional officers: Do race and sex matter? *Criminology 35*: 85–105.

Britton, D. M. (2003). *At work in the iron cage: The prison as gendered organization.* New York: New York University Press.

Byrne, J. M. (2008). The social ecology of community corrections: Understanding the link between individual and community change. *Criminology and Public Policy 7*(2): 263–274.

Cadwaladr, M. I. (1993). Breaking into jail: Women working in a men's jail. M.A. thesis, Department of Sociology and Anthropology. The University of British Columbia.

Carlson, J. R., Anson, R. H., and George, T. (2003). Correctional officer burnout and stress: Does gender matter? *The Prison Journal 83:* 277–288.

Crouch, B. M., and Alpert, G. P. (1982). Sex and occupational socialization among prison guards: A longitudinal study. *Criminal Justice and Behavior 9:* 159–176.

Dothard v. Rawlinson, 433 U.S. 321, 1977.

Federal Bureau of Prisons Web Page (2007). http://www.payscale.com/research/US/Job=Correctional_counselor/Salary

Feinman, C. (1994). *Women in the criminal justice system*, 3rd ed. Westport, CT: Praeger.

Forts v. Ward, 471 F.Supp. 1095 (S.D.N.Y. 1978).

Glaze, L. E. and Bonczar, T. P. (2008), "Probation and Parole in the United States, 2006." *Bureau of Justice*

Statistics Bulletin. Washington, DC: U.S. Department of Justice.

Gross, G. R., Larson, S. J., Urban, G. D., and Zupan, L. L. (1994). Gender differences in occupational stress among correctional officers. *American Journal of Criminal Justice 18*: 219–234.

Gunther v. Iowa State Men's Reformatory F.2d 1079 (8th Cir., 1979).

Harding, B. G., Linke, L. Van Court, L. M., White, J., and Clem, C. (2001). *2001 Directory of direct supervision jails.* Washington, DC: National Institute of Corrections.

Hawk, K. M. (1992, August). BOP programming administrator sees opportunities for women. *Corrections Today 19*: 32, 34.

Hawkins, R., and Alpert, G. P. (1989). *American prison systems: Punishment and justice.* Englewood Cliffs, NJ: Prentice-Hall.

Hayes, M. (1989). Promotion and management: What choices for women? *Probation Journal 36*: 12–17.

Hemmens, C., Stohr, M. K., Schoeler, M., and Miller, B. (2002). One step up, two steps back: The progression of women's work in prisons and jails. *Jounral of Criminal Justice 30*: 473–489.

Horne, P. (1985). Female corrections officers: A status report. *Federal Probation 49*: 46–54.

Ireland, C., and Berg, B. (2006). Women in parole: Gendered adaptations of female parole officers in California, *Women & Criminal Justice 18*: 131–150.

Ireland, C., and Berg, B. (2008). Women in parole: Respect and rapport, *International Journal of Offender Therapy and Comparative Criminology 32L*: 474–491.

Jenne, D. L., and Kersting, R. C. (1996). Aggression and women correctional officers in male prisons. *Prison Journal 76*: 442–460.

Jurik, N. C. (1985). An officer and a lady: Organizational barriers to women working as correctional officers in men's prisons. *Social Problems 32*: 375–388.

Jurik, N. C., and Halemba, G. J. (1984, Autumn). Gender, working conditions and the job satisfaction of women in a non-traditional occupation: Female correctional officers in men's prisons. *The Sociological Quarterly 25*: 551–566.

Lawrence, R., and Mahan, S. (1998). Women correctional officers in men's prisons: Acceptance and perceived job performance. *Women and Criminal Justice 9*: 63–83.

Lidster, D. (1979, March). Personal interview.

Maguire, K., and Pastore, A. (eds.). (1996). *Sourcebook of criminal justice statitics 1995.* Washington, DC: U.S. Government Printing Office.

Marks, A. (1997, April 23). Women break into some of the toughest men's prisons. *Christian Science Monitor*, p. 1.

Maschke, K. J. (1996). Gender in the prison setting: The privacy-equal employment dilemma. *Women and Criminal Justice 7*: 23–42.

Merlo, A. V., and Pollock, J. M. (1995). *Women, law, and social control.* Boston, MA: Allyn & Bacon.

Miller, T. D. (1996). *The warden wore pink.* Brunswick, MN: Biddle Publishing.

Morton, J. B. (1992). Looking back on 200 years of valuable contributions. *Corrections Today 18*: 76–87.

Nash, M. (1995). Aggravation, mitigation and the gender of probation officers. *Howard Journal of Criminal Justice 34*: 250–258.

Owen, B. (1985). Race and gender relations among prison workers. *Crime and Delinquency 31*: 147–158.

Palacios, N., and Ireland, C. (2005) Women in Parole: Respect and Rapport. Paper presented at the annual conference of the American of the Association for Criminal Justice Research, Long Beach, CA.

Peterson, C. B. (1982). Doing time with the boys: An analysis of women correctional officers in all-male facilities. In B. R. Price and N. J. Sokoloff (eds.), *The criminal justice system and women.* New York: Clark Boardman.

Platt, A. (1976). *The child savers*, 2nd ed. Chicago, IL: University of Chicago Press.

Pogrebin, M. R., and Poole, E. D. (1997, March). The sexualized work environment: A look at women jail officers. *The Prison Journal 77*: 41–57.

Pollock, J. M. (1995). Women in corrections: Custody or the "caring ethic." In A. V. Merlo and J. M. Pollock (eds.), *Women, law and social control* (pp. 97–116). Needham Heights, MA: Allyn & Bacon.

Rogers, J. W. (2000). Mary Belle Harris: Warden and rehabilitation pioneer. *Women and Criminal Justice 11*: 5–27.

Schulz, D. W. (2004). Invisible no more: A social history of women in U.S. policing. In B. R. Price and N. J. Sokoloff (eds.), *The criminal justice system and women* (pp. 483–493). New York: McGraw-Hill.

Slate, R. N., Wells, T. L., and Johnson, W. W. (2003). Operating the manager's door: State probation officer stress and perceptions of participation in workplace decision making. *Crime and Delinquency 49*(4): 519–541.

Stohr, M. K., Mays, G. L., Beck, A. C., and Kelley, T. (1998). Sexual harassment in women's jails. *Journal of Contemporary Criminal Justice 14*: 135–155.

Till, F. J. (1980). Sexual harassment: A report on the sexual harassment of students. *Report of the National Advisory Council on women's educational programs.* Washington, DC: U.S. Government Printing Office.

Torres v. Wisconsin Department of Health & Social Services, 838 F.2d 944 (7th Cir. 1988).

van Wormer, K. and Bartollas, C. (2007). Voices of *women from the criminal justice system.* Boston: Allyn & Bacon.

Walsh, A. (1984a). Gender-based differences. *Criminology 22*: 371–388.

Walsh, A. (1984b). Differential sentencing patterns among felony sex offenders and non-sex offenders. *Journal of Criminal Law and Criminology 75*: 443–458.

Walters, S. (1993). Changing the guard: Male correctional officers' attitudes toward women as co-workers. *Journal of Offender Rehabilitation 20*: 47–60.

Werner, R. (2005). The invention of direct supervision. *Corrections Compendium 30*: 32–34.

Wisely, W. (1998). $6.5 million spent in California sexual harassment suit. *Corrections Today 60*: 15.

Withrow, P. K. (1992, August). Workplace reality: Women staff tell it like it is. *Corrections Today*, pp. 88–92.

Wunder, G. (1969). Zur Situation der Bew Ahrungshelfer: Algemeines zur Arbeitssituation der Bew, *Bewahrungshilfe-Germany 16*: 91–107.

Zimmer, L. (1986). *Women guarding men.* Chicago, IL: University of Chicago Press.

14

Summary and Trends for the Future

In the tradition of feminist criminology, we have examined six major themes in this text. First, we applied an analysis based on gender, class, sexual orientation, age, and race/ethnicity to examine the experiences of women offenders, victims, and practitioners in the criminal justice system. Secondly, we considered the effects of the multiple oppressions of gender, class/ethnicity, sexual orientation, and age (youth). Third, we focused on the social construction of knowledge and how the role of women has been influenced by male-oriented social constructionism, exposing a number of myths concerning female offenders, victims, and practitioners. Fourth, this text heavily emphasized social context, especially the social context of patriarchal society. We examined how, on a micro-level, women have developed subcultures within the wider society to escape its oppressiveness. Fifth, we looked at the broader theme of globalization in that women are part of larger systems of interaction, and the international perspective portrays this. Sixth and last, the theme of empowerment received some emphasis in nearly every chapter. These six themes, as well as other insights of this text, have been presented with the goal of enabling the reader to experience paradigm shifts concerning the role and treatment of women offenders by the criminal justice system.

THEME OF RACE/ETHNICITY AND CLASS IN FEMALE INCARCERATION

The fundamental theme of this book is that girls and women who get caught up in the throes of the justice system have often been subjected to various forms of discrimination, exploitation, and criminalization starting in early childhood. The girls who are most likely to experience such deprivations and oppressions are those who are poor and from minority groups. With female delinquents, it is often their drug use and sexual behavior that bring them to the attention of juvenile authorities. It can be argued that much of the state's response is a criminalization of young women's survival strategies, surviving on the streets (Belknap, 2007). But how do they get to the streets in the first place?

The seeds of delinquency and crime often are sown in childhood in an early life characterized by abuse, often of a sexual nature. High stress levels conducive to trauma set a pattern of behavior in motion involving escape through drinking and other substance use in an environment where interpersonal violence is a way of life. More victimization follows, as well as an estrangement from law-abiding folks. We can draw this progression as a curve that extends from abuse of the child to heavy use of mood-altering substances in early and later adolescence to trouble with the law to early motherhood to incarceration. The tough upbringing of the mother now extends to the second generation as children are removed from the home. For the mother, there may be treatment inside of the correctional system; for the child, the harm may be repaired or the cycle may be repeated across the generations. This is the female's typical pathway to delinquency and crime across the life course, as studied in Chapter 4, and that relates to the consideration of the role of substance abuse and its treatment in Chapter 5. The typical male's pathway to crime is apt to occur through risk taking for excitement, leading to a similar peer-group experience that is also the male's eventual downfall.

Chapter 6, which took us into the world of the women's prison, further revealed the interconnectedness of unhealthy relationships, poverty, substance abuse, and violent victimization, in inmates' personal histories. The majority experience a second victimization within prison walls, some of which is legal and some of which is not. Nevertheless, even in the face of degrading prison conditions, some women make the best of a bad situation, forming institutional families, and working to reclaim their lives and prepare for their day of release and family reunification.

The Impact of Class

Class can be a key factor in oppression. The social class that a person is born into determines the likelihood of entrance into homelessness, unemployment, drug use, survival sex and prostitution, and even more serious delinquent and criminal acts. In adolescence, girls brought up in rough neighborhoods and with few privileges are at high risk of chronic school failure, of lack of educational goals beyond high school, to experience higher rates of physical and sexual abuse, to deal with pregnancy and motherhood, to be involved in drug and alcohol dependency, to confront the risk of AIDS, and to lack supportive networks at home. Lower-class adult women are more likely to be victimized than are middle- and upper-class ones and to be subjected to domestic abuse. Equally important, women from the lower echelons of society are less likely than others to receive the benefits of chivalry in court. Research evidence also supports the belief that girls and women of color enjoy the benefits of chivalry much less than do white girls. They tend to be viewed as more dangerous to society and to require jail incarceration and long-term institutionalization.

The interplay of race/ethnicity and class determines in part who gets prison and who is dealt with more leniently by the courts. These effects are exacerbated if women are African American or Latina and have experienced a life of poverty. In fact, if you remove the class factor, the dynamics of race may be altogether different. The success of their highly educated sisters in the professions was easy to document in the background research that shaped the concluding chapters of this book, which covered women's contributions to the professions of law enforcement, law, and corrections.

Research on women on death row reveals another factor in addition to poverty and the act or acts of homicide that determine which women get a death sentence and which women get life. This factor is sexual orientation; masculine women and lesbians—in other words, gender nonconformity—have been found to influence judge and jury to mete out the most severe punishments.

The Factor of Race

Racial oppression of women further receives documentation throughout this text. Both minority girls and women are often forced by their minority status and poverty to deal early and regularly with problems of abuse, drugs, and violence. In addition, they are likely to be attracted to gang membership. And in their affiliation with gangs, sexual victimization is almost a given. The reluctance of these African American and Latina rape victims to go to rape crisis centers or to report these attacks to the police is understandable under the circumstances.

They and other rape victims of color who are not gang affiliated are similarly unlikely to report their victimization for other reasons. A large part of this reluctance relates to larger needs and concerns in their lives, including poverty, homelessness, unemployment, difficulties in feeding their children, racism, and fear of the police.

Intersectionality

The tendency is to think about gender, class, and race as additive in their impact, so that they are calculated in terms of gender plus class plus race. Yet as we know from the sociology of social systems, the whole of gender, race/ethnicity, and class is greater than its individual parts. We need to think in terms of multiplicative rather than additive impact.

Whereas traditional stratification studies, as Andersen (2005) notes, tended to look mostly at social class, the new paradigm of race, class, and gender sees all three simultaneously and as overlapping and intersecting—that is, as a "matrix of domination" (p. 444). The new race/class/gender paradigm of the third wave of feminism, moreover, as Andersen further suggests, tends to be more interdisciplinary, stemming as it does from the full range of women's experiences and the influence of critical race studies in various disciplines.

What all this suggests is that in consideration of the background factors in female criminality, the researcher must be cognizant of the consequences of multiple oppressions and of the interactive nature of these forces.

THE NEED FOR A GENDERED SOCIAL CONSTRUCTION OF KNOWLEDGE

The major theoretical works on crime have been written by male criminologists about men and boys. Alarmingly gender blind, they added females as a type of footnote. Clearly, from the very beginning, the study of crime and the justice process has been shaped by male experiences and understanding of the social world (Chesney-Lind, 2006).

In the debate that has taken place between *sex*, which is a biologically based category, and *gender*, which refers to the socially constructed meanings that are associated with each sex, it has been argued that the claimed difference between women and men represents a political and social decision rather than a distinction given in nature (Rothenberg, 2006).

Gender is further related to the themes of domination and subordination. Women in a male-dominated society experience inequality of many resources but chiefly of status and power. Placed in subordinate categories, they become more vulnerable to victimization. Wife battering, incestuous attacks on female adolescents by fathers or father substitutes, and rape are crimes of domination against women that take place in situations of inequality.

Feminists of the second wave (1970s), as discussed in Chapter 8, helped researchers and activists conceive of rape not in either–or terms but as a series of acts along a continuum. Far from being an isolated event that could be rooted out from the society at large, the crime of rape was now seen as only the logical extension of what was already there, as a violation against women that is an exaggeration of the smaller assaults, often verbal, which subject girls and women to sexual harassment in school and in the workplace. The sexual harassment of women has emerged in the context of their employment in legal and criminal justice agencies. This context has been promoted by the cultures of the "men's club" of policing, the "good old boys" of law agencies, and male *esprit de corps* in correctional institutions and probation and parole agencies.

The consequences of the sexual violation of women across the spectrum may range from personal embarrassment to psychological and physical wounding. In considering the crime of rape, a number of rape myths were examined and refuted. These included the belief that the biggest threat to women's safety is from a stranger, and that rapes are impulsive acts committed by men who are unable to control their passions, passions that are partially induced by women's seductive behavior and clothing.

ATTENTION TO SOCIAL CONTEXT

The kinds of violence that take place in intimate relationships also reveal the importance of social context in this nation. In understanding the violence in intimate relationships, including wife and partner abuse, marital rape, and child abuse, the issues of authority and control by men over women must be carefully explored. Indeed, a man's right to chastise his wife was affirmed in the doctrine of the church as well as in early Roman law and English common law. Even into the twentieth century, domestic violence was considered a private matter, not one for intervention by the state.

Chapter 1 presented a theme that ran throughout the book: U.S. society and many others have been affected by gender in the distribution of power, wealth, and opportunities. What is so disturbing about the social construction of gender is that males have assumed the power and control over women, and that women have so often been complicit in this relinquishment of control. Many have been socialized in the United States and in nations across the world to fully accept, or to accept without complaint, a subordinate status.

For the past 3,000 years, the power of patriarchy has been pervasive. This male-dominated system with its rigidly prescribed male and female sex role behavior has only recently been challenged and its doctrine seems to be so universally accepted that it seems to be one of the laws of nature.

The laws of society have represented one of the means by which women have been oppressed under traditional norms. The belief that women had to be protected from the sordid nature of life led to restricting them from working and earning a living on an equal basis with men, keeping them from owning property for much of the history of this nation, excluding them from jury duty, and punishing in a severe way those who violated the cultural expectations.

An examination of women offenders in correctional institutions reveals the tragic story of one form of social injustice after another. Race, gender, and class intersect in America's courtrooms and throughout the correctional system. One could easily make the argument that the antifeminist and antiwelfare movements are being played out in our "halls of justice." The war on drugs has taken its toll on poor minority women and on their children, who are destined to grow up without one or both parents while their mothers serve their time. The still pervasive "get-tough-on-crime" laws have brought their effect to bear disproportionately on persons without political and legal leverage in society.

Globally, rape is a tool of dominance, power, and control. Rape in some situations, such as in war or by gangs, is an act of male bonding. Historically, little sensitivity has been shown toward rape victims. Subcultures also become important in shaping behaviors of offenders, victims, and workers in the justice system. Men socialized into the subcultures of some college campuses regard sex in terms of gaining possession of a woman. According to Schwartz and DeKeseredy (1997), "the frustration caused by a reference-group-anchored sex drive often results in predatory sexual conduct" (p. 35).

Chapter 10 examines the victimization of women globally. Sexual trafficking, honor killings, dowry deaths, genital mutilation, and rape in war are among the topics covered that relate to women's victimization worldwide. We have much to be concerned about regarding the victimization of women in the United States, but when globalization is examined, we become painfully aware of the necessity of paradigm shifts in how women are treated cross-culturally and that women's rights are human rights.

The final section of the book is concerned with the advancement of women as workers in the criminal justice professions. In recent years, women have made major strides in the legal profession, but in the law, as elsewhere, status and income disparities still exist. Policies of affirmative action have paved the way for women's participation in areas of policing and correc- tions that had formerly been closed to them. To some extent, the subculture of males in both policing and corrections has been resistant to the entrance and acceptance of women. Law enforcement and corrections have been the most resistant of the professions, perhaps due to the physical aspect of the work, inherent danger, and the existence of male bonding in policing and correctional circles. Correctional staffs, especially in men's prisons, have been quick to say that women do not belong in men's prisons and have provided stiff and consistent opposition to the acceptance of female correctional officers. And yet, research has shown that the influence of women on these areas has been largely a beneficent one.

EMPOWERMENT OF WOMEN IN THE JUSTICE SYSTEM

In searching for solutions, this text has drawn on empowerment at all levels—personal, interper- sonal, economic, educational, and political. For example, the rape reform and domestic violence intervention movements have made progress on several fronts: the legal one, women's group counseling centers, rape crisis centers, women's shelters, and other crisis intervention programs for victims. Restorative justice, the subject of Chapter 7, was shown to have the potential to provide empowerment to victims and their families, as well as to offenders, and to promote healing for victim, offender, and community—all three. The inclusion of a chapter on restorative justice from a gendered perspective is a unique contribution of this criminal justice text.

The thrust toward empowerment has also brought an effect to bear on the criminal justice professions, both in the treatment of girls and women in the system by professional women—police officers, probation officers, correctional personnel, and lawyers. For example, police officers also have become more sensitized to the feelings of women who have been physically abused by a partner and/or sexually abused. Women's entry into policing, corrections, and the law has had a tremendous impact on those fields, bringing a feminist perspective to issues of women and violence.

FUTURE TRENDS

Many trends and events of the twentieth century transformed the criminal justice system and the roles of women within it. Broadly, these events have been expressed as chivalry for white women of a certain class; harsh punishments for African American female offenders; first a stress on rehabilitation and then a cynicism toward rehabilitation; a war on drugs and on drug users; and a conservative backlash against women on welfare and women convicted of crime.

There is a truism that says we can't know where we are going until we know where we have been. What we learn from the past is that the pendulum swings in one direction, then comes back to swing the other way. So how long will it take to reverse the conservative trend of the past two or more decades?

In the writing of the last edition of this book, we stated that things may have to get worse before they get better. There was an expectation of more executions, harsher drug laws, more lethal weapons for the police, fewer rights for prisoners, and more politicians securing public support by capitalizing on the public's fear of crime, a fear largely generated by the mass media. Following that, we anticipated a paradigm shift and a return to reason and common sense. The predicted change, in part, would have been associated with the normal political cycle. But another factor that we expected to help move the nation in the direction of change is the diversity factor.

We again emphasize what we stated then: Over the past decades, the most significant change that portends well for the future is the increasing diversity of the population. This diversity is slowly being reflected in law, the legislatures, and the judiciary. Feminist women have worked for legal reform with some notable successes. Among these are the criminalizing of marital rape in many states and reforms in rape law, such as shielding the past sexual history of victims and removing corroboration requirements. The filing of lawsuits against state departments of corrections has improved career opportunities for women and minority staff, as well as vocational training options for female inmates. As increasing numbers of women are appointed to the bench and join prosecution teams, we can expect to see greater protection for victims and prison inmates (another kind of victim) in the future.

The greatest stumbling block to pending institutional change is the global economic crisis, a phenomenon that is often associated with displaced aggression in the form of heightened rates of domestic violence on the home front, greater job competition and fewer opportunities to break through the glass ceiling, and government cutbacks in much-needed social services. On the other hand, the single greatest factor in producing social change and humanizing the criminal justice system as we progress further into the new century may well be the voice of female authority. As women gain in political influence, areas for anticipated change relevant to women and the criminal justice system are:

- swifter punishments for male batterers coupled with a focus on prevention through school male mentoring programs and batterer education intervention; greater protection for battered women, legally and economically
- more protection for incest victims and less stress on reunification of violent and sexually abusive families

- legislation to provide extensive counseling services to child rape victims to prevent traumatization
- further improvements in rates of conviction of rapists as a result of advances in DNA testing and enhanced victims' rights
- less litigation and increased use of alternative forms of conflict resolution, such as restorative justice conferencing and healing circles
- greater focus on substance abuse, mental health, and medical treatment needs of female offenders; proliferation of drug courts and mental health courts in lieu of incarceration
- increased funding for halfway-house parenting programs for offenders
- as an alternative to imprisonment, much greater use of intensive community supervision programs
- within prison, strict rules restricting male guard access to female inmates
- improved educational and vocational opportunities for women in prison
- an end to mandatory minimum sentences and a return to an individualized approach to justice
- changes in the laws meting out harsh sentences to women convicted as conspirators due to their close associations with drug dealers
- a reversal in "welfare reform" laws so that women will have and be able to maintain more independence from men, if they so desire
- a greater recognition of the plight of battered immigrant and trafficked women, who will be granted legal status to remain in the country with the support of social service agencies.

Much more research is needed to explore the link between women's victimization in society—sexually, economically, and personally—and their criminality. Research is also needed to show how substance abuse and other addictive behavior figure into the equation.

References

Andersen, M. L. (2005). Thinking about women: A quarter century's view. *Gender & Society 19*: 437–455.

Belknap, J. (2007). *The invisible woman: Gender, crime, and justice*, 3rd ed. Belmont, CA: Wadsworth.

Chesney-Lind, M. (2006). Patriarchy, crime, and justice: Feminist criminology in an era of backlash. *Feminist Criminology 1*: 6–26.

Rothenberg, P. S. (2006). *Race, class, and gender in the United States: An integrated theory*, 7th ed. New York: Worth Publishing.

Schwartz, M. D., and DeKeseredy, W. S. (1997). *Sexual assault on the college campus: The role of male peer support*. Thousand Oaks, CA: Sage.

INDEX

Note: Page references with 'b' 'f' and 't' notation refers to a box, figure and table cited in the text